ON THE ROAD WITH JOHN JAMES AUDUBON

ON THE ROAD WITH
JOHN JAMES AUDUBON

By Mary Durant and Michael Harwood

ILLUSTRATED

DODD, MEAD & COMPANY, NEW YORK

Library of Congress Cataloging in Publication Data

Durant, Mary B
  On the road with John James Audubon.

  Includes index.
  1. Audubon, John James, 1785-1851. 2. Birds —
United States. 3. Birds — Canada. 4. United States —
Description and travel. 5. Canada — Description and
travel. 6. Ornithologists — United States — Biography.
I. Harwood, Michael, joint author. II. Title.
QL31.A9D87   598.2′092′4   79-22734
ISBN 0-396-07740-4

To Edward Dodd.
This book was his idea.
And to the memory of
Harold Ferrier Burns
Herbert Dudley Hale
and Reed Harwood.
They would have reveled in the adventure.

CONTENTS

ix Introduction

1 "Mill Grove," Audubon, Pennsylvania: 1804–1806

17 Louisville, Kentucky: 1807–1810

37 Henderson, Kentucky/Ste. Genevieve, Missouri: 1810–1811

79 Henderson, Kentucky: 1811–1819

111 Cincinnati: 1819–1820

121 Ohio River: October-November 1820

143 Mississippi River: November 1820-January 1821

205 Natchez: 1820–1824, Passim

220 St. Francisville, Louisiana: 1821–1829, Passim

259 New Orleans: Passim

279 To Europe and Return: 1826–1829

300 Camden and Great Egg, New Jersey:
    Spring and Summer 1829

319 Mauch Chunk and the Great Pine Forest:
    Late Summer-Early Fall 1829

330 Charleston, South Carolina: Passim

350 East Florida: November 1831-March 1832

374 The Florida Keys and the Dry Tortugas: April-May 1832

411 To Labrador: June-August 1833

485 The Gulf Coast and Texas: April-May 1837

535 Missouri River: April-October 1843

597   Going Home
619   Authors' Note
623   General Index
633   Bird Index

INTRODUCTION

We traveled by family car, covered some 35,000 miles, were on the road for thirteen months, and lived in a tent most of the way. Our purpose: to visit those places in the United States and Canada that John James Audubon had known during his travels in the early years of the 1800s. It was a journey on which he led us north to Labrador, south to the Dry Tortugas, west to Buffalo Bayou in downtown Houston, and northwest to the Montana-North Dakota border, with hundreds of stops in between—up and down the eastern seaboard and through the heartland and along its great rivers, the Ohio, the Mississippi, and Missouri. (It was one of the sorrows of Audubon's life never to have had the chance to cross the Rockies and see the west coast.)

We came to places where Audubon's name was unknown and to others where it was a tourist attraction. We met the inevitable, towns grown into urban sprawl and roadless wilderness now laced with highways. But we also found vast tracts of wild country much as it was in Audubon's day, and we discovered that many places he had known as rising new communities had vanished from the map and often from local memory—river towns gone to dust, frontier settlements gone back to prairie. America has not been cemented over after all.

The back seat of our car was replaced with shelves to give us extra space in which to pack the necessities for long distance camping and fireside research. Our basics were a typewriter, a pencil sharpener, books, two duffle bags of clothing, foul-weather gear, an old wooden milkbox packed with cooking equipment, a cooler to hold ice and perishables, a pantry box of spices and staples, dry kindling (which saved our necks more than once), sleeping bags, and a green canvas, igloo-shaped pop-tent, eight feet in diameter. A pop-tent is designed on the same principle as an umbrella, with the canvas stretched between six fiberglass ribs held in place by a locking device at the top. If the wind and the weather were with us, the tent could be assembled in four and a half minutes.

We'd slept before under the stars in sleeping bags and camped a few times in Appalachian shelters, but neither of us had any experience with a tent. Our first day out, which happened to be in a national forest in southern New Jersey where Audubon made an ornithological foray in 1829, it took us forty-five slow-witted minutes to put the tent together, and, when we left to explore for the afternoon, we didn't even know enough to tie it down. A light breeze came up, and the pop-tent bounced away through the forest, ricocheting off the pine trees (as though scoring points in a giant pinball game), until it was caught and anchored by a passing scoutmaster out with his troop. He later explained with kindly patience that a tent should always be secured against the wind. We are probably still being cited in that scout troop as a tragic example of poor woodsmanship.

We did our own cooking except for occasional lunches at roadside stands or meals served by old and new friends along our route. We took ourselves out to dinner twice—to a Chinese restaurant in Stephenville, Newfoundland, and to a restaurant in Cave-In-Rock, Illinois, where the specialty was fresh "fiddlecat" from the Ohio, a salad with fresh scallions, and cornbread fresh from the oven in cast-iron spiders. We ate well, slept well, and absorbed rhythms of the weather and the outside world of which we would not have been otherwise aware. The phases of the moon were no longer a charming celestial window dressing but served as a measure of time. Printed dates on a calendar became a technicality, made irrelevant by natural sequence. A flight of white pelicans migrating southward across the great plains as winter pressed behind them. A bloom of yellow flowers in the tulip trees as spring moved up the Appalachian chain.

John James Audubon, illegitimate son of a French naval officer, merchant, and slave trader, was born in 1785 on his father's plantation in Santo Domingo. He was raised and educated in France and in 1803, aged eighteen, was sent to the United States by his father to escape conscription into Napoleon's army. In the course of the next forty years, Audubon explored as much of the North American continent as he could, both as a merchant, his first career, and as a painter–naturalist, his second. He was a wanderer by nature, a man beset with longings for dim hills and far horizons, and he took off whenever and wherever he had the chance.

Audubon would scoff at students of nature who did their research in libraries and museums—"the closet naturalists," as he called them. He prided himself on being one of the field naturalists, out of the academic closet and into the open to study and observe with his own eyes. He was possessed of manic energies. He went full tilt, rarely sleeping more than a few hours, up and at it before dawn. Into the woods, into the marshes, up the hills, and into the mountains. Keep moving. Look, listen, track it, find it, never forget a moment of it. "I have been in the regular habit," he said in 1837 to the American painter Thomas Sully, "of writing down every day all the incidents of which I have been an eye witness on the spot, and without confiding to my memory, as many travellers have done and still do."

It's a wonder he found time to paint at all. His pen teemed with words, millions of words, and the record he left is compelling and detailed. Towns, rivers, creeks, ponds, campsites, birds, animals, insects, people, happenings along the way. Gossip, good news and bad, his jubilations and "the blue devils" of his despairs and depressions. Some of what he wrote was naive, some of it pompous, some of it bawdy, but by and large it was perceptive and often witty. On the upswing of his moods, he had a diamond-edged sense of humor and a ruthless sense of the absurd.

In 1826, he went to England with a portfolio of his life-sized paintings of American birds. He had been unable to find an engraver in the United States willing to publish his work, but in England he was recognized as a genius, found his engraver-publisher, and leaped into fame at the age of forty-one. His niche in history had been waiting for him.

The sciences were in flower. The earth and its properties were being studied systematically, and such men as Humboldt, Mungo Park, and Lewis and Clark, whose explorations were mainly scientific in character, held the attention of educated minds in the western world. Intensive investigations ranged from anthropology and ethnology to paleontology and comparative embryology, and among those disciplines emerging from myth and medieval confusion was the science of ornithology. Behold Audubon, the ornithologist.

At that same time, arts and letters were in the throes of the Romantic Revival, which had been sparked in the mid-1700s by Goethe, Schiller, and Rousseau. The values of society were discovered to be false and civilization corrupting, and the principle theme of Romanticism was the worship of wild nature. The Romantic hero lived in harmony with nature, and Jean Jacques Rousseau's novel, *Emile* —the natural man in a natural world—sent Marie Antoinette romping into the woods of Versailles with her ladies-in-waiting to play milkmaid. Pretty costumes and porcelain milk pails at Le Petit Trianon, the Queen's made-to-order rustic retreat. In England, where wild nature was exalted by Wordsworth, Coleridge, Scott, *et alia,* the stiff geometry of formal gardens went out of style, and the grounds of the great country estates were landscaped into informal "natural" gardens and "natural" vistas. Fresh air and contemplative outdoor rambles were in vogue.

North America was a romantic outpost bursting with natural wonders and new species of flora, fauna, and avifauna. William Bartram, the Quaker naturalist from Philadelphia who explored the no-man's-land of the Floridas, had already captured the imagination of Europe and America. So had Daniel Boone, whom Byron extolled in *Don Juan* as the epitome of the wilderness hero at one with nature in the fastnesses of the New World. Well-heeled Europeans began to show up on safari along the American frontier, intent on viewing untrammeled nature. Behold Audubon, the Romantic hero. Behold Audubon, the frontiersman, who stepped forth unheralded from the solitudes of the American forests.

To add to the sheen of his image—an image that his ornithological contemporaries, Nuttall and Wilson, never achieved—not only was he a naturalist, an artist, and a wilderness man, he was also at home in a drawing room or on a polished dance floor. He became a legend overnight. Although he had his critics and detractors (he still does), he remains a heroic figure in American lore. Dozens of biographies and commentaries have been written about him in close to a century and a half, and he has been eulogized in a short story by Eudora Welty ("A Still Moment"), in a play by Jessamyn West ("A Mirror for the Sky"), and in poetry by Stephen Vincent Benét ("John James Audubon") and by Robert Penn Warren ("Audubon—A Vision").

Our car library, which eventually expanded to eighty volumes and included field guides and local histories, had a comprehensive collection of Auduboniana. In particular, the American edition of Audubon's literary *chef-d'oeuvre,* the *Ornithological Biography*— seven volumes of essays on North American birds; copies of his journals; much of his correspondence; anthologies of his other writings; the two-volume set of his original watercolors published by American Heritage; and a variety of biographies. Appearing throughout these books and papers were the signposts to his forty years of travel in North America, an itinerary we condensed by zigzagging through his life, heading north in the summer to pick up his trail and south in the winter. The story of our trip, however, is presented in Audubon's chronology. And because there are three voices in this book, each is identified by initials—JJA for John James Audubon, MD for Mary Durant, and MH for Michael Harwood. Audubon's entries fall into two categories, those from original documents, which are presented as he wrote them, and those from his published works, in which his scatter-shot punctuation and imaginative spelling were corrected by his wife, by editors with whom he worked, and by later members of his family.

Thus we set out on our trip, armed with book knowledge and a checklist of landmarks. As the weeks passed, we found ourselves living in tandem with Audubon, tumbling headlong into the emotional connection that can hold a biographer for years—a lifetime. The connection, with its early conflicts and cautions, began quietly and uneventfully in Audubon, Pennsylvania, a crossroads town (renamed in his honor in 1899) that lies twenty-four miles northwest of Philadelphia, near Valley Forge.

"MILL GROVE," AUDUBON,

PENNSYLVANIA

1804–1806

JJA   In Pennsylvania, a beautiful state . . . , my father, in his desire of proving my friend through life, gave me what Americans call a beautiful "plantation," refreshed during the summer heats by the waters of the Schuylkill River, and transversed by a creek named Perkioming. Its fine woodlands, its extensive acres, its fields crowned with evergreens, offered many subjects to my pencil. It was there that I commenced my simple and agreeable studies, with as little concern about the future as if the world had been made for me.

MD   The driveway sweeps up toward the Mill Grove house between neatly trimmed hedges. A gardener on a tractor mows a vast meadow, yellow with buttercups. The spring day is sticky and hot, but in spite of that, two boys—beet red, sweat dripping off their noses and chins—pitch a frisbee back and forth in the sunstruck parking lot above the house. A solitary young man with a guitar crosses the meadow and disappears into the woods below. In a little while we will hear a faint melody in a minor key from a distant spot among the cool trees.

The house is set comfortably and snugly into the land—a classic Pennsylvania farmhouse, inviting in its lines and proportions, and built for the ages in rough-cut blocks of stone. Near the door is a cast-iron hitching-post jockey in red cap and jacket who stands with arm raised, ready to hold your horse. Across the way, a discreet sign reminds you that this is a sanctuary and all plants and wildlife are protected on the 130 acres of the Mill Grove preserve.

1

Mill Grove. *MH*

Rambler rose vines climb up the porch, and in this sudden, sultry thunderclap of spring, thick stands of peonies and boughs of bridal wreath have come into bloom. Two fat ladies in pantsuits (one in baby blue, the other in emerald green) pose in front of the bridal wreath, and the thin husband of the fat lady in blue takes their picture. They squint into the sun and giggle at the camera.

A troop of school children—little ones, second or third graders, I'd guess—are gathered at the doorstep, listening with dutiful attention to the curator. We join their tour.

The house was built in 1762, the curator begins. Audubon's father bought the property as an investment in 1774, when he came to Philadelphia on a business venture with a cargo of sugar from the West Indies. Within three years after John James came here to live, the Mill Grove estate was lost in a tangled web of partnerships and mortgages that were intended to finance a lead mine on the property and to underwrite his career as a merchant.

In 1812, Mill Grove became the property of Samuel Wetherill, a Philadelphia Quaker, and stayed in the Wetherill family until 1951, when it was sold to the Montgomery County Commissioners as an historic site.

The curator tells the children that there are swifts living in the chimney (all eyes look to the rooftop), and that the birds nesting there this spring are presumably descendants of the birds that lived there in Audubon's day. I'm sure they are. We have swifts in our chimney in Connecticut, and every spring, as faithful as the planets in their courses, they home in from their wintering grounds at the other end of the world—the jungles of the Amazon River valley where jaguars prowl and orchids grow on trees. We stare fixedly at the Mill Grove chimney, but there are no swifts to be seen. They're out flying and feeding in the midday sun and won't be back until dusk.

The children and their teacher-escorts move on into the house, to explore the displays of birds, animals, paintings, the magnificent life-sized engravings from *The Birds of America,* and other Audubon memorabilia. They are fascinated by a glass case of stuffed owls.

"I've seen that one."

"So have I."

"I've seen that one and *that* one!"

They stretch their claims to fame, pointing to a screech owl, a great horned owl, a barn owl, a barred owl, a saw-whet owl. "And *that* and *that* and *that!*"

They are momentarily taken by a gigantic canvas done in oils by JJA when he was in England in 1828—a lonely mountaintop and a golden eagle sweeping down upon a cringing lamb. He did others in the same vein. Among them, two cats fighting viciously over a dead rabbit. Another of an otter in a trap, teeth bared. All in the spirit of the sporting scenes painted in that era—nature in the raw, stags at bay, gamekeepers swathed in dead game, the spoils of the hunt stacked about in mammoth still lifes, animals and birds with bleeding breasts laid out amid guns and decanters of port.

The children scramble upstairs to explore the floors above. A Pennsylvania Dutch bedroom, the furnishings decorated with hearts and *distelfinks.* An early Victorian bedroom furnished to complement an Empire horsehair sofa that came from the house built by the Audubons in New York in 1841. Panoramic murals of his travels in North America—the plains of the Dakotas, a Louisiana swamp, the bird-rocks in the subarctic waters of the Gulf of St. Lawrence. In the attic, two low-ceilinged rooms are furnished in simulation of the studio-workshop where he painted and practiced taxidermy amid his collection of birds' eggs, specimens of snakes, lizards, and frogs, and his stuffed animals and birds.

I cross paths on the stairs with a little girl who has noticed us in their entourage, and she stops to ask me if we are bird lovers.

"Yes. Yes, indeed," I tell her.

"So am I," she replies gravely.

Voices begin to rise, someone starts a running and sliding game on the polished floor of the front hall, and there's a flurry of trips to the bathroom and to the drinking fountain. The children are rounded up by their teachers and led away for a walk on the grounds.

MH   I took to the woods myself, looking for birds—and also, inevitably, looking for links and ties to Audubon. The man he was at Mill Grove seems a strange creature: spoiled, vain, wasteful, foppish. He once said that as a young man he was "what in plain terms may be called extremely extravagant." He dedicated himself to shooting, fishing, horseback riding, collecting natural curiosities, raising fancy poultry, dancing, playing music, and drawing birds. "Not a ball, a skating-match, a house or riding party took place without me," he wrote. "I was ridiculously fond of dress [and went] shooting in black satin [knee] breeches, with silk stockings, and the finest ruffled shirt Philadelphia could afford." A contemporary who met Audubon at twenty wrote, "Today I saw the swiftest skater I ever beheld; backwards and forwards he went like the wind, even leaping over large airholes fifteen or more feet across, and continuing to skate without an instant's delay. I was told he was a young Frenchman, and this evening I met him at a ball, where I found his dancing exceeded his skating; all the ladies wished him as a partner; moreover, a handsomer man I never saw, his eyes alone command attention."

The trail I followed through the Mill Grove woods led along the brow of a slope down to the creek he called Perkioming, now Perkiomen, where he explored and hunted and sketched and skated. Occasionally I caught the dazzle of sunlight on water through the trees below me. Audubon nearly drowned in that creek during one winter's skating escapade, and the adventure made the sort of story that fathers tell and retell for their children—knowing they risk boring everyone, but unable to elude the force of the recollection once it has been stirred and set in motion.

JJA   Another anecdote I must relate to you on paper [he wrote in an autobiography for his two sons], which I have probably too often repeated in words. . . . It was arranged one morning between your young uncle, myself, and several other friends of the same age, that we should proceed on a duck-shooting excursion up the creek, and, accordingly, off we went after an early breakfast. The ice was in capital order wherever no air-holes existed, but of these a great number interrupted our course, all of which were, however, avoided as we proceeded upward along the glittering, frozen bosom of the stream. The day was spent in much pleasure, and the game collected was not inconsiderable.

On our return, in the early dusk of the evening, I was bid to lead the way; I fastened a white handkerchief to a stick, held it up, and we all proceeded toward home as a flock of wild ducks to their roosting-grounds. Many a mile had already been passed, and, as gayly as ever, we were skating swiftly along when darkness came on, and now our speed was increased. Unconsciously I happened to draw so very near a large air-hole that to check my headway became quite impossible, and down it I went, and soon felt the power of a most chilling bath. My senses must, for aught I know, have left me for a while; be this as it may, I must have glided with the stream some thirty or forty yards, when, as God would have it, up I popped at another air-hole, and here I did, in some way or other, manage to crawl out. My companions, who in the gloom had seen my form so suddenly disappear, escaped the danger, and were around me when I emerged from the greatest peril I have ever encountered. . . . I was helped to a shirt from one, a pair of dry breeches from another, and completely dressed anew in a few minutes, if in motley and ill-fitting garments; our line of march was continued, with, however, much more circumspection.

MH   No doubt.

Well, he may have been reckless and extravagant as a young man, but he also showed intensity, a capacity for single-mindedness—as in his efforts to develop techniques for his hobby of portraying birds. His early drawings, he said, were done "*strictly ornithologically,* which means . . . in stiff, unmeaning profiles." Then, "having a desire to show every portion of a bird," he tried depicting dead specimens hung by one foot with their wings and tails flopped open. "In this manner I made some pretty fair signs for poulterers"—and that didn't satisfy him either. He decided he wanted also to show birds as they looked alive, and he sketched many birds in the wild at Mill Grove. But to get the details of feathering and color he still had to work from birds that were more or less immobile. From time to time he tried to arrange a dead specimen in positions like those of the live birds he'd been sketching. "But, alas! they were *dead,* to all intents and purposes, and neither wing, leg, nor tail could I place according to my wishes."

He hung them up on threads, like puppets, which worked better but was still less than ideal. So he tried something else: while learning to draw the human figure he had used the standard wooden manni-kins, which could be posed in different attitudes, and now he in-vented a birdikin of wood, cork, and wire. When "set up it was a tolerable-looking Dodo," he said; a friend, seeing it, burst out laugh-ing, so Audubon angrily destroyed it. But he was on the right track.

"I not infrequently dreamed that I had made a new discovery," he wrote; "and long before day, one morning, I leaped out of bed fully persuaded that I had obtained my object." He rode to Norris-town, five miles away, and arrived so early he had time to bathe in the river before the shops opened. He bought an assortment of wires, hurried home, and, refusing to pause for breakfast, took his gun down to the Perkiomen and shot the first kingfisher he saw. He carried the bird up to the house, asked the Mill Grove miller to get him a piece of wood to be used as a base, and began cutting lengths of wire and sharpening the ends with a file. Now he skewered the dead bird on one end of a wire and fixed the wire to the wooden base; "another wire [that] passed above his upper mandible held the head in a pretty fair attitude, smaller ones fixed the feet according to my notions, and even common pins came to my assistance. The last wire proved a delightful elevator to the bird's tail, and at last—there stood before me the *real* Kingfisher." An *armature*—that was the answer. He was so excited he wouldn't go to breakfast even then but first completed "what I shall call my first drawing actually from nature." This was the method he would use the rest of his life.

I wonder what birds—and how many of them—Audubon would have seen in 1803 along the trail I walked today. He would have gone out with a gun, probably, which made it a different sort of enterprise. Collecting a full game bag's worth of forest species is not the same as birding with binoculars in a healthy woods with a healthy understory. You see mostly glimpses, flashes of color and motion, half a bird's back here, part of a head there. You may hear a lot of song, as I did in the Mill Grove woods, but most of the singers are lost in the glowing green leaves against the bright day high above, and no amount of craning the neck and staring through binoculars, of changing place and craning the neck some more, discovers them for more than a second or two at a time.

One rufous-sided towhee did bounce out into plain view on the trail to perform very satisfactorily. It was a handsome male—white belly, cinnamon flanks, black breast and head and back, with white markings in the wings and tail. Flaring his black head feathers, red eyes afire, he moved along in front of me, a gingery fellow in the prime of life, leaping forward with one eye on me and the other on his next bite. He fed on the bell-like buds of some ground-creeping forest flower, occasionally springing straight up to snatch a bud that hung above him.

MD Except for the curator in his office downstairs, I had the house to myself, and in the abrupt silence after the children left I walked about very quietly, as we all do in empty, unfamiliar buildings, hesitating sometimes at the door of a room to look around the corner before stepping over the threshold. The house was always full of people when JJA lived here. Not only his guests—he loved to entertain and give parties—but also the family of the tenant farmer, who managed Mill Grove and whose wife served as housekeeper and cook.

This is my second time through the house. I'm lingering. I'm looking for something, though I don't know what it is. I listen. I sniff the air. Did I really expect to see Audubon's coat swinging on a nail, and his muddy boots drying by a fire, and his flute and violin where he left them on a side table? Well, I'll admit this much—I expected a discovery. I'd hoped to tune in on something that no one else had noticed before.

I catch a shirttail glimpse of what I'm after at an attic window across the hall from the studio-workshop rooms. Attic windows have always seemed very personal to me—a secret view in a small frame from the top of the house, and when Audubon stood here and looked out through this window, he saw what I see. The green spread of the countryside, the long slope of the meadow that rolls down to the creek, the bend of the creek, the Reading Hills in the hazy distance.

But the moment passes. The picture isn't really the same. The mill and the miller's house beside the creek are gone; cattle probably grazed in the long field in the foreground, and Mill Grove hummed with activity—ploughing, planting, harvesting, the farm animals, the poultry, dogs, cats. The diggings for the lead mine, with the muck and machinery and smelting works that went with it, were just around the corner of the house in the middle of the dooryard, not far beyond the spot where the bridal wreath now blooms. Nowadays, Mill Grove is an island of tranquillity.

The late Herbert Wetherill, the last of that family to own the property, was responsible for preserving Mill Grove. He devoted himself to the custodianship of the house and the land, not only because these were his paternal acres, but also because it had been Audubon's first home in America. It was a powerful link. His grandfather Samuel Wetherill had known Audubon and had entertained him here in 1825 when Audubon dropped in on a nostalgic visit and stayed for dinner. Another member of the family, John Wetherill, had been one of the eighty-two American subscribers to the original folio edition of *The Birds of America.*

In the 1940s, Herbert Wetherill offered Mill Grove to his daughter, but she and her husband regretfully agreed that it would be more of a burden than a blessing, and thus the next alternative was arrived at—the sale of Mill Grove to the county commissioners, instead of exploiting it as prime real estate.

I've met Herbert Wetherill's daughter, Anne Wetherill Parker, who lives outside Philadelphia. Her memories of life at Mill Grove have much the same idyllic quality as Audubon's memories of the place. The country house, the farm, the poultry yard, a tenant farmer, his wife who did the cooking and baking, lots of guests, skating parties on the creek in winter, boating and swimming parties in summer. Among the family's keepsakes are a few pieces from a teaset designed by Herbert Wetherill and executed for him by the Lenox China Company. White cups with a gold band around the rim. On one side, a black and white view of Mill Grove. On the other, a picture of Audubon taken from the Henry Inman portrait painted in Philadelphia in 1833 when Audubon was forty-seven. It's the popular Byronesque pose that's so often reproduced—his face in three-quarter profile, his hair to his shoulders, his collar open, his gaze fixed up and away toward the far horizon. At the time it was done, Audubon said it was the truest likeness of all his portraits.

Downstairs at the office, I stop to talk to the curator, Edward W. Graham, who's expecting another tour group of a hundred children and fielding phone calls between my questions. He gets a request from the Philadelphia Zoo, which would like to borrow Audubon's painting of the eagle and the lamb for a zoological gala. The answer is no. There are too many canvas slashers out and about these days, the nightmare of every museum curator, here and abroad. He does not want to take the risk.

Another call comes from a distressed housewife who asks why there are blue jays in her yard every year and why do they fly at her when she goes near the nest. Ed Graham explains, with quiet patience, that birds migrate back to the same nesting area year after year, and if they fly at her, they are only trying to protect the nest and the eggs.

An earnest young woman with a sketchbook appears at the office door, ecstatic, her hands clasped at her breast. She has never seen the Audubon bird engravings before, could she copy them in her sketchbook, is that allowed? Of course, Ed Graham tells her, and he suggests that she should also see the originals in the New-York Historical Society. Yes, she vows. She'll go to New York to see them next week. No, she changes her mind. She'll go tomorrow!

Meanwhile, Ed Graham has told me that the only pieces of furniture in the house that actually belonged to the Audubons are the

Engraving of John James Audubon, by H. B. Hall after the portrait by Henry Inman. *Courtesy of The New-York Historical Society, New York City*

couch in the Victorian bedroom upstairs and the sideboard in the front room on the ground floor. Both had been among the furnishings of the house in New York City where Audubon died. The sideboard had come to Mill Grove by pure luck. Two of his granddaughters had given it to the owner of a New York City storage company. (In payment of a storage debt, perhaps?) From there, it eventually surfaced at the Illinois Audubon Society, whose members turned it around, out of the goodness of their hearts, and shipped it back east to Mill Grove.

The phone rings again, and through the office window I can see the eager faces of the next troop of school children, who have just arrived and are crowding in the dooryard. I leave Ed Graham to his tasks and go to find Michael.

MH   Audubon remembered the "rocky banks" of the Perkiomen with great fondness. He had a hideout in a rock cave at the water's edge, and he often went there to draw and read. Phoebes shared the cave spring and summer, which gave him a chance to study them closely, and with them he did the first North American "bird-banding" anyone knows about; he tied common and silver thread around their legs, so when the marked birds came back after a winter he knew he was looking at the same phoebes he had studied the summer before. It would be nice to sit in the mouth of that cave today, watching the Perkiomen, with phoebes coming and going over our heads. But the cave was broken up in Audubon's lifetime, along with much of the other stone along the banks, for the sake of a new milldam at Mill Grove. There's still a dam across the creek below the house, and maybe chunks of the cave are in it even now.

He also spoke of "sweet flowers" in bloom, and of the kingfisher perched, and of the osprey and bald eagle flying over the Perkiomen. Many sweet flowers indeed were in bloom today on the shore below the house. (Daisies and May apples I already recognize. Mary tells me the names of others as we come upon them: sweet cicely, waterleaf, yellow mustard, forget-me-nots, speedwell, dame's rocket, chickweed, hen-bit, the last of the spring beauties.) But the chattering kingfisher is now a rarity here, and the osprey and bald eagle are long gone from the Mill Grove neighborhood, except during migration. A water-pumping station stands where the mill was, and high-voltage

Mill Grove as a Wetherill farm in the 1830s, from the far side of the Perkiomen. Oil on wood panel, by Thomas Birch. *Courtesy of The New-York Historical Society, New York City*

powerlines crackle above the creek, carrying electricity to and from God knows where.

Memory is disrupted, dislocated by such transitions, and the historian's *illusions* of memory—attempted empathy—even more so. Mary and I are being a bit ridiculous, I think. Here we are, confronted by this dashing French popinjay and beau of the ball, a young man we don't recognize, and we're trying to materialize him in this changed setting by discovering signs, symbols, tokens, looking for particular birds. I even find in a bush beside the creek a bird that Audubon says he never saw at Mill Grove—the beautiful little Canada warbler, gray back, bright yellow front with a necklace of black streaks. So much for helpful coincidence.

MD   Down the road from Mill Grove we stop at the entrance to Fatland Ford, once the Bakewell farm where Audubon met Lucy Bakewell, his wife-to-be. He was nineteen, she was turning eighteen, and he fell in love with her on the spot: "my heart followed every one of her footsteps." The Bakewells, who had recently emigrated to America, were English Quakers, well born and of an intellectual turn of mind; a loving, close-knit, and disciplined family in which emo-

Mill Grove from the far side of the Perkiomen. *MH*

tional displays were frowned upon. On one occasion when the Bakewell children were very young and their father found them weeping over a book called *Simple Susan,* he threw the book into the fire.

Audubon's careless existence at Mill Grove was the antithesis of life at Fatland Ford where everyone in the household had appointed tasks and took part in the farmwork. William Bakewell was not pleased at the romance between his daughter and the frivolous young Frenchman next door. He found Audubon aimless and the parties—skating, music, singing, dancing—"Noisyish." But for Lucy, who was not a beauty—plain of face, though pretty of figure—it must have been a courtship beyond her most extravagant imaginings. Out of the woods comes the handsomest, most dashing young man in the county to lay his heart at her feet and release her from the cool orderliness of her father's household into a world of emotions expressed, passions and enthusiasms indulged.

Audubon's father in France did not approve of this romance either and wrote his business agent in America for information on the Bakewells, "their manners, conduct, means, and reason for being in that country. . . . Tell these good people that my son is not at all rich and that I can give him nothing if he marries in his present condition." Both fathers, however, were later reconciled to the match. John James and Lucy would be married in four years.

The Fatland Ford farm eventually became Wetherill property too, and the last member of their family to live there was Henry Wetherill, a physician of considerable distinction. He went with Peary on one of the Arctic expeditions and attended Mrs. Peary when her daughter was born at the expedition's base camp in Greenland. At the turn of the century, he worked in Panama on the control of yellow fever and malaria. In his old age, Dr. Wetherill became the family eccentric, camping out in the kitchen wing at Fatland Ford and driving away any relatives he wasn't keen on. We heard one story about a cousin arriving unannounced with her Garden Club friends to view the boxwood. Dr. Wetherill leaned out a window, brandishing a shotgun, and told her to pack up her friends and leave. Immediately. One terrified lady in the party is said to have taken Dr. Wetherill's outrage at face value; she ran to the car, dove into the back seat, and hid under a lap robe.

So Fatland Ford—like Mill Grove—seems to us to be very much

a Wetherill house. Even more so, in fact, because the porticoed building we see from the road is not the original house that Audubon knew when he courted Lucy. It was entirely rebuilt by one of the Wetherills in 1842. The grounds, of course, bear no resemblance to the way they must have looked when this was the Bakewell farm, or even when Dr. Wetherill was in charge in his last, erratic years. They are tidied and clipped and mowed without mercy. None of the green, inviting look, the natural landscaping, that you'll find at Mill Grove.

The present owner, one of the top brass in Philadelphia politics, has put up a sign at the end of the drive announcing that this is a private home. No visitors, please. They've been plagued by Audubon pilgrims, and probably still are, despite the sign—people who will knock on the door, anyway, to ask if they can have "just a teeny look around. . . ." We grant the owner of Fatland Ford his right to privacy and move on.

LOUISVILLE, KENTUCKY

1807–1810

MH In August 1807, Audubon left Mill Grove for the West. With him went Ferdinand Rozier, a stolid, bourgeois Frenchman eight years his senior and now his business partner—an arrangement made by their fathers during a visit home by John James. The partners had sailed together from France bearing false passports to elude Napoleon's conscription officers; it was the second time young Audubon had escaped the clutches of the draft—the "snears of the eagle" he called it.

At Mill Grove, Audubon and Rozier had settled the Audubon family's affairs as best they could. Rozier had gone to work for French importers in Philadelphia for a few months, while Audubon clerked for Lucy Bakewell's uncle in New York City. With that brief experience under their belts, the partners decided to go west to Louisville and make their fortune.

"We had marked Louisville as a spot designed by nature to become a place of great importance," Audubon explains. The "design" of nature, specifically, was the Falls of the Ohio—a rapids in which the river dropped more than twenty feet in two miles, roaring over limestone ledges that made the passage hazardous in all but high water. The Falls of the Ohio was the gateway between the upriver towns west of the Appalachian chain and the nearest convenient seaport, New Orleans. Even when there was enough water in the river to allow navigation of the falls, boats bound down from Pittsburgh usually needed local pilots to steer them through the chutes safely. Upbound boats couldn't go beyond the foot of the rapids under any circumstances, so they put into shore there; goods and passengers were carried around and loaded on other boats above. Downbound boats might be stopped above the rapids by low water, requiring a transfer the other way. So two pairs of towns grew up, one on each shore, and lived off the traffic. This center of commerce designed by nature was also a natural jumping-off point for overland travel to the interior—into Kentucky on one side and the territory of Indiana on the other. One foreign visitor wrote that in 1807, when Audubon and Rozier arrived, Louisville contained one hundred and twenty houses, was the county town and port of entry, and "carries on ship- and boat-building with considerable spirit." A little boom

The Falls of the Ohio in 1796. The beginings of Louisville are slightly right of center, and the site of Shippingport is at the lower right. *Filson Club, Louisville, Kentucky*

town, in short, with a bright future. (Had Audubon had any foresight, he told his sons later, "I might never have published the 'Birds of America'; for a few hundred dollars laid out in that period, in lands or town lots near Louisville, would, if left to grow over with grass . . . , have become an immense fortune." Prospects for their business looked so good to him that Audubon went back to Mill Grove in 1808, married Lucy, and brought her across the mountains and down the Ohio.

Audubon made that journey often and always loved it. But Lucy, having traveled it on her wedding trip, complained of its length—it was about a thousand miles—and she particularly disliked the jolting carriage ride over the mountains. The stage went from Philadelphia to Lancaster along the Lancaster Pike, through great sweeps of rolling country, and then to Chambersburg, where the Alleghenies were confronted. "We cross[ed] the Cove Mountains," wrote Lucy, "the Allegany, the Laurel, the Sideling, and many others which are very stony and disagreable to pass though they are not mentioned in the maps." Audubon's partner, Rozier, for his part hated the flatboat voyage down the Ohio from Pittsburgh—a flatboat being a square-sided scow with a shelter for passengers and cargo; it had a long steering oar at the stern and perhaps one or two sets of oars at the bow. Rozier spoke of the "terrible monotony, hardships, and deprivations," and complained about bedding down on bare boards, and about passengers often having to jump into the cold river to help heave the flatboat off a sandbar.

The two-lane state road—Route 30—on which we crossed the mountains tends to follow the old stage road, and it is steep and hazardous still. Towns and villages are scattered along the way, but on the whole, little has happened to change the wild Alleghenies. It's impressive, particularly when one drives through after dark; *there are no lights,* one realizes—the mountains are uninhabited.

We come off the western slope to Pittsburgh—gray Pittsburgh in its dramatic setting among mountains' feet, with three rivers joining in front of it. (Talk about nature's design.) And now, for miles and miles westward, the Ohio River valley bears a magnificent and awesome industrial plant—the pillars of ten thousand smokestacks, flying columns of colored smoke, sharp utilitarian angles of brick and con-

crete piled, jumbled, packed, slammed into place, and snarled together by railroad lines and superhighways. The run on the river
west to Louisville is made by towboats shoving barges; to accommodate that traffic the river bed has been dammed, dredged, and
blasted. So the Ohio River and the steep headlands that enclose it on
its upper reaches are only an adjunct to the bang and toot and roar;
they are not the scene itself.

But approaching Cincinnati, the river's shore begins to show
more and more green. The crisis is over. Between cities the river
winds through farmland and woods and past pleasant rural towns.
The river loops north to Cincinnati, then south and southwest, bends
north to take a small bite out of Indiana at Madison, and dips down
again to Louisville—to what remains of the Falls of the Ohio, at the
Corps of Engineers' McAlpine Lock and Dam.

We come into Louisville from the south in mid-November, along
the Dixie Highway, route 31W, through not just a Miracle Mile, but
a Miracle Ten Miles—shopping centers and auto dealers and motels
and Crown Burgers and Dari-Whips and more shopping centers.
"Who *buys* all that stuff?" asks Mary. The struggling storekeepers
Audubon and Rozier would be astonished at what can be sold—and
how much of it—in what looks like the human race's last stages of
consumption.

Audubon might be somewhat less astonished to see how the land
around his Louisville has been changed. When he first arrived here,
it was dotted with ponds where black terns bred and wintering
waterfowl rested, but in his lifetime the draining and filling was well
underway. Louisville is now a sprawling city of 361,000 people. It long
ago outgrew and obliterated much that was here in the early 1800s
and is rapidly tearing up evidences of its more recent past, or paving
them over, or both. And still, like a piece of good, ripe cheese, it gives
off a more than faint aroma of quirkiness, of unquenchable eccentric
personality—as befits a town given birth and nurtured for years by
a quirk of nature, the Falls of the Ohio.

MD   There's no record of the location of the Audubon-Rozier
store, and the curator at the Louisville historical society presumes
that they rented space near the waterfront—the neighborhood
where the Audubons took up residence. JJA and Lucy were living as

boarders at the Indian Queen Hotel, an establishment that's long gone, of course, and faint in memory.

I find myself looking through Lucy's eyes at old Louisville. It was known as the Graveyard of the Ohio because of the high incidence of typhus, dysentery, tuberculosis, cholera, and unnamed "intermittent fevers." The main thoroughfare was described as a Slough of Despond, and laws were being made to clean up "street nuisances" —hog pens, dead animals, stable manure, slaughter houses, tanning yards. One section of the waterfront neighborhood was denounced as a sink of iniquity: gambling dens, brothels, saloons. In short, Lucy had not been carried off to a cabin in the woods in a picturebook wilderness.

In 1808, Lucy wrote a letter to an English cousin giving polite comments on the fertile land around Louisville, the gardens that had been laid out, the welcome shown them by the inhabitants, and she made a point of saying that she and John James could be as "private as they please at the Indian Queen." Michael, in his gentlemanly fashion, takes the lady at her word and assumes that Lucy was contented here. I don't agree. I read negatives, spoken and unspoken, in every line. Granted, there's no spark or spontaneity in any of Lucy's correspondence that I have seen. She was not an adventurous observer; she wrote without a shred of humor or high spirits and always in a highly moralistic and stilted manner. (Never put anything on paper that can't be read aloud at high noon in the public square.) The Louisville letter to her cousin is a masterpiece of understated disenchantment.

She begins with her gloomy account of their trip westward—the bad roads, the fatigues, the rain, dirty Pittsburgh ("the blackest looking place I ever saw"), high winds and seasickness on the flatboat— and then goes on to say that she doesn't know whether she will like Louisville or not, since they've been there only three weeks and do not yet have a house of their own; that she's alone most of the time at the Indian Queen, "as Mr. Audubon is constantly at the store"; that she'd enjoy having something to read while she's by herself, but "there is no Library or a book store of any kind"; and as a final note of gloom, she's had no letters from home since their arrival here. To compound her distresses, as we learn from JJA, Lucy and his business partner, Rozier, did not get along.

The Indian Queen was advertised as a "house of entertainment" that excelled any other in the western country. An inside view, however, given by an English visitor, Henry Bradshaw Fearon, does not award the hotel any such four-star recommendation. He complained of the sleeping arrangements for transients—four to eight in a room, with "no conveniences," and he went on to say: "The place for washing is in an open yard, in which there is a large cistern, several towels, and a negro in attendance. . . . The public rooms are a newsroom, a boot-room, in which the bar is situated, and a dining-room. The fires are generally surrounded by parties of about six, who gain and keep possession. The usual custom is to pace up and down the newsroom in a manner similar to walking a deck at sea. Smoking segars is practiced by all without exception. . . . A billiard table adjoins the hotel, and is generally well occupied. . . . I have not seen a book in the hands of any person since I left Philadelphia."

Lucy never did get a house of her own in Louisville, and I bet she hated every living breathing minute of it at the Indian Queen. Those "private-as-you-please" riverfront quarters would be their home for two years. Their first child, Victor Gifford Audubon, was born there. When she wrote in her letter of being alone much of the time, that was only the beginning. Audubon was often away on business trips (during long absences he put Lucy in the care of friends), but he was also off and away whenever the spirit moved him, on hunting trips with his new cronies, on searches for new birds—at any season, at any time of the day or night—and one can imagine the impatience, if not the downright anger, with which each of his outings was received on the home front, where Rozier was doggedly minding the store and Lucy was undoubtedly feeling seduced and abandoned—yet one more time—back at the Indian Queen.

Needless to say, one does not pitch a tent in Louisville these days. We have found an Indian Queen of our own—Leon's Motel on the Dixie Highway. A sign in the office announces their rates without mincing words: *$5 for 2—Out by Midnight. $8 for 2—All Night. $10 for 3 or more.* In our room, the initials ED and JK have been carved into the cork-tiled ceiling; JR and BC have been written in candle-smoke. Before we leave, we'll put our initials on the ceiling too. In lipstick, perhaps. (Let's establish some traditions around here.)

On the bathroom wall a sign testifies that this building is protected by the John Allpest Exterminating Co. The sign, however, is vividly out of date. There are scuttling roaches in the bathroom, and I awoke this morning to see a large, insoucient fellow strolling home to a nook behind the mirror. My first thought: Get a can of bug spray. My second thought: Leave them lie. Spraying behind the mirror could open up God-knows-what Pandora's box of nesting roaches.

There are no blankets at Leon's Motel, but there is heat. Nonstop steam heat pouring out of the radiator, and no valve with which to turn it off. For a breath of air, I cranked open the bathroom window last night. It opened with a dull thonk onto a wooden wall and the sound of conversation. Three slow-speaking, down-country voices were discussing how and when and where to cash checks. (Couldn't determine if this were a legitimate enterprise or not.) I tried the window over the radiator. It too opened onto a black void with a dull thonk against a wooden wall. I began to feel as though we were trapped on the set of Sartre's *No Exit.*

I then tried the front window, which opened to the outside world and fresh air. The first thing today, I stepped around the corner to find out what the devil had been built across the inside wall of our room. Ah ha. Leon's motel was originally a single row of rooms that was enlarged by the simple expedient of adding a second row back to back with the first row, thus blocking off the inside windows right down the line. From what we can hear of activities next door, they're cooking in their room. So are we—our propane, one-burner stove as an impromptu kitchen for breakfasts and suppers. I'd guess that the management doesn't give a damn.

Neither of us enjoys big city research ("Let's try to get out of here in three days," says Michael) and we drive into Louisville each morning with dread. Signs that catch my eye en route: The Kentucky Mushroom Company, Black Walnut Fudge, Whisky By The Drink (lots of these), a neon flasher at a chicken and fish parlor—NOW FRYING, The Sweet Leaf Primitive Baptist Church. A hand-lettered sign in chalk on a black sidewalk billboard advertises HOG MAWS— Order your Xmas Country Hams—Save on Hamskins—KENTUCKY OYSTERS (a euphemism for hog testicles).

In the Louisville phone directory we find Audubon's name given to an animal hospital, a Baptist church, beauty salon, drugstore, an interior decorating firm, a "Bottle Shoppe," a fruit market, an elementary school, three gas stations, a Methodist church, and a used car lot.

On the city map of Louisville, we find Audubon Parkway, the Audubon Country Club, and a development called Audubon Park with street names that run the ornithological gamut: Eagle Pass; Osprey, Plover, Bobolink, Chickadee, Thrush, Wren, Teal, and Curlew Avenues; Oriole Court and Oriole Drive, which must create a continuous mix-up in the mail delivery; Cardinal Drive, Dove Lane, and two ringers from overseas—Linnet Road and Nightingale Playground.

"How about Rail Road?" I suggest to Michael.

"How about Tern Pike?" he counters. And the game is on: Coot Corners, Via Vultura, Albatross Alley, Rue Cuckoo, Junco Junction, Avenue des Avocets . . .

MH Audubon gives us no formal description of the famous rapids at Louisville, but he does tell a few nice stories about them. In winter, he says, when the Ohio was low, many of the dangerous limestone ledges were exposed and became islands. Canada geese put down there to rest because it looked safe, and Audubon liked to get to the river before dawn, hide in a pile of driftwood on one of the ledges jutting out from shore, and wait for a shot at geese. On one of those winter hunts, he watched two snowy owls in action. These big, floppy hunters—white flecked with brown and gray, feathered down to their claws, yellow eyes shaped like almonds—are native to the subarctic, and they often move into more temperate regions during winter. These migrations seem to be linked to the lemming cycle— lemmings march to the sea, a lot of snowy owls fly south; but the owls eat other things besides lemmings, so their motives are more complicated than that.

Audubon says they were regular winter visitors to the Falls of the Ohio; however, they were considered quite a curiosity in the States in his day and not much was known about them, which made his observations that winter morning particularly interesting: he saw the two owls *catch fish*.

The exposed limestone ledges were scoured out here and there into potholes, some of them quite large, and whenever the water level in the Ohio went down, fish would be left swimming in many of the potholes. According to Audubon, the owls he watched "invariably lay flat on the rock, with the body placed lengthwise along the border of the hole, the head also laid down, but turned towards the water. One might have supposed the bird sound asleep, as it would remain in the same position until a good opportunity of securing a fish occurred, which I believe was never missed; for, as the latter unwittingly rose to the surface, near the edge, that instant the Owl thrust out the foot next the water, and, with the quickness of lightning, seized it, and drew it out. The Owl then removed to the distance of a few yards, devoured its prey, and returned to the same hole; or, if it had not perceived any more fish, flew only a few yards over the many pots there, marked one, and alighted at a little distance from it. It then squatted, moved slowly towards the edge, and lay as before watching for an opportunity."

I see the scene as from a distance: a pink winter dawn, the knobby limestone ledges mostly out of water, the river tumbling through the three chutes, the young hunter crouched in his blind on the Kentucky shore, Canada geese stringing overhead, and two small dots of white poised beside pools of water.

Audubon remembers his friend Mr. Tarascon, a French emigré and successful businessman, setting up a cannon to shoot geese at the falls. Tarascon charged the gun with a load of rifle bullets, and killed birds on an island a quarter mile away, sometimes a dozen or more at a time. The geese quickly got wise and stopped using that island.

By the 1830s, Louisville was a big town, population more than 10,000, and though geese still rested on the islands in winter, says Audubon, there were very few of them. They fed at ponds nearby in the mornings, but they had become so shy that a single report of a gun would send them back to their midriver islands.

Shippingport was Louisville's "partner" community at the downstream end of the rapids. It was the French town—the "bois de Boulogne" of Louisville, as someone described it—with attractive watering places and dance halls as well as more mundane businesses,

Shippingport as sketched in 1828 by Captain Basil Hall, R.N., whom Audubon met in Edinburgh, and engraved by W. H. Lizars, who was Audubon's first engraver.

and a good many of Audubon's friends lived there. It's gone now. A canal was cut around the falls on the Kentucky side in 1830, went behind Shippingport, turned it into an island, and of course eliminated Shippingport's reason for being. Boat traffic no longer had to stop there. The town dwindled away.

In the 1920s, the Army Corps of Engineers modernized the old canal and built a dam at the falls. The dam comes across the river from Indiana above the rapids; about halfway to Kentucky it turns downstream for more than a mile along a ledge, funneling water between itself and Shippingport Island to a hydroelectric plant, where the dam zigs again to complete the crossing near the downstream end of the island. On the Louisville side of Shippingport Island is the rebuilt canal with its lock for lifting and lowering boats past the incline of the river. Tourists with a lot of patience can find the one unmarked road to the island and drive out to watch the boats and the strings of barges lock through. By pushing a button at lockside one can turn on a recording of a Corps of Engineers history of the Falls of the Ohio and of the navigation around it. Shippingport is not even mentioned. A restroom (the Corps might at least have named it the Shippingport Memorial Watercloset) marks the town and overlooks the river below the falls, or, rather, the *former* falls. The rapids have been so blocked and harnessed that little of the once magnificent spectacle remains—none of it on the Kentucky side of the river.

We have needed someone who could tell us about the falls, and we have found him—Leonard Brecher, a marvelous young-old man, aged seventy-six, stocky and short, face like an eagle's glancing brightly from under a porkpie hat. We stand with him on the one open bluff that still looks down on the falls, on the Indiana side. There's "Indian Chute," fed by a spillway in the dam, with a few boatloads of fishermen anchored or dashing their outboards against the current; limestone ledge covered with driftwood at the margins, pitted and puddled where silt has not settled thick enough for willows to root; in the middle of the river, more ledge, and running down its spine, the lengthwise zig in the dam. No more of the falls is visible than that.

"Yes, I remember a drought in 1905, 1910, somewhere in there," says Mr. Brecher, "before that dam was built, and you could walk across the river here, if you didn't mind getting your feet wet. At first the dam across the river, in this half-mile out from the Indiana side, had moveable steel plates, and they could lift out those plates with a derrick mounted on a special barge. That was how they controlled the depth of the upper pool. When the river was high, they'd open it up, and a lot of fish were swept down and got in the potholes, and all this silt and a lot of the driftwood was scoured away. Then when the water was low, they closed the dam and shut down the hydro plant, to build up the water above, for navigation. But the dam always leaked a little at the joints, anyway, so we had a steady trickle of water flowing over the reefs, and that meant there was algae and mosses and plankton on the rocks, and fresh water for the fish in the potholes, and a lot of shorebirds stopped off here on their migrations, to feed. The Corps modernized the dam in 1963. They encased all the moveable sections in concrete and put in electrically controlled gates, and the result was the dam was waterproof. The potholes dried up, the moss died, algae didn't grow, the plankton were gone, and the shorebirds didn't stop here any more. Well, I went to the chief of operations of the Corps here to see what could be done about that. I thought if they'd just put a few siphons over the dam out there on the reef, then we'd keep the rocks wet and the birds would come back. He agreed. You can see the siphons out there, and you can see that the reef is wet. The birds did come back. *Now,* what I'm trying to get them to do is really open up the gates here and let the water wash away all the silt where it's collected on the ledges. Those willows don't belong there. They grow up like weeds, give them half a chance." He pointed to thick groves of trees on the Indiana bank and in the lee of the dam out in midriver. "That's all reef under there," he said. "Ought to clear that out."

He tells us how he got interested in birds, as a boy in Louisville. He saw his first robin, didn't know what it was, had to look it up to find out, and in the act of looking it up he was hooked—as simple as that. He used to come to the falls in the old days, bringing food for a cookout on the ledges, and watched the night herons feed at the potholes. Audubon says he *never* saw a black-crowned night heron while he was in Kentucky, or even heard of one, and seems to have found yellow-crowned night herons only in the south. On the other hand, Mr. Brecher has never seen a snowy owl at the Falls of the Ohio.

When we shake hands goodbye, he says wistfully, "If I were younger, I'd like to traipse along with you." He'd be good company too.

We drive around Clarksville, Indiana, looking for General George Rogers Clark's house or some sign of it. Clark established the first permanent white settlement at Louisville in 1778 as a base of operations against the British in the west. Audubon, who admired the doughty old Revolutionary warrior and liked listening to his stories, says the general invited him out to see the ospreys that nested on Clark's place before 1810. Twenty years or so later, Audubon adds, increasing population had "driven off the [ospreys], and few are now seen on the Ohio [except] during their migrations." I find a useful lesson in that. We come into crowded place that was once the edge of wilderness, and if we disapprove of the loss of wilderness there's a temptation to blame someone we can see *now* and shout at, as if the change had taken place just in the last few years, but in fact the damage was being done at the very moment that the first cabin went up, generations ago.

On the top of an old levee at the edge of Clarksville we find an historical marker: General Clark lived here. An anachronism—not in this warren of side streets, I think; surely not here.

MD   The next day: Though Shippingport is gone and to all purposes forgotten and General Clark's estate across the river reduced to a plaque on a levee, I feel better about Louisville this afternoon. It has not been entirely leveled, re-leveled, and rebuilt. One Audubon landmark survives, handsomely—Locust Grove, the farm-estate of Major William Croghan, an Irish-born veteran of the American Revolution, who was married to General Clark's sister and was another of JJA's fast friends. He came here often to visit and brought Lucy too, upon occasion.

Locust Grove is in the Indian Hills section to the north, now a posh suburb in the country with winding roads that follow the lay of the land, lots of space and grace, and a number of old estates not yet subdivided. The house, built of brick in 1790, stands on a considerable acreage of open, rolling fields, and the flavor of the place, the gardens, and the old trees, must have been much the same as it was at Mill Grove and Fatland Ford, and it must have sent Lucy Audubon, trapped as she was at the Indian Queen, into bouts of passionate homesickness. We came to visit, however, on the wrong day. The house, an historic site, was closed, but we prowled the grounds. On the back verandah, I could peek into a window and admire a pewter jug of bittersweet on the corner of a desk, but there's no porch across the front of the house, and I didn't dare climb up to look into the parlor windows for fear Locust Grove was wired and I'd set off an explosion of burglar alarms. Everyone who was anyone was entertained here. Besides Audubon, the historic marker names Burr, Clay, Jackson, Lewis and Clark, Monroe, and Zachary Taylor, who was a Louisville boy. He grew up in a log cabin on Beargrass Creek, then in the country on the outskirts of town.

MH   Beargrass Creek was also on our Audubon landmark list; in "A Kentucky Barbecue," one of his essays of frontier life, he describes an Independence Day celebration held on the banks of the Beargrass. (It is possibly the worst piece Audubon ever wrote and is full of "comely fair ones" and their "sturdy lovers" on "prancing steeds" —just awful.) The creek has been diverted from its original bed and now runs into the Ohio near the Louisville Yacht Basin, ostensibly a rural situation—woodlands and overhanging boughs—but the water is so polluted, Mr. Brecher told us, that no birds will nest there. Meanwhile, the former mouth of Beargrass Creek is buried—filled in, cemented, dominated by a junkyard where old automobiles are pressed into cubes of scrap metal. Walls of metal bales line the riverfront awaiting shipment.

MD   Audubon's essays on birds are full of first-person anecdotes and offer a trove of place names and the names of people he knew, which often don't show up in any of his other writings. Michael, in one of those valiant projects that overtake historians and researchers, has gone through the seven volumes of the American edition of *The Birds of America* and indexed the names of people and places, from Labrador to Montana, from the Florida Keys to Houston. The index comes to 1200 file cards. Under *KENTUCKY,* we pull a card headed "Young's Inn, West Point, Ky. Volume V, page 27." The reference is in the essay on the passenger pigeon.

Audubon tells us that one day when he was on his way home from a business trip, he stopped to eat at "YOUNG'S inn at the confluence of the Salt river with the Ohio," and as he waited for dinner, legions of pigeons flew overhead "with a front reaching far beyond the Ohio on the west, and the beech-wood forests directly on the east of me. . . . Before sunset I reached Louisville. . . . The pigeons were still passing in undiminished numbers, and continued to do so for three days in succession. . . . The banks of the Ohio were crowded with men and boys, incessantly shooting at the pilgrims, which there flew lower as they passed the river. Multitudes were thus destroyed. For a week or more, the population fed on no other flesh than that of Pigeons, and talked of nothing but Pigeons."

The passenger pigeon is now extinct. How about Young's Inn?

We followed JJA's directions to the confluence of the Salt and the Ohio and found the building still standing on the river bank in the little town of West Point, about twenty-five miles south of Louisville. The original house is no longer *visible,* however. It's encased in a new skin of white aluminum clapboard siding, with contemporary windows and a square-columned, Mount-Vernonesque portico across the front.

As Michael and I, puzzled by the brand-new appearance of the old inn, were milling around in the driveway, a short, round, elderly gentleman came out the door to get the morning paper. At that moment, in fact, I was standing on his lawn, so it seemed only polite to explain ourselves.

"Of course!" he exclaimed. "Audubon was most certainly here. This was Young's Inn. I played the part of James Young in our bicentennial pageant. James Young was my great-great-great-grandfather. Please—come in, come in!"

Thus we met Mr. and Mrs. William Roberts, who gave us a cordial welcome and treated us to a thumbnail sketch of local history. James Young settled here first in a log cabin and then built the present house in 1795. He ran two ferry services, one across the Ohio, the other across the Salt, as well as keeping his inn. Mr. Roberts had a list of his great-great-great-grandfather's 1807 prices—18¢ for half a pint of peach brandy or whiskey, a hot meal for 36¢, a cold meal for 24¢, a night's lodging for 12¢, and pasturage for your horse for twelve hours, also 12¢.

They told us that Audubon was there often, according to family legend—that he used to come down from Louisville to hunt raccoon and possum with the Young boys. And Jenny Lind, the Swedish Nightingale, stayed there when she came through Kentucky on a concert tour. She stood in an open window of the diningroom to sing for the townsfolk, who gathered on the lawn to listen, and Mr. Roberts' great-aunt used to tell about it. She remembered it well. 1851 it was.

Young's Inn figured in the Civil War, as headquarters for the

Young's Inn about 1903, with five of his descendants, ranging from a grand-daughter to a great-great-grandson. *Courtesy of Richard A. Briggs, a great-great-great grandson*

Union Army on this front, and one day as General Sherman stepped out the door, a rifleman with Morgan's Raiders, lying in ambush in the woods along the Salt, took a shot at him. The shot missed and buried itself in the wood beside the front door. When Mr. Roberts put the aluminum siding on the house, he cut a hole over the spot, so you can look in and see the mark of the bullet in the old clapboard underneath.

James Young's grave lies across the way in an overgrown ceme-tery that now rests between the railroad tracks and the Dixie High-way. He was the moving force in the creation of the first Louisville-Nashville turnpike, and the bridge that crosses the Salt is the James Young Bridge, built in 1950 and dedicated to his memory as a "pio-neer Kentuckian."

Before we left, Mr. Roberts brought out a 1903 photograph of the house—a traditional American colonial building, four-square, direct, and appealing. The only change since JJA's day was a small ginger-bread porch added in the Victorian years.

Back in town there was one more rewarding moment. A fragment of a giant beech tree is kept in a glass case on the second floor of the Filson Club, Louisville's historical society. The beech had once stood on the old trail that led from the Falls of the Ohio to the Green River, in an area that later became Iroquois Park, and Mr. Brecher could remember when the tree was *in situ,* long before it rotted out and was cut down in 1932. Carved into the cross section that's preserved in the glass case is a bravura message I had always believed to be a frontier myth—the sort of warmed-over Americana that has G. Washington in children's picture books standing about in buckled shoes and a peruke with his hatchet in his hand and a flattened cherry tree at his feet. But the message was indeed carved into the trunk of the beech and is as true as tomorrow morning:

D. Boone

kill a bar

1803

MH Alexander Wilson came to Louisville for a few days in 1810. Wilson was a transplanted Scot whose home was now Philadelphia; he was nineteen years older than Audubon, and he was engaged in producing and selling the first comprehensive work ever published on North American birds. This highlights an important fact about Audubon: he was studying and painting birds at a time when very little was known and less had been published about them on this side of the Atlantic. We can go off into the woods with a field guide in each pocket and be fairly sure (after some practice) that we'll be able to identify most of the birds we see. But Alexander Wilson and John James Audubon, trying to sort out the hundreds of species around them, had in effect to write and illustrate their own field guides, doing a lot of work by trial and error, and discovering birds that no one had noticed before—or at least no *white* man had noticed. It didn't help that any given species might have several local names, or that immigrants gave European names to American birds that looked similar to what they were familiar with. Medieval beliefs were still current; it was said, for example, that swifts and swallows didn't migrate south in the fall but hibernated in hollow trees and in the mud at the bottoms of lakes. In Europe, ornithology was still a young science, but in North America it was practically brand new.

Wilson and Audubon met in Louisville; Audubon was known as the local bird nut, after all, and Wilson was looking for leads to new birds and for new subscribers to his work. Audubon didn't subscribe; he claimed long afterward that he was about to put his name on the dotted line when Rozier remonstrated in French to the effect that the subscription price, $120, was a lot of money to lay out when Audubon himself knew more about birds and painted them better than Wilson. So vanity interceded, Audubon said, and besides, he went on, Rozier was right in a way: "[E]ven at that time, my collection was greater than his." The explanation is not Audubon at his most attractive. He added that he showed Wilson his paintings, allowed him to borrow a few that were of birds new to Wilson, and at some point took Wilson on a birding tour around Louisville.

Their different impressions of this brief encounter would generate angry debate a few years later, after Wilson had died and Audubon's work was beginning to compete. Wilson partisans, citing Wilson's diary, downgraded Audubon's hospitality and contributions of information. Audubon was hurt that certain scientific debts had not been acknowledged in Wilson's published text—forgetting, surely, that his visitor must have viewed him as a talented but junior and lighthearted *hobbyist,* who was not to be taken seriously.

I find it hard to fault Wilson if he did form such an impression. The Audubon *we* see in Louisville is a young man playing at making a living while working at being . . . what? Not a scientist certainly. Not a serious artist either. Drawing and studying birds was a gentleman's indulgence, more *fun* than running a store. To put him in the rosiest light possible, he was irrepressibly larky, and even when he wrote about this period, nearly thirty years later, the larkiness came on him again: "[W]e had many goods, and opened a large store . . . , which went on prosperously when I attended to it; but birds were birds then as now, and my thoughts were ever and anon turning toward them as the objects of my greatest delight. I shot, I drew, I looked on nature only; my days were happy beyond human conception, and beyond this I really cared not. . . . All the sportsmen and hunters were fond of me, and I became their companion; my fondness for fine horses was well kept up, and I had as good as the country—and the

Audubon did this stiff little pastel at the "Chute de L'Ohio" on July 1, 1808. Compare it to his later drawings elsewhere in the book. The coloring of the original may have changed with time, but it is so ambiguous that the species cannot be identified with any certainty. Many years later JJA used the drawing as model for an immature yellow warbler (Plate LXV, "Rathbone's Warbler," in the *Birds*). *Courtesy of The New-York Historical Society, New York City*

country was Kentucky—could afford." One thinks of Lucy, closeted with the baby Victor at the Indian Queen, waiting for a house of her own, while Audubon bought horses.

"I seldom passed a day without drawing a bird, or noting something respecting its habits, Rozier meantime attending the counter. I could relate many curious anecdotes about him, but never mind them; he made out to grow rich, and what more could *he* wish for? . . .

"None of [the merchants crowding into Louisville] were, as I was, intent on the study of birds, but all were deeply impressed with the value of dollars. Louisville did not give us up, but we gave up Louisville. I could not bear to give the attention required by my business, and which, indeed, every business calls for, and, therefore, my business abandoned me."

An odd narrative that—not only larky but also littered with puzzles and nonsequiturs and Monday morning quarterbacking. This fellow Audubon is a good deal more complicated than we thought. In any event, a few months after the visit from Wilson, the partners packed up and moved farther west. We are right on their heels.

JJA [*From an autobiographical sketch written for his sons*] Rozier and myself . . . became discouraged at Louisville, and I longed to have a wilder range; this made us remove to Henderson, one hundred and twenty-five miles farther down the fair Ohio. We took there the remainder of our stock on hand, but found the country so very new, and so thinly populated the commonest goods only were called for. I may say our guns and fishing-lines were the principal means of our support, as regards food.

John Pope, our clerk, who was a Kentuckian, was a good shot and an excellent fisherman, and he and I attended to the procuring of game and fish, while Rozier again stood behind the counter.

Your beloved mother and I were as happy as possible, the people round loved us, and we them in return; our profits were enormous, but our sales were small, and my partner . . . suggested that we remove to St. Genevieve, on the Mississippi.

MD One of the most famous quotations in Audubon lore is a brief, bitter remark that Lucy made to her sister. "I have a rival in every bird," she said. So it would seem, but that was an oversimplification. There was more than a rivalry of birds to claim JJA's attentions and there was more than his footloose disposition to draw him away.

Audubon was in love with all of North America. He once wrote to Lucy from Europe that his eyes filled "with big tears" when he thought of America and her beautiful forests. When

Rozier proposed a reconnaissance trip to Ste. Genevieve, Missouri, I suspect it was the lure of a journey into new territory that caught JJA's fancy. Not the business possibilities to the northwest. One can imagine his excitement, JJA fired up to get going. Tomorrow, today, now!

Ste. Genevive was three hundred and twenty-five miles away. They would travel by keelboat downstream on the Ohio and upstream on the Mississippi. Winter was closing in, but no matter. The expedition was on. Lucy, barely settled in a log cabin (JJA liked to emphasize that it was a cabin, not a log house), was farmed out with her infant son at the home of Henderson friends, where she helped to pay her way by tutoring their children. Audubon, with Rozier at his coattails, bustled off in the dead of December. Their boat left Henderson in a heavy snowstorm. The trip proved to be a glorious romp for JJA, a bone-freezing hell for Rozier, and, ultimately, the end of their partnership.

MH   The "stores" he and Rozier took with them included three hundred barrels of whiskey, some dry goods, and gunpowder. With all that, it has been assumed, they intended to set up shop in Ste. Genevieve. However, there is a slight complication, ignored by all of Audubon's biographers.

The "patron," as he calls him, or *patroon* of their keelboat—the captain—was evidently a French-Canadian named Lorimier, who traded as far as the Great Lakes—up into fur country, in other words. And Ste. Genevieve, where they were bound, was populated by French-Canadians, many of whom doubtless had connections in the fur trade themselves. So the fact that a large part of the Audubon-Rozier stock was three hundred barrels of whiskey has interesting implications. Mary supposes that Audubon's longing for far horizons was the generating force for this winter expedition—that he could and should have waited until spring. Granted, he would start champing at the bit as soon as the idea came up. But I suggest that the generating force was a desire to get the whiskey to Ste. Genevieve before the spring thaw; the fur-traders there would head north as soon as the ice was out of the rivers, and they would pay well for trading whiskey to take with them—whiskey that, along with small-pox and syphilis, was the scourge of the Indians of the Mississippi watershed.

MD   We pick up their tracks in southern Illinois, in and around the triangle of land where the Ohio and the Mississippi converge—the Meeting of the Waters. Arriving early in November, about a month ahead of Audubon and Rozier, we find an unmarked, nearly empty campground twenty miles to the north of the river junction in a state conservation area on Horseshoe Lake—from dusk until dawn, a roar of Canada geese, thousands of them in their island roost less than half a mile away. (They sound like the roar of a crowd at a distant stadium.) In the morning and late afternoon, honking vees of geese pass overhead on the way to their feeding grounds. Occasionally we see a bullet-hole in a wing—a white circle in the dark silhouette against the sky. The nearby town of Olive Branch, Illinois, advertises itself as the Goose Capital of the World, and the local bar is The Goose Pit—where we stopped for a beer and Michael unlimbered his pool game for a couple of solo warm-ups. No one asked to join him. Folks in Olive Branch are happy to talk to newcomers, to tell the story of their lives, loves, and hard times, but they don't seem to take to playing pool with strangers.

Around the lake—farmland, swampland, woodland, and hunting lodges. The goose season opens in a few weeks. By then, says the ranger, the open fields around our campground will be full of geese, and after the season is over, the eagles will arrive. "You should see 'em," he tells us. "Five or six of 'em at a time fighting over crippled birds! We'll get thirty or forty balds. Goldens, too."

Our only neighbors at the campground are a Michigan couple, sixtyish, who live in a Hy-Lander camper and are migrating to their wintering grounds on the back roads of the Texas Gulf coast. Horseshoe Lake has been one of their stopovers for years. He and I first meet at the water faucet, each with our buckets, and he tells me about the handpump that used to draw on the well here, and you could get water year round, even after weeks of hard frost. But the powers-that-be decided that a handpump was too old-fashioned, too much trouble to use, so the system was modernized. "Now," says he, "they have to disconnect the pipe each winter because the damfool faucet freezes up." "Well," says I, "that's progress." "That's right," says he, "we're progressing backwards every day."

Our green pop-tent is set up in the shelter of a grove of young sycamore and sweetgum. We have a mockingbird, crickets, a white-throated sparrow singing shakily, and faint towboat whistles on the distant Mississippi. From our campfire the sweet and pungent smell of woodsmoke. Chicken wings crackle in the skillet. Our neighbors have gone fishing for large-mouth bass (minnows for bait), their little yellow boat slipping away through the towering rusty-gray cypress trees in the shallows. A splish-splash of oars, and they are gone. The sunset, a picture-postcard crimson, shimmers on the lake and the cypress trees turn pink. We settle down (our front paws in our sleeves like cats) to watch the day's dying.

Within striking distance of Horseshoe Lake are four places we want to see. Cache Creek, where the Audubon-Rozier expedition camped in 1810. An unnamed pond across the Ohio where JJA went swan hunting with a party of Shawnees. The Meeting of the Waters. And Tawapatee Bottom on the Mississippi, where the Audubon-Rozier expedition went into winter quarters for six weeks when the river froze over.

MH "John James Audubon was one of the most interesting and most annoying of American travel writers in the nineteenth century," remarked the historian John Francis McDermott. "He was more widely acquainted with the American scene than most men in his time but in his published works he often skillfully concealed his experiences. Like many another nineteenth century man who fancied himself as a literary person, he chose to present fact as fiction and equally often depicted fiction as fact." McDermott was commenting specifically on Audubon's earliest published recollections of the expedition from Henderson to Ste. Genevieve. Those recollections, titled "Journey Up the Mississippi," appeared in a British publication, *The Winter's Wreath*, in 1829, and were evidently written down sometime during the preceding year. During the ten or so years *after* 1829, Audubon would write a good deal more about that trip, enlarging and probably embroidering the tale. The historian and biographer, faced with all the conflicting and contradictory details JJA eventually supplied, ends by flinging hands up in despair.

McDermott decided that the version of the Ste. Genevieve trip in *The Winter's Wreath*, having been written first, was the most likely to be accurate. I think that's arguable. But it also presents some of the richest material—however apocryphal some of it may be—and as we travel through the upper Mississippi and lower Ohio river valleys it is one of the accounts we depend on most.

JJA About the third day of our journey we entered the mouth of Cash Creek, a very small stream, but at all times a sufficient deep and good harbour. . . . We soon learned that the Mississippi was covered by thick ice, and that it was therefore impossible to ascend it. Cash Creek is about six miles above the confluence of the Ohio and Mississippi. . . . The point of land, between the Creek and the junction of the two rivers, is all alluvial and extremely rich soil, covered with heavy black walnut, ash, and pecan trees, closely tangled canes, and nettles that are in summer at least six feet high. It is overflowed by both rivers during their freshes.

The Creek, now filled by the overplus of the Ohio, abounded with fish of various sorts, and innumerable ducks, driven by winter to the south from the Polar Regions. Though the trees were entirely stripped of their verdure, I could not help raising my eyes towards their tops, and admiring their grandeur. The large sycamores with white bark formed a lively contrast with the canes beneath them; and the thousands of parroquets, that came to roost in their hollow trunks at night, were to me objects of interest and curiosity. About fifty families of Shawnee Indians had moreover chosen this spot for an encampment, to reap the benefit of a good harvest of pecan nuts; and to hunt the innumerable deer, bears, and racoons, which the same cause had congregated here. . . .

MD Cache Creek, when JJA knew it, emptied to the east into the Ohio. It now empties to the west into the Mississippi through a diversion channel constructed by the Corps of Engineers after the 1937 flood, one of the worst in history to strike this vulnerable corner of Illinois. We'd been told that part of the original creek bed still existed, mostly landlocked between two levees that run parallel to the Ohio.

It took a bit of finding, but we hit at last on a rough, rutted track leading through low scrubby woodlands and up to the top of the inner levee—the *old* levee that hadn't been high enough to hold the Ohio in 1937. The road looked impassable, so we left our car near an abandoned yellow school bus that sat rusting to dust in the weeds.

Halfway up the track, a four-door hardtop came grinding by, bearing three black ladies, their fishing gear, folding chairs, and a pretty child in a new pink parka who carried the bucket of worms. When we caught up with them, I remarked that my husband and I hadn't dared bring the car; the road looked too dangerous. "Honey," said the large, middle-aged lady. "If I couldn't *ride* in, I'd *never* get here."

Cache Creek, or what's left of it—a four-pronged green lagoon among the trees—lies in a deep gulch between the levees. The outer levee looms gigantically between the creek and the Ohio. At high water, floodgates are sometimes opened—iron doors as big as the gates to a King Kong cage—and the water and the supply of fish are replenished here.

We trail the ladies down to the shore. They set up as if by ritual, quickly and wordlessly, each at her own cove on the banks. They're fishing for "mudcats, channel cats, crappies, and buffalo," the young, slim one tells me. Other than that, they don't seem to be much given to communication. The sanctity of fishing, I tell myself. Or is it an uneasiness (suspicion, hostility) toward whites? Strangers? I feel that they'd rather not have us there at all in that autumn grove by the Cache lagoon, so after the first fish is landed (a big one, but I don't want to bother them again by asking what kind), Michael and I (by a tacit communication of our own) leave them to their fishing lines and their solitude.

We find our way, by car, to the gravel road that runs on top of the outer levee; far below us, the landlocked Cache on one side and the Ohio on the other. The road is narrow here, so I stay with the car in case it has to be moved to let someone else pass. Michael disappears toward the Ohio to look for the old mouth of the Cache.

MH Down the steep side of the levee, along a zigzagged trail used by the farmer whose patch of a soybean field, just harvested, lay at the bottom. Across the field and into the thick tangle of fallen trees and stickers and vines that borders the Ohio wherever agriculture and roads and rivers have not cleared the path. The remnant creek there twists and winds against more man-made high ground—the bed of the old New York Central line, long abandoned. Blowdowns, thigh-deep mats of vines and brambles clog the way up and have overcome the roadbed itself. I stumbled and scrambled and cussed my way over tree branches and through thickets of thorns, grabbed by vines, stuck by stickers, tripped by logs, blocked by brush piles. The railroad bed beneath the tracks is washed out in places, and although I was probably no more than half a mile from the car, I was becoming very conscious of being in effect lost, or potentially so— difficult to find if I should come a cropper. The tracks led out onto a rotting trestle that looked extremely shaky, and I left them to try the river bank. From there I could see what appeared to be the mouth of the creek, perhaps twenty or thirty feet wide. I photo- graphed it from where I stood and then fought my way back to the railroad bed, along it, down the other side to the creek, and finally —covered with stickers and sweat—out onto the furrowed, stubbled soybean field, the car sitting on the levee high above me.

JJA   On the second morning after our arrival, I heard a move- ment in the Indian camp, and having hastily risen and dressed my- self, I discovered that a canoe containing half a dozen squaws and as many hunters, was about to leave the Illinois for the [Kentucky] side of the river. I learned also that their object was to proceed to a large lake opposite, to which immense flocks of swans resorted every morning. These flocks are so numerous and strong, that it is, however incredible it may at first seem, a well-known fact, that they keep the lakes which they frequent open, merely by swimming upon them night and day.—Having obtained permission to join the party, I seated myself in the canoe, well supplied with ammunition and whis- key,—in a few moments the paddles were at work, and we swiftly crossed to the opposite shore. I was not much astonished, during our passage, to see all the labour of paddling performed by the squaws; for this feature of Indian manners was not new to me; but I was surprized to see that upon entering the canoe, the hunters laid down, and positively slept during the whole passage. On landing, the squaws, after securing the boat, proceeded to search for nuts, whilst the *gentlemen* hunters made the best of their way, through the *"thick and thin,"* to the lake. . . .

[W]hat a feast for a sportsman! There they lie, by hundreds, of a white or rich cream colour—either dipping their black bills in the water; or leaning backwards, and gently resting with one leg ex- panded, floating along and basking in the sunshine. The moment that these beautiful birds saw our videttes [the first scouts], they started up in immediate apprehension:—but the plan of our Indians drove the poor swans the nearer to their fate, the farther they retreated from either shore. Men were placed behind the trees, who knew how to take a dead aim, and every shot told. Being divided, three on one side and four on the other,—the former hid themselves; and when the birds flew from the latter, they alighted within good distance of those who had first alarmed them. What would those English *sportsmen*—who, after walking a whole day, and exploding a pound of powder, march home in great glee, holding a partridge by the legs, with a smile on their lips and a very empty stomach,—say to this day's devastation amongst the swans? I saw these beautiful birds floating on the water, their backs downwards, their heads under the surface, and their legs in the air, struggling in the last agonies of life, to the number of at least fifty—their beautiful skins all intended for the ladies of Europe.

The sport was now over;—the sun was nearly even with the tops of the trees—a conch was sounded, and after a while the squaws appeared, dragging the canoe, and moving about in quest of the dead game. It was at last all transported to the river's edge, and we were landed upon the Illinois bank again before dark. The fires were lighted—each man ate his mess of pecan nuts and bear's fat, and then stretched himself out, with feet close to the small heap of coal intended for the night. The females then began their work;—it was their duty to skin the birds. I observed them for some time, and then retired to rest, very well satisfied with the sports of this day—the 25th of December.

MH No one we've asked in the vicinity of Cache Creek or in Cairo—indeed, no one in southern Illinois, so far as our luck ran—has known anything about a lake on the far side of the Ohio River where swans used to winter. But map Number One of the Corps of Engineers' chartbook for the Lower Mississippi shows a string of lakes and ponds that must lie in one of the old meander beds of the rivers here: Axe Lake, Clear Lake, Fish Lake, Flat, Buck, Prairie, Grassy, First, and Second Lakes, Lost Pond, Flat Pond, Burnt Pond, and—for heaven's sake—*Swan* Pond. That's worth following up. We cross the Ohio into Kentucky just above the junction with the Mississippi, drive southeast for less than a mile and, following a sign to "Swan Lake," leave Route 51 for a dirt road; the first turnout there leads into a raggle-taggle picnic ground on the edge of the lake. One sign, leaning against a tree, pronounces this a fishing area and asks that people pick up after themselves—a request many people clearly have ignored. Another sign orders that one PAY HERE. Between them stands an odd structure that looks a little like a lifeguard's tower; whatever its function was, it seems to have been moved to its present post as a temporary measure, for it rests at a slight tilt and overlooks very little of the lake.

We get out to explore. As I wonder grimly if we are to be charged money for our visit to the scenic spot, a pickup truck appears on the dirt road behind us, and up rolls Joe Cummins, proprietor, a stocky gent of seventy-nine summers, wearing an old fedora, camouflage hunting jacket, and no teeth.

John James Audubon is not a well-known name in these parts, so Mary introduces us by saying that we're here to look at the birds and that we wondered where the name Swan Lake came from. With that, Mr. Cummins tells *us* the story of Audubon's swan hunt with the Shawnees and wheels into a rapid-fire description of the lay of surrounding land to prove that Swan Lake was *the* lake—*had* to be, in fact. He turns out to be not the slightest bit surprised at our project.

He says that his grandfather, Caleb Cummins, came down the Ohio in a johnboat from Newport, Kentucky—opposite Cincinnati— in 1882, and settled his family near Swan Pond. (Swan *Lake* is Joe Cummins' improvement. "Swan Pond sounded like a dirty, smelly, little pond, like in Florida," he tells us.) His father Dan, says Joe Cummins, remembered swans being on Swan Lake at least as late as 1882, when the family arrived.

Perhaps the most telling commentary on the career of the trumpeter swan in the United States is this: when Arthur Cleveland Bent, summarizer and synthesizer, sat down to write his essay on the trumpeter for the waterfowl segment (published in 1923) of his life histories of North American birds, he had to refer to Audubon, writing in the 1830s, in order to say much about the plumages, feeding habits, general behavior, and wintering of the bird. Audubon himself was an observer and perhaps a participant—at Swan Lake or near it—in the sort of "harvesting" enterprise that caused his commentaries to be treated as the best available a hundred years later. Swan feathers were used for trimming on dresses, hats, and fans; and swansdown became powderpuffs. The bird was also food. Audubon thought the flesh of the cygnet "pretty good eating" but the adult swan not so good; Edward Howe Forbush nearly a century later remarked that the "older birds are about as tough and unfit for food as an old horse." Even when inedible the big birds made fine targets and fine trophies. The trumpeter is the largest swan in the world, weighs as much as thirty-eight pounds and measures more than five feet long, sometimes as much as six feet; that is, if an average-size man held the head of an average-size, freshly shot trumpeter at about his collar level, the bird's feet would brush the ground. Its wingspan is eight to ten feet across. This is an enormous, elegant, snowy creature. Its voice, said Bent, has "the musical resonance of a French horn."

Later in JJA's winter's sojourn around the juncture of the Ohio and the Mississippi, JJA noted appearances that he described in his own essay on the species. "No sooner did the gloom of night become discernible through the gray twilight than the loud-sounding notes of hundreds of Trumpeters would burst on the ear; and as I gazed over the ice-bound river, flocks after flocks would be seen coming from afar and in various directions, and alighting about the middle of the stream . . . After pluming themselves awhile [remember, we are talking about birds that—standing wings folded—are about the height of an average North American twelve-year-old boy] they would quietly drop their bodies on the ice, and through the dim light I could yet observe the graceful curve of their necks, as they gently turned them backward, to allow their heads to repose upon the softest and warmest of pillows. Just a dot of black as it were could be observed on the snowy mass, and that dot was about half an inch of the base of the upper mandible, thus exposed, as I think, to enable the bird to breathe with ease. Not a single individual could I ever observe among them to act as a sentinel, and I have since doubted whether their acute sense of hearing was not sufficient to enable them to detect the approach of their enemies. The day quite closed by darkness, no more could be seen until the next dawn; but as often as the howlings of the numerous wolves that prowled through the surrounding woods were heard, the clanging cries of the swans would fill the air. If the morning proved fair, the flocks would rise on their feet, trim their plumage, and as they started with wings extended, as if racing in rivalry, the pattering of their feet would come on the ear like the noise of great muffled drums, accompanied by the loud and clear sounds of their voices. On running 50 yards or so to windward, they would all be on wing."

The scene speaks of wildness far beyond the experience of most Americans today. As human population grew and spread on the continent, the trumpeters were extirpated region by region, killed at all seasons of the year, even when they were nesting. In the 1880s, when Joe Cummins' father saw swans here on Swan Lake—if they were actually trumpeters and not the smaller whistling swans—he was seeing only the remnants of a population that was almost gone. In 1941, a census of the trumpeter swans remaining in the United States found only two hundred and eleven individuals, and in Canada it was estimated there might be four to six hundred still alive. Fortunately, the nadir for the trumpeter had been reached; various restoration and conservation efforts have since improved the situation somewhat. In the 1960s, trumpeters were discovered breeding in Alaska—by the thousands. It always was a bird that did best in the wilderness. It has not returned to Swan Lake, to Joe Cummins' knowledge, in his lifetime.

He owns 2100 acres in the area, most of it around Swan Lake and his other ponds, but some "up in the hills." He runs this place as a private hunting and fishing preserve. Every time the rivers flood the lowlands in here, they drown the ponds and stock them. A nice arrangement. So people come in and pay to fish, and a big fish fry is held here every Saturday night throughout the summer. The ponds and sloughs attract waterfowl too, thousands of them today—Canada geese, mallards, pintails, canvasbacks, ring-necked ducks, wigeon, black ducks, scaup; the birds prefer the quiet water to the rivers and all the barge traffic, and Joe Cummins plants millet near the lake—not exactly baiting, but the nearest legal thing to it. He's built hunting blinds in strategic spots, and he rents these for $500 to $800 a season, not including the guide fees. "Lots of doctors come down," he says. "They have a lot of money, those doctors. A lot of money's going through their hands."

He tells us "The Government" wanted to take his land from him, make it into a wildlife refuge. He thinks poorly of "The Government"; most of the time government just plows you under, he believes, but this refuge idea didn't get very far. He'd already *made* it a refuge, he said. So no thanks, Uncle. " 'You sue, you'll have to take me to court right here in town,' I told 'em. And they'd never win there, you know." He says he learned to mistrust government in the days of "that De-lay-no Roosevelt and that whatchacaller, Elle-ay-nor Roosevelt," when, says Joe Cummins, they started "building up the coloreds." And now his complaint is about death taxes. That hurts him, just getting onto that subject. His wife of fifty-nine years died a little more than a year ago. They'd worked together for a long time —first in the tobacco business, and then in this hunting and fishing business, and she was as good at the job as he was. And, my, he does miss her: the confident, back-country storyteller's voice wavers as he mentions her. Then when she died, good God, he'd had to pay inheritance taxes on her share of their possessions—$70,000 just to keep the property. He shakes his head in dismay and wonder.

Well, would we care to drive around with him, see a little more of the place? We sure would; we climb in alongside in the cab of his pickup, and he winds us through the woods to the nearest blinds. We talk about the different kinds of ducks out in the middle of Swan Lake. His favorite eating ducks are the blue-winged and green-winged teal, he says. (He would hear an enthusiastic second from Mr. Audubon, who thought the green-winged teal was "probably the best of any of its tribe," and the blue-wing's flesh was "tender and savory.") After that, says Joe Cummins, he likes canvasback. Mary remarks that canvasback was George Washington's favorite. "That's right, that's *right,*" says Joe Cummins. It seems he's a history reader. "When you're making your living in tabacka, it would break your heart with nothin' to do but just sit there and watch it grow." So he took up reading history while the tobacco was growing.

We are back at Swan Lake, still sitting in the front seat, chatting, when he reaches across us, opens the glove compartment, and takes out a Smith and Wesson revolver, an old one. He breaks it, spins the magazine to count the bullets; . . . three, four; snaps it shut. It seems there's a story about the pistol. One day when Joe Cummins was about eight years old, his parents took him to a Barnum & Bailey carnival. That would be 1904 or so. Buffalo Bill Cody was in the carnival—"Beard down to here," says Joe Cummins, holding his hand below his chest. Cody had a trick where someone would throw three glass balls in the air at once, and he would shatter them with three shots from his rifle. Dan Cummins, Joe's father, was a crack shot with handguns, and he stood up in the audience and shouted he could do the same trick with a pistol. Joe Cummins remembers his mother tugging at his father: "Don't make a show of yourself in front of all these people." But Buffalo Bill told his father to come down, led him into a tent full of firearms, and let him choose his weapon. Did he want to shoot from horseback? Dan Cummins said no, he'd *done* the trick on horseback, but he hadn't ridden in a while, so he'd rather not try it. "Well, at first, the man who was throwing up the glass balls for him, he threw them up one at a time. My father said, 'Here, give 'em to me,' and he threw three into the air at once, bang, bang, bang, got 'em all, and Buffalo Bill said that was the best shooting he ever saw, 'I never seen a man shoot like that with a handgun.' They went back into the tent, and Buffalo Bill gave him this pistol here."

Joe Cummins tells us that his "grandboy," Billie Joe, a river pilot, is also a crack shot. "If he can see it, he can shoot it." His granddaughter, too, is an expert duck-hunter and fish-catcher and is one of his guides during hunting season. Best there is. He then offers an unexpected footnote to his high regard for crack shots: he tells us that he has a greater admiration for Audubon than for Daniel Boone—"because Boone was only a hunter."

Another car comes down the dirt road toward Swan Lake, and as it turns into the picnic grounds, old Joe Cummins does something else unexpected. In one small, gentle movement he checks that the safety is on and slips the Smith and Wesson pistol under his hip, out of sight. This is a region where guns are an everyday part of a countryman's traveling paraphernalia, whether it's the rifle stowed in the rack against the rear window of the pickup or the handgun carried in the glove compartment. Why would he care to hide it? We never did find out.

MD   I, meantime, unaware that the safety catch is on, sit there in the middle next to Mr. Cummins waiting for the revolver to go off and put a hole through his right hip. Or—*Wild Surmise!*—put a hole through my left hip.

But we depart the pickup truck without incident, and he plays the genial host, with introductions all around. The new arrivals, a middle-aged couple who camp and fish here every August and are back for a sentimental visit, express surprise at our Connecticut license plates. ("Say, you folks are a long way from home.") Since Mr. Cummins is knowledgeable about Audubon, I jump to the conclusion that his friends will be knowledgeable too. So I explain our mission—that we are traveling in the footsteps of John James Audubon, the bird painter, and that he hunted at Swan Lake with a party of Shawnees early in the 1800s.

I will never know what they thought *I* said, but I can never forget what *she* said in reply: "Why, sure enough." A pleased, chirrupy smile of recognition. "We met both of them here last summer."

MH   Before we leave, Joe Cummins insists on gathering some hickory nuts for Mary. The bottom land is rich in nut-trees, just as it was when it fed Audubon's Shawnee companions. The last hickory crop was a good one, and though most of the nuts have been collected already, Joe Cummins—gallant, bent-kneed, and stooping—goes through a nearby patch of woods and gathers two handfuls of the hard-shelled hickories. Then, having presented his gift, he puts in his false teeth and poses for his photograph, sitting behind the wheel of the pickup truck.

Back to Olive Branch and our camp beside Horseshoe Lake. You can get the feel of a town by shopping in the local market. By that standard, Olive Branch is poor; the market stocks lots of canned goods, some frozen vegetables, and the fresh foods are mostly on the edge of "gone-by." And, as in any depressed area, the cuts of meat on display are a further corroboration—here, a strikingly complete assortment of pig parts—feet, tails, trotters, neck bones, shin bones, pork liver. But even those, the so-called cheap cuts, are going for 79 and 89 cents a pound. (More than chicken would cost in a decent supermarket.) It's now my week to cook—Mary and I take turns, one week on, one week off—so I did the shopping tonight. ("Y'all hurry back, y'hear?" said the young man at the cash register; southern Illinois is as southern as the Deep South, but the catch phrase still took me by surprise.)

Camp cooking at best is slightly crude unless you travel in a large camper with a gas-fired kitchen including a freezer. We can't count on finding the fresh food we want in every new town; we have only a small ice-chest, and we cook on a campfire or on the one-burner propane stove. So the process is impromptu, and often depends on canned food. Tonight's dinner is one of my better extemporaneous one-dish meals—diced Spam with boiled cabbage and rice, spruced up by a couple of fistfuls of raisins and a dash of curry. Sprucing is the key ingredient in such meals—the cut-up green pepper in the pot of canned baked beans, the fried onions and dill weed in the corned beef hash.

Campfire cookery has its special limitations, of course. The fire harasses the cook by blowing smoke in his face during crucial stirring and flipping operations; pots unexpectedly tilt half their contents into the flames; food takes forever to cook over a campfire on a cold, windy night, because the wind snatches heat from underneath the pots. On the other hand, this may take place at sunset, on the edge of a glowing, backlit grove of towering cypresses; thousands of geese are roaring in the near distance and filing overhead into the pink sky; away from the fire the air in the nostrils is clean as fresh snow, and all the housekeeping before us is confined and simple—supper served by flashlight on aluminum plates, coffee in metal mugs, and all washed in a pot of hot water from the edge of the fire and then rinsed under the dam-fool faucet fifty yards away . . . moon rising into clouds and cold, and nothing for us to do but go to bed in our pop-tent, snuggle into the sleeping bags, make some notes in our journals, and—for a real *treat*—listen to the CBS Mystery Theater on the portable radio. And so goodnight.

Rain just before dawn. At 8:40 the sun is briefly out, but the air is still heavy. A mockingbird flies to the top of a sapling at the edge of the lake and begins what sounds like a Latin lesson. That's the mocker's style—takes a phrase, usually from someone else, plays with it, elaborates it; then picks up another phrase and plays with that; then another, and so on, almost endlessly. *Amo, amas, amat, amamus, amatus, amant.* Declensions and conjugations performed by a merry student.

Today we go down to the meeting of the waters, where the Ohio joins the Mississippi. Audubon tells us that not long after the swan hunt, when the nuts and game near Cache Creek grew scarce, the Indians packed up their canoes and set off southward. Audubon and two of the keelboat's crew, crossing by land to the Mississippi and finding that the ice was going out of the river, saw they could now bring the boat around the corner and start north; but they'd need help hauling the boat against the current by cordelle—a tow-line. So their captain's brother was hailed from a town on the far side of the Mississippi, and he arranged to come down to Cache Creek with six men. The next day the boat was floated a few miles to the junction, and there the hauling began. "This was slow and heavy work," says Audubon; "and we only advanced seven miles, during the whole day, up the famous Mississippi."

The junction of the Ohio and the Mississippi has been changed by man, time, and the rivers since the Lorimier keelboat turned this point and was hauled north by cordelle that winter of 1810–1811. But even in the wind and rain and fog of the day we first see it, it is a grand and moving scene. Audubon got to know this crossroads well during his lifetime. Marquette and Joliet were here too, and LaSalle. George Rogers Clark stationed gunboats here to guard against attacks by the British and Spanish. Fort Defiance was built here in 1861, to close off the South's river trade, and from here Ulysses S. Grant launched his flanking movement up the Cumberland and Tennessee rivers in 1862.

We stand in the park at the site of the long-vanished Fort Defiance, below Cairo proper, where a three-story concrete observation pavilion—stilts and three decks, shaped like the prow of a ship—rises among the trees. Before us the Ohio flows into the Father of Waters —though it is wider by far than the Father at this point. Downstream, the Lower Mississippi bends from southwest to south and shortly disappears. It is a broad, gently curving expanse of woods and water, the woods and water much greater than man's advertisements of his presence.

Out there where the rivers meet we see a towboat pushing fifteen barges of coal out of the Ohio for some port or power plant to the north. It shoves the nose of its tow—five barges long and three across —out into the current of the Mississippi; then with short bursts of power it pushes itself sideways, gradually aligning itself and its tow with the course of the Mississippi. At last it begins the slow upward climb against the current. So the Mississippi has not changed much, in that respect at least, in one hundred sixty-five years. Diesel power may make the effort seem easier than hauling by cordelle, but even the most modern diesel towboats advance at only five miles an hour against an eight-mile-an-hour current.

Upriver on the Ohio, upriver on the Mississippi, bridges link Illinois, Kentucky, and Missouri. On the riprap along the banks, a few black figures stand patiently, fishing. Around us here are willows, sycamores, green picnic tables, and a trash can labeled Pitch In. Three parkies have arrived to close down for the season the restrooms that occupy the second deck of the observation tower. They complain of the vandals who regularly storm the facilities and "take out the commodes, right off the floor." In 1973, they tell us, in the last great flood, the water rose almost to the second deck—twenty feet above the floodplain and thirty feet above the level of the rivers today.

This end of southern Illinois is called Egypt, which seems appropriate for a lowland "fertilized" by floods in the old days and still dominated by the whims of the rivers. Its principal city is even named Cairo—pronounced Kay-ro, if you please.

For his second supplement to *The American Language,* H. L. Mencken unearthed a note about Egypt that had appeared in the "Editor's Drawer" column of *Harper's Magazine* in 1858. The note goes like this: "The Southern part of Illinois has long been called *Egypt,* and some have supposed it was so called as being a 'land of darkness'—one of the benighted parts of the earth. A very intelligent correspondent of ours who lives there writes that the name had a very different origin; and he is desirous that it should be given in the Drawer, and then everybody will know it. He says: 'This portion of the State was first settled, and afterward the Northern counties. The new settlements of the North had to depend on the South for their corn until they could raise it for themselves, and hence they were in the habit of saying, "they must go down into *Egypt* to buy corn. [See Genesis, 17:2.] This is the *real* source of the name; and as to the darkness, that is all in your eye.' "

Be that as it may, these two beholders have found the Illinois

Egypt a dark, benighted place indeed—forlorn and down-at-heel, suffering from a century and a half of unpleasant relations with the Ohio and the Mississippi, which affected its uncertain relations with prosperity. High hopes and neighboring towns now fall in on themselves. To the north a few miles is a place confidently named Future City, but Future City was never finished—nor even well begun, for that matter; it is a concrete skeleton, sprinkled with broken glass. A few miles further north is Mound City. "I've never seen so many leftover old folk in my life," said Mary as we paused there the other day, and it did look as if the young had abandoned the area for someplace more promising, leaving their grandparents behind to make do among a clutter of empty buildings and boarded-up shops. We saw two octogenarians approaching each other on the sidewalk. She was black, crooked-legged, crooked-backed; he was white, unshaven, seedy looking. "How are you?" she asked offhandedly as they passed. "I'm kickin'," he said, "but not much else." "Yeah," she said —gone by him now, rolling stiffly along, her back to him, "me too." That, remarked Mary, says it for all these Illinois towns along the nether reaches of the Ohio. Kickin', but not much else.

JJA   On the approach of night, our crew camped on the bank; and having made a tremendous fire, we all ate and drank like men that had worked hard, and went to sleep in a few moments. We started the next morning two hours before daybreak, and made about a mile an hour against the current; our sail lying useless, as the wind was contrary. This night we camped out as before;—and another; and after that, a following day finding us at the same work, with very little progress, and the frost becoming quite severe again, our patron put us into winter quarters in the great bend of Tawapatee Bottom.

What a place for winter quarters! Not a white man's cabin within twenty miles on the other side of the river, and on our own, none within at least fifty! [Untrue. Settlers' cabins were scattered all over that territory, and there was a major settlement within a day's walk on the western side of the river.] A regular camp was raised—trees cut down, and a cabin erected, in less time than a native of Europe would think possible. [In later descriptions JJA spoke of snow forts built against the winter winds, but no cabin. Perhaps the cabin was in fact built, and the snow fort created around it for a windbreak.

Who's to say?] In search for objects of natural history, I rambled through the deep forests, and soon knew all the Indian passes and lakes in the neighbourhood. The natives by some intuitive faculty, discover an encampment of this kind, almost as quickly as a flight of vultures find a dead deer; and I soon met some strolling in the woods on the look out. Their numbers gradually increased; and in about a week, several of these unfortunate rambling beings were around us. Some were Osages, but the greater part were Shawnees. . . .

Our time passed away;—after hunting all day with a young Kentuckian of our party [John Pope, clerk in the Henderson store], he would join me at night to chase the wolves that were prowling on the ice—crossing the river to and fro, howling, and sneaking about the very camp for the bones which we threw away. Meanwhile I studied the habits of the wild turkies, bears, [cougars], racoons, and many other animals;—and I drew, more or less every day, by the side of our great fire. I will try to give you some idea of a great fire at a camp of this sort in the woods of America. Just before evening the axe-men tumble down four or five trees—probably ash, about three feet in diameter, and sixty feet to the first branches, or as we call them, the limbs. These are again cut into logs, of about ten feet in length, and, with the assistance of strong sticks, are rolled together, into a heap several feet high. A fire is made at the top, with brush-wood and dry leaves, kindled by a flint and steel; and in the course of an hour, there is a flame that would roast you at the distance of five paces:—under the smoke of this the party go to sleep. It happened, on the only night that my friend [Rozier] slept on shore, that being very chill, he drew himself so close to the fire, that the side of his face, which lay uppermost, was fairly singed, and he lost one of his whiskers [muttonchops or sideburns]. We all laughed at this;—but it was no joke to him, and he shaved off the remaining whisker very ruefully the next morning.

We remained here six weeks:—we had plenty of company from our Indian friends, with whiskey and food in abundance; but our stock of bread began to give way, and we got tired of using the breasts of wild turkeys for bread, and bear oil instead of meat. The racoons and oppossums, however tender, were at last disliked . . . [and bread and flour were obtained on the other side of the Mississippi]. Being now fairly settled in our winter quarters, we spent our time very merrily; and so many deer, bears, and wild turkies suffered in our hunting parties, that the trees around our camp looked like butchers' stalls, being hung round with fat venison, &c. Moreover we soon found that the lakes contained abundance of excellent fish; and many of us would walk over the ice with axes, and whenever a trout, pike, or cat-fish rose immediately beneath it, a severe blow on the ice killed the fish, which the hunter secured by opening a large hole in the ice, several feet in diameter; the fish in search of air, resorted to it from different quarters, and were shot as they appeared on the surface of the water. The squaws tanned the deerskins, stretched those of the racoons and otters, and made baskets of canes: my friend [John Pope] played tolerably on the violin; I had a flute—and our music found pleased hearers, whilst our men danced to the tunes, and squaws laughed heartily at our merriment. The Indian hunters formed the outer ring of our auditory—smoking their tomahawk pipes with a degree of composure, which no white man ever displayed at such merry-makings.

MH   Mary and I spent a good deal of time trying to find Tawapatee Bottom, where the winter camp was made. Audubon, in the *Ornithological Biography,* located it on the eastern, or Illinois, shore, but no one *there* knew what we were talking about. So we tried the Missouri side. In the first town we came to, Charleston, which is across the Mississippi from Cairo, we stopped at the library. Taped to the front door we found a notice of a Citizens Band Radio Jamboree—a big dance and feed—to be held a few days hence at the Charleston Civic Center. The sponsors were the Tywappity Yakkers. Bull's-eye. Tawapatee, it turns out, is the old name for this chunk of Missouri territory, and the bottom, of course, was Tawapatee floodplain along the river.

By now we'd seriously begun to consider the physical and psychological impact of rivers. There *are* bridges across the rivers here. And radio and television stations that reach into neighboring states. But the rivers truly separate communities, even so. Perhaps we were unlucky, talked to the wrong people; yet it was remarkable that we hadn't found anyone in Illinois who knew about "Swan Lake" just across the river in Kentucky, or anyone next to the river in Illinois who could place that memorable name Tawapatee.

All right, we've found the name. But as for the bottom itself, I already know how that sort of territory looks and feels, having fought my way almost to the mouth of old Cache Creek in the "thick and thin," as Audubon called it. We will not explore Tawapatee Bottom.

MD As these things usually go, after all our searching and our questions, once we had found Tawapatee Bottom—or Tiwappatty Bottoms—or Tywappity—the name popped up everywhere. On a U.S. Geological Survey map, in an early Missouri travel journal by historian Henry Marie Brackenridge, and in Donald Culross Peattie's book, *A Natural History of Trees* (1948), which I'd pulled out of the car so I could read up on sweet gum, the tree whose woody, spiny seed pods, the size of Ping-Pong balls, cover the ground in the fall. A sprinkling of them under your sleeping bag is like a bed of nails.

From Peattie's essay: "Sweet gum is a noble tree, that might well impress anyone new to the sight of it . . . and may be known by its beautiful star-shaped leaves . . . Crushed in the fingers, they give out a cleanly fragrance . . . In the deep gumbo soils of the Mississippi Valley, in the swamps of Missouri's Tiwappatty Bottom, Sweet Gum becomes a giant . . ."

The word Tawapatee itself is interesting. It sounds as if it might be linked to wapiti, the Algonquin word for the American elk that once ranged the continent from the Atlantic to the Pacific. Vast herds of them roved down the Missouri and into the Mississippi valley on their winter migrations, and hunting parties of Indians built pyramids of elkhorn along the riverbanks. But even by Audubon's day, the wapiti herds had been drastically diminished; they were hunted hard for their meat, and also for their teeth, which both Indians and whites considered good luck charms. In 1843, on Audubon's last journey, through the upper midwest, he would be presented with an antelope robe trimmed with fifty-six wapiti teeth, by then such a treasure that the robe was equal in value to thirty horses. The concept of elk's teeth as charms died hard. According to Peter Matthiessen's *Wildlife in America,* five hundred wapiti were poached in 1915 from the Yellowstone area alone, to supply teeth for new members of the Benevolent and Protective Order of the Elk.

This evening in the damp and in the intermittent rain at Horseshoe Lake, we have one of our eight-tiered fires going, though it's not a patch on the "great fire" JJA wrote about at the Tawapatee Bottom camp, logs three feet in diameter and a blaze that would roast you at five paces—a description written for English readers, doubtless to give them an image of the untrammeled American wilderness where trees could be felled at will, huge bonfires burned, with no gamekeepers or king's foresters to say you yea or nay.

I am the firewood nut on this trip. To me, it's the first order of business—the fire on the hearth. (Michael has become the guardian of order, the packer-of-the-car. A place for everything and everything in its place, as on shipboard.) But when we arrived here three days ago, I had an initial moment of dismay—not a scrap of wood in sight, the campground exquisitely tidy. I scanned the peripheries of the fields beyond. If I were a park attendant, I asked myself, where would I dump prunings, deadfalls, and broken branches? It would presumably be nearby, and yet discreetly out of sight.

Found. The wood dump is on a dead-end dirt road that runs through a thicket bordering the highway and is piled with sycamore, tupelo, and elm. We drive over every day, load branches and saplings crossways on the trunk of the car, and wobble back to our campsite. We have a Swedish buck saw among our gear, but learned early on that there's no need to saw wood into fireplace lengths. Stow the ends in the fire and push them forward as they burn. Or lay a big branch across the flames, let it burn through at the middle, and you have two logs. Let the two logs burn through, and then you have four.

Mr. Collins, the head ranger here (lean, taciturn, a weather-beaten face like the Marlboro man) says that one of his gravest concerns is the people who come out to Horseshoe Lake to collect the "knees" of the cypress trees to use as burl for woodworking projects. The knees, which sprout up out of the water around the base of a cypress and grow in gnarled, pointed, stalagmite shapes, are part of the root system. Their function is to absorb air, since the rest of the root system is under water. When the knees are sawed away, the tree's air supply is cut off and it can, in effect, suffer death by drowning.

This morning Mr. Collins wanted to know if we'd found that place with the Indian name. Yes, just across the river. He was perplexed. He's lived hereabouts all his life. Never heard of Tawapatee before.

Rain again tonight after we turn in. Wet sycamore leaves, big as dinner plates, fall from the trees around us and slop against the tent —as though we're being pelted in the dark by wet washcloths.

JJA After we had passed six weeks in this manner, the river began to fall very much,—the ice was heaped along both shores, so that a narrow channel alone appeared clear; and at last our patron said that this was the time to depart for Cape Girardeau. All was bustle—the cargo was once more put on board;—our camp was abandoned, and the Indians and we parted like brethren.

Our navigation was now of the most dangerous nature; the boat was propelled by pushing with long poles against the ice, or the bottom, whenever it could be touched;—and we moved extremely slowly. The ice on each side was higher than our heads;—and I frequently thought that if a sudden thaw had taken place, we should have been in a dangerous predicament indeed;—but good fortune assisted us, and at length we reached the famous Cape.

The little village of Cape Girardeau contained nothing remarkable or interesting except Mr. Lorimie, the father of our patron, who was indeed an original, and the representative of a class of men now fast disappearing from the face of the earth. His portrait is so striking and well worth preserving, that I shall attempt to draw it.

Imagine a man not exceeding four feet six inches in height, and thin in proportion, looking as if he had just been shot out of a popgun. He had a spare, meagre countenance, in which his nose formed decidedly the most prominent feature. It was a true *nez a la Grand Frederic*—a tremendous promontory, full three inches in length— hooked like a hawk's beak, and garnished with a pair of eyes resembling those of an eagle. His hair was plastered close to his head with a quantity of pomatum; and behind he wore a long queue rolled up in a dirty ribbon, which hung down below his waist. The upper part of his dress was European, and had evidently once been made of the richest materials; and though now wofully patched and dilapidated, you might still observe here and there shreds of gold and silver lace adhering to the worn apparel. His waistcoat, of a fashion as antique as that of his nose, had immense flaps or pockets that covered more than one-half of his lower garments. These latter were of a description totally at variance with the upper part of his costume. They were

of dressed buck-skin, fitting tight to his attenuated limbs, and ornamented with large iron buckles at the knees, which served to attach
and support a pair of Indian hunting gaiters that had, like the rest of
his dress, seen long and hard service. To complete his costume, he
wore on his feet a pair of mocassins . . . of most beautiful workman-
ship. These articles of dress, together with his small stature and
singular features, rendered his appearance, at a little distance, the
most ludicrous caricature that can be imagined; but upon approaching nearer, and conversing with him, his manners were found to be
courteous and polished. He had been . . . the governor of Louisiana,
while it was in the possession of the Spaniards; when this country was
purchased by the Government of the United States, he retired to this
little village, where he was looked upon as a great general, and held
in the highest esteem and consideration by all the inhabitants.

MH   Well, John James. You should see what has happened to your
old friend "Louis Lorimie"—Pierre Louis Lorimier—of Cape Girardeau. He's still held in the highest esteem and consideration in these
parts. Whatever he told you, however, or your memory invented
more than twenty years later, he was no Spanish governor of Louisiana. He began a French-Canadian adventurer trading south as far as
the Ohio. In 1778, working for the British, he and one other Frenchman and forty Shawnees attacked Boonesborough, Kentucky, and
spirited Our Dan'l off to Lorimier's trading post in Ohio. Boone
escaped a few months later, and in 1782 Audubon's friend General
Clark returned the compliment; Lorimier's headquarters were
wrecked, and Lorimier just did manage to get out alive. Next, he
went to Vincennes for a while, then to a place called Saline, west of
the Mississippi, where he traded with the Indians and became an
Indian agent for the Spanish, who owned upper Louisiana in those
days. Finally he settled here, set up a trading post and brought a lot
of Indians to the neighborhood with him, presumably to discourage
an American migration into the region. The Spanish made him a
militia captain and commandant of the district. After Louisiana became United States territory, he continued to serve in an official
capacity, as a judge of common pleas for the new government. His
first wife and the mother of his children was half Shawnee. Your
description of the little man with the big beak is completely con-

tradicted by an oil painting we saw here—done long after Lorimier died; it shows him tall and heroic, mounted on a horse, looking very grand. Frankly, we don't know whether to believe them or you. Even the entry in the *Dictionary of American Biography* says that he "was a well-formed, handsome man, fond of dress and display." But one can't always trust the *D.A.B.* in such matters either. One nice touch you'd appreciate, concerning his hair, that "long queue rolled up in a dirty ribbon, which hung down below his waist": The *D.A.B.* says that his "profusion of hair was arranged in a long plait, fastened with ribbons, which he used as a whip for his horse while riding." That sounds like *your* Louis Lorimier, all right.

JJA [O]ur patron urging us to proceed to St. Genevieve, we moved once more between the ice, and arrived in a few days at the Grand Tower; an immense rock detached from the shore, around which the current rushes with great violence. Our *cordelles* were used to force a passage at this dangerous spot; and our men, clinging to the rock as well as they could, looked as if each movement would plunge them into the abyss—but we passed on without accident. All this night, we heard the continual howling of the wolves, amidst the heavy woods that covered the large hills on the Illinois shore, opposite to this rock.

MH The Grand Tower was to take on a certain importance in JJA's ornithological career. Either on this trip or on one three years later (February 1814, which is when *he* said it happened), he invented a species of eagle here, which he called the Bird of Washington, the Washington Sea-Eagle—no practical joke, but an honest mistake. The details will interest only the dedicated birder, but in brief: There are all sorts of brown eagles in North America. Except for those exceedingly rare occasions when a European sea-eagle wanders to this side of the Atlantic, all brown eagles here are either golden eagles—in a wide variety of plumages, depending on age—or immature bald eagles. Not much was known about the many plumage variations of these birds in 1811—or in 1814. Often four eagle species were made out of two.

So, on a cold and blustery February day, Audubon said, he was lying out of the wind, flat on his back on the deck of a boat bound

KILBURN.

Grand Tower, 1854. *N.Y. Public Library Picture Collection*

up the Mississippi, with the boat's captain stretched out beside him. Near Grand Tower an eagle flew overhead, and the captain "identified" it as a Great Eagle, which he had seen before on the Great Lakes. "I was instantly on my feet," Audubon wrote, "and having observed it attentively, concluded, as I lost it in the distance, that it was a species quite new to me."

I think most ornithologists today would conclude that the eagle he saw was a large, immature, female, northern-bred bald eagle; female eagles are bigger than the males, northern bald eagles are bigger than southern bald eagles, and it was the size that seems to have caught Audubon's attention. A great many northern-bred bald eagles winter on the Upper Mississippi.

His landmark, Grand Tower—"that immense rock detached from the shore"—is on the Missouri side of the river, a round, gray stack of limestone about one hundred and fifty feet high, with a quarter acre of woods on top, looking as if it had walked away one day from the high, wooded cliffs behind. It has been federally protected since 1871, when President Grant issued an executive order preserving it in case it should sometime in the future be needed as one pier of a bridge across the Mississippi.

JJA   We arrived safely at St. Genevieve, and concluded the object of our adventure very satisfactorily. St. Genevieve was then an old French town—small and dirty; and I far preferred the time I spent in Tawapatee Bottom to my sojourn here.

MD   Ste. Genevieve, Missouri, when Audubon and Rozier landed with their barrels of whiskey (bought at 25¢ per gallon and sold at $2.00) was a prosperous town, far more prosperous than Henderson, Kentucky. Wheat was grown on the rich bottomland. There were three working lead mines nearby, a brickyard, more buildings than at St. Louis, and much river commerce. Henry Marie Brackenbridge, who lived here a few years before JJA so abruptly came and went, described Ste. Genevieve in *Views of Louisiana* and *Recollections* as a green town where the streets and houses were intermingled with gardens and orchards: "choicest fruits were grown and the finest vegetables, flowers and shrubs." He further extolled it as a town where "cookery is an art, well understood" and lauded French soups and fricassees and gumboes as far and away superior to the fried food of American cuisine. (It was ever thus, was it not?)

But Audubon's appraisal of Ste. Genevieve was merciless. "I found at once it was not the place for me; its population was then composed of low French Canadians, uneducated and uncouth . . . Rozier, on the contrary . . . found plenty of French with whom to converse. I proposed selling out to him, a bargain was made," and with the spring thaw, JJA turned around and headed home to Henderson.

Said Rozier: "Audubon had no taste for commerce, and was continually in the forest."

Said Audubon: "Rozier cared only for money . . ."

Ferdinand Rozier settled happily and prosperously in Ste. Genevieve, married eighteen-year-old Constance Roy, a French-Canadian girl from Prairie de Rocher across the river, sired ten children, was elected mayor in 1827, and lived out the rest of his eighty-seven years as a first citizen.

To read this on a printed page is one thing. It's quite another to drive into Ste. Genevieve and, first crack out of the barrel, you pass Rozier Street and the Rozier Bank. You round the town square and fetch up in front of Rozier's department store. You step into the Ste. Genevieve museum, and every other exhibit bears the Rozier name: daguerreotypes of Ferdinand R. and his wife; his head sculpted in marble a few years after he became mayor; a copper kettle and a branding iron from his household; the receipt for Audubon and Rozier's passage to America in 1806 aboard the *S.S. Polly*—"Paid in full, New York from Nantes, 525 livres." There's a case of stuffed birds said to have been mounted in 1810 by Audubon and presented to Firmin Rozier, Ferdinand's fourth child, who grew up to be a general, a state senator, a mayor of Ste. Genevieve, and author of *The History of the Early Settlement of the Mississippi Valley.* He was born in 1820, and the following year his father, down the river to New Orleans on business, spent Christmas Eve with the Audubons, who were living a hand-to-mouth existence; and Rozier brought with him a drawing of a grouse that JJA had left behind in Ste. Genevieve. We like to think there was an exchange of presents; in return for the drawing, perhaps Audubon gave Rozier the stuffed birds as a gift for the new baby. The birds in the little case are identified as "Red Tanager, Yellow-bellied Sapsucker, King Bird, Bob White, Speckled

Ferdinand Rozier. *Missouri Historical Society*

Ferdinand Rozier's residence. *Missouri Historical Society*

Snipe, Crested Fly Catcher, Baltimore Oriole, Flicker, Mud Hen, and Kinglet." They sit slightly askew on their ancient perches, and the sky-blue paint on the ceiling of the case is now flaking down upon their backs. Otherwise, taxidermically speaking, they're in fairly good condition—maybe too good to have been stuffed by Audubon more than 150 years ago.

The stand for this case of birds is yet another family memento— the safe from the Rozier Bank, which was robbed of $4000 in 1873 by a gang of outlaws believed to have been led by Jesse James and his brother. Other Rozier gifts include candlesnuffers, a Christmas-tree-candle mold, an early pocket knife, homemade handcuffs with key for securing slaves "while they were being transported," an English flintlock pistol, a petrified mushroom sponge, and a lovely photograph of the Queen of the Ste. Genevieve Bicentennial in 1935, Miss Mary Elizabeth Rozier, gazing wistfully and regally off camera —a gown of embroidered satin, yards of train draped about her feet, eight-button white kid gloves, a mitred hat with plumes, and her sceptre in her arms.

The town square, like that of a European village, is dominated by the church; at its feet, the museum, shops, restaurants, the library, houses. We arrived on a holy day, and the red brick, century-old, Ste. Genevieve Roman Catholic Church (the third to stand on this spot) was busy with Masses.

Michael stopped to take photographs, and I crossed the square to Rozier's department store, a stone's throw from the site where Ferdinand Rozier's white clapboard house-and-store once stood. We had no idea if the store still belonged to the family. It was as though I walked into a sewing machine shop asking for Mr. Singer, or into a soup factory asking for Mr. Campbell. Even as I told myself that the question was insane after all these years, I asked it anyway. "Is Mr. Rozier here?"

Yes, indeed, the clerk told me. He was in the back. At his desk. And so he was. Joseph Jules Rozier, Jr., merchant and great-great-great grandson of JJA's business partner; a smiling man in horn-rimmed glasses, working in his shirt sleeves in a tiny office stacked high with account books and files and samples cases and boxes of merchandise.

Joe Rozier had nothing new to add to what is already generally known about the Audubon-Rozier partnership, though in one family legend Ferdinand R. went off on a buying trip shortly after their arrival here, and Audubon was left in charge of the new store. "You know how Audubon was, always out in the woods, never behind the counter. When Ferdinand got back to Ste. Genevieve he found the store was locked and the door covered with cobwebs. Perhaps that did it. The last straw." Joe Rozier laughed. "The story may not even be true, but that's the way we always heard it."

He also pointed out that, appearances to the contrary, Ste. Genevieve is no longer a Rozier stronghold. Most of Ferdinand's descendants fanned out over the years, a lot of them to St. Louis. (Thirteen Roziers appear in the St. Louis phonebook.) In some branches of the family where no sons were born, the name has died out. The cousin who ran the bank, for example, had no male heirs; on his death the bank was sold to a German family in town and is now the Rozier bank in title only. As for Joe Rozier, he's pleased to have boys to carry on

Joseph Jules Rozier, Jr., at the door of Rozier's department store. *MH*

the name and, he hopes, to carry on the store. Sure, when he was a young man just out of the army, he thought about moving on, but then he looked around and decided he liked it best right here. "I expect to die here too, and be buried up in the old cemetery with the rest of the Roziers."

Jean Ferdinand Rozier's tombstone is an impressive monument decorated with Gothic motifs and a cross on top. The base and the delicate wrought iron fence around the plot are entwined with ivy, myrtle, and honeysuckle vines that show a few pale yellow blossoms, even now in November. His youngest son, Edward Amable, and his wife, Constance Roy, lie next to him. Their inscriptions are in English, though many of their neighbors' tombstones are in French: "Ci-Git . . ." ("Here Lies . . .").

We've set up camp beside a deep, forested ravine in the fifty-two-acre town park that's named for Pere Marquette, the Jesuit missionary who came this way in 1673. Ste. Genevieve was the first French settlement in Missouri and was well established by 1735. The original town, struck by floods late in the 1700s, was moved to higher ground, and a couple of houses transported in this move are still standing—the Beauvais and Amoureaux houses. The town, in fact, is rich with old buildings, some of French Colonial design, cottages and mansions made of clapboard, board and batten, brick, or sandstone, most with small identifying plaques put up by the Foundation for the Historic Restoration of Ste. Genevieve.

The character of Ste. Genevieve might have taken quite another turn had it not been for the vagaries of the Mississippi. The town began as a port, the river shifted its course, and the town was stranded inland. "Observe what this eccentric river had been about," wrote Mark Twain; "it had built up this huge, useless towhead directly in front of this town, cut off its river communications, fenced it away completely, and made a 'country' town of it. It is a fine old place, too, and deserved a better fate."

But was it such a bad fate? Here the town remains, population 4500, snug and thriving, tangible proof that less is more. The French and the later German settlers shared the same sense of thrift and pride of place. They maintained what they had, instead of rushing headlong into the devouring philosophy that "new" is better. Ste. Genevieve is alive with its sense of self, past and present.

MH   Joe Rozier's contentment here, and the evident stability and self-possession of the town are contradicted by the opinions of most of the young people we've met at our camp. They find nothing to *do*, and they complain about it. The outside world is now too close, I guess, brought into the small-town home in all sorts of instant communiqués; a lot of the young feel restless, and have the means and the freedom to behave restlessly. They drive their cars and their motorcycles endlessly on non-errands.

Of course, *they* are our sample; they are the ones who see us and stop to visit—and wonder aloud what "rich writers" are doing camping in a small dome-shaped tent and eating peanut-butter sandwiches for lunch. (So much for the clarity of their vision of the larger world.)

MD   We were invited for coffee by Joe Rozier's cousin, Mary Rozier Sharp, who was down from St. Louis for the weekend. ("I know they're in town," he told us. "I saw her at early Mass.") Mrs. Sharp turned out to be Mary Elizabeth Rozier, the pretty girl in the photograph who had been Queen of the Bicentennial in 1935, and as things also go in Rozier country, her husband, Louis Sharp, was another of Ferdinand R.'s descendants, on his mother's side. By now Ferdinand's descendants are legion, and the Sharps had not known of each other's existence, nor known that they were fourth cousins, until they first met in St. Louis two years before their marriage. Mary Sharp had a copy of an 1862 picture of Ferdinand R. to give us and despite the old gentleman's stern, almost frosty, expression, I was struck by the delicate echoes of his features that were reflected in hers—the shape of the face, the high cheekbones, the set of the eyes, the line of the mouth—a resemblance not shared by Louis Sharp or Joe Rozier.

There is some disagreement within the clan as to the number of barrels of whiskey that arrived in Ste. Genevieve with Audubon and Rozier in the winter of 1811. Mary Sharp had always heard that it was three hundred and ten barrels. "Well," said Louis Sharp, "that's not the way it was told on *my* side. I've always heard that most of the whiskey had been drunk before they ever got here."

MH   It is raining on and off. We had planned to spend the morning photographing. The light is marginal but okay for my purposes, and what we really need is an umbrella, so Mary can shield me and, more important, shield the camera. We stop in at Joe Rozier's dry goods emporium, and he sells me the needed article. This transaction fills me with delight—the Harwoods, traveling in the footsteps of John James Audubon, buy an umbrella from the great-great-great grandson of Ferdinand Rozier.

MD Following in Audubon's wake, we cross the Mississippi back to Illinois, and we home in as darkness falls to the haven of Horseshoe Lake campground at Olive Branch. We cook supper by moonrise— a moon that should be full, but as it lifts above the trees to the east, it has the appearance of a crescent moon lying on its back, and we assume that it's partially covered by a round, black cloud. Half an hour later, the blacked out section has diminished but is still perfectly rounded, and Michael suddenly exclaims, "We're looking at an eclipse of the moon."

MH From time to time today, we'd listened to local radio stations and remarked on the amount of schlock Christianity featured here-abouts—a faith reduced to cant, done up and sold in loud packages, and it literally clogs the airways. But we heard no mention of an eclipse tonight. Here we are, deluged with the most simple-minded brand of Christian exhortation, and not one word about a true wonder of the heavens.

MD Clear and cool this November night. We don't bother to put up the tent but sleep out under the moon—shining high and bright, well up and out of the path of the earth's shadow. Heavy dews rise on the lake shore, so we spread one tarpaulin under our sleeping bags, and another on top. In the morning, the upper tarp is covered with sparkling frost crystals. A brown, shaggy wolf spider, the size of a fifty-cent piece, evidently denned in with us for the night. When I shake out the tarp before spreading it to dry on our picnic table, the spider emerges from a fold. Even as I flick at the spider to chase it off, its hunting instinct proves stronger than its survival instinct. The spider pounces on a minute white gnat, holds it fast in the crook of a foreleg, and *then* races off the tarp into the safety of the long grass.

The mockingbird still sings at dawn on his topmost branch—his territorial watchtower. The mocker's song puts Michael in mind of Latin declensions. It speaks to me of embroidery stitches. The song is like a sampler—rows of elaborate stitches, no two rows alike, and each row sewn in bright silk flosses with a gold needle.

Audubon wrote several versions of his travels across the Illinois prairies that lie between Ste. Genevieve, Missouri, and Henderson, Kentucky. He covered the ground more than once.

In one account, he has himself leaving Ste. Genevieve in style: "I purchased a beauty of a horse, for which I paid dear enough, and bid Rozier farewell."

In another, Audubon said goodbye, whistled to his dog, and set out on foot during the spring thaw when the Illinois prairies were flooded and herds of deer waded through, shin-deep. So did JJA: "Unfortunately, I had no shoes—and my mocassins constantly slipped, which made the wading very irksome. Nevertheless, on the first day I made forty-five miles, and swam the Muddy River." He was given the warmest of frontier hospitality at a squatter's cabin, a dinner of venison, eggs, and "a good glass of brandy," while the two good and dear boys of the household examined his "handsome double-barrelled gun." The remainder of the trip was equally uneventful —a night in an Indian camp, a night at an inn on the Ohio, and home again.

In a third version, a travel essay titled "The Prairie," he once again whistles to his dog and sets forth from Ste. Genevieve on foot, happy as a lark. This time it is a May day (brilliant spring flowers, gamboling fawns) and at dusk he stumbles into the adventure that becomes his only story of deadly peril in the American wilderness. The kindly squatters from version two are transformed into a den of thieves. The lady of the house still serves up venison, but she's a whiskey-drinking slattern, and her two sons are no better. There's another overnight guest—a "finely formed young Indian," blinded in one eye in a hunting accident that day, but armed with bow and arrow, "butcher-knife," and tomahawk. The Indian signs to Audubon that dark doings are afoot, and Audubon loads and primes his rifle. As this tale weaves on to its finish, the Indian pretends to sleep, so does Audubon, while peeking out from under a buffalo robe to watch "the infernal hag" who's sharpening a carving knife on a grindstone and muttering to her boys about the gold watch on the gold chain around Mr. Audubon's neck. At the final, desperate moment—"cold sweat covered every part of my body"—Audubon and the Indian are rescued by "two stout travellers, each with a long rifle on his shoulder," who appear in the doorway like the good woodcutter in Little Red Riding Hood.

It's a rattling good yarn, and I don't believe a word of it. JJA may have found himself at some time or other in a chancy situation involving his gold watch and chain and let his imagination take off from there to ornament and extend the story. Perhaps he heard something similar from another traveller. Southern Illinois in those days was notorious for its outlaw bands and saw far more vicious crimes than a mere throat-cutting for a gold watch. I am surprised that most Audubon biographers give this tale thoughtful reportage—though in 1902 John Burroughs, the writer–naturalist, questioned its validity on the grounds that a frontier cabin would not contain a grindstone and a carving knife.

The very premise of the story is false: Audubon and the Indian are cast in the role of victims, cowering and feigning sleep, while the knife is being sharpened to the accompaniment of loud stage whispers from the "trio in the corner," who are still passing around the whiskey bottle. Audubon makes it clear that his would-be murderers were drunk as billy-goats. It is all too improbable. Audubon would not have been intimidated for a moment, nor would an Indian brave, whether blinded in one eye or not. They had a formidable array of weapons—Audubon's cocked gun, the Indian's knife, tomahawk, and bow and arrows. Even without their weapons, the two of them could have handled three drunks any day of the week, not to mention the plain fact that he and/or the Indian could have walked out long before, at the first hint of danger.

However, the story is well staged and well played, as much fun to read today as when it was first published in the 1830s. Audubon himself made light of his adventure tales, which were written as diverting "Episodes" to be scattered through the *Ornithological Biography* as entertainment for his readers in between the essays on American birds. He once wrote home from England asking for good stories, "any sort of thing" that could be grist for the mill, and he described the Episodes as "food for the idle"—scarcely a fair appraisal, since most of the Episodes give vivid accounts of life on America's frontiers. But how easy to make up a penny dreadful to spark the pages. Why not? (I would.)

The Illinois prairies in mid-November are brown and gold, the harvest in, the fields in stubble. You know when you're there. The road lifts from the river valley, you gain the prairie plateau, the land flattens out before you, and overhead is the wide prairie sky—a clear, cool, rich autumn blue with long fingers of white clouds from horizon to horizon.

Somewhere through here was one of the Indian traces that JJA followed down across southern Illinois, from the Mississippi to the Ohio. We stick to the secondary roads—the old roads—which might very well have been laid out on the approximate routes of the early trails, and, like all old roads, they are leisurely. An easygoing give and take with the contours of the earth. Our first Audubon landmark is the Big Muddy, which rises in central Illinois and flows into the Mississippi through Jackson County to the southwest. He spoke of it twice in his prairie travels—swimming the Big Muddy in a spring thaw, and on the second occasion riding headlong into the Big Muddy to soothe and quiet his horse, maddened by attacking swarms of buffalo gnats: "but upon reaching the shore, his motions were languid—his head dropped—and it was with difficulty that I reached a squatter's hut, where the poor animal died in a few hours."

We stop at a small iron bridge that spans the river south of Rend Lake. The Big Muddy runs through farm country here, is bordered with thick woods, and an old man sits on a dry log upstream, fishing. The water is low at this season, and it's not so much a river as a creek, but the Big Muddy sure is muddy—gray-brown water and a long slope of gray mudflats that testify to high water in other seasons.

There are no buffalo gnats here in November, but JJA's story has set me to wondering. Is it another tall tale? Can a swarm of buffalo gnats kill a horse? I look them up in *The Field Book of Insects* by the late Dr. Frank Lutz of the American Museum of Natural History, and in *Insect Pests*, a Golden Nature Guide by George S. Fichter of North Carolina State College. Buffalo gnats belong to the same genus *(Simulium)* as the black flies of the northeast and the turkey gnats of the south—a genus of stout, humpbacked, short-legged, biting, flying pests; they have a nasty habit of crawling into your eyes, ears, and nose (which we know too well from the black flies that rise in May in New England); and only the females bite—they need blood for their egg-laying activities.

But my original question remains unanswered, so later I telephone the etymology department at the University of Illinois. Yes, I am told. It is within the realm of possibility for a horse to die from an attack by buffalo gnats, which could cause a fatal anaphylactic shock. However, they have no documentation of any such occurrence. (I confess, I begin to feel guilty at my iconoclastic suspicions of Audubon's stories. Am I being a spoilsport, killing off the drama of his tales?)

JJA [*On the second day of a journey by foot across the prairie*] I was now not above forty miles from Shawnee, and my dog, who knew very well that he was near home, seemed as happy as myself. I did not meet a single person the whole day, and not a cabin was then to be found on that road. At four the same evening I passed the first salt-well: and half an hour brought me to the village. At the Inn, I was met by several friends, who had come to purchase salt; and here I slept,—forty-seven miles from home.

MD En route to Shawneetown a road sign warns: STRAY DEER. We cross Beaucoup Creek, Panther Creek, Saline River, Lawler Ditch, Eagle Creek, and drop down off the prairies into the hills. This range that cuts across the foot of Illinois is an eastern spur of the Ozark plateau, mining country. Local radio stations broadcast daily reports on which mines are working.

The salt wells that Audubon passed on his way to Shawneetown were the source of salt for communities within a hundred miles and were largely responsible for Shawneetown's start as a riverport, as a gateway to the west, as the distribution point for mail to the surrounding frontier territories, and as the first banking center in Illinois. Tradition has it that the Shawneetown Bank refused a loan to some Chicago men in 1827 because "Chicago was too far from Shawneetown to ever amount to anything." Then came a change in westward migration routes; the salt works closed, and Shawneetown began a long, slow washout. Old Shawneetown, once an Indian village, is immediately south of the junction of the Wabash and the Ohio —a battered river valley flat that has been flooded again and again over millennia, like the ragged peninsula at the other end of the state, where Cairo stands at the mercy of the Ohio and the Mississippi. A river junction can be a dangerous place to set up housekeeping, and everyone has said so right along.

"Shawneetown is subject to the inundations of the river, and in the winter and spring of 1813, the inhabitants were obliged to abandon their houses."—*The Ohio River Navigator*, 1814.

"A most unfortunate site for this town . . ."—the U.S. Land Office Commissioner, 1815.

In the flood of 1883, the floor of the First Methodist Church was lifted to the ceiling. But it wasn't until the famous flood of 1937 that the residents at last relocated in a new Shawneetown, well up the road. What's left of the old town, principally structures of brick or stone from its "golden years," is now an historic site, tragic and sullied. In their solitude the surviving buildings that crouch behind the giant levee look doubly vulnerable to the river's next rampage. They stand marooned among vacant lots and the rubble of old foundations and a random dash of mobile homes; a few of the fine old structures, sagging on their sills, boarded up, condemned, are about to tumble from neglect and a shortage of restoration funds.

MH Two items interest me. First, the salt works around Shawneetown were owned for a time by the United States and leased to private businessmen, who were permitted to operate with slave labor—slaves rented on the other side of the Ohio and free blacks kidnapped and made slaves again. Second, when Illinois entered the Union as a free state in 1818 and assumed responsibility for the "Salines," its constitution specifically exempted "the tract reserved for the salt works near Shawneetown" from antislavery laws.

Theoretically the system allowed certain slaves under certain conditions to earn their freedom while making salt, but sentiment ran high in southern Illinois against the idea and against the presence of free blacks—both before and after the Civil War; Negroes had little recourse to the law when promises of earned freedom weren't kept, as often they were not. Even today, away from the cities, "free blacks" are difficult to find in the land of Egypt. The whites on the rock bottom of this hardscrabble mining and farming country have made it abundantly clear that they still will not permit economic competition from the blacks on the rock bottom. A friend tells us that one local saying has it: "No nigger dares to stay the night in Franklin County." That's just to the northwest of us here.

MD And a couple of miles northwest of Shawneetown is the mansion built by the pre-Civil War proprietor of the salt works, who kept his slaves (under lock and key) under his own roof. The place is now advertised as The Old Slave House with lurid roadsigns inviting the tourist to come and see the torture room and the slaves' cells and God-knows-what-all. We did not stop to see it.

We do, however, take a turn down a gravel road into the Shawnee National Forest to look for one of the old salt wells. When the salt works were at their peak production, timber was leveled for five miles around to supply the firewood that kept the giant brine vats boiling. The woodlands have grown back—all grays and browns today, except for the leafy green vines of carrion-flower and the red-and-orange berries of bittersweet. The deer-hunting season opened at dawn, making this a hazardous expedition into the woods, but in the end it's a carload of weary, bleary-eyed, boozy hunters who give us proper directions to the saline spring. We find it in a low, square, log enclosure a few steps off the road. The water is smoky blue and white and yellow, the colors of cave drippings, and the smell is like rotten eggs.

Before the white man got here, the Indians worked the salt springs too, and buffalo made trails down to salt licks. (So had mastodons and mammoths.) In his essay on the passenger pigeon, JJA wrote, "I have seen the Negroes at the United States' Salines or Saltworks of Shawnee Town, wearied with killing Pigeons, as they alighted to drink from the water issuing from the leading pipes, for weeks at a time." The woods today are full, if not of passenger pigeons, of robins. They show no interest in the salt water; they are feeding on wild grapes and hackberries, and singing happily. A few cedar waxwings feed and sing with them. It sounds like a spring morning.

HENDERSON, KENTUCKY

1811-1819

MH Audubon crossed the river into Kentucky by ferryboat from Shawneetown. "Each person—25¢. Man and Horse—50¢. Wagon and Team—$1.00." And so on. "Children under seven—Free." We cross the Ohio by toll bridge and drive upriver. Our destination: the campground at John James Audubon State Park on the outskirts of Henderson.

Henderson, Kentucky, stands at the junction of the Green River and the Ohio. Like Mill Grove in Pennsylvania, it was a fulcrum in Audubon's life. He and Lucy lived here until 1819; their second son, John Woodhouse Audubon, was born here, then a daughter who died. And it was here that he went from his first successes as a businessman to his worst losses. His career went like this:

Having shed himself of one partner, he promptly took on another, Lucy's brother Thomas, then working in New Orleans. It was "Audubon & Bakewell, Commissions Merchants—(Pork, lard, & flour)." With Thomas Bakewell's connections in New York and England, and JJA's knowledge of French, they would go into foreign trade. However, war with England began the next year and pulled the plug on that project. Audubon took up storekeeping again and did moderately well—well enough to build a house and store and buy some land; it is said that he had the third biggest land holdings in town. "The pleasures which I have felt at Henderson," he wrote later, "and under the roof of that log cabin, can never be effaced from my heart until after death." He was achieving exactly what his father had wished for him, success in business. He had a comfortable marriage, with a new baby coming along every year or two. He felt good about himself. He loved his business travels: they gave him an excuse to get off into the wilderness—"the darling forests of Kentucky and Pennsylvania"—but he had no intent of becoming a naturalist and artist by profession. The capital proof of that fact was provided by the visit of Constantine Samuel Rafinesque.

Rafinesque was a brilliant, eccentric, and tragic figure in American natural science. Although he was one of the most important naturalists of his day, he died in such poverty that if friends had not smuggled Rafinesque's body from his Philadelphia boarding house, the landlord would have sold it to a hospital as a teaching cadaver to help pay the back rent. In 1818, Rafinesque was on a tour through the Ohio and lower Mississippi valleys, collecting information and specimens of plants, fish, and animals. He arrived in Henderson with a letter of introduction to Audubon, who invited him to stay as a guest —and immediately marked him as a suitable butt for practical jokes. Rafinesque wanted to see a canebrake, for example—the thickest kind of riverside tangle one could find—and by his own account Audubon got his guest so lost and scared and weary that to lighten his load and make the going easier Rafinesque threw away the collection of plants he'd been gathering in the brake. It was a filthy trick for Audubon to play—if the story is at all true; he wrote it as part of an Episode for the *Ornithological Biography,* and he may have colored the facts somewhat. However, we do know the jokes did not stop there. Years later it came to light that JJA had also gulled his guest with drawings of no less than ten "new" fishes and several nonexistent birds, including something he called the Scarlet-headed Swallow. Unhappily for Audubon's later reputation, Rafinesque didn't insist on seeing specimens but published descriptions of the ten imaginary fish—first in *The Western Review and Miscellaneous Magazine* and then in his *Ichthyologia Ohiensis,* which appeared in 1820. That same year, he also published descriptions of the birds. All of these supposed new species were based only on Audubon's drawings and on his word, and Rafinesque duly credited the source. Perhaps the most outrageous creature of the lot was the Devil-Jack Diamond-Fish, which supposedly could weigh as much as four hundred pounds, had stony scales on which one could strike sparks with a flint, and was bulletproof.

The immature rose-breasted grosbeak was drawn in Indiana Territory across from Henderson in September 1810. Not knowing what it was, Audubon called it the Variegated Grosbill. *Courtesy of The New-York Historical Society, New York City*

So it is clear that JJA had no pretensions to being a scientist at the time, and he surely didn't have the scientist's sense of responsibility about his subject. He shot and caught and drew, he kept and raised birds in his yard, he made his notes—strictly for his own amusement. As far as he knew, his destiny was to be a Kentucky businessman.

Feeling established, he had by then taken a new flyer with his brother-in-law Thomas Bakewell; they and another partner had built an expensive steam mill at Henderson, to saw wood and grind flour. It was the only mill in the vicinity, and might have flourished, given time. But the original investment was large—an estimated $15,000 or so. The mill machinery didn't run well and couldn't be made right; so there were many times when the mill wasn't earning money. Since the end of the war with England, the national economy had become unsettled and was in a treacherous condition west of the Alleghenies. Audubon's partners got nervous and pulled out on him, taking with them as much of the firm's capital as they could and IOU's for what they couldn't. The company sold a steamboat it owned, but the bank draft that bought the boat proved to have no cash resting behind it, and by the time Audubon caught up with the boat and buyer in New Orleans, someone else had made a legal claim on the boat for the buyer's debts, which took priority over Audubon's claim. Now he took on new partners for the steam mill, and—just as times seemed to be improving—banks began to fail all over the west.

Audubon, like many others, was ruined in the crash. Starting April 10, 1819, in the Louisville *Public Advertiser,* he offered to sell his "undivided half of the Henderson Steam Mill, . . . [which] has two pair of French Burrs and one pair of Laurel Hill Stones, and runs two saws, has been in operation for two years, the engine is on the condensing principle, and, with the improvements that are now making to it will be one of the best in the union; a wharf of one hundred twenty feet in length has just been completed." He also put up his lots, "situated in the very best part of the town." That summer he sold the mill and the lots to Lucy's brother-in-law, his partner and friend Nicholas Berthoud of Shippingport, and even that could not cover his losses. He was arrested for debt, went to jail in Louisville, and—to get out—declared himself a bankrupt.

A year later, writing a memoir for his children, JJA summed up the Henderson years: "This Place saw My best days, My Happiest, My

Audubon's great horned owl painting. The male, on the right, was done in 1814 in Henderson. The female was rendered later. *Courtesy of The New-York Historical Society, New York City*

Wife having blessed me with Your Brother . . . and a sweet Daughter
. . . Our Business Was good . . . but I was intended to meet Many
Events of a Disagreable Nature . . . the Building of a Large Steam
Mill, the purchasing of Too Many goods sold on Credit of course Lost.
Reduced us—Divided us . . . a Numberless quantities of Failures, put
all to an end: the Loss of My Darling Daughter affected Me Much;
My Wife apparently had Lost her spirits. I felt no wish to try the
Mercantile Business [again]. I paid all I could and Left Henderson,
Poor & Miserable of thoughts."

It would be nearly twenty years before the Audubon family was
settled again for so long in one town.

When friends visit for birding weekends in northwest Connecticut, I take them to places that excite me by their echoes of things
seen and heard before. So Audubon must have felt, showing Wilson
the terrain around Louisville; and so, I know, feels Ron Dotson, a
young public-school teacher and the president of the Henderson
Audubon Society, as he guides us along a route he has explored many
times.

Our talk is about the birds Audubon knew here. Things have
changed, of course. JJA wrote of large flocks of Canada, white-
fronted, and snow geese; of goshawks and white pelicans and goldeneye ducks on Canoe Creek; of eagles and ivory-billed woodpeckers and prairie chickens and passenger pigeons. It was a different
landscape and a different environment. At least one spectacle Audubon must have seen here still recurs around Henderson to this day:
the gathering of wood ducks by the hundreds in fall. Not far from the
Audubon State Park is a small swamp hemmed in by highways and
the spread of Henderson, which Ron tells us is one of the major
"staging" points for wood ducks headed south. "When a kid tells you
today he is going out after a duck," says Ron, "you know he's going
to that swamp to shoot a wood duck." But the swamp, as you might
expect, is in danger of being obliterated by Henderson's sprawl.
Some distance from the city, another piece of wetland, once a cypress swamp, now sprouts dead and rotting hulks of trees killed by
the salt pumped into the water by oil drilling operations. The Green
River, along whose shores Audubon found peregrine falcons wintering, is now badly polluted—as is the Ohio. No news in any of that.

As we stand on the margin of one of Ron's favorite places—a still healthy cypress swamp, now gold and gray and rusty with fall—he remarks that he likes to come to the spot with binoculars, camera, and notebook, and just sit, mostly making notes about what he sees. He might some day work those notes into a book, he says; but he simply likes the *doing* of it. That is exactly the kind of enterprise I most enjoy myself, and I am jealous of his regular proximity to the place.

MD On our ramble through the bottom land along the Green River—the little houses and shacks up on stilts, above the spring flood levels—we asked Ron where the canebrakes were, those impenetrable, swampy brakes through which JJA had led Rafinesque and been so entertained when Rafinesque lost his plant specimens. He couldn't say. He had looked for those canebrakes himself, and he'd asked a number of local people too. The cane has vanished from the neighborhood, ploughed out, washed out, burned out.

We came upon a lineup of small towboats—the *Little Ajax,* the *Nell,* the *Streaker,* the *Eleanor Gordon,*—each spanking clean, freshly painted. Moored among them against the banks of the Green River were coal barges, filled to the brim with the loot of strip-mining, floated down to this place, and now waiting to be moved out, just as in the country-and-western song (a strip-mine lament, you might call it) that we've been hearing on the car radio in these parts. The song is set in Kentucky. The lament is for the lost Eden of childhood, for the fondly remembered green countryside that's been flattened and hauled away by the coal company. The lyrics must have been written by a Kentuckian. They have an authentic ring of true loss and angry regret.

Every town worth its salt is blessed at some time or another with a leading citizen who may or may not have an official position but is a powerhouse in the community nonetheless. It's usually someone from one of the old families who has a walloping sense of tradition, who is everywhere and into everything—proposing, initiating, organizing. In Henderson, this personage was Miss Susan Starling Towles—teacher, librarian, and first family. She was a granddaughter of Judge Thomas Towles, who pioneered to Kentucky and was one of Audubon's friends here. Miss Towles died in 1954 at the age of ninety-three, but the impact of her personality and her town projects lingers on. Besides being influential in founding such organizations as the Henderson DAR, Women's Club, Garden Club, historical and geneological society, the Transylvania Society (membership limited to descendants of early settlers), and besides writing a history of Henderson, Miss Towles made John James Audubon the hero and driving cause in her life. "She did everything," said a local banker, "but bring him back from the dead."

Miss Towles gave Audubon readings at the library. She founded the first Audubon Society in Kentucky. When the state park was being developed in the township in the 1930s, she called a town meeting to suggest that there be a *reason* for the park—that it be dedicated to John James Audubon. The town and the state agreed. From that concept came the John James Audubon Memorial Museum, which stands within the John James Audubon Park grounds. "What William Penn is to Philadelphia," wrote Miss Towles, "John James Audubon is to Henderson, Kentucky. . . . Of all its honored ones the 'American Woodsman' is the best beloved, the best remembered.

"At Henderson is the mother Audubon Society of the state. The schools keep his birthday; annually the children write papers about him and take pride in the onetime citizenship that is so valuable an artistic and inspirational asset of their community . . . Many are the stories and traditions of his life here, and when the great beech on which he had inscribed in delicate letters, 'J. J. Audubon, 1814,' had to be cut down, it was a small tragedy.

"And so Henderson is happy in having a world-honored hero. For him she hopes to make a shrine that it may be a sort of Mecca to all bird lovers."

On the riverbank at the foot of Main Street is a two-acre park that was created on the site of Audubon's mill after it burned down one March night in 1913. Some say the mill once contained hundreds of sketches of birds drawn by Audubon on the interior walls. The historic society would like to see the mill reconstructed as a museum on its original site. The state, we were told, wants to reconstruct it three blocks inland on the highway. (What a bewitching thought. An 1818 steam mill in the middle of traffic.)

Nearby, down here on the river, had been the town dock, where the first steamboat to Henderson tied up. According to local legend, the young men of the town showed off by diving into the river and swimming under the boat, but Audubon did them one better. He dove in at the bow, swam under the boat lengthwise, and came up at the stern. Lucy was also remembered as a derring-do swimmer. She and John James, wrote Miss Towles, "were in the habit of swimming across the Ohio before breakfast on summer days."

At Main and Second Streets in downtown Henderson, two bronze plaques commemorate JJA. One, decorated with cardinals in bas-relief, is on the wall of the First National Bank near the site of the Audubon's log cabin. The other, on the side wall of Newberry's, marks the location of Audubon's general store, and once again we have the popular view of his face—the Byronesque, eyes-up pose from the Inman portrait. This plaque, also decorated with cardinals, is set at chest level for grown-ups, eye level for children. It has the dark red-brown patina typical of bronze, except for two shining surfaces that are polished as bright as gold by passing fingers—the wing of one cardinal and the end of Audubon's nose. His upward gaze, which seems to be avoiding the incongruity of a golden nose, looks over his left shoulder into the faces (or at the backs of the heads) of Main Street pedestrians. At night, when the street is empty, he has a patchwork view of the sky between the buildings. Catty-corner across the intersection is The Audubon House, a red-brick midtown hotel that advertises "Sleeping Rooms and Furnished Apartments" and in neon, on its street floor, LOANS.

Somewhere through here, where everything is at sixes and sevens as the shops crank up for Christmas (before any of us have even made it to Thanksgiving) and the street is being dug up for new sidewalks, the Audubons had their orchard and garden, a pond stocked with turtles for the ready ingredients of one of his favorite dishes, turtle soup, and their poultry yard. Besides domestic birds, JJA kept swans, wild turkeys, wood ducks, prairie chickens, and least sandpipers, "tiny, fat, and delicious birds" that he netted on the sandy shores of "the fair Ohio." He clipped their wings and turned them loose in the garden, "for the purpose of studying their habits in this sort of half-confined state; but they were all soon destroyed by those most destructive pests, the Norway rats, which at that time infested all my premises."

Rats were a persistent pest. Before one of his journeys, Audubon stored a wooden box of two hundred paintings at the farm of a dear friend, Dr. Adam Rankin. "Reader feel for me," Audubon wrote, "a pair of Norway rats had taken possession of the whole and had reared a Young familly amongst the knawed bits of paper which but a few months previous represented a thousand inhabitants of the air. The burning heat which rushed to my brain was too great at the moment to be indured without affecting the whole of my nervous sistem; I slept not for several Nights, and the days passed like days of oblivion . . ." In the Audubon gallery at the New York Historical Society is a Japanese illustration of this catastrophe, taken from *The Western Countries Book of Successful Careers,* published in Japan in 1878.

Further, from Miss Towles's collection of Henderson Auduboniana: "All of the big boys were at his heels, begging to be allowed to shoot some great eagle or other rare bird he had found. The grandchildren of Mrs. Stites tell how she held the wild turkey while he painted it. Another handed down a snake story. Audubon had followed a woodpecker for some distance when he saw it go into a hole high up on the side of a tree. Up he climbed to investigate. Thrusting in his hand he brought out a black snake. Down he tumbled to the ground. His friend ran to him. 'Were you scared?' he asked. 'Scared, ze devil. Vat I scared for? But if you will see one tam scared snake, you look up zat tree!' "

This is as good a place as any to speak about JJA's French accent. It's reflected in the spelling of his unedited letters and journals: "as" for "has," "hearned" for "earned," "Geay" for "Jay," "compagnon" for companion," "sheep" for "ship," and so forth. When Audubon anecdotes were told by his contemporaries, it was evidently in vaudeville French, and thus were they repeated and written down. It's surprising that his accent caused comment. America swarmed with French-speaking people. Audubon himself rarely bothered to mention in which tongue he spoke to this individual or that, except in the case of Indians. For example, the hunting party of Shawnee with whom he went on the swan hunt: . . . [M]any of them spoke French passably, I easily joined . . . their 'talks' and their avocations." Or years later, at a sealing camp of Montagnais Indians in Labrador:

The Japanese view of the discovery of rats in the chest of bird drawings, with an almond-eyed Audubon registering melodramatic horror in the best Kabuki tradition. *Courtesy of The New-York Historical Society, New York City*

"The chief of the party proves to be well informed, and speaks French."

The Henderson land grant was surveyed by the Transylvania Company in 1797 and a town plan drawn up. One passing visitor around that time described it as a muddy settlement of scattered cabins and a refuge for "horse thieves, rogues and outlaws. Neither law nor gospel has been able to reach here as yet." According to Audubon, Henderson was still an outpost of six or eight houses when he first saw it in 1810. Down through the years, despite an uppercrust of local gentry with their at-homes, musicales, church activities, and the like, Henderson was still a river town, a border town, and shoot-em-up and cut-em-up town. In the pre-World War I era, there were eighty-four saloons to a population of 10,000. "But some of the saloons down there," said one elderly citizen, "where they had the livery stables and upstairs, of course, places full of women, I don't know how many killings there were." During Prohibition, Henderson was known as Bootlegger's Heaven with "dozens of bright and shining dens of vice." We've heard that it's still a mobster town, with Mafia types from Chicago running the show. One young man, who would probably prefer to remain anonymous, said that his new pals introduced him to the gambling scene when he moved here a few years ago. "But not for this country boy," he told us. "Run up a debt, cross them, and you're dead. We used to have a murder every weekend." (This weekend they've had two murders, to date, and a beating and robbery at the Ellis Park racetrack.)

As for the general appearance of the town, it's not what we'd expected, our preconception colored by the comparatively un-spoiled ambiance of Ste. Genevieve and by Audubon's write-up from the last century: "The woods were amply stocked with game, the river with fish, and now and then the hoarded sweets of the industri-ous bees were brought from some hollow tree to our table." We had anticipated a nineteenth century flavor instead of an updated, grow-ing city of 22,500. "One ugly new building after another," said an-other citizen. "This town has a bad case of bulldoze-itis. It's a dis-grace." The destruction of the old courthouse was cited as an example. It had been a Neo-Georgian stone structure that was de-clared eminently sound by architects from a committee on national shrines, but the building was up for grabs in a county boondoggle and down it went. "I vow I'll never set foot in the new courthouse," said our informant. "But I hear it leaks like a sieve, and I'm tickled pink."

There are eight hundred and twelve acres to the John James Audubon State Park. It's north of town in an area once known as Wolf Hills, where the mound-builder Indians buried their dead. In the old days after the Ohio and the Green flooded, Henderson boys would scramble off into the Wolf Hills to look for Indian artifacts of stone, shell, bead, bone, and hammered metals that were often washed out of the grave mounds by high water. The first sizeable tract of land given to found the park was donated by David Clark, a Henderson tobacco man, who loved the Wolf Hills and asked that this stretch of virgin timber not be disturbed, that it be kept as a sanctuary for wildlife. One wonders how Mr. Clark would feel about the new John James Audubon Golf Course recently carved out of park forestland, with much attendant agitation pro and con between the local politicians and the so-called "outdoor types." Actually, this is a deluxe state park—boating, a playground, cottages to rent, a gift shop, and now golf.

The park was built in the late 1930s by the Civilian Conservation Corps and the Works Projects Administration. Route 41, the state highway, was still in open country, except for the scattering of roadhouses near the river, where bootleggers could snap back and forth from state to state depending on which way the law was closing in. The John James Audubon Memorial Museum and the park office— both of stone and wood with steeply pitched slate roofs—were designed in the Norman mode to reflect the architecture of Audubon's father's roots in the French Chateau country. The museum has an impressive collection. On the walls are ranked the beautiful life-sized engravings of his bird paintings—the engravings done in Great Britain, mostly by the firm of Robert Havell of London.

There's also a rich assortment of Auduboniana—portraits and landscapes painted by his sons, family letters, ledgers, account sheets, manuscripts, deeds; family tintypes, photographs, and correspondence; Mrs. Audubon's calling card, Mr. Audubon's calling card that identifies him as a fellow of the Royal and the Linnaean Societies of London; his watch fob with the wild turkey seal, his crayon holder, leaves and flowers that he pressed in Henderson; a wooden cog, a lock and key, and metal fittings from his mill; the amethyst pendant he sent to Lucy from London in 1826; the shell-patterned silver he bought her in London in 1836; the warrant for his arrest for debt in 1819. In one glass case are a life mask of Audubon and a silver bowl, unidentified on our visit here, except as "elegant objects" given by a member of the Havell family. A curious oversight, that, and no one on duty at the museum knew anything further. From a description in Francis Hobart Herrick's *Audubon the Naturalist*, we deduce that the silver bowl is the one JJA gave to Robert Havell in 1834 to celebrate publication of the second volume of *The Birds of America*. Also, thanks to the late Mr. Herrick, we assume that the life mask is from a mold taken by Havell in London in the late 1830s. A copy from the same mold, in Harvard's Museum of Comparative Zoology, is pictured in Herrick's book.

Audubon had more than one life mask taken. They were a fad in those days, and he described the process: "My coat and neckcloth were taken off, my shirt collar turned down, I was told to close my eyes; Mr. O'Neill took a large brush and oiled my whole face, the almost liquid plaster of Paris was poured over it, as I sat uprightly till the whole was covered; my nostrils only were exempt. In a few moments the plaster had acquired the needful consistency, when it was taken off by pulling it down gently. The whole operation lasted hardly five minutes. . . . On my return from the Antiquarian Society that evening, I found *my face* on the table."

Many people, by the way, who know something about Audubon's life and are familiar with his work are still not sure of his place in time. A startling example of this, raised to the level of an official statement, appears in a brief biography of JJA in the current museum pamphlet. It's illustrated with an imaginary sketch of the artist-naturalist in the woods, sitting on a folding campstool before an easel as he paints a large bird that appears to be a cross between a goose and a turkey. Whoever drew John James Audubon neglected to do basic research. He didn't work that way. He's also depicted in the clothing of a 1901 storeclerk: eyeshade, high starched collar, sleeve garters, necktie, vest, pipe-stem trousers, and high-laced shoes of a style worn by a great uncle of mine. The illustrator also took the liberty of

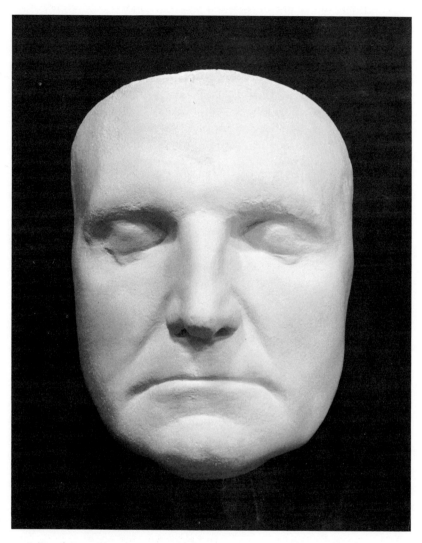

Audubon life mask. *Museum of Comparative Zoology, Harvard University*

shearing off Audubon's shoulder-length curling locks, which became his trademark, and gave him a turn-of-the-century haircut complete with center part.

We've met one of the curators from the early days of the museum: Melicent Quinn, a delightful woman in her mid-eighties, with lustrous dark eyes and an alabaster complexion. She retired not long ago from forty years as society editor of the Henderson *Gleaner*. When she worked at the museum in the 1930s, her office was in one of the tower rooms, where a portrait of Lucy hung over the desk, and Mrs. Quinn told us that the portrait once came to life. "I heard Lucy whispering. *Mmmm-oo-oo-oo . . . st-st-st-st.* I sat very still. I was there alone. Well, Lucy I thought. Are you trying to tell me something? *Mmmm . . . oo-oo-oo.* Then I heard Stewart, the guard, on the stairs and I dashed out and called him in. He heard it too. 'Fore God, said Stewart. Miss Lucy's talking! Then he looked behind the portrait and found it was a nest of wasps. But Lucy Audubon had given me the scare of my life."

"Now, let's be frank," said Mrs. Quinn about the museum. "To the average person those exhibits mean nothing. You walk around, look about, and say, 'What pretty pictures of birds.' But it would mean absolutely nothing. When I was a curator, all visitors were given a guided tour through Audubon's life as we went from gallery to gallery. It made a whacking good story. The story of a self-made man . . . I studied harder in that job than I ever studied in college. We had to. Big Brother was watching us. A member of the family, a woman, who was a bit of a martinet. A large part of the Audubon accessions came from her, and she held her power over our heads. If you don't do it *my* way, I'll take everything back. If you don't do it the *right* way, I'll take everything back."

What about Audubon? What was Mrs. Quinn's opinion of him? "As I used to tell our visitors at the museum, he had two faces that he presented to the world. The French playboy, the dandy, who dived off steamboats and swam under them from end to end to show what a French playboy could do. The other was the American woodsman, his hair to his shoulders, dressed in a leather jacket with his gun and his bundle of sketches. But genius is difficult to judge in terms of ordinary mortals. Those blessed with genius are forgiven their irresponsibilities, arrogance, their demands on other people. I myself have never known a genius who wasn't impossible. . . . Yet, whatever your opinion of Audubon, he was a marvel."

What of Miss Susan Towles? Had she tolerated any criticism of Audubon? Mrs. Quinn raised her hand in a gesture of caution. "Not in front of Miss Sue. Why, my Lord, Audubon came straight from heaven. He flew straight down on snow-white wings. Don't ever say for a moment that he left his poor partner sitting in the store for weeks while he went out tramping. Don't ever say that poor Lucy had to work like a dog, teaching, to support herself and the boys. Those were minor considerations. Audubon was charming. Audubon was an artist. When Miss Sue spoke his name, you could almost see candles burning."

Mrs. Quinn's appraisal of Audubon is not unique in this town. With all due respect to Miss Towles, Henderson nowadays does not necessarily look on him as a hero. Only one person to whom we spoke viewed him with Miss Towle's idealized devotion and even went so far as to compare his life and travels and quest to that of Christ. Otherwise, among typical comments, a Henderson newspaperman jovially referred to JJA as "that rascal." A state park attendant shrugged and laughed and said, "So far as I can see he was one jump ahead of the sheriff the whole time he was in Kentucky." A local naturalist, conversant with the many Audubon biographies, felt JJA had been sanctified far too often.

It's an interesting right about-face for a town where Audubon's name is supposedly cherished. Perhaps no man is a hero in his own land after all. And this is indeed a more cynical age, with Henderson perhaps reflecting our new attitudes toward our old heroes. We are bored by the hero with no flaws. Nothing is duller than perfection. We must know the hero's secrets, mistakes, and vices. We must see his feet of clay. Only then does the hero become real. What's more, this is the Age of the Put-Down. No sooner does a hero or heroine catch our hearts, than he or she must be leveled off to mortal proportions. (Says Michael, succinctly: "Perhaps Henderson—gamey, tough little river town that it is—has damn near been Auduboned to death.")

From the Henderson phone book:

Audubon Baptist Church
Audubon Clinic
Audubon Hosiery Mills, Inc.
Audubon Inn
Audubon Mobil Home Park
Audubon Office Furniture
Audubon Package Liquor Store
Audubon Phillips 66 Service Station
Audubon Seat Cover Center
Audubon Tire Co.
Audubon Travel Service
Audubon Wood Service

MH Late this November day I walked out along a trail into the hills and hollows of John James Audubon State Park. The trail system is just now being recut, thanks to Ron Dotson and the local chapter of the National Audubon Society. The original trails made by the CCC had become overgrown and been allowed to disappear.

I left the Norman castles—the handsome stone office and museum —and walked up a slope into the woods. A screaming blue jay ("Here he comes! Look out!"), a flicker, a red-bellied woodpecker moved away from the trail's edge, and caught my eye, their motion making them visible. I pushed ahead of me waves of robins—the stuff of many an autumn and winter pie in Audubon's day. Cardinals whistled, nuthatches honked, jays and flickers yammered, woodpeckers scolded harshly; but everywhere was the muted babble of robins, an undertone, a theme, like the distant sound of surf on an ocean beach. I made my way down into "the bottom"—so to speak—to a small lake Ron Dotson had told me about, and then I turned to go back. Carolina wrens called, and as the sun dropped behind a ridge above the lake's hollow, the leaves rustled with the scratching of busy small birds—sparrows and juncoes shuffling leaves, turning them, looking for seeds and grubs. Overhead, a flock of chucking blackbirds passed, headed south, but as usual not on any definable errand—maybe to a nearby roost And dominating it all was the *cheep* and *wees-wees*, the *pup-pup-pup, sherp-sherp,* and *cheery-up* of robins.

Soon I was back on the high ground, headed home, toward the sound of the highways. If JJA were to stand in this forest now, I thought, if he were dropped into this din of robins, he would think the world was coming to an end, because of the louder din from the roads at this end of town. Listen to those semis growl. *Roll on, Big Momma, I lahk the way you roll.* Oh, yahoo.

Great horned owls called, and I answered with an imitation, which failed to strike up the desired debate. But as if by the owls' signal, there were hundreds of robins all at once visible, visible because they were moving, not in full flight, but beginning to stir toward the south in the tops of the trees. Then some of them appeared higher up; they had cleared the trees and were on their way. What was at first an intriguing drift gradually became a surge, and I wondered how broad this stream of southing birds might be. At least as broad as the woods, I supposed. It continued as long as I was on the trail, the flood of robins rising higher and gaining momentum. Just robins, you might well say, Dear Reader. Think of them, then, as thrushes (which they are)—as a beautiful new species of thrush you've only just met; you call them Red-breasted Thrushes, and there are thousands of them passing over your head on a November evening in Kentucky.

On my way out of the woods, I met four children going the other way. I have got too old myself—I can't remember exactly when it happened—to be able to judge the ages of children with any sureness; but I'd guess they were twelve or thirteen years old. Two small boys with two bigger girls; the girls, I might say, looked as if they ought to know better. They came up the trail, the boys whooping and roughhousing and bounding on either side of the girls, and when they spotted the camera around my neck the boys were delighted. "Hey, take my pitcha! Hey, I'm a movie stah!" That sort of thing. I looked as disinterested as I could manage, but they were not deflected. One of the boys suggested that I might like to take a picture of his friend and one of the girls "doing it." I gritted my teeth and turned my head away, we passed each other, and they romped on into the woods, turning once or twice to shout back clarifications and elaborations on the theme.

MD   *Notes from our campsite:* A cold snap. Spitting snow. Night temperatures in the low forties. We've wrapped the north side of the tent with a tarp, brought out the big eiderdown sleeping bag, and go to bed with hats on—I in my woolen kerchief and Michael in his watch cap. You can lose a lot of body heat through the top of your head, like a house without a roof, but put on a nightcap, as did our forefathers in their cold and drafty houses, and your temperature rises, miraculously, within minutes. Also, I've cut the fingertips off an old pair of blue woolen gloves, so I can hold a pen or attend to cooking chores and still have warm hands. (Emmet Kelly's hobo clown gloves.)

By now, however, we're not very susceptible to cold. Our personal thermostats have adjusted from exposure, by living outside. When we go inside these days—the ranger's office, shops, the museum—it's as though we'd stepped into a boiler room. We feel ourselves going groggy and leaden in the heat. On nippy mornings when the park attendants arrive for their day's rounds, they exclaim at our continued presence. ("God Awmighty! You still here!")

What is the cutoff point, we wonder—the moment when it suddenly becomes too cold to live in a tent. One more night out-of-doors does not seem unreasonable. The light frost and the nip and snap-crackle in the air are still an exhilaration.

We're surrounded by hackberry trees. Rare in New England, prevalent throughout the Ohio River valley, and new to both of us. They belong to the elm family, as one might guess from looking at their leaves, but unlike the usual elm, with its flat, round, brown seeds designed to float on the wind, the hackberry has red-purple berries. One of the field guides we have with us is *Trees of the Eastern and Central United States and Canada* by William Harlow. Under hackberry, he wrote that the flesh of the fruit, what there is of it, has a pleasant datelike taste, and he includes a photograph of the pit, which has squarish-shaped ridges, much the same pattern as on a hand grenade. Following his lead, I collect some of the berries. Yes, a sweet, datelike flavor; and the pit matches the photo.

This morning, in the view from inside the tent, where I sit cross-legged with a cup of coffee and my notebook and my pen (wearing my Emmet Kelly gloves), the hackberry trees are thick with feeding cedar waxwings, robins, and evening grosbeaks. Oddly, these trees do not appear in any of JJA's paintings, although he saw them year after year throughout these parts and certainly must have observed all species of fruit-eating birds in their branches. Mockers and sapsuckers favor the hackberry too.

Since our arrival, the nature story in the local news has been the Spottsville Monster—Henderson County's very own Bigfoot—seven feet tall, dark green, and it walked on its hind legs like a man. A farmer out Spottsville way, some nine miles down the road from the state park, has been harassed by the monster for four months. It chased him out of his tobacco field, chased his children out of the cornfield, and prowled through his yard; his wife saw it outlined against the barn at night; one of the kids came round the truck after dark, met the monster head on, screamed, and it ran away; sixteen chickens and one goat disappeared. The farmer and his family always knew when the Monster was around—their dogs would run under the house and wouldn't come out.

It was announced on the radio this morning that just as the sheriff had formed a posse to find out once and for all what the Spottsville Monster really was, the monster turned out to be a bear. Now the sheriff has another problem on his hands. It's against the law to shoot bear in Kentucky, so they're working up a plan to remove it from the neighborhood without breaking the game laws. Tranquillizer-darts and nets.

This isn't the first Bigfoot to be seen around Henderson. A few years back, there was another on the prowl that could be glimpsed at dusk, darting through the underbrush on the Indiana shore; it was more than six and a half feet tall and covered with white fur. It proved to be an ancient, demented recluse, with a long white beard and wild white hair.

Today, Sunday, we drove down into Kentucky, south of Henderson, on what might have been a wild goose chase. Audubon mentioned a family named Sugg and wrote of having "slept comfortably" at their house on one of his cross-Kentucky trips. I'd found a William Sugg in a history of Kentucky at the library. He lived five miles northeast of Morganfield, his log house had been destroyed by fire in 1855, and his one hundred-year-old mother had died from the effect of burns. From what Audubon writes, his Mr. Sugg lived on the north side of Highland Lick Creek. I cross-referenced these two leads on an old map of Henderson County, and put Mr. Sugg someplace in the vicinity of the town of Corydon.

Upon our arrival, we found half a dozen listings under Sugg in the Corydon phone book. A trio of old timers in the window of the garage, who were watching traffic and killing time that Sabbath morning, looked knowledgeable, so I went in and explained that we wanted to ask about an ancestor of the Suggs who had settled here in the early 1800s. Which one of the family should we phone?

They checked down through the listings. Don't call that one or that one—they're Suggs by marriage and wouldn't be much help. And that one's just a boy. He probably wouldn't know much about it either. And don't bother with this one. He'll still be in bed, he had a long, hard Saturday night, last night. Now there's the fellow to call. (They pointed to a name in the book.) He's a churchgoer, up bright and early, you won't be waking him if you phone, and he'll be able to tell you something about the family besides.

The old men in the garage had steered us to the right person. We were invited to join Mr. Sugg and his family later in the day for dessert and coffee. They had not known that Audubon and their great-great-grandfather were acquainted and that Audubon had spent a night in 1824. Major William Sugg, who'd served in the War of 1812, lived on a farm (now gone) outside of town, and here was a picture of the Major with his mother, née Patience Jones, the lady who would be mortally burned in the fire—a pretty, delicate face with a little pair of spectacles on her nose and a white lace cap on her head. Her son, the Major, was a handsome man with fine features, who wore the chin-high collar and wide black stock of the era. That was the extent of the day's adventure. There were no fresh revelations on Audubon and his life in Kentucky. But we brought Mr. Sugg tidings of his great-great-grandfather, and he showed us a photograph of the man who put up Audubon for the night in 1824. A slim lead tracked down out of curiosity, and a pleasant tying-up of loose threads left dangling for a century and a half.

The return drive to Henderson, side roads. Pigs everywhere. In cornfields, woodlots, pastures. Often in the same field with sheep, cows, horses, geese. Black and white pigs; standard pink; muddy dusty heaps of flaked-out pigs, snoozing in the noonday sun, and

Major William Sugg and his mother. *Courtesy of the family*

piglets, piglets, piglets—sleeping, nursing, rooting, romping, racing and chasing, trotting about on their trotters, blinking and staring, thinking long and short thoughts. (Is this usual, this number of piglets? Or is it a bumper crop?)

A big female red-tailed hawk flew out of an oak forest near the Ohio shore. The right light, the right distance, and I could clearly see, feather by feather, the red tail fanned out like a hand of cards, as she maneuvered through the bare branches for a landing on a high limb.

We wanted to talk to someone who knew Audubon's mill when it was standing and were directed to a Henderson man, aged eighty-three, born and raised on the Green River. When I called to make a date I assumed that the voice on the phone was that of his wife, so I introduced myself and asked for Mr. Meade. "This is Charlie Meade speaking," said he. "I have a high voice like a woman, but that doesn't bother me a bit. I sang tenor for years in the Presbyterian Church and got paid for it too. I've always been a member of the Presbyterian Church."

Thus we met Charles Meade, who had a thousand memories to tell; a former bank accountant; a widower who spoke with deep regret of his wife's death four months short of their golden wedding anniversary; a small, spry, hospitable gentleman, who lives in a spruce little house he bought in 1923 for $1400—"That was a lot of money in those days."

Since his retirement, Mr. Meade has devoted himself to his lifelong hobby, photography, which he began in the era of wet plates. "I used to wash the plates in a clear mountain stream. But they're polluted now. You couldn't do that anymore." He brought out a glass plate photograph of the Audubon mill that was taken, he guessed, in the 1890s. The picture was not one of his own but was by Robert Stites, "who went to Princeton and studied dentistry" and belonged to the same family, of course, as the Mrs. Stites who supposedly held a turkey for Audubon to paint when she was a little girl.

When Mr. Meade was a child, the mill stood empty. "It was nothing but a rat warren, don't you know. We'd go back up in there and wander around, and before that it had been used as a tobacco warehouse. Back in those days, it was what they called dark-fired tobacco. Now, everything is burley, because it's light and is made into cigarettes. But that old dark-green tobacco. Takes a man to smoke *that*. Burley's still dark-fired, with sawdust sometimes, but they used to use good wood, like hickory, that burned a long time. If you go down to Tennessee this time of year, why, you can see smoke coming out of the barns. You'd think they were all on fire . . .

"Way back years ago there were quite a few hoboes coming to the kitchen door here every morning to get something. When the mill stood empty, the hoboes would go in there. Once there was a tramp up inside the mill, sick, and he had a dog with him. They had to kill the dog to get the man out. But tramps and hoboes or whatever you want to call them were always inside the mill, and I imagine they were smoking and set it on fire. It was half-gone, anyway. I don't remember when it was ever used as a mill, don't you know. That's just a myth to me. And Audubon—well, he was a wanderer and a

A print from Robert Stites' damaged glass plate of Audubon's mill in ruins.
Courtesy of Charles Meade

painter. Miss Susan Towles said he spent days and nights wandering through the Wolf Hills. I've hunted rabbit and squirrel through there. That was all virgin timber. Still is. Lots of beeches and ironwood. And I liked to go frog-hunting too, when I was a kid. I'd bring them home and my mother would fry up the legs. I used to go places I wouldn't go now, into the swamps. And we put a wire through their lips to carry them home. Once I felt something tugging behind me. I looked back and there was a water moccasin trying to eat my frog . . ."

How about Audubon and Mrs. Audubon swimming the river every morning before breakfast? Would that be possible? "It's possible," said Mr. Meade. "But I wouldn't hardly believe it. Though at low water, may be. *I've* swum the Ohio. But since they made the dams, the water's ten feet higher than it used to be. The Corps of Engineers are ruining the Ohio River as far as farmers are concerned. It wrecks our farm land. The water level rises and spreads out, and if they have a spring flood, the corn and soybeans are ruined. They're doing it for the selfish interests of the coal industry and oil, so they can put on those big diesel towboats. . . . When I was a boy we had steamboats on the river. There was no bridge here to Evansville. My dad ran a store on the Green River. General merchandise. And we went to Evansville two or three times a year to buy from the wholesale houses. Those steamboats weren't as elaborate as the one you see in motion picture, but they had colored men in ruffled shirts waiting table. My dad and I, we always sat at the captain's table."

As we leave, Mr. Meade gives us two gifts—a copy of the old photograph of the Audubon mill and a first-day cover of the John James Audubon commemorative stamp issued in 1963. We protest that he should not give away the Audubon envelope. No, Mr. Meade has another that his wife sent him. He'll keep that one. But a boy down at the post office had also mailed him a first-day cover. "You're welcome to it. I'd like you to have it."

We didn't take a close look at the Audubon commemorative stamp until later, intrigued as we were with the photo of the mill, which showed most of its siding gone, its forelegs shakily braced against the river bank, and the whole tumbling structure looking as though it would fall in at the next strong gust of wind. The stamp, which neither of us remembered clearly from 1963, pictures two

large blue-plumaged birds posturing magnificently on a dead branch
entwined with the yellowing leaves of a poison ivy vine. They have
pronounced crests and tail feathers twice as long as the birds' bodies.
"I've never seen it before in my life," said Mike. "It's a *kind* of jay,
but not from the United States."

The mystery bird turns out to be the black-throated magpie jay
(Calocitta formosa colliei), or Collie's magpie-jay, native to western
Mexico, and painted by Audubon from a gift specimen said to have
been collected at the Columbia River in the American northwest. So
Audubon called it the Columbia Jay, mistakenly included it in *The
Birds of America,* and the Post Office chose it for the stamp—thus
sending droves of American birdwatchers into confusion and/or patriotic pique. The National Audubon Society asked for an explanation
back in 1963, and the Post Office Department responded that they
had known all along that it was a Mexican species, but out of Audubon's four hundred and thirty-five bird engravings, they felt, the
magpie-jay was best suited for a postage-stamp.

Oh well. All right.

Notes from our campsite: We set forth on this trip in all innocence.
In reverence, if you will. John James Audubon—the American
Woodsman, the ornithologist, the painter of birds. A legend in his
own time and, God knows, a legend in ours. Sir Galahad of the Forest.

We've now read six full-length biographies, scores of biographical
sketches and commentaries, and his autobiographical memoirs—he
wrote several, each different. There is so much to learn, so much to
remember, so many details to mix and match, the dilemma of fact
versus fiction (sand in the eyes, red herrings across the trail), that one
despairs of ever sorting things out. But on the second and third and
fourth readings of the biographies, in the crossfire of Audubon's
correspondence (letters written, letters received), in his recollections, essays, anecdotes, and in the recollections, essays, and anecdotes of his contemporaries, the facts begin to separate themselves
from the tiddlywinks.

Now we begin to know too much, more than we know what to
do with, and we find ourselves trapped in the past—his past. We live
with our protagonist day by day, and we gossip about Audubon as we
would about any close, ill-starred acquaintance. We argue over din-

ner about Audubon and Lucy. We take them to pieces. Interpret and re-interpret. The fifty-cent picnic-table psychoanalysis. It will go on for months.

Lucy, however, doesn't come through too clearly in Henderson. One biographer wrote that a sister-in-law and a young visiting English woman both took an intense dislike to Lucy for putting on airs. But that's not conclusive. In another surviving letter to her English cousin, in which Lucy described an eight-hundred-mile trip by horseback from Henderson to Fatland Ford, she dutifully recorded their route, the dreadful roads, the gloom of the thick forests, and one or two beautiful views. But there is no light or spark to the letter except when she spoke of little Victor, aged two-and-a-half, who "rode before his Papa all the way." One line in particular strikes me as indicative. Said Lucy: "You will easily conceive I must have suffered from cold and fatigue considerably . . . but the prospect before me of seeing my family and friends . . . enabled me to endure." *Endure* looms as the key word, not only for the trip by horseback but as Lucy's summary of her life so far. I begin to see her as a capable but hardput and joyless woman.

MH   Our views and the tenor of our campfire discussion change as we become educated, of course—as facts finally take hold. A slice of what we're thinking and arguing about is transformed not only in the discussion but in the writing down, and it's hard to isolate moments in the debate. We've tried setting our notes and points of disagreement side by side—a conversation in print—and it doesn't work. But Audubon's career in Henderson certainly does offer a fertile field for this kind of conversation.

When we arrived in Henderson, we knew what Audubon would achieve, and the display of his best work and the evidences of his success that we find in the museum here reinforce that knowledge. At the same time, Mary sees this young man in Louisville, Ste. Genevieve, and Henderson, "still playing the role of the landed gentry, the rich boy from France who could do as he jolly well pleased, the spoiled darling, the prima donna. Vain, impudent, a charmer and braggart, indulging in an imitation of high life, and making foolish investments, one after another, each aimed at getting rich quick, each doomed to failure." What if he hadn't made it as John James

Audubon, she wants to know. This fellow in Henderson seems to be fixed on a straight course toward John James Nothing.

But I see a lot that's different about the man Audubon in Henderson compared to the one we've traveled with up to now. It seems to me that Audubon's biographers gloss over this, miss it almost completely—and one of them positively rages over Audubon's presumed incompetence in Henderson. I don't think he was all that incompetent; he was doing very well for a while.

The crux of the matter is the steam mill. Audubon says—bitterly, long after the fact—that Henderson and vicinity was as unfit a place for building a steam mill "as it would be now for me to attempt to settle in the moon." On such slender reeds as this biographers have propped a wholesale assertion that there wasn't enough work for the mill to do in Henderson—no lumbering industry, little grain grown for flour, no chance in the world for the business to prosper. I don't believe that. For one thing, I think Audubon exaggerated this case as he did many others in retrospection. The mill machinery drove him crazy, it was treacherous, it kept breaking down; the mechanic they hired was incompetent; there were many times when the business couldn't operate because the machinery didn't move. But Audubon worked hard at getting it to run. He leased 1200 acres across the river in Indiana Territory to give him a steady supply of lumber, and then hired a crew to cut timber there; they ran off with his tools and oxen before their contract was up. And still the mill didn't work. I'd be bitter myself after all that. In three years he'd gone from a comfortable situation—the moderately successful young storekeeper, lots of friends, growing family, nice house, up-and-coming citizen in an up-and-coming river town—to ruin, to being hounded for money by his neighbors, forced into bankruptcy, driven from his town. No wonder he was sour. But suppose the machinery had worked properly.

I'm impressed by the partners he had—people who thought, at least for a while, that the investment was worth it. I'm particularly interested in Nicholas Berthoud, an established and successful businessman, who came into the enterprise toward the end, after it was obvious how much trouble the machinery was giving. Berthoud eventually bought Audubon out, for a rather hefty sum. These people weren't stupid. The West was going to grow, everyone knew that.

Men who owned land and businesses in the towns along the Ohio stood to do very well for themselves. A mill was a basic business. It could have turned out to be an excellent investment.

I don't mean to say that Audubon was either as cautious or astute as he ought to have been. And neither does he. He says that "the times were what men called 'bad,' but I am fully persuaded the great fault was ours." Even so, all this business about his being one jump ahead of the sheriff, and so on, that's just balderdash. The idea is, why, shoot, the artist just can't handle figures or business, he's got his head so high in the clouds. But we can't have it both ways. We can't complain about his lighthearted extravagances of time and money in Mill Grove and Louisville and Ste. Genevieve and then ignore the small success he'd started with his store in Henderson, and all the hard work he put into the mill—in short, the obvious evidence that he really began to get down to brass tacks here. He's *changing* in Henderson. As far as I'm concerned, it is here he becomes a sympathetic character in his own story.

Furthermore, times *were* bad, with a lot of people taking it on the chin. Audubon would run into the effects of a depressed and shaky economy for some while yet.

MD   Lucy and the boys were taken in by the Rankins, and she began her teaching career in earnest with classes for their children and hers. Audubon left Henderson—"probably forever, without a dollar in my pocket . . . My plantation in Pennsylvania had been sold, and, in a word, nothing left to me but my humble talents." He walked to Louisville to eke out a living doing black-chalk portraits, aided and comforted by his French emigré friends in Shippingport, at the Falls of the Ohio. But nowhere in that autobiography written for his sons does Audubon mention his arrest there for unpaid debts, though admittedly the Louisville jail in those days was nothing to write home about. It was described as a "most miserable edifice, in a most filthy and ruinous condition, first cousin to the black hole of Calcutta."

Audubon never again set foot in Henderson. A year later, on a journey down the Ohio by flatboat, he passed the town and wrote bitterly in his journal: "We experienced quite a *Gale* and Put to on the Indianna Shore opposite Henderson . . . I can scarcely Conceive that I staid there 8 Years and Passed them comfortably for it un-

Thomas W. Bakewell, Lucy's brother and Audubon's sometime partner, sketched by JJA in Louisville, 1820. *From National Audubon Society*

doubtedly is one of the poorest Spots in the Western Country. . . . We left our harbour at day Break and passed Henderson about sun raise, I Looked on the Mill perhaps for the Last Time, and with thoughts that made my Blood almost Cold bid it an eternal farewell—" But in truth his last view of Henderson would come on a passage down the Ohio twenty-three years later. Time had dulled the old pains, and in a letter to his family he merely stated that they passed Henderson but did not stop: "I saw the old mill etc. and the steeples of 2 churches."

CINCINNATI

1819–1820

MH Released from jail as a confessed bankrupt, Audubon scraped along in Louisville for several months until an acquaintance, one Robert Todd, wrote a letter on his behalf to a gentleman connected with Cincinnati College, upriver from Louisville. All things considered, Mr. Todd's letter was a momentous one.

"Dear Sir—You will very much oblige me by making immediate enquiry of the Trustees of your College whether or no they wish to employ a professor of French and drawing. Mr. Audubon of this place would I think accept the appointment, if the salary would be made an object. He is emminently qualified for both or either. You have no doubt seen some of his paintings in this place and of course will be able to judge on that subject for yourself. He has nearly finished a collection of American birds, and is anxious to see Wilson's Ornithology to ascertain whether or no there is any bird in his collection which he Mr. Audubon has omitted to paint. Messers St. Clair [and others, illegible] will I have no doubt assist you in procuring them from the library. . . . The opportunity of employing Mr. Audubon must not be neglected as he would be a great acquisition to your institution."

As it turned out, JJA was acquired not by the college but by the Western Museum, which used some of the college rooms. And his job was taxidermy—stuffing fish and birds, something he'd been good at for years.

He was hired by Daniel Drake, "the Franklin of the Ohio Valley," physician, teacher, druggist, businessman, philanthropist, editor, and

111

J. C. Wild's "View of Cincinnati," painted several years after Audubon was here. *Museum of Fine Arts, Boston*

writer. As a writer, Drake was nothing if not eclectic; in the Cincinnati Historical Society I fill a page of my notebook with his topics, which include cholera, the etymology of the word "buckeye" as applied to a resident of Ohio, hypnotism, early physicians, the history and character and prospects of the West, public medical libraries, the anti-slavery movement (he was agin it, but favored resettling American blacks in Africa), the New Madrid earthquake, aurora borealis, the southwest wind, and "botanic medicine" (he was agin that too). As philanthropist and public-spirited citizen, he had a hand in the establishment of a circulating library, an eye infirmary, a society to rescue and resuscitate the drowning, a society for "the Promotion of Agriculture, Manufactures and Domestic Economy," a Commercial Hospital and Lunatic Asylum, a teacher's college, the Ohio Medical College, and the Western Museum Society. He had accomplished a good deal of this by 1819. He was thirty-four that year. So was Audubon. Drake had known where he was going in life since the age of fifteen, when he was "apprenticed" to a Cincinnati physician; Audubon had only just now sighted his own goal.

The fact of that sighting slips into JJA's story sideways. He never said much about it himself, perhaps because he chose the goal only after things went so dreadfully sour for him in Henderson. The first inkling that descends to us appears in Todd's letter, which is one reason it is momentous. JJA is now talking about a complete collection of North American bird paintings.

Lucy joined him in Cincinnati. His job at the Western Museum only lasted a few months; the hard times that had helped make Audubon a bankrupt were hard on many enterprises in the Middle West. By 1819 industries were failing in Cincinnati, and many of its wealthy citizens went broke. Daniel Drake—the Franklin of the West, the personification of the well-organized good citizen, whose foresight and direction and energy many of Audubon's detractors would doubtless like to wave in our friend's face—had to move into a log cabin, which he called "Mount Poverty." So, even though employed, Audubon did not receive all his promised salary from the museum. But he and Lucy liked Cincinnati, which was an attractive little city of ten thousand souls, and they improvised as they were becoming accustomed to doing. They found private pupils, he taught drawing at a girls' school. And, as Audubon wrote, "Our living here is extremely moderate; the markets are well supplied and cheap, beef only two and a half cents a pound, and I am able to provide a good deal myself; Partridges are frequently in the streets, and I can shoot Wild Turkeys within a mile or so; Squirrels and Woodcock are very abundant in the season, and fish always easily caught."

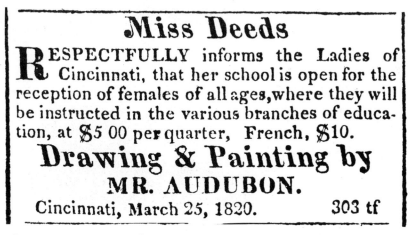

Miss Deeds

RESPECTFULLY informs the Ladies of Cincinnati, that her school is open for the reception of females of all ages, where they will be instructed in the various branches of education, at $5 00 per quarter, French, $10.

Drawing & Painting by
MR. AUDUBON.

Cincinnati, March 25, 1820.   303 tf

The Cincinnati Historical Society

And from his experience in the museum Audubon received more than money. For the first time in his life, he was exposed daily to a scientific environment and to people who treated his nature notes and drawings as more than the products of a time-consuming hobby. He and the curator, young Robert Best, put together exhibits for the museum. Best told him about odd birds and good bird-finding spots in the area. And Dr. Drake publicly praised his drawings and encouraged the ambitious *Birds of America* project.

An advertisement in the *Western Spy and Literary Cadet,* a local paper dated March 18, 1820: "The friends of [the Western Museum], who amuse themselves with shooting, are respectfully informed that Birds or Quadrupeds of any kind, in a situation to preserve, will be very acceptable. Gentlemen disposed to favor the Institution with specimens are requested to be careful to preserve the plumage of the birds unruffled and free from blood, the effusion

Bonaparte's gull in nonbreeding plumage, drawn by JJA at Cincinnati in mid-August 1820. He'd never seen the species before and named it, very tentatively, "Cincinati Gull." Many birds were named in this manner, according to the first locality where they were found, but this species had already been named for Charles Lucien Bonaparte by George Ord, a Philadelphia ornithologist. *Courtesy of The New-York Historical Society, New York City*

of which may be stopped by the application of dry earth. Any attempt to wash off the blood, will inevitably spoil the specimens. Robert Best, Curator."

I particularly like one story JJA told about this period in his life. A Cincinnati woman woke one morning to find a least bittern perched on her bedpost. The least bittern is a lovely little creature —less than a foot tall, colorful in a russetty sort of way, chestnut and buff and white and black, very ornamental—but a city bedroom is a most unlikely place for it. It is a marsh bird, best known, perhaps, for

JJA's charcoal portrait of John Cleves Symmes, drawn "for the Western Museum" in August 1820. *The Cincinnati Historical Society*

its ability to posture and shape itself to look like one of the reeds it lives among and thus become exceedingly hard to find. The lady of the bedroom surmised that the bird on her bedpost had fallen down the chimney during the night. She arose, caught the bittern, and carried it to the museum in her apron. City museums of natural history are familiar these days with such visitors—kind folk who pick up injured or starving or lost birds and would like to learn the names of the birds, and then have some knowledgeable person take the responsibility off their hands. Perhaps the people at the Western Museum found the event out of the ordinary, but they did what museums do today: directed her to the birdman on the premises.

Audubon was delighted. He relieved her of the bittern and sat down to draw, while the bird posed motionless for two hours. (In the plate of JJA's least bittern, the bird on the left—the immature—is this very individual.) When the drawing was done, he made an experiment: how thin could a least bittern get when it was really trying? He set two books upright on his table, creating a passageway an inch-and-a-half wide, and the bittern walked through it easily. He then closed the gap to an inch, and again the bittern negotiated it without trouble. This seemed marvelous to Audubon. At rest, the bittern didn't look as if it ought to be able to do that. He killed the bird to examine it further, and measured its breadth; in death it was two-and-a-quarter inches across.

The few months at the Western Museum were an instructive and happy time for him. Today in Cincinnati there are only bits and pieces left to represent that interlude—most of them in books and libraries and historical societies. We catch an occasional whiff of the old city—row-houses in brick, clinging to the steep hillsides. But the house he and Lucy rented at 414 East 3rd Street—still standing in the 1930s and pictured in a WPA writers' project tour book as one of the historic spots in Cincinnati—is now lost somewhere under the Fort Washington Distributor, a cloverleaf of downtown highway. So is the site of the Western Museum.

We cross the river to Kentucky, hoping to reach the scene of one of his birding adventures. In those days, a small army garrison was stationed in Newport, and cliff swallows built their nests on the brick walls of the arsenal. Audubon had found this species only once before, in Henderson—and most of those birds had been picked up dead from cold. So he spent many hours in Newport, collecting cliff swallow eggs (with a teaspoon, to protect the fragile mud nests) and watching the courtship, nest-building, raising of young, and the departure.

The arsenal stood on a short point of land, just where the Licking River meets the Ohio, across from Cincinnati's Riverfront Stadium,

Newport Barracks stands to the left of the mouth of the Licking River. *The Cincinnati Historical Society*

home of the Cincinnati Reds baseball team. You can see the Newport arsenal site from the bridge into Kentucky and from the little bridge that crosses the Licking River and again from a high levee on the edge of Newport: a small Washington-Monument shaft, a pentagonal wall surrounding a tree, and a road along the Licking. But as far as we can discover, there is no way to reach that road by car; we drive back and forth within a few hundred yards of it like rats in a maze, deflected by the levee and chain-link fences, and at last give up. On our way out of Newport, still smarting, we stop for gas on the far side of the Licking, perhaps a quarter-mile at most from the monument on the flat. We ask about the place. None of the natives at the gas station knows how to find it either; in fact, none of them has ever been out there.

An ad in an 1820 issue of the *Western Spy*: "RAGS! RAGS! HARD TIMES—Save Your Rags—$5.00 per 100 weight."

Suppose HARD TIMES had not intervened and caused the Western Museum to be a "poor paymaster," as Audubon would later report. (Eventually it was able to make good on at least some of the back pay owed him.) The city and the museum were congenial to JJA's nature, and a steady job at decent wages in the field of one's choice can be very seductive, regardless of one's dreams. How long would Audubon have stayed?

Well, one's "destiny" is steered by such chances, and as it happened there was nothing to hold him from the venture he had been planning for some months now. In October 1820, intending to draw and explore along the Mississippi and westward, he boarded a flatboat, Jacob Aumack, captain, bound for New Orleans. He carried his gun, drawing equipment, portfolio, very little (if any) money, and letters of introduction. One of Audubon's art students accompanied him as an apprentice-assistant—Joseph Mason, only thirteen years old but already a first-rate botanical painter.

The expedition was, in a way, a drop off into the void. Audubon was committing himself to a very uncertain future, and he felt vulnerable and scared.

OHIO RIVER

OCTOBER–NOVEMBER 1820

MD Audubon's journal for this trip (now held by the Houghton Library at Harvard) is a calfbound book the size of a ledger, with blue-marbled endpapers and the maker's label: "Book Binding In All Its Various Branches, by W. Pounsford, Three doors north of the Presbyterian Church, Cincinnati." The pages are the heavy, old-time paper made of the rags for which there were so many ads in the *Western Spy and Literary Cadet.* Beautiful paper. It never crumbles. The pages are a pleasure to touch and to turn, and a pleasure to read, because JJA's handwriting is quite legible in this instance, as though the journal were written with more care and introspection than much of his later pell-mell notes and correspondence.

Long after Audubon's death, two of his granddaughters, Miss Maria and Miss Eliza Audubon, released a few sterilized snippets for publication in *The Auk* (North America's leading quarterly of ornithology). The journal in the original is innocuous enough—field notes on birds, sprightly comments on the people with whom Audubon traveled, gloomy reflections on the pain of poverty; but the ladies felt, perhaps, that it was a crude moment in his life, which would dim the lustre of his artistic and ornithological reputation. They excised his comments on the overripe smell of a dead heron that he painted and dissected; on a "White Eye Fly Catcher" that was eaten by rats before he could draw it; on the "astonishing Leaps that Some *Maggots* took about our Table" having "Issued out of a Very good piece of Cheese to perform this"; on his embarrassment at a Natchez hotel when he absentmindedly ate with his fingers, "having not used a fork

121

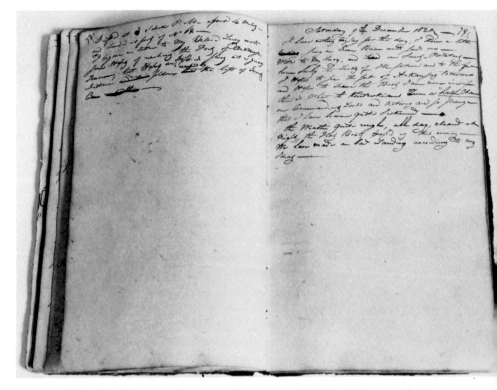

The 1820–1821 journal, open to the page on which Audubon noted, December 9, 1820, "Wrote to My Lucy and Lived on Sweet Potatoes—how surly the Looks of Ill fortune are to the poor." *Houghton Library, Harvard University*

and Scarcely even a plate since I left Louisville."

It was a three-month journey from Cincinnati to New Orleans, and Audubon was not only collecting birds to draw for his portfolio but was evidently working his passage as huntsman, providing fresh game. He himself regularly ate his specimens, if only out of curiosity and for the record. Grebes he found to be fishy, rancid, and fat; a hermit thrush fat and delicate; red-winged blackbirds, good and delicate; greater yellowlegs, very fat but very fishy; common grackle "tasted well."

By and large, the weather held on the Ohio. "The *Indian Summer*," he wrote, "that extraordinary Phenomenon of North America, is now in all its Splendor, the Blood Red Raising Sun—and the Constant *Smoky* atmosphere." A few days later, he further noted: "The Weather fair this morning. . . . The sun rose beautifull and reflected through the trees on the Placid Stream much like a Column of Lively fire—the frost was heavy on the decks and when the Sun Shun of it it looked beautifull beyond expression."

What with a long stopover at Louisville, the flatboat was a month reaching the confluence of the Wabash and the Ohio. Audubon went ashore there on a hunting expedition for the boat's mess. He had come this way before, going to Vincennes on business, and had traveled up the Wabash, making notes on nesting pied-billed grebes, nesting black terns, avocets, green-winged teal.

We too are at the Wabash in Indian summer, and we took a chance tonight on the Harmonie State Recreation Area—a stern mouthful of a name for a beautiful place—even though we thought it might well be closed for the season. More than 3000 acres on the Wabash, all to ourselves and the barred owls and the great horned owls. The "modern camping" area, which is marked OPEN, is closed. Water off, bathhouse locked, electric hookup gismos disconnected; we stormed about in the gathering dusk, trying faucets and doors. A red horizon behind the trees. Night falls fast at this time of year. No lingering twilights; the sun's trajectory is so low, it sets in seconds, and daylight is gone in a trice.

We drove on down a dark dirt road to the "Primitive Camping," as it's marked. Reward: a ridge of open fields, bounded by forest and strung together by a narrow road that's pure white in the moonlight. The fields are unmown—blue-stem grass, cinnamon brown at this time of year; spurts of white down from the seed pods shine in the moonlight. . . . A silken mist over the meadows. The low square wooden privies like little square forts in the moonlight, the vent pipes like silver periscopes. Distant lowing of cattle, hounds sending and receiving messages from one dooryard to another somewhere off to the east. MOONLIGHT. Yes, the moon *is* fair tonight along the Wabash, and we badly need a tenor and/or a soprano to carry the air for my alto and Mike's bass.

MH All to ourselves and the owls, she says, and this is, to be sure, a perfect night for owls, mild and still and bright, sounds carrying far

—particularly the sounds of Mary, who, having sung "The Moon is Fair Tonight Along the Wabash," while I groaned along in a lower register, is now disturbing the peace with songs about Indiana, Missouri, Ohio, indeed, her entire repertoire of place songs. The owls and I wait for her to run down. . . . Of course it is she who hears the first barred owl.

MD   We set up the damp tent to dry, but slept out, our sleeping bags next to the dying fire. I snugged in for ten hours—waking occasionally with the moon in my eyes, and once to the barred owl going *Whoo*-wha (and to Michael snoring inside his sleeping bag, one of the more interesting night noises I know—a muffled roar, like summer thunder). Woke just after sunrise, fire going again, Michael already up and exclaiming about the deliciously sweet and sharp smell of tulip-tree wood smoke; coffee water boiling, long dawn shadows; high overhead, orange in the first light, the cone-shaped seed pods in the top branches of the tulip trees that surround us; and the sunlight dazzling through the blue-stem down in the fields that stretch along the ridge and out of sight.

Flickers, bluebirds, cardinals, juncoes, red-bellied woodpecker; flocks of red-winged blackbirds moving south—the sun on their red shoulders; a bird song that Mike suspects to be a mockingbird imitating a Carolina wren; and an eastern meadowlark giving its "autumn song," says Mike—a short song, a traveling song, not the full melodic courting song of spring.

Oak, sycamore, and the tulip-trees, "tallest of the eastern hardwoods," I read in Harlow's *Trees* over my dawn cup of coffee. They were once called *canoe trees* because the Indians made dugouts from the massive trunks. Tulip trees were here before the last ice age, slowly seeding southward in the path of the ice front moving down the Appalachians, then seeding northward again as the ice retreated; the only other tulip trees in the world are in China.

Audubon's flatboat moves on to Shawneetown, where there apparently is some concern for the safety of the cargo, because he stays aboard, the captain nails up "the only accessible hole to our Boat," while the rest of the crew go into town for a night of shore leave. There's a fight. Ned Kelly ("a Wag of 21 . . . handsome if Clean,

This engraving of Cave-In-Rock is after a drawing by Carl Bodmer, done at high water on the Ohio in the 1830s. It appeared in *Travels in the Interior of North America* by Prince of Maximilian of Wied, 1844. *The New York Public Library, Rare Book Division*

possessed of Much Low Wit . . . Sings, dances, and fiels always happy . . .") and his buddy Joe Seeg ("Lazy, fond of Grog . . . sleeps Sound, for he burns all his Cloths, while in the ashes . . .") enjoy the Shawnee-town taverns, and "having Drank rather freely of Grog, they had a Litle Scrape at the Expense of Mr. Seeg's Eyes & Nose—" As they depart Shawneetown, Audubon notes that all in all, "the place improved but Litle."

Their next stop is "the famous *Rockin Cave*" where they put in at sunset. The following morning at daybreak, Audubon went ashore, built a good fire against the cold weather, and did a sketch of "Rockin Cave . . . one of the Curiosities that attract the attention of allmost

every Traveler on the Ohio and thousands of Names & Dates ornament the sides & Cealing. . . . This place is said to have been for Many
Years the *rendez Vous* of a noted Robber of the name of Mason. It
is about 20 Miles below Shawaney town on the same side."

We pull out our Illinois map. Audubon's Rockin Cave is Cave-In-
Rock, marked on the page with a pine tree and a tent, the symbol
for a state park with campsites. We, too, arrive at sunset and, by sheer
luck, his path and ours cross precisely. It's the ninth of November,
the same day he came ashore in 1820. The park is nearly empty, and
we have our choice of sites along the rugged limestone bluffs overlooking the Ohio—out on the promontory that juts into the sunset or
on the edge of a high meadow with an upstream view that reaches
for miles. We make two circuits of the park, undecided among all
these riches, and at last pitch the tent on the brink of the bluffs amid
cedar and oak and persimmon trees. A new moon rises. There are
stars. Mist. And the lights of the riverboats passing at our feet, as
festive as the *bateaux mouches* on the Seine. A couple of miles
upriver from our pinnacle, they gang up for the wait at Lock and
Dam No. 50, a distant bevy of little lights parked along the dark
shore.

MH   The head ranger here, young and self-possessed, lives in an
attractive woodsy house in the center of the park with his wife and
small children and a dog named Brisbane. We met them all when we
registered. Mary immediately assumed that the dog was named after
the famous Hearst journalist, and I thought of the city in Australia;
we each said to ourselves, that, ah, here was a sophisticated fellow,
one of the well-educated young who have abandoned getting-and-
spending to follow environmentally sensible, aesthetically pleasing
careers. So it surprised us to discover he didn't recognize the name
of John James Audubon, even with Henderson, Kentucky, and its
John James Audubon State Park upriver, less than a day's drive away.
"Come to think of it," he said, "I figured the Audubon Society had
to be named after *some*body, but I never did know who that might
be."

MD   The cave that gives this place its name first appeared on
French maps in the early 1700s—"le caverne dans le roc." It's two

Cave-In-Rock, with Mary seated just to the left of the entrance. *MH*

hundred feet deep, eighty feet wide, and twenty-five feet high at the entrance, and when white men first saw it they found hiero- glyphics and prehistoric drawings of animals on its high rounded walls. Those signs have long since vanished. During the years of the early westward migration, Cave-In-Rock became famous as a tav- ern, brothel, and den of murderers. Flatboat crews, stopping by for a spree, would be killed off wholesale and their cargo appropriated. If business were slack, one of the brothel girls would pretend to be stranded on a nearby island and hitch a ride from a passing boat- man, who would carry her to the Illinois shore and there be set upon by whichever Cave-In-Rock desperadoes were in residence. The career of Mason, "the noted robber" of whom Audubon spoke, ended with his severed head being handed to the authorities by a fellow bandit, who claimed the $1000 reward. There were also the mad Harpe Brothers, who disemboweled their victims, stuffed them with stones, and pitched them into the Ohio. Or (in at least one case) tied a boatman to a blindfolded horse and ran it off the bluffs into the river. The Harpe Brothers were finally chased down and their heads mounted on spikes as a warning to other highway- men. Then along came Mr. and Mrs. Potts, who opened a tavern near Cave-In-Rock—their speciality was a stab in the back when travelers bent over the Potts' spring for a drink of fresh water. And as the story goes, they murdered their only son by mistake one dark night as the young man knelt at the spring. But enough. There is tale after grisly tale.

The very formation of the land—the bluffs, the crags, the hollows, the wild volcanic thrusts and drops of the terrain—makes it ideal bandit country. There are thousands of places to hide out, to lie in wait, to scout approaching boats or approaching wagons. From our pinnacle, for example, where the pop-tent stands, a river pirate would have a commanding view. Audubon and his shipmates were lucky. On the November day they were here, Cave-In-Rock was temporarily abandoned. But it was another fifteen years before the last Cave-In-Rock brigand was executed and the territory safe for travelers.

The winding downhill walk to the cavern has steps and a bannis- ter and a drinking fountain, but the place loses none of its drama— the dark depths, the arching mouth of the cave, the river at its doorstep. It is still, of course, ornamented with names and dates and initials, many of the early ones handsomely chiseled in headstone lettering. J. Stansbury 1804. Miss B. McPeter. (I like the formality of that one.) A. R. Delano 1850-something. And on the ceiling overhead, presumably painted from a boat during high water, J. & B. C. Cole 1913, in enormous white letters. Everyone who passes stops to oh and ah and wonder at this memento from the Coles.

I sit in the sun at the mouth of the cave to watch the other visitors. A Flannery O'Connor family has arrived—one skinny, chipper little husband, two fat sisters, their pale, quiet, expressionless idiot brother, Jacky, and three small children who scatter everywhere, exploring. Their mother pays no mind to the children at all. Her pet is her brother Jacky—"My baby," she calls him, combing his hair for a snapshot, patting his face, patting his shirt collar, holding his hand to lead him over the rocks. Occasionally he wanders off toward the woods, toward the river. "Where's my baby? Jacky!" she calls him back, and he docilely obeys. Her youngest blond son has made up a game of jumping from a ledge into a pile of leaves. "Hey, Mom. Look what I'm going to do. Hey, Mom. Look what I'm going to do." She never once glances in his direction, nor does he seem to expect a response. He jumps into his leaves, still babbling for her attention. "Hey, Mom. Look what I did. Hey, Mom. Look what I did." Still no response. She's busy with her camera and tidying up Jacky, each time it's his turn to pose, while I covertly watch them from the opposite side of the cave, dissembling my curiosity with busy pretenses. I clean my dark glasses; I fuss with my binoculars. And the only one, of course, to notice my presence is Jacky. He's not alarmed or uneasy, but he has tuned in and every now and again he watches me watching.

For the last pose, the second fat sister—a vast, rolling stomach, purple pantsuit, and hennaed hair (the red-rust color you don't see much anymore)—leads Jacky onto a knoll, faces him and lifts his hands into place on her giant waistline, then puts her arms around his waist and pulls him in against her huge purple stomach; they press their cheeks together and look out at the camera. A pose from childhood snapshots! I am riveted. At the very second that the picture is taken, Jacky lifts his soft vacant gaze from the camera lens and stares across the cave into my dark glasses. *Click.*

MH   The Indian-Summer day begins gray, but by late morning the temperature is in the seventies and the sun is out; the afternoon is clear and practically windless. From time to time I look overhead for migrating hawks, see none all day, see instead a soaring monarch butterfly—orange-and-black long-distance traveler: it spirals upward for a couple of slow revolutions—fragile, vulnerable, kiting in the almost still air—then sets for the south, across the river.

MD   I have housekeeping errands to attend to this morning. Michael stays at camp with letters to be answered and bills to pay. (No matter how far you travel, you cannot shake the mortgage or the insurance premiums or the termite inspection contract.) I need a bank, a laundromat, and a light novel or a news magazine. None of these are to be found in the city of Cave-In-Rock, population five hundred, but at the Little Egypt Collector and Gift Shop I find a first-rate booklet, *The Cavern of Crime,* which gives the history of this portion of Illinois from the era of the mound-builder Indians to the present. I also come upon fluorspar in the gift shop. Chunks of it are for sale, crystals shading from translucent purple to an opaque white. I buy a sample and am given a brochure, *What the Heck is Fluorspar?.* It says the Indians carved the crystals into figurines and ear bobs, that the mining of fluorspar is the principal industry of this area of the Illinois-Kentucky Ozarks, that it's used in the manufacture of steel, the smelting of zinc, the processing of aluminum and magnesium, and is the source of the hydrofluoric acid used in aerosol sprays, teflon, and refrigerants. As I drive south to Elizabethtown, where there's a bank and a laundromat, the local radio announces the death of a miner, aged eighteen, crushed in a fluorspar cave-in. Services on Tuesday.

I explore on the way, lured by dirt roads where circling turkey buzzards patrol the hills and hollows, plank bridges rattle over the creeks, and houses are few and far between. Just about everyone keeps pigs, and hillocks of dusty piglets lie sleeping in the sun. On one dead end road, a ragged old shack, a wisp of smoke from the chimney, a pair of scrawny hound dogs napping on the broken boards of the porch, and a yard of bare dirt rooted out by a garrison of hogs—a rough, tough, mean-looking crowd, who snort and snuffle at the wobbling fence when I slow down. The dogs cock an ear, then fall back to sleep.

The whole territory through here, the thousands of square miles of the Shawnee National Forest that spreads across this peninsula, seems to be everything that the word Ozark summons up. Around this corner, or the next, you feel as though you've driven backwards into the 1930s, into Walker Evans' depression photographs of poor whites, into the cartoons of ridge-runners, crackers, moonshiners carrying squirrel rifles.

It became cloudy and cold when JJA was here. Snow flurries, rain, hail. "Never have I seen so much snow at this season in this Latitude," he wrote. We have rising winds and intermittent thunderstorms. Between squalls, a double rainbow soars out of Kentucky, lifts high over the river, and sets down lightly in Illinois. The towboats grind slowly upriver into the teeth of the weather, and in the fogs of the evening, sweep this bank with their searchlights, picking their way with care. The river is low, the channel cuts under these bluffs, and each towboat is pushing almost a quarter-mile's length of barges. One comes so close below us tonight we can see into the dimly lit wheelhouse, into the lighted windows along the lower deck that rides only a foot off the water. We stand in the dark, in the wind, looking down on the boat and watch the shimmering red and yellow reflections wash in against the bluff, and I imagine the crew sitting inside drinking coffee and swapping yarns, cozy as in a caboose. *Stop. Stop. Take us along.*

Late at night, the last thunderstorm strikes, rolling in from the Kentucky side, barreling through camp with crazed bursts of lightning, and crashing on to the east, driven by a charging wind that slams across the Ohio like a freight train. Then silence. The morning is clear, brisk, sunny. A few yards from our tent is an enormous branch that cracked and fell during the uproar. Fresh firewood delivered at our door.

It gets damp in a tent in this kind of weather, even with a dropcloth underneath and another spread inside. The rain runs down off the dome-sides of the tent as it is meant to do, but there is a trouble spot at the base, in and around the zipper that closes the doorsill of the front flaps, and we are apt to wake in the morning with the foot-ends of our sleeping bags wet and soggy. We've learned that in a heavy rain one must be careful not to have any object touch the inside of the tent—a flashlight, a book, the handle of my basket, Michael's boots. At the point of contact, rainwater running down the outside of the tent is diverted inside, along whatever object touches the canvas.

Many a morning we've warmed up the car and dried out the sleeping bags, with the heater and defroster set at high. Today, we string rope between the trees and hang out our gear in the sun. Bed rolls, bath towels, socks, pajamas, sweaters, changes of underwear. An Okie encampment.

During the thunderstorms, a nearby picnic shelter became our headquarters where we have laid out bills, correspondence, books, maps, the typewriter, the radio. It's the weekend now, and the loop through the park is the town promenade. Big town, little town, country town, there's always a promenade. Everyone out there burning up gasoline, circling and cruising, circling and cruising. A big yellow car passes twice, then stops, and the driver calls to us: "Must be pretty cold out yonder where you come from." On his third pass he stops and comes into the shelter with his boy; the Missus stays in the car. He's a burly fellow—a miner, we discover by asking—and he wants to know more about the weather out yonder in Connecticut. And what do we think about this part of the world? "It's beautiful," we tell him. And do we have mountains where we live? And what about the rivers, he wants to know. Are the rivers as big? But never does he ask us what we're doing here. Nor why the impromptu office-library in the picnic shelter. He is too polite to pry. The visit is ceremonial.

After supper, three more visitors join us at our fire—conjured up by Michael out of thin air, on the CB radio. They identify themselves by their handles—Pink Panther, Slewfoot, and The Professor.

MH "Conjured" is right. The CB radio is a little like Aladdin's lamp. Chatting at night with the local network (you got the Hawkman here), I make the acquaintance of Pink Panther, et al., and they want to "lay an eyeball" on us. Will we be in camp the next night? Sure. And so three benign genies appear out of the dark.

The Professor is a retired local schoolteacher in his seventies, tall and erect, courtly in a country fashion. He is dressed in Sunday clothes, because he is on his way home from A Viewing at a funeral parlor. His wife and two other ladies, also dressed for that occasion, remain in the car—embarrassed or amazed by this nighttime foray among strangers up in Cave-In-Rock State Park. They stare out at us through the rolled-up car windows, unsmiling, as if the Connecticut Yankees wore pistols and bandoleers. I think the Professor would as soon stay with us a while, but he is hitched to that stern line, and it is winching him home. He is gone in a few minutes.

Slewfoot, as talkative as an old gossip over the radio, is a young man who finds it difficult to string two sentences together. It seems he slew his foot in a sawmill; then, having more or less recovered from that, was badly hurt in a fluorspar mining accident when a slab of rock weighing several hundred pounds fell from a ceiling on top of him—from which he's still recovering. Most of this information is offered by Pink Panther, who joshes Slewfoot for being accident-prone. Slewfoot laughs abashedly.

Pink Panther makes up for any failures in communication by the Professor and Slewfoot. About thirty years old, he is a born story-teller, sound of wind and strong of voice and powerful of opinion, with a nice eye for detail. He's a deckhand on an Ohio River car-ferry, and is about to take the Coast Guard's difficult examination for river pilot. Talking about it, Pink Panther uses the job's romantic old title: "Pilot of the Western Waters." Unfortunately, some moderniz-ing fool in the District of Columbia—or more likely, a committee—got nervous about the broad term "Waters" and one day changed the title to "Pilot of the Western *Rivers,*" which does not have the same ring to it. The license permits one to pilot towboats on the Mississippi River system from such places as Sioux City, Iowa, and the Huey P. Long Bridge in New Orleans, and Tulsa and Chicago and St. Paul, east all the way to the Appalachians.

The Pink Panther will have no problem with any piloting exams, if I'm a judge. He is positively fierce in his delight for facts and description; he devotes a quarter-hour to pantomiming and explain-ing the fine points of "throwing chain," in which art he has appar-ently become an expert. He is not able to make *me* an expert in fifteen minutes, but I gather the skill is used when tying up the ferry to a landing and involves wrapping several loops of heavy chain around a bollard in a single motion—so the thrown chain wraps itself. One of those casual gestures that looks so easy but actually has taken the performer months of practice to perfect.

The Panther tells us a story on the owner of the car-ferry. Let's call him Captain. Captain had just got his pilot's license, says the Panther, and he was like a kid with a new toy, always wanting to drive the ferry. Captain was pilot one night when a fog came in—a thick fog. The Ohio is not particularly wide where the ferry crosses, a few hundred yards, but all the barge-traffic that moves up and down the river should and does make an inexperienced ferry driver nervous. There is also a current that can put you off your mark, if you can't see your mark because of fog. Captain says to Panther, "How's it look?" "If it was me," says Panther, "I wouldn't do it." "Aw," says Captain after a minute, "I guess we'll go. We'll make it all right." So they start across in the dark, in the fog, carrying cars from the Kentucky landing to the Illinois landing. "Oh, I could feel it happening," Panther tells us. "He headed her upstream, because he was scared of the current drifting her down." Pretty soon Captain was lost, and after a little while he ran the ferry into an island, well upstream of the landing. He got her off, and then he hit the island again. Backing out this time, he ran into the woods in Kentucky. Each time the ferry hit ground, says Panther, Captain would sing out, "Where we *at?*" Finally he got clear and, in fog still as thick as cotton batting, headed back downstream "boogiddy-boogiddy," river-ese for wasting no time. "Now keep your eye on the shoreline," calls Captain to Panther. Not being able to *see* any shoreline, Panther worried about other matters. "You look at a barge-tow," he tells us, "and you'll see on the head of the tow a red running light for the port corner and a green running light for starboard, and right in the middle, between them, is an orange light. We're going boogiddy-boogiddy downriver in the fog, and I can see this blinking orange light coming at us upstream, and I thought, Omigod, here it comes, we're going to plow into it head on. And at just that moment, there was a break in the fog, I saw the bank and the landing, and I shouted, 'There's Illinois! *Hit it!*'" Captain was so flummoxed he went into the landing wrong end to; but they were safe.

At the end of the Pink Panther's story, I almost expect Monsieur

Hulot or Charlie Chaplin—a genie like the rest of these visitors—to appear as the Captain, twittery and pleased at his narrow escape, and bowing at our laughter.

Another visiting genie has just sprung from the same lamp. The Politician—on the Cave-In-Rock city council, deputy mayor, deputy cop, park commissioner; into Democratic state politics, has met both Mayor Daley and young Ad-lye Stevenson—whom he refers to as "smart rookies," which sends my mind off for a minute, trying to figure out what he means. Rookie equals cookie?

Thinking of Slewfoot brings him to mind now. The Politician drives a truck for the fluorspar people, but he does not *ever* go underground. *No* sir. He spoke of a friend who worked in one of the fluorspar mines. One morning this friend reinforced a chamber roof with forty-five ceiling bolts pinning the spar in place and went out for lunch; by the time he got back into the mine every single one of those bolts had loosened and the spar ceiling had fallen. "He just left the mine," said the Politician, "changed his clothes, got into his car, and drove off. He said: 'That's it, I'm never going into one of those things again.' "

I wouldn't set foot in one myself. But consider all the men whose outlook and real options are so limited that they take such chances with their lives. Who, I wonder, was crippled or killed so that our house in Connecticut might have a refrigerator? I know I sound like a 1930s Liberal: gimme my guitar and I'll make up a song for Woody and Pete. Even so, are such sacrifices essential to the Survival of This Great Nation?

MD I've fallen in with the two aged parkies who do the maintenance work here. One is the silent partner, the audience, so to speak, for the other, who is a loquacious old rogue with lots of gold teeth and a backcountry Ozark accent so rich I miss about every other word (sometimes whole sentences) of his nonstop monologues. But I do catch an introductory message the first day they come by to empty our trash barrel. While his silent partner does the lifting and hauling, he sits at the wheel of the truck, laughing and shouting, and announces that he's a hard-working, sober citizen. "And don't let nobody tell you different. Why, I don't drink no more'n a quart of whiskey a day." The next time around, he shouts at me from his

window. "There's a good-lookin' woman! I'm gonna take you back to
my farm. I got hogs and a bed and a vegetable garden, and I'm lookin'
for a good lookin' woman." I tell him I'll think about his offer, doesn't
sound bad at all, I might just unpack my gear from the car and move
right on in. Then he picks up a second theme. He decides that I'm
a woman with money in the bank, because he knows a rich woman
when he sees one, he surely does. I stand at the fire holding a sticky
spatula, my hands black with charcoal, wearing a beat-up out-size
canvas jacket that's a hand-me-down from my son. "Guess I can't fool
you," I call back, and he shouts and laughs and flashes his gold teeth.

The next day we meet as I'm scrubbing my hands with a nailbrush
at an outside spigot, and the game continues.

"What's that good-lookin' rich woman doin' now?"

"Washing up," I tell him. "No rich woman ever been born likes
to count her money with dirty hands." They like that sentiment and
we have some more whooping and laughter as they ease out of the
truck with their mops and buckets to clean the bathhouses. They stop
to talk about how this land used to be before it was turned into a State
Park. Over there, on the site of the concession stand, there was a
farmhouse, and that pear tree, well, that's the last one left from the
orchard that once grew here. Old man Slaggert had the farm. And
he was *mean.* Before that, old man Davers—or Travers (I couldn't
catch the name)—and he was mean, too. *"Mean?* He was almost
mean as me," says the rogue parkie with the gold teeth. "My momma
worked there when she was an itty-bitty girl. Fifty cents a week
when Mrs. Davers had a new baby, and old man Davers was so mean,
his wife and his children ate cold cornbread for breakfast, and he ate
hot biscuits and butter."

They tell another story—"the fiddle-maker" who lived out "that
way," when they were boys. The rogue parkie points down the road.
"He was another mean one. We'd hide there by his fence and when
he come out, we'd rock him. We was always rockin' him. But one day
he lay in wait and he ketched me. He gave me a *whippin'!* He had
a whip this big." The rogue parkie holds up his thumb. "He beat me
almost to death. I had stripes all over." He shouts with laughter and
does a clog step on the path and swats the side of the bathhouse with
the flat of his mop. "But I didn't say nothin' to my folks. And the
fiddle-maker caught two more boys and whipped *them* good. . . . We

didn't rock him ever agin, I kin tell you." The silent parkie breaks
in to say that the fiddle-maker once made a violin that he took clear
to the World's Fair and he played it and won a prize. Which World's
Fair? I ask. Where? Neither of them knows. Only that it was here,
"in Illanoise."

The rogue parkie reminisces about his days as a driver of a coal
wagon for a mining company. He was hauling out of these woods, and
he had a team of six mules, with big ole harness. He gestures the size
of the collars. And he kept the brass all shining, and he kept those
mules shining and trimmed up with red, white, and blue braiding.
For a moment he's not shouting or laughing. He's back in the woods,
a young man with his beautiful team of mules, the shining harness,
and the bright braiding, and who knows what other memories. Then
he's back again with us, grinning and rolling his eyes. "On summer
days, I'd stop down there at Potts' Spring to get me a drink of water,
and I'd sure enough think about that old man killin' his boy. I'd sure
enough hear him comin' outta the woods. Comin' after me."

Once more I am invited to move into his farmhouse, but I tell him
it's too late. We're leaving Cave-In-Rock tomorrow morning. And
when are we going to come back?

"Someday, I hope."　　　　　　　　　　　　　.

"You better get here soon, or we'll be gone. Next year, we're
through. We get retired. So hurry back, hear."

I wave goodbye and start down the hill. They're still calling after
me. "Hurry back, hear." Each time I stop to wave, there's a fresh
outpouring of news, their plans. The rogue parkie is going to go and
see Hawaii, the other calls that he's going to live with a daughter in
Florida. He can breath better there. He has emphysema. I wave
again.

"You hurry back, hear . . ." until I'm out of earshot.

After leaving Cave-In-Rock, the flatboat on which Audubon traveled put ashore in a snow and hail storm ("Wetted us Compitly") near
Elizabethtown. The next settlement Audubon mentions is Golconda
—"a small Town of the Illinois—Title disputed of course the place
not improving." Golconda today is hung with banners—"Welcome
Deer Hunters," the stores and bars and streets jammed with gunners, and the Rotarians are serving them up a Bar-B-Q dinner in an

enormous tent in the center of town. Fires roaring in 50-gallon drums out front and hunters clustered around them, getting warm. We drive on downriver, keeping to back roads and small towns, where even the dogs all look to be related. Anyplace we go, anyplace we stop, we evoke the same question: "Are you here for the deer hunting?"

Audubon and company floated on, watching pintail ducks "flying southwardly" and flocks of migrating, island-hopping turkeys. At Cumberland Island, the boat put ashore, and Audubon finished a drawing of a common loon. This island, at the mouth of the Cumberland River, was a campsite for Aaron Burr in the winter of 1806–07, during his expedition to Mexico. Audubon knew it well over the years, so we stop to take a look, blundering into the area where a new lock and dam is being built by the Corps above Cumberland Island. The safety officer, an amiable young man, catches up with us as we wander among the construction and leads us to a downstream view. The wind is cold by the shore, everyone with collars turned up against the brims of hard hats, hands in pockets, shivering; great machinery swinging here and on the other side of the river; steam exhaust pluming into the gray sky; barges being shoved upstream. Cumberland Island, the safety officer tells us, was farmed until recently, and in the spring flood of '75 the river was so high that only a small piece of Cumberland showed above water—that overgrown point of land, just ahead. And it was crowded "with about forty groundhogs and birds and I don't know what-all. One of the groundhogs out there was pure white. An albino."

We drive upriver to find the man who owns the island, knock on his door, are invited in. On his hearthstone sits the selfsame white groundhog (woodchuck, as we call them in New England). It's stuffed and mounted in an upright position, its glass eyes fixed on the front window. The first and only albino groundhog our host and the guests have ever seen.

Cumberland Island was farmed in the old days, they'd float out the farm machinery, swim out the mules, plough, plant corn, and "just let 'er go." When the corn was ripe, it was put into cribs. Then they hauled out pigs and cattle and left them there to forage and fatten on what was left in the fields. With high water, steamboats could dock at the cribs, the corn would be shelled and loaded aboard.

Our host himself, a man in his middle years, had quit farming a while back, after three years of bad weather and crop failures. Now he runs some cattle and rents out the rest of his land. "I put my money into the bank now, instead of into debt. But when I retired I got fat, so I went back to work—running a johnboat for the Dog Island dam project."

He falls to telling us stories from his farming days. He has a knack for turning an eloquent phrase, inherited perhaps from his father, who was a country lawyer. We hear about a hired hand who once worked for our host: "That fellow could steal while you were looking straight at him. Why, that fellow could pick up a sleeping pig by the tail and the snout, load it onto an open truck, and drive it away, without waking that pig up. He'd steal your pigs, steal your corn, and steal the scoop to feed the corn to the pigs. He stole my chainsaw one day and said down at the store that if he'd tried it first, he wouldn't have bothered to take it away." But the worst rascals and cutthroats, our host said, were across the river in southern Illinois. "I never set foot in southern Illinois that I wasn't cheated or robbed. Old Shawneetown is still a nest of river rats and roachbugs. I've been told there are some good people on that side of the river, but the general belief to the contrary notwithstanding, I've never met one of them yet." There's the separation by the river again, said Mike later—*"hostile* separation, though, and not simple ignorance."

A couple of miles south of Cumberland Island, headed west for the Mississippi River this autumn of 1820, Audubon missed a shot at a whooping crane, "the *Largest* White *Crane,* with Black tips, but he walked off . . . on a Large naked Sand Barr—felt great anxiety to procure such for he appeared Beautifull—" The next day: "We passed . . . Fort Massacre here the Ohio is Magnificent, the river about one & 1/4 mile Wide . . . and this afternoon being Calm . . . one of those *Whimsical* sunsetts that only belong to America."

"Fort Massacre," the popular name in Audubon's time for Fort Massac, was in ruins each time he passed this way. The last Ohio River fortification to be built by the French, it had a brief renaissance under the British, again under the Americans, then suffered from the shocks of the New Madrid earthquake of 1811, and within the next few years the wooden palisade and buildings were sold for fuel to passing boats. What was left was scavenged by settlers. Audubon wouldn't know the place now. No ruins, no tangled wilderness, but a state park with a brand-new reconstruction of Fort Massac at the river's edge: stockade, blockhouses, flags flying; a little museum with an historic slide show and displays of the artifacts (Indian, French, British, and American) found on the site in a WPA archeological dig during the Depression. Now in the summer seasons there are parades, music, costumes, mock battles, craft shows.

Next door is a spacious campground in a forest of oak trees. Once again the local park is the local promenade; drive in and circle aimlessly. And once again we are asked if we're here for the deer hunting —this from a cruising motorist who stops at our campsite when he sees our Connecticut plates.

The 1300-odd acres of the Fort Massac compound are on the outskirts of Metropolis, which claims to be the town of New Thermopylae, so-named and described by Dickens in *Martin Chuzzlewit,* a claim that's also been made by Cairo, Illinois. Though why either town should mention it, I don't know. Dickens was merciless in his itemization of miry waters, slime, black ooze, decomposing ashes vile and ugly, festering elements of corruption and disease, and a landing place with naught but a barnlike hotel, one or two wooden stores and a few scattered sheds.

Metropolis also lays claim to being the home of *Superman.* His creator was a local boy. The Superman/Clark Kent image is everywhere, and Metropolis is "Gotham City."

In the middle of the night, a cold front comes through with torrential rain along its leading edge, the kind of rain that falls straight from the sky in a relentless deluge, as though under pressure from a giant showerhead. The campground is flat, the water collects in wide puddles, and by morning we are afloat in a small pond. Everything in the tent is wringing wet. We run our sleeping bags and wet clothes through a giant dryer at the nearest laundromat.

I'm depressed and gloomy most of the day—Indian Summer has finally gone for good. The warm browns, beiges, and cinnamons, the yellows, reds, and golds of autumn have become raw and harsh overnight, have turned into winter colors: gray, black, mud brown, wet rust.

Audubon's boat stops at the town of America, Illinois, "to sell some Articles." Though he doesn't specify the cargo sold or goods aboard, he does note that the townspeople are "very sickly, a miserable place altogether." America is another of the old towns laid out with much pomp and optimism; it was also the first Fayette county seat, with a brick jail and a courthouse. But the community was ravaged by fevers. One winter there were only four men in town who were well enough to dig graves and bury the dead. Then came the invention of the steamboat. The town's harbor was too shallow and river commerce began to pass it by. The county seat was moved to Vandalia, and today America is almost nonexistent—a lovely, forgotten, off-the-highway scattering of half a dozen houses and much farmland and vine-hung woodlands where barred owls whoop at midday. However, after a century and a half, the town may rise again. There's talk of building an industrial park here.

The next town downriver of America was Trinity, which Audubon also knew well over the years. Trinity has vanished so completely we could find only one person in the neighborhood (the president of the Mound City historical society), who even knew of its existence. Trinity once stood at the confluence of Cache Creek and the Ohio —stores, warehouse, taverns, hotels, billiard rooms, cabins, frame house. It was notorious as a hangout for rivermen who did as they pleased while "honest citizens feared for their lives and property." Trinity was burned down one winter's night by a flatboatman who'd been arrested and fined for selling liquor to the town proprietor's "servants and negroes." The flatboatman threatened vengeance, and after dark returned from the Kentucky side and fired the buildings. There were the further disasters of floods and a rising sandbar across the mouth of Trinity's harbor. In no time at all, the town was gone.

In our search for Trinity, I find a compensation for the end of Indian Summer. We have entered mistletoe country. Now that most of the leaves have been driven from the trees, the mistletoe is suddenly visible. We'd been on the lookout because the 1814 edition of the Ohio River *Navigator* mentioned mistletoe specifically through here. Island No. 70, upriver from Trinity, America, and Cave-In-Rock, was listed with its particulars—"Lies close to the left shore . . . Channel on right side"—and that was followed by a pretty botanical footnote: "Mistletoe begins to appear in bunches on the top branches of the trees." Exactly so. Cities may rise and fall, rivers change their courses, but mistletoe still grows in the tall trees here as it has always done.

This is the first time I've seen mistletoe *in situ*, away from florists' shops and Christmas kisses. It's not a vine the way I had imagined, as though mistletoe were an entwiner like bittersweet, woodbine, and poison ivy, which are rooted in the ground. It's a small shrub, with leaves that are always green, and is a true parasite. Its feet never touch the ground. Scattered tangles grow in round poufs through the crowns of its hosts, tupelo and red maple preferred, on whose cells the mistletoe feeds through vampire rootlets.

There's some sort of continuum moral here. A microcosmic vision of life-in-death cycles so unthinkable to man, who believes himself exceptional and immortalized and invulnerable; the mistletoe goes about making its living off the blood of its hosts and ends by destroying its source. And how beautiful it is—tufts of pale, ever green, tree-top shrubbery.

I philosophize on mistletoe. Audubon philosophizes on the Meeting of the Waters. He uses a well-worn allegory—Life is a River—but his musings are quite moving as he recalls the lost days of prosperity when he came through as a successful merchant with his own cargo. Now, he enters the Mississippi, *"poor* in fact *Destitute* of all things and reliing only on that providiential Hope the Comforter of this Wearied Mind . . .

"The meeting of the Two Streams reminds me . . . of the Gentle Youth who Comes in the World, spotles he presents himself, he is gradually drawn in to thousands of Dificulties that Makes him wish to keep apart, but at Last he is . . . lost in the Vortex—

"The Beautifull & Transparent Watter of the Ohio when first entering the Misisipi is taken in small Drafts and Looks the More aquable to the Eye as it goes down surrounded by Muddy Current, it keeps off as much as possible by running down on the Kentucky side for several miles but reduced to a narrow strip & is lost."

We head for St. Louis to pick up a boatride and will come back to rejoin Audubon on the nearly 1000-mile journey from Cairo to New Orleans.

MISSISSIPPI RIVER

NOVEMBER 1820–JANUARY 1821

MH We had decided to make the trip aboard some sort of "working" boat. We knew there were a lot of them on the Mississippi—the barge traffic. But that was about all we did know, and our first inquiries revealed that barge lines weren't licensed to carry passengers. Discouraging. We began talking about renting a houseboat instead, until someone told us that barge lines could and did take nonpaying *guests;* you only had to know someone. Through a friend of a friend of friends, the arrangements were made. We would store the car in St. Louis with the friends of the first part, take a cab to the St. Louis Fuel P&G dock at the foot of the levee below the Gateway Arch, be picked up there by a harbor boat that would ferry us out to the far side of the river, where the towboat *Ray A. Eckstein,* bound for New Orleans, would be hitching up to a tow.

St. Louis Fuel P&G is a clutter of steel cables, spooled and unspooled, of hoses and fifty-gallon drums. A Diesel-fueler of the Port of St. Louis, puffing smoke into the hazy sky, rides at the dock among a mixed fleet of towboats big and small: *Lisa Jo, Nancy Jo, Dude, R.H. Huffman, Utah.* They're odd-looking boats—should be called *push-boats.* At first glance they look like tugs, but a tug has graceful, powerfully curving lines. A towboat is mostly ninety-degree angles. It starts with a low-floating, rectangular hull, no lift to the decking, bow or stern, as flat as a wooden raft. Up at the head end, where by rights a pointed bow ought to be, are "towing knees," stout pushers sprouting straight up from the squared-off verge of the deck. A few

143

yards aft of that attenuated bow, the superstructure rises in two or three steps to the glassed-in pilot house with its coronet of radar gear, searchlights, and radio aerials. The steps up, deck to deck, are abrupt in front and long behind. From one of those long afterdecks rise huge smokestacks, venting the Diesels.

As we stand on the edge of the dock with our motley luggage around us, we are joined from time to time by other hitchhikers picking up rides to towboats. Each approaching harbor boat—miniature, boxy towboats all, with the cut-off bows sprouting the towing knees—produces a rustling-about and getting-ready by Mary and me, and the first few times that happens, the boat has not been sent for us but for someone else, and our half-lifted duffle-bag and camera pack and so on are set down again. The Mississippi flows brown and evil-looking, bearing on its bosom this day millions of puffs of an ugly cream-brown foam; where the foam comes from the people at St. Louis Fuel P&G profess not to know, though it is on the river *"all the time . . . and nobody complains about it, so it can't be doing any harm."*

Another harbor boat sidles gently to the dock, and the skipper shouts down from his pilot house, *"Ray A. Eckstein?"* We shout back Yes, and in company with a gray-haired woman in slacks, who has just arrived by taxi and turns out to be a replacement cook, we are carried across toward the Illinois side of the river. The *Ray A. Eckstein* is a big boat—almost 200 feet long, 55 feet wide, 50 high—three decks and then the pilot house, all bright with white paint and red trim, and the name is picked out, white on red, in large nineteenth-century-style caps below the pilot house. A deckhand meets us at the galley door, takes our baggage, and leads us up two sets of carpeted gangways, past the crew's quarters to the deck that houses the captain's cabin, pilot's cabin, and guest quarters, just below the pilot house. It is a trip into a unique cosmos, and the rumbling and vibration underfoot of the huge engines hint at that. But other appearances disguise it; the interior, from what we see on the way up, seems to be done up mostly in Motel Modern, lots of gold shag carpeting wall to wall and antiqued-oak furnishing, comfortably upholstered. Our suite is sumptuous—bedroom, bath, sitting room, with a color TV and a little refrigerator and more wall-to-wall shag carpeting—blue.

In the plain-Jane messroom (leatherette sofa, metal chairs, long oilcloth-covered table) I put on the mandatory orange life vest and go out on the bow for my first lesson in towboating. The *Ray A. Eckstein—Ray A.* for short—is being "faced up" to a raft of twenty barges. The mate and two deckhands horse heavy steel cables—cables almost as thick as their wrists—from the towboat up onto the stern of the tow. They loop the cables between fittings, back and forth, knitting towboat to tow, then they winch the lines tight. Now they are out on the raft of barges, checking the ties there. The barges are steel; they have much the look of freight cars, but a barge is much bigger than a freight car—200 feet long on the average and 35 feet across. Made up into a tow they are held together by cat's-cradles of inch-and-a-half cable and heavy chain and huge turnbuckles called "ratchets"—hundreds of these cat's-cradles all over a tow, connecting each barge to its neighbors on every side—not just holding the tow together but actually providing separate towing lines, so that when the tow is underway, every barge ahead pulls the barges behind, and when the towboat is backing, every

Tightening a cable. *MH*

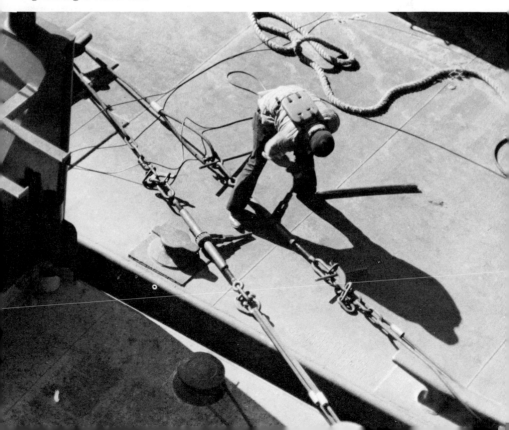

barge behind pulls the barges ahead of it.

A barge weighs more than 1500 tons, loaded, and the cat's-cradles are required to do a lot of work. So each tie is checked and tightened, barge to barge, not only now, before the trip starts, but many times a day. The deckhands carry lengths of pipe to use as levers for winding up the ratchets, and also as hammers to remove kinks from the taut cable; and if a deckhand still isn't satisfied that the cable is tight, he jumps up and down on the cat's-cradle, whangs the wire a few more times with the pipe, and tightens the ratchet again.

So it is several hours, and after dark, when the *Ray A. Eckstein* is ready to proceed downhill toward Cairo and the junction with the Ohio.

"When I stood in her pilot-house," wrote Mark Twain of one big Mississippi paddlewheeler he rode as a cub-pilot, "I was so far above the water that I seemed perched on a mountain," in a "sumptuous glass temple; room enough to have a dance in; showy red and gold window-curtains; an imposing sofa; leather cushions and a back to the high bench where visiting pilots sit, to spin yarns and 'look at the river'." This glass temple also commands the river from a considerable height. It is perhaps not so large, nor so ornately sumptuous as in that fine ship of Twain's day, but it does have the comfortable high bench at the back for "visiting pilots" like us, and a couple of easy chairs on either side. In the center, before the console, is a high-chair, a magnificent throne of stainless steel and imitation leather; it swivels, tilts, and cost the barge company $500. That's where the man "at the sticks" sits. The lovely wooden spoked pilot's wheels have long gone the way of the paddlewheels, and steering is done with stainless-steel rods; they jut at right angles from floor-to-ceiling stainless-steel columns, a pair of sticks on either hand, each rod with a rubber handle, like a bicycle. On both sides of the pilot's chair is a radar screen; the one on the right in use, the one on the left a spare, covered, used as a stand for the master's log. The pilot house glows dully with modern nightlights—the green of the radar, the red and white illuminations of dials on the console, the flicking digital readouts from the two depth-sounders, whose sensors are posted out on the corners of the head of the tow to send back to the pilot house new readings every time the depth of the channel

From the pilothouse, downbound. *MH*

varies by as much as a tenth of a foot.

At the sticks this evening is Captain Jason Keeton of Parsons, Tennessee. Jason is in his late thirties or early forties, and he's built like a barrel. He and his pilot—his brother Jimmy Keeton, on this trip —share the duties at the controls, each man standing two six-hour watches a day. Jason takes the forewatches—6 to noon, 6 to midnight —and Jimmy takes the afterwatches. Jimmy's asleep one deck below right now, and Jason is at his ease in the high pilot's chair, watching the river, one foot up on the edge of the console, one hand on a stick. Every now and then, he gets to his feet to slow the tow or speed it up a hair; he touches the throttles on the console, and the pneumatic controls puff and hiss like steam engines valving. He chats by radio with the men at the sticks of other boats nearby, and they arrange on which side they will pass: "See you on the one-whistle," "Catch you on the two." If two tows have to pass in a tight place, one or the other offers safe arrangements. "I tell you what, Cap'm. We'll just get over here and wait for you, right here at 142, below Harlow's Island."

"Got you fine on that, Cap'm. Got you fine. Well, 'preciate that Cap'm. See you on the one-whistle, then." The jargon of the river is characterized by much courteousness. It is not just that the pilots are many of them southerners; the tone reflects their caution: men steering unwieldy metal rafts worth millions of dollars do not want to run into each other.

Searchlights wash our tow—our lights, the lights of a boat astern, those of an approaching upbound boat. Jason has us proceeding very sedately. He speaks of tows breaking up, being torn apart by eddies and wind-driven wakes in busy water like this, and twenty or thirty barges "going off like a covey of quail"; the weather has begun to thicken too, and the water is low in the Upper Mississippi. There are some pretty bad stretches between St. Louis and Cairo just now. "Ain't hardly enough water in there for a long-legged rat," says one pilot over the radio. The barges and the towboat draw 8 and 9 feet. Very quickly one starts rooting for the tow. We sit in the dark pilot house and watch the digits flick up on the depth-sounder panels: 11.8 on the port bow, 13.5 to starboard, 11.3 and 13.6, 11.2 and 12.5, 10.6 and 12.2.

Because of the shallow water, Jason tells us, the *Ray A.* will not go directly to New Orleans. The boat hasn't been refueled in a while and rides higher in the water than usual, so the company has assigned it to "turn boats" at Cairo—exchange tows with another towboat, return to St. Louis over the bad ground, and start south again with still another tow.

MD   Meals were catch-as-catch-can aboard Audubon's flatboat. A Cincinnati shoemaker named Luke, "a Poor Sickly Devil who had been acting as Cook," left them early on in the voyage. Audubon's young apprentice, Joseph Mason, was then "obliged to officiate as Cook," though he did not "appear to relish the thing." Later in the trip it apparently became a matter of every man for himself: "we seldom eat together," wrote JJA, "and very often the hungry Cooked, this I performed when in need by Plucking & Cleaning a Duck or a Partridge and throwing it on the Hot embers . . . Others preferring Bacon would Cut a slice from the *Side* by the Chimney and Chew that raw with a hard biscuit."

Nowadays the majority of the cooks on the boats of the Western

Rivers are women, and their hitch is the same as the other crew members—thirty days on, thirty days off. Meals are scheduled to meet the changes of the watch, so the forewatch has breakfast at 5:30 A.M. before going on duty, and the afterwatch eats at 6:00 A.M. when they come off. Dinner begins at 11:30 A.M. and supper at 5:30 P.M. The cook is also responsible for planning menus and ordering the groceries, which are delivered en route, in mountainous quantities, by a supply boat that pulls alongside midstream. If the deckhands like the cook, they'll give her a hand and put away the groceries, though technically speaking that is not their job. If the deckhands get along with the cook only so-so, they'll put away the perishables when she's busy or sleeping. (It's a long day. 4:30 A.M. to 7 or 8 P.M., and the cook will often try to catch a nap in the afternoon.) But if the deckhands do not like the cook at all, they'll even wake her up to put away the groceries herself.

Our cook, Mrs. Ruth Carlisle, who is from Kentucky and came aboard with us at St. Louis, is a favorite with this crew. She was greeted with hugs, and one of the deckhands swung her off her feet when she stepped into the messroom. Ruth was on recall from her thirty days shore leave to fill in for a cook who'd taken ill—a Louisiana woman whose cuisine, I gather, was primarily Creole (lots of gumboes, shrimp dishes, and hot spicy seasonings), which is not popular with this crew. They're largely Tennessee, Kentucky, and Arkansas men, and they prefer Ruth Carlisle's brand of middle-south country cooking. Well, it surely is good. And there surely is a lot of it.

Mike and I are goggle-eyed at the feasts that appear three times daily. Here's a typical breakfast: hot and cold cereal, eggs, hash browns, bacon or hog jaw, sausage, hot biscuits, cornbread, milk gravy. Dinner: Baked ham, sweet potatoes with marshmallows, mashed potatoes, potato salad, beans with bacon, niblet corn, stewed okra with tomatoes, cole slaw, green salad, celery, radishes, hot biscuits, strawberry pie, cherry and orange jello mold with whipped cream topping. Supper: another huge spread. With every meal, there is coffee, iced tea, milk, lemonade, grapeade, etc. For the deckhand who's keen on cottage cheese, there's always a pot of cottage cheese out on the table. For the one who's keen on pickles, a jar of pickles. "I'm petting them," Ruth Carlisle explains.

She's an attractive, sparky, gray-haired widow; little diamond stud earrings in her pierced ears, a white gold ring set with entwinements of diamonds on her wedding ring finger—"I love diamonds," she confides. For her off-hours she's brought along a patchwork quilt she's piecing together for a friend who got tired of doing all those tiny stitches. Ruth keeps open house in her galley, unlike some cooks who treat the galley as a private domain, off limits to the rest of the crew, up to and including the captain. Daisy, one of the cooks on the river frequently cited for her wicked ways, even goes so far as to lock up the refrigerator and the pantry between meals. And there is also the crucial, highly significant question of the tending of the percolator, a task officially relegated to the deckhands. Ruth always has fresh hot coffee on the sideboard, regardless of rules and custom. Daisy, however, will not make coffee for the boys. Daisy won't even wash the pot. And when the supply boat comes alongside, you can just bet that no one puts the groceries away for Daisy.

On a typical morning when I slothfully make my late appearance, Ruth has not only been up since 4:30 A.M. (and the 5:30 A.M. breakfast a thing of the past and out of the way), but she's already put together a peach cobbler for dessert, baked a cake for in-between meals, and is well into the fixings for the noontime servings of the big dinner. Today, the main dish will be fried chicken, which Ruth tends carefully so it won't get overdone. A lot of the men don't have their teeth, she explains. Or they have false teeth. "If the food's overdone, they can't eat it. One of my boys said that Daisy's chicken was so tough and burned, his mouth hurt for a week."

I've taken to hanging out in the galley from time to time. I can identify with what Ruth is doing. I can see myself in that job—not as able, not as efficient, but somehow getting three meals on the table per day. Whereas the deckhands' work is entirely out of my ken. I can explore it intellectually but I'd never find myself out on a fifth-of-a-mile-long spread of barges, cranking up giant ratchets, tightening steel cables in the dark in a snowstorm. Since Ruth's world is a scene into which I can move and operate, and since she has thirteen people to cook for (that includes Michael and me on this leg of the trip), I sometimes set the table for her or wash dishes (there is no dishwasher) or peel potatoes. This morning I help out with salad fixings as she and I chat over our coffee and cigarettes. (Two unreconstructed cigarette smokers.)

I ask her the purpose of the steel bar that runs the length of the stove. She leans against it to demonstrate: "To keep your belly from getting burned." On the old boats, she says, there are bars all the way around, because the engines shudder so badly in reverse, the pots and pans jump off the burners. "You can't stand there and hold them down. The bars keep them on the stove."

She speaks of other cooks on the river. She's seen women who've raised five children and still can't put a meal together. They brought up their families on peanut butter and jelly. There was another Ruth knew—aged 54, who'd never cooked a steak before in her life (Saturday night on the river is steak night) and she burned them all, clean through. But a bad cook is not tolerated for long. The captain will put her off the boat and radio for a replacement. That's how Ruth Carlisle got her first job two years ago. Her application was in, a third-rate cook was fired at Memphis, and the barge line flew Ruth down from Kentucky that night to take over.

Junior, the second mate, comes in off the barges for a respite from the sleet and cold; a lean, prematurely gray, gentle, mannerly, Tennessee man. He sees today's glorious German chocolate cake on the messroom serving table and politely asks when it's going to be served.

"Now!" says Ruth, and then chides him. "That's what it's there for. I didn't bake a cake for people to stand and look at."

MH   Ruth is a good representative of this whole bunch. She has been a survivor in a difficult life—better than that, even: a cat that lands on its feet, running. Her son was ten and caught polio in Florida; to pay for his care she took factory work, fly-tying and making cigarette lighters, and on weekends she was a waitress in an Orlando nightclub. Later, in Kentucky, her husband took ill with a wasting disease, and she knew it would be expensive; she worked in a factory, making storm doors and awnings during the days, put in weekends and evenings in a laundromat, and as a cook and waitress in a Paducah restaurant. As for her job on the river, says Ruth: "It may seem like work to some people. It seems like a holiday to me."

Most of the men who gather around her groaning board on the *Ray A.* seem to share that same basic experience and character: country-born and bred, a demanding life, lots of work, a certain ornery independence and ability to make do. Most of them work twelve hours a day for thirty days at a stretch, and then take the next month ashore, free and clear. (Jason is the exception to this rule; whether on the river or at home, as master of the boat he is ultimately responsible for everything that happens on board—which he says has begun to wear on him.) Their "thirty days on" means no liquor, no shore leave (except in case of serious illness or family emergencies), no nothing—except heavy work for the mates and deckhands, a lot of boredom, high-school roughhousing and locker-room humor, a great deal of food, and a certain amount of danger on the job. The pay is good—they earn two months' wages in one month —and the company picks up their travel expenses to and from the boat. The system also allows for the man who wants to work his way up. Jason Keeton was a deckhand ten years ago.

Everyone on the *Ray A.* is white: the two pilots, two engineers, two mates, four deckhands, and the cook. That's a turnabout. In the last century most of the deckhands and engineroom crew would have been black; likely the cook would have been black; an assistant pilot might have been black. Now, we are told, you very rarely find Persons of Color working towboats on the Mississippi or the Ohio; they're not welcome.

In gray, threatening weather we pass Ste. Genevieve (thinking of Roziers past and present) and Cape Girardeau (Louis Lorimier, whipping his horse with his long pigtail). In that stretch I count twenty-three wintering bald eagles, including a couple of big immatures that Audubon would very likely have identified as Washington Sea Eagles; I saw those two not far from Grand Tower, scene of his first sighting.

Along the margins are long, sandy beaches striped by jetties. Long stretches of floodplain forest, an occasional scattering of farms. Ninety-four miles above Cairo, the St. Louis-San Francisco Railway line slides down to the river on the Missouri side and stays with us for more than forty miles, often running under high stone cliffs. Then it leaves the river for good at Cape Girardeau.

In the pilot house we've been getting short lectures in an aspect of towboating known as flanking, but it is Jimmy Keeton who pins the lesson down. The *Ray A. Eckstein* is entering the first of a string of bends above Cairo, when Jimmy says, "If any pilot of *mine* tried to

do what I'm doin' and he didn't make it, I'd fire him for tryin' it."
"Okay," I say, "what are you trying?" "I'm steerin' it," says Jimmy,
"and I should probably be flankin' it. Too late now." *Steering* a bend
with a tow-and-towboat 1200 feet long means staying under power,
driving the head of the tow around the buoy that marks the inside
of the bend, and then accelerating enough to overcome the sideways
inertia of the turning tow and—downbound—the eight-mile-an-hour
following current, both of which would like to sling the towboat right
up on the bank on the outside of the bend. "We call that chewin' out
your backside," says Jimmy. "Well," I say, "my father had an expression for situations like this. When I was in a tight spot he used to say,
'I shall follow your future career with interest.'" Jimmy likes that,
gets the note of friendly needling, and he nods and grins and says it
over to himself. Probably he knew all along he wasn't in any real
trouble, and his touch at the con is as nifty as Jack Nicklaus' with the
putter. Anyway, we come around into the straightaway with forty or
fifty feet to spare between the stern and the bank. Jimmy hops down
from the pilot's chair. "How do you like my career now?" But he
flanks the rest of the bends in this stretch—more or less floats us
through. Well ahead of a turn, he slows the tow to the speed of the
current, and as he reaches the top of the turn he backs the engines
and angles the stern of the towboat toward the inside of the bend.
This slides the head of the tow, a fifth of a mile downriver, toward
the outside bank. The current is fastest there, and by the time the
tow has reached the middle of the bend, the current has hold of its
head and carries it through, while the pilot concentrates on keeping
the towboat out of trouble. It's safe, and it's slow.

The deliberate, stately *pas de deux* of turning boats begins after
dark at Cairo. It is executed at the edge of one of the busiest river
junctions in the world, in slush showers and freezing fog laced by the
probing, bouncing, blue-white shafts of dozens of searchlights. I am
in the pilothouse with Captain Jason Keeton for about five hours
while the exchange of tows with the other boat goes on, and I feel
almost disembodied. I have no grasp at all of where we are; looking
at the chart and the radar screen doesn't help because I've never
been wherever it is in daylight and can't picture it. Every now and
then one of the sweeping shafts of light will touch the shore, glance

off the tops of trees, come to rest forgetfully on a patch of woods, and all of that—the drifting smoky beams of light, the branches and trunks, as well as the patches of water, corners of barges, and bits of steep bank picked out by the flitting spots—seems disembodied too.

After four hours we slide away from the other boat with our new tow and with a Diesel fueler clinging to us by an umbilicus that is adding 25,000 gallons of oil to the *Ray A.*'s supply. Jason hopes the weight will discourage his company dispatchers from assigning him to another short run. He yawns again and again as his watch enters its last two hours; there's not much for him to do except keep a lookout and tell towboats underway what the *Ray A. Eckstein* is up to; the crew must finish checking and tightening the tow and then lay the electric lines out to the head end and hook up the running lights and the depth-sounders. It will be about Jimmy's turn at the con by the time we actually start north.

Notes, daylight: With Jimmy, we talk about the advantages of small-town living. He lives in Parsons, Tennessee, too. "When the phone book gets more than a quarter of an inch thick," says Jimmy, "it's time to move." . . . I take a bald eagle count, from Cape Girardeau north, and—being very conservative—I see seventy-two of them, more than triple the downbound count. Is that because we are going so much slower, upbound? Headed south, we make eight or ten or twelve miles in an hour, but headed north, four or five miles is pretty good.

MD Eagles everywhere! Roosting grandly in the bare trees, displaying the Roman profile to the right, then turning the head to display the profile to the left. Feeding along the shore on dead fish or dead ducks. Gliding overhead and playing soar-and-swoop games. Two or three take off in opposite directions, wheel and head in toward each other on a collision course, a last-minute tilt—they sweep past in mid-air, wing tips almost touching, and then off again to repeat the figure—an airborne Virginia Reel.

Jason has given me a book of navigation charts to follow, *Upper Mississippi River.* (The Mississippi is divided into two parts, the Upper and the Lower; the junction with the Ohio is the dividing point.) Each chart in the book covers about six miles of river—from Cairo upstream to beyond Minneapolis and St. Paul. I sit in an easy chair at the wide front window of the wheelhouse, the book open across my lap, and watch the names on its pages come to life on the river below. Dog Tooth Bend, where Jimmy steered through instead of flanking. Thebes Bridge. Dusky Bar. Hanging Dog Light. Apple Creek, where Jason points out an old clapboard-sided railroad hotel, now derelict, beside tracks that carry only freight these days. He says that here and there on the shore are the remains of what were apple orchards before the river rearranged the landscape in one flood or another. In the autumn, says Jason, you'll find deer feeding on the fallen apples under the trees.

MH   All along the river's edge one sees levees and jetties and granite riprap and revetments—concrete slabs strung together on cables, tying down the shore. Sometimes the banks are even paved. All these labors by the Corps of Engineers to keep the river where it "belongs" have a touchingly human fallibility about them. The river breaches levees and switches channels to suit itself. It eats up the riprap and lifts the concrete weights from its banks; willows pierce and crack the pavement, the pavement is patched, the willows poke through again.

Mark Twain made the Mississippi sound almost benign in its truculent independence; it is, he said, "a just and equitable river; it never tumbles one man's farm overboard without building a new farm just like it for that man's neighbor." Consider that the Mississippi can transport that farm in the space of a few hours, destroying property lines and rupturing state lines when it does—and that (particularly in high water) it always *wants* to do so someplace along its course. We are told that downstream in Louisiana the Corps is watching with particular care the spot where the Atchafalaya River leaves the Mississippi along the course of the "Old" Mississippi. Apparently the Mississippi has an idea of going off to the westward again with the Atchafalaya, leaving Baton Rouge and New Orleans high and dry.

MD   Grand Tower, standing straight up out of the river like a giant layer cake with trees and shrubbery for frosting; Mike tries to get a sharp photograph in the sleet and fog.

Jimmy's watch, afternoon. A flock of pigeons flies out from a grain elevator and lights on our barges to feast on the free pickings of spilled grain. "I see we got us some hitchhikers out yonder," Jimmy says. "They're real river rats. Sometimes they'll ride with us fifty or sixty miles."

He speaks of the river in early spring, how beautiful it is when the trees come into leaf and the fields turn green. He talks about the loneliness of the afterwatch at night and tells us to be sure to come to the pilot house anytime we're awake between midnight and 6 A.M.

Jimmy's customary sign-off at the end of radio conversations with other pilots: "Steer easy . . ."

Audubon and his shipmates agreed at the start of their trip "to shave & Clean completely every Sunday—and often have been anxious to see the day come for certainly a shirt worn one week, hunting every day and sleeping in Buffalo robes at night soon becomes soiled and Desagreeable." A couple of weeks later he comments: "Shaved and Cleaned. One of the few enjoyments Flat Boats Can afford."

Everything and everyone are spanking clean aboard the *Ray A.* Housecleaning (mopping, polishing, vacuuming) is the deckhands' job. They also make beds and tidy up for the captain, the pilot, and the chief engineer. For laundry there's a washing machine and dryer aft, beyond the spick-and-span engine room that you cross on a hatched runway, the thundering engines to your right and left. And in the laundry room, a supply closet bursting with soaps and bleaches —a year's supply, to *my* reckoning. The crew, in fact, looks so spruce, with changes of clothes so eminently respectable, that I demand Michael give up his beige sweater with holes in the elbows and raveling cuffs, and I launder and mend his navy blue CPO shirt as a substitute.

There are other boats, I hear, that are not so shipshape as the *Ray A.* It's said that on some the cook warms over any old thing and slings the pots and pans on the table, while up in the pilothouse there's an endless round of gambling—poker or a diceboard. And at the change of watch, as one crew gets up from the gaming table to go on duty, the crew coming off takes their places. Tales are also told about some of the old-guard pilots who never take a bath. "A dying breed," says

Jimmy. "Thirty days on the river without a bath, thirty ashore without drawing a sober breath . . ."

MH   Speaking of baths, one of the hands—name of Bob, looks like Ernest Borgnine—says he almost took his Saturday night bath the other day. Wires began popping out on the tow; perhaps a barge bumped the bottom or a wave put too much strain on the connecting cat's-cradles. The inch-and-a-half cables break like dry elastic bands or guitar strings that have been stretched too far, and when they do break, it is with such violence they throw those seventy-five- and ninety-pound ratchets around as if they weighed nothing; deckhands can be hurt or killed. Bob was checking the tow for broken ties that needed to be replaced. When the action began, he ran for the river. "I got to the edge of the tow before she stopped popping," he says. He didn't much want to go overboard, anyway; if a man doesn't jump well clear, and if the pilot doesn't see him go, a moving tow will suck him right under the barges, feed him through the propellers of the towboat, and spit the pieces out astern. For that reason the deckhands generally stay off the outer edges of the tow except in emergencies.

The remark about popping cables starts a string of stories from Bob's watchmate, the sandy-haired Arkansan, Billy Nedd; Billy's been on the river seventeen years. Once cables begin to pop, a chain reaction can take place as greater strain falls on fewer and fewer cables; soon you may have the barges going off all over the river. Well, says Billy Nedd, he remembers a night a tow broke up. "It was like a Christmas party—barges flying every which way, sparks flying, and the pilot hollers at me to catch a line. *Catch a line?* I'm not going out there. I'm not catching any lines. A line would pop like thread. I once seen one of those ratchets go end over end up so high it nearly went out of sight. . . . Oh, you should see it when the barges break loose. We have about forty minutes with everyone crazy and the next watch out of bed and everything hoppin' and poppin' and dancin'."

Downbound again. A flash of recognition of how well a good pilot knows the river: the Coast Guard today reported an Exxon tanker barge aground at mile 482 on the Lower. Said Jimmy, "Oh, yeah.

Four-eighty-two. That's just below Stack Island." Stack Island and 482 are 640 miles away from where we were at the time, and between the two points are hundreds and hundreds of islands, towheads, cutoffs, bends, docks, grain elevators, gravel banks, Corps of Engineers' works, etc., etc.,—all with names; and 640 mile markers along the bank to connect to the names.

There is something easy and friendly about these southern voices around us—the aural equivalent of eating fried catfish and hushpuppies. After days of uninterrupted exposure to them, it comes as quite a shock—while seated on the high bench behind the con, watching the river go by and chatting with Jimmy—to hear over the radio the Coast Guard weather report for the river, read in accents obviously honed in some down east outpost like Rockland, Maine. So *that's* what Yankees sound like to the southern ear.

MD   Each of the watches, as a group, has a personality of its own, and each has a star performer who sets the tone. Danny the Chief Roughhouser is the star of the afterwatch, the big burly boy, the Big Rip, the black-bearded scowling clown who stalks the messroom for a quick scramble—a calculated stroll around the table, a quick dart and thump upside someone's head, a sudden shove and muttered threat to another, a lunging sortie against the chief engineer, a lunging sortie against a watchmate, Kentucky Slim. He pummels Slim into a corner. "Daddy!" Slim calls to the captain in mock terror.

But it's not roughhousing at random. Danny knows who'll play and who won't, and there are certain members of the crew on whom he never lays a finger. Big Bob is one. Jimmy Jones, the first mate. Jimmy Keeton, the pilot. Oscar, the assistant engineer. Captain Jason Keeton, however, is amused and tolerant. He enjoys the game. Danny drops into the chair next to him, they exchange banter, watching each other's eyes and hands, each waiting for the other to pounce. Danny rises, feigns departure, slopes off behind the captain's chair, then strikes. A lightning move. He bites the captain's ear. The captain bellows. Rises. Strikes back. Wings Danny with a plate of pork and beans.

"I'm not cooking again!" cries Ruth Carlisle, and laughs till there are tears in her eyes. "You two will just have to eat off the floor!"

The men on the forewatch are talkers and listeners. Well, listeners mostly. Their star performer is Billy Nedd, a man who loves nothing better than to tell stories, to sit at the messroom table with his watchmates, Junior and Big Bob, and ramble on. He's a deadpan funnyman, the compulsive talker, wide-eyed at his own adventures, which he spins out in a rhythmic, metered pattern, as the best of story tellers do, mimicking other voices, pantomiming the action.

He's spun yarns for us on coon hunting; on the bad day out on the barges when a cable split and smashed him in the face and took out his teeth; on funerals, which he hates to go to and he isn't going to any more of them, by God, except for his own and he'll have to get to that funeral, like it or not. But closest to his heart is the saga of his marriage, a continuing source of wonder to Billy—that he should be married to a woman who's six feet tall, weighs two hundred and forty pounds, with the meanest temper of any woman you'd ever want to see. "My wife's family are Germans," says he, as though to offer an explanation for her height and weight and disposition. "You can't say nothing to that woman but she snaps your head off, and you don't want to cross a woman that size." (She must make up two of Billy. He's a small man, and for all his thirty-five years, has the wiry narrow frame of a boy.)

He rolls into a story about his drinking days when he went out and got himself drunk and bought a black, $200 cowboy outfit and wheeled home, gleaming all over in that $200 cowboy suit and smoking a fifty-cent cigar. He gets out of the pickup truck, leans back against the hood, a beer can in one hand, the cigar in the other, and he calls to his wife, "Honey, fetch me an ashtray." She fetches him one, all right. She opens the screen door, shies a big old heavy ashtray across the yard, it catches him on the shin and breaks his leg. The bone cracks all the way around. He goes to bed with his leg in a cast and stays drunk for a month. Once, though, he decided to take a bath and hopped into the tub and crooked his cast over the edge to keep it dry and got stuck flat on his back under water. "My wife came in the bathroom and said, you damn fool, what're you doin'? I'm takin' a bath. You damn fool, you'll drown yourself. And that woman, that six foot woman, lifted me right on up out of the tub like a baby and threw me back in bed."

By now the table's in a roar and I'm doubled over with laughter, my head in my arms.

"Then the damn doctor gets me mixed up with somebody else. He takes the other man's cast off two weeks early, and takes mine off two weeks late. Was that other man a nigger? I asked the doctor. No, he says. Why do you ask? Because I just wanted to be sure you could tell the difference."

He drifts back to his boyhood and the girls he loved down in the mountains of Arkansas, and there he was in the privy with Ann McGee. He was fourteen, she was seventeen, going at it, when his uncle opened the privy door.

Mary (the gullible one, shocked and surprised): "What did your uncle *say?*"

B. Nedd (without missing a beat): "He said he wouldn't tell nobody if he could have some too." I bet Billy Nedd has told that story a thousand times, and there's always someone like me to play the straightman and ask the lead-in question.

"Oh, those McGee girls." He picks up the thread of his reminiscences. "No boys in the family. Just girls and each one prettier than the next. I had them all, including the mother. I went right down the line, and their daddy sat on the porch chewing his tobacco and talking to the parakeet, and he didn't know what was going on. That's God's truth. I had everyone of them in that family (pause) . . . but the parakeet and the old man."

Big Bob: "I wouldn't tell that kind of stories. I wouldn't give myself away like that."

MH   Overnight we add fifteen barges to our tow in Cairo and by 4:15 A.M. the *Ray A. Eckstein* is southbound on the Lower Mississippi, shoving before it more than five acres of barges—thirty-five loads of grain in seven strings of five. You could lay nearly three football fields end to end out there, with plenty of room for spectators on the sidelines.

This morning Mary and I are in the pilothouse before sunrise. "Here the Traveller enters a New World," wrote Audubon in 1820 as Jacob Aumack's flatboat left the Ohio and entered the Mississippi. He found himself frightened by the growing distance from his family. But to me, who has the major figure in my family with me, this feels like dawn on Christmas or a childhood birthday morning. Not only because we' e picked up JJA's trail again as we pass the confluence where his boat turned south, but for us it is a New World indeed, the wide arc of placid water, the constantly revealing bends in the river —a curtain perpetually parting, the mysterious islands we can't stop to explore, and the anticipation of hundreds of miles more of this in front of us.

We got up here none too soon. The *Ray A.* is passing the spot where Audubon camped the second night on the Mississippi, near Columbus, Kentucky, and it will take us only two hours to cover his next day's travel and pass his third camp, roughly in the neighborhood of Bayouville, Missouri, "Opposit the Head of No. 8, at the foot of No. 7"—two island names that still appear on the charts, though No. 7 is no longer an island.

MD   One of my favorite sections in Twain's *Life on the Mississippi* is a lyrical description of sunrise seen from a wheelhouse. I wanted to see one for myself, so Mike routed me out at 5 A.M. Jimmy's Watch: The wheelhouse is in darkness except for the green and yellow lights from the depth-finders and the radar screen. There's a new moon and a morning star to port. The only lights on shore are occasional Coast Guard markers. Out front on the barges, the bobbing headlamps of the afterwatch, checking ties. The night sky is clear, with low-lying black clouds like a range of hills on the horizon. The river runs wide and flat and very still. At a bend far ahead, red and green running lights appear. "I see your snout coming in now," says Jimmy to the pilot of the approaching towboat, and as we near and then pass, they talk back and forth about "buoys set wrong" at White River, Arkansas, and "left-hand drafts" and "staying with black buoys close as you can."

A peach flush touches the sky, and slowly deepens to blood-orange. The color is picked up by the river. The morning star still hangs out there with the new moon. What star is it? I ask. What planet? Venus, perhaps? But no one in the wheelhouse can tell me. They're rivermen. They don't steer by the stars.

Stick silhouettes of trees materialize along the shore. Crows are suddenly up and about. I can recognize Bob, Junior, and Billy out on the barges tightening lines, and can see my handwriting. I've been scribbling in my journal in the dark; blind, loopy handwriting that collides with the lines above or falls off the page. Crows stream upriver on their dawn commute to feeding grounds. The pink and orange colors in the sky dissolve to blue and gray, the moon and the morning star are gone. The water is silver, the clouds on the horizon pewter-gray. A grain elevator ahead—a white castle on the shore. I now can see into the trees, see driftwood and muddy banks, tangled underbrush, revetment, green fields in an occasional clearing. Somewhere through here Audubon noted: *"Ivory Billed Wood Peckers* are Now Plenty, Bears, Wolf &c but the Country extremely difficult of Access."

A white church steeple, behind a forested island, points heavenward. The sun is about to pop. The pewter clouds turn back again to pink, then to gold, and rays shine upward from the horizon like a child's drawing of a sunrise. The red sun, as though sprung from a trap, leaps out of Kentucky.

We pass the third camp, "Island No 8 at the Foot of No 7" where Audubon and shipmates put out a line, "Caught a Cat fish," and he noted that the weather was agreeable.

We enter the twenty-mile hairpin curve that passes New Madrid. "Here familly dicensions are at their Zenith, and to Kill a Neighbour is but more than to Kill Deer or a Racoon." He notes freshening winds, as "Contrary to our Wishes as that of an ole Rich Maid to the wishes of a Lover of Wealth." We have no contrary winds this morning. A glassy calm, river and sky.

MH   Forty miles below New Madrid we ease through Little Prairie Bend. Near here Audubon shot a "Beautifull *White headed Eagle"* and hurried back to the boat to start to draw it. That's the very eagle in one of the most famous Audubon engravings, the eagle with a catfish.

The chart of this stretch of river contains community names that prick the imagination. In Missouri: Gayoso, Hayti, Schult, Indian Mound, Kinfolk Ridge. Across the river in Tennessee: Cottonwood, Tennemo, and Owl Hoot.

Jason's watch now. The chief engineer, a quiet, broad-built, studious-looking man in his fifties, name of Charlie, has come up to join Jason in the pilothouse. I exclaim over the thousands of acres of

In the final version of this work, the prey—a green-winged teal—was re-placed by a large catfish. *Courtesy of The New-York Historical Society, New York City*

flood-plain forest around us, and Charlie surprises me with his re-sponse: "Ten or fifteen years from now," he says flatly, "you won't see a *tree*. They're cutting them down just as fast as they can, and drain-ing swamps to grow soybeans and rice. Soybeans go to $8 a bushel, you can just *see* those trees comin' down." He shakes his head gloom-ily. I look back at the river and its enveloping forest; a different scene does not seem possible, but then it never does.

The river is half a mile wide in many places. Above the steep banks and on former sandbars, low willows grow thick as grass. Some-times the banks are lined with a rank or two of taller trees, presuma-bly left there to help hold the banks, and then beyond them are fields for crops. But such vistas beyond the banks are few. The feeling is very much of an enclosed world, trees and water and flood levees and sandbars and islands and sky; red and green navigation marks set along the shore or perched on levees; Coast Guard buoys to mark the channel; other towboats shoving acres of barges; the courteous exchange of greetings and information by radio, Jason stepping outside on a bridge wing to wave with both arms at a passing colleague, who likely will step outside and return the salute; the rumble and grind of the *Ray A. Eckstein*'s engines, the figures of deckhands checking the tow in front of us, the flick-flick of the depth-sounder readouts on the console in front of Jason.

MD   Near the Missouri-Arkansas border is Island No. 20, and on the opposite shore Audubon's boat took refuge for two days from a rising wind. He made note of a grim riverbank camp of migrants, derelict and undone, "a family of Three People in Two Skiffs a Woman & 2 men; they are Too Lazy to Make themselves Comfortable, and Lie on the Damp Earth, near the Edge of the Watter, have *Racoons* to Eat and Muddy Watter to help that food down, are from the Mouth of Cumberland and moving to a Worst Part of the Worst Without Doubt."

I am gripped by that paragraph each time I read it. Who were these people? Did they get to where they were going? Why were they going? What did they look like? But that's all JJA tells us, except for two skimpy addenda: that the temperature rose to 70°, "Butterflies, Wasps & Bees plenty all day about us . . . , the Woman washed for us," and that the following day the temperature dropped to 22°, "the Woman of the Skiffs Mending My Good Brown Breeches." Audubon returns to his birds: ducks, geese, swans, eagles. The migrants vanish from his ken. And ours. I stare at the place opposite Island 20 on today's Mississippi. Dikes, revetments, the round towers of another grain elevator. In minutes, they and the bedraggled ghosts are left behind on the damp winter shoreline.

After supper: Everyone in the wheelhouse falls silent at a bridge approach, especially those bridges that lie at a curve, and to my untutored eye it always looks to be an impossible maneuver, as though the only way to get through would be to bend the boat and the barges into the same shape as the river. Even on a straightaway, it's a heart-stopping moment, and more so at night, like this evening's approach to the Memphis–Arkansas bridge. Over the horizon down-river, the lights of the city and its surrounding radio towers give the appearance of a distant amusement park. Then Memphis comes into focus as a city, and the bridge comes up at us out of the river, massive and intransigent. Over our heads we can read the sign at the west bank exit: "Welcome to Arkansas—Land of Opportunity." We skin between the piers on the Tennessee side where the channel is deep-est, and word goes around the pilothouse that this is where that fellow stabbed his wife with a pair of scissors, threw her body out of the car, drove to the middle of the bridge, and jumped off.

Audubon went ashore here. "We are landed immediately at the foot of Old Fort Pickering. We walked up to it through a very narrow crooked path, and found [it] in a very decayed situation; the Position a Beautifull one the Land Rich about it." The earthwork fort stood up there on the Memphis bank, right about where the bridge begins.

MH   South of Memphis on a warm, sunny morning. We have covered in a single twenty-four-hour day what it took Captain Au-mack and company more than two weeks to pass because of bad weather and adverse winds. Jason gentles his five-acre, quarter-mile-long monster under the bridge at Helena, Arkansas. Driving this rig requires a touch that the speedboater wouldn't believe. Our first morning aboard, Charlie, the chief engineer, told me that a lot of pilots and captains, leaving St. Louis, start to worry—not about the stage of the water or the shifting channel or the traffic, said Charlie, but about the bridges. The helmsman's task is to get 1200 feet of tow and towboat, 140 to 250 feet across, through, say, a 750-foot opening, usually on an angle, with a seven- or eight-mile-an-hour current shoving whimsically and threatening to drive the whole thing off line, maybe put it sideways to the bridge. A stiff wind can make things even more dangerous. Coming through at an angle, the 1200-foot rig uses up a 750-foot opening pretty fast. If it hits a bridge pier, you may have barges all over the river before you can think, and if the towboat itself hits hard, it may capsize or be ripped open and sink before anyone has time to shout.

I spend a lot of this day sitting in the sun on the deck of the bridge wings, dangling my feet over the edge, listening to the whine of the Diesels and to the groan of the cables on the tow, watching for birds, soaking up the sun and the willow bars and the woods and the smells of the muddy river and of the occasional burning-off fires near the river. I take what is probably an unnecessary number of photographs of the river's edges, trying to preserve for us and for anyone else who has never seen the Mississippi some clear image of what it is like, because we find it so *unexpected.* I don't know exactly what we thought we'd find on the Lower Mississippi, but this winding expanse of mostly flood-plain forest is not it.

MD The sun has some heat to it now, and we pass through a hatch of spiderlings that waft out from the shore on gossamer flight lines. The deck and the rails are sprinkled with them, tiny brown creatures, each smaller than the head of a pin. They are "ballooning spiderlings," the newly hatched young of certain spider families that emerge from their egg sacs to climb onto a fence post or a branch, spin threads into the air for the wind to catch, and are blown away to new territory. The afternoon sun shines at just the right angle to light up the thousands of silken threads that shimmer between the trees and the boat.

Stack Island, above Greenville, Mississippi: another Audubon landmark. Here he noted the completion of a drawing of the black vulture and added, "it stunk so intolerably, and Looked so disgusting that I was very glad when I through it over Board."

Night, after supper, the forewatch:
"Come to the window," Mike calls from the bedroom. "We're having another bridge adventure." The *Ray A.* is coming out of Walker Bend toward the Greenville Highway Bridge between Mississippi and Arkansas. The town of Greenville itself lies behind us on a loop of the river cut off in the 1930s when the Mississippi rearranged its course, so there are no city lights on the shore.

Jason is in the wheelhouse over our heads. We slide open the little window that looks onto the field of barges out front, and squeeze in together to watch the gliding approach. There are three openings in the bridge, and Jason has chosen the one on the right, the Arkansas span. The piers of the bridge loom up out of the dark water—big and solid and deathly. As the tow enters the gap between the piers,

Black vulture, finished December 21, 1820. *Courtesy of The New-York His-torical Society, New York City*

there's a gentle whomp and a reverberation that twitches up from the barges into the *Ray A*. We feel it through our feet. Seconds later, the barges heave. Shock waves ripple. Steel cables and ratchets whine, scream, and snap like basting threads. Sparks fly as thrashing metal strikes metal. A starboard double-line of ten barges breaks loose. Michael and I stand stock still at the little bedroom window. Frozen silent alarm. Frozen silent amazement as Jason pushes on in the dark, catches the loose string of barges, scoops them into the empty slot from which they've broken free, and herds them under the bridge before they make their getaway downstream.

At the same time a split cable smacks a can of gasoline that fuels the pump used to drain a leaky barge lashed directly to the bow of the *Ray A*. Gas leaks from the can. The electric line to the starboard running light has also parted. A live wire. It ignites the gasoline. Flames soar. Burning gasoline streels in the river. The river burns behind us for the length of the *Ray A*. The Mississippi is on fire! And Oh My God, I think, what about the reserve fuel for the utility boat stored in drums on the afterdeck. We're going to be blown out of the river and scattered in crumbs all over Chicot County, Arkansas.

Michael closes the window. Life jackets are in the closet. Our heavy coats are at hand. I put our journals into my basket. We are ready to move, if we have to move fast. But within the next minute, actually within seconds, Jason has shoved his five-plus acres of barges into the Arkansas shore and virtually beached the runaway inside lines of barges; the high-powered searchlights are on, giant feelers sweeping the tow, the shore, the fire, the river. There are shouted orders from the loudspeaker on the bridge. Jimmy Jones, the first mate, has materialized from the messroom to take command. Fire extinguishers are run out. The flames are foamed away, smothered, done.

We do not race up to the wheelhouse to find out what has happened. It is not an auspicious moment, Michael decides, to have visitors asking questions. So I go down to the lounge for news. Ruth is there working on her quilt, stitching together the diamond-shaped patches. Oscar, the second engineer, and Jimmy Keeton sit on the couch. All are watching TV, cool as can be. The movie version of James Dickey's *Deliverance*. I drop into an empty seat, settle back, and am into the movie with the rest of them.

Morning post mortems:

Jason explains that the breakup last night was entirely his fault. He had been talking on the radio, then stepped back to draw a shade against the searchlight of a trailing towboat, and his attention wandered. The current under the Arkansas span carried him a hair too close to shore, and the tow brushed bottom. But he did not err through ignorance of the river. He wants that understood.

As he eased over to catch the loose barges, everyone was concerned that the boat would "run into the hill," peel open, and sink like the *Lady Ree*, which was lost at the Greenville Bridge in 1972, drowning the master in the wheelhouse, the engineer in the engine room, the second engineer asleep in his cabin, three deckhands, and the cook—a man—who was out front wearing a life jacket; the force of the collision broke his neck and dropped him over the side. The boat is still at the bottom of the Mississippi. It was never found.

Up in the wheelhouse, where Billy Nedd has the housekeeping detail, he leans on his vacuum cleaner to philosophize about last night's excitement: "When I went out there and saw all those wires flying and all those ratchets bent double like licorice sticks, I said to myself, My God, what am I doing here?" Pause. He gives his audience a moment to consider the question, then delivers the answer. "The answer is money. That's what I'm doing here. It takes money to keep a big woman like my wife. Six feet tall. Two-hundred-forty pounds. That takes money."

A little bit later, the Vicksburg bridge—"another bastard." We come out of the deep bend of Centennial Cut-off (named when the river cut through here in 1876 and created the present channel), we angle sharply to starboard, and not one of us speaks a word—Junior, Billy, Mike, and me—as Jason eases through, smooth as strawberries and cream.

Next, a day of rain, and a hog-pen smell on deck. That's spilled hog pellets on the decks of a few barges, says Billy Nedd. "The spills get wet, rot, and then begin to stink like hog shit." The barge traffic also carries chicken meal, rabbit feed, bird seed, alfalfa seed, fertilizer, and grain, of course. Lots of grain. That's all we've got out front here. "Which we supply to Russia," Billy continues. "And Russia supplies us with wars."

"We've supplied a few wars in our own good time," says Bob. (We're in the messroom drinking coffee.) "That's the way it has to be. Without war, we'd be standing shoulder to shoulder all over the earth. Animals fight and kill each other. They thin out the herds. Men do the same. We're no different. We're thinning ourselves out, that's all."

MH   "See? See that? Look at that screen." Jimmy Keeton is peering out at the far-off head of our tow as it glides into the lowering fog and rain, but he gestures with his head at the radar screen on his right. "That's why you can't hardly run by radar in a heavy rain." All around us, on the screen, are rain squalls, and to our west, where the rain is thickest, the scatter blots out all other images. "We're goin' to have to get off this river pretty quick here, I bet." Fifteen minutes later, in thick fog and pelting rain, the *Ray A. Eckstein,* one of the most modern Mississippi River towboats, is parked against the east bank, and in rain and fog it waits there for nine hours, just as Jacob Aumack's flatboat would have done in 1820.

MD   The front end of the tow is alternately visible and invisible as clouds of fog wash over it. The revetment against which we're holding bursts with willows that have grown through the cement slabbing, but it's not safe to tie up to them. Willows, says Jimmy Jones, have shallow, wet roots. He's seen a willow this big around at the trunk (he opens his arms in a wide circle) come up out of the ground and fall across the barges. It's a nice point: A riverman does not need to know his stars, but he has to know his trees if he's going to use them as moorings.

Michael and I look wistfully into the wet brown woods. We'd both like to put on rain gear and leap ashore to explore the muddy road around the bend and see what there is to see. But it's too far to jump. Twelve feet. "This is going to be a long wait," says Jimmy Keeton. He fetches a tiny TV set, props it up on the control panel, and he and Mike watch the women's pro tennis finals in Chicago. Slim and Jimmy Jones play rummy and eat popcorn in the messroom, and Danny the Big Rip vacuums the lounge.

In the messroom. Junior, Billy Nedd, Bob, Ruth, and I.

The talk has turned to trapping. Possum skins are bringing in money again. Ruth knows someone back home, an old lady, who got forty dollars for possum she picked up dead on the road.

Bob reminisces on the washtubs of wild honey that his father used to bring home from the woods. I admit that I've never seen a honey tree, and Junior is amazed. How could it be possible that someone has never seen a honey tree! "But don't the bees go after you?" I ask. "How do you get the honey?"

"They're not so bad," says Junior. "The best time is early in the morning when the temperature's down and the bees are dozey. I always pull my shirttails over my head when I'm taking honey." He pulls his shirttail up over his head to demonstrate. "I don't like them biting my face. Doesn't bother me if they bite my body."

The talk moves on to hunting and venison, and Billy Nedd speaks of the many times he's seen deer swimming the river. Once they came up on one close enough to pull it aboard; it slashed the mate's face with its hooves when he tried to drag it out by the antlers. "Cap'n said, don't ever do that. Knock 'em out first. Then haul 'em aboard."

Billy has venison waiting for him at home, and a freezerful of gray squirrel. "Um! *Um!* A feast." He'll be going straight back after this hitch. No partying in Memphis, not like some of the other men, not like Bob who's already talking about that first night ashore and all the beer he can hold. But Billy's not a drinking man anymore, and besides, his wife will be at the dock to meet him. "She don't trust me out of her sight for one minute. And you don't cross a woman like my wife. *You've* seen her." He turns to Bob for corroboration. Bob nods his agreement. Billy's wife is indeed a formidable lady.

The talk shifts to children, the laughter subsides, the conversation grows thoughtful. Do *I* have children, Bob and Junior want to know. It is the first personal question any of the men has asked since Mike and I came aboard six days ago. I am enormously flattered. I take it as a token of acceptance. Yes, I have children. Two. A son and a daughter. Both of them grown and flown.

Bob: "I have five kids. One of them's a little six-year-old redhead I wouldn't swap for a billion dollars."

Billy: "But when I wanta go huntin' or fishin' or campin', I just wanta *go.* I don't wanta have to mess with kids."

Bob: "Take the young 'uns with you." (Looking quietly down the table at B. Nedd) "Take your young 'un by the hand and take him fishin' with you."

Jason comes on watch and settles into the pilot's chair with nothing to do but hold fast: "Just think," says he. "I could be at home watchin' television and fightin' with the kids." He keeps a personal log for his children, something to pass on to them in years to come, and after each of his watches Jason sits at the desk in the wheelhouse to write his careful entries.

MH Just above Baton Rouge, Jason flanks the *Ray A. Eckstein* through the sharpest bend we've seen from St. Louis south—around Thomas Point, southwest to northeast, the channel crookeder than a flexed elbow, 180 degrees in a few hundred yards; and then five miles farther on, another sharp turn to the south, under a bridge, and into Baton Rouge Reach.

We have come out the far end of more than 700 miles of very little but river. Mary and I had been told before we left the east that there wasn't much *to* the lower Mississippi—that is, not much to look at. "Just a walled chute," was the description. I suppose in a way that's right. A few bridges and car ferries. A few riverside cities. A few power plants and grain elevators and coal docks. Lots of towboats, shoving barges. And mostly just water and levees and jetties and sandbars and floodplain forest. But nothing to see? That's an amazing sight in itself—the wide, curving expanses of river, the solidly forested shore for mile upon mile, and, rarely, an Event: an isolated shack with a rusty metal roof, and an old handpainted maroon Model A Ford pickup next to it. The tableau, quickly out of sight, is followed by more miles of "nothing." This is one of the world's major waterways, yet a lot of it looks almost undiscovered. For despite the labors of the Corps of Engineers and other flood-controllers, the Mississippi is still too dangerous a river to encourage much permanent settlement within view of the water. And may it ever remain so.

One knows the river's innocence was ripped from it long ago, of course—being stabilized and channeled, diked, leveed, and turned into a sewer. And should one be lulled into forgetfulness by the water and sand, trees and caving banks of the last 700 miles, then Baton Rouge, at the nether end of this extraordinary passage, would restore perspective. Ocean-going freighters ride at anchor here, 250 miles from the Gulf, while lining the river are man's works—Consolidated Chemical, Ideal Cement, Kaiser Aluminum, Allied Chemical, Louisiana Steam Products, Exxon, Toro Petroleum.

The *Ray A. Eckstein* now sits, rumbling, near the east bank; a couple of harbor boats nibble at our tow. We drop two barges here, and various allotments are to be taken out at other places down the line before we reach New Orleans. Jason wants things to go as quickly as possible, so as the first two barges are removed from the tow, he has the harbor boats and his deck crew shuffle and rebuild what's left for easier separation downstream. I put on my heavy boots and an orange life vest and go out on the tow with first mate Jimmy Jones and Kentucky Slim and Danny, the Big Rip.

There is an aura of tautly leashed violence about the huge metal raft. As I walk out along the cracks where the barges meet, between the decked-over, shoulder-high grain hoppers, I step gingerly over the thick, humming-tight "warrs" that zigzag lengthwise from barge to barge and interlace at every junction of four corners. I can feel their threat in my ankles. I take any excuse—a better view, a more interesting camera angle—to climb up on the tops of the grain hoppers.

The deckhands go about their business, redoing such ties as need redoing. The idea seems to be to get the cat's-cradles to just this side of the breaking point—an I-dare-you infusion of toughness and violence, as the men jump up and down on the half-tight cables to stretch out the kinks, or beat at the cables with their ratchet-pipes, and then wind up the ratchets, one foot on either side of a warr, the head of the pipe above the fist arcing across in front of the orange life vest. Nothing to it, says the stance and action. Watch out, cry my empathetic ankles. And the ties can even snap right there, as they are tightened, if put together badly or unluckily.

During a lull, I ask Jimmy and Slim and Danny to pose on a grain hopper with the *Ray A. Eckstein* three or four barge lengths behind them. I have in mind Caleb Bingham's famous painting of jolly nineteenth-century American flatboatmen where a fiddle is being played while one of the men does a clogstep or a jig atop the cabin roof, and the rest of the crew looks on, grinning. Maybe I can get these three to be jolly boatmen for a minute. I don't know how to ask for that,

"Jolly Flatboatmen" by George Caleb Bingham, 1846. *State Historical Society of Missouri*

Slim, Jimmy, and the Big Rip. *MH*

so they lounge against each other, Danny on Jimmy on Slim, while I shoot with one camera, then with the other. Now, if I don't move quick, someone's going to be making the cuckold sign behind somebody's head, or the half-a-cuckold. "Okay," I shout—and immediately they relax, start to move apart, the humoring of the photographer being over—"no, wait, wait, wait. Do a jig." Slim and Jimmy smile and look embarrassed, and only Danny gives it a try—a lumbering, clownish, two-second imitation of (I should say) a dancing Turkey Buzzard. Hardly what I had in mind, but doubtless all that I deserved.

MD   Add things to see on the river, Baton Rouge:
    A little harbor boat goes by, spanking fresh paint and bright red flouncy curtains at the wheelhouse windows. "That's real cajun," says Jason.

    Seagoing vessels anchored here today are from Newcastle, Rotterdam, Palermo, Orendal, Oslo, Leningrad; the crew (both men and women) of a Swedish freighter out of Goteborg sunbathe on the afterdeck. We stare up at the Russian ships as though to solve a mystery or learn a hitherto unrevealed secret. Were their crews ever let ashore? I ask. "Sure," says Bob. "I've seen them in New Orleans losing their money to pimps and whores." Billy Nedd, out on the barges checking lines, had shaken his fist at one of the Soviet boats as we passed and called up to a sailor on watch: "You communist S.O.B. My cap'm can whup yer cap'm!" This is related at supper. "I thank you, Billy," says Jason from the top of the table. "That's exactly what I need."

Overheard from the messroom: Ruth talking to the vegetables on the stove. "Come on, peas. Heat up or go home."

MH For us this has been no bird trip. We have roared down the Mississippi at eight or ten miles an hour, not once setting foot on shore, covering in five days what Audubon took more than seven weeks to see between Cairo and New Orleans.

The flatboats he rode were quiet vessels—except for human voices and an occasional barrage of shot at passing avifauna. They always stopped on shore in bad weather, and usually they laid up at night, so JJA had plenty of land time. And there was quite a different character to the Mississippi then. The river has been trammeled and insulted by man, particularly in this century, and its edges have been hunted hard by generations of families who have fed themselves that way. In 1820, man's impact was only a scratch. With steamboating had come the woodyards and the timbering along the banks—Audubon remarked on it in his journal—but the worst of it was still a long way off. So his birding was, for much of the time, wilderness birding. And Captain Aumack's boat had turned into the Mississippi while the autumn migration was still in progress.

All that makes the ornithological aspects of his trip especially interesting—and not just to JJA. I propose to give you a feel for it, hastening to add that normally I would avoid such a thing: detailed descriptions of other people's bird trips in unfamiliar territory are usually a bore, even for me. But what Audubon saw and experienced says a great deal about where he stood as an ornithologist at the age of thirty-five, starting his life's work. And so much nonsense has been written about JJA the scientist and bird artist, as if in his great triumph he had actually *failed*—failed twentieth-century science and twentieth-century expectations of bird art, that some effort should be made to place him back in his own time and out of ours.

Start with the optical equipment. He had no sharp-focus, high-power binoculars; he used a spy-glass telescope occasionally, but he depended mostly on his unaided eyes and his aim with a gun. Then there is the matter of reference books. He mentions "Turton" during this voyage, so he may well have taken with him the bird volume in Linnaeus's *Systema Naturae*—the thirteenth edition, edited by Johann Friedrich Gmelin and Englished by William Turton. It was a book of about 500 pages, six by eight inches, listing and briefly describing all the known birds of the world; there was *one* plate of illustrations. That was a volume JJA could have stowed in his satchel. He didn't own Wilson's *American Ornithology,* and outdated though it was it remained the only major work available on North American birds; he often wished he had it to refer to, and at Natchez (where he met Lucy's brother-in-law Nicholas Berthoud and was invited to finish his voyage on Berthoud's boat), he found someone who owned the *American Ornithology* and spent the day before he left Natchez "Writting the Name and Such Descriptions of the Watter Birds in Willson as would enable me to Judge whenever a New Specimen falls my Praise [prize]"—the Instant Do-Your-Own Field Guide to the Known Watter Birds of North America.

He knew more about American birds than most—perhaps all—his contemporaries, but he knew less about them than many rank-and-file members of the National Audubon Society do today. So as he traveled he was making formal note of creatures and behavior that had not been formally noticed before—writing things down: "Saw some *Carrion Crows* and some *Turkey Buzzards* that were attracted by the scent?? of the Deer We had hung in the Woods??" That foreshadows a famous controversy JJA was embroiled in years later; after experiments, he concluded (wrongly) that the vultures do *not* use scent to find their food, and he caused an uproar with his paper that said so. "[T]he Cedar Birds Ampellis Americana fly northeast" —a good detail, considering that everything else was flying southwardly. "I saw this afternoon Two Eagles Coatiting—the femelle was on a Very high Limb of a Tree and squated at the approach of the Male, who came Like a Torrent, alighted on her and quakled shrill untill he sailed off the femelle following him and zig zaging herself through the air—this is a scarce proof I have had the pleasure of witnessing of these and all of the *Falco Genus* breeding much Earlier than any Other Land Birds. . . ." "I found the Stomack of the Great footed Hawk filled with Bones, feathers, and the Gizzard of a Teal, also the Eyes of a Fish and Many Scales—it was a femelle Egg numerous and 4 of them the size of Green Peas."

The journal of 1820–21 contains the earliest surviving examples of his writing about birds. He was to keep such journals for more than twenty years, filling them with observations and sketches, and he would eventually draw on this rich collection as he wrote the *Ornithological Biography*. His English may be makeshift and his punctuation haphazard; even so, some of the writing is vivid and expressive. After watching Mr. Aumack bring down the Great Footed Hawk, or peregrine falcon, JJA notes that "few men Can Boast of having Killed Many of them, for 15 years, that I have hunted and seen probably one hundred I Never had the satisfaction of bringing one to the Ground —I often have seen them after hearing their Canon Ball Like wissling Noise through the Air seize their Prey on the Wing particularly at *Henderson* Kentucky, where I watched for Weeks near a Pigeon House, that furnished one of those daring Robbers, with food & Exercise." Nice touch, John James. And later he describes the flocks of migrating blackbirds and grackles: they "pass Southwest constantly; forming a Line Like disbanded Soldiers all anxious to reach the point of destination each hurr[y]ing to pass the companion before him."

I've compiled a Mississippi River bird-list from his journal.

Audubon's List	Key
Diver	loon species
Dun Diver	female common merganser
Merganzer, the Large	male common merganser
Pelican	white pelican
Brown Pelican; Black Pelican;	

Cormorant; Irish Goose	double-crested cormorant
Swan	whistling swan, or trumpeter swan, or both
Wild Goose	probably Canada goose
Malard	
Sprig Tail Duck	pintail
American Teal	green-winged Teal
Wood Duck	
Little Duck the Spirit	bufflehead
Carrion Crow	black vulture
Turkey Buzzard	turkey vulture
Slate Colored Hawk	adult sharp-shinned hawk
Intrepid Hawk	Cooper's hawk?
Prairie Hawk	male northern harrier
Marsh Hawk	female and immature northern harrier
Black Hawk	dark-plumaged rough-legged hawk
Red Tailed Hawk	
American Buzzard	immature red-tailed hawk
Red Shouldered Hawk	
Winter Hawk; Winter Falcon	immature red-shouldered hawk
White Headed Eagle	bald eagle
Brown Eagle	immature bald eagle, or adult golden eagle; probably both
Great Footed Hawk	peregrine falcon
Sparrow Hawk	American kestrel
Hawk species, unidentified	
Turkey	
Partrige	bobwhite
Blue Crane	great blue heron
Large White Crane with Black Tips	whooping crane
Sand Hill Crane	
Golden Plover	
Killdeer plover	
Tell Tale Godwit	greater yellowlegs
Gull species	probably several, including Bonaparte's gull
Tern species	probably common tern
Dove	probably mourning dove
Parokeet	Carolina parakeet
Red Owl	screech owl, red phase

Great Horned Owl	
Barred Owl	
King Fisher	
Golden Wing Woodpecker	common flicker
Peleated Wood Pecker	
Ivory Billed Wood Pecker	
Red Headed Woodpecker	
Pewee Fly Catcher	eastern phoebe
Shore Lark	horned lark
Blue Geay	
Common Crow	
Fish Crow	
Crested Titmouse	tufted titmouse
Winter Wren	
Carolina Wren	
Mocking Bird	
Cat Bird	
French Mocking Bird	brown thrasher
Red Breasted Thrush	robin
Hermit Thrush	
Thrush species	He thought they might have been ovenbirds, which he knew as Golden Crowned Thrushes, but he did not get a good look
Blue Bird	eastern bluebird
Golden Crowned Wren	golden-crowned kinglet
Brown Lark	pipit—could be either water pipit, or Sprague's pipit, or both
Cedar Bird	cedar waxwing
Autumnal Warbler	likely to be yellow-rumped warbler
Red Poll Warbler	palm warbler
Maryland Yellow throat	yellowthroat
Meadow lark	probably eastern meadowlark
Red Winged Starling	red-winged blackbird
Rusty Grakle	rusty blackbird
Boat Tailed Grakle	
Cardinal	
Purple Finch	
Gold Finch	
Iowa Bunting	dickcissel? One of the longspurs? Snow bunting?

Towe Bunting	eastern towhee
Snow Bird	dark-eyed junco
Swamp Sparrow	
Sparrow, various species	"all Species of Sparrow inhabiting the Interior"

Some of these bird names reflect the fact that the pioneers in this young science of ornithology were badly confused by plumage variations, as in the eagles. In the mergansers—narrow-billed relatives of the ducks—the females are a relatively colorless lot, compared to the males. Dun Diver was what many early English authorities called the female of their goosander, our common merganser, because she was and is so different from the male. He is red-billed, green-headed, uncrested, black-backed, and white-sided at rest—and even more dramatically marked in flight; the female has the red bill, but her head is the color of cinnamon and is noticeably crested, her back is pale grayish and her flanks, dusty. That's quite a difference between the sexes and, because of it, authorities (as Alexander Wilson put it) "entirely deprived" the male common merganser of his mate. Wilson cast strong doubt on this arrangement, however, and probably influenced Audubon's view. JJA speaks of a Dun Diver on the trip, but also of killing and examining two merganser "femelles." It was a fluid science at the time.

There are summer plumages and winter plumages and first and second and third and fourth year plumages. There are permanent color variations—called morphs—within species. The gulls, the herons, the cranes, the ducks, the warblers, the shorebirds, and many others go through marked plumage changes at some point, and often do so each year.

To say the least, JJA was not wholly aware of the extent of the problem in 1820. And he was anxious to find what he called "Nondescripts"—birds that no one had ever published in the scientific literature. He believed, rightly, that new birds would be one of the strongest selling points for his collection. So when his flatboat was stopped at the Post of Arkansas, where the Arkansas River met the Mississippi, he wrote about a bird new to him: "The *Prairie Hawk* that I see here is not the *Marsh Hawk* of Willson it is Much Less-Lighter Color, the Tip of the Wings Black and only One large Bend [band] of Dark ending the Tail—they fly Much Like the *Night Hawk* and Catch Small Birds on the Grass Without Stopping their course—" He was right; it was not the Marsh Hawk of Wilson, because Wilson had described only the female or the immature, both of which are brown, while the bird Audubon was journalizing about was a male of the species, pale gray above and very light below, with the dark wing tips and the black-tipped tail. What would have puzzled him was the white rump patch worn by all the Marsh Hawks, regardless of their other colors, and the way this "Prairie Hawk" also carried its wings tilted up like the Marsh Hawk he was familiar with.

The following day Mr. Aumack had a shot at a "Prairie Hawk" but missed it. JJA must have been disappointed, especially since two days later "I had the good fortune to Kill a Beautifull *Marsh Hawk.*" It would have been nice to be able to compare the two specimens in the hand. Still, he was convinced anyway: "the *Prairie Hawk* seen Yesterday is entirely different, in Size, Color, & Manner of flying and as it is a Nondescript I hope I may meet it again."

He had more success with his Brown or Black Pelican. That *was* a new species. In fact, it was not to be described in the scientific literature by anyone until a French ornithologist published it in 1831 —more than ten years later. This wasn't a pelican at all, but the double-crested cormorant, a bird that nested in colonies—often big ones—along North American coasts and in the interior around the Great Lakes and in the plains.

JJA first noted it in his journal on November 1, when the flatboat was still on the Ohio, near Evansville, Indiana. Mr. Aumack missed a shot at two of them that were perched on a maple tree. Two more were seen before Audubon left the Ohio, and then north of today's Helena, Arkansas, on the Mississippi, he looked up from skinning a catfish and saw overhead "Several hundred of those *Black Pelicans* flying South forming a very obtuse Angle, without uttering any Noise." That "obtuse angle" is a good note because double-crested cormorants migrate in V's or files like Canada geese.

Farther south, in the White River, Audubon saw "Two Large Flocks of these *unknown Divers* or *Pelicans,*" but learned nothing more of them. Two and a half weeks later, at the mouth of the Yazoo one morning, he and Joseph "perceived a Large Flock of My un-known *Blackbirds* that I suppose Brown Pelicans—Landed below them, and after crawling on My belly for about 300 yards I arrived within about 45 yards I fired at three that were perched Close together on a dead stick about 7 feet above the Watter, at my shot they all fell as so many stones. I expected them to be all dead but to My surprise, those and about 20 swimming under them had dove, they soon rose and took Wing after running on the Watter about 50 yards at the exception of the One I had taken aim on—it would not raise, the Skiff brought up We rowed after it, diving below us up the Yazoo Nearly one Mile, Yet I could not give it up, it became Warier [wearier], & remained Less under Watter the Nearer We approach when at Last Joseph Shot at its Head & Neck (the only part in view Looking much Like a Snake) and Keeled it over—I took it up with great pleasure and anxiety—but I could Not ascertain its Genus—for I could not Make it an Albatros the only Bird I can discover any relation to."

Baffled, he nonetheless sat down to draw the bird, and three days later (the day after Christmas) he wrote with great authority: "We saw to day probably *Millions* of those *Irish Geese* or Cormorants, flying Southwest—they flew in Single Lines for several Hours extremely high." Now, how on earth did he do that? He'd never seen the species close-to before; no one, not even Wilson, had described it in the literature. However, on the same day that JJA wrote of Cormorants and Irish Geese, the flatboat arrived at Natchez and landed among about a hundred other flatboats and several steamboats. Audubon says "So busy have I been all day drawing, that I did not even go to the Shore," but we may imagine him sitting outside the cabin ("Beautifull Morning, Light frost—I began my drawing as soon as I could see"), attracting attention as he worked. He had probably completed the rendering of his unknown bird and started on a Great Footed Hawk that Mr. Aumack shot Christmas Day, but the drawing of the Nondescript lay in the portfolio. Now I picture a crowd around him, watching him draw—quite an entertainment for the rowdy waterfront at Natchez—and perhaps Audubon shows the finished drawing and polls his audience. In the crowd there's a saltwater sailor who has crossed the Atlantic, and he knows two names for it—for something *like* it, anyway: "Cormorant" is one, and the British sailors also call it the "Irish Goose," because cormorants nest by the thousands along the Irish coast, and their flesh is so tough and fishy it is fit only for an Irishman to eat.

This is only a scenario, not to be taken as Gospel. But *someone* had to tell him. And the state of ornithology in the American west was just that rudimentary. After JJA's bitch, Dash, delivered herself of ten pups, for instance, JJA and his traveling companions boiled up ten Carolina parakeets and fed them to her—"purposely to try . . . the Poisoning effect of their hearts on animals. Yesterday We Were told that 7 Cats had been Killed Last Summer by Eating as Many Paro-keets." Apparently nothing happened; he doesn't finish the story.

At Natchez, where he located the set of Wilson, he met "few Men Interested towards Ornithology except those who had heard or pleased to Invent Wonderfull Stories respecting a few species." Near the end of the voyage, at Bayou Lafourche below Baton Rouge, "We were visited by several *french Creoles* this is a Breed of animals that Neither speak French English nor Spanish correctly but have a Jar-gon composed of the Impure parts of these three—

"they Stared at My Drawing, and when a little Composed Gazed and Complimented Me very Highly—on asking them the names of about a dozen different Birds then lying on the Table they Made at once and without hesitating a Solid Mass of *Yellow Birds* of the Whole." He talks the next day about showing "the French" a few specimens of the Boat-tailed Grackle; he was told they "call them starlings but on all questions respecting them or any other birds their answer is a constant *Oh Oui.*"

If we were to take a seven-week winter float down the Mississippi on a flatboat, equipped with our excellent field guides and local bird-books and eight-power binoculars and zoom-telescopes, I be-lieve we would build a bigger species list than JJA did in 1820. But we'd miss the "Immense flocks of Parokeets" he found along the river; the last Carolina parakeet was seen in Florida only a hundred years later. And without the assistance of a miracle we wouldn't find any of the strikingly handsome, crow-sized ivory-billed woodpeck-ers. In 1820 they were not only common in the Mississippi floodplain; in places they were the most evident, *commonest* woodpeckers. Audubon writes of the woods having "Nothing in [them] More than the *Pait Pait Pait*" of ivorybills, of "the constant Cry of the Ivory Billed Wood Peckers about us—scarcely any other except a few Peleated and Golden Wings." The ivorybills were moving around in families—three to five in a group—and chatting as they prospected for food, filling the woods with their nasal, tooting conversation.

What a fall was there; few or none of them are left today, anywhere. The eighteenth-century natural historian, Mark Catesby, had noted that the bird's bill was "much valued by the *Canada Indians*, who made Coronets of 'em for their Princes and great warriors, by fixing them round a Wreath, with their points outward. The Northern Indians having none of these Birds in their cold country, purchase them of the *Southern People* at the price of two, and sometimes three, Buck-skins a Bill." But that did not constitute heavy pressure on the species. The coming of the European and his guns changed the balance. Audubon wrote later of its being shot by squatters and hunters who used "its rich scalp attached to the upper mandible" as an ornament on the shot-pouches they wore. "Travellers of all nations are also fond of possessing the upper part of the head and the bill of the male," JJA went on, "and I have frequently remarked, that on a steamboat's reaching what we call a *woodingplace*, the *strangers* were very apt to pay a quarter of a dollar for two or three heads of this Woodpecker." It doesn't take too much of that sort of progress to use up quite a lot of woodpeckers.

Our trip down the Mississippi is over. A harbor boat puts us ashore on a shellbank above New Orleans. The *Ray A. Eckstein* is in a "fleet" area, where barges are collected and shuffled around and dispatched, and the company that does the collecting, shuffling, and dispatching has a makeshift field office (locked and empty) above the shore. We scramble up the hill of shells with our gear and set everything down next to the levee on the edge of what looks as if it ought to be a road. By radiotelephone Jason has called a cab for us. Behind us, the *Ray A. Eckstein* goes about its job, too far away, now, for us to make out faces. We feel marooned.

A jet returns us to St. Louis late in the afternoon and takes less time than Audubon spent stalking and retrieving his cormorant at the Yazoo River. For two minutes just after takeoff, as the plane described a long half-circle, we could see the delta below us, the passes of the Mississippi, and the river snaking away to the north. Blue and silver entrails on a dark green carpet, giving us the sharpest sort of enticement to explore. We'll be back.

But now—we return to a blizzard, for heaven's sake. It is snowing hard in St. Louis when the plane lands. In a few days, however, with the car loaded, we'll start south once again, through the same valley by land, taking a more leisurely look at the places JJA knew.

MD   St. Louis. I am still in thrall to the boatride, even after three days ashore. I wake at night in the big sleigh bed in our friends' guestroom and hear the rumble of the *Ray A.*'s engines (traffic) and see a twinkling Coast Guard marker in the window (the reflection of a street light). Ah, I tell myself. The boat has backed down and is holding—the light on the shore is stationary, but the engines are still turning below. I fall back to sleep in my illusion.

MH   Southbound by car, we stop to find a blackbird roost at Burnham Island, north of the Ohio–Mississippi junction. From our cabin windows on the *Ray A. Eckstein* one sunset, we saw thousands of blackbirds streaming across the river, Missouri to Illinois. Jason, who watched the flight from the pilothouse, later told us that the birds were so thick in the trees on Burnham Island they seemed like the leaves in summer. He said this with the dismay and disgust common among southerners and midwesterners when they speak of blackbirds.

Immense gatherings of blackbirds can be found scattered across the middle south in winter; in the most spectacular cases hundreds of thousands, even millions of birds are concentrated in a small area, each night flooding into a patch of woods to sleep in company. Particularly in urban situations, the birds unsettle their human neighbors with noise and excrement, and there's been a lot of agitation—some of it successful—for the mass destruction of wintering blackbirds. Northeasterners, even those who know our city starling roosts, have no conception of the physical reality of these blackbird gatherings— though, of course, some northeasterners have brought political and legal pressure to bear to stop the killing. In Paducah, where the issue has been a hot one in recent winters, we did some homework in the files of *The Sun-Democrat.* A sample letter to the editor: "My family and I, like hundreds of other Paducah people, own a lot and have loved ones buried in Oak Grove Cemetery. It distresses us to see this centrally-located, wooded area, has been taken over as a roost. . . . Late, in the afternoon, about 4:30 or 5 o'clock, it is unbelievable to see the thousands of birds boiling into this area. The trees are covered, the sky is full. Hundreds of tombstones are encrusted with bird droppings so thick you can no longer read the inscriptions. This, as all know, carries a threat for lung infection."

MD February 6. Burnham Island, which lies close to the Illinois shore, is a deep, swampland forest. We take our stand along the flight line on a rutted dirt road running parallel to the river, a hundred yards or so from the island. This is bottomland. Large tracts of open fields. Many abandoned houses, though the nearest one, a quarter mile down the road, is still occupied, all appearances to the contrary. The family dog, crouched down out of the cold in the ditch by the mailbox, waits for his folks to come home.

It's three-fifteen. We're not the only ones here for the sunset flight. Eight red-tailed hawks are waiting for the blackbirds to arrive —waiting to pick off the sick and injured. They pass the time sporting in the sky; a few classic lazy circles, a turn over Burnham Island, a regal brush-off to bold crows who dare harass them. The crows are presumably here for the same reason. Easy hunting.

At three-forty, the first of the blackbirds come through. Five. A dozen. Two dozen. Within an hour, they arrive by the hundreds. Within two hours, by the thousands, not out of the sky, but funneling low out of Illinois. A few grackles, a few starlings, but most of them are redwings.

They use a big field on the inland side of the road as a staging area. It's flat black with birds, the new arrivals putting up and pushing on earlier arrivals, and a black scarf of them now funnels out to the roost, still flying low along a course that is no more than a hundred feet wide and perhaps ten feet deep. At the telephone line that borders the road, the scarf of birds ripples up and over. A few mavericks go under, then rejoin their fellows and the redwings pass on beyond us to Burnham Island and vanish through the trees; the roost is evidently on the far side, out of our view. The flight doesn't seem to indicate a huge blackbird roost—not one of those where they darken the sky at sunset. And none of those flights match the passenger pigeon migrations that darkened the skies for two and three days.

But it is a wondrous sight, nonetheless—a relentless flow of black birds with red shoulders.

They don't allow us get close or to stand underneath and look up. The flight shifts to right or to left if we try to move in on them. And though we are used to cold, by six o'clock we are frozen. It's a damp, clammy, bottomland, sun-gone cold. All I can see of Michael is his eyes between the watchcap and muffler. Still the red-winged black-birds come. I lift the earflaps of my squirrel hat to listen to the flight —thousands of wings beating per second. A low, steady, slishy mur-mur, like waves on a sandy beach, perhaps. I close my eyes to listen properly. No, not waves. It's the silken murmur of taffeta.

MH   I know there are birds flying in from the Missouri side of the Mississippi, having seen them do so from our window on the *Ray A.* But how many other streams of blackbirds are converging on Burn-ham Island, out of our sight? Flags, pennants of blackbirds, at sunset flowing out of invisibility to become specks, then birds—thousands upon thousands along this river tonight, settling in, conversing, their winter roosts mysterious and eerie, congregations of unnumbered small night souls.

MD   Columbus, Kentucky, a wooded, river bluff village, popula-tion 371, was originally called Iron Banks, the name by which Audu-bon knew it, and an historic marker tells us that the town was pro-posed as the nation's capitol after the British burned Washington in the War of 1812. ("How seriously proposed?" Mike muses.) On JJA's downstream journey, the flatboat tied up near here for the night. Three entries in his journal bring us here too. The first was a tale of grisly misadventure, told by another captain on the river, about an earlier journey on which one of the men, "having become a Luna-tic," jumped overboard at night, though he could not swim, made it to the shore of Wolf Island, but was "never seen afterward." His tracks led to the top of the bank, and vanished. The search party, however, found two other bodies (both men, both shot through the head), but did not stop to bury them. "Their stench was too great."

In a second entry, JJA wrote: "I took a sketch of the River below us comprehending on our left the Iron Banks, the Chalk Bank on our Right in the Back ground Wolff Island and Part of the Missoury shore." Since we'd passed this place in the dark on the *Ray A.*, we thought to take a ferry ride here to look for Audubon's view, but at the landing, we learned that the ferry was "broke down"—our informant, a tall, handsome, courtly gentleman with silver-capped front teeth, who carried a walking stick and wore old-fashioned buckle galoshes. In the lifetime of the Dean of the Landing (so we named him), the Mississippi has radically rearranged the shoreline. The Dean pointed with his stick. Where we saw river had once been three city blocks of the town of Columbus, now resettled out of harm's way on top of the bluffs behind us.

Fishermen were out, their pickup trucks backed to the river's edge, their boat racks down into the water, and the Dean of the Landing suggested that a few of them might very well be duck hunting, though the season is over. "Some of 'em would try it," he allowed. "That's $500 a duck, if they catch you. I couldn't afford but *one* of those." He pointed again with his stick to a spot yonder in the river where the Coast Guard, just the other day, had hauled in the body of a young woman who'd been missing for six weeks. She was found in a submerged automobile, the doors locked, no key in the ignition. "If they press it," he said in dark, foreboding voice, "they can find who did it. . . . *If* they press it."

JJA's third entry here: "My drawing finished took a Walk in the Woods, . . . Shot 2 Malards While Dash was bringing out the Last one a White headed Eagle *Dashed* at the Duck the Bitch brought it— Killed an Oppossum . . . The Game Not so plenty as on the Ohio and Much Shier—" We too walked in the woods on top of the chalk bluff upstream from Columbus. We found our first robin of the winter, and the bright red berries of black alder. And in a muddy clearing, next to the dirt road, a bizarre and unexpected woodland scene: two cars parked in the clearing, and both the cars and the clearing swarmed with cats, pussycats in the underbrush, curled on car hoods, on car trunks, at car doors, and one magically balanced on the narrow sill of a side window, for all the world like a cat in a kitchen window with gingham curtains and geraniums. Two men also strolled the bluff. "My friend here is a pilot," said one, and we instantly understood that he meant a riverman, not an airman. "Been a pilot thirty-five years." We talked about the river, and the pilot said he was running coal on the Upper these days for Northern States Power Company. We told him to give our greetings to the Keeton brothers when he next meets up with the *Ray A.*

I asked about the cars and the cats. They belonged to an old fellow and his sister whose property was once a thriving farm, and their father always said, never sell your land. Then the old man died; his two offspring kept him out of the ground for seven days before they finally buried him. It seemed they couldn't manage without him; the years passed, and they grew older and older and poorer and poorer, but still wouldn't sell any land, because their Daddy had told them not to. At last the house fell in, and that's why the cars were covered with cats. That's home. The brother and sister are living in their automobiles.

We caught sight of them farther along—two bent, unkempt, scarecrow figures in a pasture of hogs, herding a couple of steers through a barway into the next field.

MH We begin to realize the scope of what we've undertaken. At first we'd thought of these journeys as a lark, as a chance to get away from the telephone and from the fix-me demands of our old house —and best, as an excuse to drift around eastern North America, writing about birds and flowers and scenery. Then Mr. Audubon perforce imposed himself on the project more or less in person—not simply as the guide we wanted but as a quirky traveling companion. By the time we were fairly started on the expedition, it had become complicated. Once we were on the road and beyond familiar boundaries, our maps and our traveling companion and our unfamiliarity and curiosity often combined to slow us to a crawl. Now here we are in the lower Mississippi valley, *terra incognita* to both of us, and we are poking along, looking in corners and down interesting dirt roads, falling farther and farther behind schedule.

As we came south the last time, aboard the towboat, I spoke of curtains perpetually parting, each bend in the river revealing a new perspective. That's what's happening to us in the large too; our mental image of the whole continent is being mightily stretched and reshaped. We glimpse (I'm sure *only* glimpse) the grandness and variety and richness of North America—and the spiritual enormity of the tour our friend Audubon is leading. In our own way, with our own (changing) perspectives, we are experiencing something that profoundly moved him when he experienced it. In the 1830s, introducing his essay on the raven he wrote—in a sudden burst of emotion —about his North America: "Who is the stranger to my own dear country that can form an adequate conception of the extent of its primeval woods,—of the glory of those columnar trunks, that for centuries have waved in the breeze, and resisted the shock of the tempest,—of the vast bays of our Atlantic coasts, replenished by thousands of streams, differing in magnitude, as differ the stars that sparkle in the expanse of the pure heavens,—of the diversity of aspect in our western plains, our sandy southern shores interspersed with reedy swamps, and the cliffs that protect our eastern coasts,— of the rapid currents of the Mexican Gulf, and the rushing tide streams of the Bay of Fundy, of our ocean-lakes, our mighty rivers, our thundering cataracts, our majestic mountains, rearing their snowy heads into the calm regions of the clear cold sky?"

We have an unimaginable quantity of that still to get our minds around—his North America and ours.

Evening, February 9. Camping again for the first time in weeks. "I'd forgodded aboud de sboke id da eyes," says Mary. She backs away from the fireplace, fans the air with the spatula, and finds a new angle of approach to the skillet. We are in a state forest campground north of Memphis, tenting on Third Chickasaw Bluffs, which JJA mentions in his journal. February is supposed to be Tennessee's "snow month," but the temperature rose to 70 today, and the weather brought out the turtles to sun in the ditches beside the roads. It also seems to have stirred up a woodcock tonight; at least a full month earlier than we would listen for one in New England, we hear the evening performance—the nasal beeps from the ground, the bubbling, squeaking sky-dance overhead. . . .

Supper over, I sit at a table with my back to the fire; now and then the wind wafts the heat on my back and night noises on my ears. Owls? Woodcock? I have for years nursed in my imagination an impossible concert of owls: just suppose, I thought, you could hear all the owls in a county or a state singing at once. What a sound! And here's another impossible concert. Woodcock are probably up and dancing *all over* Tennessee tonight—all over the *south!* That would be some chorus: the bleating oboe notes, overlapping, would sound a drone, and over such steady bass would pour—like a cascade of liquid diamonds—the squeak and burble and twitter of a hundred thousand sky-dancing birds.

Primal spirits are awake tonight, fluttering in the dark. The hearts of voles, rivulets of wind, the loose dry leaves, flight feathers of woodcocks, uneasy stirring of blackbirds and robins on their roosts, the eyeblink and silent flight and swift, stabbing clutch of barred owl, horned owl, screech owl. We wait here, at the edge of our fire circle, listening for them.

Morning. Cross the river and turn south across northeast Arkansas —wide bottomland many times flooded, gray-brown crop fields, now and again a cluster of farm buildings, a few shanties perched on stilts, strings of drying wash, more gray-brown fields, rice paddies, old, windblown cotton bolls caught and held in briar patches. Many of the sharecroppers' long-legged shanties look empty, abandoned; but chickens scuttle under them and scratch in the shadows between the pilings. Occasionally we pass a modest-looking little house of recent vintage, or a mobile home, or a church, but most shelters have the air of timeless, picked-clean, weatherbeaten poverty; the shacks on stilts might have been built in 1930 or 1870 or 1830.

I think of Billy Nedd, who was born here. One sunny morning, as the imposing *Ray A. Eckstein* steamed down the river and Billy vacuumed the wine-red pilothouse rug, he straightened up, gestured at the shoreline, and remarked, "You know, Arkansas is supposed to be 'The Land of Opportunity,' but there ain't shit there for me except diggin' ditches and pickin' cotton." He went back to his work, chirpy as a cricket.

Audubon has led us through northeast Arkansas by pulling us toward the Post of Arkansas, at the junction of the White, the Arkansas, and the Mississippi Rivers, north of Arkansas City and six hundred river miles from the Head of Passes in the Louisiana delta.

On Sunday, the tenth of December 1820, he writes, Mr. Aumack's flatboat put in to shore about four miles above the mouth of the White River. Aumack and Audubon, young Mason and a member of the crew decided to equip the skiff with two sets of oars, row up the White to the "Cut-off," where it met the Arkansas, then stow the skiff there and walk to the Post of Arkansas.

JJA   We left at 10 o'clock with Light hearts, Small Bottle of Whiskey a few Biscuits, and the determination of Reaching the Post that Night—

At the Entrance of White River we discovered that that stream Was full and Run Violently, the Watter a Dull Red Clay Color; We soon found ourselves forced to Land to Make a Natural Cordel of several *Grape Vines* and pull up by it—the distance to the Cutt off is Seven Miles that appeared at Least 10 to us: here We Met 2 Canoes of Indians from the *Osage Nation,* Landed our Skiff on the opposite side of White River. . . . We Walked through a *Narrow Path* often so thickly beset with green Briars that We Would be forced to give back and go round—this followed through *Cypress Swamps* and round *Pounds* [ponds] and Cane Breaks untill We reached the first Settlement owned by a Frenchman Called Monsr Duval. this friendly Man about going to bed offered us his assistance put on shoes & clothing and Lead us 7 Miles through Mud & Watter to the Post; and at 9 o'clock P.M. We Entered the Only Tavern in the Country—*Wearied,* Muddy, Wet, & hungry—the Supper Was soon called for, and soon served, and to see 4 Wolfs taring an old Carcass would not give you a bad Idea of our Manners while helping *Ourselves* the *Bright Staring Eyes* of the Land Ladies Notwithstanding

however I found Mrs Montgomery a handsome Woman of good Manners and rather superior to those in her rank of Life—to Bed and to sleep sound was the next Wish for 32 Miles in such a Country May be Calculated as a full dose for any *Pedestrian per day*—Led into a Large Building that formerly perhaps saw the great *Concils of Spanish Dons* we saw 3 Beds containing 5 men, Yet, all was arrangd in a few moments and as the Breaches were Coming off our Legs, Mr Aumack & Anthony slided by into one and Joseph & myself into Another, to force Acquaintance with the strangers being of course necessary a Conversation ensued that Lulled Me a Sleep . . .

The Morning broke and with it, Mirth *all about us,* the *Cardinals,* the Iowa Buntings, the Meadow Larks and Many Species of Sparrows, chearing the approach of a Benevolent sun Shining day—dressed and about to take a View of *all things* in this Place . . .

The Post of Arkansas is Now a poor, Nearly deserted Village, it flourished in the time that the Spaniards & French kept it, and One 100 years passed it could have been called and agreable Small Town

—at present, the decripid Visages of the Worn out Indian Traders and a few American famillies are all that gives it Life, the Natural situation is a handsome One, on a high Bank formerly the Edge of a *Prairie,* but rendered extremely sickly by the Back Neighborhood of Many Overflowing Lakes & Swamps. . . .

After Breakfast We Left the Post of Arkansas with a Wish to see the Country above, and so *Strong* is My Anthusiasm to Enlarge the Ornithological Knowledge of My Country that I felt as if I wish Myself *Rich again* and thereby able to Leave My familly for a Couple of Years—here I saw a French Gentleman who but a few Weeks passed had Killed a *Hawk* of a Large size *perfectly White* except the Tail Which Was a *bright red.* Unfortunately, no remains of its Skin Legs or Bill were to be found—We travelled fast—reached the Cutt off and Landd our Skiff, having Killed *5 Crows* for their *Quills,* Never before did I see these Birds so easily approachd and in fact all the Birds We saw, 2 Hawks I did not know hovered high over us—the Indians still at their Canoes, We Hailed, and gave them a Drachem of Whiskey, and as they could not speak either french or English, I *Drew a Deer* with a stroke across its hind parts, and thereby Made them Know our Wants of Venaison hams—

they brought 2 We gave them 50cts and a Couple Loads of Gun Powder to each, brought out smiles, and a Cordial Shaking of Hands —a Squaw with them a *Handsome Woman* waded to us as Well as the Men and drank freely—Whenever I meet *Indians* I feel the greatness of our Creator in all its Splendor, for there I see the Man Naked from his Hand and yet free from Acquired Sorrow—

in White River We saw a great number of Geese Malards and Some Blue Cranes—also Two Large Flocks of these *unknown Divers* or *Pelicans—*

reached our Boats about 6 in the afternoon fatigued but Contented a good Supper, Merry Chat—and good Looks all round— Went to bed all Well—

before I leave the Trip to the *Arkansas Post* I think I will give you More of it—We saw there a *Velocipede* Judge how fast the Arts & Sciences Improved in this Southwestern Country—I want also to tell you that the Squaw on White River While Wading out to us Craked a Large *Louse* taken from under her arm . . .

about One Mile below the Mouth of Arkansas in a Thick patch of

Cane are Two *Women* the remainder of a party of Wandering Vagarounds that about 2 years ago Left some part of the Eastern State to
proceed to the *Promised Land*—these Two Wretches, Never Wash
Comb or Scarcely clad themselves, and subsist from the Scant generosity of the Neighbours—Now and then doing a little Sawing [sew-
ing] and Washing—

MD   This area, where the White and the Arkansas Rivers run out
to join the Mississippi, was a strategic location in colonial days. A
commercial and military plum—fur traders and forts. The Jesuits
settled in first, then came LaSalle's expedition, and the original *Poste
de Arkansas* was established by the French in 1686. The Spanish took
over in 1765, the French returned in 1800, and when Napoleon
needed cash and sold off the Louisiana Territory in 1803, the Americans moved in.

The Post, on a small bayou-bound peninsula that juts into the
Arkansas River, became the capitol of the newly formed Arkansas
Territory in 1819 and was a town of high hopes, soaring land prices
(up to $1500 per acre), and the promise that it would "always be a
place of mercantile importance." But when Audubon stopped here
in December 1820, the handwriting was already on the wall. The
important men in town, to whom he had letters of introduction, were
upriver "at Point Rock," where (Audubon was told) a new settlement
prospered on high, healthy ground. This was Little Rock, which
became the capitol the following year, and everyone who was anyone moved upriver along with the legislature, *The Arkansas Gazette*,
and the rafts of lawyers and land speculators who'd moved into the
territory to make their fortunes.

The Post was left to founder in the lowlands, property was sold
for taxes, and though plantations and cotton empires arose in the
surrounding country, the riverside settlement drifted back into a
French colonial twilight. Washington Irving, who visited in the 1830s,
described it in *The Creole Village* as one of the territory's many
poverty-stricken little towns of Spanish and French origin, their population "made up of descendants of those nations, married and inter-
woven together, and occasionally crossed with a slight dash of Indian." He spoke of the remains of old stockades; French buildings
with casements and piazzas and moss-grown roofs; "an old ruinous

Spanish house, of large dimensions, with verandahs overshadowed by ancient elms"; and a continuing round of Gallic gaiety, the inhabitants content in "their happy ignorance . . . their respect for the fiddle, and their contempt for the almighty dollar."

At the start of the Civil War, the post was in almost total decay —chimneys fallen in, trees growing through roofs of abandoned houses. One last stockade was constructed: Fort Hindman, built by the Confederate government and bombarded by Union gunboats that also leveled most of what had been left of the little town. The river later rampaged through and swallowed up the remains, including the original cemetery, and swept the bones of French and Spanish settlers out to the Mississippi and down to the sea. The Arkansas Post lay overgrown and forgotten until the 1920s, when a newspaper article ("Arkansas Post a Neglected Shrine") stirred interest. The site eventually became a state park and, more recently, a national park and wildlife sanctuary—221 acres, seven miles south of Gillett on the Great River Road.

Where the village once stood is an open field. A park map pinpoints Main Street, the bank, the blacksmith, the jail, the general store, Montgomery's tavern—where JJA spent the night. On the bluff are benches where one can sit and gaze across the Arkansas River at Dam No. 2, which controls the water level in the Arkansas Post Canal, and on this February morning listen to coots croaking near the shore, a phoebe calling, cardinals, a song sparrow in the reeds, and blue *geays.*

Along a path circling the point are markers with descriptions from the past—of a Jesuit's makeshift hut and the great cross on the riverbank, the Spaniards' red-oak stockade with cannon and swivel guns, the gifts of assuagement given to the Quapaw Indians: one scarlet dress coat, nine hats with silver embroidery, scissors, butcher knives, wool ribbons, sewing needles. There's a reprint of the righteous comments of an eighteenth-century French visitor, Perrin du Lac, who castigated the inhabitants for passing their time "in dancing, drinking, or doing nothing, similar in this respect to the savages with whom they live." Nature markers identify poison ivy for the uninitiated—"Leaflets three, let it be"; the osage orange, a tree whose tough yellow wood was used by the Indians to make light, strong bows; the sassafrass tree, which provided the frontier remedy for malaria and also was used to build bedsteads, because its pungent odor repelled bedbugs.

We are the only visitors here today. A sunny hush—a few birds calling—and into the empty compound come the new inhabitants of the Arkansas Post. The armadillos. The latest invaders, up from South America, through Nicaragua, Mexico, Texas, and Louisiana, and into Arkansas. Twenty years ago they were unknown here, as were all other invaders in their own cycles of time and history, intrigue and battle and possession.

The meek have now inherited these few acres of earth. Armadillos are gentle and unobtrusive creatures, cousins to the sloth, the pangolin, and the aardvark, and among the oldest mammals. They were on earth before the Ice Ages and the Cro-Magnon man, and they saw the saber-toothed tiger and the hairy mammoth come and go. In the noonday quiet, they leave their burrows in the soft, crumbling river banks, and hunch out into the open grass of the Arkansas Post to root for grubs and ants. Woodchuck-size, plated shells, long scaley tails, pink piggish snouts, and piglet ears. Neither Michael nor I have seen them in the wild before. I try to steal up on one from behind, to get a closer look. It's intent on rooting and feeding and is slow to react. Then, one footstep too close. *Snap.* It sits up on its hindquarters (watchfulness and alarm), sees me, flattens out, and gallops to safety in its riverside burrow, not a lumbering gallop, as I'd expected from an armor-plated animal, but fleet, fast, and low to the ground—into the lacing of greenbriar and honeysuckle that entangles the woodlands, and it's gone.

Armadillo is said to be tasty, much like pork. Charles Darwin reflected on this in *The Voyage of the Beagle:* "It seems almost a pity to kill such nice little animals, for as a Gaucho said, while sharpening his knife on the back of one, 'Son tan mansos' (they are so quiet)." Later, when we meet the Superintendent at park headquarters down the road, he tells us that armadillos are considered pests in these parts because they burrow into the terraces that contain the rice paddies and cause the terracing to collapse. But they are not eaten. Armadillos are newcomers and therefore not known in the traditional country fare of the South. Raccoon is the popular game dish, and the biggest local doing of the year is the annual raccoon barbecue, elbow to elbow in the Gillett high school gym.

Audubon came this way again two years later and found a small new species of flycatcher, which he subsequently named in honor of Dr. Thomas S. Traill, an English physician and naturalist who was of considerable assistance in launching JJA's successes in England— arranging exhibitions of the bird paintings, lectures, introductions. "What a fine, friendly head—" wrote JJA, "ah!—and heart, too!"

A copy of the original painting of Traill's flycatcher hangs in the Visitor's Center here. In the left hand corner, JJA inscribed the place and the date: "Fort of Arkansas April 17, 1822."

MH More than a century and a half later, after lengthy and complex investigations by several ornithologists, the American Ornithologists Union decided that Traill's flycatcher was really two species, and that Traill's name did not deserve to be connected to either one. The two "new" species are called the willow and the alder flycatchers.

The project is now to find wild turkeys. We've failed at this for weeks, despite assurances that we are *surrounded* by wild turkeys in the lower Mississippi valley. I saw a few of them in Pennsylvania years ago as they made their leisurely way along a forest floor, stirring up a great racket of rustled leaves and muttered babble. They struck me then as ludicrous. The turkey apparently shares with the domestic chicken an unwarranted attitude of high self-esteem, and it walks like a drunken divine swaying down the church aisle to conduct a service. However, there is no gainsaying the fact that the turkey is the subject of two of the most beautiful and famous of the Audubon engravings, or that for us a glimpse of turkeys here in the wet woods of the Mississippi valley would be fitting. Besides, Mary has never seen wild turkeys anywhere.

We stop to ask at the office of the Corps of Engineers beside Arkansas Post Canal. (The Corps operates a lock-assisted waterway that begins here and reaches nearly 450 miles to the northwest, mostly along the Arkansas river, well into Oklahoma—making Tulsa, in effect, a seaport, via the Mississippi.) Why sure, they tell us, we *could* find turkeys just about anywhere and any time—but if we want to get some good pointers, the person to see is Sid Jolly of the Arkansas Department of Game and Fish. He's been assigned to trap them in the state and federal refuges here, for transplant to areas of the state where the species has been extirpated. As a matter of fact, he can probably be found right this minute at Lock and Dam Number One.

In the parking lot of the lock, two Corps of Engineers types in yellow hardhats are helping an energetic figure, dressed in mud-splashed black raingear, as he tries to get a small, fat-tired, amphibious All-Terrain-Vehicle to run. The gent in the raingear has an intense, almost hollow look about him. That and the haircut, bootcamp close, reminds me of field-grade officers in the special forces or paratroops. He appears so purposeful and preoccupied and irritated that I hesitate to intrude, but over the coughing thunder of the ATV I ask one of the hardhats if that's Sid Jolly. He nods, so I wait. At the next lengthy pause in the ATV's performance, Sid Jolly gives me a brief look, and I step forward to introduce myself and state my business. He doesn't smile a welcome, but he doesn't bat an eye, either. Sure, he says, he's about to leave for an afternoon expedition, if he can just get this damned thing to run, and we're welcome to go along. He holds up pieces of tubing. "Waterproof lines," he says, and shakes out the water in them. Twenty minutes later he has given up on the vehicle and rearranged his plans to accommodate the total strangers. This rearrangement quickly stretches to cover more than twenty-four hours: we will go turkey-baiting with him, eat a supper of venison roast and turnip greens at his mobile home on the far side of the canal, and sleep in his spare room.

Sid Jolly's turkey-baiting involves carrying sacks of corn into the right habitat, finding areas open enough for him to use his broad cannon-fired nets, spreading the corn in those spots, and then checking regularly to see whether any turkeys have found the bait and left their footprints behind to prove it. Once he's got a flock into good eating habits in such a place, he rigs his nets ready for firing, builds his blind, rolls up in his sleeping bag for the night, and waits for the turkeys to arrive on their early morning rounds. If everything works as it's supposed to, he traps the whole flock at one time.

His woods-road transportation (when he needs to haul stuff) is an ancient, dented jeep, a refugee from Korea or earlier, c/o the Arkansas National Guard, which very sensibly gave up on it long ago; it is now on its third "new" used carburetor—vintage jeep carburetors in working order being hard to come by—and the jeep is running so badly that he drives it not one foot further than he must: to get it to the start of any of his routes he hauls it on a trailer behind his pickup; and if he doesn't have to carry corn or gear, he rides his trail bike and leaves the jeep at home. An operating ATV would represent a vast improvement in his stable of work vehicles, and for some time he's been after the bureaucracy in Little Rock to get him one. He could cover his turkey terrain much more efficiently. Example: his best trapping area is only a few miles from his house—but it's also on the wrong side of the Arkansas Post Canal and the White River. To get there now, he pulls the jeep on the trailer over an eighty-mile loop of roads, takes a ferry, and at last drives the jeep into the woods—where he can hear his dogs barking in their pen beside the mobile home. In an ATV he could cross the canal and be at work in a few minutes. Tired of prodding his superiors, he has at last bought a secondhand ATV himself. It is such people as Sid Jolly who redeem bureaucracies. Now, if he can only get the machine to function.

For the present, he is stuck with the jeep, which roars and bucks and belches and smokes as in a Bill Mauldin cartoon. At ten to fifteen miles an hour Sid drives the rutted and muddy trails with the door open and his head mostly down, looking for turkey tracks beside the ruts. We do the same on the other side, though we have very little idea at first what turkey tracks are. On the levees, thousands of robins and flickers and meadowlarks fly up in front of us; while in the deep woods, we flush wood ducks and pileated woodpeckers. Everywhere we are trailed by the thick, oily haze laid down by a fitful old engine —a symbol, all right. Who changed these woods I think I know: Americans shot out the ivorybills, the parakeets, the passenger pigeons, the alligators, and now (among other detritus of this non-caring and shortsightedness) the Arkansas beaver, free of their major native predators, the alligators, have been fruitful and multiplied and turned the floodplain forests that once were flooded, say, only half the year into floodplain forests that are flooded the year round. Beaver here have become the bane of a tree-grower's and a refuge-manager's existence. So alligators are now being imported from Louisiana to restore the old balance, and wildlife people are doing their bit in other ways. All at once Sid Jolly shouts, skids us to a halt, and jumps out with his Smith and Wesson pistol in two hands ramrod straight in front of him, like a cop on TV. He fires twice at the tip of a nose rippling the water through the woods toward a beaver lodge, but he does not sink the nose. He waits for another shot, knees bent, pistol steady; relaxes; the gun is returned to its holster.

We go on, through swamps and around fallen trees. Sometimes the track is blocked and both "shoulders" impassable, so Sid hooks a chain between the downed tree and the jeep and drags the obstruction to one side. He sees very few turkey signs until we are deep in the woods, and then at two of his baiting spots there are so many tracks near the bait that even Mary and I can find them easily. At last Mary sees her first wild turkeys, nine of them, about a hundred yards away. They stalk out of sight around a bend in the trail. [MD: Like nervous old ladies in black shawls, muttering "Heavens to Betsy" and "Lawks a-mercy" as they hustle away into the trees.]

Sid Jolly, now fifty-something in years, was a commercial fisherman on the Mississippi for thirty of them, selling buffalo fish and catfish to passing towboats. Part-time he worked for the state Game and Fish, mostly trapping turkeys. He lived in a houseboat; his partner and the partner's wife lived in another one. One winter, he says, ice floes filled the river and stranded them where they lay. His partner's wife had flour aboard, and he and the partner were able to get to shore and shoot turkeys, so they had turkey and dumplings but, Sid says, they got mighty sick of turkey by the time the ice went out. The "free" life can be limited and unromantic and unpoetic—and sometimes mean: a back-country politicians' feud over the pols' private hunting rights on a state "no-hunting" preserve inevitably involved the part-time employee for the state Game and Fish who kept an eye on those lands; Sid's houseboat was burned to the waterline —and all his dogs with it, he says.

He went to Alaska then. He talks lyrically of Eskimo boats, skin stretched over a frame. "You can feel the water through the skin, slipping under your feet." He settled in for a while, made friends with U.S. Air Force people in Nome; he'd been a radioman in bombers when the Air Force was the Army Air Corps. He and some of his Air Force friends started an Eskimo Boy Scout troop—the idea being to encourage the perpetuation of old Eskimo crafts, keep them alive in the new generation. "I hate to see a culture die."

He came back to Arkansas to trap turkeys for the state and live alone with his coonhounds and his pet raccoon—Miss Fit being the name of the incumbent; she's had a few predecessors. The menagerie now includes a Catahula Cur, which is a *sort* of dog, smooth-haired, silver and black, a face remarkable for its unearthly needle-toothed grin. "Isn't she the ugliest thing you ever saw?" he says lovingly.

This season is dry, but many times a year the mobile home above Arkansas Post Canal is approachable only by boat or by waterwings, and even the Dreadful Jeep cannot negotiate the wallows and shallows that intervene between Sid Jolly headquarters and the nearest road. His mobile home was acquired secondhand by the state of Arkansas from the commonwealth of Pennsylvania, which had got it from the federal government during a flood disaster. Shoddy goods, says Sid Jolly—typical of government purchases, and look who pays for them. He has thrust up tall antennas above the house, one way of making the anonymous ticky-tacky his: Sid Jolly is a radio ham.

For a dozen hours or so we shared these isolated bachelor digs, ate the delicious venison at night and huge pancakes with sorghum syrup in the morning, talked about New England and Arkansas and cheerfully debated who introduced cornbread to whom—the North to the South, or the South to the North. Sid brought Buck, his favorite coonhound, and his raccoon, Miss Fit, together in the house for an Entertainment. The coon and the dog are childhood friends; Miss Fit put her black paws on Buck's muzzle, gently, and cleaned his face. Then Sid played Chase the Boot with Miss Fit—a version of Fetch that sent the raccoon galloping from one end of the house to the other. In the early morning, as on most mornings, Sid became WB5BUQ on the Arkansas Razorback Net, checking in with at least a dozen ham radio friends.

He asked us to stay on a while. It wouldn't be but a few days before he'd be ready to trap turkeys, and he'd be pleased if we came along, joined him in the blind with our sleeping bags to wait for the dawn. He'd like it if I identified some of the small birds for him as they flitted and sang around the blind. But we are so far behind schedule *some* limits have to be set, or we'll be rambling around North America for years. We decide no. We regret it immediately, and permanently.

MD   In Gillett, a conversation with a woman who noticed our Connecticut plates. "You folks sure are a long way from home," she says.

She's sixty-five perhaps, tall, rangy, upcountry Arkansas, raised on a farm. She's still farming and expects to farm the rest of her life. She raises everything she and her husband eat in the way of fruits and vegetables. She has two tilling machines. "If one gets broke, I don't have to quit work to fetch parts from the hardware store." After living all these years on the flat bottomland, when she goes home to the mountains to visit, those little vegetable gardens in the forest clearings look like nothing at all. "Like little rag ends of a green garden spot."

"What about Connecticut?" she asks. "Can folks grow food to eat in that cold climate?"

On Sunday, December 17, 1820, it rained all day, JJA finished a drawing of a marsh hawk, and the flatboat landed at "Pointe Chico." The rain continued and for the next two days they covered only a dozen or so miles downstream, putting ashore time and again because of fog and the bad weather, and to hunt.

We are camped tonight in Arkansas in the Lake Chicot State Park, a few miles south of "Pointe Chico." The lake, another of the myriad lakes and ponds once part of the main channel of the Mississippi, was landlocked in the 1930s when the river shifted to the east and left this horseshoe cutoff behind. Our tent site is on the bank of the old channel, so Audubon passed our doorstep by boat and may well have hunted through here. Perhaps in the pecan grove where we've been gathering firewood. Perhaps along the shore where fishermen are coming in for the night.

It begins to seem as if every other place where Audubon set foot in the nineteenth century was guaranteed to become a state park, a national forest, or an historic shrine in the twentieth century.

Flowering quince and narcissus bloom in dooryards here. Gullies of pink-purple henbit (a flowering mint) in the furrows of the ploughed fields.

A commercial on the local radio, sung with a twang to a country music beat:

> Scared money don't win.
> Fast women drink gin.
> *And Beechnut's the tobacco to chew.*
>
> Girls in bars and in pants.
> A man don't have a chance.
> *And Beechnut's the tobacco to chew.*
>
> Treat your dogs with respect.
> Keep your traps oiled and checked.
> *And Beechnut's the tobacco to chew.*

From Lake Chicot, we continue southward, still in the bleak floodplain. At Lake Bruin, Louisiana, we drop down over the levee and take a ferry for a two and a quarter mile downstream ride to Claiborne County, Mississippi, and disembark on a country road that curves uphill past a large sign warning that in the State of Mississippi it is against the law to fire a gun from a car on the highway. A second sign reads "Welcome to Mississippi—The Magnolia State" and the first flowers we see are clumps of purple violets and fields yellow with butterweed *(Senecio glabellus)* as the road winds through upland farm country, neat and tidy communities, the antithesis of the forlorn desolation of the bottomland. The road carries us through the campus of Alcorn A&M (one of the early Negro colleges, now a university, and abloom with daffodils and prosperity) and on to Natchez.

NATCHEZ

1820–1824, PASSIM

MD   We are well and truly into Audubon country—the widest swathe of Audubon country in the United States. Mill Grove in Pennsylvania stands alone. So does Henderson, Kentucky. But here there are three towns on the river around which Audubon's fortunes revolved: Natchez in Mississippi, St. Francisville in Louisiana, and New Orleans. He is a known historic figure throughout the area, memorialized in plaques, monuments, and festivals, and is part and parcel of local traditions—facts and fancies. In the face of all this commemoration, the casual tourist in Natchez, St. Francisville, or New Orleans probably comes away with the impression that when JJA was here from 1820 to 1826, he had achieved his status as the hero, the consummate naturalist, the Big Winner, that he wafted through on the wings of success. But the years he spent in this part of the country were hazardous going.

Lucy and the two boys eventually came south from Cincinnati to join him, and they found themselves in dire straits, scrimping along, eking a living in one town or another, with the family parting and reuniting and parting again, and throughout, the inevitable recriminations and distresses. Prides were hurt and prides were swallowed. Lucy pulled the fat out of the fire for herself and for the boys. She had a marketable commodity—her background as an educated and cultivated woman, with the added cachet of being English born and bred. She'd done some teaching in Kentucky and Cincinnati and now turned it into a full-time career as governess and live-in schoolmistress, the classic solution for an impoverished gentlewoman, both in

Natchez-under-the-Hill, from *Das Illustrirte Mississippithal,* by Henry
Lewis. Circa 1830.

the real world and in fiction. (Jane Eyre comes immediately to mind, and the governess in Henry James' *Turn of the Screw.*)

The only constants in JJA's life were his pursuit of birds and his growing portfolio of paintings. Otherwise, as he richocheted between Natchez, St. Francisville, and New Orleans (with at least one major trip to the north), his luck changed from good to bad to indifferent and around again in dizzying succession. He earned his way as an itinerant portraitist and landscape artist; a painter of boat panels and street signs; a teacher of French, drawing, dancing, fencing. As he wrote in December 1820, "Unfortunately, Naturalists are obliged to eat and have some sort of Garb."

JJA's visit to Natchez in 1820 exemplifies this run of luck. He went ashore without a penny in his pocket, met up with Nicholas Berthoud, the Kentucky merchant married to Lucy's sister; Berthoud invited JJA to share his lodgings at the Natchez House and introduced him to several influential citizens, thus giving JJA a future entree in Natchez. He received commissions for two portrait sketches at five dollars each, but one of the sitters absented himself without paying, and on the day JJA left Natchez, his portfolio of paintings was lost on the dock (bitter misfortune), but was later found and returned to him in New Orleans (miraculous good luck).

Notes from our campsite, Homochitto National Forest, southeast of Natchez:

We seem to have wandered into a Japanese painting. Forests of tall tufted pines. A small green lake curving against a cragged hillside. A narrow point of land bending into the lake. At the end of the point, a pair of tall pines, just so, and a pair of white Muscovy ducks. One stands, one roosts, just so. And last night, out of the piney woods on the steep hillside across the lake, a full moon rose, just so, in perfect balance with the curve of the water, the point, the ducks.

Glow worms in the pine needles.

Froggers with three-pronged spears out by moonlight, hunting along the shore.

Jolly neighbors on the inlet with three little children who scamper in the dark and dance and jig on the table by the light of the

Coleman lantern. (Lovely to see.) At midnight, a whoop from their pickup truck: "Happy Valentine's day to everybody!"

There's a link with Audubon here too. He knew the Homochitto River, which runs through this preserve and gives the forest its name. On one of his stays in Natchez, when he and fourteen-year-old Victor were living there alone, both were stricken with yellow fever and taken in by a friend whose plantation lay on the Homochitto. JJA also spoke of a winter's day when he saw a greater number of peregrine falcons along the river than he had ever seen before.

The Homochitto winds through the forest a mile or so south of our campground. No peregrines are there this winter. The river is low. A wide sandbar slopes down to the thin channel of running water, and across the sand bar, bird tracks, animal tracks, and a network of tunnels burrowed under the sand by small creatures (shrews?) fanning out from the safety of their brush piles in search of food and/or water. Scattered over all, thousands of beer cans and bottles. Thousands! Enough to start an instant junk yard or recycling plant on the spot. This appears to be a popular picnic and cookout stop, a lover's lane, and general what-the-hell gathering place. What a pity. The pine woods, the sand bar, the river. . . . And it's a wilderness slum.

Because we're traveling by car and living in a tent, we were not aware of the pecking order in the camper and trailer world. A prickly question of status. Who is seeking it and who has got it. I learn this today from the wife-and-mother of our neighbors to the left who have a pop-up trailer rig and a fair-sized tent. The talk turned to Airstream trailers, the big glossy ones that look like silver bullets, and she tells me (without a trace of humor) that the people who own Airstreams are "stuck-up."

MH In conversation with a couple from Rochester, New York (they are touring the south in a camper, looking for a place to retire), we hear that the lady has been very upset to discover John James Audubon's true colors. He *shot birds,* she tells us—sometimes a lot of birds in a day—and *enjoyed* it. She read this somewhere recently.

I'm not surprised. It has become common to see Audubon assailed as a bird-butcher, in a My-God-look-at-this-skeleton-I-found-in-the-closet tone of voice. You can run across it in *The New York Times* ("The Man Who Loved Birds But Shot Them") as well as in the *National Enquirer* ("Conservation Society Was Named For Him, But Famed Artist Audubon Killed Thousands of Birds for Sport"). A few years ago, a children's editor turned down a suggested book about JJA on the grounds that such a sportsman was a poor example to set before children. And even two of his modern biographers—the least friendly of them, to be sure—take the same moralistic stance.

It's ridiculous. It's a standard applied *ex post facto.* It denies historical progression. It's like laughing at George Washington's wooden false teeth. Most important, it ignores the many demands of scientific inquiry in an era when the science of ornithology in North America was almost brand new.

Work backward from the present. Today there are millions of acres of wildlife refuge in North America. Almost all non-game species of birds are protected by law everywhere on the continent and cannot legally be killed without collecting permits, which are issued sparingly. Game birds are protected by a variety of laws that generally open only brief shooting seasons.

These refuges and laws were created because of the decline and sometimes disappearance of regional populations of various birds, even the extinction of entire species. Shooting was often to blame for the declines and disappearances—sport and market gunning for food or feathers or trophies. Habitat destruction played a part too and so —recently—have environmental poisons. Whatever the causes of bird destruction, our perceptions about it and our goals have changed over the years. We preserve, or try to preserve, far more than we kill.

Who's responsible for this? Thousands of North Americans have labored actively for the cause, to be sure. But still we might, after all, view birds differently today in North America than we do. In many other parts of the world there is no effective bird conservation at all. And how many people in the United States and Canada are actively involved in saving *reptiles,* for example, or *butterflies?* The very existence of the American bird-protection effort is noteworthy. The source of this effort is Audubon's work, which still merits the praise given it by his contemporary Baron Cuvier, who called it "the most magnificent monument which has yet been raised to ornithology."

JJA was properly proud of having helped bring the science of birds out of the museum closet on this side of the Atlantic. Alexander Wilson had made a start, certainly, but Audubon popularized birds in a way that no other individual has ever done on this continent— perhaps even the world. It is Audubon's name, not Wilson's or anyone else's, that is most closely associated with our bird-conservation movement; he is the ornithologist for whom people name towns and housing developments and liquor stores and gas stations and national conservation societies. He is the focus, the wellspring of our bird-protection.

Even today no naturalist could produce such a major work as Audubon's without using dead specimens—although Audubon could depend now on the millions of skins collected by others and preserved in museum cabinets, and wouldn't have to do much collecting himself. In any case, he needed many specimens, because bird plumages within any given species vary widely, individual to individual, sex to sex, age to age, and season to season. Science demands that these matters be studied with birds in the hand, and that nests and eggs be taken, and that birds be taken captive and examined and watched, as captives. Science especially demanded such "sacrifices" —if one wants to think of it that way—in Audubon's day, when nobody knew very much about North American birds.

Furthermore, as time went on, Audubon collected specimens for many other scientists besides himself, particularly European bird-men. He used the extra skins to raise money and gain influence when both were desperately needed to keep the *Birds of America* engraving project afloat in England.

So you can't have the "magnificent monument to ornithology" without dead birds, captive birds, collected nests, and eggs.

"Well," one might argue, "that's all very fine, but how about the *slaughters* he took part in, not as a scientist or artist but as a man who liked to shoot down a lot of flying objects—proving his skill with a gun over and over, and glorying in it?" It's true he did that. We'll run into this from time to time as we follow him. But *everyone* thought wildlife on our fecund continent was too numerous to be destroyed; when Audubon was alive, a frontier and a vast wilderness existed here. A man who traveled on foot and on horseback most of his life must have known far better than one who flies or drives automobiles the amazing size of this land; technology has truncated its grandeur, but grand it still is. What could be extinguished that had so much wild land to live in and flee to? Going gunning then, and being good at it, was a legitimate sport—just as golf or bowling is today. Few men foresaw any trouble ahead. Audubon was one who eventually recognized what was happening —because he observed so much of North America, its wildlife and its human civilization as he produced his masterwork. Consequently, he changed his behavior, and tried to get others to change theirs. But once again—blamed in outraged tones for his love of sport—he is the focus, the major figure. And he would not have been this, had he not produced *The Birds of America* . . . which required the shooting of many birds . . . and which led by degrees to strict limitations on the shooting of all birds in North America, whether for science or for fun.

From the River opposite Natchez, that place presents a Most Romantick scenery, the Shore Lined by Steam vessels Barges & flat Boats, seconded by the Lower town, consisting of Ware Houses, Grogg [Shops], Decayed Boats proper for the uses of Washer Women, and the sidling road raising along the Caving Hills on an oblique of a quarter of a Mile and about 200 feet High covered with Goats feeding peaceably on its declivities, while hundreds of Carts, Horses and foot travellers are constantly, meeting and Crossing each Other[.] reduced to Miniature by the distance renders the whole really picturesque; on the Top of this the Traveller comes in sight of the town as he enters avenues of regularly planted Trees Leading to the different Streets running at right Angles towards the River . . . advancing, he is Led into Main Street; this as well as the generality of the place too Narrow to be Handsome, is rendered Less Interesting by the poorness & Iregularity of the Houses, few of which are Bricks—and at this season very much encumbered by Bales of Cotton —the Jail, Court House are New and tolerable in their form the Lower part of the [Jail] is a Boarding House of some Note. there are Two Miserable Looking Churches; I dare not say unattended but think so—

the Natchez's Hotel is a good House built on the Spanish plan, i.e. with Large Piazas and Many Doors and Windows . . . and is the rendez vous of all Gentile Travellers and Boarders—Several Large tavern which I did not Visit furnish Amply the Wants of the Strangers that at all times abound from different parts of the Union—this place now Contain about 2000—inhabitants and Houses, has a Bank in good Credit—a Post Office receiving the Diferent Mails Thrice per Week, a Public reading Room and 2 printing offices—

. . . the remains of an Ancient Spanish fort are perceivable, the Center is now Honored by the Gallows and the Ditch [moat?] serves as buriing ground for Slaves—. . . about 2 Years ago a Large part of the Hill above the Lower Town gave Way, Sunk probably 150 feet and Carried Many Houses into the River—. . .

this sunken part is Now used as the depot of Dead Carcasses, and often times during the Summer emits such Exalasions as attract hundreds, Nay I was told Thousands of Carrion Crows [black vultures] —an Engine is now Nearly in Operation Intended to raise the Watter of one of the springs . . . to suply the City—This indeed is much wanted, Watter hauled from the River is sold at 50^{cts} p^r Barrel taken out of the Eddy very impure—

MH   The Lower Town was also called Natchez-under-the-Hill, a seamy waterfront. Alexander Adams' biography, *John James Audubon* (Putnam, 1966), relates as typical of the place a story about a minister of the Gospel—passenger on a steamboat—who was mugged and robbed of his savings in the Lower Town and complained to the captain of his steamboat. The captain lashed heavy chain around the frame structure in which the thieves were holed up, fastened the other end of the chain to his steamboat, and started to back the boat out from shore. The money was returned.

Cotton money and river commerce improved Natchez in JJA's lifetime, and the city escaped the worst of the Civil War; it wasn't leveled like some, and it kept its antebellum character. The railroads passed it by. It is no longer a port where one could find the equivalent of hundreds of flatboats and steamboats tied up to the bank, loading and unloading. "The Mississippi might as well be the Yangtze for all the effect the shipping has on Natchez," a local attorney tells us. As in the old days, the Lower Town has a single street. It consists of brick and frame houses, and is merely seedy and rundown and partly abandoned—not venal. A restaurant of certain pretensions, with a

Natchez-under-the-Hill. *MH*

Gay Nineties decor, has been opened there, to capitalize on the gaudy history of under-the-Hill, and perhaps the place will be rescued so well it will eventually bear no resemblance at all to what it was.

Natchez on top of the hill is greenery and blooming shrubs and few buildings taller than the tree-shaded, elegant old mansions . . . the sounds, through an open door, of after-school piano practice; fish crows conversing gently, *ca-ca, ca-ca,* mockingbirds doing their Latin recitations, their musical stitchery. One would like to be able to package some of the city's quiet gracefulness for export.

MD Every spring, when the camellias and azaleas are at their height, the Natchez Garden Club and the Pilgrimage Garden Club "invite the lovers of history and of romantic traditions to step into the past for an enchanted visit." (I quote from the Pilgrimage Tour brochure, *Natchez on the Mississippi—Where The Old South Still Lives.*) "Ladies in hoop-skirts will welcome you into antebellum houses, furnished with priceless antiques, which still echo the colorful legends that made the Old South famous." Many of the old houses are still owned by the original families. Others now belong to new families, are maintained by new Southern money, and I gather that much of it that's loose hereabouts these days comes from oil, as once upon a time it came from cotton. Natchez, socially and historically top-drawer, is evidently a place to buy into once you've made your fortune and can afford the swank of keeping up an antebellum estate.

During the Pilgrimage, a Confederate Pageant, billed as the outstanding social event of the gala month, is presented at the city auditorium. "The King, Queen, and court, the tableau groups, the dancers, all are members of the Natchez social world, who, for this brief period, turn back the clock a century or more to those far-away, courtly days."

The program for the pageant is enticing, and one scene leaps out at us from the pages of the program.

AUDUBON, THE DANCING MASTER

(Performed by the Martha Hootsell School of the Dance)

In the early part of the 19th century, John James Audubon made some of his finest bird studies in Natchez. During a lengthy sojourn here he taught at Jefferson College and also gave painting and dancing lessons to the young people of the plantation neighborhood . . . Here he appears with his class—carefully chosen young people of Southern families of affluence and distinction . . ."

The Pilgrimage and the Pageant, alas, will be held next month, so we must content ourselves with a secondhand account of the Audubon ballet—the young men in black (pin-tail coats, rhinestone buttons, lace jabots), the girls in yellow (off-the-shoulder dresses with accordian-pleated skirts). Audubon is dressed in rust and the role is taken by a ballerina. The music and dances are of the period. A waltz, a polka, a gavotte, a minuet. Audubon demonstrates, the *corps de ballet* follows his lead. During the minuet, Audubon shines in a solo of arabesques, while the class dances round him. The ballet closes, as it began, with a waltz to the music of *Southern Roses.*

Audubon's "Natchez" dancing classes were actually held in the nearby village of Woodville, Mississippi, and they were far from sedate. We have Audubon's word for it. "I marched to the hall with my violin under my arm, bowed to the company assembled, tuned my violin; played a *cotillon,* and began my lesson . . . How I toiled before I could get one graceful step or motion! I broke my bow and nearly my violin in my excitement and impatience! . . . I pushed one here and another there, and all the while singing to myself to assist their movements . . . After this first lesson was over I was requested to *dance to my own music,* which I did until the whole room came down in thunders of applause in clapping hands and shouting. Lessons in fencing followed to the young gentlemen and I went to bed extremely fatigued."

Twenty-five years later, when JJA was famous, the Woodville paper published a memoir of those evenings—riotous revelry with John James Audubon, the young people wild with delight when it was time for their elders to take the floor. "Shouts greeted their appearance, tears of laughter streamed down their cheeks as they watched the solemn antics of fathers and grandfathers taking their first steps from that funny Mons. Audubon." An added entertainment was the fun of watching Audubon trying to control his temper as he labored amongst his pupils with cries of "Sacre bleu" and other Gallic imprecations. There also was said to have been a rival teacher, one Monsieur Muscarilla, who was so outraged at Audubon's having cornered the dancing class trade in the neighborhood that he accused JJA of being nothing more than a vulgar stuffer of birds. Audubon supposedly retaliated by describing Muscarilla as a *parvenu puant*—a stinking upstart. With that, a duel threatened, until one of the local gentry told Muscarilla that JJA was the best shot for miles around. Muscarilla reportedly packed up his dancing slippers and moved on.

The temperature has risen. Hot and sultry, as we take to the sidewalks of Natchez. The Audubons lived for the winter of

1822–23 in a little frame house at 118 South Union Street, a narrow back alley of a street behind the old business section. Their particular guardian angel at that time was a Natchez physician who saw to it that there was food on the table, clothes and school tuition for the boys, drawing materials for John James, and who introduced Lucy into St. Francisville, Louisiana, where she made her way as a schoolmistress for the next ten years. Natchez friends also arranged a teaching job for JJA at the Elizabeth Female Academy, in the nearby village of Washington, Mississippi, where his name is recorded on a historic marker among the roadside trees where the school building once stood. But he left the job after six weeks. A seven-mile walk each way and not enough time for his hunting and painting.

Natchez tradition has JJA teaching at yet another school in Washington village—Jefferson Military College—as is noted in the Confederate Pageant program. His biographers agree that he did not, and Audubon himself never spoke of such a job in any of his memoirs. He would have, if it were so. A teaching position at Jefferson would have been a feather in his cap. A Natchez attorney who is on the committee to restore Jefferson College as an historic site has done exhaustive research through the school's old files and account books. He found no record of Audubon's having taught dancing there, or French, drawing, fencing, or anything at all. He also told us that Jeff Davis was said to have been associated with the college too, but there was no record of that, either. (His law partner suggested dryly that perhaps no more research should be done. "Or the college won't be *worth* restoring.")

Natchez legend also has it that a gingko tree, formerly in the yard of the Union Street house, was planted by Audubon himself. I am a cynic in these matters. Why would a man who was scratching out a living for his wife and family, who had to depend on the kindness of new friends, take the time to plant a tree in the garden of a house he did not own? But I perhaps am an iconoclast beyond what is fair and possible. The ceremony of planting a gingko tree was the sort of bravura, gentleman-of-leisure gesture in which Audubon might have indulged. God knows, he was given to such gestures. When there wasn't a penny to spare, JJA was wont to ship Lucy exotic potted plants, modish stockings ("for thy dear ankles"), a crate of Queensware, a set of silver, dresses in the latest fashion, an amethyst pendant.

Whether he planted the gingko or not, the pleasing part is the trust that perpetuates the legend, a memory that goes back to the autumn of 1822. The house is gone, the garden paved over, the gingko tree chopped down, but the tradition rolls on. Audubon once planted such a tree, there is the place where it once stood, and neither he nor the tree is forgotten.

We go on to Washington Street, the air drenched this humid day with perfume from the pale yellow blossoms of the sweet olive trees *(Osmanthus fragrans)* that bloom in gardens and at doorsteps in this pretty neighborhood. Number 508, a white brick house, belonged to Emile Profilet, merchant, who befriended Audubon time and again. It is believed that JJA did much of his painting in a room over the old kitchen. "Though he couldn't possibly have chosen a worse place to paint," we were told. "It was a very small room. Very small windows. Very dark."

We go up to the bluff that faces north, overlooking the city. Audubon painted this view in 1823, when he had the great good fortune to receive a commission of $300 for an oil of the city of Natchez. But as his luck tended to run in those days, his patroness died before the picture was completed—an heroic canvas, eight feet by four feet. Her heirs did not want it and refused to pay. Emile Profilet hung the painting, for sale, in his downtown store. Still no buyers. Audubon went on with his life. Profilet sent the painting to France to show his relatives a view of the American city in which he lived, and, not incidentally, a view of his store, which stood in the center of the view. Eventually, Profilet brought the painting back to Natchez, hung it once again in his store, and this time it was bought by Dr. Stephen Kelly, who took it to Melrose, his plantation estate. The painting is still in the family.

The bluff where Audubon painted the panoramic view of the city carries Bluff Street and the edge of a black community. The ravine at the foot of the bluff is now Route 84. Overhead, there is a magnificent sky today—rich clouds, the sun in and out behind the gray and white rounded cumuli and now and again touching the distant buildings of Natchez with bolts of sunshine. The view has not changed all that much. JJA would know where he was.

Last notes from our campsite, Homochitto National Forest:
Wild Mississippi skies tonight. Black, tumultuous clouds. Rain flurries. A tornado watch to the north of us. (Natchez House, where JJA
stayed with Nicholas Berthoud in 1820, was blown away by a tornado
in 1840.) Mike's rigged up a plastic tarp to serve as a cook tent, the
corners tied to trees with lengths of rope. Gusting winds lift the tarp.
It billows. Snaps, crackles, and lashes. Tears loose at the grommets.
Mike has retied it at the corners three times; the tarp becomes
increasingly tattered, and the cook tent smaller and smaller. Our
dinner (his week to cook): sweet potatoes wrapped in aluminum foil
and baked in the coals of our fire; a sausage and onion dish; a green
salad. (After dinner, in the dark and in the commotion, Michael
manages to sit down in the sausage skillet.)

Nothing like bad weather and a tornado watch to empty the
campground. No one is left but us, the two Muscovy ducks, and an
old couple in a trailer that sits back off the lake in the tall pines. They
appear to have been here for months. They've rigged a front porch
alongside and low fencing around their site to create a front yard. I
assume they're among the inordinant number of old people who can
no longer afford to live at home and have sold the farm or the little
house, moved into a trailer, and taken to the road. They go where
the weather suits their clothes and their pensions, north in the summer, south in the winter, camping out at half-price on their Golden
Age passes. Here at Homochitto, we pay two dollars a night, they pay
one. That's thirty a month for rent. Not bad. Not bad at all. The old
people on the road nowadays outnumber the young. The old people
are the footloose rovers—the vagarounds, as Audubon would say—
and I wonder who's left at home to babysit with the grandchildren
and serve on the Board of Deacons.

ST. FRANCISVILLE, LOUISIANA

1821–1829, PASSIM

MH   It is 130 river miles from the bridge at Natchez to the bridge at the head of Baton Rouge Reach; between the two, nothing carries traffic across the Mississippi except the Feliciana Free Ferry, thirty-three miles above Baton Rouge. The ferry connects two old communities well known to Audubon and now barely more than names on a map—Pointe Coupee and Bayou Sara—but officially it runs between New Roads and St. Francisville, Louisiana.

As we wait on the New Roads side, a small boy visits from the camper-pickup ahead of us in line. He's been attracted by the sight of my CB antenna. It isn't long before he's telling us about the major recent event in his life. His sister's boyfriend, he says, went off hunting last December; four people, including somebody's father, piled into a small boat with four dogs and started across the river. The boat was hit by a barge, and everyone on board was lost. Two of the bodies haven't been found yet. That recalls a remark by Sid Jolly—the professional hunter talking about the amateurs: "Who else would go across the raging Mississippi at high water in a dinky little boat with a three-horsepower outboard, just to shoot turkeys?" But the boy's story, told here at this rare river-crossing, puts me in mind of something more momentous than the foolhardiness of certain hunters. I remember thinking—sitting in the pilothouse of the *Ray A.* during the barge-shuffling in Baton Rouge Reach—that in order to know someone well you have to feel the pace of his environment. The same thing could be said about the dominant physical characters and limitations of his familiar spaces. I try to imagine the spiritual impact of

220

a lifetime with this broad and sometimes dangerous river, where the roads run alongside for miles and miles as if hunting for a crossing; where the waters of half a continent flow endlessly by, and millions of tons of that half-continent's riches pass routinely through the view each year; where the river, with its floodplain, is an important source of food and water and income, and is also a major dispose-all.

In a simpler and less populated time, when the river's fruits were more bountiful and the offal and need for sanitary engineering less, when the river frequently jumped its banks and the swamps harbored yellow fever, this territory around Bayou Sara, Pointe Coupee, St. Francisville spoke to Audubon in some special way. Over a span of eight and a half years—during which he became an accomplished and well known painter of wildlife—he spent a total of about two years here. On three occasions he left in high dudgeon; but, as he said after the first such departure, to leave these "sweet woods" was painful, "for in them we allways enjoyed Peace and the sweetest pleasures of admiring the greatest of the Creator in all his unrivalled Works. I often felt as if anxious to retain the fill of My lungs with the purer air that Circulate through them."

In June 1821, escaping a precarious artistic existence in New Orleans, he and his young protégé, Mason, came up by steamboat to Bayou Sara, a busy river port at the junction of the river Bayou Sara and the Mississippi. JJA had agreed to spend the summer and fall at one of the many nearby plantations, Oakley, tutoring a young lady in drawing, music, dancing, and other skills. He'd earn $60 a month and also be able to work on his birds.

It was an ideal place for an ornithologist. At Bayou Sara Bend, on the east bank where JJA and Mason disembarked, the bottomland woods and marshes that dominate the delta down to the Gulf meet higher ground of loblolly pines and upland hardwoods. Here and there the land is cut in narrow ridges and steep gullies, thick with vines and briars—"machete country," Mary calls it. So within a relatively small area there was a wide variety of habitats and birds.

Audubon and Mason walked up the steep road away from the river to the village of St. Francisville, built along the top of a ridge, and from there they walked a few miles farther inland to Oakley. Fresh from the delta flatlands, Audubon was fascinated by what he saw along the way—"the Aspect of the Country entirely New to us distracted My Mind from those objects that are the occupation of My Life—the Rich Magnolia covered with its Odiforous Blossoms, the Holy, the Beech, the Tall Yellow Poplar, the Hilly ground, even the Red Clay I looked at with amazement[.] such entire change in so Short a time appears often supernatural, and surrounded once More by thousands of Warblers & Thrushes, I enjoy^d Nature."

Oakley's regular inhabitants, besides the slaves, were the master, James Pirrie—good-hearted and an alcoholic; his wife, who had met and hired Audubon in New Orleans; their married daughter and son-in-law; and Audubon's pupil, Eliza, fifteen years old. Five other children were recently dead, possibly from yellow fever, though Audubon doesn't say.

His employment began happily enough. It required him to spend only half his time with Eliza; the other half was his own, so he and Mason could do a lot of exploring and collecting in the sweet woods. For nearly two months, his journal is full of birds and other wildlife; there are a few brief entries on other matters, but not a word about the job. At last, near the end of August he describes his anatomical studies and drawing of a rattlesnake. The "Heat of the weather," he says, "Would not permit me to Spend more than 16 hours at [the drawing]—My amiable Pupil Miss Eliza Perrie also drew the same Snake; it is With Much pleasure that I now Mention her Name expecting to remember often her sweet disposition and the Happy Days spent near her."

A few days later, he adds a postscript about a bird he'd written up earlier—and that is his last entry for six weeks. Nothing more about birds, nothing about his amiable pupil; and when he takes up the pen again, evidently on October 10, it is only to note that he's sent "Mrs. A." $100. Suddenly, on October 20, he and Joseph Mason are on a boat for New Orleans. JJA has left Oakley under something of a cloud.

"Three Months out of the 4 we lived there Were Spent in peaceable tranquility," he tells his journal now; "giving regular Daily Lessons to Miss P. of Drawing, Music, Dancing, Arithmetick, and Some trifling acquirements such as Working Hair &c . . . Seldom troublesome of Disposition, and not Caring for or Scarcely ever partaking or Mixing with the constant Transient Visitors at the House, *We*

Were Called *good Men* and Now & then received a Chearing Look from the Mistress of the House and *sometimes* also one Glance of Approbation of the More Circumspect Miss Eliza."

He briefly describes the inhabitants and some of the visitors (including one Mrs. Harwood of London, "a *good* Little Woman Very Kind to us in Mending our Linen &c—her Little Daughter a sweet Child about 5 Years Old, Hated by Mrs P." I'd like to know more about *them*. Relatives of mine?), but considering the outcome we are drawn past that to what he says about Eliza: "Miss P. had no particular admirers of her beauties but several very anxious for her fortune." She was idolized by her mother and had "a good form of *body*, not Handsome of face, proud of her Wealth and of herself cannot be too Much fed on Praise—and God Knows how hard I tryed to Please her in Vain—and God knows also that I have vowed Never to try as much again for any Pupil of Mine—as usual *I* had to do 2/3 of all *her* Work of Course her progresses Were Rapid to the Eyes of every body and truly astonishing to the eyes of some good observers."

In September Eliza fell ill. Being one of two surviving children in a family that had just lost five offspring, she was evidently much spoiled and worried over through her convalescence. And all this apparently coincided with something else, because "her Phisician the *Man she Loved* would not permit her reassuming her Avavocations near Me and told the Mother that it would be highly Improper Miss Eliza Should Draw, Write &^c untill some Months. . . . I saw her during this Illness at appointed hours as if I was an Extraordinary ambassador to some Distant Court—had to Keep the utmost Decorum of Manners and I believe Never Laughed Once With her the Whole 4 Months I was there."

About October 10, Mrs. Pirrie "dismissed" him. He asked if he and Mason couldn't stay on another eight or ten days as visitors, to tie up loose ends in their natural history studies, and Mrs. Pirrie said that would be fine. So he was still on moderately good terms with the Pirries, and he remained that way with the *men* of the household. Not so with the ladies, however. A "remarkable Coolness had taken place from the Ladies toward us," particularly from Eliza's married older sister, Mrs. Smith, who "took an utter dislike to Me," derided his painting and laughed in his face. JJA returned coolness for coolness; when Mrs. Pirrie offered Joseph Mason a suit that had belonged to her late son, Audubon instructed him to refuse the present, "Knowing too Well how far some gifts are talked of." The behavior of the Pirrie ladies seems to have bothered Pirrie and Smith too, and doing what they could to make up for it, they joined Audubon and Mason in their room after supper on the last night at Oakley. Then came the formal goodbyes to the ladies. "My Entry before the Circle possessed none of that Life and Spirit I formerly Enjoyed on Such Occasion, . . . yet I walk^d in followed by Joseph and approaching to Mrs P. bid her good bye as simply as ever any Honest Quaker Did, touch^d Slightly Mrs Smith's Hand as I boughed to her—My Pupil Raised from the Sopha and Expected a Kiss from Me—but None were to be disposed off, I pressed her Hand and With a general Salute to the Whole Made My Retreat. . . . as Joseph Was following me he received a Voley of farewells from the 3 Ladies of the House put after him Ridiculously to Affect Me, but the Effect Was lost and it Raised a Smile on My Lips—We Joined again the Two good Husbands in our Lodging Chamber—they remained with us untill bed time; Cordially parted with us."

This is a most remarkable sequence of events—and obviously JJA left out key connectors. The sequence does not stop there. About seven weeks later, when he was in New Orleans, he wrote the following: "My Lovely Miss Pirrie of Oackley Passed by Me this Morning, but did not remember how beautifull I had rendered her face once by Painting it at her Request with Pastelles; She Knew not the Man Who with the utmost patience and in fact attention *Waitted* on her Motions to please her—but thanks to My humble talents I can run the gantlet throu this World without her help."

There's no law that says a man has to tell the truth, the whole truth, and nothing but the truth in his journal. As a writer of journals myself, I know how much is left out and that usually one describes an event to suit the feelings of the aftermath. I think JJA has laid down a few smoke screens and false trails about his stay at Oakley. The simplest interpretation of his story is probably the most likely. JJA, the romantic enthusiast, had fallen into an affectionate friendship with his amiable pupil Eliza, flattered her, flirted with her, kissed her in greeting and in pleasure at her achievements—he was a great kisser of ladies—began to turn Eliza's head, and got lots of winsome attention in return. I'm sure he would have been convinced

Audubon's pastel drawing of Eliza Pirrie. *From National Audubon Society*

throughout that all this flirting was completely innocent and harmless; but between a handsome, talented, flamboyant Frenchman and a not-so-pretty fifteen-year-old girl, such daily flirtation could have its serious overtones and consequences. Eliza's doctor—beau or not—and Mrs. Pirrie would have caught wind of this and decided when Eliza was ill that her health would not be improved by lovesickness, so some effort was made to restrict and formalize the teacher–pupil arrangement while Eliza recuperated. JJA could see what was up, was offended by it, perhaps even protested his innocence, and the ladies began to see him as annoying and slightly ridiculous. His appointment wasn't supposed to last much longer, anyway, and Mrs. Pirrie, using the excuse that on doctor's orders Eliza wouldn't be able to study with him for months, decided he'd best leave earlier than planned. Audubon had neither the temperament nor the experience to extricate himself gracefully from the situation, so he helped make matters worse in the last few days of his visit and departed Oakley as the Injured Victim. ("Daylight . . . Saw us Loading our Trunks and Drawing Table. Vaulted our Sadles and Left this abode of unfortunate Opulence without a single Sigh of regret.")

I confess I don't have complete confidence in my scenario. I go back into Audubon's talk about Oakley's inhabitants, looking for more clues:

James Pirrie was one of those drunks who goes crazy under the influence of liquor—"Never associating With any body on such occasions," says JJA, "and Exibiting all the Madman's Actions. . . . When Sober; truly a good Man a *Free Mason,* generous and Entertaining—his wife Raised to opulence by Dint of Industry an Extraordinary Woman—Generous I believe but giving Way for Want of understanding at times to the Whole force of her Violent Passions—fond of quizing her husband and Idolatring her Daugh[t]er Eliza."

"Quizing" does not have the same meaning today as it did then; it meant *needling,* making fun of. Mrs. P. was not the sweet little woman. But Audubon clearly admired her. And as for her older surviving daughter, Eliza's sister: "I cannot say that I Knew or rather I never did Wish to Know [her]," says JJA; "of Temper Much like her Mother, of Heart Not so good Yet God forgive her the Injuries She did me—

"her Husband a good, Honest Man and Citizen Viewed all the faults of her he Wedded With Patient Kindness and felt his reward through his own Correctness of Conduct—I admire him Much—"

Next Audubon speaks about Mrs. Harwood of London and the daughter that Mrs. Pirrie didn't like, and goes on to mention "a Certain Miss Throgmorton" who "Was also good deal Disliked, the poor Girl was nearly drove off as We Were by the Ladies—although she had been Invited there to Spend the Summer."

The onion unpeels, making the eyes tear. I feel as if we have arrived at the end of a disastrous house party to carry away one of the survivors. "What happened?" you ask as you tumble his luggage into the car. "Jesus Christ!" he begins—and you have entertainment if not elucidation all the way home.

Oakley. *MH*

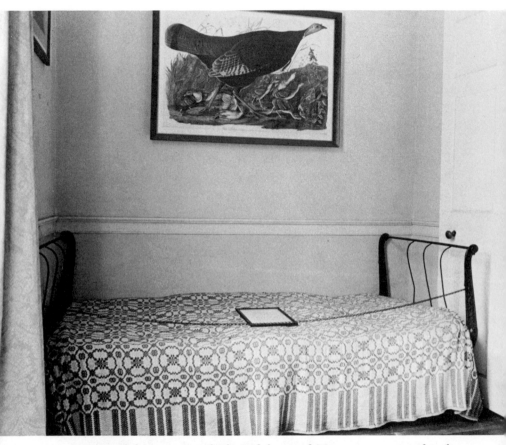

Interior of the room in which Audubon and Mason are supposed to have slept. *MH*

The white house, built in 1799, is surrounded by live oaks and azaleas so thick they hide it from view along some of the approaches. The front is dominated by two stories of dark, airy, open porches with slender columns.

Thirty years ago, Oakley was near ruin. Old Miss Lucy Mathews, last of the Pirrie line and granddaughter of JJA's pupil, Eliza, was living here in a couple of the rooms—old Miss Lucy Mathews and her hound dogs. We have seen the "before" pictures, the way it was when Miss Lucy was mistress: walls, ceilings, and furnishings badly decayed, clutter in the corners, a house ready for the burning. People who came here in those days still talk about the dogs and their fleas and how callers had to pick the fleas off themselves after they left. The state bought Oakley, apparently just in time, and made it the center of the Audubon State Commemorative Area—a hundred acres of mostly old woods, with a pond and a picnic area and a few outbuildings and a gift shop. The house was lovingly restored and furnished in the style of the late Federal period in which it was built. Audubon prints decorate the walls. There's a curator on the scene whenever the house is open, to lead visitors through and to watch over things; she's new on the job, which is a state-government appointment, and is learning about John James Audubon as she goes. She loves the work and is captivated by the idea of Audubon, but she is distressed by any of his pictures that show predatory birds with their prey, and she cannot stomach the thought of JJA's having done dissections. She grimaces and turns away her head at even mentioning these things.

The second-floor room that JJA and Mason are said to have shared in 1821 is on the same floor as the drawing room, and is the size of a servant's bedroom—literally big enough only for two beds on either side of a sunny window. A print of the famous turkey hen and chicks is hung on one wall, above a wrought iron camp bed the shape of a sleigh. The original painting for that engraving was probably begun during the 1820–21 river trip to New Orleans, and the turkey cock— Audubon's "signature," as his contemporaries saw him—may well have been painted in these parts, a few years later.

But many are the homes and communities, from Henderson south, that lay claim to being the very place where the one or the other turkey was painted. A little reflected glory. Stanley Clisby Arthur, a Louisianan who wrote a biography of JJA, remarked that the places in Louisiana bragging the original turkey drawings as their own are as numerous as the beds where Lafayette is said to have slept when he came to New Orleans. It's all of a piece with the hand-painted "Audubon" china treated as icons in dozens of fine homes in the south today. These sets of china were allegedly painted by the Master Himself, and as someone in St. Francisville commented to us, if Audubon had painted all the dinner plates he is reported to have painted, he wouldn't have had time to do anything else. In fact, I doubt he painted a plate in his life, even in hard times. Never in all the millions of words of his that we've read does he mention such a thing.

We leave the house and walk back into the woods, along paths that twist among the shrubs and live oaks. What magnificent trees the live oaks are—massive in the trunk, heavy-limbed, knotted and gnarled, obviously wrought by nature as foundations for tree-houses, with handholds and footholds everywhere to encourage climbing children.

This is a nature walk provided by the State and the path is worn bare and smooth. But overhead there are pine warblers trilling; JJA painted his "Pine Creeping Warbler" pair here at Oakley, and Mason did their perch—the branch and needles and green cone of a loblolly. Carolina wrens are tootleetootleetootling, cardinals and blue jays are flashing through the woods, downy woodpeckers are drumming; Audubon's paintings of these species were done in the area, if not precisely here. A pair of pileated woodpeckers is working on a nest in the hulk of an old beech. Quite likely JJA made near Oakley at least the working sketches for his splendid painting of four pileated woodpeckers. High overhead a red-shouldered hawk circles and soars; Audubon portrayed red-shouldered hawks in three works I know of, including two that became Havell plates, and all three come from this area. I feel a little as if we have been dropped into an Audubon painting.

Splendid peacocks and peahens stalk the grounds of Oakley and roost in the live oaks. The cocks, courting, marking out territory, screech mournfully and strut in tiny dance steps and rattle their fanned, erect tail-plumes. A pair of picnickers, frightened by the near approach of two of these birds, stand up out of the way on a picnic bench; still eating their sandwiches, they keep a sharp eye on the birds.

From here, JJA's trail in this region becomes more difficult to follow. Case in point: Beech Woods plantation, north of St. Francisville. Beech Woods was the property of Mrs. Robert Percy, who invited Lucy to set up a school, where JJA also taught off and on. For three years, while JJA bounced from pillar to post to England, it was the closest thing the Audubon family had to a permanent residence.

Swallow-tailed kite, painted by Audubon in West Feliciana, 1821. *Courtesy of The New-York Historical Society, New York City*

Yet very little about it remains. Audubon's journal for 1822–24, when he was a familiar at Beech Woods, existed as late as the 1920s and has since vanished. What survives is an undocumented but believable and tantalizing story from *Audubon the Naturalist: An Intimate Portrait* by Stanley Clisby Arthur who tramped all through this territory in the 1920s, visiting and photographing places Audubon had known.

Audubon was learning to paint in oils here. He seems to have considered this art form far and away more difficult and admirable than the medium he was inventing for himself—pencil, crayon, pastel, water color, pen and ink, egg white, whatever would serve. He spoke of the latter as *drawing;* oils were *painting.* At Beech Woods in the summer of 1822, says Arthur, evidently quoting from a journal, Audubon "continued to exercise myself in painting with oils and generally improved myself. I undertook to paint the portraits of my wife's pupils but found their complexions difficult to transfer to canvass." Mrs. Percy thought Audubon had got her daughters' skin too yellow, too jaundiced. Audubon demurred—but one can't tell whether out of frustration or from pride at having conquered a difficult painting problem. Evidently they disputed this matter for a while, until Audubon finally blew up and stormed out of Beech Woods. A few nights later, when he quietly came back to the plantation and snuggled into bed with Lucy, a servant alerted the Widow Percy, who burst into the nuptial chamber and ordered JJA out. A humiliating event. Your wife stays, you impecunious, impetuous, horny artist. *You,* however, go. And the wife, the major support of herself and their two sons, must swallow the humiliation. So must the artist—for the sake of his family and for lack of other places to go in a pinch: after JJA and son Victor caught yellow fever in Natchez, Beech Woods was where they came to recuperate. Audubon and Mrs. Percy made up after a fashion, but Audubon *père et fils* left again as soon as they could, within a few weeks.

They went to Shippingport, Kentucky, where Victor was apprenticed as a clerk to his uncle Nicholas Berthoud and over the winter JJA turned his hand to whatever offered in the way of a living—painting portraits, street signs, panels to decorate riverboats. In the spring he went on to Philadelphia, where he showed his portfolio around and looked for an engraver. He made good friends there during the visit; but he also made some important enemies—particularly one Thomas Lawson, the best engraver of bird drawings in North America. Lawson had engraved Alexander Wilson's birds, and was now engaged in a new and enlarged edition of the *American Ornithology,* under the editorship of the ornithologist Charles Lucien Bonaparte, twenty-one-year-old nephew of Napoleon. Bonaparte thought Audubon's drawings were excellent and wanted to use them in the new work, but Lawson is said not to have liked them. William Dunlap, author of *History of the Rise and Progress of the Arts of Design in the United States* (1834), reported that Lawson told *him* Audubon's birds "were ill drawn, not true to nature, and anatomically incorrect." Lawson also said as much to Bonaparte, who argued with him and finally declared he'd buy the pictures for the book anyway. "You may buy them," Lawson is supposed to have replied, "but I will not engrave them."

Another engraver advised JJA to forget about having his work published in North America, and Bonaparte said the same; instead he should go to Europe, where the job would be done right. With that bug in his ear, Audubon left Philadelphia for New York City, where he read a scientific paper to the Lyceum of Natural History, was made a member, and exhibited his work. After this he set off up the Hudson to Albany, crossed the state to Niagara Falls. He had had an idea of painting the falls but decided that any rendering could only be "puny" set against the thunderous reality. (Years later the English Shakespearean actress Fanny Kemble met Audubon in Boston and wrote, "He gave us a description of Niagara which did what he complained no description of it ever does—conveyed to us an exact idea of the natural position and circumstances which render these falls so wonderful; whereas, most describers launch forth into vague and untangible rhapsodies, . . . he gave me, by his simple words, a more real impression of the stupendous cataract than all that was ever writ or spoken of waterfalls before, not excepting Byron's Terni.")

He took passage on a ship across Lake Erie, was robbed of most of his money before he embarked and was tossed about in a gale at the entrance to Presque Isle Harbor before he landed. (Mary and I walked on the stone jetty at that entrance one summer day, while retired folk in camp chairs filled their plastic pails with perch and bluegills. Audubon would have been pleased by the loudspeaker-voice from the tour boat that passed us there— calling attention to some Bonaparte's gulls.) With the few dollars they had left, he and a companion hired a wagon to carry their baggage to Meadville, in northwest Pennsylvania. There Audubon set up as a portrait painter for two days (local tradition has stretched that to as much as a year) and then, with a little cash in his pocket, walked to Pittsburgh. He stayed for about a month and a half, doing portraits, drawing birds, and teaching painting to another talented adolescent girl—to whom he gave a sketch-book filled with his paintings of insects and reptiles when he left at the end of October and headed "home" to Beech Woods.

Evidently he had by then decided to commit himself to the European venture. For the next year and a half he stayed at Beech Woods, working on his portfolio of birds, teaching music and drawing and dancing, building a grubstake for the voyage. But Mrs. Percy and JJA held no high opinion of each other, and the Audubons' humiliation rankled. Lucy would later write her husband in England to suggest that when he returned he might do well not to stay at Beech Woods. He agreed, saying that he'd den in with his friend Bourgeat on the plantation next door and never step over the boundary line by so much as one foot. And when Lucy—for reasons uncertain—later moved her school to the Beech Grove plantation of the William Garrett Johnsons and wrote JJA about it, he approved wholeheartedly: "[I]f I wanted to go to bed to thee there, I would not be sent back 15 miles on foot to Bayou Sarah instead!!!"

Except for this whiff of the place and some of Audubon's bird paintings, Beech Woods plantation is mostly local recollections and phantoms. Beech Grove, where he stayed for a few weeks before taking Lucy to England in 1830, is even more shadowy. Each plantation site is still very much "country," but the plantation houses are gone. At Beech Grove, the gate posts bear the name; the old mansion —burned down—has been replaced by a prosperous-looking modern house, and cattle browse in the pasture. We can find no sign at all of Beech Woods—no winding drive between live oaks and azaleas, no cellar hole. Near the spot where the house must have stood, the dirt road forks to reach two shanties: a barber chair in one yard and a barking dog in the other, and no one to answer my knocks or show a face at a window.

MD St. Francisville—"La Villa de San Francisco"—was named in the late 1700s for the patron saint of the Spanish Franciscan monks who had chosen this site on the bluff as a safe burial ground well out of the reach of the Mississippi River. The district was called Nueva Feliciana—"The New Happyland"—and is now divided into West Feliciana Parish and East Feliciana Parish (parish being the Louisiana equivalent of a county). Once again, as I've had to do all up and down the Mississippi River Valley, I must cast out Plymouth Rock and the Pilgrim Fathers and think in terms of a Spanish and French colonial history. In this instance, the territory was ceded to England by France in 1763, ceded to Spain by England in 1783, became the independent Republic of West Florida in 1810 when the Felicianas revolted against Spanish rule, and seventy-four days later the little republic was annexed by the U.S.A.

Bayou Sara, at the foot of the St. Francisville bluff, was once the biggest cotton port between New Orleans and Memphis but was wiped from the map by loss of commerce, by fire and flood. Nothing remains but the ferry landing and one roadhouse. Add it to the lengthening list of vanished or dying towns that Audubon knew as busy communities (the Arkansas Post, Shippingport, Trinity, America, Shawneetown)—an historic reversal that always catches us off guard, set as we are in our visions of unchecked and uncheckable urban sprawl.

The same road, however, runs up from the Mississippi to St. Francisville; population, 1600. You are on Ferdinand Street. The Grace Episcopal Church and cemetery (live oaks and Spanish moss) to your left; Court House Square to your right; several little streets of old, well-kept buildings (white clapboard, flowering trees, wisteria in bloom); and two blocks down on Ferdinand Street, the West Feliciana Historical Society, which sponsors the Audubon Pilgrimage, held annually in mid-March—*A Visit to the Past in Audubon's "Happyland."* Like the Natchez Pilgrimage, though on a smaller, less elaborate scale, there are tours of historic buildings in town and plantations and gardens in the surrounding countryside.

Audubon's "Happyland"? Well, in spite of the rows with Mrs. Pirrie and Mrs. Percy and the chagrining dismissals from their households and, heaven knows, the gossip and giggles that must have flown through the community, West Feliciana was indeed a kind of Eden to JJA. He painted at least seventy-six, possibly a hundred, of his bird portraits here; he had dear friends, particularly among the hunting companions with whom he roved in Tunica swamp, along Thompson Creek and Bayou Sara, and up in the hills through the Sleepy Hollow Woods, often for days at a time. Among them was Dr. Nathaniel Wells Pope, a young physician whose wife had the proper family connections in West Feliciana, but his new medical practice was not a success. The Popes were hard up, had moved down the ladder into a log cabin in the woods, and were no longer, Martha

Henry Lewis' rendering of Bayou Sara, from *Das Illustrirte Mississippithal.*
Missouri Historical Society

"Bayou Sara Catroom," circa 1828, by Charles A. Lesueur, French artist and naturalist. Lesueur was the author of monographs on reptiles, crustaceans, and American fishes; he taught drawing at the Robert Owens community, New Harmony, Indiana, 1826–37, and was a friend and champion of Audubon. *Collection of Leonard V. Huber; photographed at the Museum of Natural History in Le Havre*

Pope implied in a memoir, counted among the elite.

Her memoir, nonetheless, gives a warm impression of halcyon days in St. Francisville with JJA as a frequent guest, and her starry-eyed reminiscence of him would have set Mrs. Pirrie's and Mrs. Percy's teeth on edge.

"Audubon," wrote Martha Pope, "was one of the handsomest men I ever saw. In person he was tall and slender, his blue eyes were an eagle's in brightness, his teeth were white and even, his hair a beautiful chestnut brown, very glossy and curly. His bearing was courteous and refined, simple, and unassuming. . . .

"He kept his drawings in a watertight tin box, which remained in my parlour for months. His reputation was spread far and wide, and often our home was filled with visitors who came to see his drawings and paintings, which he would spread out on the floor for inspection, and he never seemed weary of unpacking and explaining them. He was very sociable and communicative, being the center of attraction in every circle in which he mingled. . . .

"After spending a short time with his family he would start out again on his lonely journey in the woods, with his knapsack on his back, alone and on foot, often remaining in the open until his clothes were tatters, and his hair in long curls on his shoulders. His hair was beautiful!"

Martha Pope also wrote: "While he was wandering in the forests his noble wife was working in order to assist him in having his pictures engraved. It grieved him exceedingly to have it so. Every time he returned home he found her fading and drooping and he could not help but compare her to 'a beautiful tobacco plant cut off at the stem and hung up to wither with head hanging down,' as he put it in his quaint way of using similes." It's safe to say that Lucy did not find this the least bit quaint. But the key words in that passage are "noble wife." Lucy is always described as noble. Audubon's biographers never fail to stress her selfless devotion to her husband's life work, though when Lucy first found herself pressed into teaching, she did not have John James in mind. She was concerned with the basics: bread and butter and a roof over her head and her children's heads. And how he adored her, the wife and mother who could support the family while he rambled and gambled on his future. She gamely adapted herself to the amorphous position of governess and walked that nasty narrow line between servant and invited guest, forever at the whim of the mistress of the house and never the mistress of her own household. She kept her books in order, paid off loans, paid her debts as she went, while JJA dismissed or forgot loans and old debts. Those were niggling trifles from yesterday. I admire her gallantry and her grit, but I must admit that I have come to the conclusion that I am not fond of Lucy Audubon. I get the strong impression that she was among those self-righteous people who never let you forget just how noble they have been, who subconsciously welcome catastrophe as an opportunity to prove, once more,

Lucy Audubon, aged forty-five, in a pose chosen by the artist to emphasize
her eyes and minimize her nose. After a miniature by Frederick Cruikshank,
London, 1831. *Courtesy of The New-York Historical Society, New York City*

Lucy Audubon in her early eighties. *Courtesy of The New-York Historical Society, New York City*

how forebearing and self-sacrificing they can be.

Lucy and John James had now been married close to twenty years. He was as dashing and good-looking as ever, the cock of the walk, and she was still the little gray hen. Martha Pope wrote frankly that Mrs. Audubon was not handsome—"Her face was spoiled by her nose, which was short and turned up"—and that Lucy's chief attractions were her eyes, expression, gentleness, and intelligence (qualities that others always spoke of too). Over the years, Lucy had grown from a conscientious young girl into a sternly conscientious woman with a stern philosophy of life. As she told John James again and again and again: "The world is not indulgent." He needed her Calvinistic scourge, and she needed his manic, whirlwind passions and demands. She could recite his faults and her martyrdom, and he could say, yes, yes, I am mad, bad, and dangerous to know, and without you I would be nothing. I am the rascal. You are the pearl. And they would collide in luscious anguish. There was a strong emotional bond between them, and I'm sure there were times when he was away on his interminable journeys, leaving her alone for months, sometimes years ("I have a rival in every bird!"), that Lucy must have said to herself, that's it, it's finished, he will never touch me again. But he had only to walk in, speak her name, there would be tears from both of them, and she would melt at the first kiss.

JJA often talked with the Popes about the bad times in Kentucky and used to say: "I mean to get me a coach-and-six and ride through the streets of Louisville yet." Though there's no record of his having made a comparable remark about St. Francisville, JJA surely reveled in the vindication of returning here from abroad as a celebrity. He had been transformed in a twinkling from the explosive itinerant teacher and bird painter into a charmingly eccentric famous person, and the late unpleasantness with the Pirries and the Percys was forgiven or forgotten as the years passed and his fame grew. But even today, as in Henderson, there are those who judge him with a cold eye. A history scholar here, with whom we compared notes on JJA and Lucy, said without apology: "I find the Audubons tiresome." An autobiographical sketch in the Audubon Pilgrimage brochure opens with an arresting choice of words. JJA is described, flat out, as: "The quasi-naturalist, sometime dancing master, unkempt wanderer, and trying husband . . ."

Well, you've got to hand it to him. Though he's been in his grave since 1851, he can provoke an emotional response, pro or con, to this day. Audubon's shade is restless still.

Martha Pope, of course, was not the only one to recall him with loving adulation. St. Francisville's memories of JJA were fondly re-told and recorded. His alligator hunts with Augustin Bourgeat. The girls in his dancing classes begging for locks of his hair to keep as souvenirs. Little Mary Ellen Johnson sitting on his lap while he painted his bird studies. The swimming lessons he gave to the chil-dren in the Beech Woods plantation springhouse. The day young Robert Percy was with him in the Sleepy Hollow woods when JJA called in a turkey gobbler with a "yelper" made from the second joint of a wing bone and that very gobbler was said to have been the model for the famous wild turkey engraving. And another day when he and Dr. Pope returned from a fishing trip bearing a snapping turtle whose skull measured eight inches across and whose shell was "large enough for an infant's cradle."

In the 1930s, Audubon Pageants were held at Greenwood planta-tion—music, singing, dancing, a whistler who did bird songs, a wood-land scene with Audubon and number of the birds from his most popular engravings (the birds played by children in costume). During those years Mrs. George Lester of West Feliciana toured the state with copies of Audubon engravings and gave lectures to acquaint Louisianians with his work. And in 1941, the first Audubon Pilgrimage and house tour was held.

His name is everywhere. The Audubon Amoco Service Station, Audubon Lion's Club, Audubon Girl Scout Council, Audubon Li-brary, Bryant's Audubon Pharmacy. On the outskirts of town is the Audubon Holiday Inn ("Welcome to Comfort, Convenience and Ele-gance in Audubon's Happyland")—a mid-Victorian decor, the Beech Grove Room, the Bayou Sara Lounge, and an Audubon Gallery with a permanent exhibit of *The Birds of America* in a fine recent edition printed in Amsterdam. Farther along the highway is an open field offered for sale by the Audubon Realtors. Next to it, the Audubon Lounge ("Dancing Fri & Sat The Rhythm Masters Coors Beer Pizza Sandwiches") and the Audubon Package Liquor Store (ICE).

A few more miles southeast, bear left down a country road, and
you come to the Audubon Lake Camping Resort—108 acres, nature
trails, a 45-acre lake, boats available, a swimming pool, a recreation
and amusement hall—this place said to be the spot JJA spoke of in
August 1821, during his stay at Oakley. JJA: "We left this morning
after an early breakfast to go and explore a Famous Lake . . . where
we were to find (as told) great many Very fine Birds—the walk to it
was pleasant being mostly through Rich Magnolia Woods."

Here we make camp. We have steered clear of the crowded
trailer sites by the lake, with their hookups to water and electricity,
and are living under the trees on the edge of a large green open
meadow. Our only neighbor is a portly, cheery fellow who works at
the paper plant down the way, from which sulphurous fumes waft
through the countryside when the wind is wrong. He's been here in
a tent for six months, ever since he parted from his wife. In the late
afternoon after work, he flies kites from our mutual meadow and
remarks, with a big grin and shrug, that that's what his wife told him
to do. "Go fly a kite, she said." In the tops of the tall trees that circle
this meadow, dead kites—one red, one yellow, doomed by wind and
chance—snap and moan in the breeze.

A gift of fresh scallions today from the garden of the owner of the
campground—a Missouri man who says he's still grateful for having
had the luck to move to Louisiana twenty years ago. "The first
twenty-five years of my life I did nothing but shovel snow to get to
the garage."

Green tree frogs, the first we've ever seen. Pale jade green above,
yellow below. Fat, round, sticky fingertips with which they can cling
to smooth surfaces, even upside down. In all, not more than an inch
and a half long, and they fold down as thin and as flat as a Patek
Phillippe watch. Prodigious leapers, six and eight feet at a bound. A
voice, say our field guides, like a distant cowbell. Either they are not
calling, or we are not tuned in. Have heard no cowbell music, only
distant cows lowing back and forth—deep throaty intervals, like
foghorns in colliloquy.

So far as we know, this is the first time we've camped amid fire
ants. *Solenopsis geminati,* the scourge of the southland. They slipped
into the U.S. from Argentina by way of Mobile in World War I.

They're a constant torment and trouble to field workers and will devour the young of ground birds, poultry, and small mammals. Otherwise their diet is beneficial to man—the larva of houseflies, weevils, cutworms, much the same diet as that of the armadillos, whose burrows riddle the soft earth of the wooded ravine behind our tent. The fire ant is a day worker. The armadillos here seem to do their foraging only after dark, clanging about in the underbrush, the noisiest of night visitors. (Prisoners at the state penitentiary, north of here in the Tunica Hills, make pets of the armadillos.)

Fire ants are said to work in gangs, a swarm of them crawling onto an intruder in their nest, and at a secret signal—Get Ready, Get Set, BITE—all will sting at once. The local country remedy is a wet plaster of chewing tobacco. I sweep them out of the tent every morning and evening, along with beetles and inchworms and woolly bear caterpillars, who find their way in though the tent is buttoned up and zipped down after each housecleaning. Other than that, we co-exist peacefully. Mike hasn't been stung, though I have, once, given as I am to walking around barefoot. The fire ant's bite is a sharp, fiery sting, like a jab from a red-hot needle.

A list of those flowers blooming here in mid-March, which appear in *The Birds of America* and were painted as background either by JJA or by Mason:

Cross-vine, in the trees above our tent. *Bignonia capreolata.* Trumpet-shaped blossoms, scarlet on the outside, yellow on the inside, a cousin of the orange trumpet vine of the northern states. Shown in one of JJA's pictures of the yellow warbler. A few sprigs also copied by Havell into the engraving of blue jays.

Jessamine. *Gelsemium sempervirens.* The sweetest of scents, the truest yellow of yellows, the vine in one of JJA's most dramatic paintings—that of the mockingbirds defending their nest against a tree-climbing rattlesnake. (The published engraving caused a major controversy. Critics claimed that the shape of the fangs was incorrect and that rattlesnakes did not climb trees. Audubon was right on both counts, the critics wrong.)

Toadshade, *Trillium sessile,* in the underbrush behind our campsite where the armadillos root and clang. Not found in New England. Three leaves with asymmetrical spots and streaks, a three-petaled, deep-red flower that stands erect like a pronged cup and never opens completely. Pictured with the upland sandpiper and with the ruffed grouse.

Red buckeye throughout the woodlands. *Aesculus pavia,* a shrub with spikes of jungle red tubular flowers, pictured with the Carolina wren.

Swamp maple, *Acer drummondii,* scarlet, winged samara on gray leafless branches, brilliant in the gray-green swamplands. Pictured with the bobolink.

Rose vervain, *Verbena canadensis,* pink flower clusters, shown with Henslow's sparrow and savannah sparrow.

Silver bells, *Halesia diptera,* a shrub with white, waxy flowers, shown with yellowthroats.

The Cherokee rose, *Rosa laevigata,* a climbing, twining, ever-green vine that blooms in rambling cascades from trees and fences. Originally imported from China for southern gardens, and now the state flower of Georgia. It escaped into woods and fields and has become a pest in many places. Give it an inch and it will take the acre. An exquisite rose—a flat, fragrant, five-petaled white flower the size of a demitasse saucer. Pictured with what Audubon called the Oregon Junco, now known as a variety of the dark-eyed junco.

Audubon, by the way, had no interest in flowers, except as decorative adjuncts to his paintings. His journals contain almost no flower names, no detailed descriptions of color, size, and shape. I am tantalized by (and impatient with) his skimpy entries. "Many pretty flowers in bloom." Or, "Saw a purple flower today." A maddening and curious blindspot, that. Particularly for a man with such a relentlessly inquisitive eye.

The barred owl, said Audubon, seemed to be more abundant in Louisiana than in any other state. "At the approach of night, their cries are heard proceeding from every part of the forests around the plantations . . . and they respond to each other in tones so strange, that one might imagine some extraordinary fete about to take place among them." He also spoke about wilderness treks, when he was about to cook a piece of venison or "the body of a squirrel," and a barred owl would alight within a few yards of the fire "and eye me in such a curious manner that, had it been reasonable to do so, I

would gladly have invited him to walk in and join me in my repast
. . . his society would be at least as agreeable as that of many of the
buffoons we meet with in this world."

We've been hearing barred owls all through the Ohio and Mississippi valleys, but—pleasingly and fittingly—they still sing in unnumbered chorus in the forests round and about the Audubon Lake
Camping Resort. "Who cooks for *you?* Who cooks for *you*-all?" The
questions ring clear, the interpretation you'll find in just about anything you may read about the barred owl, whether in a signs-of-
spring editorial in *The New York Times* or in a scientific essay. In
Audubon's day, this reading of the barred owl's cry had evidently not
become commonplace. He described it merely as *whah, whah,
whah, whah-aa.* Alexander Wilson didn't describe it at all, except to
say the owl screamed during the day like a hawk. But country people
who knew the song must have heard the question in the barred owl's
call all along. Benjamin Wailes of Natchez, whose interest in natural
history was said to have been inspired by his early friendship with
Audubon, gave the following account in his *Report on the Agriculture and Geology of Mississippi* (1854): "A hunting party, encamped
for the first night in the woods, were grouped around the campfire,
making arrangements for the preparation of the evening repast,
when an owl perched overhead, and seemingly much interested in
their proceedings, startled the party with this inquiry: Who, who
cooks, who cooks for y-o-u a-l-l?—At least, *so they understood him.*"

This call, along with the wild turkey and the mourning dove, was
one that Audubon would later enjoy imitating at social gatherings in
England when he was asked to perform examples of American bird
songs for the assembled guests. I've seen Michael startle and amaze
fellow Americans when he lets loose with *his* sterling rendition of the
barred owl in full voice.

Visually, the barred owl is, to me, the most elegant of its tribe.
Seen from the front, it wears a brown and white muffler slung loosely
across its throat, and below the muffler a loose gown of the same
brown and white pattern. Years ago, when I first heard the barred
owl's name, I thought—as many people do—that it was a Bard Owl:
a singer, a poet, a strolling musician. However, it's the alternating
brown and white bars of the plumage that gives the owl its name.

The owls are enjoying these moonlit nights in West Feliciana

Parish. One lives nearby in the marshy woods next to Audubon Lake, and its call is being answered—I am *sure* it is an answer—by a rooster somewhere to the west of it. Why shouldn't he answer? The rooster may be territorializing too. "This is my barnyard and these are my hens."

But I prefer to think of it as a conversation between the owl and the rooster. In the pioneer days, wagon-train emigrants remarked on the astonishing behavior of foot-sore, weary oxen who chanced to get in amongst buffalo at night, and they would thunder off across the plains, galvanized by the freedom and the excitement of the herd, as wild as the wildest. I think of the rooster reacting in the same spirit, calling out at night in reply to the owls, the domesticated creature talking to the untamed creature, an atavistic cry in the moonlight.

"Who-cooks-for-*you?*"

"Cock-a-doodle-*doo!*"

MH   The Audubon Pilgrimage lasts three days, Friday through Sunday, and the morning programs are full of parades and ceremonies. On Saturday, March 13, we join the gathering crowd at Courthouse Square, the center of these activities. The morning is sunny, to the relief of the Pilgrimage Committee; the past few days were cold and damp, and yesterday's attendance was poor. Already Mary and I *care* that the pilgrimage goes well. That's one of the nice things about a small town—ours or theirs; browse around a few days with a pleasant purpose and you make some friends and know some faces and begin to recognize local names, family connections, and topics that matter.

The morning here at Courthouse Square has another familiar quality: the sense of anticipation, excitement, good humor, and neighborliness that vibrates in the atmosphere of such events. Everyone has come to cheer.

Today's festivities begin with a parade—people in costumes to represent the region's history; the Washington Artillery Saluting Battery of the Louisiana National Guard with three field cannons; the St. Francisville High School marching band; and the U.S. Navy Steel Band, riding on a flatbed trailer.

In the normal fits and starts the parade winds along a short route through town, then back to the square where it began; it lasts only about an hour. Some of the spectators—hostesses for various houses on the tour—are dressed in antebellum costumes (hoop skirts and pantalets). The National Guardsmen have come with fistfuls of colored coins from the recent New Orleans Mardi Gras; they fling these from the trucks, and the children of St. Francisville dive for the coins, perilously close to the wheels.

The three cannons are now being set up in a lot across the street from the bank, which is one of the town's handsomest buildings—two stories, flat-roofed, with great arched windows on both floors; in each of the upper windows, the arches are filled by two large sheets of plate glass, top and bottom.

The U.S. Navy Steel Band, in red-white-and-blue uniforms, goes on playing as the cannons are placed—"Matilda," "Mary Anne," "Blowin' in the Wind." The St. Francisville High School players drift and collect on the sidewalk alongside the flatbed trailer, listening, watching, admiring; the steel-drummers are very good, very professional. There is to be a flag pageant now, and a representative of the historical society will present a new official flag for St. Francisville and West Feliciana Parish; she will read a short speech, and then we shall have a twenty-one-gun salute.

The audience has its back to the cannons, and when the first volley is fired, one lady in the crowd—who is holding a paper cup of hot coffee—startles, screams, tosses the cup into the air; coffee splashes on her neighbors. But even when expected, the guns *are* awfully loud. At the third or fourth volley, out of the corner of my eye I see a wavering reflection: the salutes are shaking the glass in the tall arched windows of the bank's upper story.

WHAM! The glass quivers. WHAM! "Those windows are going to *break*," I say to Mary. WHAM! They shake again. WHAM! A crack appears in one window. WHAM! A piece of glass pops from the pane and tinkles on the pavement. WHAM! Mary turns and looks back at the dais, to study the faces of the dignitaries; all are staring in alarm at the windows. WHAM! Another splash of glass on the pavement. I have begun late, but I am counting volleys, and the Washington Artillery Saluting Battery of the Louisiana National Guard is only halfway home.

WHAM! More glass falls, new cracks show in the thin panes. WHAM!

An entire pane hops from three sides of its sash and teeters, waves, trembles out into space over the sidewalk. WHAM! Why is no one stopping the artillery? WHAM! I suppose for the same reason I don't shout *Stop* myself. WHAM! But *someone* must be in charge. Can't he see what's happening? WHAM! The loose pane of glass continues to sway. WHAM! Glass is still breaking out, in less dramatic fashion, from the other windows. Think what this is going to cost. WHAM! The long arms of the law—of the St. Francisville sheriff, to be precise—appear in the about-to-fall window and—WHAM!—gather it to safety. WHAM! Someone has already cordoned off the sidewalk under the windows. WHAM! Silence. The sharp smell of burnt gunpowder drifts over the crowd. The salute is over.

(We learned later that the possibility of damage to windows had been discussed, and a trial had been made in advance—but with charges considerably lighter than those used in the ceremony. Naturally.)

After lunch in the parish house of Grace Episcopal Church, we take the house tour and pause to look at some plant or other at a front yard, and a young woman in hoopskirts invites us to see the garden. With her little daughter—also in costume—tagging along and Mary and our guide talking about flowers, we go around back. The shady garden and its gazebo overlook a deep glade, thick with vines and live oaks and willows and garlands of lavender-gray wisteria in bloom.

Prothonotary warblers nest in the gazebo, says our guide. *Where?* cries yours truly, who has never seen a prothonotary warbler. Oh, they'll nest in *anything,* she says. She points to the containers hung in the gazebo—old enamel coffee pots and a large glass jar on its side; and hollow gourds have been put out for them on the other side of the house. All empty, of course, now; the season's a bit early yet.

This is not what you'd call the classic nesting territory of the prothonotary warbler. Tree-holes near water are said to be preferred. And it's disconcerting to learn that a bird I've waited many years to find in the northeast (it seldom wanders closer to New England than southern Jersey and western New York) is so ridiculously easy to come by here and is as vulgar and tame in its domestic habits as a house sparrow.

Back at the West Feliciana Historical Society, our new friend
Mary Ellen Young rubs a little salt in the wound. She's seen prothonotary warblers try to build a nest in the pocket of a pair of her husband's khaki pants hanging on the clothesline. Another year, she had
to chase one out of the house, where it appeared to be prospecting
for a home.

Well, for all the good its plenitude and tameness has done me, it
might as well be rare and shy. Our traveling companion JJA counsels
patience: "I have observed their arrival in Louisiana to take place,
according to the state of the weather, from the middle of March to
the first of April." George H. Lowery, Jr., in his *Louisiana Birds* says
the warbler arrives in small numbers the first week of March. Today
is March 13. Any day now . . .

March 19. What a brilliant orange-yellow head! Saw my first prothonotary at the edge of Audubon Lake, early this morning, after
hearing it sing. And what an elegant texture too. The bird looks as
if it might have arrived *poured,* like cream. Golden head, the gold
gracefully shading into the pewter wings and tail; not a wingbar or
any sharp, contrasting mark anywhere, except the bright black eyes
in the bright yellow face. No painter I know of has ever done the bird
justice, and that includes JJA.

MD   Sweet olive blooms in gardens throughout West Feliciana,
as it did in Natchez, drenchingly fragrant. "Our sweet olive," says
Mary Ellen Young. "When you walk out in the morning, there it is
to greet you." She takes an unabashedly personal view of birds and
flowers, as I tend to do. I recognize the relationship. "Our trillies,"
she says, speaking of the toadshade trillium. "Our golden warblers,"
when she speaks of the prothonotaries. But when it comes to robins,
ah, that is another matter. "They are *your* robins," she explains to
me, because their homeland is in the north where they nest and raise
their broods. Here, they are merely winter visitors, feasting on the
red berries of pyracanthus and holly, and here it's not the first robin
that counts, but the last. "That means good weather is on the way,"
says Mary Ellen. "We're delighted to see them go."

To think of all the songs, the prose, and the poetry—from Long-
fellow, Thoreau, Lowell, Emily Dickinson, Holmes, Burroughs, et al.

—that eulogize the robin as the herald of spring ("When the red-red-robin comes bob-bob-bobbin' along") and not a word of it means anything at this end of the continent.

Today we went in search of a waterfall, an Audubon landmark we had known nothing about until now. Our lead came from an article in the historical society's files—"Audubon in West Feliciana," written in 1912 by a local resident, Miss Sarah Turnbull Stirling, who, like Miss Susan Starling Towles in Henderson, had gathered stories about the Audubons. Miss Stirling included the memoir of a sentimental journey John Woodhouse Audubon made to West Feliciana some twenty years after the family left. Victor, it must be remembered, was here only briefly before going north to Shippingport to his mercantile apprenticeship, so this was John's terrain, his home from the age of eleven to sixteen.

"How he rushed around to places of 'Auld lang syne,' remembering everything." He visited the plantations where he and his mother had lived and he met with childhood friends. "He quite disdained a horse and walked to all the old haunts. . . . he did not think there were as many birds as when he was a boy, and would exclaim again and again at the 'beauty' of the Magnolia Grandiflora and said it was the most beautiful tree in the world. . . . His face would beam with delight as he related the sports of his boyhood, and he would exclaim 'West Feliciana is one of the brightest spots on earth to me.'" He found his way to the place where his father had watched "the habits of the beaver" and took particular note of the red clay from which his father had made a "fine paint." He went to "Bayou Sara Creek," where he and his father used to bathe and fish, then on to the Roberts' property where there was a waterfall known as the "silver bath"—"a favorite resort for the men and boys of that day."

The Roberts' property, upcountry in the hills, is still in the same family, and old Frank Roberts now lives there alone. He has no phone. We'd have to drive out and hope that he'd be around. Mary Ellen Young got directions from her son, who's in real estate and knows every corner of the parish. North of town, a dirt road that winds to the top of the ridge. To the right, a negro cabin (a herd of burly hogs rooting among the trees), and just beyond, to the left, an old dogtrot farmhouse set back on a low rise, a few gray weatherworn outbuildings to the side.

There were no signs of life about the place, so we walked up past the orderly vegetable garden to the house where a tiger tomcat slept on the porch, and I, as the lady of a party arriving unannounced at the home of an old man who wasn't expecting visitors, waited on the steps where I was joined by the cat, who smoothed his whiskers and arched his flanks against the timbers that supported the porch roof. Mike knocked and called Hello and finally Frank Roberts came to the door in immaculate khaki pants and khaki shirt and rubber boots, and he said he'd been taking a nap, that's what took him so long. He was as welcoming to strangers as his cat, who turned out to have been a stray and Frank Roberts had taken him in because there was no reason not to.

The Roberts have lived here close to two hundred years, he told us. His great-great-grandfather came down from Georgia with a wagon and mules. No, he hadn't heard of John James Audubon, but whatever our reasons for wanting to see the waterfall, he'd be pleased to show us the way. And where had we come from, where was our home? He was unable to identify the word Connecticut, though we repeated it several times, nor did he understand New England, only England, and concluded that we'd come from abroad, and he wanted to know about the English climate and how had we brought our car across the ocean. So Mike spread the road atlas on the hood, and showed Frank Roberts New England and Connecticut, up north.

There were several big fire-ant hills near the vegetable garden, and Mr. Roberts said he scalded them out with boiling water and he'd known them to eat baby chicks and pick a new-born calf clean to the bone. His corn, okra, and cabbages had just sprouted and the deer would be coming in soon to eat the shoots. He'd have to put up a scare-pants pretty quick.

Across the road, a path ran along the spine of a steep ridge, and Frank Roberts led the way, bounding ahead through his woods, light-footed as a boy. He pointed out yaupon, cypress, and huckleberry as we passed. "Huckleberries make the best pie there is." Then he pointed below through the trees, and we caught sight of a brook and heard the sound of splashing water. It was a fine place in summer, he said, to take a bath and cool off. "Once you're in it, you can't leave."

Michael and I scrabbled down into the gorge and followed the narrow stony stream bed to the falls. The water, cold and clear, sluiced through a cut in the rocks and fell to a shallow, sandy-bottomed pool twenty feet below. Magnolia trees grow on the opposite bank, one bough spreading outward over the pool, and when they come into bloom in late spring, what a sight that must be. Waterfalls are mesmerizing. We lingered, looking up at the frothing column of water that sprang away from the ridge and leaped into the catch basin at our feet, both of us smitten by the possibility of a ghostly image of John James Audubon and his young son naked in the "silver bath."

We took a wide loop back to town through the Sleepy Hollow Woods. Another ridge-top dirt road, deep wild gullies to the side. Live oaks and sycamores hung with Spanish moss. Silverbells, dogwood, red buckeye. Jessamine, cross-vine, and wild wisteria topping the trees. Vines to the tenth power.

MH JJA often had a terrible time identifying and describing bird songs. Here in West Feliciana Parish, where he spent so much time observing and listening and watching, I can hear the ruby-crowned kinglets all over the place; it's a sweet, perky, insistent song, quite loud for a character only about as long as my thumb. Audubon says he didn't hear one sing until he got to Labrador in the summer of 1833. That can't be right. He must have heard the song many times here, from wintering and migrating kinglets; however, it mixes in nicely with other common songs—of the tufted titmouse and Carolina wren and yellowthroat—and he often failed to link singer to music. Good binoculars are useful for making such connections, and of course he lacked binoculars. But he could frequently get close to singing birds. If *I* can, he could. On the other hand, chance plays a huge role in the study of birds. So he must simply have missed, for many years, an ordinary experience—an eye-level encounter with a singing ruby-crowned kinglet; the same sort of missed connection has happened to me with various bird species, for no good reason and for years at a stretch.

Frank Roberts on his porch. *MH*

The Silver Bath. *MH*

Time marches on, all right. Just downstream of Bayou Sara and St. Francisville, Gulf States Utilities is building a nuclear power plant —with fearful urgency. There has been some opposition to the project in the parish, we understand, but it's not enough so far to bring things to a halt. Tonight, having seen bright lights in that neighborhood from the ferry landing, and later hearing the roar of distant engines as we finished supper, we put two and two together and went to investigate. It turns out the contractor is working nights to get the nuke built. From a bridge at what must be the fringe of the site, we watched monstrous earthmoving equipment grinding across freshly flattened and graded earth, in the glare of floodlights.

MD You know, Audubon was startlingly prescient on the subject of *Progress*. As we watched the armies of the night levelling and rearranging the West Feliciana landscape, I thought of an impassioned outcry he wrote against mankind's "increasing ravages on Nature." He predicted that neither the stream, the swamp, the river, nor the mountain "will be seen in a century hence as I see them now." Rivers would be turned from their courses, the hills reduced to swamp level, and the swamp itself "become covered with a fortress of a thousand guns." There would be no more fish, he wrote; no more deer; the magnolia would almost vanish from Louisiana forests; millions of birds be driven away or destroyed by man, and "the eagle scarce ever alight."

MH March 21. A calm and sunny day, which we spent housekeeping. I have not yet seen a second prothonotary. My first of two days ago must have been much in the van; either that, or I am *still* missing the bird. Robins, yellow-rumped warblers, dark-eyed juncoes remain in Louisiana today; along the east coast and in the Appalachians all have begun to move by now, and surely each morning here I must be seeing twenty-four-hour segments of a stream flowing north, not just winter residents. Well, at least, having come all this way myself, I have a much better feel for the great distances these little migrants have to cover in a short time each spring.

My uncertainty about birds is a metaphor for our experience in West Feliciana Parish. Two weeks may be long enough to absorb the flavor of a strange community and its history, but as to the specifics, that is a different matter. Here is a basic problem for historian, biographer, reporter. Something embarrassingly obvious and essential may be missed.

That was a basic problem for Audubon, too, most of his life; covering so much ground and so much unfamiliar scientific territory, he was usually short on time. He sometimes discovered rarities and didn't come across ordinary things and so drew conclusions about birds based on evidence that later turned out to have been insufficient.

Altogether, the historian who reaches for the essence of people risks clutching chimeras. Each generation has its peculiar attitudes, and those who write about a person or an era from the perspective of a different generation have to look through a double prism, at least —a dizzying effort. Biography written even so short a time ago as 1900 bears little relation to "modern" biography at its best: critical, psychological, scholarly, documented, indexed. So, when looking for specific information, one hates to have to depend on formal biographies written in the middle of the last century, for instance; much of it is pure puffery, childlike hero-worship. Then, when history is reduced to local common denominators—as when an illustrious personage becomes a key part of a community's self-image—it takes on a hearsay, gossipy quality that may eventually lead it miles away from the truth. On top of everything, the biographer brings personal blind spots to the task, or hasn't read enough, or has taken inaccurate notes, or too frequently goes by intuition instead of research and cross-checking. It's as easy as spilling the salt. Example: just this week we found a locally written biography of Audubon in which the lady author speaks of JJA's use of *thee* and *thou* when he wrote to Lucy, and she ascribes it to his French background—a leap of faith, unprovable. Audubon's most important English teacher was his Quaker wife, who probably thee and thou'd him plenty. I have this cautionary tale very much on my mind as we leave St. Francisville. I've spent the last few days blundering around looking for JJA in the litter of facts and suppositions we've collected. Mary seems much more sure than I am of how they add up—what sort of a man he was. For me he fades in and out all along our route.

NEW ORLEANS

PASSIM

MH   New Orleans was a city Audubon knew well. But he disliked cities, and this place was no exception: "New Orleans, to a man who does not trade in dollars or any other such stuff," he once declared, "is a miserable spot." He came here to live for brief periods only to scratch for said dollars and to paint new birds and to gain a reputation. He was nearly penniless when he arrived in the winter of 1820–21. He remarked that in earlier years (when he had come here on business) he could at least afford to go to the theatre. Now he couldn't even spend a dollar to attend the "Quartroon Ball"—a high point of the local social season, coming-out party for the mulatto mistresses-to-be of New Orleans' white gentlemen. He stood outside for a while to listen.

Still, New Orleans could entertain even the threadbare stranger. JJA wrote about a Sunday when "The Levee early was Crowded by people of all Sorts as well as Colors, the Market very aboundant the Church Bell ringing the Billiard Balls Knocking, the Guns heard all around. What a display this"—he was obviously thinking of Lucy— "for a Steady Quaker of Philadᵃ or Cincinnati." The room that he and Joseph Mason rented for $10 a month, on Barracks Street near the corner of Royal in the oldest part of the city, was "between Two Shops of Grocers and divided from them and our Yellow Landlady by Mere Board Partitions, receiving at once all the new Matter that issues from the thundering Mouths of all these groupes."

They lived near the French Market—"the Dirtiest place in all the Cities of the United States," said JJA—which was kept regularly sup-

The Levee at New Orleans, from an 1828 drawing by Captain Basil Hall, R.N., engraved by W. H. Lizars.

plied with freshly shot birds. Sometimes he could find a good specimen there to draw, although most of the birds hung for sale were either too damaged by shot to be useful to him or had been partly plucked. Even when he came across something in good condition the experience could be frustrating. He found "Grey Snipes" (probably willets, a species he had only just met) but "the Stupid Ass who sold me one Knew Nothing, Not even where *he* had Killed them." Naturally, he would rather have done all his hunting himself, but he couldn't do that and still earn a living and make a name for himself where it counted—in the city—and perhaps convince the federal government to hire him as naturalist for an exploring-surveying expedition. So, besides prowling in the French Market, he employed other men to do his hunting for him, around the rivers and swamps and beaches and bays of southern Louisiana.

Meanwhile, once he was established in New Orleans, he didn't do badly as an itinerant maker of black-chalk portraits or as a drawing teacher. In fact, his success—though mild and short-lived—sometimes surprised him. On one occasion, going to the studio of the painter John Vanderlyn to get a letter of recommendation, he had to show his work to prove he was worthy. This took place in front of a second visitor, a stranger, and when Audubon left, with letter in hand, he was feeling humiliated by what he'd been through. But the other visitor followed him from the studio and stopped him on the street to compliment him on his drawings and ask the price of a portrait. "I thought how Strange it was," wrote JJA, "that a poor Devil Like me Could steal the Custom of the Great Vanderlein—but fortune if not *blind* certainly Most have his Lunatic Moments."

When he and Mason came back to New Orleans from Oakley and St. Francisville, he rented a furnished room on St. Anne Street, until he found a house on Dauphine Street, anticipating the arrival of Lucy and the children. They joined him a week before Christmas 1821, but the family was together only three months before JJA's prospects once again soured and he and Mason left for Natchez, seeking greener pastures.

So we are here to look for three houses in the *Vieux Carré*, or French quarter of New Orleans, and to browse around the city. Most of this metropolis—all but the Vieux Carré, really—ought by rights to be a full-time swamp, and the entire area frequently flooded. The French quarter was built on the only natural high ground, and everything else is on drained wetland and fill. A lot of it is six feet below

Nouvelle Orleans, circa 1820, by Himely after Ambroise Louis Garneray. *The Historic New Orleans Collection, 533 Royal St.*

sea level. More than twenty huge pumps and two hundred miles of drainage canals are needed to keep the city dry in normal circumstances, never mind floods or hurricanes. And if it weren't for levees along the Mississippi at the south and flood-diversion canals and seawalls on Lake Pontchartrain to the north, the city would often be drowned: one can look down into the streets from ships passing on the river at flood, and hurricanes sweep high tides from the Gulf across thirty miles of marsh, into the houses of the suburbs. Altogether an interesting prospect to live with. It must be largely responsible for the no-tomorrow character and spirit of the city. The bayous through the vast surrounding marshes are lined with trash. Canals and ponds and bayous and marshes have been used as dumps; egrets and herons stalk among the drifts of garbage, just passing through, like the humans here. At the heart of the city (the Vieux Carré, the city that Audubon knew, beautiful old French and Spanish brick town houses cramped gently together, narrow streets and delicate iron grillwork and green-glowing inner courtyards) there's a carny spirit, a sinister, whores-and-trash-on-the-midway carny spirit, people putting on the dog and the tourists and each other.

MD   To live in the French Quarter means tourists, tourists, tourists. It's geared for tourists, caters to every taste. The Voodoo Museum, the old Absinthe House, St. Louis Cathedral, ice cream parlors, Antoine's, steaming night life, Topless Everything, porn shows, cheap souvenir shops, million-dollar antique shops, the state museum in the Cabildo, where the Spanish government was once housed and where JJA's *The Birds of America* is now displayed.

Doors and shutters are open to saloons and music, one set of shutters open to a pale figure in a bed in a tumbled darkened room. Other windows are shuttered tight and bolted against the light, eyes, prowlers. Crowds overflow from the sidewalks. Tourists, tourists, tourists. Beats and street people, the very young and the very old in rags and tatters. Drunks, dudes, fags, pimps, peddlers, drug heads. A ravaged beauty (patrician features, real jewels on her fingers, scabby veined legs, sneakers cut down into slippers) who elbows angrily (snarling) through sightseers ganged up at the mouth of a saloon to hear Dixieland. In the street, black boys dancing to the music for coins. Across the way, a balcony musician with lounging friends, a

Black-necked stilt by Audubon, painted at New Orleans, May 2, 1821. *Courtesy of The New-York Historical Society, New York City*

loop of Spanish moss hanging from the neck of his banjo. On the next corner, an old black man with a tambourine, his wife singing in a voice like Leadbelly's, the tambourine for rhythm and to catch the coins.

The French Market, where JJA browsed for unfamiliar birds, has been largely remodeled into cafes, boutiques, rest rooms. Tourists, tourists, tourists. Beyond, one small section is still a market. What fruits and vegetables there! Vine-ripened, shining tomatoes, lacquer-green bell peppers, plump lavender garlic buds, striped green melons, flats of red strawberries . . .

MH   No game is exposed for sale, though walking down the long, roofed aisle of the open-air market, sun-dazzle on the street to either side, food-dazzle in the middle, one can imagine the marsh-hares and raccoons and deer, the ducks and snipe and owls and robins, each split, gutted, tied up by a foot. That business ceased not so long ago. West of here in the Garden District, where the khaki-colored trolleys run along a grassy track, and houses of some years and dignity stand surrounded by gardens in the shade of old trees, a widow of an old New Orleans family, her parlor guarded by a Doberman, told us over cocktails that her mother had spoken of game for sale in the French market and of men crying game through the streets of the Garden District, though of course anyone with money and leisure shot his own. Said our hostess, "I cannot think of a man of my father's generation who did not go hunting, and my father used to bring home hogsheads of ducks." But now game is rare in New Orleans. Just recently a friend had brought her a brace of snipe, she said. "It was like being given a string of diamonds."

One of Audubon's three New Orleans homes is gone. The other two, seen only from the outside, are as small and unprepossessing as one would expect for domiciles of an indigent artist. Neither is open to the public.

We went to Audubon Park—"New City Park" when it was created in 1871, but renamed in 1876 by the City Council "in consideration of the distinguished ability of the late John James Audubon as an ornithologist and an artist, his many virtues as an exemplary gentleman and the high honor he reflects upon this his native state."

(More about this "native state" business momentarily.) It's four hundred acres fronting on the river in the southwest corner of the city: golf course, small zoo, aquarium (closed due to vandalism), open-air theater, swimming pool, tennis courts. The only sign of JJA about the park is an heroic bronze statue on a ten-foot granite pedestal—the artist in buckskin, shoulder-length hair, shot-pouch and powder-horn hanging at his side, tablet in one hand, brush in the other, head back, eyes on a presumed bird in one of the surrounding trees. This figure came to stand in the park through the devotion of Mary Fluker Bradford, daughter of a St. Francisville pupil of Lucy Audubon. Mrs. Bradford wrote a brief, chatty biography of JJA in 1900, earned $1000 for it, and donated the proceeds to start the Audubon Monument Fund. Ten years later she had $10,000 and commissioned one of the best sculptors of the day, Edward Virginius Valentine. The statue is now partly hemmed in by chain-link fence and barbed wire while close by are two of the planet's few score remnant whooping cranes, residents in the zoo.

MD   Even before he lived in New Orleans or in West Felician, the Louisiana countryside and its Spanish-French colonial flavor had

Audubon's "little house" on Barracks Street, New Orleans. *MH*

Valentine's statue of Audubon, Audubon Park, New Orleans. *MH*

spoken directly to JJA. It's very likely that the appeal was one of nostalgia, a remembrance of things past. It would be the closest he would ever come to going home again to Santo Domingo (now the Republic of Haiti), where he had been born out of wedlock and where he lived until he was almost six years old. The ingredients in both places were much the same—the climate, the lush terrain, the well-heeled insular plantation life, the tempo of existence, the easy living in a slave-based society. As a bastard child, JJA spent a lifetime hiding his guilty secret behind a smokescreen of prevarications, even to the point of pretending not to know the year in which he had been born: "The precise period of my birth is yet an enigma to me." He may have reasoned that if he could hide the year and the country of his birth, he could hide the facts. He would invent another birthplace, and so, early in his career, he chose the familiar ambiance of Louisiana. That would be his native land from then on.

Whatever Audubon's memories of his father's household and the plantation life on Santo Domingo, he left only hints of his childhood impressions: the dark foliage of orange trees overhead, the golden fruit, the sweet blossoms "upon which fed that airy Silph the Hum Bird," the colors of the sky and the land—azure blue and emerald green. Other than such veiled poetic recollections, he admitted nothing to the world at large, except in the case of legal documents such as landing papers and his naturalization papers, in which he swore to being born at Aux Cayes on the island of Santo Domingo.

Louisiana, as JJA's birthplace, made its first formal appearance in an autobiography he wrote for his sons in 1820 when he was thirty-five years old. He devised an elaborate myth in which he had his father, on a visit to Louisiana, meeting and marrying a lady of Spanish extraction, "as beautiful as she was wealthy," and after his birth, he then had his parents moving to his father's Santo Domingo plantation, where the story ended with his mother's murder during a Negro insurrection. It was a tale with all the elements of high romance: beauty, wealth, and tragedy on a tropical island. In conversations with Martha Pope in St. Francisville, he described the mythical house in which he had been born: "It was on the banks of the Mississippi river, in lower Louisiana, and was surrounded by orange trees." Lucy Audubon, in the biography she wrote after his death, perpetuated the myth: "The naturalist was born on his father's plantation near New Orleans . . . and his earliest recollections were associated with lying among the flowers of that fertile land, sheltered by orange trees, and watching the movements of the mockingbird, the king of song, dear to him in after life from many associations." (Note that the Hum Bird recalled by JJA had been transformed into a mockingbird, one of the most beloved creatures in Louisiana lore.) From there, JJA's myth took wing, and the exact spot was eventually determined. Audubon was said to have been born on the shore of Lake Pontchartrain in the plantation house belonging to Bernard de Marigny, scion of a wealthy New Orleans family, and photos of the very house were printed in books and magazines.

The true story of Audubon's birth is a plain and pathetic one. It begins with his father as a seagoing rover. Captain Jean Audubon joined the French merchant marine as a cabin boy and went on to a swashbuckling career—sea battles against the English navy, imprisonment twice by the English, service with the French fleet at the battle of Yorktown, and a successful trade in sugar, coffee, and slaves as he sailed the mercantile routes between Santo Domingo, the United States, and France. Captain Audubon was married to a wealthy widow of surprising equanimity. She accepted his long absences from their household in Nantes and had no quarrel with her husband's second home in Santo Domingo, where Captain Audubon kept successive mistresses in residence over the years and sired possibly as many as five offspring.

Audubon's mother was neither Spanish nor wealthy, nor did she die in an insurrection. She was French, her name was Jeanne Rabin, and she died at Captain Audubon's plantation of an undisclosed illness, aged 27, about six months after John James was born. Further facts on Mlle. Rabin are uncertain. According to Francis Hobart Herrick, author of *Audubon the Naturalist* (D. Appleton-Century Company; first edition, 1918; revised edition, 1938), Mlle. Rabin's parents had been French colonials in Santo Domingo, and family descendants there still spoke of JJA as a relative. According to Alice Ford, author of *John James Audubon* (University of Oklahoma Press, 1964), Mlle. Rabin had come to Santo Domingo from France as a chamber maid for a colonial family and then had moved into Captain Audubon's menage.

Shortly before World War I, a bill from a Santo Domingo physi-

Supposed birthplace of Audubon. Bernard de Marigny's house at the Fontainbleau plantation, Mandeville, Louisiana. *From Mary Fluker Bradford's* Audubon, *1897*

cian came to light in France among Audubon family papers. The bill had been rendered to Captain Audubon by a Doctor Sanson, of Aux Cayes, for house calls from December 1783 to October 1785. Sanson cared for the entire plantation from master to slaves—giving ipecac, purges, tincture of rhubarb, smallpox vaccinations, and treatments for mange-mites. Mlle. Rabin appears as a chronic patient well before her pregnancy and JJA's birth. She was bled, dosed with Hoffman's mineral water, and treated for erysipelas. Dr. Sanson attended the delivery of her son on April 26, 1785, later treated her for an abscessed breast, and treated her for the next six months before her death with unnamed medicines for unnamed ailments. The truth of Audubon's background and a copy of the doctor's bill were published for the first time in the Herrick biography, and written on a corner of the bill in an unknown hand was this comment: "Tres curieux Mlle. Rabin & son enfant."

Young Audubon was called Jean Rabin, after his mother, and upon her death, her place was then taken by a former mistress of Captain Audubon, who resumed her previous position as the lady of the household. She was of mixed blood, French and Negro, and two years later gave birth to a daughter, Rosa. In 1791, on the brink of the Negro revolution in Santo Domingo, the Captain's two little love children, Jean and Rosa, were whisked to safety in France and into the welcoming arms of the ever-unperturbed Mme. Audubon. Captain Audubon legally claimed the children as his own; he and Mme. Audubon formally adopted them. Jean Rabin then used the name Jean Jacques Audubon, which he anglicized in America to John James Audubon.

It's interesting to note that as a schoolboy JJA had already begun re-identifying himself. He took to using the name LaForest, which he appears to have invented, and Lucy always addressed him by that name, though no one else did so far as is known. Later, fired by his craving for re-identification, he toyed with another fantasy: He was the Lost Dauphin—Louis XVII, son of Louis XVI and Marie Antoinette, rescued from prison and sworn to keep the secret of his royal birth forever after. The fantasy of secret nobility is a fairly common neurotic symptom: Beethoven, one of the greatest neurotics in the annals of Western culture, disavowed his alcoholic father and claimed to be the illegitimate son of the King of Prussia. At any

rate, JJA set the Lost Dauphin story into motion in his cryptic confi-
dences to Lucy, who may have taken him seriously or may have been
only humoring him, but some of his family later chose to believe
the story, several of his biographers flirted with the idea, and it
has not yet been completely put to rest, in spite of the evidence of
twentieth-century research. For a thorough investigation into
the Lost Dauphin myth, I recommend the thirty-six page fore-
word that Francis Herrick wrote for the 1938 edition of *Audubon
the Naturalist.*

*Notes from our campsite, Fontainebleau State Park, Mandeville,
Louisiana:*
    Mandeville is north of New Orleans on the far shore of Lake
Pontchartrain, which we cross on "The Longest Causeway in the
World"—23.87 miles long, out of sight of land in the middle of the
lake and not without its horror stories, such as the dark night when
a barge hit the causeway, knocked out a span, and the next vehicle
to come through, an eighteen-wheeler, barreled off the broken span,
into space, and into a watery grave.
    The park, two miles east of Mandeville, covers 2700 acres—forests
of magnolia, oak, pine, hickory, and sweet gum; marshes where daffo-
dil-yellow pitcher plants are now in bloom; the moss-crusted ruin of
a sugar mill that stands in a grove of live oaks off the long drive
curving down to the lake. We like to think that from all the campgrounds in the New Orleans area we chose this one of our own free
will. But evidently not. Other forces seem to have been in motion—
a ghostly nudge in the ribs, a beckoning whistle from beyond the
grave. Because now that we're here, our tent pitched on the edge of
what had been a flooded meadow during Mardi Gras (heavy rains,
the water rising, campers fleeing in the dark, their possessions abandoned for days, while others of the Mardi Gras diehards and hop-a-
longs, who'd rolled into the bushes for the night, crawled up into the
big trees with their sleeping bags and huddled on the broad
branches), it turns out that the Fontainebleau State Park is the former Bernard de Marigny plantation, where Audubon was once said
to have been born.
    The myth that grew up around Marigny's plantation here was the
doing of Bernard de Marigny himself. He must have told his story to

hundreds of people. We have a direct account of it from the Reverend Gordon Bakewell, Lucy Audubon's nephew, who wrote that Marigny said Audubon's mother had been a guest at his plantation on Lake Pontchartrain and while there, she had given birth to John James. "Marigny was present at the time, and from his own lips," wrote Bakewell, "I have repeatedly heard him assert the above fact. He was ever proud to bear this testimony of his protection given to Audubon's mother, and his ability to bear witness as to the place of Audubon's birth, thus established the fact that he was a Louisianian by birth."

This tale was outright nonsense. Bernard de Marigny and Audubon were the same age, both had been born in 1785, which does not put Marigny in the position of having been able to play the gracious host to anybody's pregnant mother at that particular time. Furthermore, the Fontainebleau estate did not belong to the Marigny family in 1785. Bernard bought it when he was grown.

Bernard Xavier Philippe de Marigny de Mandeville was of French noble blood. He once remarked that the Marigny family had been *marquises* before the Bourbons had ever been heard from. He had a European education and one of the finest private libraries in America, had inherited a fortune from his father, owned large tracts of New Orleans property, served in the Louisiana legislature, and was a gambling, duelling, profligate Creole gentleman of the old southern school. He is credited with introducing America to an exciting new French dice game, then known in Europe as *Hazard,* now known to us as craps. He designed and built a New Orleans suburb, the *Faubourg Marigny,* in which he is said to have installed a bevy of mistresses, each of whom he presented with a lot and a cottage on a street that he called *rue d'Amour.* When his wife complained of his infidelities, Marigny replied: "Madame, I wish to inform you that I possess in the highest degree every vice of a gentleman!"

After buying the property on the far shore of Lake Pontchartrain, he developed it into a sugar plantation, built the sugar mill that now lies in ruins, and then turned his talents to designing and building the town of Mandeville as a fashionable summer resort for the *bon ton* of New Orleans—a lakeside hotel, chic little villas, a church, a marketplace, lots of gambling facilities and lots of good food prepared by chefs imported from Paris. Marigny's taste for high living, however, outstripped his income. He spent his declining years in poverty, in a cottage, cared for by a faithful old Negro woman, and he died, aged eighty-four, from a fall on his own doorstep.

He and Audubon met early in the 1820s when Audubon was living in New Orleans, poor and discouraged, and it is known that Marigny gave JJA financial assistance. What is not known is the extent of communication between the two men. Did JJA confide the story of his Santo Domingo origins? Or did Marigny learn it from another source? Perhaps, for example, from John Davis, gambler and theatrical entrepreneur, who was a close friend of Marigny, his partner in the development of Mandeville, and who also was an emigré from Santo Domingo. There's a coincidence to chew on. Davis could have known the Audubon and Rabin names, known all the old gossip from the Santo Domingo plantation community; it's likely that he too met John James in New Orleans. ("Jean Rabin! Jean Jacques Audubon! So here you are, after all these years . . .")

I've found what I believe to be another link between Marigny and Audubon. In 1821, when JJA was pounding the pavements trying to raise money, he received a surprise commission for a nude drawing of a Mme. André. He made no specific reference to this in his day-to-day journal entries, but eventually wrote a long account of his adventure intended for Lucy's eyes only. "Be careful about participating any part" and "Keep it Snugg." The manuscript showed up by chance only twenty years ago. The story JJA wrote is overdrawn and much of it sounds make-believe to me. A heavily veiled beauty approaches him on the street, commissions the nude drawing, the sittings are arranged with much secrecy, with JJA trembling like a leaf, temples pounding, pulse racing. When the drawing is completed ten days later, she bestows upon JJA one "delightfull Kiss," gives him a "souvenir gun" and permission to kiss her hand in parting. Audubon did not mention Marigny in connection with the mysterious Mme. André, but the lady lived on *rue d'Amour* in the *Faubourg Marigny*. Another coincidence to chew on, and I see Marigny in this adventure, offstage someplace, amiably commissioning the drawing to give JJA a helping hand. And a nude drawing at that, not bird figures. It would have been in character. A witty and sophisticated gesture.

"One of the family Marigny" (presumably Bernard, because his

Bernard de Marigny in his youth. *The Historic New Orleans Collection, 533 Royal St.*

Bernard de Marigny in his old age. *The Historic New Orleans Collection, 533 Royal St.*

father was dead) is supposed to have described Audubon's mother to ten-year-old John W. Audubon as "une dame d'une beauté incompa- rable et avec beaucoup de fierté." If that report is true, it's evident that Bernard de Marigny knew Audubon's secret and took on the part of fellow-conspirator fairly early in their friendship. Yes, I am leaping from speculations to conclusions, but my point is this: There would be no reason for Marigny to step forward and offer a cover-up story unless he knew that Audubon was badly in need of a legitimate mother and a legitimate birthplace. One can only guess at his motive, even so. I suspect it was a matter of good fellowship toward friend Audubon—and a laugh on the world. Audubon's origins were at question as his fame grew. One Boston art critic remarked that Audu- bon was one of those men who had never been born at all, but was erected—like a public monument.

Bernard de Marigny's story caught on. His former plantation at Mandeville became a semi-shrine, and an article about it appeared in *The Auk* in 1901—"A Visit to Audubon's Birthplace," by O. Wid- man. The place was no longer a sugar plantation, Widman wrote, but "a third-rate stock farm . . . no trace of its former splendor. The foundation of the mansion, in which Audubon first saw the light of day, is still there, but the walls have crumbled into a heap of bricks, which fill the cellar. The whole is overgrown with rank vegetation . . . but Nature's grandeur is the same . . . the Mocker sings as cheerfully as it did then, and the Vultures soar as dreamily as of old."

In 1906, F. Claiborne of Louisiana wrote an essay on Audubon that also placed him on the Marigny plantation: "The youth of Audubon must have been deeply impressed with the mystic charm, the soli- tude, the poetic meaning of the forests of Mandeville. . . . There his infant steps became familiar with the woodland path. . . . Among the boy Choctaws of his own age, by whom he was surrounded, he must have learned to start the arrow to its mark, to impel it through the *sarbacane,* or blow-gun, and to derive those elements of woodland skill which made him the peer of trapper or pathfinder."

The Claiborne article quotes a Louisiana poet, Adrien Roquette, who had eulogized Audubon as a brother poet to the Choctaws: "The creole Audubon, the wondrous artist,/Since infancy married to aus- tere solitude/ . . . The free child of the forest, the untutored Ameri- can,/He had only his faithful dog and his hunting knife,/His long carbine with the redoubtable voice,/And his light maple-bark canoe."

In 1918, when Herrick presented the facts of Audubon's background, there were ripples of dismay. A Mandeville author, who did a historical compendium of the town in 1919 under the Indian pseudonym of "Ialeske-Chata," expressed heartsick outrage: "As a Louisianian, 'Ialeske-Chata' would have been immensely happy to find out that John James Audubon, the naturalist, was born in Mandeville, but . . . The death knell is from: 'Herrick, Francis Hobart' . . . Mr. Herrick wrests a most beautiful pearl from the crown of our dear Louisiana . . . Where in God's world is the use to have brought out all this miserable stuff." However, the myth dies hard. Three examples: In 1930, *The National Geographic* printed an article on Louisiana that gave Mandeville as Audubon's birthplace. In 1975, a write-up on Audubon in a Louisiana newspaper did the same. An article in the *New-York Historical Society Quarterly,* April 1946, threw out all evidence from all sources and went out on a limb with the dumfounding statement that his birth and childhood were still a mystery, except for the fact of his adoption by a French seafarer named Audubon, and that the identity of his real father was as yet unknown.

A final footnote: The Reverend Gordon Bakewell, to whom Marigny so often told his Audubon story, was a rector of the Grace Episcopal Church in St. Francisville. Descendants still live there. Among them, his great-great-granddaughter, who is therefore a great-great-grand-niece of Lucy Bakewell Audubon. She has an enchanting oil portrait of Gordon Bakewell as a young boy. The body was painted by John Woodhouse Audubon, but the face was done by John James. He had a gift for painting children's faces, could catch the direct gaze of innocence combined with a look in the eye that expressed the serious business of being mannerly and quiet while sitting for a portrait. (At the age of 89, Gordon Bakewell said of the picture: "It is as fresh in color . . . as if painted only yesterday, but by no means foreshadows the old, delapidated 'critter' who stands before you.") When we visited his great-great-granddaughter in St. Francisville, we asked what she thought about the Lost Dauphin legend. "It was ridiculous," she exclaimed. "No one on *our* side of the family believed it for a moment."

Today in Mandeville, the original section of Marigny's fashionable spa has the fragile air of gentle decay, many overgrown gardens, the pretty old houses buried in thickets of trees, shrubbery, and vines. The Audubon-birthplace myth is generally forgotten here. The young woman on duty in the library had not heard it before. We looked in the phone directory; Audubon's name is not memorialized by any of the local businesses.

We visited on a front verandah one afternoon with a Mandeville maiden lady in her eighties, with twinkling eyes and a quick sense of humor. Marigny's grandson, she said, the last of the family locally, had run a barroom on the lakeshore drive. As for the people in Mandeville who were no longer aware of JJA's mythical birthplace down the road: "Sakes!" she exclaimed. "Some people don't even know yet that Audubon is dead!"

Notes from our campsite:

Raccoon and possum come out of the dense forests at night and into our firelight, stepping over our feet, rummaging into pots and pans, the coons onto the table and into our plates, given half a chance. "Scat!" We stamp, clap, growl, "A-a-a-rgh!" and send them packing. Our immediate neighbors, a young couple visiting from France, have never before laid eyes on raccoon or opossum. A hue and cry rises from their campsite as the bold, bizarre denizens of an alien forest emerge from the darkness and search the luggage.

Dozens of feral cats also live here. They stick to the territory in and around the trash barrels, fighting for food and wailing and crooning in seasonal combat. In the small hours, when the animals have the run of the place, we awake to blood-chilling fights. Coon versus possum? Possum versus feral cat? Feral cat versus coon? Throaty cries, as they tear at each other. Someone wins. The other moves on. We fall back to sleep.

Two Carolina wrens have their hearts set on nesting in the trunk of our car. When it's open, they fly into the dark recesses with beaks full of tiny twigs. We shoo them out. Shut the trunk. They look for an entrance under the car. On a sunny morning, when the sleeping bags were hung out to air, the wrens chose mine (it's the same forest green as the car) and began a nest in a fold, slipping in sideways with their twigs and revealing the pretty brown and white gingham pattern on the undersides of their tail feathers. When I took down the sleeping bags, they flew into the empty space, fluttering, searching, with chirrups of distress.

From the forest at our doorstep, the calls of the pileated wood-peckers—WICKA, WICKA, WICKA—a raucous cry that sounds like rainforest birdsong or monkeys screaming, the sort of cries used for atmosphere in the background of South American or West Indian dance music. The red-bellied woodpeckers speak in quite another voice—a trill with an upward lilt that sounds like the purring trills of a mother cat speaking to her kittens. Both the pileateds and the red-bellies have nest holes in a tall dead pine near our tent, and yesterday a flock of blue jays, always the first to announce bad news, converged on the pine tree, shrieking and squawking and flying at the trunk on bombing runs. The red-bellies joined them, diving at the tree, trilling with agitation. A narrow, dark gray, double S-shaped form was slithering upward, miraculously adhering to the straight up-and-down, bare surface of the tree trunk. A rat snake, I'd guess, a tree climber with a fondness for eggs and chicks. It lost its grip only once, the top third of the snake's body suddenly looping backwards into space. It collected itself, snapped back like a whiplash against the tree trunk, and slithered onward. The dive-bombing continued, though none of the birds got close enough to be within striking distance of the snake's darting tongue. The jays lost interest after a while and flew off to other excitements, leaving the woodpeckers to fend for themselves. (There was no sign of the pileateds during the uproar.) Thirty feet above ground, the snake slid into a nest hole, and one last attacking red-belly hung around, peeking in and jumping back. It too finally lost interest. All was quiet again, the drama done.

TO EUROPE AND RETURN

1826–1829

MH In the spring of 1826, John James Audubon, aged forty-one, sailed from New Orleans to England and to fame. Mary and I will not follow him, except through his letters and journals; we will meet him back east when he returns in 1829.

He didn't know what to expect in England and was extremely uneasy. Little in his American experience could prepare him for the European passion for natural history; there, this was natural history's Golden Age. Science teetered on the brink of Darwinism and evolutionary theory. Any person with pretensions to learning and sophistication took an interest in and knew something about plants or shells or insects or birds or fish or *everything* in nature. JJA arrived in July bearing letters of introduction from influential men to other influential men, and within two weeks the virtually unknown artist of America had been invited for the first of many times to exhibit his paintings and was acclaimed as a genius. By the end of the year he had found an engraver in Edinburgh, William Home Lizars, and the publication of *The Birds of America* was underway. He was taken up by the landed gentry and nobility. Major figures of British art, letters, and science were his friends and admirers. He was admitted to membership in learned societies. He gave drawing lessons to Sir William Jardine and Prideaux John Selby, two of the leading British ornithologists and bird artists. "I came to this Europe," JJA wrote in December, "fearful, humble, dreading all, scarce daring to hold up my head and meet the glance of the learned, and I am praised so high. It is quite unaccountable and I still fear it will not last. These good people

Scenes on shipboard, 1826, from Audubon's journal. *Courtesy of Henry B. Martin*

*at work on the fore castle
Larboard Side*

Drawn on shipboard, 1826. Courtesy of Henry B. Martin

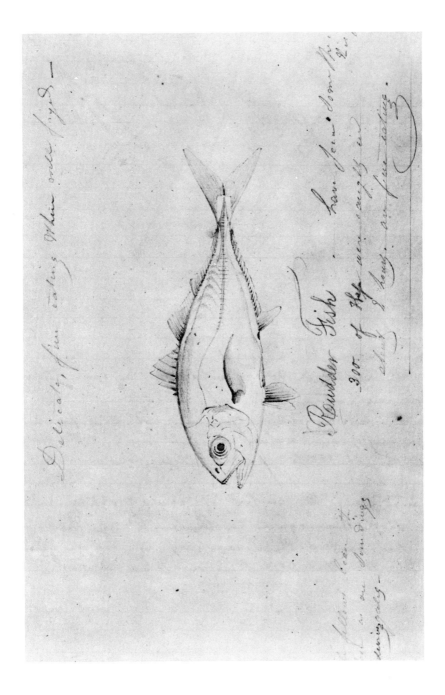

certainly give me more merit than I am entitled to. It is only a mere glance of astonishment or surprise operating on them, because my style is new and different from what has preceded me." He was right about that. But the novelty was not frivolous: it was substantial, and that made a difference.

Consider what he was up to. He wished to publish a complete collection of the known birds of a continent. This collection had to appeal to the best academic ornithologists of Europe or it would never be taken seriously; thus Audubon often presented a species from various angles, in various attitudes and plumages, and always with important characteristics carefully displayed, so that his work could be used as a reliable reference. He also wished to paint the birds unclassically—that is, not as they might look standing in a museum case, dead and stuffed, but as they looked when alive and in action in their environment; he wasn't painting only for science but for an audience whose interests in nature were both inquisitive and romantic. And last, he was going to present all these birds the size of life.

What was then remarkable has become accepted as routine Auduboniana: "He portrayed all the birds life-size." But the decision to do so was a crucial one, and combined with his desire to show the Compleat Bird—plumages, postures, place, and behavior—gave the production an extraordinary character. Suppose he had been content to make drawings and publish engravings in which the birds were *not* life-size. All of them could have been presented in any shape and pose he wished. The great blue heron, for example, which in life may stand more than four feet high, could have appeared in a statuesque, upright stance, regardless of the size of the page. The trumpeter swan, despite its great length, could have been shown in flight, from the side, its slender neck extended. For practical reasons, there had to be some limit on the size of the engraved sheets; no one would buy the work if it was too cumbersome. So the engravings would be printed on a size of paper called Double Elephant, thirty-nine-and-a-half inches by twenty-six-and-a-half inches, and since Audubon was not content to scale the birds down, he had thereby forced on himself certain demanding artistic constraints. Some birds would fit easily in the available space, but others did not, and they had to be posed to stay within the boundaries of the page. Many of the most eye-catch-

ing engravings truly fill the page with strong shapes: birds in arresting, eloquent activity bursting from the margins. I think particularly
of the great blue heron, shown fishing; the trumpeter swan on the
water, reaching back for an insect on the surface; the whooping
crane catching a baby alligator; the great white heron about to swallow a fish. Audubon also achieved the same effect with medium-sized
birds—ducks, for example—by putting a pair of them together on the
page; again, the large sheet was filled to the margins by action and
detail. With the smaller birds he often took advantage of the space
to present groups or families in some interesting situation—mockingbirds mobbing a rattlesnake at a nest, for example; robins feeding
their young, ten hummers at a trumpet vine, a flock of parakeets in
a cockleburr. Or he might isolate within a great expanse of white one
or two birds, perhaps in flight with prey or posed on a beautiful plant.
The combined impact was staggering—the size, the action, the colors, the variety, the details of birds and flowers and insects and
backgrounds, and the artist's delight at his subjects.

To be sure, some critics complained then and some complain now
that those active birds Audubon drew didn't look like that in life; they
were "distorted." Audubon was highly conscious of the limitations of
his art, but he would remark about his birds' postures that birds in
life were far more interesting than mere profiles or faded skins. We
needn't debate the point here, though I intend to in a while. Distorted or not, the end product was tremendously exciting to look at.
It was also very costly to produce and difficult to sell and consequently a risky idea—typically extravagant; some of JJA's friends
tried to talk him out of it before he started publishing, but it was the
keystone of his plan, and had been for years.

The failed merchant and entrepreneur of Kentucky became the
successful promoter and salesman of a remarkably expensive and
uncertain product. He billed it as a work of 400 hand-colored engravings of birds, all life-size, and priced it at £174, or $1000 American; it
was to be finished in fourteen to sixteen years. Success depended on
his getting enough subscribers in advance to float the project, then
on keeping the subscribers confident and satisfied as the work appeared bit by bit, so they didn't renege; the entire structure could
come tumbling down like a house of cards if word got out that it was
losing significant support.

He had to be fast on his feet during the first few years of the venture. He traveled a great deal in England, Scotland, France, meeting people, selling subscriptions, collecting installments of subscriptions, exhibiting, currying favor with persons whose opinions counted. He painted canvases of birds and quadrupeds as gifts and sources of funds and as advertising; he sat for portraits and allowed life-masks to be taken of his face and submitted to examinations of his head by phrenologists. He began to establish himself as a generous source of curiosities, collections, and information from North America.

He had an advantage in all this which he played for all it was worth: he was regarded as "an Original," a singular character. Forty years later, a writer in the London *Athenaeum* recalled when Audubon's "portfolio excited delight in Edinburgh, London, and Paris . . . The man also was not a man to be seen and forgotten, or passed on the pavement without glances of surprise and scrutiny. The tall and somewhat stooping form, the clothes not made by a West-end but by a Far West tailor, the steady, rapid, springing step, the long hair, the aquiline features, and the glowing angry eyes,—the expression of a handsome man conscious of ceasing to be young, and an air and manner which told you that whatever you might be he was John Audubon, will never be forgotten by anyone who knew or saw him."

MD   Audubon's original journals from this period have disappeared or been destroyed, except for a small portion that covers the first seven months of the European adventure—May (at sea) to December 1826. It shows a man markedly changed from the author of the 1820–21 journal: he was more polished, more self-aware, more open and garrulous on paper, more literate; his mastery of English in the few intervening years is astonishing, and everything is laid out in rich, yeasty entries—his gift of perception, his sense of humor, his vulgarity, the "blue devils" of his depressions, the deliriums of success, the pangs of inadequacy. He had turned a corner and was on his way, sometimes cocky and confident, sometimes panicked and in black despair. But whatever the mood, he was full of himself and declared that anyone keeping a journal should write down "all *he sees, all he thinks,* or all—yes, out with it—*all he does.*"

This journal wasn't published until 1967: *The 1826 Journal of John*

James Audubon, transcribed by Alice Ford, University of Oklahoma Press. An earlier, bowdlerized version had appeared in *Audubon and his Journals,* edited by his granddaughter Maria R. Audubon, Charles Scribner's Sons, 1897; this was reprinted in 1967 by Dover Publications, New York City. I have just finished reading the two journals, the books side by side on the picnic table, to compare entries day by day. It has been an eye-opener.

Miss Maria Audubon, the granddaughter who released a few sterilized snippets from JJA's 1820–21 journal, rewrote, deleted, invented whole passages, rearranged facts, and presented John James Audubon the way she wanted him to be. Given the era, one can understand the expurgation of salty remarks and personal comments and revelations, but Maria whittled him down into a namby-pamby near-anemic. Here are four samples. (There are hundreds to draw on.)

JJA on shipboard: " 'A whale! A whale! Run, Mr. Audubon, there's a whale close alongside.' The pen, the book, were abandoned, the mice frightened. I ran up, and lo! there rolled most majestically the wonder of the oceans. It was of immense magnitude. Its dark auburn body fully overgrew the vessel in size. One might have thought it was the God of the Seas beckoning us to the shores of Europe. I saw it and therefore believed its existence." *Maria's version:* "I had a beautiful view of a whale."

JJA on his uneasiness at a dinner party: "I chewed my food as rapidly as if I had stolen it." *Maria's version:* "At dinner . . . I enjoyed the conversation of Lady Douglass much."

JJA after a day of unprecedented acclaim: "Burst my brains, burst my coarse skull." *Maria's version:* "This was a day of much excitement."

JJA after watching a game of marbles played by four unwashed truant boys whose carefree spirits reminded him of his own youth: "I arose after giving them enough to purchase a shilling's worth of marbles." *Maria's version:* "As I gave them some money to buy marbles, I recommended that some of it be spent in soap."

Having thus emasculated Grandfather, and despite the pleadings of Audubon scholars of her day, whom she tantalized with peeks at the original journals and with transcriptions copied into a small black notebook, Maria then destroyed unnumbered papers that she found most telling and distasteful. Presumably she burned them, and I see

Miss Maria on the hearth, her mouth pinched in maidenly alarm as she tossed the offending pages into the flames. From here on, unless other Audubon papers are still under wraps in private collections, there are no more original journals extant, only those editions sifted through Maria's Victorian sensibilities. (Maria, by the way, once paid a visit to Mill Grove when the Wetherill family still lived there. Anne Wetherill Parker, who was a small child at the time, cannot remember any details about Miss Audubon, only a general impression. "What was she like?" I had asked. Mrs. Parker smiled gently. "Very old. Very dour.")

Given the original English journal plus all other Auduboniana we have gleaned, JJA now comes into focus at this moment in his life. Detail builds upon detail.

He knew how to plait willow baskets, how to make Indian moccasins out of snakeskin, and how to weave hair into rings and watch chains and the like. He was an expert carver—roasts, game birds, etc. He played chess. Despite New Year's vows and other promises of abstinence, he was never able to shake off his addiction to snuff. He was a member of the Ancient and Honorable Fraternity of Free Masons. When agitated he had a habit of pacing up and down, snapping his fingers. He had "some acquaintance with legerdermain," was ambidextrous, and one of his parlor tricks was to write with his left hand. One of his common expressions was *Nous verrons*—"We shall see"—delivered as a philosophical shrug. Sometimes people didn't get his name straight and would identify him, for example, as Mr. Ambro or Mr. Anderson. Upon occasions when it was not appropriate to carry a gun, he often carried a sword cane. He disliked grinding his own colors: "It makes me hot and fretful, and, I am convinced, has a bad effect on the mind of any artist."

He was familiar with the work of the masters, and his comments include mention of Raphael, Titian, Correggio, Van Dyke, David, Hogarth. He was well read, not only in natural history but also in poetry, essays, and novels. He spoke of Byron, Milton, Dryden, Cowper, Samuel Johnson, Voltaire, Ben Franklin, Sir Walter Scott, Smollet, Cervantes' *Don Quixote,* Dante's *Inferno,* Sterne's *Tristram Shandy,* St. Pierre's *Paul and Virginia,* and Goldsmith's *The Vicar of Wakefield.* That last was evidently the source of his use of "fudge" as a mild expletive, a choice that puzzled us at first; it's so unFrench and nonAmerican. "Fudge" turns out to be a byword with Mr. Burchell, a leading character in *The Vicar of Wakefield,* and since JJA mentions Mr. Burchell by name in a literary allusion, the connection seems fairly certain.

He admired good preaching. He loved the theatre ("I often find myself when there laughing or crying like a child") and spoke of performances by traveling players in Kentucky as well as the best companies in London and Paris. His journals name (among others) Molière's *Tartuffe,* Goldsmith's *She Stoops to Conquer,* John Gay's *The Beggar's Opera,* Sheridan's *The Critic,* Rossini's *Semiramis,* and *Punch & Judy.* He knew his Shakespeare; when in London, for example, he went to Covent Garden to see *Othello,* starring Edmund Kean and Charles Kemble, and found the production "terrifyingly well performed."

He was a showman and a dramatist himself. He set forth to meet the world in the persona of "An American Woodsman." Sometimes he gave that as his occupation when he signed a hotel register, rather than signing himself as an artist or naturalist. Just as Ben Franklin had dressed for the role of an unadorned American Quaker and had appeared at the French court in homespun, carrying a stout wooden staff in lieu of a walking stick, JJA dressed for his role as the simple and unaffected woodsman—frontier clothes, wolfskin coat, hair long to his shoulders. He wrote to Lucy that his "beautifully long and curly hair" did as much for him as his talent for painting.

His hair, his hair, his hair! He was extravagantly vain and often described his own good looks. His "erect stature." His "muscles of steel." His "handsome figure . . . aquiline nose and fine set of teeth." But his hair—"fine texture and luxuriant, divided and passing down behind each ear as far as the shoulders"—was the reigning vanity in his life. He described himself at work, "my neck uncovered as usual, my sleeves up to my shoulders, my hair all flowing." He wrote of hurrying down a street, his locks "flowing freely" from under his hat, "and every *lady* that I met looked at them and then at me." At an exhibition of his paintings: "the eyes of the ladies were again, I perceived, searching the lines of my face and the undulations of my locks." In a chance encounter with a pretty maid in a public garden, she "praised my curled locks, and called me The Handsome Stran-

Self-portrait, September 1826. Audubon and His Journals, *1897*

ger." When friends in England persuaded him to cut his hair to a fashionable length in 1827, he entered a black-bordered notice of mourning in his journal and compared himself to the victims of the French Revolution, whose hair was shorn before they were taken to the guillotine.

He often drank a whiskey and water with his breakfast and another at bedtime—his grog, as he called it. At the end of the day he sometimes drank too much grog, or wine or porter or whatever was going around the table, and wrote turbulent, wildly scrawled, riotously punctuated accounts of anything that came into his head—lots of Elizabethan humor with an emphasis on farts, and heavy-footed allusions to the pleasures of "horizontal patterns" (his phrase). Needless to say, such passages were excised by Maria, along with almost every reference to the bottle and the glass.

He jumped from one side of the ledger to the other, from the roughneck frontiersman to the sensitive, poetic, and breathless artist-naturalist; from the seeker of forest solitudes to the drawingroom charmer; from the bawdy jokester to the prim, affrighted Puritan (when accosted, for example, by prostitutes in English streets); from the jailhouse visitor who deplored the cruel conditions of prison life, to the anti-Irish reactionary who harangued against the Irish peasants, calling them blackguards, drunks, and starving beggars, whose emigration to America would be "the *upsetting* of our country unless we dispose of them through the medium of sulphur or of good ropes"; from the lover of freedom who empathized with the American Indians' loss of their land and way of life, to the sometime slaveholder who apparently accepted the bondage of the Negro as part of the God-given order of things. (The Audubons owned slaves during their palmy days in Kentucky, and he spoke casually of buying and selling slaves. Lucy, as the lady schoolteacher in residence in West Feliciana —English Quaker or not—acquired three new slaves that we know of, Cecilia and her two sons Ruben and Lewis, who were eventually handed on to friends in New Orleans when she left Louisiana.)

Not only did JJA weave a tangled web of false stories about his birth, he also had a predilection for telling white lies. Spurious claims to having studied art under Jacques Louis David, court painter to Louis XVI and Napoleon. A capricious claim to being English—"Hi em en Henglishmen"—made to an incredulous fellow Frenchman whom he met on the road in the Alleghenies. The curious claim of being older than he was, especially in later life, when he would add years to his age. And the question of his height. In a passport issued to JJA in 1830, his height was given as five-eight-and-a-half. He himself said he was five-ten-and-a-half. So did Lucy. But he had also written that he and his father were of the same height, "say about five feet ten inches," which in any case was a generous description of Captain Audubon, who had been measured by the French Navy as five-five. (A suit of JJA's deerskins—trousers and a shirt—are in the ornithology department of the American Museum of Natural History in New York City, and if they were taken out of the glass case and tried on by men of different sizes, perhaps the question could be resolved.) JJA also promoted his father to the rank of Admiral, though the senior Audubon had been retired from the French navy as a *Lieutenant de Vaisseau,* equivalent to our Lieutenant Commander. (His title of "Captain" was the customary one for a man who commanded trading ships.)

JJA was an implacable neurotic. Moody, strenuously insecure, with an insatiable craving for approval; feelings easily hurt, quick to imagine slights when no offense was intended, and a cherisher of old wounds never forgotten. When ill at ease he was often afflicted with drenching sweats and tongue-tied stiffness, or would retreat into a haughty, angry silence.

As a friend he was wholehearted, sentimental, and affectionate. In return, he needed your unstinting approval and attention. He was one of those people who expects an immediate answer to a letter; if you did not respond instantly, the sincerity of your friendship was in doubt. And he was an indefatigable correspondent. To think what he would have done with the telephone! Monumental long-distance bills—JJA burning up the wires, calls in every direction at any time of the day or night, to recite his woes or his triumphs.

He adored children. There was instant rapport, epitomized for me by a lovely line written about his first visit to the household of a new friend: upon walking in the door, JJA found "some little children, clean and pretty enough to be kissed, so I kissed them." Children were always in his arms, in his lap, tagging at his heels. In England he gave money to little beggar girls selling nosegays and to a boy doing tumbling tricks alongside a moving stagecoach. To another child begging barefoot in the streets of Edinburgh the week before Christmas he gave a bundle of clothing and five shillings. (Strangely enough, these acts of charity were deleted by Maria. Perhaps she didn't like children.)

He was also drawn to pretty women in general and young girls in particular. The unexpurgated English journal fairly sobs aloud. He is electrified by the rustling of a silk gown, by hair the color of sunset, by playful curls, eyes of placid blue, dark eyes seen through a veil, dark eyelashes, brilliant eyes, by the rosy hue of English girls, their "well-shaped forms." There are intense friendships with the daughters of households in which he is a guest—exciting but safe; they are well-chaperoned. He is the delightful and very interested giver of drawing lessons and kisses, the flattering, attentive companion for country strolls and carriage rides. In his journal he writes about these beautiful daughters—the one who touched the keys of her piano and her hands reached his ear and his heart; another for whom he picked a rose that "died on her bosom"; others who inspired "young night thoughts." The contretemps in St. Francisville over Mrs. Pirrie's daughter, the fair Eliza, becomes very clear. He thrived on ambiguous flirtations with this "female angel" and the next, on the exchanges of letters and little gifts, on the adoring sonnet written to him by so-and-so's smitten daughter.

Robert Buchanan, who compiled *The Life and Adventures of John James Audubon,* which was published in England in 1868, commented astutely on JJA: "He was more like a child at the mother's knee, than a husband at the hearth—so free was the prattle, so thorough the confidence." That pre-Freudian analysis caused a stir within the family, but Buchanan was on the mark. JJA sent his English journal to Lucy in installments. His romantic encounters in dewy gardens and country drawingrooms were held up for her to see —with the most innocent countenance and tone of voice. And whatever did Lucy make of JJA's prattle about his oh-so-brotherly attempts to win kisses from her youngest sister, Ann? Ann and her husband, Alexander Gordon, lived in Liverpool, and JJA took to popping by for visits. Her refusals to share kisses with her brother-in-law ring out through page after page of his journal, and it begins to sound like Restoration comedy: a chase around the embroidery

Lucy's sister, Ann Bakewell Gordon.

frame, teacups rattling, a lapdog barking. One of JJA's entries is a lulu: "Ten o'clock: pears and plums and wine have been tasted, but none of the nectar that flows on thy sweet sister's lips."

Poor Lucy. She had been telling him for years that the world was not indulgent, and now the world was being indulgent as the very devil. While she plodded along in St. Francisville at her schoolmarm duties, not only was he being wined, dined, lionized, and honored beyond either of their wildest dreams but he was also in high gear playing the cat among the pigeons. Yet he suffered loneliness and homesickness away from her. He missed Lucy fiercely, had terrifying visions of her dead and in her shroud, fell to the floor in a deep faint at thoughts of the miles that separated them, and he said goodnight to her, out loud, every evening from his bed. He kissed her signature when her letters arrived, wept into his pillow when they didn't. "I am on thorns without news of thee." "My dearest beloved sweetheart." "I thought of an evening when we were walking, gently arm-in-arm together toward the waters of Bayou Sarah, and I watched thee bathe thy gentle form in its current." "Oh my Lucy, what I would give now in my possession for a kiss on thy Lips and—"

MH   By spring 1829 he had been gone for three years, and the separation had put great strain on their marriage. Trouble had been surfacing between them when he sailed for England. Lucy seems to have believed that if he was to achieve what they both wanted, he *must* go; but still she felt abandoned, and she resented having to scrimp and having to take full responsibility for the welfare of their sons. She was encouraged in such sentiments by various friends and family, who were exasperated by JJA's instability, "enthusiasms," and wanderlust. (The Reverend Gordon Bakewell, in his reminiscences of JJA, quoted an anonymous member of the clan who had once said, "He neglects his material interests and is forever wasting his time, hunting, drawing and stuffing birds, and playing the fiddle. We fear he will never be fit for any practical purpose on the face of the earth.") Lucy evidently made plain to her husband (partly in retribution and pique, partly from caution) that she wasn't sure she'd just drop everything and hurry off to Europe as soon as he crooked his finger. When the publishing project was actually upright and tottering forward, she must have been unnerved by the reality of the time it would take—fifteen years or so more before it was done, fifteen years in which something irreparably awful could happen to wreck the project. She hesitated to put herself once more completely at the mercy of Audubon's success or failure, his glooms and exaltations. Would she come to England? She wasn't sure. Throughout JJA's stay in Europe, the skirmishing weaves through their communications.

"I will arrange everything for thy comfort," he wrote to her from London in 1827, "and in arriving at my House, My Lucy may set either on an easy sofa or before a good Piano or laid down in a soft bed to be kissed by her 'Old Man'—I feel so much as if it is the case that my heart bounces at the Idea—Thyne and *Thyne Only* forever." But for the first couple of years, such offers were mostly rhetorical. JJA was living the life of a high-class traveling salesman, boarding in rooming houses when he wasn't somebody's guest; there wasn't any money to establish a home to which Lucy and the boys could come; and the engraving project suffered a number of serious setbacks.

Lizars' colorists struck, which led Audubon to young Robert Havell in London—one of the luckiest and most productive conjunctions in the history of art. They were to make each other's reputations, but there were still numerous procedural difficulties to be ironed out. For a variety of reasons JJA lost subscribers he'd worked hard to get. And the longer he stayed in Europe, the more he experienced the negative side of being a public figure: his work was criticized by some and treated lukewarmly by others, while gossip and jealousies and vanities—including his own—got in the way. There were times when it appeared that the littlest push might bring down the whole house of cards.

Yet the house stood; and once the project was established, then the idea of Lucy and the boys coming to England began to look more reasonable. Lucy was riled however. At least that's the way she appears to me. For all these years he'd made her suffer privations and indignities, but at the same time he'd come to depend on her for guidance. Now he had an independent footing for his enthusiasms. Many people—famous people—thought his work wonderful. He had gone off and become a success *without her,* and Lucy wasn't comfortable with that. Was he still her LaForest, did he still need her, or had she been outgrown? Lucy wanted him to give it all up. She wrote that

Detail of the engraved plate of the hawk-owl. *American Museum of Natural History*

she was anxious to have him come home and live a humbler and happier life. Furthermore, she said, the boys were opposed to moving to England, a land "where neither freedom nor simplicity of habits exist . . . altogether uncongenial to their mode of life."

By January 1829, JJA had decided to act. He had to go home soon anyway, because he needed many more drawings. There were North American birds he had read about but had not seen or rendered; while he had been in Europe, other naturalists had been off collecting new and undescribed species, and those birds must be included too, if the work was to be complete; and there were perhaps as many as a hundred species that he now wanted to redo before Havell engraved them because he thought the old drawings weren't good enough. He decided he'd concentrate on the northeast at first—ground he hadn't explored as thoroughly as he had the Ohio and Mississippi valleys.

"My Dearest Friend," he wrote, "Thine of the 8th November reached me about a fortnight ago, and ever since I have been debating what was or would be the best thing to do, as I plainly read in it, the same that has filled every other that has come from thee since I left America i.e. the *uncertainty* of thy *ever* joining me in Europe. —I have therefore come to the following conclusion . . . I will sail for America (New York) on or about the 1st day of April next . . . I had no wish to go there so soon, although as I have often repeated to thee I always intended to go on account of my work; but I have decided in doing so *now* with a hope that I can persuade thee to come over here with me."

He landed in New York on May 5. (Andrew Jackson had been President just two months.) Lucy remained in Louisiana, and the tug of war between husband and wife continued. Audubon had much drawing to do, and it had to be done in spring and summer when the needed birds were in the northeast. At best, after he was finished with that, he would rather not cross the Appalachians to fetch Lucy; if something went wrong in London, he might have to return there immediately, so he didn't dare be out of touch with England—certainly not as far away as Louisiana. Meet me in Philadelphia, he urged Lucy; or if you must, meet me in Louisville, or Pittsburgh, or Wheeling, Virginia. Otherwise, we may never meet again anywhere. "We have been married a good time, circumstances have caused our voyage to be very mottled with Incidents of very different nature but our *happy days* are the only days *I now remember.* [T]he tears that now almost blind me are the vouchers for my hearts emotions at the recollection of those happy days." But Lucy, pouting, would not agree to come even so far as Louisville. "For God sake my Lucy," he pleaded, "do not be troubled with curious Ideas such as my liking the Birds better than thee &c &c &c. Come and be mine." "[S]he complains of my want of affection," he wrote Victor; "of the coolness of my style of writing &c—and thinks that my not going to [L]ouisiana for her is quite sufficient proof for all these her doubts and fears."

Well, distressing as all this was, finding a solution would have to wait for a while. He had work to do.

CAMDEN AND GREAT EGG,

NEW JERSEY

SPRING AND SUMMER 1829

MH It appears that JJA—still under sharp attack from the Philadelphia partisans of the late Alexander Wilson—designed his summer's expeditions to cover a lot of territory previously explored by Wilson. It would not do, surely, for him to miss anything his predecessor had seen, and it would be a feather in his cap whenever he outdid Wilson in Wilson's territory.

He began by setting up headquarters at a boarding house run by a Mr. Armstrong in the village of Camden, New Jersey, across the Delaware River from Philadelphia. From Wilson's published accounts—and doubtless from his own experience in the Philadelphia region as well—Audubon knew that the Delaware River valley was a good place to watch the spring migration of warblers, which he particularly wanted to do.

Curiously, only two of the warblers he painted for *The Birds of America* can be definitely ascribed to this place in that spring: the ovenbird (which he didn't think of as a warbler and called the Golden-Crowned Thrush or Wagtail) and the blackpoll. But these four weeks or so in Camden were useful anyway. Many mornings he walked out with his gun and returned with specimens to study and draw and preserve: warblers, the eastern wood pewee, the Acadian flycatcher, the whip-poor-will, the common nighthawk, and doubtless others—two hundred individual birds in all. And in a Lombardy poplar that grazed the window of his room a pair of warbling vireos courted, built their nest, and raised their young. He watched their progress and kept a careful record; on one occasion, trying to discover why the vireos were away so long on each trip they made after grass for their nest, he followed them from tree to tree until they reached an old haystack, out of town; there was the source.

Today's Camden, of course, is a far cry from the little village of 1829. The Camden County Historical Society, located in what was once a high-class part of town, has bars on the windows, an iron gate across the front door, and you must ring for admittance. Neither Audubon's visit here nor the site of Mr. Armstrong's boarding house are revealed in the local lore and records. And the place name, "Mickle Swamp," where he collected nighthawks and whip-poor-wills, has also disappeared. Apparently the southwestern part of today's Camden, down to the Delaware, was then owned by Mickles, and the river-edge may have included the swamp JJA talked about. If so, it has fallen victim to the warehouse-railroad-storage-tank sprawl, like so many riverside stretches in North America; the surviving patches of swamp carry rivulets of sludgy, poison-green water.

From his base camp in Camden, Audubon made two major foraging trips after birds that breeding season of 1829. The first took him east to Great Egg Harbor on the Atlantic shore of New Jersey. Alexander Wilson had been there before him.

Wagons from the Jersey coast came into Philadelphia every day —men bringing fish and birds and eggs to the city markets—and Audubon hired one of these "fishermen-gunners," as he called them, to take him to Great Egg Harbor. They left at sunset, traveling for a while in the company of a veritable caravan of wagons, the drivers walking beside the line of carts, swapping news and prices and yarns. Their route was a sandy road that crossed the flat mid-Jersey lowlands where now there are labor-camp farms worked by migrants. Billboards advertise nudist camps ("Families and Couples Invited"). Nursery gardens advertise "Grave Blankets—$3.00 Up."

Audubon's wagon reached Great Egg Harbor not long after dawn, and he looked up a "thoroughbred fisherman-gunner" who agreed to take him in as a guest and to be his guide. In fact, the "good man rubbed his hands with joy, as I spoke of shooting and fishing, and of long excursions through the swamps and marshes around." JJA arrived in mid-June and stayed three weeks; he wrote an Episode about the visit for the *Ornithological Biography*.

JJA   At daybreak on Monday, I shouldered my double-barrelled gun, and my host carried with him a long fowling-piece, a pair of oars, and a pair of oyster-tongs, while the wife and daughter brought along a seine. The boat was good, the breeze gentle, and along the inlets we sailed for parts well known to my companions. To such naturalists as are qualified to observe many different objects at the same time, Great Egg Harbor would probably afford as ample a field as any part of our coast, excepting the Florida Keys. Birds of many kinds are abundant, as are fishes and testaceous animals [shellfish]. The forests shelter many beautiful plants, and even on the driest sand-bar you may see insects of the most brilliant tints. Our principal object, however, was to procure certain birds known there by the name of Lawyers [black-necked stilts], and to accomplish this we entered and followed for several miles a winding inlet or bayou, which led us to the interior of a vast marsh, where after some search we found the birds and their nests. Our seine had been placed across the channel, and when we returned to it the tide had run out, and left in it a number of fine fish, some of which we cooked and ate on the spot. . . . [T]he seine was spread out to dry, and we again betook ourselves to the marshes to pursue our researches until the return of the tide. Having collected enough to satisfy us, we took up our oars, and returned to the fisherman's house, where we dragged the seine several times with success.

In this manner I passed several weeks along those delightful and healthy shores, one day going to the woods, to search the swamps in which the Herons bred, passing another amid the joyous cries of the Marsh Hens, and on a third carrying slaughter among the White-breasted Sea-Gulls; by way of amusement sometimes hauling the fish called the Sheep's-head from an eddy along the shore, or watching the gay Terns as they danced in the air, or plunged into the waters to seize the tiny fry. Many a drawing I made at Great Egg Harbor, many a pleasant day I spent along its shores; and much pleasure would it give me once more to visit the good and happy family in whose house I resided there.

MD   *Notes from our campsite, Belleplain State Forest, Belleplain, New Jersey:*

May 19. Laurel is in bud. Rusty-pink sprouting tendrils of fox grapes weave over fences and underbrush. One rosy-red moccasin flower blooms on the path. (*Who will pick it?* I wonder, as picked it must be, inevitably, by someone.) A nuthatch begs for food at the table. A wood peewee calls *Woe is me-e-e-e-e*. ("Like the last sighs of a despondent lover," says JJA, "or rather like what you might imagine such sighs to be, it being, I believe, rare actually to hear them.") A great horned owl at dusk. A whip-poor-will. Mike strums his guitar to the rhythm set by the whip-poor-will's call and whenever the bird falls silent keeps strumming on the beat to test the bird's internal metronome. Each time the whip rejoins their duet, it makes its entry almost precisely on beat—*Whip-poor-* WILL. State troopers patrol the park every couple of hours through the night. Local boys cruise through between patrols, grooving out on the sandy forest road, their car radios tuned to fevered deejays.

Great Egg Harbor is about ten miles south of Atlantic City; this state forest is inland and to the south of Great Egg. The territory through here was once Tuckahoe Indian country. One evening in 1692, so the story goes, the Tuckahoes held a council, agreed they were being crowded by the six white families who had settled around Great Egg Harbor, and forthwith packed up and departed, leaving their forests, marshes, rivers, and seashores to the newcomers. When Audubon came to Great Egg in 1829, it was a fishing and farming village of more than 2,000 inhabitants. The town, which is perched on a hilltop overlooking the marshes to the west and the inlet and harbor at its feet, is now called Somers Point; population, 8000. We stopped this afternoon at the historical society to ask if there were any local accounts of Audubon's visit or any clues to the "good and happy family" with whom he stayed. Everyone was busy at long tables studying genealogical charts, land records, and ancient wills. No one seemed to know anything about JJA's visit. For that matter, no one seemed to know or much care that Audubon had been here at all. But given as I am to making unsolicited suggestions, I asked if they had considered decorating the walls of the reading room with prints of the birds Audubon had drawn at Great Egg. No one pounced on my suggestion. "The osprey? The laughing gull? The vesper sparrow? We could give you a list." No one asked for our list, so we left them to their genealogical sleuthery and went on to the

Somers' Mansion, a brick and stone country house built in 1714 on a knoll that is now cut off at the knees by the main road of the town.

The Somers family settled here shortly after the Indians left, were in residence when Audubon came through, and lived on in this house until the 1930s, when it was restored by the Works Progress Administration and became an historic site. Only a thumbnail scrap of the original land remains as part of the property—barely enough to hold the house and a patch of lawn—where once the Somerses commanded the entire hillside down to the water's edge, to the Somers' boatyard and sail loft, and out to Somers' Beach where Alexander Wilson explored a rookery of snowy egrets in a grove of red cedars. When we went out on the captain's walk—a second-floor balcony that surveyed the Somers' domain and its approaches from the sea —we had our first sense of what Great Egg Harbor looked like in Audubon's day. True, the view is mangled by undistinguished buildings and gimcrackery, and two toll bridges slice across the inlet, but in the middle distance is marsh, thousands of acres of untouched marshland, which has not been filled in and built upon. Upstream on the Great Egg Harbor River is a power plant cooling tower, a round fat structure that looks like a prehistoric hand-thrown jug wrought by a giant potter. It suits the view.

The narrow barrier beach, a string of outer islands that runs for forty miles down the Atlantic shore of southern New Jersey, was once accessible only by boat. Fishermen used it, and gunners; wreckers camped here, ready to salvage cargo from ships that came to grief along the shore; naturalists such as Wilson and Audubon explored it. Today we drove out from Great Egg via Roosevelt Boulevard. The barrier beach is now almost solid megalopolis from Atlantic City to Cape May at the tip end of the state, most of them townships of recent vintage that sprang up with the coming of the railroads. Ocean City (population 11,000), on that stretch of beach that lies across the mouth of Great Egg Harbor, oozes respectability and healthy retirement funds. It's a community of powerboats and conscientious citizens who polish their doorknockers, weed the cracks in the sidewalks, and sweep the curbside gutters in front of their houses on Ocean Drive and Starboard Lane and Seaspray Road. Ocean City was founded as a camp meeting and temperance resort. It's still dry. A local policeman ticked off the rules: "No bars, no liquor stores, no drinking allowed in cars. But don't let 'em kid you. Everyone has booze in this holy town."

The beach this afternoon was strewn with seawrack and bikinied bodies, lovers entwined on the sand, greased and oiled folk of every age and shape spread-eagled in the sun. Sanderlings, turnstones, a couple of winter-plumaged plover, and lots of dunlin poked and fed at the water's edge. Two girls passed with a bounding red setter. The birds scampered away—like wind-up toys. The dog bounded on. The birds rose, veered, then settled in his wake and fed, wave-chased, in the wet sand.

The next day. We must get out on the marshes that bound Great Egg Harbor. We must find a boat. So far, no luck. Nothing for hire but oceangoing fishing boats complete with skipper and first mate. All we want is an outboard.

This morning we explore, by car, a deep peninsula of marshland. Fog and mist. Highway signs read: Turtle crossing, Turtle Exit, Spare Our Turtles. The tide is out, slick mud flats, muddy serpentine tidal streams that squiggle through the reeds (the kind of terrain where boy scouts or fishermen stumble upon bodies and an officer of the law is subsequently pictured in the newspapers pointing to a tarpaulin-covered corpse).

The marshland looks empty, except for fog-bound distant bridges that loop across the landscape from solid ground to solid ground. But raise your binoculars, scan the flats, and birds spring into your field of vision. Semi-palmated plovers, snowy egrets, killdeer. Lower the glasses, and they are gone. We find a clapper rail at its morning bath —Susannah in her Biblical garden. It stands in a tidal stream dipping up water with its beak and splashing the water down its back. It preens and scrubs, working its curved bill through the feathers on wings, back, and breast. A final beakful of water to rinse off, a final shake, the last touch-up preening, and the bath is done. The clapper rail stalks out of its pool and vanishes into the marsh grass. Black skimmers fly out of the mists. Magnificent plumage: a black cape across the back and the wings; a hood pulled down over the eyes like an executioner's mask; poking out from beneath the mask, a long red bill. Brant stand about in dignified consortiums, splendid-looking birds (far handsomer than Canada geese, their larger cousins)—

Salt-marsh, brant, and egrets. *MH*

brown coats, brown and cinnamon and white vests, black shoes and stockings, black hoods and mufflers.

MH   We push on in the search for our elusive boat, and ask at two boatyards next to the Tuckahoe River, which feeds into Great Egg Harbor. One place used to rent outboards, but insurance costs got too high. At the other we are offered a rowboat. A rowboat? We walk down to the edge of the river; the falling tide boils seaward at an ominous rate, so thank you no. We cross to the other side of the harbor and drive inland along the Great Egg Harbor River. At last, dead ahead, a sign advertises a marina, bait, *boats to rent.* [MD: Once again, like the Mississippi and the Ohio valleys, where so many people didn't know place names and landmarks on the other side of the river, people we spoke to here didn't know there were boats to rent on the other side of the harbor. Captain George has been here for years. Are rivers and harbors such impassable boundaries?]

We turn off the tar onto a dirt road toward the river, the marshes, the harbor. It leads us through woods, past tall trees covered with blooming lavender wisteria, and bursts into the open on an embankment of landfill stretching half a mile across the greening marsh to the edge of a creek. At its end stands Captain George T. Elmer's marina and fishing establishment, rag-tag and down-at-heel, on the periphery of a cluttered turnaround-parking area with a slapped-together outhouse in its center. Captain George's OFFICE—as it is dignified by the sign—is an ancient beached houseboat with screened porch attached. Most of the screening is torn and hangs in swags, and the porch furniture within, tottery and coming unstrapped and unstuffed, looks as if it had been scavenged from the marsh after various hurricanes. Captain George cheerily invites us in and sits us down on the best of the chairs. He's smallish, gray-bearded; apologizes for the general disorder and jokes about the torn screen. "Never have got around to fixing it. It blew out in a storm. We leave it that way to let the mosquitoes out." He agrees that for a fair price he can supply us a boat with an outboard the next day. I ask about charts of the marsh and the bay. Even from the roadmap and a quick look around, it is obvious the area is a maze of salt creeks and ditches. No, he doesn't have any charts, for sale or otherwise.

"Isn't it awfully easy to get lost out there?"

"Oh, yes," he says, grinning.

"Well, what do you suggest?"

"Just keep looking behind you." He laughs.

He offers us a beer and pops one for himself. "Australian beer. Best there is."

We talk a bit about what Mary and I are up to. It seems to me he isn't familiar with more than just the name Audubon, but he is the sort of man who would have "rubbed his hands with joy as I spoke of shooting and fishing, and of long excursions through the swamps and marshes around." He likes the sound of our adventure. He has a sneakboat out back he wants to show us—an old-style waterfowling boat whose prototype is said to have been invented on the Jersey shore in 1836, just seven years after Audubon was here. Captain George's sneakboat looks a little like a flattened kayak, decked over except for a waist-wide hole near the center, and it can be either sailed or rowed. It sits in the grass, badly in need of another coat or two of sky-blue paint, but in shape it is a thing of beauty.

He suggests we spend the night in his domain. His son and daughter-in-law live in a houseboat near the dock, and his marina manager, Ray Somethingorother—a tall, saturnine, dark-haired, dark-moustached man, who has joined us on the tattered porch and seems only to mutter when he talks—sleeps in the beached houseboat-OFFICE. So we'd have company. But the afternoon is well advanced, and our gear would have to be fetched from the state forest. So—tomorrow night, instead.

MD   This morning we come back with our camping gear. A few old folks are fishing from the dock—one, an elderly lady with neatly marcelled hair and a shiny new folding chair. Three other oldsters potter around a beached boat; the drill seems to be scrape and paint. But no one is in a hurry. Captain George sits on the unscreened porch of the houseboat-OFFICE and drinks his Australian beer.

We shove off from the dock and putt out into the channel, round a bend, and Captain George's marina sinks down behind the reeds and grasses. Sun and clouds. Sun and clouds. The water is gray-green, the marshes are gray-green, and the world is so flat down here, you

The laughing gull astern of our boat. *MH*

can see a sailboat fifteen miles away. Our craft is a shabby old workboat, chipped and scarred, that probably hasn't felt the touch of a
paint brush in ten years, and the floor is crusted with oil and sand and
dried-up bait—exactly the right kind of boat for this day and this
outing.

We drop anchor. Ocean perch and striped bass are said to be
running. Mike puts out a line, and we catch the attention of a laughing gull. JJA, who had remarked on the great number of them breeding here in 1829, said that he "observed some of them whilst on the
wing, and at a considerable height, suddenly check their course, as
if to examine some objects below." Our laughing gull does just that.
He checks his course at the stern of the boat and hangs here, pinned
to the sky, tipping his head from side to side, taking our measure—
the fishing line, the package of melting squid, the landing net. Seen
head-on, he's round and plump and has a double chin, a friendly
demeanor, and a blatant curiosity. His plumage is basically white
below, charcoal gray and black across the wings, and an all black
head, as though he had been picked up by the feet and dunked into
a bottle of India ink. He decides to join us and settles onto the water
behind the boat with a fussy rearranging of wings and feathers, like
a cat settling in on a pillow. But Mike catches nothing and the gull
eventually pegs us as sure losers. He departs for greener pastures. So
do we.

We move south, prowling into side coves and making a slow,
circumspect approach toward an osprey nest on a listing telephone
pole in the marsh. When JJA was here, he saw upwards of fifty of the
"fish-hawk" nests in the course of a day's walk. Now, a single osprey
nest becomes a neighborhood attraction. Captain George told us that
when the phone lines went underground, the pole was left for the
ospreys, the nesting platform built to lure them in, and local people
of good will hope that they won't be shot out of the sky by some damn
fool showing off his star-kissed marksmanship. All we can see is the
head of the brooding bird that sits in the great rattletrap heap of
twigs and branches and heaven knows what else on top of the phone
pole. (Ospreys' nests are often littered with odds and ends that catch
the birds' fancy and have been found containing barrel staves, shark
eggs, feather dusters, rubber boots, tin cans, rag dolls, rope, shingles,
crows' wings, old trousers.) The brooding bird makes soft chirping

cries. Its mate soars in, circles, lands. They chirp back and forth, then change places. The bird that's been relieved of nest duty stands for a moment on a cross beam, its wings lifted like a swimmer at the edge of a pool, stretching its muscles, surely, to get out the kinks. Then it dives into the air and coasts across the marsh.

We putt on into the labyrinth of marsh islets, find a narrow channel meandering inland, cut the engine, and drift with the incoming tide. Sunlight, shadow, sunlight. (I loll in the prow, one hand trailing in the water. Up the lazy river in the noonday sun. We have the sandwiches and the iced tea, but where are the parasols and mandolins?) At eye level other creeks and drainage cuts are invisible. The superstructures of faraway boats (a wheelhouse or a net boom) slide across the horizon as though pulled by strings. The marsh erupts with birds. A whirl of terns. Clapper rails sounding off in the reeds. (I'm tuned into engines today; the clapper's call sounds to me like a one-lunger motor running down and stalling out.) A greater yellowlegs comes in for a mid-marsh landing. We drift into willet territory —boldly patterned wings lined above and below with brown and white stripes. They land with tremulous flutters like butterflies, holding their wings up over their backs for a second or more, then folding them down, and the brilliant brown and white feathering vanishes into their speckled brown-gray plumage, and the birds themselves can vanish before your eyes, camouflaged against the background of reeds. They resent our intrusion. A hue and cry. We drift on. They fall silent behind us.

"Biddle . . . eej-*jee.*" The song of the seaside sparrow. When JJA was here he had a number of these birds made into a pie, "which, however, could not be eaten, on account of its fishy savour." The seaside sparrows are up, nervous, fretting, and flying from stalk to stalk. Mike repeats their call to himself, emphasizing the final buzz, trying to fix it in his memory. "Biddle . . . eej-*jee.*" Farther back in the marsh, sharp-tailed sparrows skitter and disappear, as nervous and shy as seaside sparrows. Glimpses of orange and yellow and gray striped faces. "B-ggg-jeeee . . . bejeezzz" they sing, taking the Lord's name in vain, and Mike repeats that call too, trying to fix it in his memory bank. It's a thinner song, he decides, than that of the seaside sparrow. The two songs, in fact, are so close that Mike and his birding friends have lumped the seaside and the sharp-tailed into one catch-all category—the C-Sharp Sparrow.

Egrets are everywhere. Their white sinuous necks, primal and reptilian, rise out of the marshes. I scan the flats with my glasses. Egrets land, take off, stroll, feed, or stand stock-still in frozen profile like posterboard cutouts. The tide moves us softly past one egret that's so close we can see with naked eye its black bill and yellow triangular mask. The fishline is out again. A strike, and Mike pulls in a catfish. We now pick up a yellow jacket, which flies along with us, buzzing and hunting among the squid smells in the bottom of the boat. We drift on, bump against the shore, push off with an oar, and drift on again with the tide, sometimes floating sideways around a slow bend.

A long-billed marsh wren fumes and reveals its nest, a round ball of woven grasses, the entrance more or less at the center where a belt buckle would be on a waistline. The nest, looking at first glance like a clump left by high tide, is suspended between two low branches of marsh alder. Consider the logistics of weaving a hollow grass ball with nothing to work with but a beak. (With nothing to work with but your *teeth.*) To my ear, the sound of the long-billed marsh wren's call falls somewhere between a squeaky hinge and a stutter. When I later cross-check with JJA, who painted marsh wrens here at Great Egg, I find my interpretation coincides with his: "Its song, if song I can call it, is composed of several quickly repeated notes, resembling the grating of a rusty hinge." He further says: "The males are extremely pugnacious, and chase each other with great animosity, until one or the other has been forced to give way. This disposition is the more remarkable, as these birds build their nests quite close to each other. I have seen several dozen of these nests in the course of a morning ramble, in a piece of marsh not exceeding forty or fifty acres." Precisely. We have drifted into a marsh-wren housing development. Last year's nests. This year's nests. A lot of the dummy nests that the long-billed marsh wrens will build—two or three or four for every nest that's actually occupied.

Another bend. We see a few houses ahead with powerboats and sailboats at their docks. Houseboats are moored in little coves. Enviable places. From the woods a bobwhite calls his name, and we are turned back at last by a low bridge and a highway.

Long-billed marsh wrens, finished June 22. *Courtesy of The New-York Historical Society, New York City*

MH The water becomes fresher the farther inland we go, of course, and quite likely Audubon went well beyond here, looking for birds—particularly the tall and spindly-delicate "lawyers," whose plumage resembled the old formal courtroom dress of counselors-at-law. But black-necked stilts have not nested in New Jersey for many, many years—more than a century, as far as anyone can tell; they seem to have been almost as sensitive to the white man's presence as the Tuckahoe Indians. So, there are no stilts to look for beyond the bridge; the tide is turning and the sun is going down; the highway interrupts the mood, too, implying more civilization upriver.

MD As we head in, one of the ospreys skins through, harrassing the egrets in its nesting territory, not with a hunting dive, but with the brakes on. A coolly calculated last-second sideswipe. Egret head-feathers crest and white wings flash. A skein of curlews passes over-head with high trilling calls like tiny police whistles. They fly in squadron formation, streel off into crack-the-whip, and repeat these figures from horizon to horizon. As Mike once said, man bangs the air in his motor-driven planes; slams through it. A flock of birds that veer, mesh, curve, and sweep up one side of the sky and down the other give a sense of the *look* of the air—the invisible patterns of wind currents and thermals.

We have no trouble finding the winding backwater that leads to Captain George's dock. We have been out for five hours. We have seen only one plane and one helicopter all day. And we did not meet or pass any other boat underway.

MH I am more than a little embarrassed by my day's catch—a single small catfish. Now when we arrive back at the marina, to the pleased greetings of Ray the manager and Captain George—neither of whom seems surprised we made it home—we find three sep-tuagenarians in aluminum chairs and one restless ten-year-old fishing from the marina's floating dock and doing rather well. After our tent is set up in a corner of the turnaround, I go down to the dock and join in. As the septuagenarians depart with a bucketful of catfish, the ten-year-old and I stand side by side in the fading daylight, casting hooked bits of squid into the swirling tidal creek and filling a bucket of our own. Ray brings down a pole, and he too contributes to the collection. The ten-year-old's mother appears and patiently, over a twenty-minute stretch, eases him away from the dock toward home; he is not interested in the eating, only in the fishing, so he leaves his share of the catch with us. For a few minutes Ray and I continue to cast and catch, because that is the way fishermen are, even though the bucket has a dozen or more fish splashing around in it. Our fishing is an excuse to extend and enlarge a pleasant moment; the beautiful day is ending, the birds of the broad marsh are calling from all points of the compass; in the diminishing light, colors become deeper and clearer before us; the creek eddies and spins past, sucked seaward by a falling tide.

Captain George is preparing to dine at a table on his unscreened porch; his wife has come from their house in town, bringing a weakfish in tomato sauce, ready for the oven. There's a nice coincidence, that weakfish. Walking beside the caravan of Jersey wagons on his way here, JJA asked the company of "fishermen-gunners" whether he'd find ospreys on the Jersey shore, "and was answered by an elderly man, who with a laugh asked if I had ever seen the 'Weak fish' along the coast without the bird in question. Not knowing the animal he had named, I confessed my ignorance, when the whole party burst into a loud laugh, in which, there being nothing better for it, I joined." And so when he was here he drew his magnificent osprey carrying a weakfish in its talons.

Ray is so reserved that he often seems to be talking only to his teeth. But he does talk, and I am becoming tuned to his rhythms and sounds. I had put him down for a Maineman, he's so dark and weathered, but it turns out that Maine is the only state he's never been in. When he and I finally concede that we have caught more than enough fish for supper, he offers to show me how to skin a catfish. Mary and I have decided to roll the fillets in a corn-meal batter—Ray and Captain George have their own ideas—and then fry them. But we have no corn-meal, so Mary goes to a nearby gas-station-and-general-store to find some. While she is off, and while I am making a couple of drinks, Ray rigs up a skinning board. The trick to skinning a catfish is to hook it by the head somehow—Ray uses a nail at one end of the board; then cut through the skin behind the head, grab the end of the skin with a pair of pliers, and pull toward the tail. I

Audubon's osprey, carrying a weakfish. *Courtesy of The New-York Historical Society, New York City*

am delighted. Audubon used a very similar method himself, a century and a half ago, and wrote about it, going down the Mississippi in 1820. "Skinning the Cat Fish . . . was done by cutting through the Skin (which is very Tough) in Narrow Long Strips and tearing those off with a Strong Pair of Pincers." It is easier described than done, however, and I make a botch of my first few attempts. Ray sips at his drink and takes back the pliers. The job is soon finished, and he has skinned more than enough fish for three.

He will not pool his dinner with ours; I think he has more faith in his recipe. But he looms around our campfire as Mary cooks, accepts a dividend on his drink, and with Mary breezily asking questions, talks about himself. He is, she remarks later, the quintessential rover in American lore. Born on a Snake Indian reservation in Saskatchewan, part Indian and part French and German, he has been (among other things, surely) a lumberman, rancher, cook, janitor, marshall, prospector, guide, short-order cook, oil-refinery hand, and now a marina manager. Up and down. "I've tried every kind of job. Except"—an old joke with him—"I never practiced medicine or law." The constants in his life have been fishing, hunting, and traveling. He's been married five times and has left wives behind from sea to shining sea—one in Hawaii, two in the West, one in the Midwest, and the last in Key West—plus a scattering of eight children. He's lost track of most of the children, it seems. He tells us a story about drinking in a bar on Larimer Street, Denver; the bartender said to him, "Hey, Ray, there's a big Marine looking for you." He couldn't for the life of him figure why that should be so, but it worried him. The next time he came into the bar he had taken the precaution of jamming a pistol into his belt. Sure enough, there was the Marine, a strapping young man. Ray had never seen the fellow before in his life. "Are you Ray So-and-so?" "Yes. Who are you?" "I'm your son." He still doesn't know exactly how the Marine found him. And now they've lost track of each other again.

While he seems to take comfort from our affectionate domesticity around the fire, he holds himself just on the fringe of the light; withholds his speech, yet it bursts from him at the same time. He looks weary, and says he is already thinking about moving on. He's intrigued by all our gear, though a bit lofty about it too. "I only take salt into the back country." But as it develops he is not really so spartan as that; he also carries a bedroll, frying pan, teapot, green tea, a gun, ammunition, an axe. He says it takes two men with axes only two days to build a log cabin. At last he leaves the light of our fire and heads for the dark OFFICE to cook his supper and then to read —from a stack of *National Geographics*, appropriate for a man with a wandering foot.

I wake in the dark. Clapper rails are calling *chuh-chuh-chuh-chuh-chuh-chuh-chuh-chuh*, one to the other, sounding now just across the creek, now far out in the marsh. I lie in the sleeping bag, assessing how I feel. Pretty good. Rested okay. Time to get up? I check the watch; my God, only half-past three. I'm used to waking early, but this verges on foolishness. I lie back, thinking about it, testing to see whether there is sleep left in me. *Audubon* would get up—spring to his feet and rouse everyone with him. Beyond the tent walls, the rails chug to each other. I listen for the hollow *thunk-a-CHUNK* of the deep-voiced bittern, don't hear it, and realize that my mind is already up and exploring. The body dresses and follows. I can sleep next year.

I zip the tent closed behind me and walk back along the raised dirt road, away from the marina. Fog has closed in, smelling of salt and mud; wrapped in it, the marsh lies black and mostly invisible. The rails chatter amongst themselves. I wonder where they got the name "clapper." To my ear their calling bears not the slightest resemblance to handclaps, although that is the standard explanation, and I suspect the reference originally was to a mechanical clapper, such as a wood or metal piece used in mill equipment. *Chuh-chuh-chuh-chuh-chuh-chuh-chuh-chuh-chuh* . . . toneless and long-winded.

The first wrens are awake, spluttering musically. And now there is one of those damned C-Sharp Sparrows. I have just spent a long afternoon listening to both species carefully so I can separate them by ear, and a few hours later I'm right back where I started. I stop in the dark, straining to put sound and memory neatly together and produce—*voilà*—a name. No dice.

At the edge of the trees I pause to listen for owls. Not a sound in the woods. I cup my hands at my mouth and imitate great horned owls, barred owls, screech owls. That's my entire owl repertoire. No answer. I turn and start back. The willets are calling stridently in the foggy dark, a distant, ringing reveille, *pee-willet, pee-willet, pee-willet.* Perhaps they have been disturbed by prowling foxes; something is yapping out there. Quite likely there is a good deal of violence being perpetrated within my hearing, although all the sounds are ambiguous as to that. I remember one night years ago when, standing at the freshwater head of a small salt marsh, I heard a sudden desperate squawking and screeching almost at my feet; after that there were a few splashes, followed by silence—in which I stood breathless, poised, quivering.

Pee-willet, pee-willet. The morning is coming, the morning is coming. Even now the barn swallows are up and doing business, chittering close above my head, chasing gnats. Near as they are, I can only just see the swallow shapes. Back at camp I start a fire to heat water. Campfires beguile the boredom of such pot-watchery in the dark. The sky brightens, the fog begins to lift. In the distant trees up the road, not a hundred yards from where I stood to imitate them a while ago, a pair of great horned owls hoots, one bird singing about two steps higher up the scale than the other. And a good day to you too, *Madame et Monsieur.*

The rising sun thins the fog to haze and enlivens the gnats. I sit, notebook in my lap, facing the creek. The old workboat that took us through the lovely marsh yesterday rides quietly beside the dock with its six-horsepower kicker cocked up, at ease, on the stern transom. It is partly ours now. It is ready to go out again, and waits patiently. I am strongly tempted to accept its nodding invitation.

I love salt marshes. Even when I'm a thousand miles from the nearest bit of it, my mind's eye sees the sweep of green-brown prairie, a few distant lone trees and bushes standing on the drier hummocks; I can feel it underfoot—quaking, slippery, crunchy, the spiky plants scraping my ankles—and smell the rich, sulphurous, peaty mud. Yesterday was the most wonderful marsh day of my life. Mary and I are often too busy working, one or the other of us at least, just to *drift* for a day together and share our foraging as amateur naturalists. Now that we are on the road on this project, the chance has arrived, and I have my eyes open for wildflowers to photograph for her, while she scribbles pages of notes on birds. In truth, these are caresses of the spirit.

MAUCH CHUNK AND

THE GREAT PINE FOREST

LATE SUMMER–EARLY FALL 1829

MD   Soon after he returned to Camden from Great Egg Harbor, Audubon set out again in the footsteps of Alexander Wilson, this time into Pennsylvania's Pocono Mountains. His destination was the town of Mauch Chunk (now called Jim Thorpe) and the Great Pine Forest, where the Lehigh River snakes through deep gorges and is fed by hundreds of mountain streams—an area that was also once known as The Shades of Death because of the settlers who died there, having fled to the forests in 1778 to escape the British and the Senecas after the Wyoming Valley massacre.

"I left Philadelphia," JJA wrote in an Episode, "at four of the morning, by coach," with drawing supplies, journal, extra clothes, money, "twenty-five pounds of shot, some flints . . . my gun *Tear-jacket*, and a heart true to nature as ever." The coach traveled the eighty-eight miles to Mauch Chunk in sixteen hours, passing "through a very diversified country, part of which was highly cultivated, while the rest was yet in a state of nature, and consequently much more agreeable to me." After a night's sleep at a local inn, he went out with gun and journal to see what he could find. But Mauch Chunk was a coal-mining and lumbering community in the first flush of a booming prosperity. On Broadway, along the river, were stone houses, a grist mill, a newspaper, a fireproof office building, and the Lehigh Coal and Navigation Company, with more than three dozen (wonder of wonders!) mail runs leaving town per day. It was not a neighborhood for birds. Most of the trees had been timbered out, so JJA arranged to be taken by wagon about fifteen miles out of town

The Lehigh gorge at Mauch Chunk. *MH*

where the forest was still standing (if not for long). There he stayed, for six weeks, in the cabin of Jediah Irish and family, and he saw Mauch Chunk again only on his way back to Philadelphia.

We follow Audubon northward at the end of May, dropping off the superhighways and onto back roads as soon as we clear Philadelphia and its satellites. "Instant refreshment," says Mike. This is Pennsylvania Dutch country, settled in the early 1700s and still "highly cultivated" as it was when JJA passed through en route to Mauch Chunk. Old farms in apple-pie order, fields of sprouting crops roll across the hills, each planting a different shade of fresh springtime green, houses and barns set off the road in groves of trees and in nooks by rivers. A venerable countryside that speaks of traditional ways and one-man-one-machine crops, the antithesis of the bleak labor-camp farms in New Jersey, where migrant workers hunched in rows on the tail beams of gigantic planting machines that towed them up and down the endless furrows as they set seedlings into the ground. Here, you can be pretty sure that the man in the field is the man whose name is on the mailbox. Fenstermaker . . . Heinzelman . . . Knappenberger . . . Schwenk . . . Saeger . . . Ziegler—where we see a man with a scythe, presumably the self-same Mr. Ziegler, trimming off the edge of a meadow. He's stocky, muscular, looks about seventy, and he works with the grace of a dancer; forward on the left foot, flex the knees, swing the scythe out and across, swing it back with a step forward on the right foot, and repeat. The scythed grass lies behind him in evenly spaced, crescent-shaped rows.

North of the Allentown-Bethlehem complex the mountains begin in earnest, and spring is just catching up on the heights—the first showing of apple blossoms and lilacs. We cross Chestnut Ridge and drop into a pocket of Carbon County industries. Smoke, coal yards, railroad yards, refineries. Stunted scrub growth on the mountains. The onion-domed Greek Orthodox churches of Slavic communities. Then the pall of industry is left behind, the green forests begin again, and we are at Mauch Chunk, a thread of a town built along a deep ravine that runs down to the Lehigh River gorge. The "rude mountains," as an 1850 gazetteer described them, "are of such height that the sun is invisible to many of the inhabitants during the short days." Mauch Chunk means "sleeping bear," a name given by the Lenape Indians to a rounded mountain across the river. The town's new name of Jim Thorpe was given in honor of the great Oklahoma-born Indian athlete who died in 1953.

This is another of the towns that has risen and fallen since Audubon's day. It would become the particular province of Asa Packer, a journeyman tanner and carpenter from Connecticut, who heard that barge captains were needed on the Lehigh, arrived here by sleigh in the dead of winter, made his mark, made his fortune, and founded the Lehigh Railroad in 1853. His lavish Victorian country house on the hill is Mauch Chunk's major historic site.

Two railroad lines were eventually routed through. Packer's fellow tycoons summered here, the town became a popular resort: The Switzerland of America. Swank hotels, donkey rides to the top of Flagstaff Mountain with its view of the Delaware Water Gap and the Blue Ridge Mountains to the south. A pavillion in Flagstaff Park was billed as The Best Dance Floor in the East, and after World War I and into the 1920s all the big bands came here to play. A trolley line was built to carry sightseers up to Flagstaff Park, excursion trains came out from Allentown for Moonlight Dances, and the original switchback gravity railroad that ran down into town from the Sharp Mountain mines became a tourist ride. Then the coal began to peter out. The millionaires moved on and the excursionists left. The old hotels went out of business, the best dance floor in the East closed down, the switchback railroad and the trolley line were dismantled, and the Victorian Romanesque railroad station that once saw a hundred trains a day now sees only one—and that one is said to have an uncertain future. But the living symbol of Mauch Chunk's decline is its new name.

As the story goes, after Jim Thorpe's death, his widow shopped for a town that would take his name and his mortal remains for burial; in exchange she had devised a business scheme that promised to create a tourist center around his memory and a manufacturing center for sporting goods. The Borough of Mauch Chunk, ready to grasp at any economic straw, accepted her offer. But though Jim Thorpe had been one of the most famous men in America around the time of World War I, his name was no longer a drawing card. The wishful plans came to naught, and we were told that Mrs. Thorpe was *persona non grata* in town. Older residents still feel they were hoodwinked, and there's been agitation to get the old name back again. They are Mauch Chunkers, first, last, and always—the Molly-Polly Chunkers, the Muck-Chunkers; meantime the younger generation is content to leave it as it is. There the conflict rests, and Thorpe's grave in an open field north of town gets scarcely a passing glance from passing motorists.

To us, the very uneventfulness of Mauch Chunk is appealing: the one main street that winds uphill like a European mountain-village road; the mountain stream that tumbles downhill beside it; the compendium of American architecture that begins at the bottom of the hill with Pennsylvania rubblestone and moves on up the street through Federal, Victorian, and Turn-of-the-Century; the sidehill fortress of the Carbon County Jail, built in 1869, where some of the Molly Maguires were executed during the labor wars of the 1870s. As Mike photographs, I step into the shade of row-houses where a gray-faced man stands on his front porch, one foot up on the railing, watching us, watching the town go by. He's killing time until his daughter comes to take him to watch his grandson play Little League baseball, and he talks about himself. He spent thirty-eight years in the mines, all but six of them underground here (he gestures to the wall of mountain on the far side of the creek). But he's been out of work for fourteen years now. Black lung. He keeps a tank of oxygen in the house. Even takes it with him in the car when he's not feeling well. "See those blue marks under my skin?" He proudly bares his arm. It's crisscrossed with dots and dashes that look like an abstract tattoo. "Those there are anthracite cuts. They never go away. I'll have 'em the rest of my life."

We came across this in others here—their pride in their long experience with brutal work, their pride in their fathers before them who went to work on the coal breakers at the age of nine and put in twelve hours a day, six days a week. Old photographs in the public library show rows of small boys bent over a conveyor as they picked and sorted the coal that spewed from the crusher above them. A couple of the boys look over their shoulders. Peaked, dusty faces under coal grimed caps. None of them smiles at the camera.

Notes from our campsite, Hickory Run State Park:
We're about twenty miles north of Mauch Chunk (or Jim Thorpe, if you must). The Hickory Run park is in the Penn State Forest, a 15,000-acre preserve within the mountain fastness of what Audubon had known as the Great Pine Forest. This enclave in the wilderness preserve is our first full-blown encounter with American camping fever at its hectic zenith. Lines of cars and trailers waiting to register at the gate. A pickup truck in front of us towing a flatbed carrier on which rides a pair of glistening, beribboned, His-and-Her matching motorcycles. A pretzel and potato chip truck drives through to make a delivery at the canteen. (A canteen? In the Great Pine Forest?) We crept to the outlying fringes of the campground, a walk-in, carry-in site, and staked out our small territory of separateness where the rhododendrons grow shoulder to shoulder and sassafras is in bloom along a rushing bedrock stream. The woodland in the center of the campground is topheavy with trailers. Marquees have been erected, lawn furniture set out, flags unfurled, tablecloths laid, chef's aprons donned. Two immaculately got-up ladies, their hair coifed and sprayed into the shape and consistency of cotton candy, stand toe to toe and douse each other from head to foot with mosquito repellant,

then recline in their portable chaise-lounges to survey the Out-of-Doors. The energetic unload baseball equipment, badminton sets, frisbees, whiffle ball, giant dart games, ring-toss games, wading pools, scooters, tricycles, bicycles. Also, motor bikes and motorcycles. Two young men on Yamahas scout the peripheries of the ladies' room for possible pick-ups, find no one enticing, and roar off to the canteen. (It's a curious phenomenon, the need for a snorting, noisemaking machine. See my chrome. Hear my combustion. I and my mighty, gasoline-powered digestive tract are one. Take that, neighbors. *Bla-a-at!*)

But the morning parade to the bathhouses rings a familiar bell. The men in undershirts or no shirts at all, towels over their shoulders. The women stepping out of the woods in their bathrobes with pocketbooks on their arms. I've seen them before. Yes, in the days of train travel. The morning parade to the restrooms in the old Pullman cars. So this is where they've gone to.

Off the beaten tracks, dwarf ginseng is in bloom. Wild pink azaleas. Spikey red and yellow spreads of lousewort. Starflowers. Painted trillium—three snowy petals with a red heart. Rhodora, the azalea Emerson extolled in poetry—"Beauty is its own excuse for being," he wrote. I see the rhodora as one of nature's unfortunate colors, a shade of pale magenta I associate with cheap lingerie. And throughout the mountain woodlands, deep pink, red-veined moccasin flowers are just coming into bloom. A country family (who asked us in for cake and coffee when they found us exploring on their back road) didn't know our familiar names for these plants, neither moccasin flower nor lady's slipper. They'd always called it old duck. A son-in-law went into their woods, picked one, and brought it back to show us why. Take the flower off its stem, strip away the curling sepals, and set it afloat in a cup of water. The narrow neck of the flower looks like the neck of a duck, and the pouched petals that we compare to moccasins and slippers look like the plump body of a duck with its wings folded. Britton and Brown's *Illustrated Flora of the Northern United States and Canada*, 1913, gives "old goose" as a nickname, which I'd never understood. The mystery is now explained.

From the maze of bird calls in the forest, I single out a scarlet tanager in a hickory tree near our tent site. He sings a run of notes that begins gently enough, but as he nears the end of each run, the tanager gives his whole heart. He bends his knees, raises his scarlet neck feathers into a ruff, beats his black wings in a rapid flutter, and leans into his song.

Why do the park rangers trust us, the thousands of us, with fires in the forest? I ignite the damp wood with doses of lighter fluid and fan the explosions with a twelve-inch pot top. If I were a ranger, I would lose my mind worrying over the hordes of fire-hungry campers with their kerosene, gasoline, Jiffy Light, and the rest of it, crazedly striking matches under juiced-up kindling and charcoal.

MH Audubon's host in the Great Pine Forest was millwright and woodcutting field boss for the Lehigh Coal and Navigation Company. According to a local history, the company needed wood for barges to carry the coal to market; once there, of course, the barges were broken up and sold as lumber. JJA implies that at least some of the later lumbering was done for the sake of the wood alone. In any case, as the Mauch Chunk operation expanded, Jediah Irish had been sent out into a vast, wet, mountainous tract of virgin pine and hemlock; he had directed the opening of a new wilderness settlement as his headquarters, built the first sawmill, and begun the cutting, working upstream along the steep hillsides above the Lehigh. Writes Audubon: "The Lehigh about this place forms numerous short turns between the mountains, and affords frequent falls. . . . The pass here [where the Irish cabin stood] is so narrow that it looks as if formed by the bursting asunder of the mountain, both sides ascending abruptly, so that the place where the settlement was made is in many parts difficult of access. . . . [Jediah Irish] told me, pointing to a spot one hundred fifty feet above us, they for many months slipped from it their barrelled provisions, assisted by ropes, to their camp below." More mills went up, and the trees came down at the rate (says the local history) of four hundred acres a year; JJA tells us that fully a third of the forest was gone by the time he saw it, that the cutting went on all day, and on "calm nights, the greedy mills told the sad tale that in a century the noble forests around should exist no more." (Actually, it took only half that time. A Mauch Chunk oldtimer remembers hearing about a small patch of the original timber said to have been still standing in 1935, and he went to look for it, but it had been cut down. The "noble forests" have been succeeded by a mixed deciduous and evergreen forest, and stretches of the Lehigh there are wilder and emptier of man and man's works than they were when JJA knew the place.)

Despite the cutting, bear and deer and trout and turkeys and grouse—and many other birds—were "tolerably abundant" in 1829, and JJA enjoyed himself. He liked the rough communities of the frontier and being associated with the people who made them tick. He was very much taken with Jediah Irish: "Reader, to describe to you the qualities of that excellent man were vain; you should know him, as I do, to estimate the value of such men in our sequestered forests." Irish was "tall and powerful," a "fine-looking woodsman," "young, robust, active, industrious, and persevering. The long walks and long talks we have had together I can never forget, nor the many beautiful birds which we pursued, shot, and admired. The juicy venison, excellent Bear flesh, and delightful trout that daily formed my food, methinks I can still enjoy. And then, what pleasure I had in listening to him as he read his favorite poems of Burns, while my pencil was occupied in smoothing and softening the drawing of the bird before me!"

I love that vision of the artist at work while his host reads aloud; Mrs. Irish tidies up after a dinner of venison, bears prowl outside, a nearby creek rushes past toward the Lehigh below. JJA did some wonderful work in that cabin (wherever it was; we found not the slightest trace or lead to the settlement). This included a batch of warbler paintings—a pair of Canada warblers on a sprig of blooming great-laurel, two magnolia warblers in a purple-flowering raspberry bush, two female black-throated blue warblers (an olive-and-yellow "species" so very different from the black-blue-and-white males that both Audubon and Wilson missed the connection and called them Pine Swamp Warblers), female Blackburnian warblers (so much paler than males that both men did it again, naming the females Hemlock Warblers), and a lovely pair of fall-plumage pine warblers in a spray of canoe-birch (JJA called them Autumnal Warblers, thinking they were a new species, then later changed his mind and left them out of his text). The other fruits of this visit include his magnificently detailed raven, a trio of black-backed three-toed woodpeckers on a rotten tree stub, a lively group of pileated woodpeckers, his red-breasted nuthatches, and probably the beautiful immature gos-hawk that later was paired with a much earlier drawing of an adult to make up the plate of that species.

"I am at work and have done much," he wrote from Camden on October 11, having just left Mauch Chunk, "but I wish I had eight pairs of hands, and another body to shoot the specimens; still I am delighted at what I have accumulated in drawings this season. Forty-two drawings in four months"—he was speaking of everything comp-leted since the spring (and his addition was off), "eleven large, eleven middle size, and twenty-two small, comprising ninety-five birds, from Eagles downwards, with plants, nests, flowers, and sixty differ-ent kinds of eggs. I live alone, see scarcely any one, besides those belonging to the house where I lodge. I rise long before day and work till nightfall, when I take a walk, and to bed.

"I returned yesterday from Mauch Chunk; after all, there is noth-ing perfect but *primitiveness,* and my efforts at copying nature, like all other things attempted by us poor mortals, fall far short of the originals. Few better than myself can appreciate this with more despondency than I do."

The accomplishments of the summer seem to have made him less worried about the possible disasters that might be occurring in the engraving project in England. He wanted to see his boys, who were both in Louisville, and if Lucy weren't there to meet him as he hoped, then he'd be halfway to St. Francisville. So in October he headed west. Victor and John were fine—though Victor had changed so greatly in five years that Audubon didn't recognize him. But his wife was not in Louisville.

Lucy must have felt desperate. The little gray hen with her feath-ers ruffled, she had refused to make any attempt to join Audubon that summer, and her letters—such as they were—were whiny and bitter. She was, in effect, saying to Audubon, *If you really love me, you will risk everything and come to me and carry me off to London with you.* The ultimate test. She knew that JJA was riding the crest of a wave as artist and entrepreneur. He had even gone so far as to threaten never to see her again. Wasn't there a good chance, despite all his assurances that he loved her, that he might just finish what he said he had to finish in the northeast and then get on a boat for England?

Had she torn it? Did it really matter if she had?

In the middle of the night, cusp of November 16–17, the steamboat left JJA at Bayou Sara landing. The village above was almost empty because of a yellow fever epidemic, but he managed to borrow a horse, and in the dark he tried to find his way to the William Garrett Johnson plantation. He quickly lost himself, and didn't get on the right road until dawn, but at six he was there. "A servant took the horse. I went at once to my wife's apartment; her door was ajar. Already she was dressed and sitting by her piano, on which a young lady was playing. I pronounced her name gently—she saw me—and the next moment I held her in my arms. Her emotion was so great I feared I had acted rashly. But tears relieved our hearts, once more we were together."

They sailed from New York for England the following April. During the next twelvemonth, the first volume of the life-size engravings —one hundred sheets—was finished, the second was started. Audubon began to publish a text to accompany the art. He knew he was no ornithological scholar, he said, but "meantime I am aware that no man living knows better than I do the habits of our birds, . . . and with the assistance of my old journals and memorandum books, which were written on the spot, I can at least put down plain truths, which may be useful." He hired a young Scottish scientist, William MacGillivray, to edit what he wrote and also to provide technical descriptions of bird anatomies and plumages. He immersed himself in the writing. Lucy (who was his copyist) wrote to the boys, "Nothing is heard, but the steady movement of the pen; your father is up and at work before dawn, and writes without ceasing all day." The first volume (of an eventual five) of the *Ornithological Biography* appeared in March 1831.

Four months later the Audubons took ship for home. JJA believed the time had come to seek North American subscribers to his work. And as before, he needed more birds. In the autumn, Lucy went to stay with their sons in Louisville, and he began an expedition he hoped would take him—with the help of friends and admirers in the national government (including Representative Edward Everett of Massachusetts, Secretary of the Navy Levi Woodbury, and Secretary of the Treasury Lewis McLane)—to Florida, Mexico, the Rocky Mountains, California, and the mouth of the Columbia River.

It was actually a much shorter expedition than that, as matters turned out: he went to Charleston, South Carolina, and from there he made two trips into the Floridas, as they were known—one to the northeast corner of the territory, the second out through the Keys to the Dry Tortugas and back. But he was accompanied by an assistant artist, George Lehman, a good landscape painter who had already done some settings for him during the summer of 1829, and by a hunting and bird-stuffing assistant, Henry Ward, an Englishman. With their help he produced at least forty-four paintings—enough to keep Havell busy for nearly two years—and returned with more than a thousand skins for his and others' collections. He added greatly to knowledge about the ranges, life histories, and behavior of many species, and also collected adventures and stories about people, which he could turn to good use as leavening in the *Ornithological Biography.* He sold some subscriptions. He added to the expanding network of friends who collected specimens and information for him, including a man who would become one of his closest and most influential confidantes. He found another excellent "assistant artist," who would for years supply beautiful settings for his birds. The newspapers and journals kept track of his comings and goings; in particular, he made regular reports of his southern travels to G. W. Featherstonhaugh's *Monthly American Journal of Geology and Natural Science.* The good press enhanced his public reputation just at the moment when his engravings and writings were becoming available in North America. Not a bad sum total for a few months' work.

JJA [*to Lucy*] We left [Fayetteville, North Carolina] in a cramped
Coach and passed over a flat level and dreary Country crossing at
every half mile or so Swamps all of which might be termed truly
dismal—no birds, no quadrupeds no prospect (save that of being
Jostled)—The waters were all high—it took us three hours to cross the
Pedee River in a Canoe &c &c but at last on Sunday last [October
16] . . . we arrived at Charleston—put up at a boarding house . . . I
delivered my letters [of introduction] to Mr Lowndes who received
me as all strangers are when they present a letter of that kind and
we parted.—I pushed almost out of town to deliver another to the
Rev^d Mr. Gilman—There I found a man of learning, of sound heart
and willing to bear the "American Woodsman" a hand—he walked
with me and had already contrived to procure us cheaper Lodgings
&c when he presented me in the street to the Revd Mr Bachman!
—Mr Bachman!! why my Lucy Mr Bachman would have us all stay
at his house—he would have us to make free there as if we were at
our own encampment at the head waters of some unknown Rivers
—he would not suffer us to proceed farther South for 3 weeks . . . We
removed to his house in a crack—found a room already arranged for
Henry to skin our Birds—another for me & Lehman to Draw and a
third for thy Husband to rest his bones in on an excellent bed! . . .
  Out shooting every Day—Skinning, Drawing, Talking Ornithology The whole evening, noon, and morning—in a word my Lucy
had I thee and our Dear Boys along I certainly would be as happy
a mortal as Mr. Bachman himself is at this present moment, when he

has returned from his Congregation—congratulated me on my days work and now sets amid his family in a room above me enjoying the results of his days work.

MH From this moment forward, John Bachman was Audubon's closest friend. He had been born in 1790 in Rhinebeck, New York, where he also had his first parish; he is said to have accepted the call to St. John's Lutheran Church in Charleston in 1815 for the sake of his health—tuberculosis. He had been an enthusiastic naturalist since childhood, had known and gone birding with Alexander Wilson, but, not having in Charleston the regular companionship of a first-rate ornithologist, he had let his interest slide. Enter John James Audubon. "Look here, my friend," wrote Bachman, two months into their acquaintance, "before I forget it, why are you always talking of 'a load of gratitude'—now suppose we say no more about this. Your visit to me gave me new life, induced me to go carefully over my favorite study, and made me and my family happy." The two men shared a deep, mystical feeling about birds as (in Bachman's words) "the most beautiful of God's works"; each enjoyed the act of hunting and the act of discovery; each was open and emotional about good friends.

For the rest of Audubon's life, in visits and in correspondence, they encouraged, praised, needled, and corrected each other—about birds, quadrupeds, shooting skills, painting, illegible handwriting and other bad habits, which Bachman listed as obstinacy, grog, and snuff; Audubon was addicted to all three, Bachman to at least two. "[H]ammer away at the middle my friend," wrote Bachman in reference to his list, "& I will work on myself at the two extremes."

Bachman appointed himself Audubon's chief agent for the South and enthusiastically hawked the engravings and the *Ornithological Biography* wherever he went. They supplied each other with streams of information, specimens, skins, live creatures for observation. Audubon often quoted his "learned and generous friend" on birds, and eventually, with Bachman leading the way, they collaborated on a major work about North American quadrupeds. Audubon's two sons married Bachman's two eldest daughters; the fathers rejoiced at grandchildren—and suffered together as the Bachman girls went through long illnesses (tuberculosis again) and died within months of each other.

So theirs was a friendship of uncommon closeness and intensity. It had its nicknames: Audubon had complained about the first coach ride to Charleston; he had been thoroughly *jostled,* he said, and Jostle became a password between them. Audubon was Jostle and Old Jostle, his son John Woodhouse was Young Jostle, and Bachman was Jostle the Third. The friendship had its enthusiastic do-you-remembers. "Just ask your father," wrote Bachman to John W., "whether he remembers Chisolm's Pond—when I missed, I always had for an excuse that *my gun was too short,* and when he did so, he always said that the Cranes were a *quarter of a mile off.*" And to JJA himself: "Do you not remember, as if it were yesterday, with what triumph we brought home the first 'Blue Herons?' With what a shout we made the forest echo, when we picked up the 'Yellow-crowned Heron,' which you were so anxious to draw: and how we rejoiced when . . . we at last found out where the 'White Cranes' fed; how you cheated me out of a shot; and how we hung up the fellows by their long necks on the bushes."

Audubon also remembered shared pleasures. My favorite is the November shooting expedition to Cole's Island at the mouth of the Stono River, southwest of Charleston, recounted in the *Ornithological Biography.* Audubon and Bachman and party had watched the arrival of migrating flocks of long-billed curlews, which settled for the night on sandbars off the shore. In the dark the hunters returned to their camp, a small summer house.

JJA   Fish, fowl, and oysters had been procured in abundance and besides these delicacies, we had taken with us from Charleston some steaks of beef, and a sufficiency of good beverage. But we had no cook, save your humble servant. A blazing fire warmed and lighted our only apartment. The oysters and fish were thrown on the hot embers; the steaks we stuck on sticks in front of them; and ere long every one felt perfectly contented. It is true we had forgotten to bring salt with us; but I soon proved to my merry companions that hunters can find a good substitute in their powder-flasks. Our salt on this occasion was gunpowder, as it has been with me many a time; and to our keen appetites, the steaks thus salted were quite as savoury as any of us ever found the best cooked at home. Our fingers and mouths . . . bore marks of the "villanous saltpetre," or rather of the charcoal with which it was mixed, for plates or forks we had none; but this only increased our mirth. Supper over, we spread our blankets on the log floor, extended ourselves on them with our feet towards the fire, and our arms under our heads for pillows. I need not tell you how soundly we slept.

MH   There were other reasons, as well, for Audubon to think fondly of Charleston. He made many friends among the gentry—Poinsetts, Rhetts, Lees, Ravenels—who often were good naturalists themselves, who competed for his company, and who supplied him with bird specimens and notes and joined as "merry companions" in the hunting expeditions. "I must confess," he wrote Lucy, "that no where in America have I met with so much attention, kindness, or hospitality."

And as he became increasingly aware of the enormity of his project and the uncertainty of lifespans, he felt pressed to produce more paintings for Havell, faster, faster; in the Bachman household he found not only a careful observer in Bachman, someone who could contribute to the knowledge of North American birds, but also an exceptional artist to take away some of his drawing burdens—Maria Martin, John Bachman's sister-in-law, a meticulous and graceful painter.

We came to Charleston in our second spring on the road, to meet Audubon, who had traveled south from Baltimore that autumn of 1831.

Warm at dawn this seventh day of May at our campground in Francis Marion National Forest, north of Charleston, and very warm in the city by the time we arrive. We are here to look for Auduboniana in the Charleston Museum, but we walk for a while, first. What a clean and airy city this is—and *short*, if I may say so: Charleston is still an old town, and it isn't dominated by concrete-and-glass towers, the obelisks of modern architecture. Common egrets flap slowly overhead, with chimney swifts chittering around them. Mockingbirds feed on the little lawns of eighteenth-century townhouses and perch on wrought-iron fences to sing. A cardinal pair flirts in a dark back garden. Very nice, very southern-gentle. [MD: And the sidewalks around St. Michael's church on Meeting Street are thronged with flower vendors, most of them elderly Negro women, who sell cornflowers, field daisies, coreopsis, colic root, California poppies, and handwoven baskets made of sweet grass, palmetto, and the needles of long-leaf pine.]

The Charleston Museum is in a wonderfully ramshackle building —semicircular portico out front, cluttered and old-fashioned and disordered and inviting inside, just like an attic. It is filled to the brim with things natural and things historical, and like the old stuffed birds on display—feathers faded and brittle, bodies aslant—most of the collection is dusty and looks out of sorts. So the museum is itself a piece of history. The building was erected as a temporary structure in 1899 to house a reunion of Confederate war veterans, and has been "temporarily" occupied for years by the museum, which is at last preparing to move to new quarters. We are told that one end of the roof leaks badly; in fact, the chief naturalist, Albert Sanders, remarks that the staff suspects the building is held upright only by the collections stored inside, and once that's all moved out, the place will fall in on itself.

We are led into the gloomy backstairs library to explore the Bachman–Audubon correspondence. Some loving soul has carefully prepared a typescript of John Bachman's letters, and now we browse through it, taking notes. Look at this: Bachman liked to sit in front of his fire and imagine Audubon in Charleston. "Here you come," he writes to his friend in 1840, and in the reverie imagines asking a servant to close the house to all other visitors: "—shut—shut the door old Tom—tie up the knocker—& tell any lie you please—" Then, in his mind's eye turning to Audubon: "& now for the yarns—aye & the quarrels too."

John Bachman's church, St. John's Lutheran, still stands on Archdale Street, next to the stone Unitarian church, whose pastor, Samuel Gilman, introduced Audubon and Bachman. The surrounding neighborhood is old and quiet. St. John's rises to oversee it, a tall, frame building painted white, with a cupola on the steeple. Bachman is buried under the altar, and quite rightly: the church was dedicated in 1818, early in his ministry there, and when he died in 1874, he had been its pastor for six decades. He was eighty-four; he had outlived Audubon by twenty-three years.

St. John's Lutheran Church. *MH*

The Reverend John Bachman. *Charleston Museum*

As I photographed the church today, two white ibis flew directly over the steeple. I thought, *The friends return?*

MD We've seen two portraits of John Bachman, one painted when he was a young man, the other when he was middle-aged. Both show his dimples and warm smile, which must have been the most irrepressible of smiles, since neither artist could paint Bachman without it—a smile so distinctive, the blue eyes so direct and lively and *interested,* that I am sure I would recognize him immediately if our paths could cross. Not so with JJA. He never looks like quite the same man in any of his portraits. He was always overly posed, with no hint of a relaxed expression on his face, no spontaneity, and his poses were usually that of the hero: the lifted chin and impassioned eye, like the stills of oldtime matinee idols. He did two self-portraits of which we know. One, done in England, is a dramatic profile. The other, done in St. Francisville, is a burning, introverted view of himself—thin, drawn, intense, his eyes fixed almost angrily on us (as so often happens in self-portraits, of course, when the artist stares at his own face for days in a mirror and repeats the same baleful stare in his picture).

John Bachman's house and grounds at 149 Rutledge Avenue are gone now and the site is covered over with the concrete complex of a new high school. But from Bachman's letters and from a granddaughter's memoir in the Charleston Museum, I feel as though I would also recognize the house (as I'd recognize the man himself) if we could round a corner and suddenly come upon it. From his study window, Bachman's view of the garden was framed by the piazza and the jessamine vines. The garden was famous for its lilies. Roses grew in profusion. Verbenas, mignonettes, pinks, iris, camellias, Japanese quince, syringa, orange trees, azaleas, dogwood that had been transplanted from the country. Wisteria and trumpet vines. An arbor of clematis. Pink crape myrtle trees that had been placed there by Audubon and Bachman, and a magnolia with the names of three generations of friends carved on the trunk. Beyond the garden was the poultry yard, duck pond, chicken house, and the cotes for Bachman's pigeons—fantails, pouters, carriers, and tumblers. A vegetable garden. Fig trees. Beehives. Beyond that, the slave quarters. (The estimable Bachman, I regret to say, was pro-slavery. Also anti-Indian.) The household burst with children, guests, visiting relatives, servants, pets. (Beauregard, the Newfoundland dog; cats and kittens; the tame bear that almost hugged one of Bachman's daughters to death and was forthwith "executed.") A pier table on the second floor held the first good impression of Volume I of *The Birds of America*, bound in Russian leather, which had gone with JJA from England to France and later was presented to Bachman. "When we were especially good," wrote his granddaughter, "our reward was to have the giant volume spread open on the rug on the floor, and lying flat, we turned the leaves carefully to find the great wild turkey and all the other wonders."

This expansive and welcoming household was exactly the kind of family that pulled in Audubon like a magnet and, as Bachman once wrote him (when there were at least twenty-two people in residence) "we are pretty closely packed but have room in some corner of the house & heart for you." If JJA would come to visit, which they all wished might be soon, "I will sooner pack some of them in the fowl house than not accommodate you."

The family, however, was not without its despairs. Of the Bachmans' fourteen children, five died young of TB, and Mrs. Bachman was an invalid. A classic Victorian ménage à trois was established: John Bachman, the invalid Mrs. Bachman, and Maria Martin, Mrs. Bachman's unmarried sister, to run the household. It was the traditional role for a maiden aunt, but Maria Martin was an enormously interesting woman for her time. Besides being housekeeper, smoother of fevered brows, and a fine artist-naturalist who worked along with Audubon and her brother-in-law in Bachman's basement workshop amid bird specimens—freshly killed or decayed or preserved in spirits—she also helped John Bachman prepare his sermons as well as research his scientific papers, some of which she illustrated, and did some paintings of reptiles for *North American Herpetology* by John Edwards Holbrook, a Charleston physician and zoologist. Maria Martin was not afraid of adventure nor was she given to the vapors. Once, on a ride down the St. Lawrence River, as the open boat plunged and bucked into a stretch of deep rapids, Miss Martin —to her brother-in-law's amazement and delight—"gave us the boat song."

I think of poor Lucy Audubon grumbling about her boat ride down the Ohio River to Louisville, and her horseback ride to Fatland

Ford from Kentucky. That was not Maria Martin's style. No wonder Bachman and JJA called her Our Dear Sweetheart. Her contributions to JJA's paintings included nests; beetles; butterflies—the buckeye *(Junonia coenia)*, the white peacock *(Anartia jatropha)*, and day moths *(Pseudohazis eglanterina)*; flowers—flame azalea, loblolly bay, strawberry shrub, mistletoe, cleome or spider-flower, hibiscus, and western dogwood, together with a picturesque assortment of dead, mossy, lichened branches on which various birds were to be perched. Sometimes her botanic drawings were sent separately to Havell in England, and he then would create a balanced composition using her background materials and JJA's birds.

Blessed rain this afternoon that cools down the city. At the door of the museum as we leave for the day—our umbrella! Where is the Rozier Umbrella? I had it last. I streak through the museum in search. The library, the office, the Indian exhibit, the birds, mammals, reptiles, minerals. Found—in a dark corner at the top of a staircase, where I'd hung it on the bannister.

MH "What about Bachman's warbler?" I had asked Albert Sanders, the museum naturalist, hoping he'd tell me that I could find it any morning at such-and-such a spot near the city. But it remains one of the rarest and hardest to find species in the New World—as it was when John Bachman discovered it. That was an early high point in his friendship with Audubon. When Audubon first appeared on the scene, his host was a tag-along birder, just getting his eye back and his mind on the business. But it didn't take him long; and shortly after JJA left for Florida, Bachman wrote him: "I have gone carefully over my Ornithology [presumably the Wilson and Bonaparte *American Ornithology*], and have perfected myself in the Fringillas [finches, sparrows, buntings, and the like] and I think that you will not catch me napping on that point—Would that I knew the Sylvias [in those days, warblers, wrens, and kinglets] as well. However, the Spring will do wonders, and we will astonish you with new specimens."

And so he did. In the spring of 1832 he discovered a brand new warbler and a "new" sparrow. The sparrow actually had been described nine years earlier by a German zoologist, Martin Heinrich Lichtenstein, but in America it was not yet a known species. Audu-

bon, back from the Florida Keys in June, promptly named it after
Bachman (Bachman's Pine-Woods Finch, now Bachman's sparrow).
The new warbler—an olive-green bird with a brown cap—Audubon
named for William Swainson, an English ornithologist who was an
important and influential friend in Europe.

Only a few weeks later, after JJA had left for the north, Bachman
shot another warbler, a female, that he thought might represent still
a third new species. During the next several months he collected a
number of other birds that puzzled him. These he wrote about to
Audubon, who of course asked to see the skins; and, early in 1833,
Bachman sent him a box of specimens. But the new warbler and two
other skins stayed in Charleston; Bachman had donated them to the
local Philosophical Society's collection, of which he was curator, and
didn't want to let them go. Instead, he sent paintings of the birds by
Maria Martin. This didn't satisfy Audubon, and he said so. At the
same time, Bachman had asked for and just received a generous
collection of skins from Audubon and his son John W. So, albeit
reluctantly, Bachman sent the missing specimens to Boston, where
JJA and Lucy and John were spending the winter.

Audubon studied the warbler. It was olive on the back, yellow in
front, with a suggestion of a dark hood or cap on the back of the head
and a faint patch of black flecks on the breast. He didn't recognize
it; perhaps it *was* new. Wilson however, had figured something that
looked a bit similar; was Bachman's bird possibly the female or young
of what Wilson called the Mourning Warbler? Such was the skeptical
tone of his response to Bachman.

As it happened, Bachman in the meantime had collected more
evidence. "Now take a seat along side of me," he wrote Audubon at
the end of March, "and deliberately & patiently go with me over the
description and history of this beautiful bird. I have a secret to tell
you in your ear, softly my friend, I have the male, it is fairly drawn,
it is in full plumage. I have the skin well put up & if Maria's drawing
does not suit you, you may draw it over, for the bird was shot by Jostle
the third, and it is now the property of old Jostle and if he cannot
swear to it I can." Bachman had gone to visit in-laws some fifty miles
northwest of Charleston, and on his way home by carriage, he said,
he had "heard a soft & pleasant note that was new to me. I leapt out
of the chair in a crack, to use an elegant expression coined in some-

body's brain." (JJA of course used that "elegant expression.") "I saw the bird on the upper branches of the largest Tupelo Tree, I shot it and it lodged in the Moss. Goodbye says I & went sorrowing to my chair. 3 miles further the same sweet note like music from the spheres came over me, I saw and watched the bird for a quarter of an hour." Then he fired his gun again and brought this one to the ground. It proved to be a boldly marked version of the female he'd sent to Boston—a male with black cap, black bib, otherwise yellow front and olive back. "Now my friend," concluded Bachman in justifiable triumph, "draw this male & female, it will be an ornament to your book." Which Audubon did, and named the species Bachman's Swamp-warbler.

In his brief write-up, Audubon expressed the hope that soon the details of the bird's life history would be discovered, but even today information about it remains very thin. Bachman's warbler has been known to nest in apparently small local "colonies" here and there in the southeast; it builds its nest near the ground and (like many warblers that nest low) it often goes to the tops of the tallest trees to feed and sing. But no one has done a field study of its breeding and life history, and there is some evidence that the species is diminishing in numbers, so we may never learn much about it before it vanishes. The U.S. Forest Service seems determined to cut timber in the one place where the warbler is best known—I'On Swamp, north of Charleston, near our camp. Only thirty-seven nests of this species have been found and reported—ever, anywhere—and thirty-two of them were in I'On Swamp.

If I wanted to try for a look at the bird anyway, advised the museum naturalist, I should get in touch with Jay Shuler in McClellanville, out that way; writer, photographer, guide for visiting naturalists, he was the chief organizer of the battle against the Forest Service's lumbering project, and if anyone knew of recent sightings of Bachman's warbler, he would. So I telephoned, and we were swept into the orbit of Jay Shuler and his wife Martha.

We have been given free run of the Shuler house, which, rising on pilings as thick as elephants' legs, overlooks thousands of acres of salt marsh—please use their shower, their washing machine, their guest room, drop in any time for a meal, please come for dinner tonight, let's go birding in the Cape Romain National Wildlife Refuge

Bachman's warbler, painted by Audubon in 1833. The flowering shrub is franklinia, painted by Maria Martin. *Courtesy of The New-York Historical Society, New York City*

offshore and then birding and botanizing in I'On Swamp, etc., etc., etc. We spent most of today with them. One snapshot: Aboard Jay's boat, bound for the marshy, sea-isle refuge, we find two oystercatchers on a shellbank. I've usually seen this stocky, duck-size shorebird at very long range, almost always a mile or more off across a body of water and just barely identifiable through a high-powered telescope, but these oystercatchers stayed put (apparently near their nest) only fifty feet from the muttering, circling boat, while we paused to study them—black and white plumage, brilliant orange-red button eyes, and incandescent orange-red bills as stout and blunt as old hand-forged nails. [MD: And knobby, gangling, pink legs. Says Jay: "As though they'd dressed up for a party and forgot to put on their stockings."]

A second snapshot: In the large Shuler livingroom, after dinner, salt marsh looming outside, we are talking very late—birds, bird-painters, I'On Swamp (where we did *not* find a Bachman's warbler), environmentalist philosophy, the market for writing, the courses of four careers. And Audubon and Bachman; Jay is intimately knowledgeable about their relationship and enjoys it as much as we do. During one moment of shared recognition—I forget about what, but a pause of nods and grins—I sense that we are just then all conscious of the echoes of the instant Audubon–Bachman friendship in the instant Harwood–Shuler friendship.

MD Painted buntings at the Shulers' feeder. Martha's gift of homemade sausage meat. And conversation about the pronunciation of Audubon's name. We say it, as most northerners do, in a flat, anglicized form, *Oughta-bon.* From Kentucky on down through the south, we'd noticed that the French pronunciation is used, *Owe-du-bon.* But hereabouts Bachman is pronounced *Backman.* "That's Charleston for you," said Jay. "German names are anglicized. But French is French."

We've also paid a visit on a great-granddaughter of John Bachman, Mrs. Francis J.H. Coffin, who lives in the old part of Charleston down near the Battery. She's a charming, sparky, independent-minded woman in her eighties, an authority on Maria Martin's paintings, who has been consulted by Princeton University and the New York Historical Society for identification of Maria's work in the Audubon engravings, and who has also been writing a biography of Maria. Mrs. Coffin has a picture of her that was taken in later years. It is not flattering. It emphasizes Maria's long flanged nose, her large, thin-lipped mouth, and heavy-set face with a heavy-hearted look. Said Mrs. Coffin, who herself has delicate features: "If I publish that picture of Aunt Maria in the biography, my sister says she'll never speak to me again."

Mrs. Coffin has a few of Maria's drawings, but otherwise the sketchbooks have been divided among the family over the years or have gone into museum collections. The volume of *The Birds of America* that used to be on the pier table on the second floor of the old Bachman house was sold by two of his daughters, who were pressed for money in their old age. Mrs. Coffin has made her own collection of bird prints: Prideaux John Selby, John Gould, George Edwards, Mark Catesby, and the Havell engravings of Bachman's warbler and Bachman's sparrow. We gather that Catesby is her favorite, because, as she explained, he not only painted his birds, but engraved and colored them himself. In fact, she is not an Audubon fan. "As I said in my book, Audubon was a volatile Frenchman." Then she laughed. (The conspiracy of the researcher-author.) "I can't say anymore. I mustn't give my secrets away. It's all in my book." However (exactly as did Millicent Quinn of Henderson), she went on to speak in discreet general terms about the temperament of genius and the privileges demanded by those who are gifted with genius—their assumption that genius entitles them to rude manners, irre-sponsibility, and vulgarity. It was a reflection of Audubon that had been passed along in letters and in stories. In family gossip. (And gossip, as Andrew Field wrote in his biography of Nabokov, is the tenth muse of the historian.) Mrs. Coffin also told us that Cousin Florence (that would be John W. Audubon's daughter by his second wife) said that her grandfather had never painted birds on china, but if it pleased people to think that Audubon had done so, then let them think it. [Mrs. Coffin has died since our visit on that splintering hot May day in Charleston. Another direct thread to the past is cut, and the communication between the Audubon and Bachman descend-ants spins out thinner with each new generation. Is there anyone left who speaks of Cousin Florence and Aunt Maria Martin? Or shares stories about Grandfather Audubon and Great-grandfather Bach-man?]

Notes from our campsite, the Francis Marion National Forest, twenty miles north of Charleston:
We're a quarter of a mile from the Intracoastal Waterway that cuts through the marshes here and is as busy these days as an interstate highway, with cabin cruisers that were wintered in Florida now beating their way north for the summer. They pass in glossy herds of threes and fours.

A handful of fellow campers here. Spacious sites in a grove of tall, leggy pines. And, to borrow a phrase from JJA, "all free gratis," courtesy of the Forest Service of the U.S. Department of Agriculture, whose signboards announce that they are dedicated to the "management of the Nation's forest resources for sustained yields of wood, water, forage, wildlife, and recreation." Not only is the survival of Bachman's warbler threatened by timbering here, but another of their natural resources is in serious trouble. There's a sign on the campground pump warning us not to drink the water. An elderly couple from northern Maine who come here every May, drawn by a curious predilection for hot, muggy weather, told me that the well beneath the pump has been polluted for years. I cross-checked this tale at the ranger's office. That's right. Three years of a high coliform count that the Department of Agriculture can't seem to track down, but they're thinking about drilling a new well one of these days. *Good God.* The ultimate laissez-faire of a controlling bureaucracy.

Wildflowers in bloom within view of our tent: orange butterfly weed; yellow-and-pink goat's rue; two downy, spiked varieties of lavender verbena; yellow-eyed grass; and yellow sundrops.

Down the road in I'On Swamp, Indian pink *(Spigelia marilandica)*, which I have never seen before but knew by sight from JJA's paintings of the Henslow's sparrow and savannah sparrow. It's a flower that is neither pink nor a member of the pink family, but is a fire-engine red cockscomb of trumpet-shaped blossoms with yellow mouths and belongs to the same family, *Logonia,* as yellow jessamine.

George Lehman did several landscapes in the Charleston area that served as backgrounds for JJA's birds. The snowy egret and the common snipe were placed against views of plantation houses, the lesser yellowlegs and the little blue heron against wooded river and

Long-billed curlews painted by Audubon in October 1831, with the view of Charleston by George Lehman. *Courtesy of The New-York Historical Society, New York City*

marsh terrains. JJA's long-billed curlews are set on a rocky, reedy spit of land against Lehman's painting of Charleston harbor on the Cooper River. Two white steeples rise above the skyline of the town. Offshore is a string of barges at anchor, boats under sail, and the battlements of Castle Pinckney, one of the three island forts that guarded Charleston harbor. Approaching from the sea, there was Fort Moultrie at the mouth of Cooper River on Sullivan's Island, then Fort Sumter, and then Pinckney.

Today we went in search of Lehman's view and also explored Sullivan's Island, where JJA had gone on a hunting expedition with Dr. Henry Ravenel—"had a splendid breakfast Dinner," he wrote to Lucy, "and was conveyed to & fro in a 6 oars boat all free gratis. —Doc^r Ravenell is a great Conchologist and will give me a fine mess of shells—I wish in return that Victor should ship to him by way of New Orleans a box of Ohio shells as soon as possible." Audubon left no description of Sullivan's Island, but Edgar Allan Poe (another beloved national eccentric) used it as his setting for his mystery story, "The Gold Bug." He'd been stationed at Fort Moultrie from 1827 to 1829, having enlisted in the army at the age of eighteen, impoverished by gambling debts, and he knew the island well. "It consists of little else than the sea sand, and is about three miles long. . . . It is separated from the mainland by a scarcely perceptible creek, oozing its way through a wilderness of reeds and slime, a favorite resort of the marsh-hen. . . . No trees of any magnitude are to be seen. Near the western extremity, where Fort Moultrie stands, and where are some miserable frame buildings, tenanted, during summer, by the fugitives from Charleston dust and fever, may be found, indeed, the bristly palmetto; but the whole island, with the exception of this western point, and a line of hard, white beach on the sea-coast, is covered with a dense undergrowth of the sweet myrtle so much prized by the horticulturists of England. The shrub here often attains the height of fifteen or twenty feet and forms an almost impenetrable coppice, burthening the air with its fragrance."

Nowadays, Sullivan's Island is approached by a spanking new, oleander-lined highway that carries you up and over the reeds and the slime and the oozing creek, but the flavor of the place is still that of a jerry-built settlement that's been struck by hurricane after hurricane over the centuries. Fort Moultrie, like Fort Sumter, was abandoned as a coastal defense fort after World War II. Both are now National Monuments administered by the National Park Service, under the Department of the Interior. And the National Park Service has money to burn—at least in South Carolina. Fort Moultrie is being restored and refurbished, archeologists are sifting every crumb of sand as they go, and next door is a palatial new information building —a sweeping stone structure with an entry like the hall of the mountain king, an auditorium for lectures and slide shows, and a Ladies Room done up to the nines with brick walls and floors, black ebonized stalls, foot-pedal flushers, pumpkin-orange counters, a wall-to-wall mirror, and decorator lighting (as I believe it's called in the trade)—clear, globular bulbs the size of grapefruit with incandescent filaments in imitation of early electric lighting. Meanwhile, back at the Francis Marion National Forest, the Department of Agriculture can't even come up with clean drinking water for its campground.

Charleston Harbor, we learn from the Fort Moultrie rangers, is a hotbed of restoration and building activities these days. Up the way at Hog's Island, the Navy is constructing a museum of their own. However, they've changed the name of the site to Patriot Point. "The Hog Island Naval Museum" simply would not do. ("The Navy has no soul," says Michael.) And the Sons of the Confederacy, the present owners of Castle Pinckney, have restoration plans in mind; the Pinckney fort is now a fallen ruin, best seen in a bird's-eye view from the heights of the Cooper River Bridge.

We've brought along Volume I of the American Heritage edition of JJA's original watercolors for *The Birds of America,* which has a double-page print of the long-billed curlews and Charleston harbor. The Fort Moultrie rangers pore over the print for landmarks and clues and bring out charts and old maps to try to pinpoint the spot from which Lehman did his painting—a refreshing right-about-face from our quirky reception at the Charleston Historical Society three days ago. "Is that meant to be Charleston?" said the young librarian. She gave the picture a cursory glance and waved us on to an older woman, who received us with mannerly indifference, though she went so far as to say that the two church steeples were probably St. Michael's and St. Philip's. But she too was not familiar with the picture or the view, and we presumed, therefore, that genealogy was the strong suit at the Charleston Historical Society, just as it was at Great Egg. Of course, dear Mrs. Coffin knew the curlew-Charleston picture well and had made a pilgrimage of her own, once upon a time, in search of Lehman's vantage point. She had concluded that the harbor scene was painted from a boat. The Fort Moultrie rangers come to the same conclusion.

We go back to the mainland and nose down to the shore wherever we can. It's thickly settled here, some lovely old houses, miles and miles of new ones, and misty glimpses of Charleston far across the Cooper River. No doubt of it. Lehman anchored a boat in the harbor and did his painting from there. His sky is a gray wash of lowering clouds—an overcast gray day like this one.

EAST FLORIDA

NOVEMBER 1831–MARCH 1832

MH Having concluded that for the time being they had exhausted the ornithological possibilities around Charleston, Audubon
& Co. took a schooner to St. Augustine in mid-November. The second
night out, the wind blew dead ahead and hard, and the captain—
doubtless not keen to beat along the Georgia shore in the dark—
made for St. Simon's lighthouse and the sheltered sound behind St.
Simon's and Jekyll Islands, to wait for a change in the weather. In the
morning JJA went ashore on St. Simon's and presented his card to
Thomas Butler King, who owned a cotton plantation called *Retreat*
on the south end of the island. King recognized Audubon's name and
welcomed him generously—JJA was given a shave by the plantation
barber, walked with King around the grounds, was invited to stay for
a month's shooting and drawing; JJA reported that "I was fain to
think I had landed on some one of those fairy islands said to have
existed in the golden age," but he was also anxious to get on to
Florida, and he declined the offer. King asked him at least to stay for
dinner and to send word to Lehman, Ward, and an Army captain on
board the schooner that they were invited too. Audubon gladly accepted, but the schooner captain weighed anchor and sent Henry
Ward ashore to tell JJA that the ship was leaving. (Audubon capsul-
ized the voyage for Lucy: "The winds were contrary and so was the
Cap^n as poor a 'shoat' "—worthless fellow—"as ever I have seen.")
So King hurried to the beach with them, and before they left he had
subscribed to *The Birds of America*. (As often happened, it then took
JJA years to collect the subscription price.)

St. Simon's Island is now a deluxe resort, and T. B. King's *Retreat* has become the Sea Island Golf Club. Cars are parked in the shade of venerable trees near a small, ruined building of "tabby"—a strong, concrete-like mixture of water, sand, lime, and oyster-shells. The ruined building was once the plantation's slave hospital. Near a fairway lies the graveyard for slaves and their descendants. The pro shop is in an old tabby barn. This May day, golfers practice their woods and their irons beside the remnants of the manor house—vine-covered chimney, cornerstones, brick walk. The little daughter of one of the golfers tries on tiptoe to drink from an adult-size water fountain; Mary lifts her up so she can reach it; the child drinks, is put down, races away; now she is in the ruins of the King mansion, picking a bunch of daisy fleabane, runs to Mary with it, prettily presents it, races away again.

We explore a woods road, which turns out to be the road to the club dump. Beyond it is the shore—the broad, flat beach where JJA and the hospitable Mr. King said their goodbyes. Shorebirds dash along the sand as we walk the beach; in the mouth of St. Simon's Sound, where the schooner must have drifted with sails flapping, waiting for Audubon to come aboard, a sleek shrimper, wings of nets akimbo, lies at anchor.

Ruins of the *Retreat* mansion with golfers in the background. *MH*

Thomas Butler King. *Courtesy of Mary Strachan Blun*

That night, Audubon told Lucy, the wind "blew like great Guns," and at dawn they were at the inlet to Matanzas Bay, off Anastasia Island, in sight of St. Augustine. It wasn't until the next night, however, that they actually reached the city. "The entrance of the Port here is shocking," said JJA; the inlet and the city couldn't be more than four miles apart, but sandbars lay in the way. As the schooner rode at anchor in the inlet—presumably waiting for the tide—Audubon & Co. went onto Anastasia Island and "collected some hundreds of shells—in some places we could have taken them up (Live ones) by the shovel full—Saw great number of Water Fowls, Pelicans &c." Of course, Mary and I have to explore some of that beach too. A road now connects St. Augustine to the island, and where it touches the outer beach we find the full complement of bathers, motorcycles, a beach buggy, dogs at play, a bored life guard in a red truck. (Not many interesting shells, to our unpracticed eyes, but we do see a shell collector.) We walk in the direction of the inlet and away from all this activity. Sanderlings and ruddy turnstones and ring-billed gulls feed at the spumy margin and unwillingly give way before a rising tide. In the dunes we find a rutted, sandy track; least terns, carrying fish, beat lightly past, and willets stand and fly around us *silently;* both species must have young in nests nearby. Pelicans cruise overhead. Later, inside on Matanzas Bay, the sun half a fist from the horizon, we begin supper at a picnic table above a salt marsh, among shorebirds, rails, marsh wrens, gulls, herons, egrets. If you sit with us and squint, to blur the scene a bit, you can see our friend Mr. A. and his companions exploring that marsh. "The boat is anchored, and we go wading through mud and water, amid myriads of sand-flies and mosquitoes, shooting here and there a bird, or squatting down on our hams for half an hour, to observe the ways of the beautiful beings we are in pursuit of."

St. Augustine is in the background of this scene, as it is in one of the Audubon engravings, setting by George Lehman. The bird in that engraving, by the way, is an Old World species, the greenshank, a long-billed shorebird that stands about a foot tall. Audubon said he collected three of them in Florida Bay, on the other side of the peninsula, a few months after he was here. It has become fashionable to downgrade Audubon's science, and modern ornithologists declare he was mistaken about this species—or, rather, that at least one of two experienced British birdmen, Henry Ward (who first identified the dead birds) and later William MacGillivray (who very likely saw the skins in London and seconded Ward) were mistaken. There is no other acceptable report of greenshanks in North America, which is apparently the main reason for the pooh-poohing; but when the species is afoot on a sandbar it could easily be overlooked, passed by as only our greater yellowlegs. That's what JJA thought the three birds were before he shot them: "They had been shot merely because they offered a tempting opportunity, being all close together, and it is not often that one can kill three Tell-tales [greater yellowlegs] at once." But then he had the birds in hand, and at that proximity the field marks would make it absolutely impossible to confuse them with yellowlegs. My goodness, a new species, says Audubon. Nonsense, says Ward, turning them over, these are greenshanks.

Compared to other Florida cities, St. Augustine is a shade less garish than most. But it turns a profit from its tradition, and we find it crammed with people, here to see the Castillo de San Marcos National Monument—a large Spanish fort that was ancient in Audubon's day—and the Oldest Store Museum and the Zorayda Castle and the Oldest House and Ripley's Museum and the Oldest Wooden Schoolhouse and the Old Sugar Mill and Potter's Wax Museum and the restored sample of the old city, San Augustin Antiguo.

JJA called it a "would be a city," the "poorest hole in Creation," and thought the Spanish inhabitants lazy and the surroundings dull. "We . . . feed principally on Fish and Venaison and have little more in sight than the Breaking Sea Surf in our Front and extensive Orange Groves in our rear—As far as I have been in the Interior of this place the Country is wretchedly sterile, Sandy and covered with almost impenetrable Spanish Sword plants. . . ." But the birds were "aboundant," and in less than three weeks, with Lehman's help, he had produced drawings at a fantastic pace, drawings of seventeen species, including (he wrote Lucy) "a *new one* which proves to be a *new Genera* for the United States—a kind of Exotic Bird probably very common in South American but quite unknown to me or to anyone else in this place—it is a mixture of Buzzard [vulture] and Hawk." This was the caracara, common indeed to Central and South

America and uncommon on the southern fringes of North America; the scientific name of the North American subspecies honors JJA: *Caracara cheriway audubonii.*

In his text, he writes of first seeing the bird flying high overhead; he thought it looked new, so he followed it for about a mile, until it landed among some vultures on the carcass of a horse. He tried to get close enough for a shot by sneaking along a ditch; that left him too far away, so he stood up, and all the birds flew away from their meal. The new one circled directly over him; he fired and missed, but it sailed only a few hundred yards before it found something else to eat and landed again. JJA had to approach it across an open field. "I laid myself flat on the ground, and crawled towards it, pushing my gun before me, amid burrs and mud-holes," until he was only about seventy-five yards off. Now, Audubon did something he often did: instead of shooting, he lay there and watched the bird. After a while the caracara saw him and took off again. Audubon's second shot missed, and that was the last he saw of his quarry for the day. It returned on the next, however, and he went after it in much the same way and with similar results—good observations but no specimen to paint. Two or three days later, he heard that it was in the neighborhood again. This time he sent Henry Ward to collect it, and Ward tended strictly to business; he was back with the trophy in about half an hour. Audubon began drawing right away and was glad he did. The caracara's colors faded rapidly, and when the drawing was finished twenty-four hours later the specimen bore a poor resemblance to the bird in life, one reason Audubon preferred to paint from freshly shot and wired-up specimens instead of from dried skins or stuffed birds.

"I made a double drawing of this individual," he wrote, "for the purpose of shewing all its feathers . . ."—once again, painting with science in mind; but "double drawing" is a poor description of a magnificent and lively piece of work, done at startling speed.

Our base of operations in east Florida is the home of the Fred Wetzels, who live a few hundred feet from the bank of the St. John's River in Jacksonville. When I first met Fred he was assistant curator at Hawk Mountain Sanctuary in Pennsylvania; now he teaches biology in a Jacksonville private school. But he is primarily a bird-painter, a good one, and through him—since he doesn't mind talking about his work—I try to squirm inside the head of John James Audubon.

Surely bird artists are as different from each other as reverends or writers or biology teachers. But they must share characteristics too. Among bird painters one common denominator should be the ability to see detail and shape in an instant and then remember it. Fred is apt to say, after a bird has flown past, something like, "Did you notice all those light feather-edgings on the back? The plumage must be very new." I noticed no such thing, and even if I close my eyes to bring back the image, I don't see what he saw. One autumn afternoon at Hawk Mountain, a partially albino red-tailed hawk sailed over us. The aberration in coloring was dramatic beyond dreaming, and when Fred got home that night he set up his paints and began working without even pausing for supper; he didn't want to lose the slightest nuance of what his mind's eye retained. The painting was finished before he went to bed, and in the morning, to the astonishment of birders who had seen the hawk, the wet canvas hung in the sanctuary headquarters.

This month he is painting—in watercolors—for a one-man show. Late in the afternoons he comes from teaching and goes immediately to his studio, a first-floor sun room full of orchids, and works through the evening, stopping only for dinner. He sits at a steeply slanted drawing board, with an extension lamp on either side shining close to his work—a tall, lean, angular fellow, wearing large horn-rimmed glasses, dark hair falling over his forehead. He is now painting—largely from memory—a peregrine falcon, which he has posed on top of a freshly killed bufflehead. Last night he sketched the falcon and the setting, and he painted most of the head; tonight he is working on the body, meticulously picking out the edgings and shadings of the breast feathers. "It never gets any faster," he says. The care and patience with which he proceeds illuminates Audubon's capacity to race through swamps for six or eight hours, paint and write up observations all afternoon and evening, and rise early to start racing through swamps again.

Four nights ago Fred began painting a killdeer, and the next evening was nearly finished with the figure; but he was stopped by the setting (time to call in George Lehman or Maria Martin), and seemed generally dissatisfied with his mental image of the work. I asked why he didn't do a *bathing* killdeer. "Because it's not in my memory bank" he said. He paints only what he sees. Audubon went at it that way too, and he was aggressively, even pompously assertive about the approach, because in his day so many bird paintings were done from skins alone without any mental or visual reference to the bird in life. JJA, however, did not work as Fred does, out of his head, drawing a recalled image; he set the wired bird up to match his image of it, and then began to draw. This method has displeased some critics: the eminent twentieth-century German ornithologist, Erwin Stresemann, who thought JJA was really no great shakes as an ornithologist in any respect, remarked that since JJA "was unable to remember form and movement and render them artistically, he frequently attached dead birds to a board in theatrically distorted positions and so copied them 'after nature.' " That fairly represents the attitude of many modern birdmen.

As Donald Culross Peattie said, "They charge him with scientific untruth, but what they really cannot endure is his personality." That's the key, I think. Audubon was an artist, not an illustrator, not a camera. Every artist *translates* life, presents an idiosyncratic vision of the world. JJA painted birds, to be sure, and he strove to paint them accurately, but in his best paintings his art transcends the birds; they were the matter through which he presented himself and his vision of the world.

Fred—an admirer of Audubon the artist—tells me about going to see the paintings for *The Birds of America* exhibited at the New-York Historical Society. "I walked into the exhibit hall, and there at the far end was a painting in which a red berry hung at the tip of some plant. I forget which bird was in the painting, but I remember stopping dead in my tracks and thinking, 'My God, the painting is about that berry.' "

MD From Fred Wetzel, two bird-banding stories. The first concerns an impassioned bander who recklessly climbed to a great horned owl's nest to band the owlets—not in daytime when the adult birds doze, but at twilight when they are awake and alert. A parent owl struck and ripped his shirt. Struck again and ripped the flesh on his back. Then ripped his scalp and one ear. The last thing the zealous bander remembered was his own blood pouring forth. He fell from the tree and woke up in the hospital, where repairs were made to his scalp and his ear, what was left of it. He now, says Fred, has a "sort of an ear."

The second story concerns a veterinarian's wife who was banding a Louisiana heron. All herons must be handled with care and adroitness. Keep a firm grip on the bill. She didn't. The heron drove its bill into her forehead. The lady and the heron were taken to the hospital as a single unit, to have the bill removed.

From St. Augustine, JJA went plantation-hopping—a succession of visits with three planters to the south. The winter of 1831–32 marked a lull in the Seminole Wars and JJA's hosts were at the peak of their prosperity. Four years later, when the last and probably the bloodiest of the Seminole wars broke out, the plantations where he stayed would be laid to waste. We tend to think of the Seminole Wars as a relatively brief series of conflicts between the U.S.A. and the Indians. Not so. It was a three-hundred-year-old conflict—massacres, treachery, and destruction that had begun with the Spanish conquests in the 1500s and would not be finished, once and for all, until 1842. A few years after Audubon's travels in Florida, Philip Hone, a former mayor of New York and gentleman about town, who had seen an exhibition of JJA's original paintings, wrote in his diary: "This is beyond a doubt the most magnificent collection on this subject in the world, and ought to be purchased by our government to form the nucleus of a great Natural Museum. A few thousand dollars spent in this way would be more honorable to the country than the millions which have been squandered upon the disastrous Florida war."

Today, April 25, when we follow JJA southward out of St. Augustine on the old shore highway, we have two guides to lead us from plantation to plantation: JJA, of course, his letters and commentaries, and *Audubon in Florida* by Kathryn Hall Proby (University of Miami Press, 1974)—a title, by the way, that was misunderstood by a young clerk in a bookshop who thought I was asking for "Autobahns in Florida" and led me to their department of roadmaps and atlases.

Patrols of brown pelicans above, masses of red and orange gaillardia in bloom along the road. The Slipped Disc Lounge, a scattering of condominiums, Devils Elbow Fish Camp, Fort Matanzas National

Monument, Marineland, and we come to the Washington Oaks state gardens, once a plantation belonging to General Joseph Hernandez.

Hernandez, who came originally from the island of Minorca, as did many of the Spaniards in and around St. Augustine, was an attorney (he had studied law in Havana), a militia officer, and the Florida Territory's first representative in the U.S. Congress. In 1837, it was General Hernandez who broke the Seminoles' resistance when he captured their war chief, Osceola, by tricking him into a parley under a flag of truce. Hernandez is remembered today as a hero of the Seminole Wars and a first citizen, though there were those among his contemporaries who described him as overbearing, foolish, and contentious. Whatever the truth about his personality, we do know that the General and Audubon did not hit it off. "General Hernandez," JJA wrote to Lucy, "has received me *rather* cooly, and I daresay is not likely to be troubled with our Company." However, good manners prevailed on both sides, and in mid-December JJA was invited to bring Ward and Lehman for a visit. Hernandez owned three plantations on the Matanzas River, and JJA doesn't tell us which of the three he visited, but tradition has it that Washington Oaks was the place.

The site of the old house is now a green lawn. It is lush and shady under the trees, the gardens are winding-pathed and very groomed. A portly German gent plays the heavy local birder for Mike, rumbling out his rich lists of warblers seen so far this morning. In a rocklined pool, a few steps away, a green heron chases minnows among the banded water snakes. The heron has made a pet of itself, one of the gardeners tells us, and follows the men about at their work. Two of the snakes are also pets—Susie and Charlie by name—their lives, however, in daily jeopardy at the hands of the tourists, who all too often kill any snakes in their path. The metal plant markers are a ready source of weapons. A tourist will pull one out of the garden bed, club the snake, and display his kill as a copperhead. But there are no copperheads at Washington Oaks, the gardener tells us. "We have a few diamondbacks around, but they keep their distance. They try to get out of your way as fast as they can. Our dangerous venomous snakes are the coral snakes, because they hide under the low foliage, and when one of the men reaches in to pull weeds, the coral snake will strike. So that's the

General Joseph Hernandez. *St. Augustine Historical Society*

only snake we kill. And they don't just bite. They chew."

Our informant is an older man who'd been a corporation accountant in Pennsylvania. The job was killing him. His doctor said he'd be dead in a year. So he moved to Florida, joined the state park system, learned gardening on the job, "And that"—he snaps his fingers—"was eighteen years ago." The green heron now stands stock still at the brink of the pool, ready to pounce. "Pussycat fishing," says the gardener.

MH There are no jolly stories from JJA about hunting adventures with the general. Hernandez did not share his guest's passion for wildlife, but a number of Audubon's essays, particularly on North American waterfowl, include references to things he observed during that visit. There's one note I particularly like, about the ruddy duck. "On small ponds they often dive and conceal themselves among the grass along the shore . . . I saw this very often when on the plantation of General HERNANDEZ in East Florida. If wounded, they dived and hid in the grass; but, as the ponds there were shallow, and had the bottom rather firm, I often waded out and pursued them. Then it was that I saw the curious manner in which they used their tail when swimming, employing it now as a rudder, and again with a vertical motion; the wings being also slightly opened, and brought into action as well as the feet." A nice picture, that: JJA poised thigh-deep in the pond—not unlike a fishing heron—watching the ruddy ducks swim past him underwater along the bottom.

However polite Hernandez was, JJA must have found something lacking under the general's roof. For when he received an invitation to go elsewhere, he took it. On Christmas morning, he and his assistants walked fifteen miles south to Bulow Ville, while the master of the plantation, John J. Bulow, sent a wagon for their luggage.

This new host was young, rich, generous, worldly, well educated and well read, a collector of books, and (from available evidence) probably an Indian sympathizer in the Seminole Wars. Having inherited the plantation on Bulow Creek when he was a schoolboy, by the time he turned twenty-one—about 1828—he was in full charge of the place, working three hundred slaves or more in the cultivation of cotton and sugar. When JJA visited in 1831, Bulow was building a large and costly sugar mill near the creek. An acquaintance described him as "very wild and dissipated" and a graduate "in all the devilment to be learned in Paris, France." That may be a slight exaggeration, but Bulow evidently did like his drink. He is said to have "kept an eight-oared barge and traveled in state with his guns and nets and tents and cooks and used to have a grand time of it." Obviously Audubon's sort of fellow.

A few days after JJA & Co. arrived, Bulow suggested they might like to go down Bulow Creek to the Halifax River in one of his boats and hunt for rare birds. So off they set—Bulow, JJA, probably Henry Ward, six Negro hands to row. The day was beautiful and the wind was at their stern. The birds were scarce, though some were collected for skinning. When nightfall came they put in at a live oak landing near the mouth of the Halifax, where wood was being cut for the U.S. Navy. The next morning, JJA and four of the hands went off shooting, looking particularly for brown pelicans; he wanted a superb example of the pelican to paint and two dozen more for his collection of skins. They found a pelican roost, and JJA dropped "two of the finest specimens I ever saw," but someone's error in gun-loading cost him the rest. By the time he returned to the live oak landing, JJA was discouraged by the general scarcity of birds, and Bulow suggested they start up the Halifax for home. A falling tide and a strong northeast wind were against them, however, and after nightfall, still short of the mouth of Bulow Creek, they ran hard aground on a mudbank hundreds of yards from any shore. They weren't dressed or equipped to spend the night there, and hadn't "the least hope of being able to raise a fire, for no trees except palm trees were near, and the *grand diable* himself could not burn one of them." After a miserable night trying to sleep in the bottom of the boat, they found themselves at dawn still stuck fast, the water in the river very low, and all hands cold and hungry. There was nothing for it but to get out and push the boat across the mud toward a bend in the river where a few burnable trees stood on a small patch of dry ground at the edge of the salt marsh—about a quarter-mile away. The "mire was up to our breasts, our limbs becoming stiffened, and almost useless, at every step we took. Our progress was as slowly performed as if we had been clogged with heavy chains." Two and a half hours later they were ashore—and two of the Negro crewmen collapsed. JJA got a fire going quickly ("in a crack"); the men were wrapped in blankets and fed hot tea—the only provisions left. "We all got warm again, and tolerably gay, although the prospect was far from being pleasant: no road to go home, or to any habitation; confined in a large salt marsh, with rushes head high, and miry." They now got back in the mud and shoved the boat upriver until they reached Bulow Creek, where they found enough water to float her. "[O]ur spirits rose . . . to such a pitch, that we in fun set fire to the whole marsh: crack, crack, crack! went the reeds, with a rapid blaze. We saw the marsh rabbits, &c. scampering from the fire by thousands as we pulled our oars." But water had drained from Bulow creek, as well, after at least two days of northeasterlies, and before long they were wading and pushing the boat again. So they finally made for shore, left the boat, and struck out for Bulowville along the ocean beach, the slaves packing the collected birds. The chill and the exhaustion of the last stretch of the escapade is plain as Audubon writes: "Pretty walking along the sea side beach of Florida in the month of December! with the wind at northeast, and we going in its very teeth, through sand, that sent our feet back six inches at every step of two feet that we made."

JJA's party finally left Bulow Ville in mid-January, having made it headquarters for about three weeks. "During the whole long stay," Audubon said, "there was no abatement of [Bulow's] kindness, or his unremitting efforts to make me comfortable, and to promote my researches." We have no reason to think they ever saw each other again.

When the fighting between whites and Seminoles broke out four years later, the militia occupied Bulow Ville—over Bulow's strenuous objections. Many men in his situation, occupying the frontier between the Indian community and the white civilization of the scattered Florida towns, got along well with the Seminoles, bought all the plantation meat from Indian hunters, opposed the national government's plans to move the Seminoles to lands west of the Mississippi River, and thought the warfare was madness—particularly since the plantations were usually major casualties. According to tradition, Bulow was a close friend and drinking companion of Coacoochie, a local Indian prince. So now here comes the militia—a detachment called the "Mosquito Roarers," to be precise—invading the Halifax region to protect the planters from the Indians in December, 1835. "Mr. Bulow . . . was very much disgusted by the presence of troops

at his place," the commanding officer told a Congressional committee later, "and very uncivil." Uncivil indeed, particularly when the
officers decided the Mosquito Roarers should be quartered at Bulow
Ville and must fortify the plantation as a refuge for the people of the
region. Bulow set up a cannon and fired blanks at the soldiers as they
approached.

"[S]o rude was he in his reception of the officers," said another
witness, "that they took possession of his house and would not admit
him to their mess *at his own table.* He was pressed as a soldier, and,
it is said, put under guard." Cotton-bale breastworks were set up
around his plantation, and for nearly a month it was a DP camp. Then
the Mosquito Roarers went on a foraging expedition and were badly
mauled by a superior force. Bulow Ville was abandoned, and within
days the Seminoles had sacked it. "We gazed . . . on a scene over
which ruin brooded," reported a reconnoitering officer. "The noble
mill and mansion are utterly destroyed, and an extensive library of
splendid works is scattered over the field, torn or fired . . . Here we
rescued a Milton and Shakespeare and mean to make them companions of our otherwise weary way."

Young John Bulow died three months later in Paris—how, the
record doesn't say. He wasn't yet thirty years old. Audubon said his
host had "rheumatic pains," so Bulow may have died of heart disease.
The family tradition is, apparently, that he died of drink. I doubt it.
But he may of course have drunk himself to death in a fit of rage and
sorrow over the unnecessary destruction of his patrimony.

Mary and I joke about the number of these Audubon-related
places that have become parks and historical shrines. But in fact it
is a fair measure of Audubon's time and place in our history. In East
Florida, comfortable as he was in the keeping of the stuffy General
Hernandez and the spirited John J. Bulow, he was on the very edge
of wilderness during a short pause in white–Indian wars. Here at
Bulow Ruins State Park, that fact should leap out at us. No one took
over Bulow Ville and rebuilt it; we have come upon a plantation that,
only four years after Audubon described it as "immense," died in a
type of North American war that self-aggrandizing history and the
horse-opera cinema have transmogrified so that few people now
know what really happened. The fruitful climate of Florida has
obliterated the openness of the plantation; but distilled here, as if we

could rest a hand on it, is the national character in 1835—brave, stupid, rich-quick, inventive, cruel, and pioneering.

MD   There is a picnic grove with children's swings where the mansion stood. Screened shelters for cook-outs. A concession building with rest rooms and a Pepsi Cola machine. Bulow Creek is now a "canoe trail"; there is a nature walk through the old slave quarters (a single delicate spiral of ladies'-tress orchis blooming in the pine needles), and deep in the forest, a little museum with an exhibit of farm implements and machinery from the big days of sugar cane, cotton, and indigo, and a collection of remnants from the ruins— shards of Ironstone and Staffordshire, an ale bottle from Dublin, a bootscraper, a bone-handled fork, a clay pipe, the lid from a blue and white Canton teapot.

Vines, mosses, ferns, live oaks, and pines. Above the ruins of the sugar mill, a canopy of palm trees and the dry rustling of the fronds scratching together. The mill itself, magnificent in its desolation. Arched doorways and towering round columns. Green fingers of mosses and vines creeping in, up, and over the stones. A haunting and melancholy place. It outdoes in reality the jacket cover of any Gothic novel. And what a hellhole it must have been in this climate when the boiling vats in the mill were fired up.

A sudden thought that deserves comment: Audubon was coolly received by General Hernandez, but warmly received by John Bulow. From this evidence, we form our personal opinions of both men. The General, says Mike, was a stuffed shirt. Young Bulow, however dissolute he may have been, shines as the best of companions. Our cup of tea. With these ipso facto appraisals, I realize how proprietary we've become about JJA. It's all very well for us to criticize Audubon. He belongs to Mike and me for the time being. But we will not accept displeasure with his company from other people who knew him. We dismiss them as inadequate, as fools.

In a letter to Lucy at this time, JJA made a cryptic comment: "I write this Laconically because I have reasons for so doing as long as I am at St. Augustine; a place which I assure thee is far from being *generally* pleasant." Mike spots this sentence, and I seize upon it. Is this a sly reference to General Hernandez? Was he reading JJA's

Bulow Ville ruins. *MH*

outgoing mail? Had he pinned him as a Seminole sympathizer because of Audubon's friendship with Bulow? If so, was he the one who
made St. Augustine unpleasant for JJA? We leap to conclusions. The
letter reinforces our dislike of Hernandez.

Now, to catch up with Lucy.

From Audubon's replies to her letters, it's clear that she was
woeful and discontent. He wrote her time and again to keep up her
spirits. Keep up a good heart. Be gay. Be happy. Do not despond.
Take care of thy dear sweet self for my sake. Of course she was lonely.
He urged her to pass her time reading and writing and visiting
friends from the old days. "Do not suffer thy spirits to depress thy
Phisical faculties . . . Depend upon it we must yet see better days. My
name is now ranging high and our name will stand still higher." Lucy
also seems to have been in terror of something dire happening to
him, because he assured her repeatedly that he would come back
safe and sound, that he was not likely to drown at sea and that he was
taking good care of himself. She must do likewise.

Oh dear. Poor Lucy. She had given up her snug haven in St.
Francisville and it was now pillar to post again, living out of a suit-
case, visiting around with whichever of her family could take her in.
There had been a problem at Thomas Bakewell's in Cincinnati, because his household was large and he didn't have enough room for
her to stay very long, and when she returned to Louisville, she was
uncomfortable at William Bakewell's, because she didn't approve of
his business arrangements with John and Victor. Audubon replied
that she must manage to live quietly with her brother's family; William had a good heart and "never mind the roughness of *the Bark!*"
He also wrote that he could not cut short his trip. No, he had to finish
what he'd set out to do, but in a letter from Bulow's plantation, he
said: "I am now on my last Journey after Birds in North America."
As the years went by and the trips rolled on, I wonder how many
times Lucy charged him with that broken promise.

One can sympathize with Lucy Audubon, and I don't mean to
make light of her woes. But I do mean to refute the popular
image of her as the noble, supportive wife. She was as human as
anyone else. She had her frailties. She did not suffer in silence,
and we now have two instances (his English trip and the Florida

trip) when Lucy wanted John James to quit in the midst of his project and come home.

MH "I have been on the Head Waters of the St John by land from the Alifax River," wrote JJA to Lucy, characteristically dropping the H, "across the wildest desolate tract of Pine Barrens, Swamp and Lakes that I ever saw—I remained 2 days at *Spring Garden* . . . and went by Water to the St John—had an island named after me—a Compleat Mass of orange Trees and Live Oaks." In the *Ornithological Biography* he gave more details. He and "an amiable and accomplished Scotch gentleman," an engineer who built sugar mills for the Florida planters, mounted Indian horses and headed west across the pine barrens from the Bulow plantation, forded the three broad forks of Haw Creek, entered hillier, more varied terrain that was dotted with many shallow lakes, and arrived at the plantation of Colonel Orlando Rees, where they spent the next two nights, as Audubon explored the back country by boat. He later remarked in a formal essay that on the way in from the Halifax River they had seen "scarcely a bird, and not a single quadruped, not even a rat; nor can one imagine a poorer and more desolate country." To Lucy he was even more caustic; he'd read William Bartram's *Travels,* and Bartram—being mainly a botanist—had been delighted with Florida, called it a garden. "Kentucky," said JJA, "nay the worst of Kentucky is a Paradise compared with this *Garden of the United States.*" But by his own account, the day he spent on the water near Spring Garden in the company of his host was flowery and idyllic indeed, with alligators to look at and many birds, including a new one, the glossy ibis, which he shot—and then, because of the swampy ground, couldn't collect. They stopped on a little island not far from the head of the St. John's River, where they spread a cloth, ate a meal, and Audubon smelled the wild orange blossoms and watched the hummingbirds. The island had no name, Colonel Rees told his guest, so it would from now on be Audubon's Isle.

We head inland ourselves, Bulow Ville to the old Rees plantation, part of our journey taking us on Route 304, a dirt causeway built across the bogs and barrens, roughly parallel to the Indian trails that Audubon traveled on horseback. The land is poor looking, all right, but it is certainly no less in that respect than, say, the barrens of Cape

Cod or southern New Jersey. Haw Creek, of which we cross all three branches, is greatly diminished. Audubon said that each of the streams was between a quarter and a half mile across, and that was in the dry season. Doubtless Florida's desperate water problems, poor water management, and the drainage of wetlands are reflected in Haw Creek as elsewhere: a small child could toss a rock across any one of the branches today. And what water remains is pretty well covered with a beautiful plant—though a dreadful pest—that has put down its roots in southern waterways since JJA was here: the water hyacinth.

MD In a popular contemporary biography of Audubon, the author—who wanted to add a touch of local color to the narrative —described a Louisiana bayou in the 1820s as a sheet of floating water hyacinths; a pretty, botanic anachronism. Water hyacinths were introduced from Brazil as decorative planting at the New Orleans Cotton Exposition of 1884 and took off for the wild from there. The flowers bloom in spiked clusters, each flower two inches across, six lavender-blue petals, the top petals touched at the center with a yellow blaze that's marked with deep purple veinings. Utterly beautiful and an insidious pain in the neck wherever they run rampant and interfere with boat traffic. Millions are spent annually to keep waterways clear of them, but here at Haw Creek it's live and let live, and the stream winds like a purple ribbon through the trees.

I'm working up an imaginary pastoral scene furnished entirely with flora and fauna that Audubon never saw in this country. In the sky, I have flocks of European starlings and European house sparrows and a cloud of gypsy moths. There's a grove of eucalyptus trees, kudzu vines, lots of boll weevils, Japanese beetles, and fire ants, and a pasture full of gray, hump-necked Brahman cattle. Feeding at the heels of the Brahmans, as their hooves kick up insects out of the zoysia grass, is a flock of cattle egrets—birds native to Africa that made their appearance in the New World in the late nineteenth century—arriving perhaps by cattle boat or by storm winds. No one knows. And now, for a slather of purple in the foreground, masses of water hyacinth.

Native plants in bloom this April day are purple passion flower in a damp ditch. Fragrant wild pink roses. Purple skullcap, yellow co-reopsis, and rattlebox trees with clusters of sizzling red-orange flowers—the most intense color of any in the spectrum and the most visible in any landscape. A wood stork flies overhead, white plumage, jet black wing tips, its toes pointed, the wings held steady, as it sky dives on the wind. JJA: "Now in large circles they seem to ascend toward the upper regions of the atmosphere; now, they pitch to-wards the earth; and again, gently rising, they renew their gyrations . . . the most beautiful evolutions that can well be conceived."

The dirt causeway ends at Haw Creek Ranch—Brahmans graz-ing, cattle egret at their feet—and we turn south. Audubon made this trip to Spring Garden expressly to see a "curious spring," of which he had heard "wonderful accounts." It was one of many sulphur springs in this area but unique for its size, a circular, sandy, shell-strewn basin almost sixty feet in diameter, the water bubbling up in the center from its subterranean source at a rate estimated by Colo-nel Rees to be 499,500 gallons per minute. The name Spring Garden no longer exists. Rees' plantation is now a privately owned resort park called Ponce de Leon Spring in the town of De Leon Springs. The Indians, who had once brought their sick and wounded here, called it the Spring of the Healing Waters, and based on Ponce de Leon's account of his quest for the Fountain of Youth, he is believed to have made his way here by boat from the St. John's River, seven miles away. Spring Garden changed hands many times over the centuries in the conflicts between the Indians, the Spaniards, and the English. When Colonel Rees took over the property there were ves-tiges of a plantation and sugar mill that he then restored and refurb-ished, and all of this was again destroyed by the Seminoles four years after Audubon's visit. The new owner rebuilt in 1854. The Union troops destroyed it again in 1864. It was rebuilt in 1875. Then along came the railroad. The town of De Leon Springs was platted, a bathhouse built on the edge of the spring, and a pavillion for picnics and dances. Excursion trains brought customers and thus began the spa and pleasure grounds that we visit today. Central Florida's His-toric Wonderland. The brochure makes much of the Old Spanish Sugar Mill and its date is boldly proclaimed as 1570, all historic facts to the contrary. There is the Hangman's Oak, the Indian Mound, the twenty-seven-hundred-year-old cypress, camellia and azalea gardens. Campsites, paddle boats, canoes, rowboats, scuba diving in the Spring Creek run, and SWIMMING IN THE FOUNTAIN OF YOUTH. A cartoon on the cover of the brochure pictures a bearded Spaniard in a sixteenth-century helmet; he is pop-eyed with joy at finding himself transformed by the magic spring into a roly-poly, diaper-clad baby, while a shapely Indian maiden, who looks like a Varga girl, gives him a winsome smile.

We pay our admission at the gate and join the procession of automobiles, round the corner of the tree-lined drive, and park on a wooded bluff overlooking The Great Spring. A crowd of cars, vans, and pickup trucks have been drawn into a semicircle to create a hillside amphitheater. At our front fender, an electric generator that's stowed under a flowering hibiscus feeds the power cables that twine down to the red hot center of this encampment—a VW van with turntable, amplifiers, and a bonfire of music. Mobs, *mobs* of young people bake in the beat—sunning, lolling, gazing, mooning, waiting. At the periphery, they turn cartwheels, pitch frisbies, drink beer from kegs in washtubs of ice, sip wine from paper cups, wreath their necks with leis of Spanish moss. Pot on the breeze. Peacocks in the trees. My God. If Audubon could see this! The hillside of brown bodies and enough girls in bikinis to satisfy his insatiable eye for "graceful female forms." A garden of earthly delights. At the foot of the bluff is a new bathhouse, a hamburger stand, a covered dance floor, and the big gray-green circular spring. It's now enclosed with a cement wall and ringed with a cement deck, but the natural floor of the spring remains: white sand, still strewn with shells. Whatever the mysterious workings of the watertable that feeds it, the sulphurous smell that Audubon found "highly nauseous" is gone. I kneel at the edge and scoop up a handful of water to taste it. There's no sulphurous flavor, either.

Only a few people are in the pool, mostly small children and oldsters. (This is not where the action is.) We take a turn past the Sugar Mill, now the Grill and Griddle House. Old gears, cogs, sugar vats lie in the grass. The music is still aflame on the hillside and follows us to the gate. Audubon's visit is not mentioned in the park brochure, but he was remembered by the town fathers when they laid out De Leon Spring a century ago. One block away from the park entrance gate is Audubon Avenue, a shacky little road leading

Ponce de Leon Spring. *MH*

off into the trees and labeled with a rusting green and white metal street sign.

MH In February 1832, JJA sailed past Jacksonville and the Wetzels' door. After returning to St. Augustine from Bulow Ville, he and Ward and Lehman hitched a ride on the U.S. Schooner *Spark*, which explored far up the St. John's River on a search for stands of live oak that the Navy might reserve for its future ships. JJA was ecstatic at the invitation: "What will my Philadelphia Friends say or think when they read that Audubon is on board of the U.S. Schooner of War . . . going around the Floridas after *Birds?*" But neither he nor the Navy found what they were looking for. A "useless expense, of time, and labour," reported the lieutenant in charge, "the Land on both sides of the River (alternately) consisting of Pine Barrens and endless Swamps." Game was scarce, and they dined largely on possum and alligator meat. As for JJA, who hadn't had a new bird to draw in a month and was frantic with the inactivity, there was "Scarcely a Bird to be seen and these of the most common sort—I look to the leaving of [the Floridas] as an Happy event." The leaving of it occurred rather sooner than he had expected. He had a falling out with the schooner's commander, got off the *Spark*, and by hired boat and then shank's mare JJA & Co. made for St. Augustine. After waiting around "that miserable spot" for another week or so, they caught the Charleston–St. Augustine packet that had brought them in November, and fled north. As on the down voyage, a gale drove the *Agnes* inside the protecting sea-isles, which this time gave JJA an opportunity to visit Savannah and sell some subscriptions. From there he rode the mail coach to Charleston, arriving tanned and wearing a full beard—"gray as a badger & not over clean," Bachman reminded him years later. "I think a Buffaloe Bull after having wallowed in the mud or a grizzly bear 47 years old must have claimed you as par nobile frater."

THE FLORIDA KEYS

AND THE DRY TORTUGAS

APRIL–MAY 1832

MH   So far, Florida had been a disappointment. JJA didn't like the terrain; the birds were scarce; and what he had found he had had to suffer for. He wrote to Featherstonhaugh of "scrambling through the vilest thickets of scrubby live oaks and palmitoes, that appear to have been created for no purpose but to punish us for our sins." As for botanist William Bartram's well-known description of Florida as a garden, snorted Audubon, "A garden, where all that is not mud, mud, mud, is sand, sand, sand; where the fruit is so sour that it is not eatable, and where in place of singing birds and golden fishes, you have a species of ibis that you cannot get when you have shot it, and alligators, snakes, and scorpions."

Charleston had much more to offer than that. There was Bachman's hospitality and company, and birds to shoot and draw. But though he was able to report gleefully to Lucy in mid-April that he had made "9 *Beautiful* Drawings and collected an immense deal of information &c," he went on to say that he and his "lads" would be returning to "that poor Country the Floridas" in a few days, sailing for the Keys and the Dry Tortugas aboard the revenue cutter *Marion.*

The cutter's orders were to proceed to Key West and examine the Tortugas Light House, where alterations had recently been made, and not to start back from that vicinity until May 20 or so—in other words, to stretch a trip of two or three weeks into an excursion about six weeks long. So it was back into the spiky brush, the mud, mud, mud, and the sand, sand, sand, as the *Marion* island-hopped out the Keys and the Tortugas.

JJA   Having landed on one of the Florida Keys, I scarcely had time to cast a glance over the diversified vegetation which presented itself, when I observed a pair of birds mounting perpendicularly in the air, twittering with a shrill continued note new to me. The country itself was new: it was what my mind had a thousand times before conceived a tropical scene to be. As I walked over many plants, curious and highly interesting to me, my sensations were joyous in the highest degree . . .

I was on one of those yet unknown islets, which the foot of man has seldom pressed. A Flycatcher unknown to me had already presented itself, and the cooing of a Dove never before heard came on my ear. I felt some of that pride, which doubtless pervades the breast of the discoverer of some hitherto unknown land. Although desirous of obtaining the birds before me, I had no wish to shoot them at that moment. My gun lay loosely on my arms, my eyes were rivetted on the Flycatcher, my ears open to the soft notes of the Dove. Reader, such are the moments, amid days of toil and discomfort, that compensate for every privation.

MH   Gadzooks! Our traveling companion may have found his tropical expectations at last satisfied, but the Keys are not what we hoped they'd be. The setting is exotic—immense sky piled high with cumulus, glowing turquoise water, and a chain of low, dark-green mangrove-and-coral islands curling southwestward for as far as we can see. And down the spine of this chain are shore-to-shore beach houses and motels and gas stations and souvenir shops, fed by what must be, hands down, the most dangerous highway in all of North America—for a hundred miles, Key Largo to Key West, two lanes of concrete, U.S. 1, negotiated by opposing columns of vehicles: roaring semis hustling supplies to the end of the line, tourists browsing, locals in a hurry, puttering neighborhood traffic. It's crazy. Accident Alley. We are told that the natives play it smart and do their *serious* traveling on Route 1 at two or three in the morning when they drive at eighty or a hundred miles an hour. In daylight—hell, then they only go seventy or so, when trying to get around a line of cars poking along at fifty, while the oncoming traffic looks for holes in the guard rail. Myself, I'd rather be on the *Marion* with JJA, poking from island to island and taking two weeks to get to Key West. We're there in less than a day and arrive April 15, two and a half weeks ahead of JJA, whose ship dropped anchor at last off Key West after sunset on May 4, 1832.

MD   Key West: the lure of land's end. Sea, sky, trade winds. A tropical English–Spanish culture steeped in a history of pirates, smugglers, turtlers, revenuers, fishermen, wreckers. Now, an artist's colony, homosexual colony, hippie colony, Cuban colony—thousands of refugees from Castro's Cuba, many of whom made it here on homemade rafts, tires lashed together, scraps of cloth sewn into sails.

A naval base, the naval air station. Shrimp and lobster fishermen, treasure hunters, the flotsam of losers, drifters, and beach bums. Earnest handicraft peddlers. Gift shop and boutique entrepreneurs. Pensioned retirees. A well-heeled winter colony with the requisite country club, golf club, yacht club, and garden club activities. And funneling onto Key West via Route 1, day and night, a land mass of tourists.

Barely below the surface is the seamy world of heavy trade in contraband (hard drugs, guns, illegal aliens, you name it) and the machinations of secret agents of every persuasion (federal connections, Cuban connections, South American connections, underworld connections). One young man who scrounged a living here this winter on the scabby underside of Key West described the island community as "spooky." Then said he, sweepingly: "*Every*one is an agent." An ex-cop, who retired from the local force at his wife's insistence ("Too many shoot-outs") told us that the second biggest crime, after drug-running, is murder. "Seven unsolved murders in the past two years. They could be solved, but nobody's trying very hard. They pick up their pay checks and don't give a damn."

I like Mark Twain's summation of Key West. He was here in 1867 and wrote that it seemed to be a pretty little tropical-looking town with handsome shade trees, very cool and pleasant, and that the chief business, so far as he could determine, was mostly gin-mills catering to the soldiers from Fort Taylor. Twain concluded: "If I have got Key West sized up right, they would receive War, Famine, Pestilence and Death without question—call them all by some fancy name, and then rope in the survivors and sell them good cigars and brandies at easy prices and horrible dinners at infamous rates."

But JJA had no complaints. Much of his pleasure here was due to

Key West in 1838, looking north. *Monroe County Public Library, Key West*

Dr. Benjamin Strobel, an Army physician, a Charleston man, and a brother-in-law of Mrs. John Bachman. Strobel was at the harbor to meet him when the *Marion* arrived, saw him almost every day, and admired him without reservation. He wrote that Audubon was the most enthusiastic and indefatigable man he had ever known, that "It is impossible to associate with him without catching some portion of his spirit," and that Audubon's engaging manner (frank, free, affable, polite) and his French savoire faire enabled him to accomplish many things: "Every one appears to enlist at once in his service." Dr. Strobel also wrote a splendid account of JJA in top form, striking out on a circuit of Key West at two-thirty in the morning and in the lead through bogs, thickets, mud, mosquitoes and sandflies as the heat rose under a broiling sun; other members of the party fell by the wayside and stole home by horseback, while he plunged on until eleven A.M. But to JJA, said Dr. Strobel, "this was an every day affair." While he was here, Audubon drank molasses and water as a pick-me-up and thirst quencher. We've tried it. Not bad.

MH   On at least one of these expeditions Audubon was the follower, not the leader. Major James Glassel at the Army barracks in Key West made available to Audubon the services of a sergeant named Sykes, who knew the island well. Sykes impressed JJA as "a perfect woodsman," by guiding him from one side of the island to the other through the worst of tangles "in as masterly a manner as ever did an Indian." In Charleston Audubon had seen a pigeon's head that Dr. Strobel sent to Bachman, and he believed it was a new species. Sykes knew the bird and where to find it. So off they went into the thickets, to be tripped by branches, stuck by thorns and cactus, bitten by mosquitoes. Suddenly Sykes crouched, then darted ahead, raised his gun, and fired. " 'I have it,' cried he. 'What?' cried I. 'The pigeon' —and he disappeared. The heat was excessive, and the brushwood here was so thick and tangled, that had not Mr. Sykes been a United States soldier, I should have looked upon him as bent on retaliating on behalf of 'the eccentric naturalist' [Constantine Rafinesque, whom Audubon had "guided" through a canebrake]." JJA crawled after him, found him with the prize in hand, and took it eagerly. It was a small pigeon, not quite twelve inches long, creamy white below and a rich red-brown on top, with a broad white line below the eye and a bright iridescence on its head and neck and upper back. "I never felt, nor did my companion, that our faces and hands were covered with musquitoes; and although the perspiration made my eyes smart, I was as much delighted as ever I had been on such an occasion." He wrapped the pigeon in a "winding sheet" of paper to protect it, and on they went, but shot no other bird that day.

When they emerged from the thickets onto the beach at last and sat to rest, JJA took out the bird to study it again. "[A]s I now more quietly observed the brilliant changing metallic hues of its plumage, I could not refrain from exclaiming—'But who will draw it?' " (Audubon's rendering, in fact, is not one of his most successful.) It was a new species, and he named it the Key West Pigeon, or Dove; the name stuck, more or less—now it's the Key West quail-dove—even though Key West was the very northernmost edge of its range, which includes the Greater Antilles, Cuba, Haiti, northwestern Bahamas, southwestern Puerto Rico. Apparently it used to be a fairly regular summer visitor to Key West but now is considered rare over almost all its territory and hasn't been seen at Key West since 1897.

No use looking for it then. Another of JJA's new pigeons from the Keys—the blue-headed quail-dove—hasn't been reported here since Audubon saw a pair on the beach at Key West; he said the locals believed more could be found on the Mule Keys, nearby, but that a day's diligent search made there by himself and friends didn't turn up a one. It's a Cuban bird, and the people who referee these matters for the American Ornithologists Union have decided JJA's record is "unsatisfactory"; they have stricken the bird from the North American list. Again, it seems unlikely that Audubon would either have mistaken something else for the blue-headed quail-dove or lied about seeing the species. But he apparently made his lovely drawing from some captive live birds in Key West—and then ate the subjects and found them as tasty as bobwhites, which means "extremely agreeable to the palate"; so it is possible that the "wild" birds he saw on the beach were escaped captives brought in as poultry from Cuba. Anyway, no blue-headed quail-doves to search for either. A third pigeon, the little Zenaida dove, has been seen very rarely in the Keys since Audubon's day; it too is a more southerly species. So the only "new" member of the family Columbidae that Audubon or Harwood could still find here is the white-crowned pigeon, but I haven't seen it yet. I'm looking.

MD   The three big names in Key West are Ernest Hemingway, Tennessee Williams, and John James Audubon. Sloppy Joe's bar advertises itself everywhere as Hemingway's favorite hangout, and the Hemingway house is a registered National Historic Landmark. "Covers One Acre Including Pool and Guest House—BRING YOUR CAMERA . . . HEMINGWAY WROTE HERE." Tennessee Williams' property is described as a "quaint Conch Cottage and guest house with a great spreading travellers palm in front," and when he dies it too will probably become a heavily advertised tourist mecca.

At Greene and Whitehead Streets is the Audubon House, a white clapboard building that's now a museum supported by a private foundation. "It's 1830 . . . and you are there! Authentic antiques and rare art treasures restored to its original elegance the home where the famed naturalist and painter John James Audubon lived in 1832 while painting wild life of the Florida Keys," reads the museum brochure. "The Audubon House was built in 1830 for Captain John H. Geiger, skilled pilot and master wrecker who selected the original furniture from the cargoes of ships from many lands wrecked on the Florida Reef . . ."

A tour hostess guides you through. The new collection of antiques

Audubon House. *MH*

Audubon's white-crowned pigeons in the branch of a Geiger tree. *Courtesy of The New-York Historical Society, New York City*

is awesome. Queen Anne, Chippendale, Hepplewhite, Regency. In the front hall hangs a portrait of JJA's "sociable host, the jovial Captain Geiger." On the second floor is an original elephant folio edition of *The Birds of America.* We go out on the gallery that overlooks the garden, and there below (how perfect!) an orange *Cordia* is in bloom, the tropical tree that JJA used as background foliage for his painting of the white-crowned pigeon. They say he did that painting in this house, and there at the end of the gallery is the little room furnished to represent his studio. From its window, yes, another view of the lovely flowering tree. According to a booklet on tropical plants that was written by a research botanist at the University of Miami, it was Audubon himself who gave the *Cordia* its popular name—"Geiger Tree"—in honor of his Key West host.

It all dovetails so nicely. Not a piece is missing. But the truth of it is, the whole lovely story is based on Key West lore. There's not a shred of evidence that Audubon ever set foot in this house. Nor was the nickname of "Geiger tree" his doing. That apparently was of local origin, perhaps inspired by the publication of the engraving that so handsomely pictured the Captain's flowering *Cordia.*

First of all, during his two weeks at Key West, JJA lived aboard the *Marion,* as he had promised Lucy he would do throughout the cruise, because she worried about his catching fevers ashore. Dr. Strobel also makes it clear that JJA lived on the *Marion.*

Secondly, here's what JJA had to say about his painting of the white-crowned pigeons: "I have placed a pair of these Pigeons on a low, flowering tree, which is rather scarce on the Keys. . . . *The Rough-leaved Cordia* . . . I saw only two individuals at Key West, where, as was supposed, they had been introduced from Cuba. . . . Both trees were on private property, and grew in a yard opposite to that of Dr. Strobel, through whose influence I procured a large bough, from which the drawing was made." In 1831, Dr. Strobel had rented a house at 205 Whitehead Street and was presumably still living there in 1832 when Audubon came to Key West. Captain Geiger, at Greene and Whitehead Streets, was a neighbor.

In the third place, JJA never mentioned Captain Geiger in any letters, essays, or memoirs on Key West. He spoke only of Dr. Strobel, Sergeant Sykes, and Major Glassel, who put his barge at Audubon's disposal and from whose cool verandah JJA saw a frigatebird, on the wing, rob a tern of its fish.

But this is the stuff from which myths are made. Audubon immortalized the Captain's beautiful trees in one of his paintings. Audubon was a celebrity. Everyone likes to have a firsthand link with a celebrated person. Therefore, how easy (how tempting) to move Audubon bag and baggage off the *Marion* and out of the hands of Dr. Strobel, Sergeant Sykes, and Major Glassel, into Captain Geiger's new house. After all, if Audubon painted a man's trees, it must follow that he was the man's guest. And there you have it: The Audubon House.

None of this is news to historians. The evidence has been sifted many times before, and there are Florida researchers who have said nothing, out of courtesy to the foundation—though we know of one visiting Audubon scholar who challenged a museum hostess with the facts and threw the house tour into confusion.

What about the historic implications? Is it honorable to make claims based on folklore and hearsay? Or should the foundation be applauded for memorializing JJA's journey to Key West? Should we not be grateful that the Geiger house was saved and restored? It was on its last legs in the 1950s, tumbling, unpainted, and forlorn; it was still the family home, the residence of Captain Geiger's grandson, who'd also been a wrecker and harbor pilot—Captain Willy Smith. He's remembered around town not so much as a recluse, the way the museum hostesses tell it, but as an old bachelor who fell into bad drinking habits after repeal—a little man who was never seen without his captain's hat, drunk or sober, and he just let the house go. He didn't care. He lived in the shambles with an old mulatto woman to cook for him. (It sounds like Eliza Pirrie's granddaughter at St. Francisville, living in the shambles of Oakley with her flea-ridden hound dogs.) The oldtimers in Key West are amused that it should be called the Audubon House, when he didn't own it, and that the other historic shrine should be called the Hemingway House, when he didn't build it.

The final question, however, is this: Does it matter that history is bent and stretched to suit the immediate moment? I find a philosophical parallel in Florence Audubon's remark that her grandfather never painted birds on china, but if it pleases people to think he did, then let them think it. If it pleases people to believe that Audubon lived under Captain Geiger's roof, just so. What harm is done? Let them believe it.

A footnote: Since our visit to Key West, the elephant folio of *The Birds of America* was stolen from the Audubon House—alarm wires cut, the giant edition spirited away, but shortly afterwards recovered by the FBI, three volumes in Marion, North Carolina, one volume in New York City. This was not a unique event. The first folio of one hundred engravings from a complete set of *The Birds of America,* which Audubon had sold to Union College in Schenectady in 1844, was stolen from the college library in 1971, and again a rescue was effected by the FBI, with drawn guns at a motel in Queens, New York. Fine arts is big business, and big business attracts the underworld. The last sale of an Audubon elephant folio was in 1977 at an auction in London; the take-home price: $325,000.

If you have lost the herd instinct, camping along Route 1 on the Keys is crowded and sometimes downright ugly, except at the two state parks, where you must apply for a reservation months ahead of time. There simply isn't room for everyone on this string of islands, so tenuously linked by the two-lane thread of concrete. We've heard speculation of what could happen if a severe hurricane struck—a disaster-film scene of thousands of cars trapped on the highway and causeways as everyone tries to make it back to the mainland, the sea slashing through and carrying them off forever in one gulp—including Route 1, you understand. No compromises. All of it would go.

There will be no series of notes from the three high-density campgrounds at which we put in down here. One sample evening will suffice.

April 19. Key West Seaside Park. "20 Acres of Fun & Sun." Mike and I huddle together, eyes streaming, bandannas tied across our noses and mouths—books, bathtowels, road maps, anything we could lay our hands on slammed over our dishes of food and the cooking pots on the propane stove—as a gummy, petroleum-based, gray, poisoned fog of mosquito spray settles wetly over Seaside Park. We had only five seconds' warning. A flashing rooftop light, a howling siren, *"wow-wow-wow,"* and the county mosquito control truck was upon us, careering through the campground at top speed and laying its wake of noxious vapors. It takes half an hour for the air to clear.

The mosquitoes, who share with us this six-by-ten plot of ground that we have rented for the night at a barbaric price, beat it smartly into the shelter of the oleander bushes behind the tent, and then sally forth again to pick up where they left off.

The brochure for Seaside Park has a list of do's and don'ts concerning pets and unattended children and mini-bikes, and let's maintain cleanliness and beauty, please wrap all garbage, no laundry lines at campsites, "use clean bathroom habits," and after 10:00 P.M., campers, it's Quiet Time.

Well, down here in the backwaters of the tenting area, Quiet Time is severely interrupted by a couple of night watchmen quartered in a popup trailer next to us. Shortly after midnight, they have a rouser of a fight down by the canal, draw blood, and one of them pitches the other fellow into the drink. Their venom spent, they sit (from 2 A.M. to 4 A.M.) six inches from our tent wall with their drinks and their remorse and their pledges of fast friendship forever and I-don't-want-your-blood-on-my-hands-old-buddy. A virtuoso performance from both of them, though it loses its poignancy, at least to this audience, on the third, fourth, and fifth times through. As a spin-off from the disorder of the night watch, a zombie population of shaggy young men creeps into Seaside Park after dark to sleep on the counters in the lunchroom and in the laundromat, their rolled sweaters or sneakers for pillows. In the morning, with a supersensory skill like that of the mosquitoes fleeing the spray truck, they vanish seconds before the Big Boss arrives in his Big Cream-Colored Hardtop. He is aware of disarray after hours and buttonholes *me*, under the illusion that I am a respectable citizen, and asks sharply: What went on here last night? (Who watches the watchmen?) He is slick and sleek, dressed to the nines in freshly pressed resort wear. His fingernails are clean. I switch allegiance instantly, go over to the side of the watchmen and the zombies, and plead ignorance of any breach of the peace. (If the boss wants to know what's going on at his campground, let him get up out of his air-conditioned, mosquito-free bed and come down here and find out for himself.)

JJA went exploring by barge among the outer islands off Key West. We do the same by charter boat—the sea, which we call turquoise, the "curious light pea-green" that had so struck JJA. On his painting of the great white heron, which he placed against a view of Key West, JJA made a special point of this in a message written to Havell at the bottom of the picture: "have the water of a Pea-green tint." In certain lights, the color of the sea is so vibrant and so rich that the color of the sky is drained to a wishy-washy blue. We go out to an old lighthouse on a curved sliver of coral. Mike wades ashore to bird. I tumble overboard to snorkle with the skipper: purple jewel fish, yellow and black rock beauties, flamingo-tongue snails, pink and white jellyfish—the underwater exotica that JJA did not see, or at least did not mention.

We go on to Ballast Key and Woman Key, islands where JJA chased down seabirds, "a burning sun over my head and my body oozing at every pore." (One of the oldtimers, a former fisherman and prohibition-era rum runner, told us that the climate here is so debilitating that where it takes three stevedores to load a piano aboard ship in New York, it will take twelve men to offload the piano at Key West.) The outer islands are lovely, isolated and inviting. Our skipper delivers fresh water to a solitary campsite—one tent, a fire on the beach. Ah, that's more like it.

MH   In less than an hour's foraging on Ballast Key, under the gun of a falling tide and a captain anxious to depart, I find thirty species of birds—herons, shorebirds, warblers, blackbirds. Remarkable. I'll bet that a week on one of these keys would produce a hundred species or more. And what a pleasure it would be to sit on such an isolated beach for a few hours just to watch the brown pelicans fishing, corkscrewing down into the shallows like strings of bombs. Maybe with a little patience I might even find a white-crowned pigeon or two. Where *are* those birds? I'm still looking.

MD   We chug softly into Key West harbor as the sun is setting. The dock is deep with people. Sunset watching is a tradition here, and this is the gathering place, the last horizon. The tide is out. Twenty hands reach down to our boat to pull us aboard Key West. A trio—guitar, banjo, and singer—plays at the dock's edge, and we sift into the mob of sunset watchers to listen. "The fuzz," someone shouts. The banjo player stops in mid-measure and walks away. "Why?" I ask the stringy stranger to my left. Because the Key West township doesn't want to encourage crowds. That is, "hippie" crowds; tourist crowds are okay. So they put in a local ordinance forbidding more than two musicians at one time in a public place.

The cops sit in their cop car. The sun sinks gorgeously into the pea-green sea. Fangs of flame, galactic explosions, tarrying tints. The guitarist and the singer go on with their music.

JJA   Early in the afternoon of the 9th of May, 1832, I was standing on the deck of the United States revenue-cutter Marion. The weather was very beautiful, although hot, and a favourable breeze wafted us onwards in our course. Captain Robert Day, who stood near me, on looking toward the south-west, ordered some person to be sent to the top to watch the appearance of land. . . . It was the low keys of the Tortugas, toward which we had been steering. No change was made in the course of the "Lady of the Green Mantle" [as the wreckers nicknamed the *Marion*] . . . Now the light-house lantern appeared, like a bright gem glittering in the rays of the sun. Presently the masts and flags of several wreckers shewed us that they were anchored in the small but safe harbour. We sailed on, and our active pilot, who was also the first lieutenant of the Marion, pointed out to me a small island which he said was at this season the resort of thousands of birds, which he described by calling them "Black and White Sea Swallows," and again another islet, equally well stocked with another kind of Sea Swallow, which he added were called Noddies, because they frequently alighted on the yards of vessels at night, and slept there. He assured me that both species were on their respective breeding-grounds by millions . . . "Before we cast anchor," he added, "you will see them rise in swarms like those of bees when disturbed in their hive, and their cries will deafen you."

You may easily imagine how anxious I was to realize the picture; I expressed a wish to be landed on the island; but the kind officer replied, "My good sir, you will soon be tired of their incessant noise and numbers, and will enjoy the procuring of Boobies much better."

MD   The Dry Tortugas are a cluster of small islands in the Gulf of Mexico that lie at the tag end of the long, curved chain of the Florida Keys. They were named by Ponce de León—*las Tortugas*—for "the great amount of turtles which there do breed." The later

name, Dry Tortugas, was given by mariners because there is no fresh
water. Our destination is Garden Key—Fort Jefferson, now a National Monument, and (without checking the facts) I venture to say
that it is the most remote arm of our national park system. A polka
dot in the sea, sixty-eight miles from Key West. A park bulletin warns:
"All food, water, and supplies must be brought from the mainland.
Visitors must provide for their own independent existence."

The sea is so treacherous here, as it funnels in and out of the Gulf
through the Straits of Florida, that professional fishermen, who know
every channel and cove, will not venture into open water if the wind
and the tide are running against them. Flying is safer and surer, so
we go by charter seaplane from Key West. At 2500 feet, the skeleton
of the Keys is laid bare. Drowned reefs. The ocean floor ribbed with
shifting underwater dunes and incised with the sharp lines of propel-
ler tracks left by boats that scraped bottom. Occasional green islands
with white coral beaches hold their heads three or four feet above
the green water. Threaded through the reefs and the shoals are deep
channels of blue sea. The deeper the channel, the deeper the blue.
As we pass the Marquesas atoll, our pilot shouts and points down.
Below is a treasure divers' workboat anchored over a buried ship that
sank three hundred and fifty years ago—*Nuestro Senora De Atocha*
—laden with gold and silver and tobacco for King Philip IV of Spain.
Ahead on our southwestward course the Tortugas lift from the sea.
Garden Key is all but covered from beach to beach by Fort Jefferson
—a giant, six-sided, rosy-red, brick star lying open to the sky.

What a way to travel. We drift down like a feather, ride in on the
low surf, and jump off the pontoons into the warm sea. There is
nothing to match the exhilaration of wading ashore onto a tropical
island. Mike and I and our pilot form a bucket brigade from the plane
to the beach and unload our gear: camera bag, binoculars, telescope,
bed rolls, tent, ice chest with food, and six gallons of water (which we
husband so carefully we will have two gallons to give away when we
leave tomorrow afternoon).

Nothing was here but the Tortugas lighthouse when JJA stopped
at Garden Key. The construction of Fort Jefferson began in 1846
under the aegis of the Army Corps of Engineers and was never
finished, because of a series of misjudgments, the sort of drawing

Fort Jefferson National Monument. *National Park Service*

board snafus that seem to dog the Corps down to this day. To begin with, there was no bedrock under Garden Key. It was only a heap of coral resting on sand, and as the fort rose, so did it sink and settle. The walls and the mighty system of cisterns designed to hold 1,500,000 gallons of rain water shifted and cracked. There was also a problem with sewage, which the Corps had confidently routed into the moat around the fort on the assumption that the moat would be scrubbed clean twice a day by the tides. The average tidal rise and fall, however, was too slight and too gentle for the job, and the resulting build-up of sewage in the moat created a foul and unhealthy open cesspool. Further, the eight-foot thick walls, designed to withstand cannon fire from enemy ships, were made obsolete before the fort was completed by the perfection of the rifled cannon, which could take down anyone's walls in jig time. So there it stood, "The Gibraltar of the Gulf," the largest fort in the United States, and it was of no use to the Army whatsoever. Fort Jefferson served for a while as a federal prison, later as a coaling station in the Spanish-American War and in World War I, and in 1935 it became a national monument.

MH   Now, late in the day, I'm seated on the eastern parapet of this handsome and unfinished monument to man's folly, looking out toward Bush Key and its noisy colony of thousands of Black and White Sea Swallows—sooty terns—and noddy terns. The near beach is only a couple of hundred yards off, at most. I'll be going over there tomorrow with a crew of researchers led by the park biologist of Everglades National Park and Fort Jefferson National Monument, Bill Robertson. He's been studying the terns on Bush Key for years, and he has published (in the *Bulletin of the Florida State Museum*) an erudite and good-humored history of the terns of the Dry Tortugas. Bush Key, he says, is where Audubon found a large colony of noddy terns and so called it Noddy Key; the island JJA called Bird Key, where he found his sooty terns nesting, no longer exists; a Dry Tortuga survives at the suffrance of weather and waves, and Bird Key was gradually washed away. Now the two species nest together and will go on that way until their shared environment no longer suits the one or the other; they seem to move around.

Overhead, a dozen or so frigatebirds—long-tailed and crook-winged "man-o'-war birds"—are hanging, swinging gently in the wind. "[F]ar up into the air," wrote an admiring Audubon, "far beyond the reach of man's unaided eye, he soars . . . in the pure air, but thither can fancy alone follow him. Would that I could accompany him!" Right, JJA, but what is that bird *doing* riding the wind so gracefully up there? Frigatebirds are predators (JJA described them as Marine Vultures), and they feed on tern chicks, so their presence here is logical—except the chicks haven't begun to hatch yet. Frigatebirds also fish on the wing at the surface of the sea—so skillfully, someone once said, that in picking up their prey they don't even ripple the water. But I haven't seen any of these frigatebirds go fishing. They soar overhead, drifting slowly, head-on into a stiff easterly wind. Maybe they are waiting for some other bird to catch a fish, so they can steal it; they do that.

Brown pelicans swoop past me, close, at eye-level, using the wind currents deflected by the walls for lift, like surfers riding a wave. Below, in the parade-ground within the fort, a few dozen insect-eating birds of various sorts—cattle egrets to warblers, all migrants headed north—hunt for food and gradually die of starvation because there is so little food for them to find on Garden Key. The longer they stay, trying to recover from the exhaustion and hunger that forced them to land here, the less likely it is they will get off. Most of them will simply drop dead; but sharp-shinned hawks and American kestrels, also migrating, hunt here and pick off the exposed weaklings.

Outside the thick red brick walls the streaked sea reaches away —sandy blue, aquamarine, brown-blue, sandy, aquamarine, dark, pale, dark, pale—to meet the blue sky. On my right, fishing boats and yachts ride out the easterly that has held them for five days now in the same "small but safe harbour" that protected the wreckers' ships when JJA was here. The noddies and sooties descended from his noddies and sooties trade low over the water in company with laughing gulls, while overhead the frigatebirds hang and cruise and watch. Do they sleep like that, I wonder.

The driftwood of our campfire, burning briskly in the easterly half-a-gale, is hard, gnarled, small limbs and twigs—the bones of sea-trees, mangroves, that did good duty. Behind us the great fort, crumbling from age and weather and neglect, glows palely in the light of the sun that sinks now into Loggerhead Key. The east wind flings our tin plates from the wood picnic table, snatches the high-pitched gabble of terns from Bush Key and delivers bits of it at our backs. When we finish supper we stoop into our tent, which dances and whips and snaps and jounces. We have tied it down outside to a tree and the fireplace and the picnic table, and now we bring the water jugs inside to weigh down the edges, but that does little good.

I am up and at 'em at 1:30 A.M., convinced that dawn is imminent. The wind, blowing hard and rocking the tent, keeps me wakeful, and still bears bits of tern cries like faint short-wave messages from Bush Key.

The ornithological traveler sometimes finds himself in an environment so different from what he knows that birds he's hitherto only dreamt of seeing are suddenly as common as—well—as prothonotary warblers in a West Feliciana garden. That happened to JJA on his Keys expedition and it's happening to me.

Bill Robertson's headquarters for the morning is a luxuriant patch of purselane thirty yards from the beach on Bush Key, and on one side of us, a dozen steps away, noddy terns brood eggs on their nests in the head-high bushes; all around us in the little purselane meadow are sooty terns, brooding eggs on *their* nests, and the nearest of them are likewise only a few steps away. I've spent some time in nesting colonies of other members of this family—common terns, roseate terns, arctic terns—where the invading human is screamed at, mobbed, bombed with excrement, and pecked on the head; the calmness of the sooties and noddies is astounding. That in itself would be sufficient reward, but these two species are also new images for *my* memory bank, such as it is, and I get close looks at them. For one thing, Bill Robertson's project this morning is to capture and band nesting pairs of noddy terns, which is relatively easy to do. Audubon says that his party even caught a few noddies bare-handed, but Bill's party uses a long-handled net; the bird is either pinned on its nest in a bush or is scooped out of the air. Then it's carried back to the center of the purselane meadow and examined, weighed, banded with a Fish & Wildlife Service numbered aluminum leg ring and two colored plastic bands (in varying combinations that make each bird individually identifiable without another trapping), and then marked with a dot of dayglow red paint on the back of the head, which says

Terns on Bush Key, with Fort Jefferson on Garden Key beyond. *MH*

Catching noddies. *MH*

at a distance to the person with the net, "This bird has been banded, so don't chase it." Finally it is released, on its nest. Bill and his assistants handle the beautiful and gentle noddies with a casualness that could only come from long exposure to the species, but it is an extraordinary-looking creature and must have reminded JJA of what he called "Nature's superior & Inimitable softness and beauty of coloring," which he despaired of capturing on paper. Most of the feathers are as fine as silk thread, and the color shades subtly from dark ashy brown below to silver gray on the neck and head and at last to white on the forehead; under the eye is a sliver—a little scimitar—of brilliant white against the gray.

The sooty terns are white below, inky black above, except for an inverted trapezoid of white on the forehead. It was a rare treat for Audubon too to get so near and see so much of a species new to him. Put ashore on the now-vanished Bird Key one morning, he sat for several hours and watched quietly; the sooties were only briefly disturbed by his presence, and they settled down around him, some laying, some brooding, some courting: "The male birds frequently threw their heads over their back[s] as it were . . . ; they also swelled out their throats, walked round the females, and ended by uttering a soft puffing sound as they caressed them [an Audubon euphemism for copulating]. Then the pair for a moment or two walked round each other, and at length rose on wing and soon disappeared. Such is one of the many sights it has been my good fortune to witness." A modern ornithologist may be too jaded to appreciate it, but in Audubon's day this was pioneering stuff.

We're in the Tortugas in mid-April, several weeks earlier than Audubon, yet these noddies and sooties seem to be at about the same stage in their breeding cycles as they were in May of 1832: birds are courting, they have eggs in nests, and no chicks have hatched yet. Bird protection has surely had a crucial impact on the birds' timing, because it means egging is no longer allowed. In that spring of 1832 there were commercial eggers here from Cuba, carrying away thousands of tern eggs—*tons* of tern eggs, JJA was told; and the crews and passengers of other ships (including "Our Lady of the Green Mantle") did their bit too. Audubon himself considered these tern eggs delicious and said that the *Marion*'s men collected large numbers here every day. That sort of thing disrupted the breeding schedule, to say the least, and stretched it out a good while. The terns kept laying new sets, but even so one wonders how they managed to bring off any young at all under such pressure. At any rate, things are different for them now. All they have to cope with is life and death and weather, and people with nets, leg bands, and spray paint.

MD   This is the life. This is the good life. I sun, I swim, I nap, I read, I make a flower list: wild poinsettia, which Lehman painted for JJA in the Keys as background foliage. Sea-grape trees. Gumbo-limbo trees. A yellow, parrot-beaked, seaside pea. Moonflowers, which belong to the morning-glory family but bloom only at night and die at dawn.

I prowl the fort, around the outside on the narrow wall between the moat and the sea. Then up the spiral stone staircase to the third tier (the terrepleine) to look through my binoculars to Bush Key across the channel, where Michael is spending the day with Bill Robertson and his research team at the tern colony. I admire the windmill dance and jumping-jack leaps of the young researcher who wields the long-handled net in pursuit of birds. (If you didn't know what was going on out there, it's the damnedest performance you ever saw.) Then, down to the parade ground again. It's nearly three hundred yards across to the opposite wall, where each shadowed arch frames an empty cannon emplacement that looks out onto the piercing brilliance of the sea.

The historic celebrity here is Dr. Samuel Mudd, the physician who set John Wilkes Booth's leg and was convicted as a conspirator in the Lincoln assassination. A signpost points the way to *Dr. Mudd's Cell,* a dark stone room below ground level. He was later pardoned, largely in recognition of his round-the-clock labor during the prison's yellow fever epidemic in 1867. Another conspirator, Sam Arnold, described prison life as *horrible.* "The bread was a mixture of flour, bugs, sticks and dirt. Meat was rotten to such an extent that dogs ran from it. No vegetable diet, and the coffee was made into slop by those who had charge of the cook house." An 1863 article in *Harper's Magazine* had already reported a grim prison system at Fort Jefferson—no money for limes or fresh vegetables, so the Tortugas Amateur Dramatic Club was organized to raise money to buy them from the mainland. Seventeen prisoners took part in a minstrel show, with their audience other prisoners and the prison staff. Irish jigs, songs such as "Rock Me to Sleep, Mother" and "Old Kentucky Home"; a "yellow-haired Negro, a magician and performer on the conch shell" did a turn, and Tambo, the Mulatto, sang popular breakdowns and walk-arounds—"Ham Fat" and "The History of the Flag." (Listen, spirits. Are you still here? Can't you do the minstrel show just one more time?)

These spring days, the sick and starving at Fort Jefferson are migrating cattle egrets that set down, looking for insects and small rodents, but find this tiny island picked nearly clean of their kind of food. I discovered one egret in a shallow corner of the moat, limply fluttering at the edge of the water. Another, barely alive, had hidden itself behind a pipe at the door to the ranger's office. Another was behind a cactus, sitting low out of the sun as though roosting, but too weak to move. Their normal weight is 350 to 400 grams, and their stomachs normally large enough to hold forty grasshoppers, a couple of beetles, and a mouse. Here, the dead birds have dropped in weight to not much more than 160 grams, and their stomachs have shrunk to the size of walnuts.

A summer tanager, mostly an insect eater, sings and prances, merry as can be, in the big gumbo-limbo tree at the edge of the parade ground. It's expected to starve here, if it doesn't leave now while it has the strength. Overhead, the magnificent frigatebirds, whose food supply is secure (fish and their neighbors' young) continue to float as evenly and steadily in place as a flight of Japanese kites, as though the rangers send each bird aloft tethered to a long string. Down by the dock, brown pelicans (who dine on fish and shall not want) roost on pilings or ride on the soft sea. The Reverend Sirs, as Audubon called them. Dour, solemn faces, chins sunk down upon their chests, long beaks that cry for pince-nez glasses—a pontifical image that's marred, however, by those pelicans who are afloat, their long beaks dipping in and out of the water. Each carries a perpetual drip at the end of the nose.

MH We are headed northeast up the Keys on Route 1 again.

Both coming and going, the *Marion* stopped at Indian Key, which is about a third of the way out to Key West and lies a few hundred yards south of what eventually became, because of the highway, the

Brown pelican. *Courtesy of The New-York Historical Society, New York City*

main line. Indian Key was then an important island, all eleven acres of it, because it guarded a good channel from one side of the Keys to the other. It was a wreckers' headquarters, a field office for the U.S. Customs Service, and had a boarding house, operated by one James Egan. JJA was delighted by the place—"the beautiful rocky islet named Indian Key," with its "gorgeous flowers, the singular and beautiful plants, the luxuriant trees." He made friends immediately with the inspector of customs, Alfred Thruston, who put a "beautiful barge" at his disposal, together with Thruston's "pilot," as JJA described him, a Mr. Egan—whether the boarding house Egan or not, no one knows. Egan proved to be, like Sergeant Sykes of Key West, a kindred spirit—a "first-rate shot" who "possessed a most intimate acquaintance with the country. . . . In a word, he positively knew every channel that led to these islands, and every cranny along their shores." And Egan would cheerfully keep pace with Audubon's manic energies.

The artist's party was put up at the Egan house where in keeping with the spirit if not the letter of his promise to Lucy, they slept in hammocks on the piazza. Early each morning they were off in their boats after new birds, Egan leading the way; sometimes the hunt went on through the night and the next day. Audubon was in *heaven.*

One wet night, wakeful with excitement and chilliness and the drumming of rain on the shingles, he roused everyone at four. "Determined not to lose a day," he then organized breakfast and put together an expeditionary party that pushed off at six after "unknown birds," despite what JJA described as "a gentle shower" which ended an hour later. (It must have been exhausting to be hitched to the Audubon Express. Mary tells me *I* behave the same way when I'm chasing birds, but I don't, not by a long chalk.) That day produced an example of what fueled his engine. The hunters saw a concourse of resting terns on a distant sandbar. They approached in their boats, fired two charges of shot, and splashed ashore through the shallows to see what they'd killed. Thirty-eight of the birds proved to be roseate terns—birds a bit bigger than robins, gray-backed and black-capped, with long, forked tails and (since it was spring) pinkish breasts. This was a *find.* JJA knew such a species existed, as it nests here and there around the world. But he had never seen "even the skin of one stuffed with tow," and the latest synopsis of North American birds, by his friend Charles Bonaparte, didn't mention the species. Suddenly "I had my cap filled to the brim with specimens." He says he "felt delighted," and I'm sure that's putting it mildly; he was looking at a bird new to him and to the North American list; his discovery added to the knowledge of the species' worldwide distribution; and he knew he could now look for breeding grounds nearby, find nests and eggs, and collect observations of the live birds. Delighted indeed.

As for us, we motored north along Accident Alley this blazing day a century and a half later and arrived at Upper Matecumbe Key—where we intended to rent a boat and putter out to Indian Key ourselves. But the state of Florida has closed Indian Key to the general public, and it took me the better part of the afternoon in an outdoor phone booth to find out who in Tallahassee and locally we had to ask permission from, and then to get that permission. So we go out tomorrow. Now, at the end of the day, I have insisted on putting in at a motel; no more driving on Route 1, and no flinty coral campground for me tonight. We have found a likely-looking establishment, where Mary will go in and register while I rest as prostrate as I can get behind the wheel. Mary opens her door, steps out facing aft. "Look," she says, pointing behind us, "isn't that a white-crowned pigeon on the wire?" That snaps me out of the car, and even before I lift the binoculars to look closely at the bird on the power line I can see she's right. I study the pigeon briefly, then turn to grin at her delightedly, but she's already gone into the office—*as if the pigeon didn't matter,* and my grin sails right past the spot where she should have been and lands on two people who are seated in aluminum chairs on a patio about fifty feet away. They obviously find my pleasure interesting but odd, so I keep right on turning until I am facing the pigeon again. Handsome bird. JJA said that he found this species to be the shyest and wariest of any he knew and that the "sight of man is to them insupportable." Well, they've adjusted to man and his works, I'd say. This white-crowned pigeon sits above Route 1, unperturbed, and surveys traffic.

MD   The town on Indian Key is another ghost on our list. It had a life span of some twenty years. It was on the map in 1825, was the Dade County seat before the city of Miami (the present county seat) had even been dreamt of, and in 1840 it was wiped out in an Indian massacre, never again to be permanently settled. The state bought Indian Key in 1972 with restoration possibilities in mind, but has closed it to the public in the meantime because souvenir hunters and amateur archaeologists were digging in the ruins.

The sky is cloudy this morning—blessed relief from the unremitting sun. We are dispatched from the rental dock by a bejeweled boat boy: a necklace of gold and ebony beads, one silver Assyrian earring, gold bracelets hung with Mako shark's teeth, two gold rings in a Cretan pattern. He lacks only an ankle bracelet. We pick up Indian Key Channel on a hairpin course that takes us under Route 1 and out onto the Gulf, threading our way through what JJA described as "immense, muddy, soap-like flats that stretch from the Outer Keys to the Main." We beach the boat in a sheltered cove of the island and wade ashore. Mangroves, cactus, palms, seagrapes, yellow ox-eyed daisies, rouge plants in flower, lavender verbena, and the flowering poles of Yucatan sisal hemp (first planted here in the 1830s by Dr. Henry Perrine, a botanist and former U.S. consul to Mexico, who was among those killed in the massacre). Busch beer cans; a single pink plaid leg from a pair of slacks; the ashes of a campfire. Small crabs, furtive as cockroaches, rustle and scrabble in the seawrack. JJA said they were known hereabouts as "soldiers" and that their number was so great, "game could not be suffered to lie a few minutes on the ground without being either much mangled or carried into their subterranean retreats." Snails inch their way on the undergrowth, as JJA had foretold: "Whilst at Indian Key, I observed an immense quantity of beautiful tree snails . . . some of pure white, others marked with spiral lines of bright red, yellow and black. They were crawling vigorously on every branch of each bush."

There are the coral foundations of long gone buildings. Cisterns. A scattering of bricks. All of it overgrown and slowly decomposing, as nature reclaims a chunk of real estate. The only other living things that we find besides crabs, snails, and a smattering of birds, are the spiders. Silver argiopes *(Argiope argentata)* and red crab spiders *(Gasterancantha canciformis)*. The argiope lives at knee level in the sunstruck leaves of the sisal plants, its body an inch long and shaped as though enclosed in a white merry-widow corselet with a ruffled black, white, and orange hem; long slim legs with harlequin bandings in brown and white. At the center of each web, where the argiopes hang in wait, upside down, are thick zigzag reinforcements, like darns in socks. It's a family trait—the same zigzag darn is woven into the webs of the big black and yellow argiopes that appear in August, by the dozens, in the tall grass around our springhouse in Connecticut.

The chunky, bright red, wooly crab spider lives overhead in the trees. Its body is about half an inch long with a shell-like abdomen edged with red spines. Its web is ornamented with white tufts.

We duck and bob as we explore. The island is a maze of shimmering webs and silken guy wires. How did this enchanted place escape the Florida land grabs and developments down through the years?

MH Sometime on this voyage, Mr. Thruston's handsome sailing barge carried JJA & Co. through Indian Key Channel and west-northwest away from the main string of the Keys, across Florida Bay to Sandy Key, which lies off Cape Sable and the Everglades, near the western end of the Florida mainland.

They reached Sandy Key on a rising tide not long before sunset. JJA reports that the "shelly beaches" of the little island were covered with shorebirds—meaning that the mudflats where the birds fed were well under water. Other birds perched on branches and still others soared overhead. The numbers "so astonished us," says JJA, "that we could for a while scarcely believe our eyes." Roseate spoonbills "stalked gracefully beneath the mangroves." Four species of herons and white ibis by the thousands nested in the trees. There were brown pelicans and two kinds of gallinules, cardinals, crows, and pigeons. A huge flock of marbled godwits—the biggest flock of these large, brown shorebirds that JJA had ever seen—rested on the beach; Audubon's party needed supper, so four or five guns were fired in one volley, killing sixty-five godwits; enough meat for two days. The hunters built a rude lean-to, cooked and ate supper, hung up their mosquito-netting, and went to sleep—"lulled to rest," says our traveling companion, "by the cacklings of the beautiful Purple Gallinules!"

When they woke, doubtless before dawn, the tide had fallen, the water receding across the shallows for miles, so that what had been an island in a bay became a piece of dry ground just a shade higher than an apparently endless expanse of rippling mud flats surrounding it. "Our boat lay on her side, looking not unlike a whale reposing on a mud bank. The birds in myriads were probing their exposed pasture-ground." JJA would have liked immediately to go out chasing the feeding birds across the mud but was advised that was a bit dangerous, and Mr. Egan promised that shortly the birds would move to Sandy Key. So the hunters foraged for eggs, ate breakfast, and waited. As the tide came in, so did the birds, pushed by the rising water, and before long they were within gunshot and "the work of destruction commenced. When it at length ceased, the collected mass of birds of different kinds looked not unlike a small haycock." Quickly Audubon and Ward and others fell to the job of skinning out all the specimens, and with the high tide the barge sailed away from Sandy Key, bearing a rich harvest.

Nowhere in the twenty-three-mile crossing from Indian Key to Sandy Key is the water more than a few fathoms deep today—quite as it was in 1832, when, says JJA, "the tortuosity of the channels rendered our course fully a third longer" than if drawn directly, point to point. It's nasty water, we've been told, not only difficult to navigate, but liable to stir up quickly in bad weather because it's so shallow. Mary and I have decided we do not care to strike off on a sixty- or seventy-mile-round-trip across unfamiliar ground in a small boat. So we will approach Sandy Key from the mainland to the north.

Map-reading, book-reading, in preparation. I am delighted to see that our friend the American Woodsman, Sir Galahad of the Forest, apparently managed to slip one past Lucy and MacGillivray and the bowdlerizing Maria Audubon. In connection with this Sandy Key trip, he fell to talking about Mr. Egan and "balacoudas," those fast and dangerous predatory fish with the sharp teeth. On "more than one occasion 'some of these gentry'" had followed Egan (he told Audubon) when he was up to his waist in the water, spearfishing for something else, "until in self-defence, he had to spear them, fearing that 'the gentlemen' might at one dart cut off his legs, or some other nice bit, with which he was unwilling to part."

The extensive complex of campgrounds in the Everglades is nearly deserted this last week of April. Only two other sites are occupied in the area where we've pitched our tent and where the basso roars of the alligators echo across the swamp. As the heat rises and the mosquitoes hatch, the tourist season dies and won't pick up again until November. (Said a lady from Pennsylvania: "I wouldn't live down here if they gave me a villa.")

We get permission to go ashore on Sandy Key from the naturalist at Everglades headquarters, which keeps the island a refuge, posted against all intruders; at Flamingo we hire a motorboat and a guide named Jack—an amiable if jittery sixty-year-old in a straw cowboy hat. Our boat-ride out is properly twisting: the distance from Flamingo on the chart is nine-and-a-half miles, but between us and the island are acres of reefs and flats, so even at high tide in a shallow-draft skiff we must go nine-and-a-half miles out toward the Gulf of Mexico just to get within four-and-a-half miles of where we want to be; then we turn sharply left, skirting a flat called First National Bank on the chart, and point toward our destination. The water is tepid. Just below the surface is an eerily lush pasture—flats thickly covered by spongy weeds and green grasses that bear gelatinous plumes, as if they flowered jellyfish.

JJA describes Sandy Key as being about a mile long and at its widest a hundred yards broad, shaped like a horseshoe, with the inside of that curve facing what he understood to be Cape Sable, which would mean that the key was oriented toward the north-northwest. "The vegetation," he says, "consists of a few tall mangroves, thousands of wild plum trees, several species of cactus, some of them nearly as thick as a man's body, and more than twenty feet high, different sorts of smilax, grape-vines, cane, palmettoes, Spanish bayonets, and the rankest nettles I ever saw." Today's Sandy Key is a good deal smaller and has somewhat different greenery; it seems to have lost most of its eastern arm or been reshaped at that end by weather; its western end has been separated by a hurricane; and the inner curve of what's left faces more northeasterly, toward Flamingo. But, looping in on the back side, we can see birds all over it. In fact, there is too much action to take in. The low trees are festooned with birds; birds rest on the "shelly banks" and feed in the shallows, sail in the wind just over the top branches. Beyond the island I can see dozens, perhaps hundreds of what JJA called Great White Herons; they dot the silver sea to the northeast like white fence pickets. So we may have great squadrons of waders and shore-birds waiting for us within the island's curve on the other side.

Our boat is only fifty yards from shore when the gas tank runs dry and the engine stops. Jack switches to a second tank, but the engine will not restart. For five minutes he and I yank uselessly at the starter rope. Hard by are all those birds and that dramatic island. What's more, I've been told we've got to be back to Flamingo before dark or the Coast Guard will do I don't know what to us. So we paddle and pole the boat nearer to the beach, Mary and I slide off the bow into the water and wade up the bank, while Jack goes back to tinkering and yanking on the motor. Trying to look in all directions at once, we walk along the water's edge toward the narrow waist of the island, where a break in the greenery along the spine promises a view of the shorebirds on the other side.

As I climb the rise I slow down almost to a tiptoe, peek over the top of the bank, and there they are, all right. Among other things, I am within about fifty steps of a small flock of roseate spoonbills, an extraordinary looking bird, head like a short knob-handled canoe paddle surmounting a body feathered in delicate and beautiful pinks. They are feeding in the shallows and don't seem even to look up when my head appears on their horizon.

Mary has been deflected by an unfamiliar plant and is down where she can't see what I can. "Psst," I say, and direct her up the slope with a crooked finger, a grin, and a stealthy point toward the spoonbills.

MD   I creep up the bank and peer through the bushes. I have never seen them before, but even with my untutored, unornithologi-cal eye, I know that these rosy birds with the improbable, long, flat, warty, gray beaks are spoonbills. They look like a troop of woefully ugly girls who've been dressed up in feathered Folies Bergères costumes. The white herons on the shimmering horizon line remind me of figures in a ballet, poised motionless before the music begins.

On the branch of a mangrove tree far down the curve of the beach, two bald eagles perch side by side, looking out across the flats in the majestic privacy of their own thoughts. We sit side by side on the low saddle of the island, partly hidden by the bushes around us, and I suddenly notice that we're talking in whispers.

On Sandy Key. *MH*

MH   Because it's so physically isolated and protected, Sandy Key is as close as we're likely to get to the natural show Audubon saw. Near at hand with the roseate spoonbills are a few willets, ruddy turnstones, black-bellied plovers and laughing gulls, most of them racing about, feeding. At least a hundred of the great white herons stand just this side of the miragic, silver edge of the earth, along with a scattering of great blue herons. (Although Audubon discovered the great white heron in the Keys, and named it as a full species, it has recently been deprived of that status and is now considered merely a "morph"—a color phase—of the great blue heron.) Spindly and tall above the shallows, where the receding tide seems to cover just their feet, the big herons look half asleep. Postprandial suspended animation? Far away on the broadening, rippled flats I see a large, brown bird—long bill slightly upcurved; it's too distant for me to make a positive identification, but I think it's a marbled godwit, perhaps a descendant of birds JJA & Co. missed with their barrage out here; for JJA's sake I'm willing to add the name to our Sandy Key list. Here comes a reddish egret, splashing through the shallows. It lopes along like a horse, like a drunk on a spree, wings outstretched and waving wildly. I've heard that the "umbrella" of those outstretched wings shades the water surface for the egret and makes its prey easier to see, and the big, darting shadow must also frighten small fry into dashing unwisely across dangerous open terrain toward new hiding places. This egret now crouches, runs in the crouch, slows . . . straightens, then races away, wings akimbo; poises with wings still partly open, like an Irish setter on point; closes wings, leans forward, straightens, and stands at rest—not having caught a thing.

Brown pelicans cruise above the cove; double-crested cormorants roost and open their wings to dry. (Audubon called their ancestors Florida Cormorants, a species in their own right, but that too was contradicted by his successors.) On the trees and in the water are common egrets, snowy egrets, reddish egrets, cattle egrets, little blue herons, Louisiana herons. A prairie warbler sings in the spikey, gnarled underbrush at my back. A palm warbler appears, and a red-bellied woodpecker, and swallows of some kind. From where we sit, all these birds—more, I think, than I've found in any similar place —seem contained in a tiny, disconnected world, set apart by shoals and mudflats and mirages and space. "I find this very moving," I tell Mary. "Yes," she says. "It's like discovering the elephant graveyard."

MD Jack, anchored offshore, is still wrestling with the dead motor. And if he cannot get it started? Well, Mike and I agree that would be just fine. Someone will eventually come out from the marina to look for us. In the meantime, since it's my week to cook, I make plans for our supper. We have provisions in the cooler, which we brought along—lock, stock, and barrel—as the easiest way of transporting our lunch. So there's stew beef and fresh squash aboard. Slice thin, skewer on sticks, and broil over a fire. Serve with bread and butter, cheese and apples. If we are here for the night, we have extra sweaters and jackets to roll up in. We're set. I'm looking forward to this.

When the Everglades became a national park in 1947, the fishing families at Flamingo moved out to Sandy Key, and Flamingo was rebuilt; none of the old town remains. When Sandy Key became a wildlife refuge, the fishing families were moved back to various towns on the mainland. After Sandy Key was divided in two by hurricane, the new island thus created was named Carl Ross Key, in memory of a former fisherman-resident, who had asked that his ashes be buried out here. When the day came, Jack has told us, a flotilla of local boats formed the winding funeral procession that escorted Ross's remains across Florida Bay to his island grave.

I walk along the shore toward the channel at the northern end that runs between the two keys. A pair of osprey with eggs in the nest —or maybe young—whine and scold. Another pair stare wrathfully as I approach their dead tree roost. I have a moment's apprehension. Will osprey dive at intruders as common terns do? I make a wide circle, but keep moving; the osprey shy out and fly to a dead branch poking up from the shallows. I pass a roost of cattle egrets sitting on their branches in their typical stoop-shouldered posture: ancient Dickensian clerk-accountants. The channel is too deep and too wide for me to wade over to Carl Ross Key, a dream-picture deserted island. A reef of sand and coral. A few palms for shelter from the sun. Open sky. Open sea. While Sandy Key remains a wildlife sanctuary, Ross Key is now a National Park campsite and is furnished with a plastic, portable, Park-Service-issue privy in a synthetic shade of green that doesn't match anything else in the landscape and sits four-square and incongruous with one palm tree bending over it, ever so slightly, in mild curiosity. A lone camper is in residence. He's out of eyeshot from the channel, but we saw him earlier from the boat—no shoes, no shirt, a pair of ragged, faded, blue trousers. And his food? With fresh water and a few staples, Jack told us, there's blue crab, coconut, prickly pear, and fish.

Out there in the mirage where the tops of distant green clumps of mangroves rest on tremulous slivers of white sky, birds— perhaps terns? or pelicans?—dive and, before they reach the green water, vanish. On an expanding mudflat collect cormorants and gulls and shorebirds and pelicans and herons. A spoonbill near me clacks its bill as it eats. ("They move their partially opened mandibles later- ally to and fro [in the water and mud] with a considerable degree of elegance," JJA said, "munching the fry, insects, or small shell-fish . . . before swallowing them.") Too much to see, too much to experi- ence; the tide is running out, so is the day, and I've written down almost nothing about this place—not to do it justice. I've been sitting here transfixed in one spot, mostly just staring or watching through binoculars, and occasionally taking photographs. And from behind me comes the whine of the outboard motor.

MD   Damn. We're not stranded. After an hour and a half, bless us all, Jack has brought the Evinrude back to life—the $40 guide, tremble-handed, bloodshot-eyed, breathless, absentminded. He carried nothing along with him in the way of contingency supplies, not even a canteen of water, and he has accepted only a bite of cheese and a couple of swallows of iced tea from our larder. ("I'm waiting for those two fingers," he said, and when we got back to Flamingo, he hit the cold beer cooler first thing and drank down two cans worth without taking a breath.)

He shouts and waves. The day is waning. Time to go, and as we wade out I admit to the forefront of my mind the nagging worry that I'd pushed aside—the very real possibility of Jack working himself into a stroke from the effort of pulling on the starter rope again and again in the blistering sun. When we'd left him, his face had gone purple, and his arms were shaking. But he is casual about his trials with the Evinrude. It was a matter of switching the tops of the gas tanks, because the top to the spare didn't fit tightly enough to maintain pressure, which, he says cheerfully, he should have figured out in the first place, since a lot of the equipment on the rental boats is not shipshape. (Lord, I'd even had a vision of an afterdark rescue with the Coast Guard steaming to the island and Jack being carried away on a plank.)

Royal and Caspian terns—big, blocky, white birds with silver wings, black caps, and heavy red or orange bills—fly alongside as we plow slowly homeward. A wild pink sunset gathers. A line of black dolphin-shaped clouds leaps across the horizon. Flying fish break out of the bay and skim over the low waves like skipped stones. A couple of loggerheads, the only species of sea turtle that still nests regularly on our southern coasts, lift their heads above water level, look at us with dark, deepset eyes. *Blip,* and they're gone. A butterfly, moving across the bay at six inches above the water, catches up with us, circles the skiff once, and moves on. I pick cactus needles out of Mike's back and shoulders. He'd nestled against a prickly pear, and every now and again he twitches, pulls up his shirt, marks the spot with a finger, I pull out another. The seats of our pants and the cuffs of our shirts are matted with the sticky viscous leaves of a pretty, five-petaled, yellow flower that must have been the rank nettle JJA spoke of on Sandy Key. Stickleaf, it's called. Or, poor man's patches. *Mentzelia oligosperma.* It doesn't sting like nettles or prickly pear, but the matted leaves *will not let go.*

As we approach Flamingo, the Sunset Boat is pulling out for a short evening run, its deck lined with the last dwindling few of the tourists to brave the Everglades at this time of year. One of the advertised delights is the sky-darkening twilight flight of the water birds heading to their roosts for the night. Jack up to now has made no comment about the possibility of our having been beached at Sandy Key with a dead engine. While we'd been looking forward to being marooned, he'd been equally intent on anticipating ways and means of getting the devil out of there and back to the mainland. Now, with safe harbor and those "two fingers" just ahead, he admits that he'd been uneasy. But he figured that if we hadn't returned by dark, his buddies would have come looking for us.

Indeed? As we pull in, the manager of the marina walks down the dock to our skiff. "You just coming in?" he asks in surprise. "I thought you got back two hours ago."

MH   Driving to camp in the late twilight, white moonflowers opening in the dark beside the road, we turn on the radio and pick up a news broadcast in Dutch. The only recognizable words are Rhodesia, CIA, and Goodyear-Goodrich.

TO LABRADOR

JUNE–AUGUST 1833

MH   Audubon stopped in Charleston for a while before going north by coach. Lucy and the boys joined him in Philadelphia, and late that summer they toured eastern Maine and New Brunswick together. The birds were scarce, but the Audubons made a number of new friends, and JJA was urged to come back in the spring and explore north all the way to Labrador—where, he was assured, there would be many, many birds.

Victor, the older son, sailed for England in October to oversee the publishing venture, and the rest of the family moved into a rooming house in Boston. John W. was rapidly becoming an able assistant, a first-rate bird-stuffer and an increasingly accomplished painter of birds; and Lucy, as in England, was secretary, amanuensis, and first editor. JJA found Boston most congenial and responsive to his talents. He socialized with the likes of Colonel Thomas Handasyd Perkins— merchant, philanthropist, and president of the Boston Athenaeum— President Quincy of Harvard, and the actress Fanny Kemble, who wrote in her journal that Audubon was "enchanting. . . . one of the great men of his country; . . . there is a simplicity, a total want of pretension about him that is very delightful." He went birding with Thomas Nuttall, whom Audubon classed as "a gem," though Nuttall was a so-to-speak rival, just then publishing an important handbook on North American birds. Senator Daniel Webster (another sub- scriber who required much time and much prodding before he paid for his subscription) sent JJA a brace of freshly killed Labrador ducks —a species that was rare then and has since become extinct; Web-

411

Boston, from City Point, by W. J. Bennett, 1833. *Museum of Fine Arts, Boston*

ster's gift was the basis for the Labrador duck engraving.

Audubon was at the peak of his—what? *Form,* perhaps. Not success, though he was getting there; and not his powers as a painter, because he would go on getting better and better for another dozen years or so. But he seemed able to manage a complex and risky business with rising confidence, and to focus his energies with less flouncing and fretting.

Perhaps I make too much of the incident involving the golden eagle; after all, it is awfully easy for someone who has steeped himself in the relics of another man's life to let imagination in the guise of instinct or intuition run away with the facts. But for what it's worth: In early February 1833, Audubon purchased a beautiful golden eagle —in perfect mature plumage and alive. He wanted to kill the eagle and draw it, and he also wanted to let it go; clearly, in any event, he was so taken with the perfection of the bird that he did not want to mar it, whatever else he did. He tried to kill it by asphyxiation, he said, burning charcoal in a small room; that failed, and failed again when he added sulphur to the fire. Finally he pierced the eagle's breast with a long straight-pin, posed the specimen on wires as usual, and spent "nearly the whole of [one] night" doing the outline, and then "worked so constantly at the drawing that it nearly cost me my life. I was suddenly seized with a spasmotic affection, that much alarmed my family, and completely prostrated me for some days." Three of Boston's most prominent physicians were called in to attend him: Dr. George Parkman, Dr. George Shattuck, and Dr. John Collins Warren, professor of anatomy and surgery at Harvard.

He speaks of spending sixty hours on the painting; another time he mentions having taken two weeks to finish it. I see a man pressing at his outer boundaries—of endurance, spiritual awareness, and craft. He had worked himself to exhaustion on other occasions, but here he was so wound up by his sense of the eagle's perfection and by the challenge of reproducing it on paper that he was willing to drive himself beyond his physical limits until he had a seizure, blew a fuse. And the painting itself is similarly courageous, outreaching. He posed his eagle in the act of just rising from its strike on a white hare. The bird has fastened to its prey and has begun to labor upward, body at forty-five degrees to the horizon, head thrown back, beak open. Audubon presents the eagle side-to, its great wings bent sharply at the wrists in mid-stroke. Few painters, wishing to show the power and splendor of the eagle, would depict it in this manner; instead the bird would be painted with its wings flared, soaring, or perched on a branch, majestically surveying the countryside. But Audubon didn't just paint an eagle; the thing is an exultant shout of triumph. And there in the background is a huge, hurriedly painted sky; beneath it, beneath the eagle, lies a range of snow-covered mountains; nearer is a rocky crevasse, spanned by a fallen tree, and crossing that chasm—seated, inching along on the fallen tree—is a small figure in buckskin, wearing a visored cap, clearly Audubon himself. Over the figure's shoulder is slung a gun and the wings-open body of an eagle. The figure is only halfway across the chasm, still in danger. *I DARE!*

The fallen tree appears in the Havell engraving. But the figure is gone. Why, no one knows; Havell often added or subtracted material, usually on order. And although the story of painting the eagle was published in Great Britain as part of the golden eagle essay in the *Ornithological Biography,* it too was deleted later.

MD "The die is cast," Audubon wrote to Bachman, "I go to the coast of Labrador this season." His port of departure would be Eastport, Maine, on the brink of the Canadian border. Lucy, farmed out with a sister and brother-in-law in New York City, fretted about his health, as well she might after the winter's seizure episode. (That was also the winter when Henry Inman painted the popular Audubon portrait that's been copied so often. In the original it's evident from the sunken line of the mouth that JJA had lost many of his teeth and was graying at the temples. I don't like to see any of this.)

He wrote to Lucy from Eastport that his health was much improved: "[I]t would appear a hard life is the one best suited to my Constitution.—No snuff—no Grog—and plenty of exercise."

Traveling with him on the voyage through the Maritimes and north to the Labrador coast would be five young men, "all spirit and hopeful expectations." His son John. Joseph Coolidge from a local seafaring family. Thomas Lincoln, whose parents had been hosts to the Audubons the previous year in nearby Dennysville, Maine, where their colonial clapboard house still stands—though no longer in the family—and where people in the neighborhood remember visiting as children and having Tom Lincoln's letters from the Labra-

The golden eagle painting. *Courtesy of The New-York Historical Society, New York City*

Eastport and Passamaquoddy Bay by William Henry Bartett. *From* American Scenery, *1840*

dor expedition read aloud to them by his grandson, the late Dr. Lincoln. Also two Harvard medical students, young George Shattuck and William Ingalls. Seventy years later, Dr. Ingalls said that though he couldn't remember how he and George Shattuck got to Maine to join Audubon, he presumed that in their high pitch of excitement they "took a run on the Mall and then leaped from Boston to Eastport, and if you do not believe this you have no imagination."

Eastport was once among the busiest of the New England harbors —fishing, smuggling, and a European trade that took American ships to the Labrador waters to buy fish, which they would then transport to the Mediterranean for sale. The town is now impoverished by the downhill slide of the fishing industry, but for all its empty docks, abandoned canneries, and high unemployment rate, Eastport is spruce and tidy, built upon granite and hanging on by its teeth at the edge of Passamaquoddy Bay. We went there looking for news of Captain Henry Tilton Emery, the skipper of JJA's chartered schooner, the *Ripley*. With one stop at the historical society and two

Captain Henry Tilton Emery. *Courtesy of Joyce Emery Kinney*

phone calls, we met Joyce Emery Kinney, the Captain's great-grand-daughter; and we found a portrait of him over the mantle in her diningroom. He is shown with gray hair, gray muttonchop sideburns, and the quiet gaze of a man of authority. JJA had taken to him immediately. "Cap^n Mr Emery is a fine looking small Yankee . . . a gentleman of some education and a first rate Seaman . . . a better man is rarely to be found." Dr. Ingalls remembered Captain Emery steering a dory into an unfamiliar harbor: "lead-line in hand, and *eating* tobacco, standing aft, eyes everywhere, excited yet weary, slow, easy, pull hearty, accomplished."

Mrs. Kinney told us that her great-grandfather had been born in 1783, which made him JJA's senior by two years, that in the course of his seagoing career the Captain had once been captured by Spanish pirates off Puerto Rico, that he had served as selectman in Eastport and later as a state legislator, had also operated a tide-powered mill on Deer Island, had died shortly before his eighty-second birthday, and was buried in the Eastport cemetery, where she showed us his grave—an impressive stone shaft enclosed by a wrought iron fence. (Much like Ferdinand Rozier's grave.) Mrs. Kinney also had the Captain's brass spyglass and we took turns with it, looking through the window into her garden. ("Think about this," said Mike. "Isn't it likely that Audubon looked through Captain Emery's spyglass too?")

"[D]epend upon it," JJA wrote Lucy, "the Yankees are the lads for the Ocean—They are firm, cool, considerate, human & generous when ever these qualities are called for." He was in fine fettle and raring to go, yet at the same time he wrote Lucy that he could not refrain from shedding tears at the thought of leaving his own dear country and his "Dearest, best beloved Friend, my own love and true consoler in every adversity . . . Oh my Dearest Lucy this appears to me one of the most agonizing day I ever felt—" To Victor in England he wrote a long letter of advice on managing the family's business in the event of his death during the voyage. The *Ripley* sailed from Eastport on June 4, 1833. "Everyone of the male population came to see the show, just as if no schooner the size of the Ripley had ever gone from this mighty port to Labrador. . . . The batteries of the garrison, and the cannon of the revenue cutter, saluted us, each firing four loud, oft-echoing reports." [MH: Audubon was particularly susceptible to sea-sickness, which gives his Labrador project an extra dimension. I find it difficult to imagine going to sea for several months to do a lot of close work, knowing in advance I was going to be physically ill much of the time.]

Mike and I sailed on June 24 on the *Bluenose,* the car-and-passenger ferry that runs between Bar Harbor, Maine, and Yarmouth, Nova Scotia, a distance of a hundred miles. A glassy sea undulated gently in a long swell, and I (as prone to seasickness as Audubon) stretched out on a hatch cover on the foredeck to sleep off the effect of an unnecessary seasick pill that I'd taken in anticipation of a rough crossing. Mike shared the bow with three other birders—a college student from Massachusetts, a young physician on a bicycling trip, and an airline pilot from Louisiana. They added considerably to the pilot's Life List: two petrels, greater shearwater, common guillemot, the fulmar, the Arctic tern. The *Bluenose* is famous among the birding fraternity, and the airline pilot was going across to Nova Scotia largely because of the birds he might see on the boat ride.

From Nova Scotia northward, we tracked JJA mainly by his Labrador Journal—the only available version, however, being the one that Miss Maria Audubon edited with her shears and her blue pencil. She then destroyed the original. What could he have said that so offended her! She was not able, however, to smother completely his intensities and his exclamatory voice. What's missing is the salt in the stew: his outspoken personal voice. At any rate, all hands were "shockingly seasick" as the *Ripley* rounded the southeastern coast of Nova Scotia in a fresh northeast wind that carried them past the hamlet of Lower Argyle, where we camped in an open meadow by the sea: a distant dock piled with lobster traps and a soft rise of hilly ground to the west where scarecrows stood on guard over a vegetable garden, the three skiffs in the bay multiplying into eleven by dusk and a full moon rising over the trees where ravens had gone to roost. "A dreary, poor, and inhospitable-looking country," said JJA. To our New England eyes, it was a homecoming. Andrew Wyeth hills and meadows. Church-centered villages and clapboard houses with steep peaked roofs, many of the buildings trimmed with the extravagant gingerbread of the Carpenter Gothic era, the trim picked out in brilliant color combinations: mustard on yellow, apple-green on yellow, black on white, red on yellow. A blue house with white trim and a purple roof. But no dooryard flower gardens or shrubbery. No lilacs. No housecats on the steps. The roadsides were strewn with sea-moss laid out to dry in the sun and to be turned and tended like hay. The gathering of moss—*mossin'*, as the Nova Scotians say in their down-east accents—has been an important cottage industry here since World War II. The particular saleable moss is carrageen, which grows only on a few rocky coastlines in North America and northern Europe and is used as an emulsifier in chocolate syrups, hand lotions, ice cream, instant puddings, canned milk, cheese, medicines, et cetera. Why, only that very morning before we arrived at Lower Argyle, the assistant principal of the junior high school had gone out mossing with the fifth grade teacher at 4 A.M., and in a couple of hours they'd filled their boat with seventy-eight dollars worth of carrageen. ("That's a lot of money here," we were told. "That's a lot of money anywhere," I replied.)

JJA made note of gulls and petrels nesting on Mud and Seal Islands, which lie about twenty miles offshore of Lower Argyle. We went out for the day (sun and a calm sea) with Captain Ashton Spinney, fisherman, lobsterman, mosser, and substitute lighthouse keeper at White Head Light, a big, sandy-haired, open-hearted man whose family has been here some two hundred years. He turned our expedition into a gala, bringing along his little boy, a splendid lunch of fat sandwiches packed by Mrs. Spinney, and a duckhunting companion, George Godwin—whose name we already knew because the pilot aboard the *Ripley* was a Mr. Godwin from Nova Scotia, though Audubon did not give his first name, so there was no telling which of the Godwin seagoing ancestors he might have been.

On Mud Island, the spruce trees, their tops flattened by the wind, were full of herring gulls and black-backed gulls. Yellow silverweed bloomed in the tide pools, purple iris in an open bog, and pink sorrel in the woods. Clotted mossy hummocks were underfoot and gulls' eggs and fluffy gull chicks everywhere, both the eggs and the chicks of the same shade of gray flecked with dark spots to camouflage them perfectly among the lichened rocks. But Mike discovered no petrels; what appeared to be their underground nesting burrows were empty.

On Seal Island, we found an empty village with a church. The only year round resident, besides the lighthouse keeper and family,

The church above Canso and the Strait. *MH*

was a Mrs. Hamilton, whose father and husband had been keepers there. A hardy, spry, dark-haired woman in her nineties whose regular companions were her ancient dog and the radio-telephone installed in her parlor by the Coast Guard. "If she went into an old folks home on the mainland, the way they want her to," said Ashton Spinney, "she'd die off in a fortnight." The tide was out, so on our way back through a maze of little islands—where sheep had been put out to graze and fatten and where the lambs bounced, as though on pogo sticks, from cliff to cliff to watch us pass—Captain Spinney stopped to do a bit of mossing with a long-handled rake, working among the rocks from his tender—canary yellow with green trim along the gunwales. (Nova Scotian boats are as joyfully painted as the houses.)

The *Ripley*, in "a horrid sea," beat its way eastward to the Strait of Canso, which separates Nova Scotia and Cape Breton Island. We followed after along the shore: rocky headlands, upland fields white with carroway, low coves and salt meadows; bogs where mahogany red pitcher plants bloomed in company with sundew, another of the insect-eating plants, a tiny carnivore with thumbnail-size leaves that bristle with red spines, each spine tipped with a shining globule of digestive juices. We camped by a still lake lined with pointed spruce, where loons laughed in the dark, a rippling chortle, and then they cried *Ha-ha, Ha-ha.*

On June 11, 1833, the weather cleared, and the *Ripley* sailed through the Strait of Canso in company with twenty other vessels, all fishing boats also bound for Labrador. The land, wrote JJA, rose on either side of the strait like an amphitheater; he was reminded of some parts of the Hudson River. "Many *appearances* of dwellings exist, but the country is too poor for comfort; the timber is small, and the land, very stoney. Here and there a small patch of ploughed land . . . saw some Indians in a bark canoe, passed Cape Porcupine, a high, rounding hill, after which we entered the Gulf of St. Lawrence." The Strait of Canso still has its hills, a few old houses in flowering meadows with a vegetable patch, but Cape Porcupine is gone—blown up with dynamite, and the boulders used in the construction of the Canso Causeway at Cape Porcupine's ruined feet. The Causeway is two hundred and eighteen feet deep, it connects Nova Scotia and Cape Breton Island, it cost twenty-three million to build in 1955, and it created a deep water, ice-free harbor for Cape Breton, a major shot in the arm for the island's economy. Heavy industry moved in—a power-generating plant, a heavy-water plant, a gypsum plant, a pulp-wood plant, a refinery, and oil tankers sailing under Monrovian registry. But this bulwark of stone across the strait drastically changed the fish migration patterns of southern Nova Scotia, and all these years later, the Canso Causeway is still a bitter subject of contention.

The *Ripley* sailed northward up the western coast of Cape Breton. "The country looked well," said JJA, "the large undulating hills were scattered with many hamlets, and here and there a bit of cultivated land was seen." The sea was calm. They put in briefly at Jestico Island for a look-see and found it sprinkled everywhere with the blossoms of wild strawberries. We crossed the causeway to Cape Breton, passed through a miracle mile on a four-lane highway lined with the usual look-alike chain stores and discount houses and the omnipresent Colonel Saunders Kentucky Fried, then curved up the coast and followed a dirt road running parallel to the *Ripley*'s course. At a wild pond, where Mike stopped to watch the progress of a female ring-necked duck with ducklings, I found wild strawberries in fruit. They like a southern bank with full sun and are far tastier than the professional strawberry. It's a special sweetness sparked with a nip of spice. To completely relish wild strawberries, have patience. Gather a handful and then eat them all in one gulp—two dozen make up a mouthful. I moved on from the next patch of strawberries to the next. A field mouse scuttled under my feet and gave away the location of its down-lined hay nest. A few yards farther along I stumbled (actually stumbled) over the rotting, stinking body of a large otter spread-eagled on the bank amid the strawberry vines and purple skullcap. I turned my back on the otter and picked onward, my momentary turn of stomach overcome by my strawberry lust.

At Port Hood, we camped in a Wyeth meadow (more strawberries in fruit) overlooking the town and, in the blue sea offshore, Jestico Island, now called Port Hood Island. The village historian, the venerable Mr. Perley Smith, told us that Jestico had been the old name for this area, given by the French and now almost forgotten. He thought it came from *Just-au-corps,* the word for a close-fitting jacket, though why the French should have chosen it, he could not guess. Mr. Smith took us for a tour in his car, proceeding slow and grandly up the middle of the road, oncoming cars veering into the grass to allow us the right of way. Our last stop was a graveyard on a headland above the shore, where he showed us his family plot and the grave of his great-grandfather, who died on the ice on a sealing expedition. Mr. and Mrs. Smith's own headstone was already *in situ.* "I'm not here yet, but I like to know where I'm going," he told us. We admired his grave and his destined view out across the sea to Jestico Island.

It was at this place that the *Ripley* left the Cape Breton coast and sailed north to Les Iles de la Madeleine, or the Magdelene Islands, as the British chose to call them. To catch up, we had to double back in our tracks and hopscotch northward by ferry via Nova Scotia and Prince Edward Island.

MH   The Magdelene Islands lie on a map of the Gulf of St. Lawrence like the skeleton of a small bird's wing. Except for Ile d'Entree, which sits off by itself at the southern end, they are essentially one island—mountaintops connected to their near-neighbor mountaintops by dunes and sandbars; but in Audubon's day, and indeed until quite recently, the links of sand were tenuous and made for hard going, at best. Much of the communication between villages was by boat, except in winter, when the ice froze solid enough for riding. Most of the place names on the Magdelenes come in two languages, reflecting the long tug of war between France and Great Britain, but French is the first language.

We approached from the south aboard a small ocean-liner of a ferry, which was to dock at Grindstone, Cap-aux-Meules, at the elbow of the spidery archipelago. The sun had set, and during the long twilight smooth and graceful hills lifted slowly from the Gulf. Mary and I had fallen in at the rail with two young Montreal Frenchmen—friendly, full-bearded, one black beard, one red. The red was the handsomest beard I've ever seen—Commander Whitehead (suggested Mary) at age twenty-five. The ferry passed the little green dome of an island, Ile d'Entree, to starboard and a sandbar reaching out from Amherst Island, Ile du Havre Aubert, to port, and entered the harbor at Cap-aux-Meules. As the great sandstone cliff—once the source of grindstones—loomed above the sparkling lights of the port in the near dark, Red Beard began to dance, in sheer joy at the drama and romance of the sight.

The exceptional beauty of these islands has inspired the provincial government to develop them as "Quebec's Bermuda." The once isolated villages and beaches are being tied together by a broad gravel highway, the Route Principale, and we disembarked at Cap-aux-Meules into a mob scene of vacationers, go-go cafes, motels, Dixie-fried-chicken, and souvenir shops. At the provincial park near the harbor, our hearts sank; the campground was full to the brim, as the ranger at the gate mournfully told us in French; he had no alternatives to suggest. We drove around helplessly in the night (lights gradually going out around us) looking for a place to lay our heads. The motels were also full, and when our wandering brought us past the hospital for the third time, I began to wonder if we shouldn't try *there*. But at last we saw a CAMPING sign that pointed us away from the hoopla of Cap-aux-Meules and onto a dark coast road, where we found Mon Rivage campground. That was crowded too, but the management was indifferent to how many people came in or where they settled down. We pitched our tent, by the light of the headlights, in a clump of juniper, dove into our sleeping bags—

"with the quickness of thought," as JJA would say—and were asleep with thought to spare.

MD   On June 12, the *Ripley* anchored in Pleasant Bay off Havre Aubert, and from shipboard JJA saw "many houses, a small church, and on the highest land a large cross, indicating the Catholic tendency of the inhabitants." The next morning, Audubon and his troops went ashore: "We landed between two great bluffs, that looked down on us with apparent anger, the resort of many a black Guillemot and noble Raven . . . We walked through the woods and followed the road to the church. Who would have thought that on these islands, among these impoverished people, we should have found a church; that we should have been suddenly confronted with a handsome, youthful, vigorous, black-haired, black-bearded fellow, in a soutane as black as the Raven's wedding-dress, and with a heart as light as a bird on the wing? Yet we met with both church and priest . . . He is a shrewd-looking fellow, and, if I mistake not, has a dash of the devil in him. . . . Pere Brunet said he lived the life of a recluse, and invited us to accompany him to the house where he boarded, and take a glass of

The shore at Havre Aubert. *MH*

good French wine." The land, the priest told them, was poor in every respect—soil, woods, game—and the one hundred and sixty families on the islands made their livelihood from cod, herring, and mackerel fishing.

At the village of Havre Aubert, with its new modern church, the high ground overlooking Pleasant Bay still carries a wooden cross—this one, a recent replacement, is painted white and wired for electric light bulbs and was erected in 1963 to commemorate François Doublet, who made the first attempt to colonize the islands three centuries earlier and named them for his wife, Madeleine.

We followed the winding path up the hill, savannah sparrows yipping at us as we passed, swallowtail butterflies, a dozen at least, fluttering across the rough headland meadow, battling a north wind off the sea from Labrador. There was no way to guess which of the coves, far below us, was the one where JJA had come ashore. As he remarked about Ile d'Entree, the coastline changes often, the soft, red sandstone cliffs "constantly falling into the sea."

A lady from Montreal joined us at the foot of the cross. A plump, blonde, English-speaking French-Canadian. So, we were Americans. She was in Washington, D.C., she told me, on the day the astronauts landed on the moon. What's more, she had been in Miami the very day they flew over Africa. Yes, she was putting on her lipstick at the mirror at the exact moment the news came over the radio. And that, she said, is not the sort of thing they tell you in the papers. Indeed, I replied, it is not.

Had she been to France, I asked, curious to know her attitude toward the Motherland, in view of Quebec's independence movement toward a separate, French-speaking nation. She shook her head stiffly. She had not enjoyed her travels in France, and she did not like the French. "They make fun of our accents. They call us the hillbillies from Canada, and I don't like to be laughed at for the way I speak French."

Well, one man's accent in any language is another man's joke, and JJA had been amazed and amused by the inbred patois with which the Magdelene islanders spoke French. The first person they met upon landing at Havre Aubert was a woman dressed in coarse French homespun with a close, white, cotton cap tied under her chin: "At a venture, I addressed her in French, and it answered well, for she responded in a wonderful jargon, about one third of which I understood, and abandoned the rest to a better linguist, should one ever come to the island." That wonderful jargon still confounds French-speaking visitors here. At Le Musée des Iles in Havre Aubert, Mike and I crossed paths with our Montreal friends of the ferry, Red Beard and Black Beard, who were having a rollicking holiday, up most of the night in the cafes and discotheques at Cap-aux-Meules, but oh, they groaned, the accent of the local people. Incomprehensible. A Magdelene man in a bar had been so angered by their inability to follow his end of the conversation that he'd threatened to take them outside and beat them up if they persisted in not understanding his French.

Le Musée des Iles is the creation and pet project of the present priest at Havre Aubert, Pere Frederic Landry, an enthusiastic historian and sailor; on the afternoon of our visit, he was away on parochial rounds, traveling by boat, which he prefers to a car. In the museum's display of local church history, however, we found the name of JJA's handsome, dash-of-the-devil priest—J. H. Brunet, who was here for only three years, 1830–33.

On JJA's one day ashore at Havre Aubert, they also organized an egging expedition with Captain Emery as the hero of the moment, which was perhaps the reason for its being deleted from Miss Maria's published version of the journal, but JJA gave an admiring account of this event in his essay on the black guillemot in the *Ornithological Biography:* "It was a frightful thing to see my good Captain, Henry Emery, swinging on a long rope upon the face of a rocky and crumbling eminence, at a height of several hundred feet from the water, in search of the eggs of the Black Guillemot, with four or five sailors holding the rope above . . . When the friction of the rope by which he was suspended loosened a block, which with awful crash came tumbling down from above him, he, with a promptness and dexterity that appeared to me quite marvellous, would, by a sudden jerk, throw himself aside to the right or left, and escape the danger. Now he would run his arm into a fissure . . . Whenever he chanced to touch a bird, it would come out whirring like a shot in his face . . . After much toil and trouble he procured only a few eggs, it not being then the height of the breeding season. You may imagine, good reader, how relieved I felt when I saw Mr. Emery drawn up, and once more standing on the bold eminence waving his hat as a signal of success."

MH The guillemots and ravens no longer nest in the cliffs above Havre Aubert, but like JJA, who was surprised to discover the forests "rich in Warblers, Thrushes, Finches, Buntings, etc.," we have found many birds on our rambles around the Magdelenes. Among the thrushes is the robin, which seems to me to sing more sweetly on these islands than I've heard it anywhere, almost as if there were *vocal* as well as ecological niches for birds to fill—as if the robin sought to replace the wood thrush, which doesn't travel this far north. Hermit thrushes recite their pensive verses: the pure introductory whistle, the fluttery improvisations. The veeries and the Swainson's thrushes sing together in each other's hearing—and mine, causing lots of concentration scowls; Audubon found veeries here, but never knew the Swainson's thrush. That and the very similar gray-cheeked thrush eluded him, probably because they both look and sound as if they might be races of the veery. He also failed to see the mourning warbler here, a beautiful little bird with a gray head and black throat and yellow-olive body. Alexander Wilson found only one specimen—on migration, near Philadelphia—and named the species; Audubon apparently missed it altogether, and did his painting from a museum skin. But the other day, I made a tape recording of a mourning warbler that sat in the open to brag about itself, fifty yards from the edge of a road.

This is a magical place, with snipes courting, fan-tailed, in flight overhead; a short-eared owl hunting along a marsh edge in daylight —great jerky, floppy flight; least sandpipers trilling from tree-top perches; dozens of blue herons stalking the flats; green northern wild orchids blooming on boggy roadsides; golden buttercups as big as quarters. And the landscape! For days I tried to pin down what it reminded me of. It is often rugged and steep, with abrupt valleys and momentous headlands that appear at a distance to be mountains but are actually never more than a few hundred feet high; one has constantly to adjust one's perspective to a smaller scale. This miniature alpine terrain is patched with dark green spruce forests, wildflower meadows, and red sandstone cliffs; the houses are brightly colored; the hills are bound together by dunes, long tawny beaches, sweeps of green marsh and red-brown mudflat, so that one is constantly coming on new, distant, colorful vistas. Les Iles look *planned,* make-believe. At last the image came to me: they're like a beautiful electric-train layout, or a land-developer's model. They might have been lovingly made of papier-mâché, painted, then spotted with toy houses here and there, and toy boats set down along the shore.

I could cheerfully spend the summer here, learning Magdelenes French and studying birds. We've already discovered places worthy of weeks of diligent birding, including an area at the northeast end of the archipelago, on Grosse Ile, that Audubon wanted to see but didn't get to—many thousands of acres of dunes and bogs and lakes and marshes, a summer's worth of exploration. We went to look at what JJA had missed and got a tantalizing whiff of the possibilities. But like our predecessor we are propelled northward.

He had planned, the day after his visit to Havre Aubert, to see Grosse Ile, but as the wind turned "fair for our passage to Labrador, the ultimatum of our desires," the *Ripley* set course in that direction instead. They would pause on the way, some twenty miles north of the Magdelenes, at the "Bird Rocks," two red sandstone rocks that held thousands upon thousands of nesting seabirds. So we are bound to the Bird Rocks ourselves, we hope.

The day before yesterday, we drove out to Grande Entrée—northeasternmost port in the islands—to look for a fisherman who might be planning an expedition to the vicinity of the Bird Rocks, and we were directed to a boat the name of which we understood to be something like Arrow Gay-dew and turned out to be *Harold G. II.* Its owner, we were told, was Aristede Cyr; he and one other fisherman were the only people who fished for lobsters near the Bird Rocks.

Aristede Cyr received us seated in his living room—a stocky, wooly chested man dressed in pants and shoes. Apparently he is a Grand Seigneur of Grande Entrée; he not only fishes, but has built many of the fishing boats in the island's fleet. He speaks little English and we less French, so the three of us labored pleasantly to make our dialogue amount to something, and Aristede was all nobless oblige. Certainly he would take us to Les Rochers des Oiseaux, and he would certainly *not* accept any money because he was going there anyway to pull his lobster traps for the season. So, if we would just be at the dock at three A.M. two mornings hence, we would go to Les Rochers.

The early rising meant that we had to buy an alarm clock in French. The right name is *réveille-matin,* and—as any one of half-a-

dozen French teachers of my acquaintance could have predicted—
I didn't know that. Somewhat more surprisingly, neither did Mary.
"Une horloge avec une cloche qui sonne," she ventured. A clock with
a bell that rings. *Horloge,* of course, connotes a big clock—a clock in
a steeple, for instance—but the ladies in the shop caught on immediately and sold her a large alarm clock. [MD: The clock was made in
the USSR and is called the Allegro, which proves that Russian industry can be as frivolous in its choice of brand names as the decadent
Western capitalists. However, the alarm ring has only one level—
LOUD, and its message is clear: Get up and get up now, *tovarich.*]
Having tested the alarm several times before going to bed and waked
everyone in Mon Rivage campground, we set the clock for one A.M.
when we woke everyone again, rose, struck the tent, packed the car,
ate breakfast, and drove nearly forty miles to the harbor at Grand
Entrée. We got there well before three, of course, and watched the
breaking of the fishermen's morning.

Already the men were beginning to arrive at the harbor, parking
cars and pickups near the lobster-processing plant, where a single
light shone above a door. Their boats lay darkly, side by side and end
to end against the wharf. Now cabin lights, pilot-house lights came
on—squares of warm yellow in the dark that drew my heart to them
the way Mary's heart was drawn to the Ohio River towboats passing
under the cliffs at Cave-in-Rock. Coziness, energy, commitment to
work, the sea, human company—all are part of what they spoke.
From my journal, as the dawn came:

Fog blowing under a clear starry sky, and shifting beams of light
from cabin hatchways. The fishermen come down, in ones and twos,
engines are started, there is a good deal of hawking and spitting. The
sky pales slowly. Boats leave. The fog lifts, vanishes, except as a rim
of dark scud, then returns. The white and orange boats—deck lights
lit, lobster cars stacked in the stern—rumble; snatches of conversation in French and English. In the fog, it is a long dawn, and Aristede
Cyr is late.

"My boat is broken," explains Aristede after breakfast. Last week,
off shore, the engine caught fire, the fire spread, and for a while (we
hear later from one of his friends) there was some question whether
he and his first mate and Jean-Claude Cyr—son and crew—should

abandon ship. When he set our date, Aristede had thought the engine would be fixed before this morning, but guessed wrong, still had a dead boat, and took the opportunity to sleep a few extra hours. Wish *we* had. But now he has invited us to move aboard the *Harold G. II* to wait, and we have accepted.

At the moment I am sitting on the edge of the wharf while below me he and various friends work on the engine; naturally a good deal of the work involves everyone standing around staring at the machinery, as if that would fix it or as if the answer to what ails it were about to appear in script on the machinery like Mene, mene, tekel, upharson. The *Harold G. II* will not be repaired today. A mechanic was called from the other end of the islands, and he has not come as promised. Maybe tomorrow.

MD   Aristede Cyr evidently is a man of certain aloofness, who keeps his own counsel. He arrives at the point with a majestic indifference to the hustle and bustle, marching forward, eyes front, with his first mate and his son in his train. He has said nothing to any of his friends to explain our presence aboard his boat—despite their obvious curiosity—not even to Captain Desraspe of the *Donald G. III*, the other fisherman who hauls lobsters at Les Rochers des Oiseaux and always travels there in company with the *Harold G. II*, for their mutual safety. Captain Desraspe at last comes aboard late this afternoon, after everyone has left, to ask if Aristede is there. No, he is not. That is of course perfectly evident. So we explain who we are and why we're here, and he joins us in the pilot house to chat and tell tales of seal-hunting on the ice in below-zero weather. His English is excellent, and it is heavily salted with old downeast expressions that these men have learned from Mainemen and Nova Scotians: "By jeez," pronounced "Boy jeez," and "terrible dear," a phrase he uses again and again when speaking of the expense of gasoline, engine parts, paint for a boat—and my favorite, an expletive that I don't think I've ever heard spoken, only read in stories of another day and another lingo: "By Jupiter."

MH   In our second afternoon as guests on board the *Harold G. II*, there is a sudden flurry around the boats of Captains Cyr and Desraspe. The engine, it seems, is *fixed,* and as far as I can make out we

Aristede Cyr. *MH*

are off to Les Rochers des Oiseaux immediately. Mary knocks back her seasick pill, we climb aboard with the mate and Jean-Claude, and within minutes the two lobster boats are on their way out into the Gulf of St. Lawrence, Captain Desraspe and the *Donald G. III* in the lead. Aristede stands in his pilot house, watching the water but concentrating on the sound of his engine; when he pushes it up to steaming speed, he exchanges a glance with the mate, shakes his head. He seems not to like what he hears. If we travel to the Bird Rocks this afternoon, we will be returning in the dark, and he doesn't like that combination. In a minute he says to me, "I am sorry. We do not go to the Rochers des Oiseaux today. We pull trawls near here. We go tomorrow."

All the lobster fishing I've seen before this was in New England. There the standard rig is one trap on the bottom at the end of a rope, and one or two painted pots floating at the upper end of the line to mark the location. Aristede's traps are set in strings of ten—"trawls" —with a buoy at either end of the string. The islands' short lobster season will be over tomorrow, so after they pull each of his near-shore trawls, they cut the traps from the line—"pot-warp," the line is called in Maine; the traps are stacked in the stern, and the warp is coiled and tossed in a corner. It seems to me, as we go along, that the fishing is very poor, that what he's taking in lobsters will scarcely pay for his fuel; it is probably just as well the season is done.

Back in the harbor, after the traps have been heaved up on the wharf and then into Aristede's pickup, I help the mate and Jean-Claude offload the coiled pot-warp and then wash down the decks. I don't like standing around watching others work when I know how to do something that needs doing, and, besides, this is the proper sort of duty for a boat-guest. I think perhaps it has impressed Aristede; in any event, as we finish cleaning up, he asks if Mary and I would like some lobsters for supper. "Oh, oui," I tell him, "but we must pay for them." "No, no, no," says Aristede, dismissing the topic, and goes off toward the lobster plant. Will the man's hospitality never cease? We puzzle over what to do, and Mary comes up with the solution: "The *champagne.*" Brilliant. Our neighbors the Wetherills (he's a member of the clan that bought Mill Grove from JJA one hundred and sixty years ago) sent us off on this part of our journeys with the sort of present one almost never buys for oneself, just for other people's special occasions, such as *bon voyages*—a large bottle of excellent champagne. The occasion for us to drink it has not arisen, and it rests amongst the jackstraws of gear behind the front seat of the car, still in its gift box. I fetch it out and stand it on the wharf beside the boat. Here comes Aristede with a cardboard carton. "For you and your wife to eat," he says with great ceremony, holding out the carton. I take the carton under one arm and reach down with the other. "For you and your wife to *drink,*" I say, handing him the box.

He draws in his breath with the word "Moët," which is printed on the box, opens the top, and pulls the bottle part way out. And now —in the unmistakeable accents of a Maineman—"Boy Jeezus Chroyst!" he says softly. "Champagne!" Laughing with delight, both at *his* delight and at his leap into a familiar tongue, I open his carton. My turn to say Boy Jeezus Chroyst: three, four, five—Good Heavens —*six* chicken lobsters. A feast!

There is beaming on all sides. And now Aristede—not one to extend the moment—jumps into his pickup, backs it down the wharf and turns for home and supper, while we begin rustling up the equipment for boiling a few lobsters on board the Arrow Gay-dew.

Jean-Claude Cyr, slight and smooth-cheeked, looks younger than his sixteen years. ("He is very small for his age," his father has said to Mary with a regretful nod. "He may be small, but he is very smart," she answered, pointing her hands at her temples.) He speaks less English than his papa—in fact, almost none, and yet he manages to seem more open and extroverted with us. On our way to Les Rochers des Oiseaux in the dawn, he says to me over the whine of the engine that Les Rochers are "très beaux." The more I think about this aesthetic judgment, the more out of the ordinary it seems. Those rocks are not just a place for Jean-Claude to fish with his father, not just a seamark and a hazard to navigation. They are also very beautiful. *Très beaux,* eh? I watch our northern horizon with much interest, just as JJA did.

In Audubon's journal—his and his granddaughter's—he writes about the approach to the main tower of the Bird Rocks: "At eleven I could distinguish its top plainly from the deck, and thought it covered with snow to the depth of several feet; this appearance existed on every portion of the flat projecting shelves. Godwin [the pilot] said, with the coolness of a man who had visited this rock for ten successive seasons, that what we saw was not snow—but Gannets! I rubbed my eyes, took my spy-glass, and in an instant the strangest picture stood before me. They were birds we saw,—a mass of birds of such a size as I never before cast my eyes on." In his essay on the gannet he added that he had "imagined that the atmosphere around was filled with flakes," but through the glass "saw that the strange dimness of the air before us was caused by the innumerable birds, whose white bodies and black-tipped pinions produced a blended tint of light grey. When we had advanced to within a half a mile, this magnificent veil of floating Gannets was easily seen, now shooting upwards, as if intent on reaching the sky, then descending as if to join the feathered masses below, and again diverging toward either side and sweeping over the surface of the ocean." Back to his journal: "The whole of my party stood astounded and amazed, and all came to the conclusion that such a sight was of itself sufficient to invite anyone to come across the Gulf to view it at this season. The nearer we approached, the greater our surprise at the enormous number of these birds." The rock, his pilot said, was three- or four-hundred feet high and about a quarter-mile long. So large, and covered with birds from top to bottom? That would be a great many birds and a *très beaux* sight, indeed.

Aristede sees the big rock first, in spite of fog—when we can't find it even with binoculars. But now there it is, and not white on top at all, much as I may try to make it so; a lighthouse has been built there, along with two grand houses for the two keepers and their families, and instead of a layer of white birds on its flat summit, the rock is capped in green—grass fertilized by thousands of years' worth of dead birds, broken eggs, fish remains, and guano. It stands only a shade over a hundred feet high, not three or four hundred; probably it wasn't even remotely as big as the pilot made it out to be in 1833, but quite likely it was bigger than it is now, at least in some ways. The rock shows many signs of peeling away, rotting into the gulf in great red-brown sheets and chunks, like the sandstone cliffs of the Magdelenes behind us. And the bird colony remnant is only a pale echo of the community that astounded Audubon and his friends.

This is probably true of every "bird island" in the western Atlantic. Think of what's been extinguished *forever* from our coast in only a century and a half—Labrador duck, great auk, probably the Eskimo curlew. Long after JJA's day the assumption was still commonly maintained that in creating these birds the Lord God Jehovah was *setting the table* for mankind, and that whatever man took from that table, good old God would replenish. The great auk, for example, a bird that couldn't fly, *covered* some islands during the breeding season; year after year a man could collect sufficient to salt down for food for a whole winter just by walking ashore with a stick and laying about him. The auk's eggs were delicious too. And its feathers were useful. Three centuries of increasing persecution by European settlers and their descendants, and the auk was gone. Gone: period.

Les Rochers des Oiseaux were raided for the gannets, according

On the main Bird Rock. *MH*

to the *Ripley*'s pilot, who had done it himself for ten years. Gannets are marvelous flyers, but on the ground they are clumsy, and their takeoffs are slow and labored. So they too can be killed with sticks, on or just above their nests. "The Labrador fishermen and others ... annually visit this extraordinary resort of the Gannets," JJA quotes the pilot as saying, "for the purpose of procuring their flesh to bait their cod-fish hooks." Godwin remembered a time when he and five other men had killed five hundred and forty gannets in one hour on the rock. "The dead birds are now roughly skinned, and the flesh of the breast cut up in pieces of different sizes, which will keep good for bait about a fortnight or three weeks. So great is the destruction of these birds for the purposes mentioned, that the quantity of their flesh so procured supplies upwards of forty boats, which lie fishing close to the Island of Brion [nine miles to the west] each season."

In 1860 one observer estimated that 100,000 gannets still nested on top of the rock and 50,000 more on the sides. In 1887, not quite twenty years after the lighthouse was built, the entire gannet colony was estimated at 10,000, and in 1904, at less than 3000 with none nesting on top. The numbers are somewhat higher than that now, I judge, aided by the active bird protection that began early in this century, but not a patch on the former colony.

However, since I never witnessed what Audubon observed here, Les Rochers des Oiseaux are one of the most dramatic ornithological spectacles I've ever seen. Aristede has lobster trawls set on all sides of the main tower and, about a mile away, around North Bird Rock as well—two wave-cut remnants not twenty feet high. We spend over an hour slowly making our way past them, while the trawls are pulled and the empty traps stacked in the open stern cockpit. The little turrets of North Bird Rock are thick with gannets and black-legged kittwakes and common murres, while the air above all the rocks is an eddying veil of flying birds. On the big Bird Rock the gannets still line the broader flat ledges, spaced as regularly as cabbages in a garden, just as Audubon described them; the kittiwakes and murres and a few razorbills crowd where they can on the narrow shelves and in grottoes.

I catch Jean-Claude's eye after we have partially circled the big rock. *"Très* beaux," I tell him. "Truly. Vraiement." He grins.

A human figure on top of the rock waves to us. The keepers would surely be pleased if we came ashore to visit. What a desolate station on which to serve—the sense of desolation sharpened by the knowledge that on top of the rock is the grave of a little girl, a keeper's daughter, who fell from the rock and died. "The sea beats around it with great violence," Audubon writes, "except after long calms, and it is extremely difficult to land." A bit less so now perhaps, in Diesel-engined boats, while that little dock at the base and the long stairway climbing steeply to the top must help some. But these conveniences do not attract Aristede today. "We do not land," he tells us. Godwin had advised Audubon the same; bad weather was upon them, and the wind was rising. Audubon's young men wanted to make a try anyway, so John W., Tom Lincoln, and Coolidge went off in a whaleboat rowed by four sailors and disappeared around the far side. They didn't get on the rock, but they did shoot some specimens and collect a few eggs knocked into the water by birds in panic takeoffs. "An hour has elapsed," says JJA; "the boat . . . is now in view; the waves run high, and all around looks dismal. See what exertions the rowers make; it blows a hurricane, and each successive billow seems destined to overwhelm their fragile bark." Worriedly he watched them through a telescope, as they approached—now riding the crest of a wave, now plunging down into the trough, almost out of sight. "My son stands erect, steering with a long oar, and Lincoln is bailing the water which is gaining on him. . . . [A] rope is thrown and caught, the whale-boat is hauled close under our leeboard; in a moment more all are safe on deck, the helm round, the schooner to, and away under bare poles she scuds toward Labrador." In his painting of the gannet, JJA's background has the big Bird Rock in the distance, with its veil of birds; the sky is dark, as at the approach of a storm, and a streak of bright weather on the southeastern horizon illuminates the distances, the isolation, the vulnerability of men at sea.

MD The hill of lobster traps on the *Harold G. II* grows upward and outward from the pilothouse wall—back, back, back to where we sit on the stern transom. There has been no explanation as to how we will get from the afterdeck into the pilothouse (and to our extra sweaters, foul-weather gear, and lunch) once this structure of wet, barnacled, seaweed-slippery lobster traps has been completed. After we are penned on the transom, Jean-

Audubon's painting of gannets, which he began within days of visiting the Bird Rocks. *Courtesy of The New-York Historical Society, New York City*

Claude indicates that we are now to climb up the face of this perilous structure, crawl over the top of it, edge across the roof of the pilothouse (where we must remember not to touch the exhaust pipe, because it is *hot*), and then lower ourselves in through the starboard window: an interesting and exhilarating journey on the open sea as the boat pitches and slides from crest to trough like the *Ripley*'s whaleboat. The traps under my knees and hands are as slippery as wet ice. (And bobbing in the waves at the foot of North Bird Rock is a herd of seals, every eye upon us.) When I reach the window, Captain Cyr takes a deathgrip on my ankles to save me from dropping off the roof into the ocean and wrestles me inside—ankles, waist, wrists and elbows, into his arms and the pilothouse. Mike sends his camera and binoculars forward with Jean-Claude and follows after.

MH   I wanted to know Aristede Cyr better. Behind that majestic air of authority lay substance. I could *see* that he built magnificent fishing boats, and I'm sure that he knew a great deal more. He told me, for instance, half in French, half in English, that the rock of the Bird Rocks was the same as the rock of Brion island, nine miles west. They must once have been one piece, he suggested. The idea (expressed by scholars too) would be interesting to discuss. What could I say? Oui, Oui. Most unsatisfactory. We (I more than Aristede) lacked the key mechanism for exploring it between us.

On the way home, after the mate had served up a huge pot of boiled lobster (and we had caused the fishermen's noses to wrinkle by dipping *our* lobster meat in melted butter—a convention they had never seen) Jean-Claude wanted to look through my bird book, the Chandler Robbins field guide. That caught Aristede's attention, and soon he was leafing through it too. Finally, while the mate took the helm, we three sat on the deck of the pilothouse, Aristede in the middle, and went through the book, page by page. Aristede or Jean-Claude would spot something and put the point of a finger on it; I'd look interested, and one of them might say, "En hiver," meaning that they saw it in winter. Or I'd say, "Ici"—either as a statement or asking whether the bird occurred in the islands—and point to a picture. Hands held *here* and *here* measured out approximate sizes of the birds in life, faces registered surprise or agreement or lack of knowledge. We smiled, nodded a lot, and shrugged. But after half an hour, we had used up the book, Aristede went back to the helm, Jean-Claude took a nap below, so did Mary, and the mate flipped through the field-guide by himself as the *Harold G. II* headed home.

On June 17, eleven days out of Eastport, the *Ripley* was at anchor near the rocky Labrador coast, at a so-called "American Harbor," west of Natashquan. (The Hudson's Bay Company had a fishing station at Natashquan and kept out American ships.) For the next several weeks the expedition looped eastward—to Wapitagun, Little Mecatine, Portage Bay, Bras d'Or Bay—stopping to explore, collect, and draw.

"Every morning," says JJA, "the cook was called before three o'clock. At half-past three, breakfast was on the table, and everybody equipped. The guns, ammunition, botanical boxes, and baskets for eggs or minerals were all in readiness. . . . At four, all except the cook, and one seaman, went off in different directions. . . . Some betook themselves to the islands, others to the deep bays; . . . on landing [they] wandered over the country till noon, when laying themselves down on the rich moss, or sitting on the granite rock, they would rest for an hour, eat their dinner, and talk . . . I often regret that I did not take sketches of the curious groups formed by my young friends on such occasions, and when, after returning at night, all were engaged in measuring, weighing, comparing, and dissecting the birds we had procured; operations which were carried on with the aid of a number of candles thrust into the necks of bottles. Here one examined the flowers and leaves of a plant, there another explored the recesses of a [loon's] gullet, while a third skinned a gull or a grouse."

As they went along, they collected quite an aviary on board—living birds to study. At one time or another they carried young cormorants, a loon, black guillemots, common murres, young merlins, young great black-backed gulls, and puffins. Doubtless there were others too. The puffins "were agreeable pets," said JJA, "only that they emitted an unpleasant grunting noise, and ran about incessantly during the night, when each footstep could be counted."

Audubon himself did not go ashore as often as his companions did. He used the daylight to draw by. His table was set beneath a hatch fitted with a glass skylight that could be opened when the weather permitted. After he had been on the Labrador coast five weeks he would complain that he had done only seventeen drawings—*only* one drawing every two days, under the most difficult conditions. Sometimes he couldn't work, because of the leaping of the ship. Then there were days like July 8: "Rainy, dirty weather, wind east. Was at work at half-past three, but disagreeable indeed is my situation during bad weather. The rain falls on my drawing-paper, despite all I can do, and even the fog collects and falls in large drops from the rigging on my table; now and then I am obliged to close my skylight, and then may be said to work almost in darkness." The weather was usually dreadful—foggy or rough—so that when the sky more or less cleared on July 2 JJA remarked that it was a "beautiful day for Labrador," and on July 20 he exclaimed, "Labrador deserves credit for *one* fine day!"

He was deeply moved, and disturbed, by the landscape. It "is so unlike any thing else that I have ever seen before," he wrote Lucy, "and so far beyond my means to describe that to let it alone may (for the present at least) prove the most prudent." But such prudence quickly gave way before the strength of his feelings. "We have however been deceived as to the quantity of Birds represented to be met with here—Birds are rarer than even on the St. John's River of the Floridas," except for, he said, "those of a few species of which thousands may be seen. . . . Scarcely not a day have we been without a constant fire—We see snow in all our walks—Musquitoes and Caraboo flies in thousands at every step—a growth of vegetation that would astound any European Gardner and yet not *a cubic foot of soil!*———Granit—Granit—Granit—Moss—Moss—Moss—and nothing but Granit rocks and Mosses of thousands of species."

"The country, so wild and grand," says his edited journal, "is of itself enough to interest anyone in its wonderful dreariness. Its mossy, gray-clothed rocks, heaped and thrown together as if by chance, in the most fantastical groups imaginable, huge masses hanging on minor ones as if about to roll themselves down from their doubtful-looking situations, into the depths of the sea beneath. Bays without end, sprinkled with rocky islands of all shapes and sizes, where in every fissure a Guillemot, a Cormorant, or some other wild bird retreats to secure its egg, and raise its young, or save itself from the hunter's pursuit. The peculiar cast of the sky, which never seems to be certain, butterflies flitting over snow-banks, . . . Then the morasses, wherein you plunge up to your knees, or the walking over the stubborn, dwarfish shrubbery, making one think that as he goes he treads down the *forests* of Labrador. The unexpected Bunting, or perhaps Sylvia, which perchance, and indeed as if by chance alone, you now and then see flying before you, or hear singing from the creeping plants on the ground. The beautiful fresh-water lakes, on the rugged crests of greatly elevated islands, wherein the Red and Black-necked Divers [loons] swim as proudly as swans do in other latitudes, and where the fish appear to have been cast as strayed beings from the surplus food of the ocean. All—all is wonderfully grand, wild—aye, and terrific."

He was also impressed by what man was doing to that stretch of coast—the egging, trapping, sealing, fishing, hunting. "Fur animals are scarce," he noted (for example), and "every year diminishes their numbers. The Fur Company may be called the exterminating medium of these wild and almost uninhabitable climes, where cupidity and the love of gold can alone induce man to reside for a while. Where can I go now, and visit nature undisturbed?"

Much of the *Ripley*'s voyage in Labrador was made in company with the Royal Navy cutter *Gulnare*, which carried a party of scientists surveying the coast. So JJA had the luxury of testing his impressions of the land and its tenants with accomplished, educated men. One evening he and his lads paid a visit to the officers' temporary camp on shore. "We talked of the country where we were," says his journal for that day, "of the beings best fitted to live and prosper here, not only of our species, but of all species, and also of the enormous destruction of everything here, except the rocks; the aborigines themselves melting away before the encroachments of the white man, who looks without pity on the decease of the devoted Indian, from whom he rifles home, food, clothing, and life. For as the Deer, the Caribou, and all other game is killed for the dollar which its skin brings in, the Indian must search in vain over the devastated country for that on which he is accustomed to feed, till, worn out by sorrow, despair, and want, he either goes far from his early haunts to others, which in time will be similarly invaded, or he lies on the rocky seashore and dies. We are often told rum kills the Indian; I think not; it is oftener the want of food, the loss of hope as he loses sight of all that was once abundant. . . . Nature herself seems perishing. Labrador must shortly be depeopled, not only of aboriginal man, but of all else having life, owing to man's cupidity. When no more fish, no more game, no more birds exist on her hills, along her coasts, and in her rivers, then she will be abandoned and deserted like a worn-out field."

On July 26, the *Ripley* entered the long bay at Bras d'Or, within sight of the Strait of Belle Isle between Newfoundland and Labrador: she stayed for more than two weeks: "Bras d'Or is the grand rendezvous of almost all the fishermen that resort to this coast for codfish. We found here a flotilla of about one hundred and fifty sail, . . . mostly from Halifax and the eastern portions of the United States. There was a life and stir about this harbor which surprised us after so many weeks of wilderness and loneliness—the boats moving to and fro, going after fish, and returning loaded to the gunwales, others with seines, others with capelings for bait. A hundred or more were anchored out about a mile from us, hauling the poor codfish by thousands; hundreds of men engaged at cleaning and salting, their low jokes and songs resembling those of the Billingsgate gentry."

MD   To catch up with the *Ripley,* we once more had to double back via ferry to Prince Edward Island, to Nova Scotia, and thence to Newfoundland—island-hopping through the Maritimes, though in truth one is mountain-hopping from peak to peak across the drowned valleys of the upper reaches of the Appalachian chain. We drove to the Strait of Belle Isle at the top of Newfoundland by way of the western coast road (there is no eastern coast road), and the ferry route—a half-inch line of dots that we'd hunted down with a magnifying glass in our atlas at home—materialized into reality at the port of St. Barbe. A blue sky shone overhead, the road was lined with the ox-eye daisies that had followed us through Newfoundland to the ferry slip, and across the strait lay the dark mist-bound shore of Labrador.

When this trip was in the planning stage, we could find out nothing about southeastern Labrador, not a scrap of information on the ferry schedule, grocery stores there, campsites, or alternate lodgings. The Quebec government's tourist board knew only what they (and we) could see on the map, and they referred to that distant corner of their province in British fashion as The Bush. A travel agent I consulted in Connecticut knew even less. "No one," she told me flatly, "*ever* goes to Labrador." (She said the same about the Dry Tortugas.) Well, we can testify that on this day, July 18, eighteen other people were going to Labrador on the afternoon run. The ferry ride is a short one, but can be tumultuous. Our car was chained down to the deck of the *Marine Coaster,* a small broad-beamed, ferry-freighter that makes two trips per day when the channel is open. In winter, the Strait of Belle Isle is a jagged plain of ice; today the sea, calm as a swimming pool, lolled and sparkled in the sun. The *Marine Coaster* picked its way through a field of giant red balloons—the marker buoys on fishing nets—and we sailed from the blue skies of Newfoundland into an overcast of mare's tails that reached out from the Labrador shore as though to swallow the boat alive. The sky thickened, lowered, and we were into the fogs of the Laurentian highlands. We disembarked at Blanc Sablon—a long wooden dock, cod trawlers, the ferry office, the fishery office, a curving road around a mountain leading up from the sea, and the view opened before us, due north. Bogs, lakes, far mountains, dark clouds casting their shadows. A break in the overcast, and a sheen of light swept the blue, gray, smoky greens, and purples of the landscape.

A wide dirt road, which is not on our maps, runs along the coast. To the east is Newfoundland-Labrador and the village of Blanc Sablon, a cluster of small frame buildings stacked on granite, mud streets, a general store, and behold, a Gulf station that takes Gulf credit cards. To the west is Quebec-Labrador and hand-lettered signposts point the way to Le Musée, the Dumas Motel, and L'Auberge au Jeunesse (Youth Hostel). We drove west for seven miles and came to the village of Lourdes de Blanc Sablon, also not on our maps though it's a considerable settlement: the museum, L'Hôpital de Notre Dame (with a small ambulance), a new, towering, modern church (with a bowling alley in the basement), a firehouse (Service de la Prévention des Incendies), and an outdoor hockey rink (the local team is The Jets). Two miles farther is the village of Bradore Bay, which *is* on the map and has an airport, the Dumas Motel, another general store (we'd brought a week's supply of staples, not knowing what to expect), and a branch of the Quebec Sûreté in a new pre-fab building—a new Jeep patrol car and two handsome bilingual police officers (moustaches and knife-edged creases in their immaculate khaki uniforms). We stop to ask where we could make camp. "Anywhere," one of the officers replies with a half bow, and he gestures sweepingly to all Labrador.

The wind blows continually, so for our campsite we choose a deep U-shaped sandpit in the mountainside near the port of Blanc Sablon. A narrow track leads up through the mosses. We park next to the sandpit, slog down into the excavation with our gear, and set up camp about fifteen feet below wind level. Like any other place on earth, once you get there, it is no longer remote. It becomes the center of your universe. Our center is our sandpit. The rest of Labrador goes on forever. The coast road at the foot of our hillside is the line of demarcation. Step over it, walk into the fog past the wooden crosses of the bleak little roadside cemetery, and you could wander forever, northwards to nothing.

Fog. You have never seen fog, until you see the fogs of Labrador. They are blown in from the ocean where the icy Labrador current, flowing down from the Arctic Sea, meets the balmy Gulf Stream just before it bends eastward to Europe. Cold meets hot. Fog is brewed on the instant. "Sterile and stormy Labrador," said JJA. "[C]omfortless, cold and foggy, yet grand." In summer, the temperature rarely goes above 55° Fahrenheit; in winter, it goes down to 55°F below zero. And summer is only six weeks long. Labrador is known as "the land that God gave Cain"—a phrase we hear again and again that was coined by Jacques Cartier in 1534 when he wrote that Labrador was "composed of stones and frightful rocks and uneven places . . . not one cartload of earth . . . nothing but moss and stunted shrubs . . . I am inclined to regard this land as the one that God gave to Cain."

Perhaps He did. The Labrador peninsula is among the oldest land on the planet. It is on the Laurentian Plateau, which curves northwest to the Beaufort Sea above Alaska, and it was the first part of the continent to be permanently elevated above sea level—before there were any life forms on earth. So far as is known, the Norsemen were the first Europeans familiar with the Labrador coast. By 1000 A.D. they had a settlement in Newfoundland at L'Anse-aux-Meadows across the Strait of Belle Isle. Basque whalers were here by the 1300s, followed by Portuguese, French, English, and Scandinavian sailors fetching fish for Catholic Europe. The Normans and Bretons were the first to settle in with fishing stations, and by the time Cartier arrived the place names along this stretch of coast were already established. Blanc Sablon, the village named for the fine white sand on its beach. Longue Pointe, or Long Point, the promontary to the west, now called Lourdes de Blanc Sablon (except by the old timers). And Bras D'Or, "the golden arm," so-named because of the lucrative fishing and sealing in these waters, with the town at its zenith in 1600 —two hundred houses and a population of one thousand people.

Labrador was a chance name given in 1500 by a party of explorers from the Azores out to claim islands for the King of Portugal. One of the leaders of the expedition was a *lavrador,* a landed proprietor or gentleman farmer, as we would call him; he was the first to sight the landfall of Greenland, so his shipmates dubbed Greenland the *Tiera del Lavrador,* The Land of the Farmer. Since Eric the Red had already given Greenland its name centuries earlier, European cartographers eventually shifted the title of Tiera del Lavrador over to the continental area of eastern Canada. Down through the years in the course of translation from Portuguese to French and to English, though it is no longer The Land of the Farmer, it is still The Labrador in the spoken word. On the *Marine Coaster,* we heard it from a toothless, weather-lined Blanc Sablon man who'd been working in Newfoundland and was bitter at the massive unemployment "in The Labrador," and we heard it from a traveling repairman for the fish-processing plants on the coast, who was heading to "The Labrador" with spare parts for a broken scaling machine. Now that we have arrived, we hear it from most people we talk to.

Important archaeological discoveries have recently been made on this stretch of coast by teams from Newfoundland and Quebec, each of them digging, you understand, in their own province on their own side of the line. Between them, they have uncovered three burial mounds built by the Archaic Indians seven thousand years ago —the oldest known burial mounds in the world, pits five feet deep, excavated by the Indians with such tools as caribou horn. The bodies were laid in place with grave offerings: quartzite knives and spear heads, whistles made from bird bones, walrus tusks, bone and walrus-ivory sharpened into pointed awl-like tools, pestles, toggling harpoon heads of caribou antler, harpoon line holders of walrus-ivory. The dead were dusted with ceremonial red ocher, then covered with a cairn of boulders, and, as the millennia passed, by creeping vegetation. The Quebec dig is in the village of Bradore Bay, where a display of bone and ivory artifacts is laid out on paper towels on a couple of folding tables in the post office.

The Bradore Bay post office is in the basement of the general store. Here we met Leonard Hobbs, storekeeper and postmaster. "When is the post office open?" we had stopped to ask. "Whenever I'm in it," he replied with a twinkle in his one good eye, which is of a brilliant, piercing blue. He's a man of perhaps fifty; stocky, sturdy, dressed in a purple lacework shirt of some synthetic fabric or other, and bell-bottom pants. A man who hurries from task to task, a jog step as he goes. A man of instant camaraderie, who becomes our source of much information and our general host—just as JJA and company had been welcomed by Mr. Jones, master of the sealing station at Bradore Bay in 1833: "a rough, brown Nova Scotia man, the lord of this portion of Labrador."

Mr. Jones' house (his country seat, as JJA spoke of it) fronted the Strait of Belle Isle "and overlooked a small island, over which the eye reached the coast of Newfoundland, whenever it was the wind's pleasure to drive away the fogs . . . [Mr. Jones] has seen much of the world, having sailed nearly round it; and although no scholar . . . he was disgusted with it. He held his land on the same footing as his neighbors, caught Seals without number, lived comfortably and happily . . . and cared about nothing else in the world. Whenever the weather was fair, he walked with his dame over the moss-covered rocks of the neighborhood; and during winter killed Ptarmigans and Caribous, while his eldest son attended to the traps, and skinned the animals caught in them. He had the only horse that was to be found in that part of the country, as well as several cows . . . The only disagreeable thing about his plantation or settlement, was a heap of fifteen hundred carcasses of skinned Seals, which, at the time we visited. . . . notwithstanding the coolness of the atmosphere, sent forth a stench."

At dinner one evening Mr. Jones gave JJA an account of traveling by dogsled in winter: "The dogs are so well acquainted with the courses and places in the neighborhood, that they never fail to take their master and his sledge to their destination, even should a tremendous snow-storm occur whilst underway; it is always safer to leave one's fate to the instinct which these fine animals possess than to trust to human judgement, for it has been proved more than once that men who have made their dogs change course have been lost, and sometimes died, in consequence. . . . Mr. Jones lost a son of fourteen, a few years ago, in a snow-storm, owing to the servant in whose care he was, imprudently turning the dogs from their course; the dogs obeyed the command and struck towards Hudson's Bay; when the weather cleared the servant perceived his mistake, but alas! too late; the food was exhausted, and the lad gradually sank, and died in the arms of the man."

Detail from Audubon's horned larks. On July 29 ("Another horrid stormy day" in Bradore Bay) he reported, "I have to-day drawn three young Shore Larks . . . the first ever portrayed by man." *Courtesy of The New-York Historical Society, New York City*

Audubon poked a bit of fun at Mrs. Jones for her cultural pretensions—the "vile" Italian prints that hung on the walls and her conversation about music, which she said was her forte: "Her instrument had been sent to Europe to be repaired, but would return that season, when the whole of her children would again perform many beautiful airs; for in fact anybody could use it with ease, as when she or the children felt fatigued, the servant played on it for them. Rather surprised at the extraordinary powers of this family of musicians, I asked what sort of an instrument it was, when she described it as follows: . . . '[It] is large, longer than broad, and stands on four legs, like a table. At one end is a crooked handle, by turning which round, either fast or slow, I do assure you we make most excellent music.' The lips of my young friends and companions instantly curled, but a glance from me as instantly recomposed their features. Telling the fair one that it must be a hand-organ she used, she laughingly said, 'Ah, that is it; it is a hand-organ, but I had forgot the name, and for the life of me could not recollect it.' " However, concluded Audubon: "I felt glad to find that she possessed a feeling heart, for one of her children had caught a Siskin, and was tormenting the poor bird, when she rose from her seat, took the little fluttering thing from the boy, kissed it, and gently launched it into the air. This made me quite forget the tattle about the fine arts." Also: "During our stay at Bras d'Or, the kind-hearted and good Mrs. [Jones] daily sent us fresh milk and butter, for which we were denied the pleasure of making any return."

But Audubon forever cherished Mrs. Jones and her interest in music. Years later, he would express the wish to visit Bradore Bay in wintertime: "Under the hospitable roof of Mr. Jones, while the tempest might be hurling southward the drifting snows, I could live in peaceful content, cheered by the matchless hand-organ of my kind hostess."

The descendants of the master of the sealing station still live in Bradore on the same patch of ground. "Right over there," says Mr. Hobbs, pointing off into the fog. "That's the Jones' house." We squint through the gray gloom and barely make out the square shape of a two-story, white clapboard building not more than thirty yards away. As strangers and unexpected visitors, we go to the front door of the house instead of the kitchen door and are ushered in through a small oblong parlor where a smiling girl, very blond, rather plump, whom I guess to be a great-great-great-granddaughter of JJA's Mr. Jones, passes the afternoon on the sofa in the casual embrace of her gentleman caller. The house is unfinished inside—no plaster or wallpaper. The walls and ceilings are bare board darkened to a smoked, heavily lived-in patina; most of the furniture is homemade, country-carpenter construction. The kitchen is the heart of the house, the biggest room, and it is full of Joneses, three or possibly four generations. The current patriarch (a great-grandson of Audubon's friend) is a lean, stooped, dark-eyed man in his mid-seventies.

They are pleased at our visit, but express no astonishment that two strangers should arrive from the United States with news of the doings of their forebear. The Joneses have had a lot of historiographic attention recently from the archaeological team that excavated the foundations of the original Jones house, which stood fifteen paces from their present back steps. The original house, in turn, had been built on the foundations of a French fort that was abandoned and fell into ruin after the English won Canada in 1759. Mrs. Jones brings out

In the foreground, the remains of the Jones house where Audubon visited. In the background, the present Jones house at Bradore. *MH*

a model of the fort, presented to the family by the archaeologists—
a long, narrow, white-painted, wooden structure with three chimneys and sharply peaked roof. A small moss-covered hill that was also
excavated turned out to be a pile of thirty French boats left behind
more than two hundred years ago. But none could be saved, a son-in-
law tells us; the wood crumbled at a touch. Also, when the coast road
was put through a few years back, the construction crew unearthed
layer upon layer of seal and whale bones, the evidence of centuries
of hunting expeditions. The entire town apparently rests on an im-
measurable boneyard.

No one in the household has heard of John James Audubon, but
whoever he might have been, they like his comment—that Mr. Jones
was the lord of this portion of Labrador. They correct JJA on one
point, however: the master of the sealing station was not Nova Scotian born. He was a Welshman and had come to Labrador by way of
Nova Scotia, and he so loved the wildness of this land that he vowed
never to leave for the outside world. However, in his old age, Mr.
Jones capitulated and moved to Quebec City, where he is buried.
"I've been to Quebec," says the son-in-law. "I've seen his grave."
They don't know the story JJA told about a son who was frozen in a
blizzard. "That boy would have been your great-uncle," Michael says
to old Mr. Jones, who accepts this thought without comment. The
drama of sudden death in a cold climate is an everyday matter to
him, but for a moment he turns and looks away out the kitchen
window, perhaps thinking of someone from his own lifetime who
froze, starved, or drowned out there. Mrs. Jones tells us a story from
the recent past about a neighbor, alone and frightened in a winter
storm, her husband away on a hunting trip, who took her new baby
in her arms to go to the next house only a few yards distance. But she
lost her way in the storm and was found frozen the next morning; the
baby, by a miracle, was still alive. The son-in-law speaks of the terrible day when thirty-eight men, out hunting seals on the Strait of
Belle Isle, were swallowed by the sea as the ice shifted and heaved
and turned over.

The son-in-law escorts us to the excavation of the old Jones' house
—square-cut foundation stones set in a low rectangle, the stub of a
chimney at dead center, set in a natural garden of mosses, lichens,
and white-flowering Alpine smartweed. (And yes, on a clear day, one

can look across to Newfoundland.) We were then joined by another Jones, whom we take to be a grandson of the patriarch in the kitchen and the brother of the young lady who is entertaining her beau in the front room. The grandson was home on holiday from his job in Labrador City to the north—a mining center with some 20,000 in population, which was opened up and settled about twenty years ago but also has not yet found its way onto most maps. Young Mr. Jones (who wears a diamond-studded wedding ring) is well-spoken, outgoing, and enthusiastic about future plans for Bradore—a reconstruction of the French fort, a museum, a provincial park. "Come back in four years," he tells us. "You won't know the place."

Change, however, is received with mixed reactions. Leonard Hobbs at the general store speaks with regret of the passing of the dogteams. Ski-Doos are killers, he says. An accident or a breakdown out on the tundra and you're done for. With a team, you were never lost: "Dogs can home." And nowadays, because of the insidious Ski-Doos, the game is in shorter and shorter supply. The Ungave Bay caribou no longer make their annual migration to the coast. "Let a caribou set foot out of the northern mountains, and someone's there with a Ski-Doo and a rifle. We know every inch for two hundred miles inland. The caribou don't stand a chance."

He spoke of a hunting trip seven years ago, his blue eye sparked with anger and disgust. He was on the shore of a river, inland to the north. The caribou passed on the far side, and a gang of Ski-Doo hunters was lined up on the near side. "It was a massacre. They weren't shooting for food. They couldn't cross the river to get the meat. They shot for the sport of shooting." That was Mr. Hobbs' last hunting trip. He never went out again, but he misses the treks with the dog team, setting out at three in the morning into the frozen wilderness; the hunting camp, the good taste of food eaten around a campfire: "Even a cup of tea tastes better outside."

Almost everything is store-bought now, the food frozen or canned. There are no more gardens where once beans, potatoes, and other root vegetables were grown. The crafts learned from the Eskimo in centuries past are almost forgotten—the making of sealskin boots, sealskin foul weather gear, sleds and harness. There are many products from communist countries, such as our new North Korean rubber boots, which we bought from Mr. Hobbs for $6.95, one-third the price of Canadian-made boots. And fresh produce is in limited supply. Mr. Hobbs never knows what his wholesalers will send him. The onions and potatoes in his bins have gone brown and grown roots; meantime, he receives a shipment of fresh bananas, pears wrapped in tissue paper, pink Kleenex, disposable baby diapers, and Jiffy Pizza Delight. But there's never any pipe tobacco for sale; the men here are not pipesmokers.

Most of the new buildings are store-bought too—pre-fabs. The old houses were built of wood in a straightforward clapboard construction, no log cabins as on the western frontiers. A number of the old wooden houses in Bradore, incidentally, reflect an Italianate Renaissance architecture that was repeated down through succeeding generations, so that it's impossible in passing to know if a house of this style was built in 1810 or in 1940.

Summer in Labrador, like Alaska and Siberia, is notorious for its deer flies, black flies (the ones that seek out eyes, ears, and nostrils), mosquitoes, and no-see-ums or sand flies, the smallest of the winged bloodsuckers, some of them only four-one-hundredths of an inch long. They're also known as punkies, from the Lenape Indian word *ponk,* meaning fine ashes or powder, to describe their infinitesimal size. JJA spoke constantly of harassment by insects, of being driven back to the boat time and again by the gnats and mosquitoes, "as troublesome as in the Floridas;" of "hungry and abundant" mosquitoes, even in fog as thick as rain, driving him below decks where he "continued fighting them till daylight"; of the young men suffering from the "Caribou flies" on their hunting expeditions: "Tom Lincoln who is especially attacked by them, was actually covered with blood, and looked as if he had had a gouging fight with some rough Kentuckians."

Luck is with us. This past spring was so dry in Labrador that insect larva did not have enough moisture to survive, whereas in the south —Florida, Georgia, the Carolinas—we were made miserable by insects, the same list as above, and because no-see-ums are small enough to get through mosquito netting, I slathered the screening on our tent with salad oil to keep them out.

The dry weather last spring also lowered the water level hereabouts. Where JJA spoke of bogs and morasses into which they sank to their knees—sometimes to their armpits—we found the footing comparatively dry. But it is an unpredictable terrain, nonetheless, like walking on a trampoline. A spongy, springy surface of lichens and mosses, and strewn throughout, like a field of golf balls, the round white puffs of reindeer moss. Add to this the little trees—pygmy-sized larches and the alpine birch that grows like a creeping shrub, the leaves smaller than my thumbnail and toothed around the edges as though trimmed with tiny pinking shears. "The stubborn dwarfish shrubbery," said JJA, "making one think that as he goes he treads down the *forests* of Labrador."

On July 2, he wrote of the "probing beautiful dwarf flowerets of many hues pushing their tender stems from the thick bed of moss." Some were included in his paintings. (All of them again in bloom this July.) Lincoln's sparrow is pictured with bunchberry, cloudberry, and bog laurel, which JJA said were new to him "and probably never before figured," not knowing that bunchberry and cloudberry were also native to and known in northern Europe and that bog laurel had been classified by German botanists in the previous century. The willow ptarmigan is pictured with Labrador tea, roseroot, and beach pea. JJA, by the way, did know beach pea and laurel by name, though most other flowers, as in his earlier journals, were merely noted as pretty or plentiful. "I wish," he wrote, "that I were a better botanist." Agreed.

But even the local people, as we have found in our travels everywhere, have no names for many of their wildflowers, which seems doubly strange in Labrador where the season is so brief and the flowers so astonishing in the desolate grandeur of this landscape. There seems to be no word of identification for the arctic senecio *(Senecio frigidus)* that grows as high as your shoulder, wrapped in a white, woolen web from which the green plant bursts into leaf with a yellow, sunflower-like blossom as big as a saucer. "Would it be a buttercup?" said Mr. Hobbs' mother. No, not a buttercup. "Well, then," said she with a second helpful thought. "Would it be a lily?"

Nor is there a local nickname for seaside mertensia *(Mertensia maritima),* also known as oysterleaf because of its flavor; big, round, plump circles of it bloom on the beach, some a foot and a half across and frosted with salt dew, the flowers at the outer rim of the circle hatching from pink to blue, a sure clue to the forget-me-not family to which mertensias belong. From above, the plants look like leafy blue-green sofa pillows bordered with pink and blue ruffles.

On the other hand, the small, flowering, berry plants do have identifying names, because there is a use for them. The berries are eaten by animals, birds, people. Cranberry, partridge berry, gooseberry, blueberry, bearberry (though the bears are gone), curlew berry (though the Eskimo curlews have vanished from this coast). The cloudberry, which was identified to JJA as "baked apple," is still known as baked apple, because of its flavor. Five white petals, a few fat, unripe, orange berries just beginning, and a favorite throughout this part of the world. Leonard Hobbs shipped three tons of baked-apple berries to Newfoundland a few years back, but says the crop is finished because of Newfoundland pickers who were boated over a season or two ago and ripped the vines out of the ground in their greed and haste, whereas his Labrador pickers knew better and had always taken care when gathering baked apple.

Labrador tea, of course, is named—the white flowering shrub in whose branches the young fox sparrows and white-crowned sparrows play overhead at our sandpit. The French botanist, François André Michaux, who traveled this area in 1811, noted that the Montagnais Indians understood the beneficence of Labrador tea and also wild fruits as guards against scurvy, while the colonists on their persistent diet of salt meat and seal suffered all manner of scorbutic complaints. Nutritional diseases and poor health have always plagued the white man here. It was survival of the fittest in the roughest and most bleak terms until only a few decades ago. The illiteracy rate was high, the life span short, and the survivors, as a whole, were not the hearty, healthy, seafaring folk one would imagine in a romantic image of the Labrador wilderness. A visiting physician we met on the *Marine Coaster,* who had served with the Grenfell Mission twenty years ago when they made their rounds by boat in summer and by dog team in winter, said that centuries of intermarriage in isolated villages had also taken their toll. Nine times out of ten, he could guess a patient's home village by his or her birth defect or chronic illness. But medical attention was slim, at best. Distances were so vast that most villages

saw a Mission doctor only once a year and then only for a few hours.
No one, he told us, touched a drop of cod liver oil, a mainstay of the
economy; it was shipped away to be refined and fed to other people's
children.

The first telegraph line in 1905 was viewed as black magic and
an instrument of the devil. One generation ago, an outhouse was
unique—a frivolous gewgaw. Leonard Hobbs was the first person in
Bradore Bay to install a bathroom, and that was in the late 1950s.
But the villages are finally slipping into the twentieth century.
Electricity. Telephones. (If we had a phone in our sandpit, we
could call Blanc Sablon for a delivery of cold beer.) The airfield.
The hospital. Oil or electric heat instead of the wood that once was
carted home by dogteams from the forests miles and miles inland.
Compulsory schooling, though there is no high school; those who
want to can leave for government boarding schools, an arrangement that does not sit well with many families who fear their chil-

Our campfire at the sandpit. *MH*

dren will learn bad habits in the outside world—drugs and dissatis-
faction with the village life they come home to.

Except for southern Illinois, we have never seen so many bad
teeth as we do here. Black, ragged smiles—broken, missing, and
decayed teeth. A clean, even, white smile in anyone over the age of
thirty usually means dentures. Nor have we seen so many bright blue
eyes, the intense blue of a gas flame. (Leonard Hobbs is not alone.)
For the rest, the color is usually deep brown—mournful French eyes,
and the brown eyes that bespeak old blood lines from intermarriage
with Eskimo or Indian women.

Notes from our campsite:
    The ice for our cooler is given to us (free) by the Quebec Depart-
ment of Fisheries, whose plant down at the Blanc Sablon dock manufactures a ton of chipped ice per day for the shipment of fresh fish.
Our firewood in this treeless land is scraps of seasoned lumber—the
tag ends of two-by-fours and two-by-eights that were shipped here
to build a switching station for Télébec, the Quebec phone company.
No one else has apparently scavenged any of this first-class trash
that's scattered at the building site, and you could frame up a small
house with the abandoned lumber. There's an anti-litter sign at
Lourdes de Blanc Sablon: "Aidons-nous à garder notre village
propre." (Help us keep our village clean.) But Labradorians are as
willful with trash as any other culture, the usual disrespect for one's
countryside, and here there's so *much* countryside to absorb it. (Consider the reeking hills of seal and whale detritus absorbed over the
centuries.) We've dragged back a few useful objects found in the
mosses and in nearby ditches. For our fireplace: a wire refrigerator
shelf that serves as a grid and is supported by a ten gallon pickled
beef can at one end and a large pail, which looks to me like a milk
bucket, at the other. Next to it is a drying rack made of lumber on
which we hang gloves, socks, and sneakers. We unearthed a pair of
half-buried pallets (flat wooden racks used in shipping large objects)
and one of them serves as a platform to keep books, dry boots,
binoculars, etcetera out of the sand, the other as a storage platform
for cooking utensils and for dishwashing, complete in its appoint-
ments with a turquoise drainboard that Mike found this morning

during a chase after what he thought was a saw-whet owl, but turned out to be a fog whistle. (In the old days, the fog warnings on the Strait of Belle Isle were given by a small cannon, fired every five minutes.) Mike also scavenged home a long strip of dark blue carpeting, which serves as a big doormat and keeps the sand out of the tent.

We have a pantry and dining area sheltered by a tarpaulin, the back edge tied to roots protruding from the bank of the sandpit and held aloft at the front edge by aluminum tent poles. The tarp tilts downhill at one side to create a controlled sluiceway, under which we can place a large jug and collect plastic-flavored rainwater. Otherwise, we have two water sources—the Gulf station at Blanc Sablon or Mr. Hobbs' well of iron red water at Bradore Bay.

Our first site for the pop-tent had been calculated against the prevailing southwest wind. We should have heeded JJA: "Nowhere else is the power of the northeast gale . . . so keenly felt as here . . . One would imagine all the powers of Boreas had been put to work to give us a true idea of what his energies can produce . . . these horrid blasts, that now and then seem strong enough to rend the very rocks asunder. The rain is driven in sheets . . . I can hardly call it rain, it is rather a mass of water, so thick that all objects at any distance from us are lost to sight."

We had a bruiser of a storm in the Homochitto Forest in Mississippi; the thunderstorm that charged out of Kentucky and struck our campsite at Cave-in-Rock like a runaway freight train; and the rain-out at Fort Massac on the Ohio. But last night's storm crowned them all. A northeaster that slammed out of Greenland, drove across the Labrador Sea and the Torngat Mountains, skinned down the Laurentian Plateau, funneled into the open end of our sandpit, and walloped us amidships. We dragged the tent to a sheltered cove along the north edge of the sandpit, the two of us slipping, sliding, floundering in the wind and the rain, wet to the skin, shouting to be heard—a vaudeville skit of Campers In A Storm, our arms full of billowing canvas that threatened to fill, explode from our grasp, and take off for the Great Lakes.

Thank God we had a fire going, a leaping, snapping, crackling bonfire. It had taken me half an hour earlier in the evening to get it started, not that we needed it for cooking. I could have used the propane one-burner. But I wanted the light and life of a fire in the wide Labrador darkness. I began small: a tiny sheltered heap no bigger than a bird's nest made of damp typewriter paper, with wooden matches for kindling, lighting it again and again, on my hands and knees to blow at a palsied inch-high flame, nursing it along like primitive man with a single spark in a filament of moss. One more wooden match, one more shred of paper, then two slivers of wood, another pinch of paper, another sliver, until I had a cupful of fire, then more and finally more, until there were coals and the blaze at last took hold. The persistence of fire! It burned on, lashed by rain, scaled flat by the wind, a swirling curtain of sparks blowing up into the storm, every sodden piece of two-by-four ablaze within minutes after going on the flames.

According to JJA's Labrador Journal, the *Ripley* had a "capital cook, although a little too fond of the bottle." However, food stores aboard were chancy: the butter rancid and the cooking oil "only fit to grease our guns." But they had beef, ham, ship's bread, and they ate well off the country. Eskimo curlew, "fat and juicy." Hashed eider duck. Lobster and codfish. Willow ptarmigan, "tender . . . an agreeable aromatic flavour." Though these are fishing villages, there's no fresh fish for sale, so the day after our arrival Michael made connections with the boss of the fishing fleet at Blanc Sablon—a short, fat, hearty party. "My dear sir," he exclaimed. "You're too late. The fish have already been split and salted. But come back early in the morning and you shall have your fresh cod." We returned two mornings later. The cod cargo ship at the dock was surrounded by smaller vessels that had just come in, the crew pitchforking fish aboard her, the men working in the time-honored assembly line manner that JJA wrote about here: the first man beheading and slitting open the cod; the second man cleaning the cod, the liver into a barrel, the entrails over the side; a third man removing the vertebrae, then tossing the fish into the hold, where another team salted and packed. Mike's connection appeared from the foredeck.

"My dear sir," he again exclaimed. "You didn't forget." He picked up a fresh cod about two feet long, cracked off the head across a thwart, and presented it to Mike.

"What do I owe you?"

"You owe me nothing. It's yours."

Mike walked back to the car up the long narrow dock wearing an ear-to-ear smile (it was his week to cook) and bearing the huge headless cod with fingers hooked into a bloody gill. We had several feasts of fresh cod fillet rolled in a batter of egg and bread crumbs and fast-fried in a deep skillet.

This afternoon we went out beyond Bradore to the eastern shore of the bay where the *Ripley* had anchored among a flotilla of one hundred and fifty sail, the water in the harbor coated with fish oil, the bottom covered with the refuse of codfish. JJA: "The very air I breathe and smell is impregnated with essence of codfish." The bay will probably never see the like of that again. Today, there was no essence of codfish, no one on the water, no one on shore, only Mike and me on the tidal flats making our selection through a couple of acres of mussel beds, every now and then coming upon tail flippers from butchered seals—rounded pairs of them still fastened together with gristle, and looking like pairs of big brown mittens. Washed in from winter sealing kills? From recent kills of seals caught in nets? To the fishermen, seals are the enemy, and though the killing is limited by law, who is to know, who will find out? Said JJA of the Labrador seals: "These rise to the surface of the water, erect the head to the full length of the neck, snuff the air, and you also, and sink back to avoid any further acquaintance with man." They were a staple here in the old days, before food was shipped and flown in. Armies of seal gathered on the ice. "When we needed meat, we went out on the harbor and took them with a stick," Mr. Hobbs told us. Then he shook his head. "I don't think I could hardly eat it anymore."

On our way back to camp, the backwash of flippers and the usual seawrack of garbage gave us second thoughts. Were the mussels edible? Was the bay polluted? Mike pulled up at the Lourdes de Blanc Sablon hospital, and I darted in to ask. No one was around except a roly-poly, smiling, elderly French-Canadian priest who appeared in the hall on a parochial visit to the sick and disabled—the most genial of men, smelling sweetly of sherry or brandy. "No, no, Madame. We have no water pollution. I eat mussels from the bay and they are delicious."

This evening, I serve steamed mussels, brown rice, and a canned wax bean salad. We sit in our sandpit, feasting once again, our portable radio tuned in bell clear to WCBS in New York City. Beirut is burning, the president announces that the economy has stabilized, a heat wave with temperatures above 100° F smothers the east coast. News from another planet. Our bonfire lights the dark corners; both of us are dressed for July in Labrador: Mike in long winter underwear, wool shirt and sweaters; I in a turtleneck cashmere sweater, a woolen shirt over that, an Aran Island sweater over that, and my son's hand-me-down canvas coat over that. We are snug, well-fed, and pink-cheeked, God wot.

The heater in the car has been a boon for drying damp sleeping bags, and the defroster vents on the dashboard provide a quick drying shelf for socks and gloves when we're away from camp. In this climate, comfort means dry feet and warm hands. The other day, after a cold clammy walk along the shore, Mike sat next to the fire, his watchcap down over eyebrows and ears, his beard sparkling with mist, a poncho wrapped around him like a blanket, and his bare feet soaking in an iron kettle of hot water and soapsuds, as he roared with laughter and declared that he never thought the day would come when he'd enjoy a foot bath. I have managed one extemporaneous bucket bath by the fire since we've been here, but otherwise bathing is not part of the daily drill.

We've had one laundry day, however, thanks to Mr. Hobbs, whose kindnesses to us are beyond telling. He has two washing machines and a dryer, so we laundered and spun-dry to a fare-thee-well and made free with his kitchen to cook lunch—family and neighbors coming and going, to visit, to eat, to use the laundry facilities, to chat, exchange news. This is the ritual pattern. There's much visiting from house to house. No one knocks or announces himself. (After all, they've known one another since at least 1600.) And when the long winter closes in, kitchens are packed with people visiting and passing the time. Thus, no one questioned our presence. Mr. Hobbs is keeping bachelor hall while Mrs. Hobbs visits a son in Ontario, and there was a stack of dirty dishes in the sink, which I washed up as a thank-you present. Otherwise, the house was ship-shape, and Mr. Hobbs took us for a tour of the one hundred and fifty houseplants he waters every day in his wife's absence.

This, you understand, is the grandest house in town. Brand new, a modern kitchen, two baths, a diningroom, livingroom, sun porch, and though we didn't see the second floor there must be four bed-rooms. When Mr. Hobbs' parents were his age, a wind-up victrola was a symbol of status. I suspect that Leonard Hobbs, like JJA's friend, the master of the sealing station, is the present lord of this portion of Labrador—a man of property. His former house, an old unpainted clapboard building next door in which he installed the first bathroom in town, is maintained as a rental to the archaeologists when they're here.

The second most impressive establishment in Bradore is the Dumas Motel, also brand new, with lots of dark woodwork inside, a taproom with tavern tables, and rock bands from Newfoundland on weekends. The taproom is usually full of customers, the front yard full of pickup trucks. (Decals are a popular item on pickups here, the side panels decorated with large, gaudy pictures of mallards, black bears, moose, red fox, Indian princesses, palomino horses, tongues of flames.) I'd stopped at the Dumas out of curiosity to ask the price of lodgings for two. Twenty-eight dollars, I believe. I wasn't listening closely. The manager and his wife, a team of gimlet-eyed French-Canadians, were as welcoming as a nest of rattlesnakes. With the antagonism between the French and the English coming to a boil, and the French tense and chauvinistic about their language, their homeland, their rights and privileges to be autonomous, I'm sure that in many instances through the Maritimes the French took us for the loathed Anglo-Saxon Canadians. Or perhaps they knew us for Ameri-cans and were frosty just the same. However, we get the impression that the petit bourgeousie as a group (one must always except the individual) are tight-lipped and hostile, not only with strangers, but also with each other. Students and professional men we've met along the way were of a different stripe. A sophisticated turn of mind, charming and friendly, at ease with foreigners.

MH   Every now and again the base of the fog rises a few feet and gives us a glimpse of our surroundings, then crouches down and hides it all. So far we haven't had more than a few hours when we could see more than a few yards in any direction. This stops us from plung-ing off on foot over the terrain north of the coast road to look for nesting loons and the like, and it makes even ordinary sightseeing difficult. We've walked along the shore of a lake, but haven't the

slightest idea how big the lake is—frog pond or Lake Erie; a glum
Quebec-French family—*Mama, Papa, et fils*—put out in a rowboat
to fish, and vanish—splash, splash—in a few seconds; for all we know,
they've fallen off the edge of the world. And how high are the hills?
How wide the bay? And does this remarkable, ankle-high, knee-high
forest go on across the boggy, bouldered landscape forever?

We've driven as far as we can to the westward, hoping to see
something. (When we stop and Mary leaves the car to look for wildflowers away from the road, we keep in touch by voice so I don't lose
her—a disconcerting exploration.) Our westering was ended by a
combination of the road and the visibility. The road, we've been told,
will be completed someday from one end of the coastal Bush to the
other and thence to Civilization; now and here it stops at the first big
river to the west and is a stone and gravel track about a lane-and-a-
half wide, which the young bucks of far-eastern Quebec (having no
other road to travel and knowing this one by heart) negotiate at sixty
miles an hour in their pickups—fog or no fog. Headed west, carefully
negotiating a steep rise on a roadbed of head-size rocks, where a cliff
evidently drops a hundred feet to the sea on one side and rises high
above us on the other, I feel the wheels spin and start to slide near
the top of the hill; back off a bit and try again, cautiously. But still we
slip and slide. The blanket of fog makes our position seem particularly hazardous. So we back up a quarter of a mile until we find a safe
place to turn around. I don't know what we expected to find on the
other side of that hill, anyway, except more fog. [MD: The old priest
at Lourdes de Blanc Sablon has told us there are times when his heart
is in his mouth as he's being driven along this road, on his way to
celebrate Mass in an outlying village.]

Even in the fog there are ornithological delights. We've
moved into a subarctic environment, and overhead—mostly un-
seen—whirl buzzing flocks of redpolls—Christmas-tree ornaments,
little gray-brown birds with black chins and jaunty red caps
pulled down over their foreheads, and the males with a rosy
bloom on their white breasts. I find them in Connecticut once
every few winters, if I'm lucky. As they pass over us here in the
fog I follow the sound with my eyes, watching for a descending
flock; occasionally a pair drops down, dives into an alder thicket,

and usually vanishes as I approach for a close look.

Other birds we see only in winter or on migration are singing all around us: fox sparrows, white-crowned sparrows, Lincoln's sparrows. I've been communing with the Lincoln's sparrows a good deal. That's the only new species JJA and his party discovered in Labrador. At the American harbor west of Natashquan, hunting through a small valley out of the wind, Audubon heard an unfamiliar song and shouted for the young men; they chased the bird, it proved very shy, but at last Tom Lincoln shot it. "I named it *Tom's Finch,*" says JJA, "Three cheers were given him, when, proud of the prize, I returned to the vessel to draw it." This is far from being *my* first chance meeting with Lincoln's sparrow. I've seen it in spring in New York City's Central Park as it pauses to eat and rest on the way north to Canada.

At low tide above the mudflats of Bradore Bay I saw, I *think,* an arctic tern. (I hesitate to declare it positively; a birding acquaintance who qualifies as an expert claims there are seventeen field marks by which one can distinguish the arctic from the very similar common tern; still, it seems to me that I would have to have the bird posing three feet away, in good light, before I'd be sure.) Dr. Ingalls, at the age of nearly ninety, wrote of an experience with Audubon and the arctic tern—a memory of the moment and the man he had held for seventy years: The entire party was on a seabird nesting island with JJA and Ingalls standing near each other, watching the birds. An arctic tern, said Ingalls, "flew toward me swiftly, falling very near my feet seeming to be in consternation or fright; with flashing swiftness another Tern descended and in his dart came within a very few inches of the terror stricken bird. The next day on our return towards night from our excursion, I darkened a little the table at which Mr. Audubon sat. He looked up and saluted me with 'Hollo, Sangrido' (he gave me this name the first day), 'he is here, he is scared, afrighted, he is looking up at you, you cannot help him.' Now, the dear man had his chalks upon the table and upright in front of him was a pine board upon which was secured in position by means of long thin pins, the bird whose likeness he was transferring to the cardboard before him. When you look at this picture you will see with wonder *expression,* even after reading this lame description."

A whimbrel passes over our camp—Hudsonian curlew, as it used to be known—a duck-size, long-legged shorebird. It flies toward the salt water, fades into the fog. I watch it go, wishing it would turn into an Eskimo curlew; that little northern cousin, once present here in enormous numbers on migration, is evidently nearly extinct, if not gone altogether, but I cannot stand in this gloomy landscape and not *hope* to see one. It was a lively, interesting creature. JJA's journal for July 29 says: " 'The Curlews are coming;' this is as much of a saying here as that about the Wild Pigeons in Kentucky. . . . The accounts given of these Curlews border on the miraculous, and I shall say nothing about them till I have tested the fishermen's stories. . . . [August 3–4:] I have seen many hundreds this afternoon, and shot seven. They fly in compact bodies, with beautiful evolutions, over-looking a great extent of country ere they make choice of a spot on which to alight; this is done wherever a certain berry, called here 'Curlew berry,' proves to be abundant. Here they balance them-selves, call, whistle, and of common accord come to the ground, as the top of the country here must be called. . . . [E]very one of the lads observed . . . the great tendency these birds have, in squatting to elude the eye, to turn the tail towards their pursuer, and to lay the head flat. . . . [It] feeds on the berries it procures, with a rapidity equalled only by that of the Passenger Pigeon; in an instant all the ripe berries on the plant are plucked and swallowed, and the whole country is cleared of these berries as our Western woods are of the mast. In their evolutions they resemble Pigeons also, sweeping over the ground, cutting backward and forward . . . , and now and then poising in the air like a Hawk in sight of quarry." JJA's friends the Joneses (among many others) shot "a great number every season, which they salt for winter food." In that way, from Labrador to South America and back, the species was gobbled up within the century; and man, on what remains of his frontier, has learned no lessons from that experience, nor from others like it: no caribou herds visit this shore any more; no great seal herds appear on the ice now; the whales are scarce and growing scarcer; the cod are so few they are hardly worth fishing for—certainly not in the old way, with hand-lines and small nets that a few men could haul. And yet if these creatures were to appear in desirable numbers they'd likely be hunted hard again, if only for the fun, if not the profit in it.

Labrador deserves credit for *one* fine day! Not an hour after dawn, the fog literally rolled away toward the east (whence it will doubtless shortly return), and the air was clear as glass. We spent the day dashing around the Bradore vicinity, looking at the wondrous landscape that has been hidden from us for five days. Yes, the knee-high forests do seem to go on northward to the horizon, and grow taller than knee-high only in sheltered valleys. There is a pond or a lake or a puddle of water in view practically wherever one looks, and so the terrain is like nothing else we've ever seen—mosses, mosses, mosses, all right, in hundreds of shapes and colors, and granite, granite, granite, in piles and megaliths and swelling ribs that burst up through the moss, and splashes of blue water sparkling here and there all over it.

The clear day coincides with our trip to Paroquet and Greenly islands, just offshore; JJA and his lads went onto Paroquet to collect some young puffins just before they sailed for home. The local name for puffins is parakeet or sea parrot, and Paroquet Island is a traditional breeding site. The "air was filled with these birds," says JJA's journal, "and the water around absolutely covered with them, while on the rocks were thousands, like sentinels on the watch. I took a stand, loaded and shot twenty-seven times, and killed twenty-seven birds, singly and on the wing, without missing a shot; as friend Bachman would say, 'Pretty fair, Old Jostle!' " That sort of sport is now illegal, and the Canadian government has made Paroquet a bird refuge. When we asked our dapper friends of the Quebec Sûreté where we might find someone to take us out to the islands, they warned us not to go out with anyone carrying a gun; if our guide were arrested, we would be too, as accomplices. But the shooting goes on anyway. One indolent, swaggering young blood (who had asked us why we would ever want to come to a place like this) let it be known that he might try some puffin-hunting in the fog and treat himself to a good dinner. And despite the laws against egging, we heard of another local sportsman who collected a few hundred puffin eggs this summer for his winter's food supply. "No matter how many are killed," one man told us, "they always seem to be as many left." Whether that's true or not we have no way of knowing. The fisherman who took us out on the water did not like the state of the wind and tide around Paroquet, and wouldn't land us there, so we did no close inspection. We saw only a few puffins as we circled the little island, and they seemed very skittish, but the lighthouse-keeper we met on Greenly told us that on fine days the puffins mostly go off fishing or stay in their burrows; it's just before bad weather breaks that they line up on the rocks—"so many of them, they'd almost knock you down." When the government did its most recent puffin survey, he said, "they" wouldn't say how many nesting birds they counted; more than they *expected,* he'd wager. Fishing and shooting rules, and the rule-makers, are not popular at this end of the Quebec Bush.

MD   We were taken out to Paroquet and Greenly Islands today by Leo Paul Beaudoin, of ancient Labrador lineage, a thin, dour, woeful man, who indicated the long boats pulled ashore on the ribs of rock that form the narrow harbor of Lourdes de Blanc Sablon and said that those boats would never be in the water again. The fishing, what's left of it, is now the province of the factory ships, trawlers, and draggers that work in fleets down the length of the continental shelf. Local fisherman with small boats cannot compete and most of them here are on welfare. Mr. Beaudoin counts himself among the lucky ones; he can turn his hand to carpentry.

In the little museum in Lourdes de Blanc Sablon—which has a collection of fishing and hunting gear, tools, and household objects from the early days—a prominent display is devoted to the *Bremen,* a German plane that fell out of the skies onto Greenly Island during a trans-Atlantic flight in April 1921. The aviators, Baron Hühnefeld, Major Fitzmaurice, and Captain Koehl (who were unscathed) lived at the lighthouse for three weeks before their rescue could be effected, and this corner of Labrador found itself suddenly on the map and in the newspapers, worldwide. It was an epochal event, not yet surpassed even by Brigitte Bardot's visits to Bradore Bay to protest the seal hunting on the Strait of Belle Isle. And what a treat the three aviators had been for the keeper of the light. Company! Heaven-sent company to break the monotony. The keeper we met on Greenly, who ran down to the white beach to greet us, begged us to stay longer, to come back tomorrow and stay for the day, and was ebullient with pleasure at new faces and fresh conversation. It's a lonely station, though two keepers and their families live there.

(Which I had deduced through my binoculars when I spied two clotheslines. "Right!" the keeper exclaimed. "No woman would hang her clothes on another woman's line!")

Greenly is also said to be haunted—flickering lights along the shore, carried by the spirits of departed French settlers who buried their valuables on the island when Canada was ceded to Great Britain in 1768, and the French ghosts come back from time to time to search for and reclaim their treasures. Another ghost appeared there in the 1920s—the wandering shade of a previous keeper who had committed suicide and whose footsteps were heard and his silhouetted figure seen on the staircase leading up into the light tower; the priest came out to Greenly the next day, exorcised the room in which the suicide occurred, and the keeper's ghost was laid to rest.

On the mainland, far out on a sunstruck, crystalline, ice-green, silk-smooth lake bounded with jagged boulders, we saw a solitary common loon—a distant, black, beaky periscope. JJA wrote that his son and Tom Lincoln had lured loons to the shore of a Labrador lake by tolling them in—"by running towards them halloing and waving a handkerchief, at which sight and cry the Loon immediately swam towards them, until within twenty yards. This 'tolling' is curious and wonderful. Many other species of water-fowl are deceived by these manoeuvres, but none so completely as the Loon."

We tried it—waving bandannas and halloing. The loon paddled toward us about six inches from its chosen place in the middle of the lake, then circled away, sliding through the water as though on wheels, and paid us no further attention.

The two resident police officers have made an arrest. The word is flashed up and down the coast road from Blanc Sablon to Lourdes de Blanc Sablon to Bradore Bay. The criminals are a trio of dope peddlers who robbed a bank in Sept Iles, some five hundred miles to the west, and came to Blanc Sablon by coastal steamer under the hazed illusion that they could hide out in this community of villages where no one is anonymous. They will be loaded aboard the afternoon plane and returned to Sept Iles. We go to the airport to witness The Happening. The airfield is crowded; a murmur of anticipation, side glances to the dirt track from the village: Where is the Sûreté jeep?

The silver plane slips out of the sky and descends into our midst. Visiting expatriate relatives and Canadian fishery bureaucrats debark from its side. At departure time, six passengers board. We are still waiting for the Sûreté. On cue, after the travelers have been fixed into their plane seats, the jeep arrives, the officers unpack their quarry and march them to the plane in handcuffs. A scruffy looking lot, these bandits. Pale, gaunt, unwashed, uncombed, dirty blue jeans, ragged T-shirts. Not a sweater or jacket among them. Their appearance alone would identify them instantly—on the run, living threadbare. They walk to the gangway, heads bowed, climb aboard, stumbling and awkward, their wrists bound behind them in the short link of their handcuffs, and are taken into custody by an officer on the plane. Our Sûreté officers, their assignment complete, turn smartly, march to their jeep, and drive away in single parade formation.

In passing at Lourdes de Blanc Sablon, I met again with the elderly genial priest, who asked if we enjoyed our mussels. "But without a good sauce," said his lanky, ascetic curate, "one cannot eat mussels."

"Ah," said I. "We had a sauce of freshly minced garlic, tarragon, and butter."

"Ah," said both priests, eyes closed in appreciation. "Ah . . ."

We've been aware of only five other tourists since our arrival last week:

A pair of dejected, shivering backpackers (boy and girl, English-Canadians), who had been here twenty-four hours and were heading home on the next ferry.

A French-Canadian student with a motorbike, who was staying at the Youth Hostel in Bradore.

A French-Canadian couple, also at the Youth Hostel, though they were no longer youths. Fortyish, I'd say. Both with aristocratic profiles, both with an exultant, eyes-only-for-each-other manner, their hands clasped on wind-seared walks across the rocks, the beach, the moors—he, leading the way, poncho streaming behind him like a cape. They behaved like a couple on a stolen weekend. (If so, what a long way to travel for a rendezvous.)

This morning in the early slanting light, the red spore stalks of the mosses turn patches of our hillside to scarlet. I depart this campsite much against my will. The majesty of the view from the cliffs above, codboats in the strait, the sweep of the sea, the shoulder of Newfoundland to the south. We leave the fireplace standing with a stack of firewood beside it and stow the blue doormat under the wooden pallets for safekeeping. Perhaps someone else will find our camp and use it before winter sets in. Perhaps—a wishful thought—we'll come back someday and find it magically waiting for us.

MH   When we recross the Strait of Belle Isle, bound southward, three hotshot young Canadian birders are also on board the *Marine Coaster*, doing a bird-count. Naturally the strait is chocked with fog, so we have plenty of time to chat about such matters as the local bird names. In JJA's day the razorbill, for example, was called a "Tinker" in the Maritimes, and it still is. The thick-billed and common murres were both called "Turres" (rhymes with Sirs), at least earlier in this century, but I gather some distinctions have since been made, so now one kind is called "Turre" and the other "Murre"; we've heard about this before, but there seems no agreement on which is Turre and which is Murre. The little dovekie, seen in winter, is "Bullbird." The sandpiper tribe is made up of "Sanders," and a least sandpiper is a "Beachy Bird." The short-eared owl is the "Lopper." The locals, say our Canadian companions, also believe the great black-backed gull is the fully-mature version of the herring gull; that's interesting, because in 1833 Audubon entertained the same notion.

When JJA wrote Lucy late that July, he intended to remain in Labrador until September. But two weeks later he changed his mind. The weather, the terrain, the difficulty he had drawing on board in rough water, the lack of new species, the need for resupply (Lincoln and Shattuck were now shoeless, for instance), the failure to find a guide to lead them inland from Bradore—all discouraged him; and he was bone tired. "I now sit down to post my poor book," says the journal for August 10, "while a heavy gale is raging furiously around our vessel. My reason for not writing at night is that I have been drawing so constantly, often seventeen hours a day, that the weariness of my body at night has been unprecedented . . . At times I felt as if my physical powers would abandon me; my neck, my shoulders, and, more than all, my fingers, were almost useless through actual fatigue at drawing. . . . When at the return of dawn my spirits called me out of my berth, my body seemed to beg my mind to suffer it to rest a while longer . . . Yesternight, when I rose from my little seat to contemplate my work [probably the Eskimo curlews] and to judge of the effect of it compared with the nature which I had been attempting to copy, it was the affair of a moment; and instead of waiting, as I always like to do, until that hazy darkness which is to me the best time to judge of the strength of light and shade, I went at once to rest as if delivered from the heaviest task I ever performed. The young men think my fatigue is added to by the fact that I often work in wet clothes, but I have done that all my life with no ill effects. No! no! it is that I am no longer young." These are unsettling portents: at the age of forty-eight John James Audubon is slowing down.

The next night the *Ripley* was at sea, and he was only thirty days, he hoped, from Lucy. "Seldom in my life have I left a country with as little regret as I do this," says the journal. "Now we are sailing in full sight of the northwestern coast of Newfoundland, the mountains of which are high, with drifted snow-banks dotted over them, and cut horizontally with floating strata of fogs reaching along the land as far as the eye can see. . . . John and Lincoln are playing airs on the violin and flute; the other young men are on deck. . . . Twenty-three drawings have been executed, or commenced and nearly completed. Whether this voyage will prove a fruitful one remains to be proved; but I am content."

MD We follow the *Ripley* down the northwestern coast of Newfoundland. Herds of shaggy wild horses among stands of pink fireweed. Split cod drying on wooden racks in the coves below. A fisherman walking up through a buttercup meadow with a stack of dried cod, like a load of firewood, tied to his back. Much of the coast road still under construction and thick with titanic earth-moving machinery, deep with potholes, boulders, car parts, and many body shops along the way. Newfoundlanders drive hell for leather.

Midway down the coast, the *Ripley* rounded the Cape of St. George, a soaring, land's end of red, sea-beaten cliffs that appears as a mere fleck on the map of Newfoundland, this giant, forested, mountained island of looming headlands and royal-blue fiords. Today, July 26, purple harebells bloom in the rocks on the Cape of St. George and we find a sunlit pastoral scene of grazing sheep, horses, and colts, chickens everywhere, and cows come home to be milked, their mistresses kneeling beside them with milking pails at the edge of the road. A Holstein hide dries on a rack in a farmyard. In another, there's a roof-raising. In every cove, one fishing boat at least and lobster traps on the shore.

Newfoundland is edged with fishing villages; many, along the southern and eastern coasts, can be reached only by boat. It has a vast interior wilderness—no roads, no settlements, lakes and valleys still uncharted—and because there are so few roads to the interior, you never lose your sense of the sea. The deep, thunderhead-blue sea is always at your feet, the barricade of the mountains at your back.

Newfoundland is the tenth largest island in the world, a fifth again larger than Ireland—and also has no snakes. (Nor skunks either.) It is pronounced "Newfun*land,*" and they have a rhyming mnemonic for visitors, to help them remember: "It's Newfun*land.* Under*stand?*" Any pronunciation with the final syllable as *lind* instead of *land* is particularly frowned upon, as in *New*funlind or New*fund*lind.

It was the outback of eastern Canada for centuries, the isolated island with a take-out economy—fishing, lumbering—and not enough agricultural land to put in your hat. It's still a poverty pocket and still viewed as the outback. One Newfoundlander said to us: "An urban center is any town with fifteen hundred people and a fried chicken bar." Every Polish joke you've heard has been transposed into Canadian terms and is told as a Newfie joke—with a number of regional originals, of course. Cartoon booklets of Newfie jokes are sold on the Maritimes ferry boats.

The people are descended from French, English, Scottish, Irish, Channel Island, and Portuguese settlers, often with a strain of Indian blood, and the accent we heard along the western coast was a sing-song potpourri. One blond, blue-eyed boy, who spoke of his mother as "me mudder," pointed to the controls on my tape recorder and asked, in Scotch, Irish, and French: "Wha' ee tha bootin la?" (What is that button there?) He and his friends (dark-eyed, dark complexioned boys, each with his own family accent) who'd surrounded us at a fishing cove, asking to have their pictures taken, asking to talk into the tape recorder, had never seen old-fashioned wooden kitchen matches and took them to be a new American invention. I gave each of them a handful as a present.

JJA made only one stop in Newfoundland. The *Ripley* anchored in St. George's bay on August 14 at the village of Sandy Point, which stood on an elongated tongue of sand that served as a natural seawall for the harbor—"a beautiful and ample basin," said JJA, "wherein more than fifty line-of-battle ships could safely ride, the bottom being of clay." Across the harbor on the mainland, there were signs of cultivation and a settlement of Mic-Mac Indian huts. During the next two days it was all ashore in search of birds, plants, shells, and "the usual *et ceteras* attached to our vocations." JJA brought back to the *Ripley* a red pitcher plant, which he added to his painting of the red-throated loon drawn in Labrador. The pitcher plant (whose name he did not know) is now the official flower of Newfoundland, by proclamation of Queen Victoria.

Sandy Point, because of that fine harbor (said hereabouts to be the second best on the Atlantic coast), was *the* town between Cape Breton and Labrador. It was the fishing capital of western Newfoundland and it saw them all: the first European fishermen-settlers; the pirates of the mid-1700s; the British and French warships during the disputes over fishing rights throughout the 1800s; and the fighting ships of the twentieth century, up through World War II. It is yet another ghost town on the Audubon list. The docks, barrooms and stores, churches and schools (Church of England and Roman Catholic), the Convent of the Sisters of Mercy, the houses, streets, and little farms—gone.

The population began its shift to the mainland after the railroad came through in 1896, many families settling in and around the village of St. George that stands where the Mic-Mac Indian huts had been. (Apropos the coming of the railroad in the 1890s, a local fisherman commented: "That's the way it goes in Newfoundland. The railroad had been invented fifty years before, but it took all that time to get to us.") Later, more people left Sandy Point when the herring fishing died out, and then the sea came through, cut the point off from the mainland, and left the village stranded on an island. By the mid-1960s only thirty families remained, the government resettled them ashore, and the town was officially abolished.

From the shore today, we can barely discern the shallow silhouette of Sandy Point, which is no more than ten feet above water line at any tide or at any given place. An expedition has been arranged. Our escorts are two young men from the nearby village of Seal Island, who are taking the trip for the pure fun of it. Our trip leader is Philip Bennet, a rollicking charmer (and a descendant of a French sailor named Benoit, since anglicized to Bennet, who settled on Sandy Point around 1750), and Phil Bennet's friend Bob, quiet, shy, sturdy, who is the owner of the expedition boat, a big dory with an old Acadian engine amidships. Would they let us pay for the gasoline? Not on your life, said Bob. We could get to Sandy Point and back on a cupful of gas, we could ride St. George's bay for the day on a gallon. The Acadian is a one-cylinder engine that revolutionized fishing on these coasts. It was the Model-T Ford of its time—small, easily repaired, low fuel consumption, and it got you there and back, *unka-unka-unka,* no faster than men could row, to be sure, but farther than men could row in a day's pull. Mike has already had a run in the dory—a cod-jigging voyage with Bob and Phil. Rub-a-dub, three men in a tub, and they all went aground on a sandbar, and had fine noisy tales to tell upon their return—no codfish and soaked to the skin. We join them again today from our campsite in the spruce forest of Barachois Provincial Park. Clouds, wind, rain. At Sandy Point, we tie up to the rotting pilings of a ruined dock and clamber ashore.

JJA and company were lit ashore one evening with paper lanterns and escorted to a ball given in honor of the *Ripley.* The dance was held in a fisherman's house, wooden benches and stools around the wall, "the belles of the village . . . flourishing in all the rosy fatness produced by an invigorating northern climate, and in decoration vying with the noblest Indian queen of the West." Tom Lincoln brought his flute, JJA his flageolet in a waistcoat pocket, and John Audubon his violin. John opened the ball with an overture of patriotic music—"Hail Columbia," The Marseillaise, and "God Save the King." Tumblers of rum were served between dances and equally relished by the ladies, to JJA's astonishment. The young men stayed until two-thirty in the morning, John playing on in company with the Sandy Point fiddler. JJA, much fatigued, was back aboard the *Ripley* and abed before midnight.

In two other memoirs of Sandy Point that I've seen, dances and balls are the common thread. The Sandy Pointers loved to dance. Any excuse, and the party was on. Edward Chappell, aboard His Majesty's Ship *Rosamond* in 1818 wrote about a "rustic ball given by the fishermen's daughters in a hut on Sandy Point," the young ladies, said he loftily, "dressed in the most burlesque finery for the occasion." In a local history of Sandy Point, compiled this year, interviews with the former residents now living on the mainland had reference upon reference to music and the dances they held—"kitchen rackets" with a fiddler, Saloon Dances given whenever a warship anchored, the food provided by the ladies, the music by the sailors, and everyone over eight years old at the party.

Even the old roads are overgrown now and the site of the village gone back to meadowland. Many of the buildings were salvaged and the lumber carried to the mainland in winter across the ice. We explore the foundations of a former church and the tangled cemetery next to it. The first Sandy Point cemetery, down by the harbor, has been washed away. The vandalized hulks of a few old frame houses still stand, roofs open to the rain. A few horses that have been swum out here to graze for the summer skitter away at our approach. We walk through the broad sweep of meadows and into the spruce forest to the end of the island, rain running off the ends of our noses, and the horses get into our lunch bag, which I'd left stowed under some

Sandy Point. *MH*

loose boards. They eat the almond granola, the bananas, unwrap the peanut butter sandwiches but find them not to their taste, and leave the mouthed remains for us.

MH Philip tells me that all seafowl are considered good eating in these parts and fair game, in and out of season—except perhaps gulls. Loons, herons, ducks, geese, spotted sandpipers, which they call "tickle-asses." He says the taste was learned during the Depression, but its antecedents are a far sight older than even the community of Sandy Point. On migration, he says, birds of all kinds are shot, just for practice: "Anything that moves."

MD JJA bought a barrel of salmon for ten dollars when he was here, and for seventeen dollars he bought seven Newfoundland dogs to take to friends in the States. They were enormously popular dogs, both in America and in England, and JJA had a Newfoundland with him on his Florida trip. In 1818, Edward Chappell wrote that upon the coast of Labrador "most of the Fisheries are plentifully supplied with these dogs, and they prove of great utility in dragging home the winter fuel. They are also employed in Newfoundland for the same purpose, where they are usually yoked in pairs. Such is the disregard of these creatures for cold, that when the thermometer of Fahrenheit has indicated twenty degrees below Zero, they have been known to remain in the sea during an entire hour. The fisherman feed their dogs upon salted halibut, or, indeed, any other sort of food . . . Their docilety is so remarkable, that they will leap from the highest cliff into the water, in obedience to the commands of their master. To many they are ever gentle and good natured; so much so, indeed, that it has been very customary, of late years, to cross their breed with an English bull-dog, whereby they are rendered more fierce and surly towards strangers."

These dogs are a rarity here nowadays. "And there's not a man who would deny that a Newfoundland could move more wood than a horse," a veterinarian told us. They also pulled the wagons of fish from the docks to the stage and were invaluable on the fishing boats because of their unflagging instinct to retrieve—lost gear, men overboard. The vet (the only veterinarian in all Newfoundland) had a Newfoundland dog named Caesar, a gentle fellow of one hundred and sixty pounds who stood twenty-eight inches at the shoulder, and who had made a name for himself one summer by retrieving spruce logs that were being floated to the mill by a lumber company. Caesar, unbeknownst to the family, was wrestling the logs ashore and neatly stacking them on his master's property, which took some explaining and a demonstration by Caesar when lumber officials came by to accuse the vet of stealing their logs.

When the *Ripley* was anchored in St. George's Bay, JJA also spoke about the Mic-Mac Indian women collecting baked apple, the fruit of the cloudberry *(Rubus chamaeorus)*. As we head down the coast en route to the ferry, everyone is out picking. Bogs are dotted with folk, bent and intent, not just those trying to stretch a dollar, but those who've arrived in late model automobiles. (We have yet to taste a cloudberry that's ripe, and so cannot vouch for their baked apple flavor.)

MH   Once out of St. George's Bay, the *Ripley* ran into a southwest gale, and lay to under bare poles for two or three days. Everyone in JJA's party was dreadfully seasick. When the storm abated somewhat, Captain Emery made sail and beat southwest for the Gut of Canso, but before they reached it, the wind died. The wait there, within whiff of solid ground, was evidently too much for JJA and his young men. They were "sick of sea-sickness, the sea and all its appurtenances." So when the wind came up again, the *Ripley* was turned around and pointed for the port of Pictou on the Nova Scotia mainland, where the expedition would disembark. "The great desire we all have to see Pictou, Halifax, and the country between them and Eastport, is our inducement," says the journal. But now the wind turned contrary again, and so did the tide; after a night and half-a-day of fighting them, the schooner was still a few miles from harbor. Put us ashore *anywhere,* said Audubon, so the captain rowed them to a nearby island—the name of which sounded to JJA like Ruy's Island —where two men who were haying agreed to carry the baggage and Ingalls and Coolidge by boat around to Pictou, while the rest of the party walked. "[W]e all shook hands most heartily with the captain —to whom we now feel really attached—said farewell to the crew, and parted, giving three hearty cheers."

We have driven from St. George's Bay to Port-au-Port, ferried to

North Sydney on Cape Breton—another millpond voyage—and driven down across Cape Breton, into western Nova Scotia. The last part of the journey is made in the fringes of a hurricane, and the storm is blowing itself out by the time we reach "Ruy's" Island—which is really *Roy's* Island, but if you were writing a phonetic interpretation of Roy as pronounced by a down-easter, how would *you* spell it? Roy's Island is newly connected to the main by causeway; it has only a few houses on it. The shallow bay inside is an ugly brown and covered with whitecaps. The wind whips off the mainland, carrying spits of rain and spray out over the bay and north across the gulf. We stand on high ground and look out to where the *Ripley* waited, hove-to and sails flapping, while JJA and his friends were landed. How JJA would have hated this day's weather on the water! "We were now, thanks to God, positively on the mainland of our native country, and after four days' confinement in our berths, . . . we felt so refreshed that the thought of walking nine miles seemed like nothing more than dancing a quadrille." We, like they, enjoy our reunion with the familiar: Audubon mentions the smell of new-mown grass, the sounds of crickets and blue jays, and the sight of a hummingbird. For me, as the day clears, it's the voice of a song sparrow, and a catbird tootling. And in a Pictou waterfront parking lot, at a picket fence over which white and pink hollyhocks peep like shy children, a female hummingbird sips and buzzes around the blooms, chases a bumblebee, and "quite fills our heart with delight," as it did Audubon's.

Professor Thomas McCulloch must have been the attraction that drew JJA specifically to Pictou. They had mutual friends in Scotland, and quite likely Audubon was carrying letters of introduction to McCulloch. The professor was one of Canada's leading educators, a naturalist, Presbyterian minister, and controversial political figure. That evening they called on Dr. McCulloch and visited Pictou Academy, which McCulloch had founded in 1816. In those days, natural history commanded far more attention in progressive academic curricula than, unfortunately, it does today, and one of the gems in Pictou Academy's crown was its natural history collection. Audubon thought it the finest private collection he had seen in North America, and the next morning—he and his lads having returned for "an excellent Scotch breakfast" with the McCulloch family and to revisit

The Reverend Thomas McCulloch, by Daniel Munro. *Dalhousie University Archives*

William Eager's "Pictou from Fort Hill," drawn in the 1830s. *Killam Library, Dalhousie University*

the collection—he remarked that he coveted certain specimens. McCulloch promptly "had the cases opened, the specimens taken out, and he offered them to me with so much apparent good will that I took them." Take anything you need, McCulloch told him; do you see anything else you'd like? JJA did, but he was too embarrassed by the professor's generosity to ask for more. [MD: Another instant bond between the two men, incidentally, was their fondness for snuff. Professor McCullough, wrote JJA, *"loves it."*]

Audubon also made the acquaintance of the most dedicated naturalist among the professor's four sons—the youngest, Thomas McCulloch, Jr.—who was to be from that moment a faithful correspondent, sending bird and quadruped skins and notes on behavior from the north to JJA, who reciprocated in kind from the States.

MD The McCulloch house, which JJA described as "much like a small English villa," remains on its knoll, a handsome stone building erected in 1806. Within, it's a little jewel of a house—handcarved woodwork and plasterwork ceilings in Adams and Regency patterns. The former owners, Mr. and Mrs. Murdoch McCuish, sold the house and land to the province of Nova Scotia for preservation as an historic site, rather than let it go into a suburban development—bearing some such name as McCulloch Estates. Mrs. McCuish, now a widow in her eighties, has quarters in the house for the remainder of her life, and she still cares for the garden, hauling water from the McCullochs' old well. Red poppies grow there, iris, scarlet weigiela, mock orange, rhododendron, bleeding hearts.

The architecture of the house is not so much that of an English villa as of Scottish domestic design—granite or sandstone with dorm-

The McCulloch house. *MH*

ers—the prevailing architecture in Pictou's early houses, which was also interpreted in clapboard. Like Ste. Genevieve in Missouri, Pictou cherishes its past, and the Pictou Heritage Society is on its toes, researching, documenting, and preserving old buildings—the early ones on the harbor up through successive architectural styles to the High Victorian houses built on the hills above the waterfront as the town grew.

MH JJA and his companions went east to Truro, and then on to Halifax, across the waist of Nova Scotia by coach, at night. In the moonlit hours of the morning a key piece of the coach's equipment broke and fell off. While the piece was looked for and repairs made, "Ingalls took charge of the horses, and responded with great energy to the calls of the owls that came from the depths of the woods, where they were engaged either at praying to Diana or at calling to their parents, friends, and distant relations." We tried calling owls on the Truro-Halifax high-road ourselves at night, but this major thoroughfare is now no place for that—too much noise, too much forest gone. And away from the highway, if any owls were present, they weren't talking to us.

We follow JJA next from Halifax across Nova Scotia to Windsor, high up the Bay of Fundy. There he had watched the "tide waters of the Bay . . . rise sixty-five feet"—a sight that inspired an Episode for the *Ornithological Biography.* We find that the rise and fall of the tide is much ballyhooed by the Chamber of Commerce but is apparently far less dramatic than in 1833. A causeway has been built across the watercourse where JJA sat to watch the tide come in ("At half-flow the water rose three feet in ten minutes, but it is even more rapid than this"), and the causeway has created a huge sandbar that chokes the old channel and spoils much of the effect. We did not comprehend the astonishing rapidity of tide changes in the Bay of Fundy until we had driven clear around the head of the bay and were camped high on the cliffs of Parrsboro, directly across from Windsor. There you may see a lobster boat floating at its mooring near a cobblestone-shaped, spruce-covered island; ten minutes later the boat is on its side on a mudflat. The going tide recedes almost as quickly as the sun slips through the last few seconds of its setting.

MD   They sailed by steamer from Windsor, Nova Scotia, back to Eastport, Maine, at the end of August 1833. In his reminiscence of the Labrador expedition, written in 1902, Dr. William Ingalls said: "I cannot realize that seventy years have passed since we were together on that truly wonderful shore." And of Audubon, he wrote: "I think there is no exception to the fact that those who have spoken of him have testified to his great amiability and manliness, his humanity, and it has always seemed to me he was one of those men who on meeting, one would at once say, 'Bless you, dear man.'"

Many years after the Labrador expedition, when Tom Lincoln was asked by his son what sort of person Audubon had been, he gave a classic down-east reply: "He was a nice man, but as Frenchy as thunder."

THE GULF COAST AND TEXAS

APRIL–MAY 1837

MH   After the Labrador expedition, JJA was off again, but on more routine rounds: New York, Philadelphia, Baltimore, Washington, D.C., Virginia, Charleston for the winter, England and Scotland for a year with Lucy and the boys. JJA was painting, canvassing for subscribers, and working on the *Ornithological Biography*, which was being published in Edinburgh—the reviewers, said he, "all agog" for the next volume. Fame, however, has its hazards. JJA had been arrested in Philadelphia on the complaint of a former creditor from the bankrupt days in Kentucky, and another creditor filed suit in Charleston. Bankruptcy laws precluded any furtherance of these suits, but the threat heightened JJA's dreams of burning and sinking ships, and such morose concerns as lost paintings and cancellations by his subscribers. Money was still short, while the mountain of business and editorial and production details for *The Birds of America* was never-ending. A fire in the winter of 1835 in a New York City warehouse destroyed many of the Audubons' possessions—books, drawings, papers, some copper plates of the *Birds* engravings, guns, collecting equipment.

Meantime, an expedition along the Gulf Coast was in the planning stage. He wrote Bachman from abroad for news from the south. Would the Seminole War and the Texas Revolution wreck his hopes of traveling along the Gulf?

"With regard to Florida," replied John Bachman, "nothing will be done by naturalists for at least two years. Your Indian friends, the cut-throats, have scalped almost every woman and child south of St.

485

Augustine, save those on Key West. They have burnt and plundered every plantation; and although they will probably be, in a great measure, put down next winter, yet there will, undoubtedly, remain many small predatory bands that will make no bones of scalping an Ornithologist *secundum artem* [strictly by the rules of that art]; and would ask no questions whether he were the friend or enemy of William Penn. Of Texas, I think better, and thither, or along its borders, you may, I think, venture—for the Texans are our friends. I suppose Genl. Gaines will keep the Comanches quiet."

However rollicking and beamish a friend he was to Audubon, and however good a pastor he was to his Charleston flock, which included many Persons of Color, the Reverend John Bachman was what we would call today a racist. But he was in the flow of his times, his views were socially acceptable. JJA's views on the matter of "his Indian friends" were socially acceptable only insofar as they reflected the white world's romantic vision of the "noble savage," who lived in simple harmony with the other beautiful inventions of his Creator. This ideal was given shape and texture by Jean Jacques Rousseau in the eighteenth century. Before him, William Penn had admired Indians as free beings of few wants: "We sweat and toil to live; their pleasure feeds them, I mean, their Hunting, Fishing, and Fowling." Penn had been scupulously fair in his dealings with them, but for most whites the Indians were Noble Savages only until some invading European wanted their land; with that, they abruptly lost their nobility and were proclaimed cut-throats. Audubon had written in a frankly friendly way about the Indians of the Ohio and the Mississippi Valleys, with whom he had camped and hunted and broken bread. He was sensitive to the reasons for the decline and fall of the Indian spirit—as he showed in his Labrador journal, which by now Bachman would have read. Quite likely the two men had argued about it more than once over their grog. In 1836, Audubon remained faithful to his instincts. He was in England "on thorns" at the reports of the murderous Indians in Florida, and yet wrote to Bachman: "[M]uch do I regret the total forth coming extirpation of a race of beings all of whom Must for ever be acknowledged to have *once* been the only Lords of the Land alloted to them by our God!" (The man is incorrigible, Bachman must have thought.)

On JJA's return to America, the basic issue was not whether he would be scalped in Florida, but whether he could get to the Gulf Coast at all. Would the Navy have a vessel for him? All the cutters were committed to the Indian war. Andrew Jackson, the outgoing president with whom JJA dined in the White House, and Martin Van Buren, the president-elect, could make no promises. The Audubons' winter was spent in the elastic Bachman household in Charleston; Lucy, the two boys, JJA—hunting, writing, drawing. They were joined by Edward Harris, a gentleman farmer, horse breeder, European traveler, and naturalist, who lived in Moorestown, New Jersey. (Two buildings that survive on the remains of his former estate are now a Quaker retirement home.) Harris had rescued JJA both financially and spiritually years before when the artist's fortunes were at a desperately low ebb; he had bought all the paintings JJA would sell, and in response to this generous act, Audubon had made a generous gesture—he gave Harris his entire collection of early drawings of French birds. Since that time, Harris had been a patron and promoter of Audubon. JJA's one real regret about the Labrador voyage was that Harris had been unable to come, but Harris would be on the Texas expedition, and JJA was delighted.

They were packed and ready to go when news came of Osceola's capture in Florida. To all intents and purposes the war was over. Audubon, Harris, and John W. headed south to prod the Navy for a cutter. In Alabama they crossed the "Trail of Tears"; the Indian removal westward was in full swing. At a village whose name JJA could not remember when he wrote the Bachmans a week later, they saw a hundred Creek warriors "confined in Irons, preparatory to leaving for ever the Land of their births."

JJA Some miles onward we overtook about two thousands of these once free owners of the Forest, marching towards this place under an escort of Rangers, and militia mounted Men, destined for distant lands, unknown to them, and where alas, their future and latter days must be spent in the deepest of sorrows, afliction and perhaps even phisical want—This view produced on my mind . . . reflections more powerfully felt than easy of description—the numberous groups of Warriors, of half clad females and of naked babes, trudging through the mire under the residue of their ever scanty stock of Camp furniture, and household utensiles—The evident re-

Edward Harris. Audubon said he wished Harris had been his brother. *W. U. Harris Collection, Montgomery, Alabama*

gret expressed in the masked countenances of some and the tears of others—the howlings of their numerous dogs; and the cool demeanour of the chiefs,—all formed such a Picture as I hope I never will again witness in reality—had Victor been with us, ample indeed would have been his means to paint Indians in sorrow—

MD   At the Pensacola Naval Station, Audubon presented his letter of introduction from the Secretary of the Navy, Levi Woodbury, and was assured by the commanding officer that a cutter could be made available quite soon.

JJA wrote a long letter to John Bachman about Pensacola; "a small place at present; principally inhabited by Creole Spaniards of the lowest Class, and some few aimiable & talented families of Scotch, and Americans." Building lots, peddled by New York land speculators, were selling at great sums, but JJA doubted that Pensacola would amount to very much, because the back country was "so poor" —nothing but sand and pine barrens for eighty miles inland.

He also remarked on "two powerful fortifications" that guarded the entrance to Pensacola Bay. We camp early in April in the shadow of one of them, Fort Pickens, which is now being restored. Creeping among the ruins and across the sandy parade ground is a sheet of scarlet flowers—Drummond's phlox, named for a young Scotsman sent to America in the 1830s by the Glasgow Botanical Society. He walked over the Rockies and through the western country collecting new plants. This little flame-colored phlox that would be the parent stock of our hybrid garden varieties was one of the last specimens he shipped back to Scotland before dying of fever on a botanic expedition in Cuba, and the American wildflower was given his name— "that it may serve as a frequent memento of its unfortunate discoverer." I knew the story of Drummond's travels, and I'd written about his phlox before, but today is the first time I have seen the plant. This evening acres of them bloom, doubly scarlet in the sunset light. (Michael is hauling driftwood up from the beach. I run down the seawall, shouting and calling: James Drummond's phlox! James Drummond's phlox!)

This stretch of the coast, the Gulf Islands National Seashore, is particularly lovely—the pine barrens, a chorus of spring peepers from a nearby bog. The remainder of the evening, however, is de-

Seminoles drying fish on the white sand beach of Santa Rosa Island at Pensacola. By George Catlin, 1834. *National Collection of Fine Arts, Smithsonian Institution*

stroyed by the bombardment of racket surging and heaving from the Naval Air Station across the inlet as the night flights take off, each plane's engines equal to the monstrous fartings of ten thousand motorcycles revving up at the same time. We get the full effect as each pilot juices his plane for takeoff, the tail end pointing in the direction of the park.

JJA and Harris stayed the night "at a rascally house" called Collins' Hotel. ("May your star never shoot you there," he wrote to Bachman.) The name Antoine Collins shows up frequently in the archives of the Pensacola Historical Museum on Seville Square—a small, charming enclave of the old town, deep in the heart of the present city. When Florida was ceded to the USA in 1821, Collins was a prominent citizen, a ringleader in organizing a petition to Congress asking for land for a school and another petition asking that Pensacola *not* be attached to the state of Alabama. A social note: Collins' Hotel was also the scene of a ball, one evening, that erupted into a bloody free-for-all—brickbats and swords—with all who were so engaged hauled into court.

(To our pleasure and theirs, Michael and I arrive at the historical society bearing the news of JJA's visit here. There is no record of it in the archives, so the curator makes a Xerox of our copy of his Pensacola letter for their files.)

MH   From the abstract of the log book of the US Revenue Cutter *Campbell,* N. L. Coste, Esq. commanding, New Orleans, 1837 (found in the National Archives, Washington, D.C., and penned in a fine, flowery hand):

March 23   Crew employed at painting out Side & receiving Sundry articles of Mr. Audubons.

March 26   At 9am got underway & drop'd down to Slaughter House point & anchored. Mr. Audubon, Son, & Mr. Harris joined us on an Ornithological expedition.

Lieutenant Napoleon Coste, skipper of the *Campbell,* had sailed with JJA once before—as first officer on "Our Lady of the Green Mantle" in the Florida Keys and Tortugas five years earlier. Accompanying the *Campbell* would be a small schooner, the *Crusader,* which would act as tender to the cutter. Our first checkpoint is the

The Balize, or beacon, at the mouth of the Mississippi River, 1849. *N.Y. Public Library Picture Collection*

Mississippi delta where the *Campbell* waited for the *Crusader* to join the expedition; JJA & Co. went shooting, and Captain Coste put Mrs. Coste on shore to await his return at "a Fishers house."

The Mississippi delta oozes out into the Gulf of Mexico in the shape of a hand, fingers spread, heel on New Orleans. Through the delta run thousands of creeks and bayous and oil-company canals, and a series of passes that connect the river to the open water of the Gulf. As you sail downriver from New Orleans or drive, about 65 miles of squiggles either way, the road ends at Venice. Below that is the oil industry's staging area, called The Jump—an expressive name for the entry into a swampy no-man's-land that is traveled only by boat or helicopter, and veined with passes. Clockwise, as they enter the Gulf, the important ones are Main Pass, Pass a Loutre, South Pass, and Southwest Pass.

Most of the eastern delta is now a nature preserve. The lower section is a state hunting ground, in season, and the upper section is the Delta National Wildlife Refuge of the U.S. Fish and Wildlife Service—nearly 49,000 acres of water and marshy islands. Delta is one of the most isolated of the federal refuges. We had to call ahead by radio-telephone to make arrangements with refuge headquarters at the former quarantine station at Head of Passes, and although the refuge people would give us a lift back, we had to hire a boat to take us the seven miles downriver from Venice. (That, it turned out, was billed at oil-corporation prices: thirty dollars, more than four dollars a mile. Well, explained the Cajun whose son would drive us, the oil companies were paying $120 a day for hired boats.)

We camp upriver at Fort Jackson, another coastal defense post that has become an historic site. [MD: Perhaps the Pentagon in a hundred years will be a picturesque ruin with campsites and picnic tables.] Fort Jackson, completed in 1832, was sold by the government as surplus property in 1927, reverted to a jungle with mud-filled tunnels infested by snakes, and was dug out and partially restored in the 1960s. Tonight we build our cooking fire (of salt-rime riverside driftwood) inside a round shell of cast iron—the remains of a Civil War mortar—and sleep in a manmade valley behind the ruined breastworks.

April 1. A fine, clear, cool morning, mosquitoes out, along with hundreds of common and boat-tailed grackles, red-winged blackbirds, snowy egrets. Having been ferried out to the refuge (by a dark, fat, silent young man with pointed teeth like a bat's), we are now taken for a tour of the refuge in a small motorboat by a knowledgeable young Arkansan, who sucks on a pinch of snuff tucked inside his lower lip.

JJA mentioned nothing in the way of birds here except four gull-billed terns; and we are not overwhelmed with birds ourselves. But a lovely sight along our winding way through the marsh: perhaps a dozen avocets feeding in shallow water are chased and displaced by one of the smaller, less robust black-necked stilts. The stilt stretches itself into a posture so erect that it becomes *taller* than the avocets.

[MD: A raccoon wades across a sandbar from island to island. A big brindle swamp rabbit hops across the marsh. A banded water snake, midstream at Octave Pass, turns and faces up to the boat, ready to challenge our right to cross his bow.]

The oil companies pump out petroleum all over these nature preserves, and two aspects of this coexistence are quite striking. The first is the unobtrusiveness of the well-heads in the marsh; I expected something more massive and hateable. The second is the relative cleanliness of the passes and canals. Here and there you see a huge rusting tank that a storm has torn away from an installation in the Gulf and which no one picks up, presumably because no one can identify where it came from. Otherwise, the refuge is an oil company's dream picture, though if the federal and state governments weren't involved in the eastern delta, things would probably be different.

MD   The *Campbell* and the *Crusader* entered the Gulf by way of Southwest Pass, sailed westward, and crossed the bar into Baratraria Bay. The pass into Baratraria runs between two islands—Grand Isle to the west, Grand Terre to the east. They anchored at Grand Terre.

4th April	Mr. Audubon & Company went on Shore Shooting Birds.
5th, 6th, 7th, & 8th	Crew variously employed in ships duties. Mr. Audubon & Company on shore shooting.

There are no westward roads across the bayou country here. We return to New Orleans and head south again down Bayou Lafourche, pronounced "Lafoosh." The bayou, only a stone's-throw wide, is lined with fishing boats, mostly shrimpers. The *Cajun Lady, Cherami, Frenchie, La Lumette, Cajun Power, Le Bon Coeur, Petit Caporal, Bayou King.* Roadside signs advertise hog cracklings, coon for sale, live crawfish, red and white beans, frogs legs—"The Prettiest Legs in Louisiana," and "Crawfish Etouffe & Bisque for-to Go."

Notes from our campsite, Grand Isle State Park, Louisiana:
The weekenders have departed—the surfcasters, the nuclear families and their folding lawn furniture, the sunburned maidens,

the brawny boys, the lovers, the children, the cruising no-muffler Impalas—leaving a glittering sandscape of aluminum cans and the iridescent detritus of shrimp and crawfish that the herring gulls fight over, charging, snapping, and mantling like birds of prey over their kill. The wide, beautiful shoreline is adrift in food, underclothes, sneakers, blue jeans, hairbrushes, baby bottles, sandwich wrappings, Polaroid film boxes, Polaroid film strips.

A new crescent moon on its back. The vibrant sunset that blooms over the Gulf and is pulsed by blinking red lights high in the sky on a refinery radio tower. Eight miles out in the mist is a sulphur mine —a man-made island that twinkles like an offshore casino. Enticing, bubbling blue and white and red lights. The ultimate tinsel town. On the inland side of the beach, the shallows of the marsh are sprinkled with lights from an onshore sulphur refinery. Clapper rails nick and tshush in the reeds, as though it were still their territory. Retreat is sounded at the Coast Guard Base, and at 10 P.M. taps trembles across the marsh, barely heard above the southwest wind. We turn in, dutifully. (It's only a recording. But taps can break your heart, any time.)

Six A.M.—reveille.

The morning flights of helicopters begin, buzzing out to offshore operations. Grackles and red-winged blackbirds come out to join the gulls to scavenge among the leavings of the Big Animals on the beach. Redwings dive into trash barrels to rummage and claw, then perch in a circle on the rim of the barrels and call *okaree* as though on a branch in a damp northern meadow. (My redwings—*my* New England redwings—as beach rats.)

Grand Isle is locally pronounced in English, but Grand Terre is pronounced in French, still the first language of many people in these parts. On our CB radio, we can pick up Cajun conversations from shrimp boat to shrimp boat out in the Gulf. An assistant librarian in the Library here—the French-born wife of a Grand Isle man —is strangely timid, however, at speaking in her native tongue with the Cajuns. She finds them hard to understand, not only the accent, but also their vocabulary. For example, the archaic *chevrette* for shrimp, instead of the present day *crevette*. It embarrasses her not to understand, and she thinks they're embarrassed too, not to speak

English in an English-speaking nation.

On the other hand, we met an expansive and voluble French woman in New Orleans—an anthropologist working with the Society for the Preservation of French in Louisiana—and she cried nonsense and bah at such language dilemmas and timidities. The Cajuns love to talk their language, she declared. And if you don't understand, you only have to ask and they will explain. She gave as an example a phrase that had baffled her at first hearing—*"Maison de Chaud."* A hot house perhaps? No, no. Maison de show—a movie theater. She also spoke of a Cajun family in which an aunt had married an American sailor. He never learned French. The aunt never learned English —though they managed to have ten children—and no one in the family ever learned his name. He was *L'Américain*—The American —till the day he died.

MH   When you want a good, quick, short course about wherever it is you happen to be on the American coast, one place to ask is the local Coast Guard Station. In this case, we'd been searching for navigation charts to help us visualize JJA's voyage from the delta to Galveston, and there were none for sale in the village of Grand Isle. However, the Coast Guard would have charts, which is how we found ourselves talking to Chief Petty Officer Timothy S. Torrence, a snappy dark-haired Texan who said he liked Grand Isle so much that when the time came for him to retire he was going to set himself up in a sporting goods store with a local partner and stick around. The hunting and fishing couldn't be beat, and Chief Torrence found the people and history of the place fascinating.

Among the things he told us: This is an area where Spanish, Portuguese, German, French, Italian, Indian, and black blood lines are mixed up in various strains, while racial and clan feelings run high; ancient rivalries and feuds still control much of the community existence. The people of Grand Isle will have little to do with their neighbors in Golden Meadow, and refer to them as "Sabines" and "Indians"; the people of Golden Meadow call the Cajuns of Grand Isle "Pirates" because of the contributions to the breeding stock made by Jean Lafitte and his colleagues. We had already heard that —for all crossing of bloodlines—there are no out-and-out blacks on this part of the coast. Apparently they were driven away after the

Civil War, and this is still one of those places where it would be worth their lives to move in. A sidelight on the matter came from Chief Torrence: bottle-diggers going through local trash heaps constantly come up with skin-lightener-formula bottles, some dating as late as the 1930s.

We asked him about an expression that had puzzled us for months. In the Mississippi valley, back-country whites often refer to themselves and each other as "coon-asses." We thought that the word might have its roots in the slang "coon" for Negro, but no one we spoke to seemed to know anything about it, the chief included. Long afterward I finally caught up with a plausible explanation. Louisiana was settled by Acadians, French colonists driven out of Canada in the mid-1700s. "Acadian" was modified to "cajun." Then the Spanish moved in, and they rendered "cajun" as "ca-hoon" and the plural as "los ca-hoon-os." It is a short jump from there to the Anglicized "coon-ass."

Chief Torrence spoke about the hummingbird migration he sees in early April—hummers, exhausted and hungry, swarming in the clover on the Coast Guard lawn, as thick as honey bees. They appear and are gone, he said, in about forty-eight hours—and the birdwatchers with them, he added. The hummer is still known here by its French name—*oiseau mouche,* a bird with the quality of a fly. JJA saw such a migration too, hummingbirds "entering the United States in crowds in the beginning of April, advancing eastward along the shores of the Mexican Gulf. The weather having become very cold one morning, many were picked up dead along the beaches, and those which bore up were so benumbed as almost to suffer the members of my party to take them with the hand."

How about other local birds? Audubon included many of them in his essays, particularly in those on the water birds. The chief started to make a list, caught himself up, and telephoned a hunting companion, a native. Out of our three-way conversation came quite a string of names:

Doe-gree, said Timothy Torrence. Ah, yes, *dos gris.* The lesser scaups—gray-backed ducks, flotillas of them now riding the placid waters of Baratraria Bay. JJA didn't mention the *dos gris.* Until late in life he was not clear in his own mind about our two species of scaup duck, and he evidently missed them on the Gulf Coast. Perhaps they'd moved north by the time he got here.

Bec croche—the ibis, with the curved beak. The only common ibis in Louisiana in JJA's time was the beautiful white ibis, and the "creoles of Louisiana call this species 'Bec croche,' . . . although it is also generally known by the name of 'Spanish Curlew.' " That too needs an explanation. Syphilis, for example, was known as the French disease to the Spanish and the Spanish disease to the French. Similarly, the gray-green moss that hangs from southern trees was called French beard by the Spanish, and Spanish beard by the French. How about Spanish Curlew? Again, a derisive name. The true curlews, shot by the tens of thousands, provided a delicious, delicate meat, the food of gourmets. The flesh of the *Spanish* curlew, wrote JJA by way of explanation, "is of a dull-orange colour, is extremely fishy, although the birds are often sold in our southernmost markets, and are frequently eaten by the Indians."

Gros bec—great blue heron. JJA said the Creoles gave the name instead to the black-crowned night heron. Same principle. Big beak.

Bec-scie—merganser. Saw-beak, which refers to the saw-like ridges on the merganser's mandibles. Another match. "In the lower parts of Louisiana, [the common merganser] is called 'Bec-scie-de-mer,' probably because there it is found only on the large salt-water lakes, and about the mouths of the Mississippi, and to distinguish it from the Hooded Merganser, which there is more usually seen on fresh water."

Za-Za (as it sounds to me)—wigeon. "This lively and very handsome Duck is abundant during winter at New Orleans," says JJA, "where it . . . is best known by the name of *Zinzin.*" That stops me for a moment. Why so close, yet different? Of course. It's the same name. My Anglo-American ears are not yet tuned to Franco-American, certainly not to Cajun French as relayed by a Texan.

Canard gris—gadwall, of which only the male is gray. JJA recorded another name altogether for the gadwall: *Violon*—"on account of the whistling sound of its wings."

Canard cheval—canvasback duck. Exactly the same, and a splendid name for it, the "horse duck." In profile on the water, the canvasback wears a silver-white saddle between its black tail and its black breast, chestnut neck, and red head. The oldest duckhunters of New Orleans, says JJA, who had known the *Canard Cheval* all their lives, told him that "it is not more than about fifteen years since [the market for the ducks] began to rise, from a very low price to two dollars the pair, at which it sold during my visit in March 1837." Audubon himself did not think much of the celebrated canvasback as food, certainly not when compared, say, to the green-winged teal or the mallard in certain seasons, and he took some pleasure in needling the "epicures of our middle districts," whom he blamed for puffing the reputation of the canvasback and skyrocketing its cost in New Orleans.

Canard Français for the delectable mallard. JJA gives no Louisiana name for the mallard—nor does he mention any *Spanish* duck.

"Pain-in-Ass for the mockingbird," relayed Timothy Torrence, laughing. But *why*, I asked. A little more conversation, then the relayed cryptic explanation in a new name: "Eat All Things." Chief Torrence explained that his Cajun friend grows fruit. Doubtless the fruit taken in summer by mockingbirds is a fair exchange for the insects they eat year-round, but it's difficult for a grower to believe that at harvest time.

From the eastern point of the sand spit that forms the Grand Isle State Park, one can look across the mouth of Baratraria Bay to Grand Terre. Audubon called it Baratraria Island, which, as Chief Torrence told us, had been an alternate name for Grand Terre in early days. Audubon described it in a letter to Bachman.

"This Island is about 10 miles long but scarcely a mile broad—it is low, and mostly marsh (hard however) with many ponds, Lagoons &c—it possesses one sugar plantation and a few dilapidated Government buildings . . . This was 'Lafitte's' (The Pirate) Strong hold. —The remains of his fortification, and the ground on which his houses stood are yet discernible.—Some say that much money is deposited there abouts—I wish it was in the Charleston Bank placed to *our* Credit!—The Island is flat, and in [1831] was overflowed by the waves of the Gulph impelled by a Hurricane to the depth of 4 feet above the highest ground . . . The soil is good enough to produce cotton or sugar.—and the place healthy and pleasant; and yet I should not like to be imprisoned at large upon it the remainder of my Life—It abounds with *Snakes* not however injurious excepting a very small *ground* Rattle species.—We have

placed several in rum for Docr Holbrook, and *Crabs* for yourself!—
No Insects of note except *Musquitoes* and sand flies of which we
could spare enough God Knows."

The government buildings on Grand Terre Island these days belong to the Division of Oysters, Water Bottoms, & Seafood of the
Louisiana Wildlife & Fisheries Commission, which has a laboratory
there. Written permission from the New Orleans office is required
for a visit. This we have, and are given a lift across the bay in a
Fisheries Commission boat.

The director of the lab on Grand Terre is Ralph Latapie, Jr.,
slender, black-rimmed glasses, dark blond moustache and goatee.
He's an enthusiastic historian of Barataria Bay and southern Louisiana, and he shows us some of his Grand Terre notes. About the same
time JJA and Ferdinand Rozier were starting out in business at Mill
Grove, Lafitte was building his "Strong hold" on Grand Terre—
houses, storehouses, a small fort. In 1814, just before the Battle of New
Orleans, the federal troops burned down the whole shebang, not just
because of Lafitte's crimes of piracy, but on the assumption that he
was about to side with the British. Instead, the pirate and his men
defended the Barataria Bay approaches to New Orleans, and fought
beside the federal troops in the famous battle itself; the government's
side of the deal was a full pardon for Lafitte and his men, which came
from President Madison less than a month after the battle of New
Orleans—and only five months after his establishment had been
sacked by the feds. Lafitte soon returned to the old life, moving his
base of operations into disputed Texas territory, where he gathered
a thousand followers. There he was left in peace until some of his
colony attacked American property, whereupon the government
sent a naval force out against him. Lafitte, with a band of his closest
associates, sailed peaceably away in a favorite ship, and that was the
last ever heard of him.

The next proprietor of Grand Terre was Jean-Baptiste Moussier,
who ran cattle and horses, and also grew sugar cane. In 1831 his
widow sold most of the island to the Consolidated Association of
Planters of Louisiana, and that organization had sugar plantations
here until the Civil War. After that, as Ralph Latapie drily puts it,
"They lost their help." Grand Terre's plantation days were over.
Meanwhile, Madame Moussier had sold the western tip of the island

to the federal government and a coastal-defense fort was built there, Fort Livingston.

Ralph Latapie lists the years when hurricanes have struck at Grand Terre: 1831, 1856, 1886, 1893, 1909, 1915 (two), 1926, 1956, 1961, 1964, 1965 (a very bad one, "Betsy"), and 1974.

MD   Most buildings along this coast, except those inland and sheltered by trees, are hurricane-proofed against high seas. The bathhouse at the state park, for example—a natural wood structure with a round central pavillion and two wings—stands ten feet off the ground on wooden pilings (and looks like the palace of a Polynesian chief). On some buildings, the pilings that constitute the first floor are masked with breakaway walls that will wash out with no damage to the rest of the building. Even trailers and mobile homes on Grand Isle are held aloft in giant cradles of timber, and this by law, because mobile homes, it was discovered, when picked up by the sea, destroy everything in their paths—slamming through town like battering rams.

MH   The state bird of Louisiana is the brown pelican, though in certain official depictions the pelican is portrayed as white, for the sake of graphics one supposes. (And what the hell, a pelican's a pelican, right?) JJA found the brown pelican to be breeding abundantly on this coast, and in the 1930s—a hundred years later—estimates of breeding populations ranged between 10,000 and 85,000. It remained a common bird in the state until the 1950s, when, like the osprey, the bald eagle, the peregrine falcon, and other North American species that hunt on or near water, it went into a sudden, drastic population crash. By 1962, there were no nesting brown pelicans in the state of Louisiana. This rapid decline, like the others, coincided with the massive introduction of organochlorine pesticides (DDT, endrin, dieldrin, et alia) into the environment. In 1968, Louisiana was almost out of pelicans, so the state created two brown pelican colonies with young birds brought from healthy Florida populations. In all, 665 pelicans were imported. One of the colonizing attempts, in western Louisiana, failed completely. The other, here at Grande Terre, has been somewhat more successful. Eight young were hatched and fledged by the imports in 1971, 14 in 1972, 26 in 1973, 104 in 1974, and just as things were looking up, only 13 young were brought off in 1975. "A notable die-off of white and brown pelicans occurred in the winter and early spring of 1975," says a report on the progress of the program. (White pelicans winter in Louisiana, though they don't breed here.) "Pesticides," the report continues, "were judged to be a significant contributor to this die-off. The colony was reduced to about 225 to 250 brown pelicans, a loss of approximately 30 to 40 percent." Brown pelicans start breeding in November and keep trying until July; by the winter of 1975, when the nesting season began, there were only about 40 pairs on the colony site.

"I've seen pelicans fall right out of the sky," Chief Timothy Torrence told us. Ralph Latapie adds this picture: when a brown pelican is in the terminal stage of endrin poisoning, it stands with wings akimbo, feet apart, head between its feet, trying to remain upright. Then it dies.

Mary and I go for a walk. Two walks, really, which now and then intersect; but we start together toward the remains of Fort Livingston. Seven brown pelicans sail ever so slowly upwind, flapping only occasionally. Near the old fort, just off the beach, porpoises thrash in the shallows after boiling schools of small fish, with laughing gulls dancing attendance on them, trying to snatch the leaping fry in mid-air. There is for me a moving conjunction here—the gulls, the porpoises, the fry, the brown pelicans. Listen to our friend Audubon, for he has observed something similar, first in Florida, then here:

JJA [The laughing gulls] were all busily engaged on wing, hovering here and there around the Brown Pelicans, intent on watching their plunges into the water, and all clamorously teasing their best benefactors. As with broadly extended pouch and lower mandible, the Pelican went down headlong, so gracefully followed the rosy-breasted Gull, which, on the brown bird's emerging, alighted nimbly on its very head, and with a gentle stoop instantly snatched from the mouth of its purveyor the glittering fry that moment entrapped!

Is this not quite strange, reader? Aye, truly it is. The sight of these manoeuvres rendered me almost frantic with delight. At times, several Gulls would attempt to alight on the head of the same Pelican, but finding this impossible, they would at once sustain themselves

around it, and snatch every morsel that escaped from the pouch of
the great bird. So very dexterous were some of the Gulls at this sport,
that I have seen them actually catch a little fish as it leaped from the
yet partially open bill of the Pelican.

MD In Europe, particularly in England, during the late 1700s
and early 1800s, ruins became so fashionable that they were often
built on country estates, planted about with a tangle of vines and
shrubs, and a "hermit" was hired to live amid the broken arches and
fallen stones.

I understand completely. The romance of a ruin. I am sitting at
the top of a flight of granite steps that once led to the parapets of Fort
Livingston and now lead to nothing. Fort Livingston had not been
built when JJA was here. With a few more hurricanes and high seas,
it will be gone again, and this shoreline of Grand Terre much as it
was when he roved the island bagging birds, rattlers, and crabs and
pickling them in rum. The bastions that faced the sea were swept
away years ago. Only three walls of the fort remain—red brick over
an exposed foundation of coquina, the building material of this territory—a soft white limestone of shells and corals.

Nature has provided the tangle of wild plants—Cactus, wild garlic, and orange lantana in bloom, thistle gone to down, yellow rattlebox. A muskrat with crisp, white whiskers swims in the moat—busy
feeding in the green slimes and weeds. Shrimp boats pass with all the
gulls around them, and eight miles out, the offshore sulphur mine by
daylight is a gray, spider-legged shadow on the horizon.

MH The *Campbell* and the *Crusader* proceeded westward with
stops at several small islands in Atachafalya Bay: "Mr. Audubon &
company on Shore Shooting." On April 19, they anchored in East
Cote Blanche Bay, and for the next three days, while the crew was
employed in tarring the rigging and replenishing the water supply,
Mr. Audubon & company were again on shore shooting. We follow
after by way of Houma (Terrebonne Parish) and Morgan City (St.
Mary Parish). The day is hot and sunny. We stop to watch a flock of
about fifty white pelicans flapping and soaring together on a thermal,
then a second flock, and some stragglers, soaring high up into the
bright blue sky in a communal dance. Louisiana herons in their

delicate finery (the species Audubon lovingly nicknamed "Lady of the Waters") feed in roadside ditches, and egrets too, picking their way among the trash.

At Centerville, we turn south and follow the country road along Bayou Sale—the "salty bayou," now pronounced Bayou Sally. We camp at the end of this peninsula on Cote Blanche Bay at the Burns Point town campground. All free-gratis, it's a gathering place for local people. Everyone seems to know everyone else and also know the identities, or at least have strong suspicions about the identities, of the young vandals who've been shooting out the lights and burning the picnic tables in their campfires.

Most of the land here, bayou and farm country in JJA's day, is now leased to Exxon and Atlantic-Richmond and Cities Service for pumping and refining natural gas—white shell roads leading out to huge towers in the marsh, blinking red lights on top; just up the road here, the roar of engines performing I don't know what task inside unrevealing low buildings; rumbling mining operations on steel rafts far out in Cote Blanche Bay; the refineries and pumping towers flaring-off zillions of cubic feet of natural gas. Poor Louisiana is right now one great power factory, being pumped dry, and just beginning to worry about the future.

But last night the brilliant stars overhead would have done credit to a New England December sky, and here in these wet woods white spider lilies are in bloom. The morning chorus of sweet-voiced southern cardinals calls you to see the sunrise, and so I got up this morning to find the sunrise heavy with fog. I walked back toward the roar of the enigmatic engines—no other direction to walk—and saw a great horned owl perched in the open at the top of a snag in a patch of wooded marsh. On a nearby snag perched an American kestrel, littlest of our falcons. Predator of the night and predator of the day meet, both hunting, as one is leaving and the other coming on the morning's stage.

MD When the *Campbell* and the *Crusader* put in at Cote Blanche Bay, their mooring was "at the entrance of a canal of a sugar plantation." JJA and companions rowed ashore and walked inland along the margin of the canal, "in single file, like culprits . . . Hark! What's that? . . . a parcel of men coming to greet us . . . seven or eight

Negroes. Who lives here my good fellows? Major Gordy, massa. Well, now show us the way to the house."

The planters along Cote Blanche Bay had been at the mercy of pirates for years, and by JJA's own testimony he and his companions —muddy, unshaven, and armed with hunting rifles—looked like a troop of pirates themselves. And so Major Gordy concluded as the strangers approached from his landing on the bay. JJA's first view of the Major was of "an elderly man, of tall stature and firm aspect, leaning on what I would call a desperate long gun . . . something not so very friendly as I could have wished was expressed in his countenance. As he rested his heavy frame on his monstrous rifle, he neither moved his head, nor held out his hand."

Explanations and introductions were quickly made. JJA presented his "unequivocal credentials, from the head departments of the United States." With that, the Major "invited us to consider his dwelling as our own," and hospitably dispatched gifts to the ships— a barrel of sugar, another of corn meal, pails of fresh milk, fresh butter, potatoes. The following morning, he entertained JJA and friends at a breakfast along with several neighbors, also planters, several of whom already knew John James Audubon's name and fame. "After we had been introduced to all around, we seated ourselves, and made a vigorous attack upon our host's eggs and bacon."

On our way to Burns Point yesterday, Michael and I initiated our search for the Major, his plantation, and his canal at the nearest library, which was in Franklin. We learned that the Gordys were an old and important family in the township, and we were given the name of the local historian, Mrs. Clyde Alpha, who could tell us anything we wanted to know. Small towns being what they are, word got around that we were asking questions. When we phoned Mrs. Alpha today, she greeted us heartily: "You must be the Gordy people. I've been waiting for you to call!" She gave us her afternoon to lead a zestful exploration into Gordy country.

Flossie Alpha, known as "Miss Flop," her childhood nickname, is a wonder—a stout, gray-haired, indefatigable ransacker and recorder of history. She immediately identified with our project, having done the same kind of thing herself. On one of her historical expeditions, for example, she took her eighty-eight-year-old mother to retrace the family's covered-wagon migration down the eastern seaboard to

Louisiana; they met lost relatives and were given boxes of family mementoes along the way. Miss Flop also has Mennonite forebears in another branch of her family and recounted their migrations and settlements down through the centuries—more history, in fact, than I could absorb at first hearing. (And I was paying attention. I have Mennonite forebears too in my melange of ancestors.)

We begin at the Franklin Court House archives, where we scan the records of Major Michael Gordy's property. His household furnishings—the silverware, bedsteads, armories, crockery, candles, the plantation bell, etc. His slaves—James, Preston, Harry, Sheppard, Little Bill, Aaron, Saul, John Guina, etc. Ploughs, saddles, mules, horses, etc. One hundred bottles of claret. Casks of wine, whiskey, and "prime port."

Then into the car and west on Route 90, once more turning down the country road bordering Bayou Sale as it meanders out to Cote Blanche Bay. Our Burns Point campsite is not more than a mile from the cove where JJA came ashore at Major Gordy's lower plantation.

The Gordy house is gone, leveled in a clean sweep by the present owner, though his wife (or so we hear from an old man working with a roto-tiller near the road) had doted on the place. As described to us, the house was in the classic planter style: outside chimneys at each end, a verandah across the front, a "dog trot" (breezeway) through the center, and "a cute little staircase." JJA described it as a mansion, as he did for anything larger than a cabin, and he rhapsodized over the Major's Indian corn "at least six feet high . . . a fine garden, a yard well stocked with cattle, together with a good number of horses and mules . . . a mill for grinding corn and making sugar." Now a modern ranch-house stands on the site.

The canal would be south of this spot, between here and the bay. We move on down Bayou Sale road, Miss Flop bounding ahead, scouting the terrain like a bird dog. Eureka, she has found it. Mike and I have passed the old canal bed a dozen times in the past two days—a wide, sloping declivity in the ground that meets the road at a right angle, a neatly clipped lawn and vegetable garden on one bank, a rough field on the other. What remains of the canal bed is overgrown with clumps of live oak and yellow pea trees. We would need a machete to follow it down to the bay.

Miss Flop believes this to be the first canal dug in Louisiana. She is overjoyed to find it. So are we. JJA walked through here, precisely here, on a late April afternoon, led by the Major's guard of slaves, either on *this* side of the canal, next to the field (we run down through the canal bed and up the opposite bank), or on *this* side where a clump of blue toadflax blooms next to a drainpipe. A miserable, gray-muzzled hound slinks off at our approach on his territory, tail between legs, poor old fellow.

But there is more. Miss Flop leads us onward to an abandoned graveyard: "Not a pocketful of people even know it's here!" She tracks ahead into a grove of live oaks, Spanish moss, palmettos, black cherry, and poison ivy. The graveyard has gone to wrack and ruin. The above-ground mausoleums are open and empty. We peer into the curved vault of Major Gordy's tomb—within, dead leaves and twig nests made by some woodland creature or other. Most of the tombstones were carted away years ago and were laid, face down, into a walk between house and barn on the property of a man "with enough money to pay for walks of his own twice over." He was an illiterate, oil-rich farmer, "who had to draw a picture of his name," but at the bank in town he could pass a $50,000 check across the counter and it would be honored. At any rate, when the news got out that his fine marble walk was made of gravestones, he dug them up and dumped them into the nearest bayou.

Miss Flop has given us her afternoon and would probably give us her evening too, should we ask for it. But it is six o'clock. Hunger pangs have set in. We return Miss Flop to her family.

Her exuberance at finding the Gordy canal is catching. Or is it JJA who has caught us alive? Hours later, Michael suddenly exclaims that when he saw the canal, he was *really excited.* Why, most folks living along Bayou Sale these days don't even know Audubon's name. It was our own highly charged, irrefutable, transient moment of footsteps within footsteps. Right on the money.

MH JJA wrote about visiting Rabbit Island, at the entrance to Cote Blanche Bay, where "not a single Rabbit or hare is to be seen," and since the island isn't too far away, we've been exploring the possibility of getting there. Word travels through the campground, and we are put in touch with a Texaco boat driver, Guy DeCuir, who's on holiday, and it is one of the luckiest meetings of our trip.

The square face of this outgoing Cajun looks as if it were the texture of sculptor's clay—very plastic, not quite finished; the sculptor is still working. It looks out from under a dark peaked cap with one of those crossed golf-sticks patches on the brow. Middle height, middle years, a prodigious beer drinker. [MD: Nice, sing-song Cajun accent—French patois with soft southern accent. And Cajuns are friendly. Not like so many of their Canadian cousins we chanced to meet on our Labrador voyage.] He comes back with me to the campground and we talk. Very little left of Rabbit Island, he tells us. Not so long ago he used to hunt dove out there, but now there's not much more than a shell-bank. It wouldn't be worth our trouble.

Something gets him onto the subject of auto dealers; anyway, it's obviously one of his favorite stories. There was a fellow who bought land for 30 cents an acre, just down the road, years ago. He was a dirt farmer, and he never got very far ahead. He wanted a car, but he couldn't make any substantial down payment for one, and the bank wouldn't loan him the money. He went to the dealers in the area—Ford, Chevrolet, DeSoto—and they wouldn't even discuss any sort of an arrangement. But a Plymouth dealer trusted him, and sold him a car on terms the farmer could handle. Well, sir, that farmer—as was the way with farmers in coastal Louisiana—struck oil on his 30-cents-an-acre land, and became a millionaire. [MD: I believe this was the same farmer who used the tombstones as his walkway.] Came time for him to buy a new car, he retraced his steps around the various auto dealerships and had the pleasure of telling off everyone who had refused his money when he was poor. He bought only Plymouths until the day he died.

We agree that that is a most satisfying story, and Guy DeCuir insists on showing us the farmer's first oil well and his modest white frame house. And so we meet the Amarode girls.

MD   There are four of them, aged six to fourteen, fair-complexioned, small-boned, dressed in shorts and T-shirts, and trotting along the road. One carries a cane knife. Another carries a jar full of something she is being careful not to spill.

Guy DeCuir slams to a stop, hails them in an expansive, beer-buzz, avuncular roar of greeting, and asks what they're hunting after. He *knows,* of course. We don't, and we would never have guessed.

The Amarode girls are out to cut thistles (hence, the cane knife) and to eat them (hence, the jar, which holds a dressing of white vinegar and pepper). They take us in tow for the thistle hunt, while Mister Guy, as the girls address him, loafs at the wheel, grinning and pleased that he's sprung a bayou surprise on us. The Amarode sisters are bright and friendly and chatty, the best company you could want on a walk down a back road. Sue, aged thirteen, who is nicknamed Kill-dee (because she has long, skinny legs like a killdeer) is their nonstop talker. She explains about the thistles. They can be eaten only in bud. After they bloom, the stalk is too tough. And only one variety can be eaten. We come upon a patch. It's the southern bull thistle *(Cirsium horridulum)*, a forbidding plant with a basal rosette two feet in diameter, and the stems, the new leaves, and the bud covered with hairy white spines as though wrapped in a web—as if it were the lair of a giant spider.

The oldest sister, Lynn, wields the cane knife, smartly trimming off the outer branches and the outer spiny skin of the central stalk. What's left looks like a stick of plump, fresh, all-green celery. Kill-dee holds out the jar of vinegar and pepper. We dip and taste. The flavor of fresh-cut, fresh-trimmed *Cirsium horridulum* is like a bite into a mythical plant that holds the essence of green vegetables. A delicate flavor that combines the best of broccoli, asparagus, zucchini, and green beans.

While Lynn chops and trims and everyone dips and nibbles, Kill-dee chats on. She wants to be an actress when she grows up. (She poses with hand on head and hand on hip.) Did I believe in flying saucers? I had never seen one, but I was ready to believe. *She*'d seen one. With her mother one night in the car. She'd fallen asleep and her mother woke her up to be witness and it was a big, blinding light like the headlight of a train that came across the bayou and stopped in front of the car and hung there blazing and then it turned off and it was gone. And did I believe in faith-healing? I had never seen that either, but I was ready to believe if I did. Because her little sister Kim once got a sliver of glass in her eye, and the woman who healed her said: Satan! Release your hold on this child! And the sliver fell from Kim's eye. Kim tries to join the conversation. Her lisp is incomprehensible. "She's tongue-tied," Kill-dee explains. "She was born that way. They had to cut her tongue loose." She points into her mouth to show the place. So does the little sister, with smiling pride in her uniqueness and particular complication. And what church did we go to? Mister Guy had asked the same question. "What religion are you?" he had said, as someone else might ask where you live or what you do for a living.

Further, I learn that coon with sweet potatoes and white beans is *sooo* good, and the meat is very clean because coons always wash their food before they eat. But when you dress them, you have to be sure to get out all the glands. The same with possum, though possums are the hardest to dress, especially the females, because they have lots more glands. And nutria tastes a little like chicken, a little like rabbit.

Mister Guy is growing restless. It's time for another cold beer. He announces an outing to the Great Bend general store up the road— and a round of Cokes, his treat, for the Amarode girls. As they pile into the car, Lynn is suddenly summoned home across the field by their mother. "We have a new baby," says Kill-dee. "Mama needs Lynn to help." I am impressed at Lynn's response. At fourteen, she is second in command of the household and the baby. She is needed. She turns and races home without a murmur of protest.

MH   Guy DeCuir invited us to join him after supper at his friends' place down the road. They lived in Morgan City, but had a "ca-been" here, and we'd enjoy talking to them about the bayou country. They knew it well. They were trappers.

And so, after supper, we walked into Martin and Marjory De-Hart's trapping shack on the bank of one of the little creeks that feeds Hog Bayou, east of Bayou Sale. The DeHart establishment is no more than it has to be. A few rooms in a line, railroad style; siding peeling white paint; a galvanized iron roof; and perched on stilts over the creek, their drying shed—kerosene stove going all the time, furs (turned inside out, scraped, stretched on frames) hung up to dry; others stacked on shelves. On one side of the shed, a low, roofed porch, which also serves as a boat landing. Moored at a small dock is a sizeable, chunky fishing boat Martin DeHart built and a twelve foot bateau, square-ended, made of plywood and carrying a small outboard motor on its stern thwart.

We sit around the kitchen table—Marjory, Martin, one of their sons (who has a broken arm), Guy DeCuir, Mary and I—drinking beer (the empties tossed into the kitchen midden outside the floor-to-ceiling window) and telling of our lives and adventures.

This went on for several hours. I tried to tape our conversation on a cassette machine set between my feet under the table (no room *on* the table), and all I got was the spirit of our babble, Cajun French, Southern English, and two boisterous eastern voices—everyone talking at once. After we'd been there a while, Martin DeHart looked across the table at his wife and suggested that maybe we'd like to go with them when they ran their trap line the next day. She agreed. They got no argument from us, and Guy popped another beer, grinning and pleased at having brought us all together. Our bayou host.

The DeHarts have what Mary considers a decent attitude about the proper rising hour. They would like to get going about eight or nine, but they'll wait for us if we are later. None of this on-the-dot at the dock at 3 A.M. So the sun is up and we've had breakfast by the time we return to the bayou.

Martin DeHart, bustling about equipping the bateau for the morning's work, is a slender man with a small, sharp, bristly goatee, small moustache, small cigar usually sticking out from under the moustache. He wears forest-green pants, a long-sleeved khaki shirt, and an olive-drab cap, all Army-Navy surplus. Over the pants he has pulled a pair of full-length waders. A .22 pistol in a holster is strapped to his waist.

Marjory DeHart is stocky, has a strong, broad face, and eyeglasses. She has tied on a straw hat decorated with spikey straw flowers, and wears an orange pullover jersey, cinched in at the waist with a belt, knife in a sheath at her side, heavy brown pants, and ankle-high rubber boots. Marjory has been trapping since she was in her early teens. In fact, this line we are about to run is based on *her* trap line —her dowry—which has passed from one generation to the next and will stay in the clan forever; Martin, son of a trapper himself, can work this territory only because of Marjory's ancestral rights and her established use of those rights.

We zoom out into the sun of a bright morning and into one of the many oil company canals, which often are cut through the marsh on a plan of rectangles, like city streets. Our plywood bateau is flecked with its original coat of red paint, and stained red with animal blood. Mary and I ride amidships, seated on a burlap-covered cooler that was installed for our benefit.

Into the broad, winding Hog Bayou. A Louisiana heron flying slender and graceful. Killdeer bobbing, racing, flying along the margins. Tree swallows overhead. A long-winged harrier hunting, wings cocked in a shallow V. Kingfishers perched. Shorebirds in a flock, high. Duck and teal ahead of us, with coots. We leave Hog Bayou for a narrow side street, shut down the motor, and Marjory "pulls" the boat, standing up, pushing the long home-made oars, which are tied to upended spikes on blocks on either side. Martin walks alongside, picking up empty leg-hold traps and tossing them into the bow. He says that the unwritten rules about whose turf is whose out here are sometimes broken. He lost thirty traps and thirty nutria this winter, stolen. (We don't know yet what a nutria looks like, only that it's a South American import, the coypu, now well established in Texas and Louisiana marshes and a trapping staple because it bears a valuable skin and it breeds like the proverbial rabbit.) Human thieves aren't all you have to worry about, Martin goes on. There was a bear in the marsh this winter, eating as many as a dozen trapped nutria a day.

"Look at this," he says from under a willow. A raccoon in one of the traps. It looks so innocent and charming. Mary and I both turn away when Martin draws his pistol and shoots the raccoon in the head. He springs its leg from the trap, tosses animal and trap separately into the bow, holsters the pistol, walks on ahead. The light goes out of the raccoon's eyes almost immediately, and they turn a bright empty green. Blackbirds and yellowthroats sing in the reeds, vultures soar overhead, Marjory works the oars, steadily, easily; the bateau slides slowly down the canal. Now Martin has the first trapped nutria of the day, shoots it, releases the body from the trap, tosses trap and animal into the bow, walks on. A nutria looks like a cross between a woodchuck and a muskrat. About twenty-two inches in length, with a long bare tail. Marjory washes the nutria beside the bow, as one would hold a baby in a bath, then, lifting the animal by its tail, shakes it to get the water off. She drops it alongside the raccoon, steps back, takes up the oars again. How about mink? No, she says. The price is too poor, so they leave them to breed. "Don't catch nothin' you can't use, that's our philosophy," says Marjory.

Martin has been tracking off into the marsh for an otter that got away with trap, chain, and stake. Returns, shaking his head; they've lost the otter. Marjory tells us about an otter they caught recently, a female about to bear young. "I was soft-hearted," she says apologetically. "I wanted to let her go." "Yeah," says Martin, "but she bring twenty-two dollars." Matter of factly. Marjory, however, has strong feelings against trapping pregnant females of any species, and she tells us that when she skins females, she always checks the womb for embryos—for her own peace of mind that they're not destroying too many of next year's animals.

Beside the canal, a pair of downy woodpeckers performs a noisy in-flight wings-up display around a tree. All around us are birds: white-throated sparrows and chickadees and robins and cardinals and Carolina wrens; they pop up, dart away, sing. A flicker dashes off in bounding flight.

Marjory jams a stick in the mud bank and moors the bateau to it; she has spotted a thistle, her first of the year, and she wants it. "Thistle sure will kill your thirst," she says. Martin agrees; he tells us it's the drink for alligator-hunts. When she was pregnant for the first time, Marjory says, she had a terrible craving for thistle, and she had her daddy and her sister out cutting it for her. She's at work with her cane knife now, hacking at the cluster of new plants. "Watch out for the snake under that thistle," jokes Martin from the other bank, and at that moment a cottonmouth slides away at her feet. She gives chase with the cane knife, but the snake disappears. They laugh at the close call. Martin has a loop of traps to cover here, back in the marsh, so she gets in the bateau to chat and eat one of her thistle stalks. After a while Martin arrives at the bank a bit farther down the canal, a nutria hanging from one hand, his drawn pistol in the other, and fires at the water, where a cottonmouth is swimming across the canal, head up.

They have traps on both banks of the canal here, so I offer to row while they each work a side. Not much of a knack to pushing the boat along, though for a conservative rowboater it feels awkward to be standing up *and* facing forward.

Marjory does not like guns. On her side of the canal she dispatches the trapped animals with the flat of her cane knife across the skull, or with a stick. The day's take is not particularly good, this being the end of the season, but the dead animals do pile up in the bow—mostly nutria—and blood mixes with the water that is slowly leaking into the bateau. Mary bails. A sora rail cackles nearby as Martin fires his pistol.

We pass a budding willow tree, and Martin, from the bank there, points out a big king snake—five feet long, speckled-yellow on black —coiled on a low branch. With a stick he coaxes the snake into motion, and it writhes and ripples around the limb and intertwines with itself like a braided coffee cake, then splashes into the canal and slides quickly up the bank again. "We don't kill king snakes," says Marjory. "They're harmless."

MD We reach the end of the trap line at a wide stretch of bayou so densely packed with water hyacinth that the bateau cannot get through. Marjory and I are dropped off on the right hand bank to cover the last hundred yards of shore—mud, willow, cane—while Michael and Martin take the far side. Marjory is in the lead; I slog along behind in Mr. Hobbs' Labrador boots. She points to bear tracks in the mud, a nutria's nest in the reeds, a cottonmouth just ahead, coiled and hissing. She cracks it to the side with a long stick, a killing blow to the head, and flicks it with the stick into the bayou. I now know a cottonmouth when I see one—gray-brown, chunky head, and a wide, white mouth. A few steps farther: "There's another one, Marjory!" Crack, splash, dead and disposed of. There are three nutria in the half dozen traps ahead. They'll often struggle and fight you, Marjory says, so she approaches with a certain caution. How about raccoon? The one they caught at the start of the run hadn't struggled. It seemed to know, and stared up at Martin and the pistol. "Sometimes," says Marjory, "the young coons will cover their eyes. You hate to kill them."

When she cracks the skulls of the nutria I surprise myself by feeling no emotion one way or the other, though that first dead furred body in the boat at my feet had made me wince and catch my breath. We retrace our steps to the bateau, sinking into our mud track, Marjory carrying the nutria by their long rat tails, I following with the traps. Another cottonmouth lies up on the bank out of our path, taking stock of us and we of it. "He won't bother us none," says Marjory, and we muck on toward the boat. The men have one nutria, six traps, and saw no snakes. Martin starts the engine and we head home.

In a little while, Marjory tells me, the marshes will be abloom with iris, water hyacinth, yellow lotus, and magnolia. "And all along the road, yellow and pink buttercups." (It's not until we get to Texas that I discover what she means. "Buttercup" is the country nickname for the southern evening primroses—butter yellow and boudoir pink.)

Marjory knows every bend and corner and twig of these bayous and canals, and she watches it pass, now that the work is done, with an open, smiling face. Her home. Her own country. Then, looking me square in the eye, she tells me in a direct, no-nonsense voice that is at the same time an inner, content, whole-life voice: "I am in love with the marshes."

MH   We pass a trapping camp, approachable only by boat. Martin and Marjory wave at the two people visible there; the camp belongs to Marjory's uncle. Out into the broad curves of Hog Bayou again, the water mud-gray, clumps of cloud riding above the flat, marshy horizon. We are near home now, and suddenly the whine of the outboard lowers to a mutter; Martin has spotted a raccoon asleep in a tree, about two hundred feet away, fifty feet up. He steers for a tangle of fallen trees there, takes up his rifle, and uses the jackstraws of tree-hulks to climb ashore. We can see the animal's silhouette now ourselves. It lies on a limb, asleep in the sun. Martin fires, the animal falls. Martin scrambles back into the boat with the coon by a leg; he hasn't wasted a bit of motion in this whole operation. Now the motor whines high, and we are soon back at camp. Marjory, Mary, and I are put ashore, and Martin tosses the day's haul out of the sunlight and up onto the porch-dock—fourteen nutria, two raccoon, one muskrat. They are left lying there while we have lunch: rabbit and turnip stew with white beans, cooked by the son with the broken arm.

Family has been arriving. Another son, tall, lank yellow hair; he brings the dozen nutria he has shot this morning and adds them to the collection on the porch. Marjory and Martin's daughter, with her husband, and their two-year-old girl, who wears an orange Neversink for safe wandering around the camp and toddles among the grown-ups with the dead muskrat in her arms as if it were Winnie the Pooh.

Martin DeHart. *MH*

After the meal, Martin and Marjory—with some help from the son-in-law—skin out the animals, which is nearly as simple as stripping off a sticky glove, after you've made the proper cuts here and there. Marjory stretches the skins inside out on a board shaped like the round end of an ironing board; there, with a two-handed scraping knife, she cleans flesh and fat from the skins. Now each is washed, and the loose water is shaken off. Once the skins are clean, they are hung on clotheslines in the sun. The skinned nutria corpses go into the creek; Marjory says the meat's too tough to be edible except as hamburger, and evidently they've got plenty of it in the freezer at their house in Morgan City. Only one of the raccoon carcasses looks good enough to keep, and it is hung for the time being by a foot from a porch rafter.

MD Do they eat armadillo? (Marjory had shown me their burrows in the marsh.) No. The skin smells so bad when it's cooking, it kills your appetite. Like goat. Though young goat is good if you dress it carefully. Don't let the hide touch the meat, Marjory explains, or the meat will taste the way a goat smells.

And coot? Yes, the gizzard and breast make good stew. Mike and I had been told in and around New Orleans that coot was inedible —except to blacks and country people, and JJA had said the same, putting down coot as cheap food for "negroes and the poorer classes [who] purchase them to make 'gombo'." But I'll take Marjory De-Hart's word for it; I bet she turns out a fine coot stew. She has a sound point of view on the taste of food. Her vegetable garden, out front by her poultry yard, is grown organically. "The way they're intended." No chemical additives, like the grow-fast chemicals her neighbor uses to get fat, early-ripe vegetables. "They taste like cotton-wool," she says. "And they're probably poison besides." She and I stroll between the rows, and she pulls up some crisp young carrots for me to try as a sample.

MH What will the DeHarts do now that the trapping season is over? They'll sell the last of the dried skins, which they do every two weeks during the season, for about $800 each load. The skins, incidentally, will be shipped to Germany, made into coats, and shipped back to the United States; so much for the North American fur indus-

Marjorie DeHart scraping a nutria hide. *MH*

try. Marjory has a regular job in a bakery—a job she sticks with because it offers medical insurance for the family. Their food bills are low, what with the poultry yard, the garden, and wild game; it's the medical bills that kill you. Martin can fish for catfish and crab now, which he likes to do, but last year that didn't produce much, so he may go to work as a carpenter in Morgan City. Or perhaps he'll drive a boat for one of the oil companies. "But Martin likes to be his own boss," says Marjory.

MD From the abstract of the *Campbell's* log book:

25th April At 2 PM made Galviston Island. At 4 crossed the bar & anchored in the harbor in 4 fathoms water. At sunrise fired a Salute of 24 guns in Honor of the Texian Government. Was returned by the fort at

Galviston. Also by the Texian Man of War Schnr Invincible. Mr Audubon & Company in Company on Shore Shooting.

We move westward. A moist, overcast day, the air smelling of petroleum products. A starling gives his bobwhite whistle. We pass L'Oasis Lounge; the Glad Tidings Full Gospel Church; an Old Maud Fertilizer ad on a billboard, a mule as the logo; "We Clean Duck" outside a house trailer. Acres upon thousands of acres of marsh and prairie. Cattle grazing. Occasional roads to landings—Boats. Bait. Fishing Equipment to Rent. Gun Clubs.

Grackles and coots walking on the matted water hyacinths that clot the wide ditches on either side of this levee road, Route 82—the Hug-The-Coast-Highway, as the tourist brochure proclaims it. A marsh hawk hunting. Occasional dead steers—huge bloated bodies, as though inflated for Macy's Thanksgiving Day parade. A white egret takes off over the marshes like a flying bed sheet.

The Louisiana tourist brochure promises campsites. As dusk nears, we ask at gas stations, general stores, on CB. There are no campsites for fifty miles, so this evening finds us at Broussard's Motel ($12.00) in Cameron. Our kind of motel. Linoleum floor, a chenille bedspread (in a dead pea-pod green), a Gideon bible, fresh paint. A marsh breeze billows the curtains.

There is a slow water leak around the porcelain foot of the basin in the bathroom, and I am grateful to whatever housekeeping gods there may be that it is not my plumbing headache. I do not have to concern myself with having the basin pulled out, pipes repaired, new flooring and linoleum put down. I have become thoroughly imbued with the irresponsibilities of transience and the pleasures of irresponsibility. The freedom of passage. This may seem to be a trifling moment in a rented room, but it is my epiphany on the road to Galveston. I have caught road-fever from John James Audubon.

We sit outside in the dark on the steps of our little front porch to enjoy the breeze from the prairie-marsh, palmettos rustling, Spanish moss wafting. Our landlady is throwing a party, a ladies' night. The guests, dressed in pantsuits, are dropped off one by one by the men of their households, who wheel away into the Louisiana night. Greetings are exchanged at the door, and to each "How are you?" our landlady answers with the same reply: "Ah'm all right, ah guess. Ah'm not dead yet." (Much laughter.) What is the event that's being celebrated? It couldn't be a birthday or a shower. There are no presents. ("Well, shoot," I tell Michael. "Mrs. Broussard's giving a party and didn't invite us.")

We leave Cameron on Route 82. A ferry ride across the inlet that leads from the Gulf into Calcasieu Lake, the inlet busy with rock barges, shrimp boats, ring-billed gulls, terns. A farewell billboard bids us to COME AGIAN (sic).

The road continues to hug-the-coast. I look inland through my 7 × 50 binoculars. On the horizon not a tree or a radio tower or a barn, but now and then the spires, domes, and minarets of a distant refinery—Gulf Coast byzantine. A boat-tailed grackle tears at a dead snake on the highway. Coots in the open ditch alongside run tip-toe on the water as they take off; pitter-pat, wind-up-toy feet. Gray and brindle humpnecked Brahman cattle in the fields. A palomino mare with her honey-beige colt sleeping at her feet.

A second ferry boat ride—across Sabine Pass into Texas. A sky highway carries us above the silver mosque-cities of the refineries south of Port Arthur. On all refinery gates, warning signs: No Smoking Beyond This Point, and the air is heavy with a gaseous, oily smell. The entire area smells as though it could go up at the striking of a match. We drop down again onto the coastal plain. Dazzling spreads of Gaillardia in bloom—Indian Blanket, they call it—daisy-shaped red and orange fire-wheels. Blue-eyed grass also blooms, bigger and richer than our New England variety, I admit. Texas-sized blue-eyed grass.

A third ferry ride from Port Bolivar across the passage through which the *Campbell* must have sailed in 1837. We are greeted and escorted by troops of laughing gulls, mendicants who ride the wind alongside the ferry's upper deck and lunge for whatever is tossed to them.

"Welcome To Galveston—Happy Days on the Gulf Coast"

There seems to be something here for everyone. The Sea-Arama Marineworld. Tours of historic houses. Tours of Fort Crockett, the yacht basin, the shrimp fleet docks. Surf and surfers on the beach at the foot of the town. A seashell club. An historic display and panoramic view from the top of Galveston's one and only skyscraper. A new convention center. A tourist bureau, with hostesses. Seawall hotels and motels with "Welcome Honeymooners" out front. A skin parlor on an old fishing pier advertises topless go-go girls, a swimming pool, and "Foosball," whatever that may be.

Old folks, however, seem to be a major business here. There's a new geriatric clinic; lots of ancient couples tottering about together, holding hands tightly as though the wind might blow the other away; lots of little widows with perfectly coiffed white curls doing their banking errands; a library poster reads: Welcome Senior Citizens; a church carillon plays "Rock of Ages" at funeral tempo.

Edna Ferber once described Galveston as a city with a ghostly charm, "where the humidity was like a clammy hand held over your face. . . . The scent of tangled gardens hung heavy on the muggy air. The houses, pockmarked by the salt mist and the sun and heat and

Ruins of Lafitte's fort on Galveston Island, circa 1820. *N. Y. Public Library Picture Collection*

mildew, seemed built of ashes. Here was a remnant of haunted beauty—gray, shrouded, crumbling." Galveston, she concluded, reminded her of Miss Havisham, the spectral bride in *Great Expectations*.

That crumbling ghostly charm is a thing of the past, however, now that there's plenty of money in circulation along the Gulf Coast; in the old residential section, gardens are manicured and the houses exquisitely restored. A forty-block area is assured of preservation under the Historical Zoning District Ordinance. They're trying to hold the line in town. The new subdivisions are outside the city limits —Pirates Cove (in honor of Jean Lafitte's settlement here), and Pirates Beach, Spanish Grant, Gulf Palms, et alia. Not long ago, the road along the twenty-nine-mile spine of the island was not even paved much beyond the city limits. Now it's hardtop from end to end, and the developments will creep onward. But a chunk of four square miles of shore and marsh country has been recently preserved as a state park (our destination)—the Galveston Island landscape that JJA would have seen.

When he was here, the Battle of San Jacinto had been fought just a year before, April 21, 1836—the Mexican army routed and the war of Texas independence ended. The town of Galveston was a "Texian" naval base, but it amounted to nothing else at the time. The directors of the Galveston City Company didn't hold their first meeting until April 1838, and the first wharf wasn't built until 1839.

JJA Went ashore on Galveston Island, and landed at a point where the Texan garrison is quartered. We passed through the troops, and observed the miserable condition of the whole concern. Huts made of grass and a few sticks, or sods cut into square pieces, composed the buildings of the poor Mexican prisoners, who, half clad and half naked, strolled about in a state of apparent inactivity. We passed two sentinels under arms, very unsoldier-like in appearance. The whole population seemed both indolent and reckless. We saw a few fowls, one pig and a dog, which appeared to be all the domestic animals in the encampment. We saw only three women, who were all Mexican prisoners. The soldiers' huts are placed in irregular rows, and at unequal distances; a dirty blanket or a coarse rag hangs over the entrance in place of a door. No windows were seen, except in one or two cabins occupied by Texan officers and soldiers. A dozen or more long guns lay about on the sand, and one of about the same calibre was mounted.

MD   A new day. Another age. The Texas Gulf Coast is the gold coast. Every morning, local radio stations announce calls for workers —welders, pipe-fitters, carpenters, truckers with their own rigs. "There are jobs lying in the streets," says a young man from Chicago, who's browsing Galveston in a third-hand camper with wife and children. He's been in construction, oil rigging, security work, and the like. One of those who are temperamentally unsuited to sticking to anything or any place for very long. Here, he's free to quit any time he pleases. He can pick up another job tomorrow.

On a side street in town: "Hello there, Connecticut." A gray-haired, suntanned man in chinos pops his head in at the car window to say that he's a New London boy. Well, he used to be, anyway. Hasn't been home to Connecticut since he joined the Navy at seventeen.

He gives a thumbnail sketch of his life—and his financial double-timing. When he retired from the Navy, still a bachelor, he settled in Galveston ("Can't take those New England winters"), but grew restless on the beach, so he joined the Merchant Marine as an AB seaman. In fact, he is on his way to the union hall to pick up a short run. He explains the rulings of the Maritime Union: members can work only a certain number of days per year, so that other members get a chance for jobs. Therefore, at the end of this upcoming short run, they'll have to fire him, because he will have used up his allotted number of work days, and once he's fired, he can pick up $90 a week in unemployment compensation. "I already have my Navy pension," says he jauntily, "but I might as well work all the angles."

Notes from our campsite, Galveston State Park:
We've moved three times in four days, looking for surcease from the wind and swirling sand on the Gulf side of the park. We are now settled in on the bay side overlooking the marshes, with a picnic shelter and no neighbors. As in Labrador, our firewood is seasoned lumber scraps from a building project (a new park pavillion).

A covey of bobwhites lives nearby under a sprawling stand of Lindheimer cactus. I've flushed them twice, walking by—an explosion of bobwhites.

The heronry below our campsite remains an unapproachable sanctuary. We see the birds dropping into the encircling wall of tamarisk trees (called salt cedars here), but if one tries to steal up on the congregation within—snapping twigs underfoot and pushing through the thicket of intertwined branches—they lift and leave. From our campsite, the heronry sounds like a chicken run.

Baby rabbits abound. After dark, the marsh road is alive with them, blinded by headlights, leaping every which way. An obstacle course of baby rabbits.

May 2, 1837. JJA on Galveston Island: "We . . . found a few beautiful flowers, and among them one which Harris and I at once nicknamed the Texan Daisy." I splutter at this entry. Yes, yes. Go on. Don't stop there. But once again, his eye is blind to flowers. Not an iota of detail—color, size, or shape—though I'd guess that his "Texan Daisy" was the red and orange *Gaillardia,* but certainly not the little pink-tinged "lazy daisy" that blooms here in the sand. That's not a flower that would have struck JJA as uniquely Texan. Nor would it have been Drummond's evening primrose (another flower named for James Drummond, the Scottish botanist). Crawling vines, yellow flowers two-and-a-half inches across that open at dusk. You can watch it happen. The buds are tightly furled inside a cage of four narrow green sepals. As the moment approaches, the bud fattens, the sepals pull at the gluey catch that holds them closed at the top of the bud. Then the signal is given, as though a button were pushed—*GO!* The sepals fly apart, snap down and backwards and are clamped against the stem, elbows in. The buds burst into flower: big wet newborn yellow petals wrinkled at the edges. In a matter of minutes, the petals expand, dry, and the wrinkles are smoothed away.

The first evening we were here, when I noticed the primroses blooming behind the dunes, I thought at first glance that the ground was littered with yellow paper napkins. (Conversely, if I should ever see sand dunes littered with yellow paper napkins, will I think they're evening primroses?)

An elderly Michigan woman, one of our nation's gypsy-vagabond senior citizens, with whom I fell into conversation in the ladies' bathhouse, spoke about a state park in Louisiana where she and her husband should have stayed put—away from the salt and sand and wind of the Galveston beach. It was beautiful back there, she says. Trees. Outside laundry tubs. "And redbirds till you couldn't rest."

It was a country idiom new to me, but instantly luminous. The mind boggled by redbirds, the eye plundered by redbirds. No peace amid such plenty. *Redbirds till you couldn't rest.*

JJA says, "The muskrat is the only small quadruped found here, and the common house-rat has not reached this part of the world." Without even asking around, it's safe to assume that the house rat has found Galveston Island. And nutria now live in muskrat territory. We see their tracks in the mud at marshes' edge—another animal to add to the list of creatures (cattle egret, starling, boll weevil, Japanese beetles, etc.) that JJA never saw in America.

On the beach, a dead dolphin washes ashore, rolling in the waves like a log. A dead sea turtle, its bottom shell crusted with barnacles, rots on its back in the sand a-buzz with flies. As far as the eye can see in either direction, there are dead and dying jellyfish. Wind sailors, the cerulean blue jellyfish of the genus *Vellela*—round, opaque blobs four inches long, looking like balloons blown from blue bubble gum—that have oblique crests that act as sails, often carrying them off course onto the beaches of Maine and sometimes as far as England. Those still alive draw in clots of blue tentacles across the wet sand as they expire.

Moon jellyfish, whose range carries them from the arctic to the tropics—low glistening domes, big as hub caps.

Portuguese men-of-war—pink-crested air-filled floats a foot long, streamers of blue tentacles stretched out behind them. The freshly beached men-of-war, still alive, raise the outer edges of their floats and point toward the water, reaching for the sea. Their venom can be as powerful as a cobra's, if it gets into a cut or a scratch. An eight-year-old boy recently died from the stings of the man-of-war in these waters.

On the Labrador trip in 1833, JJA (aged forty-eight) complained of fatigue, of not being able to keep up to his old pace, and morosely declared that he was, after all, no longer young. On the Texas-Gulf Coast trip, two entries again touch on his flagging stamina (at age fifty-two). *Galveston Bay:* Friday, April 28, 1837. "Feeling myself rather fatigued, I did not return to the bushes with the rest, who went in search of more venison for our numerous crew." And on the following Monday, "I was much fatigued this morning, and the muscles of my legs were swelled until they were purple, so that I could not go on shore." He'd been troubled with a swollen leg on his Florida trip five years earlier. We read over his shoulder and try to read between the lines. Whatever it was that ailed him (it sounds like a circulatory problem), it was getting worse.

MH   The birds he found on Galveston were all familiar. In fact, the entire Texas trip produced no new birds. Nonetheless, it had its reward. He wrote to his fellow ornithologist, Thomas M. Brewer, in England: "One thing that will interest you most, as it did me, is that we found west of the Mississippi many species of ducks breeding as contented as if in latitude 68° north. There is, after all, nothing like seeing things or countries to enable one to judge of their peculiarities, and I now feel satisfied that through the want of these means many erroneous notions remain in scientific works that can not otherwise be eradicated. We found not one new species, but the mass of observations that we have gathered connected with the ornithology of our country, has, I think, never been surpassed. I feel myself now tolerably competent to give an essay on the geographical distribution of the feathered tribes of our dear country, and I promise that I will do so, with naught but facts and notes made on the very spot."

Across Bolivar Roads to Point Bolivar, opposite Galveston, for shorebirds. A multitude, a vast multitude of birds rests on sandspits and feeds in a wide stretch of shallows—shallows created by mistake by the Corps of Engineers, I am told. A classic example of an unlooked-for side effect of constructing a stone jetty: deflected currents, carrying sand, now dump the sand in what was once tolerably deep water, and presto, more beach. The greater part of the birds before us are avocets—2500 of them, by my estimate. Now *there's* a sight, thousands of long-necked, long-legged shorebirds: long, upturned bills, tawny-golden from head to shoulders, white and black below that. Most of them just rest, facing into the wind, and preen themselves, but a few are working the sand of the shallows with the characteristic sideswiping motion of the head. A helicopter puts them up. They swirl, circle, drift, and set down, go back to what they were doing. . . .

March 7. Gray, cold, north-windy with rain. But the eastern meadowlarks are singing the opening lines of "Bring on the clowns" and "Here lies love."

Their sweet song has always seemed to me a song of leisure, phrases delivered languidly from a high roost on a balmy spring morning. So I was disconcerted, even disappointed the other day to hear the song apparently being uttered in the midst of a wild, quarrelsome, speeding chase through the dunes, three meadowlarks involved.

Thunder before 7:30 in the morning, and wind sliding easterly, increasing in force. The low baccharis bushes toss in the drier parts of the marsh. . . . Later, P.M., rain has stopped, wind is down a bit, and I walk out to a distant observation tower. On the way I hear the far-up winnowing of snipe—the first since the Magdelenes. . . . Standing on the platform of the tower, watching Forster's terns in the marsh below, I look up to catch sight of a roseate spoonbill passing directly overhead, not very high. Apparently the big, pink bird hasn't noticed me either, until just this moment, and is as surprised as I am; it looks down and back at me, under its body, and keeps going.

March 10. At last the wind has moderated, the air turns soft, clouds drift in the blue sky. Ducks and waders hurry on various errands over the marsh. The red-winged blackbirds sing. And the eastern meadowlark perched nearest us carols a phrase from "Collegiate! Collegiate! Yes, we are collegiate!"

MD   From the abstract log of the *Campbell*:

> May 9th   At 1 AM got underway & ran up to Red Fish bar and Moored Ship. . . . Mr. Audubon & Party & Captn Coste left for the City of Houston in the gig & Crusader.

They sailed up Buffalo Bayou, which empties into Galveston Bay, and put in at Allen's Landing at the junction of Buffalo Bayou and White Oak Bayou—the heart of Houston. This is where the city began in 1836 when the Allen brothers, Auguste and John, New York land speculators, bought a mosquito-ridden swampland, laid out a town tract, and named it after Sam Houston, hero of the Battle of San Jacinto and the first president of the new Republic of Texas. The landing now lies under the massive shadow of the Main Street bridge. At water's edge is a curved esplanade that follows the curve of bayou; an historic marker; an American flag; tubs of flowering shrubs. A patch of lawn on the steep bank rising to the city above is bordered with chinaberry trees in lavender fragrant bloom. Audubon came to Houston by way of Buffalo Bayou, passing, en route, the San Jacinto battleground. The bodies had been left unburied after the battle, and JJA, the week before in Galveston, had been promised a gift of Mexican skulls, still lying about for the picking.

There had been heavy rains in the spring of 1837. JJA wrote that Buffalo Bayou had risen about six feet "and the neighboring prairies were partly covered with water; there was a wild and desolate look cast on the surrounding scenery. We had already passed two little girls encamped on the bank of the bayou under the cover of a few boards, cooking a scanty meal; shanties, cargoes of hogsheads, barrels, etc. were spread about the landing; and Indians drunk and hallooing were stumbling about in the mud in every direction. These poor beings had come here to enter a treaty proposed by the whites."

At the top of the bank, JJA and his companions saw before them "a far-extending prairie, destitute of timber, and with rather poor soil." The town itself could be taken in at one glance—tents, a liberty pole (erected in celebration of the first year of independence), half-finished houses without roofs, the capitol building and its floors, benches, and tables still open to the weather. They waded through water above their ankles to the President's mansion, a two-room log house, the floor deep in mud, a large fire burning, camp-beds, trunks, a small table with paper and writing materials.

"We first caught sight of President Houston as he walked from one of the grog-shops, where he had been to prevent the further sale of ardent spirits to the Indians . . . he is upwards of six feet high, and strong in proportion. But I observed a scowl in the expression of his

Capital i

American Quarter house.

Capitol 90 feet front — 1...

Dec

Houston with the completed Capitol, sketched by Mary Austin Holley in December 1837, eight months after Audubon's visit. *The University of Texas at Austin*

eyes that was forbidding and disagreeable." However, Houston received JJA graciously, offered to be of any assistance within his power, and asked his visitors to join him in a drink, which they did, with a toast to the success of the new republic. Audubon ends his account of Sam Houston on an ambiguous note: "Our talk was short; but the impression which was made on my mind at the time by himself, his officers, and his place of abode, can never be forgotten."

JJA & Co. returned to their boat at Allen's Landing "through a melee of Indians and blackguards of all sorts," and departed the city of Houston. Buffalo Bayou in those days was described by one traveler as "a most enchanting little stream," by another as the home of duck, crane, and heron, with magnolias on the high land, gray and red squirrel leaping from branch to branch, mockingbirds and cardinals "imparting life and language to these wonderful solitudes." Audubon remarked on the number of ivory-billed woodpeckers.

The bayou served as the town's drinking water until the 1880s, and as a secondary water supply until the turn of the century in spite of outcries about cattle yards, dead cattle, privies, town sewage, mill waste, and a smallpox graveyard, which were poisoning the stream. In 1894, the Houston Cotton Exchange characterized the bayou as "an immense cesspool, reeking with filth." In 1914, fifty-seven miles of the bayou was dredged to create the Houston Ship Canal and efforts were made to clean it up—on order of the U.S. Government. No clean-up, no federal funds. But Houston has yet to control its sewage problem. The city has grown too fast in the years since World War II—a building boom that took off with the advent of air-conditioning, which also accounts for the general building boom throughout the south. As one man explained it to us when we were in Mississippi delta country: "In the old days you could only work six months out of the year. The other six months we sat on the verandah, drinking and fanning and sweating." (And before the introduction of air-conditioning, the British foreign office considered the consulate in steaming Houston to be a hardship post, like Calcutta.)

The city continues to grow. At last appraisal Buffalo Bayou was still an immense cesspool, and the Attorney General of Texas brought suit against Houston as the worst polluter in the state; seventy viruses, including polio and meningitis, had been identified in the bayou's water. After that came the crisis of the Culex mosquitoes, carriers of encephalitis, that were breeding at an epidemic rate in city sewage. The bayou also made the headlines a couple years ago when a floating corpse was found there—the body of a Mexican-American, last seen in the custody of the Houston police.

We lean over the wall at Allen's Landing to look down into the great gray-green, greasy Limpopo of Buffalo Bayou, wending its way between warehouses and commercial buildings as it flows eastward through the city to the Ship Canal and Galveston Bay. This little park under the bridge appears to be the haunt of the downtown bums. One ragged derelict paces thoughtfully along the bank. Another sleeps in the sun, lying on his face, out cold, as though he'd been pole-axed. Another sits slumped under a chinaberry tree. Another sits uphill on the greensward with his shoes and socks off, picking out the dirt between his toes.

We made a valiant effort to stop at the nearby Sam Houston Park —a restoration of old houses with historic collections—but were carried past it twice by the surge of the Gulf Freeway traffic. We finally clawed our way onto a side street and stole up on the park from the rear, but could find no place to leave the car. The only lot we saw was reserved "For Employees Only." So be it. Fate did not intend us to see the Sam Houston Park. We clawed back onto the Freeway and were carried out of town on the rip-tide of rush hour traffic. No quarter given. He who hesitates is mangled.

The city map shows a suburban development called Audubon Park, which lies under the eastward airspace of the Houston International Airport. "Audubon" is a skillful choice for a housing tract. Buyers and investors like a name they've heard before—a name with good vibrations—as the Allen brothers knew in 1836, when they gave this city the good, sound, patriotic title of HOUSTON.

How many Audubon housing tracts are there in the United States? This one, like its counterpart in Louisville (and all the others, one would assume) has bird names for the streets. In this instance: Waxwing, Redbird, Flamingo, Heron, Egret, White Swan, Peacock, Falcon, and so on. The main thoroughfare commemorates the Golden Eagle. The mourning dove's name, however, has been amended to a more cheerful and sunnier spelling. It is recorded as

Morning Dove Court. God forbid that anyone should mourn in Houston.

From the abstract log of the *Campbell* on the return voyage to New Orleans:

May 19th   Strong breezes with a heavy head sea. Mr. Audubon & Party all Sea Sick.

MD   Before we go any futher with Audubon's fortunes and travels, I want to stop here for a moment to catch up again on Lucy. They now have been married for thirty-five years. She had gone to England with John James on three business trips and worked alongside him as an editor and copyist for his ornithological essays as they were being published in Edinburgh. But even with her husband's fame and international recognition, Lucy does not seem to have relaxed her stern view of life as a toil and a trouble. She remained capable, diligent, and joyless. I find it significant that in none of the letters we have seen from Bachman to JJA is there any personal, affectionate, easy-going message to Lucy. Formal greetings to Mrs. Audubon, but nothing more. I have a hunch that she regarded Bachman as another rival for her husband's attentions. I find my clue in a letter to Lucy from John James in which he tells her, in effect, that she should trust John Bachman, that he is a good fellow. Had she then been complaining about Bachman?

Lucy's hair had turned gray, and she wore dark, false curls pinned to her cap, a vanity she at last abandoned in her mid-fifties, and JJA wrote to the boys that Mama now wore her own natural curls and looked all the prettier for it. A letter from Edinburgh during their last visit puts Lucy into final perspective for me. She had been ailing (an unidentified illness), and Audubon wrote to the boys to say that Mama was feeling better and on the road to recovery.

Dear Lucy, ever the harbinger of gloom. She couldn't let it go at that. She took up the pen and struck in a querulous postscript. "Papa thinks I am very well, but I am as weak as a cat and good for nothing." Before the letter was mailed, Audubon added a gentle, ameliorating postscript of his own: "Mama is simply low-spirited just now."

MH "What a strange realization of a Dream this finishing of a work that has cost me so many Years of Enjoyment, of Labour and of Vexations," wrote Audubon to Bachman from New York in July 1837 as he made ready to sail for England again, "and yet a few more months will I trust see it ended aye ended, and Myself a Naturalist no *longer!* No More advertisements of this poor me. No more stares at my face whil[s]t traveling—No I have some Idea of revising even myself and altering my very name, not to be pestered any more."

But that was hardly likely. The *Birds* project had survived by the skin of its teeth and by dint of the monumental efforts of the entire Audubon family and of such good friends as Bachman and Harris. Only about one-hundred-and-seventy-five complete copies had been sold by 1839, when it was finished, "everyone believing," as Lucy wrote to a cousin, "that afterwards it would be cheaper; and already the mistake is beginning to be felt, since the coppers are all put by, in the application of some for a few extra plates which cannot be had even now."

There would be no more editions of the Havell engravings, and that source of income for the Audubons was about gone. JJA had achieved a masterwork, and his reputation if not his living was assured; the best he could do now was trade on that reputation. So he and Bachman would publish a folio on the North American quadrupeds, and he and the boys would issue a seven-volume octavo edition of *The Birds of America,* with small versions of the engravings reproduced by lithography and the bird essays from the *Ornithological Biography.* The price of the "small work," as JJA called it, was one hundred dollars a set, which he hoped would assure a large sale. He rented a house at 86 White Street in downtown New York (the address now holds a small parking lot between buildings). When he wasn't drawing animals, he was back on the road, a salesman once more—in the next three years traveling through New England and to Charleston, Baltimore, Washington, Richmond, Philadelphia, New Brunswick, Quebec, and Ontario. Success was sufficient so that he finally bought a piece of land—above the Hudson, north of the city

Audubon painted these black rats in September 1842. *The American Museum of Natural History, New York City*

The western fox squirrel was done in January of the year Audubon went to the Yellowstone. *Courtesy of The New-York Historical Society, New York City*

—and a house was built there. The family called it Minnies Land, after the Scots term of endearment for a mother; the boys had taken to calling Lucy Minnie, and their Minnie had the first permanent home of her own since the Henderson years, more than two decades earlier.

The more or less stable economic situation also encouraged JJA to make one more expedition, mostly for the sake of the *Quadrupeds.*

St. Louis, from *The Ladies Repository,* January 1845. *State Historical Society of Missouri*

Pierre Chouteau, head of the American Fur Company, had offered free transporation up the Missouri River from St. Louis. So, wrote Audubon, "It is now determined that I shall go towards the Rocky Mountains at least to the Yellowstone River, and up the latter Stream four hundred of miles, and *perhaps* go across the Rocky Mountains."

But he had to scrimp and borrow in order to make the trip, and he needed the financial help of Edward Harris, who would again accompany him. From St. Louis he wrote home, "I do sincerely hope that Victor will be able to meet all his money calls, without *ever* PLEDGING MINNIES LAND."

Besides Harris and himself, the party included a top-notch taxidermist, John Graham Bell of New York, artist Isaac Sprague of Hingham, Massachusetts, who was along to assist with the drawings, and young Lewis Squires of New York, who would be Audubon's secretary and aide-de-camp. They reached St. Louis March 28, and there they waited nearly a month for the ice to break up on the Missouri. (Almost nothing is left of the city as JJA knew it. The rabbit warren of the waterfront neighborhood was leveled in the 1940s to make way for the Gateway National Park; the only original building left standing on the edge of the park's open plain is the old cathedral, the Basilica of St. Louis.) Meanwhile, there was lots of publicity and newspaper coverage of Audubon's forthcoming expedition. On April 25, the river clear, they boarded the American Fur Company's sidewheeler *Omega* and started up toward Fort Union, the fur company's outpost at the confluence of the Yellowstone and the Missouri, some 1800 miles away.

St. Louis from East St. Louis. The cathedral, left of center, is the only building shown that survives from Audubon's day. *MH*

Their fellow passengers included more than a hundred trapper-engagés contracted to the fur company—"of all descriptions and nearly a dozen different nationalities," says JJA's journal, as strained through his granddaughter's Victorian cheesecloth, "though the greater number were French Canadians, or Creoles of [Missouri]. Some were drunk, and many in that stupid mood which follows a state of nervousness produced by drinking and over-excitement. . . . [They] came in pushing and squeezing each other, so as to make the boards they walked on fairly tremble. The Indians, poor souls, were more quiet, and had already seated themselves on the highest parts of the steamer, and were tranquil lookers-on." Harris remarked in *his* journal that one of the engagés who had signed on for the trip had then been arrested as a murderer and counterfeiter, and he thought the trappers were "the very off scouring of the earth, worse than any crew of sailors I ever met with."

"[A]s the boat pushed off from the shore," says JJA's journal, ". . . the men on board had congregated upon the hurricane deck with their rifles and guns of various sorts, all loaded, and began to fire what I should call a very disorganized sort of salute, which lasted for something like an hour, and which has been renewed at intervals, though in a more desultory manner, at every village we have passed."

Two days later they left behind the capital of Missouri, Jefferson. By 1837 Jefferson had had two steam-driven mills (more successful than Audubon's?), a courthouse built of hammered rock, and a state penitentiary. In 1840 it held more than a hundred buildings, including five hotels. The first state capitol burned and its successor was raised in 1842 at a cost of $350,000—no mean price for those days. "The State House stands prominent," says JJA's journal, "with a view from it up and down the stream of about ten miles; but, with the exception of the State House and the Penitentiary, Jefferson is a poor place, the land round being sterile and broken."

Among the penitentiary prisoners that summer of 1843 were three ministry students from the Mission Institute in Illinois. They were abolitionists, and they had come into Missouri in 1841 to convince slaves to flee to Canada through Illinois. One slave peached, and the three students were sentenced to twelve years in jail. Their wives were petitioning for pardons as JJA passed, and the pardons

The Missouri, left, joins the Mississippi a few miles north of St. Louis. *From Henry Lewis'* Das Illustrirte Mississippithal

Jefferson City, capital of Missouri. *From C. A. Dana's* The United States Illustrated, *1855*

were at last granted after the "criminals" had served four or five years.

The State House of the 1840s is gone now; it was destroyed by lightning in 1911 and the present version was finished in 1917. The state pen Audubon saw is still in place and in use, and a warehouse of square-cut granite that stood near the riverbank—back of the railroad tracks today—is upright and being restored.

Eight days from St. Louis the *Omega* reached Fort Leavenworth —then Louisiana Territory, now Kansas. Leavenworth today is the longest-sustained U.S. Army post west of the Missouri, having been established in 1827. Though the Army's fabled prison is there, the post has much the look of a venerable college campus, and some of the buildings around the old parade ground were standing when JJA passed.

Beyond that post there would be no more white settlements to salute. They were in wilderness, with only an occasional Indian village or fur-trading post within sight of the river. To put this voyage of 1843 in perspective, remember that two years previous the first wagon train had left for the Pacific coast. The *Omega* was making only the fourteenth annual steamboat trip "to the mountains." John C. Fremont, who had gone this same way aboard a fur company steamer in 1839, remarked, "Once above the settlements of the lower Missouri, there were no sounds to disturb the stillness but the echoes of the high-pressure steam pipe, which travelled far along and around the shores, and the incessant crumbling away of banks and bars, which the river was steadily undermining and destroying at one place to build up in another."

The Missouri was a difficult river to travel, particularly up-bound. The snowmelt in the Rockies and the spring rains combined to open it for steam navigation as far as the Yellowstone for only about three months of the year. This gave the fur company an opportunity—just barely—to get a boat loaded with supplies and trapper-engagés up to the farthest outposts of its fur-collecting system and back to St. Louis before all the water was out of the upper river. Audubon described the master of the *Omega,* Captain Joseph Sire—a partner in the fur company and himself a refugee from Napoleon's draft—as "a persevering Man who loses not a moment," and under the circumstances, no wonder.

The *Omega* had to stop frequently to cut or take on firewood; the preferred species were ash, cedar, and cottonwood, which Captain Sire called *liard,* French for black poplar. Occasionally only driftwood was available, which gave off scarcely enough heat to make steam. Sometimes wood was ripped from an abandoned riverside cabin or trading post.

Each night on the upper reaches of the river, the boat was moored to the bank and the boilers were cleaned out. "The water is literally half mud," wrote JJA to Minnies Land, "and . . . the deposit is beyond belief. I drank some yesterday taken out of the stream and felt its weight on my stomach for upward of one hour."

From time to time the boat was also stopped by wind. "[T]he wind, which had risen with incredible force," wrote Captain Sire in his log, "and the strength of the current (for the water commenced to rise again last night) made us give it up. I had the boat put to shore and set the men to cutting wood for the return trip. Instead of subsiding the wind increases. It is rather a hurricane. I am momentarily in fear that the smokestacks will fall down. . . .

"The wind continues to blow as hard as yesterday. I set the men to cutting *bois de liard* again. At about 3 P.M. the wind seems to soften. . . . I will have the boilers fired up so that we may be ready if it falls enough. We set out, but Great Heaven, how slow we go! Often we drift backward by the force of the current." And a few days

Fort Leavenworth, 1849. *State Historical Society of Wisconsin*

Captain Sire of the *Omega. From John Thomas Scharf's* History of St. Louis City and County

later: "All day long the wind blows as only it does on the upper Missouri. Often we scarcely move at all."

Then the water would fall again, causing new problems. "I plainly see that the High prevailing winds are more against us than anything else, although *L'Amour propre* of our Pilots, is nearly as bad for us," wrote JJA. "Instead of sending the yawl [ahead] to sound for a . . . channel, they keep poking about running us on the same bar, several times and when we are once fast, then we have to stick [and] lose a day or so, or if we get off have to retrace our steps for a mile or two." (Audubon notwithstanding, the pilots did use the yawl to find channels ahead, and that too meant dawdling along the river.) "No one going down to New Orleans even 20 years ago can have an Idea of the Snags, Sawyers, and Planters that are found in this Upper Missouri they show [their] brittly prongs as if some thousands of mammoth Elk Horns had been planted every w[h]ere for the purpose of impeding the navigation."

And yet, this voyage to the mountains by the *Omega* was by weeks the fastest yet. In 1841 the *Otter* had needed eighty days to get up to Fort Union and twenty-one to get down. In 1842, the *Shawnee* had spent seventy-six days on the upbound trip and twenty-two coming down. Despite everything that slowed her, the *Omega* reached Fort Union in forty-nine days and then made her downstream run in fifteen.

Still, that was a seven-week up-voyage—westward across Missouri to the corner of Kansas at Leavenworth, then northwest along the breadth of present-day Iowa and Nebraska, through South and North Dakota to a point just short of the Montana line. It was both tedious and frustrating for the Audubon party much of the way. Every hour of this season that they did not spend collecting and drawing and taking notes was precious time wasted. The boat plugged along, sometimes making no headway at all, and then it laid up against the shore—but in terrible weather or at night or only long enough for a hundred-and-one engagés to fill the boat with firewood. There were relatively few chances for the naturalists to do any extended hunting for birds or quadrupeds; and even though they were assured that game was abundant in the territory they passed, wildlife seemed exceedingly scarce near the river, where they had to do most of their hunting. Yet what must have made all this terribly tantalizing was

An engraving after Carl Bodmer's "Snags on the Missouri." *St. Louis Art Museum*

what they *did* discover, particularly of new birds for JJA's United States list: Harris' sparrow, Bell's vireo, Smith's longspur (named for a Baltimore physician, friend to Audubon), Le Conte's sparrow (named for another friend), the clay-colored sparrow (which JJA called Shattuck's bunting, after George Shattuck of the Labrador adventure), the Missouri Red-moustached Woodpecker (now considered one of the "common flickers"), and—a special triumph—the Missouri Meadowlark, our western meadowlark, to which he gave the scientific name *Sturnella neglecta*—the neglected meadowlark. [JJA: Although the existence of this species was known to the celebrated explorers of the west, Lewis and Clark, during their memorable journey . . . no one has since taken the least notice of it. . . . They say, on the 21st June, 1805, "There is also a species of Lark, much resembling the bird called the Old Field Lark, with a yellow breast and a black spot on the croup. . . . The beak . . . is somewhat larger and more curved, and the notes differ considerably." . . . We found this species quite abundant . . . , and its curious notes were first noticed by Mr. J.G. Bell, without which in all probability it would have been mistaken for our common species.]

Now, JJA was a guest, and he admired Captain Sire, but there must have been times when he said to himself, or *sotto voce* to one of his traveling companions, "What's the hurry?" He had been at the mercy of others' needs—government or commerce—on earlier expeditions. "What opportunities, good Reader," he once wrote, in a heartfelt passage cut from the *Ornithological Biography* before it was printed, "have been lost in making the most valuable observations on the habits of our birds by scientific men being attached to what may be called Galloping Parties?"

On May 12 the *Omega* tied up to the bank across from what is now the vicinity of Decatur, Nebraska, in view of Blackbird Hill; the bluff was named for a powerful Omaha chief who died of smallpox about 1800 and was buried there, by his request, overlooking the Missouri valley from horseback—"whilst the animal was alive," says Audubon. Hunting for the bluff ourselves, we asked directions of a farmer at a grain bin, of a young Indian woman walking with two children, of a roadman on an earthmover. There's no grave marker on the bluff, the roadman told us, no monument to Blackbird's memory. The spot is Indian reservation, "but it doesn't belong to the Indians, you know. Belongs to a white man." That's true of much Indian reservation land. "He's dead now, the man who owned it, and it's in a nest-egg. It's a pretty spot," he said. "You can see the world from there."

We walked up a steep, deeply rutted, dusty track. The world to see was all river and bottomland: dry cornfields, green trees, farms reaching to the east across Iowa into the hazy distance, into the smell of dry leaves and standing hay. A nice place to be buried, Blackbird Hill, a nice prospect for any spirit.

MD   "This evening," wrote JJA as they passed what would one day be Sioux City, "we came to the burial-ground bluff of Sergeant Floyd, one of the companions of the never-to-be-forgotten expedition of Lewis and Clark." Edward Harris also spoke of this place, and so did Captain Sire in the *Omega* logbook, though for a practical purpose—they had stopped to cut wood three miles below Sergeant's Bluff, and Sire noted that there was enough wood for another year at that particular location.

Sergeant Charles Floyd died on August 20, 1804. On the previous day, as recorded in the Lewis and Clark journals, he had been "taken very bad all at once with a bilious colic . . . he gets worse and we are much alarmed . . . All attention to him." On the twentieth: "Sergeant Floyd as bad as he can be, no pulse, and nothing will stay a moment on his stomach or bowels . . . Sergeant Floyd died with a great deal of composure . . . We buried him on the top of the bluff a half mile below a small river to which we gave his name. He was buried with the honors of war, much lamented."

A cedar post was fixed at the head of the grave, and over the years it was replaced by passing travelers. Everyone voyaging on the Missouri knew the grave as a landmark and understood the significance of his burial place—the possibility and the nearness of death away from home in unknown country. Floyd's Bluff became a symbol of the wayside burials that lined the routes to the west.

Attention was paid. When the Missouri washed away the bluff in 1857 and exposed his bones, they were rescued and reburied. When the new grave was obliterated a half century later, his bones were once again removed and interred in another site on safe, high ground and the site marked with a granite plinth. It's still far enough out of town not to be too cluttered or demeaned, but Sioux City creeps up —rusticated apartment houses, a shopping plaza, a minigolf course, a truck depot for the Army Reserve—and the highway passes close by. At the edge of the bluff one looks down on the river and the soft cottonwoods growing on the shore. Beyond, to the westward in Nebraska, is a classic midwestern, city–country view: the enormous silver screen of a drive-in movie, TV and radio towers, water towers, grain elevators, a stockyard, windmills, a cultivator raising dust in a distant field. Upriver, the statue of Chief War Eagle lifts his peace pipe over Sioux City.

We know nothing more about Sergeant Floyd than his name and the brief story from the Lewis and Clark journals, but I am caught by the poignancy of the place. No one else was here when we arrived and stood on his bluff and surveyed the view. Then another car breezed in off the highway, and three youngish men, overweight and wearing the pallor of office workers, strolled out to the grave for a quick look-see, one of them announcing with a ho-ho laugh that Sergeant Floyd was said to have died of nothing more exciting than a bad case of appendicitis, and the others laughed along with him at the contradiction of the splendid memorial for such an uninteresting death. I found myself shaken by rage. Fat, soft, whey-faced fools!

MH As far upstream as Sioux City, Iowa, the Missouri is dredged and maintained for the barge traffic. Higher, above Yankton, South Dakota, there are six Corps of Engineers lakes and six hydroelectric power dams. One of these dams, in Montana, was begun as a simple flood-control project in the 1930s; the rest, between Williston, North Dakota, and Yankton, South Dakota, were built in the 1950s and 1960s with both power and flood-control in mind. Between them they "impound more than fifty per cent of the upper 1500 miles of the Missouri River." So it's a changed river we travel with—drastically changed even in our lifetimes. The great reservoirs behind the power dams fill most of the old river bottoms from edge to edge; everywhere that the Missouri cut through the prairie badlands in its floods—the meanders, the shifting channels, the swales—are full. Captain Sire would be amazed at all the water under his boat in these lakes. But of course because of the dams he couldn't travel under power to the mountains on his river, not without an Army amphibious "Duck." (Is this *really* an improvement? Once you've built such a system, it becomes one, I suppose.)

Elm Creek, above Fort Randall Dam, South Dakota. In this place we hear no cars, no airplanes, nothing at all but our own thoughts and those of a few crickets and steers. After driving more than twenty miles to reach the campsite—already shut down for the winter—we are more isolated than we've been since Labrador. Downriver, about at the bend, there are Bijou's Hills, named for a pioneer fur-trader, so we are very near where JJA and company camped twice. The spring camp was made after a day of some excitement. Audubon had borrowed Harris' double-barreled shotgun, and on his first shot it misfired, blowing off a part that "passed so near my ear . . . I was stunned, and fell down as if shot."

The *Omega's* master had a terrible time that May day, crossing sandbars, and we can understand why. The river is still shallow here, and we had to walk out half-a-mile on the flats, gumbo to our ankles, to reach water deep enough to fill a half-gallon bottle, an iron kettle, and a leaky five-gallon jug for the sake of cooking and washing. JJA described "the turbid waters of this all-mighty stream" as looking "more like that of a hog puddle than any thing else I can compare it to." [MD: Missouri River water boils up to a gray porridge, then settles fifty-fifty: half mud, half water. The privies here are full of black widow spiders, each of them hanging upside down in her web, the red hourglass on the belly brilliantly visible.]

Morning. I could hardly be happier. Great horned owls calling distantly around the camp before dawn, and geese gabbling nearby. The spines of the hills are bold and flat against the first light of day, but soften, become more complex, as the rising light picks out the folds; the only sounds other than of the birds and insects and cattle and the crackle of our driftwood fire (heating coffee water) are sibilants of the endless wind.

MD Mrs. Maresh, in a hunting cap—flaps down and tied under her chin—ragged men's pants, and shirt and cracked shoes, runs a farm above the river, growing wheat, barley, and corn. In the background as we talk is an old woman, a bundle of rags, in rubber boots tied with string. They live in a house that looks as though it won't survive the next high wind, already beaten to its knees, its windows blown out. There was once a town up on the bluffs, she tells us, called Bijou Hills, with a bank, blacksmith, movie theater, schoolhouse, post office; everyone went shopping there. Now all we can find of it are two abandoned privies and three houses. Everything else has been swallowed by the prairie—the cellarholes filled and grown over.

MH We are well into "badlands" terrain—a topography featuring steep bluffs and sudden knobs, flat-topped buttes, deep clay ravines, and long swells of prairie. Its colors are tans and grays and blacks; even green leaves look dusty.

We walked out into it today at the famous Great Bend of the Missouri. Audubon and friends crossed the waist of the bend on foot while the Omega took nearly a day to travel the long way round. The Corps of Engineers has built Great Bend Dam below the spot, but the lake formed thereby does not overcome the high ground in the center, so the bend persists.

At the top of the hills we were surrounded by a view that is still as moving as when JJA saw it—"one of the great panoramas this remarkable portion of our country affords. There was a vast extent of country beneath and around us. Westward rose the famous Medicine Hill"—the highest hill in the vicinity, doubtless used by the Indians for "medicine" then and used for different kinds now, bearing a white cross on top and two television towers—"and in the opposite direction were the wanderings of the Missouri for many miles." The river shone silver in the bright sun for us, and we looked down into the gorge at the western end of the Great Bend. There Audubon and his party made camp, shot a black-tailed deer, and cooked the venison on pointed sticks over the fire. "The Camp of the Six Cottonwood Trees," Edward Harris called it. Surely the campsite is drowned now. We saw no black-tailed deer, but three antelope appeared on the top of the next rise, studied us alertly, and vanished before we remembered to try attracting antelope the way Audubon had on one excursion that summer—by lying on his back and kicking his legs in the air. "In about twenty minutes [the buck] had come two or three hundred yards," and when JJA could see the animal's eyes, he leveled his gun—still with his shoulders down and legs in the air —and fired. He missed.

Iron Nation campground, below Antelope Creek. The *Omega* steamed past, "laboring over the infernal sand-bars until nearly four [in the] afternoon, . . . actually cutting our own channel with the assistance of the wheel." JJA had been given a dead buffalo calf that morning, and the severed head of another; Sprague and he spent most of the day drawing that head, and the whole calf was skinned out by Bell and pickled as a specimen.

The water in front of our tent this dusk is gold where calm, and blue where ruffled by the wind. On the far side, against the pale aqua and gold western sky, is a silhouetted hill, a few groves of trees, and Iron Nation Church, in the Lower Brule Indian Reservation.

The river is beyond that ridge; we're on a backwater, amid profound quiet. Except for the sound of a very occasional car on the road above us, there is no noise on the faint northwesterly wind but the rasp of a few crickets, a few singing Missouri Meadowlarks, and— once—a killdeer.

MD As I gather driftwood—feather-light, bone dry, water-smoothed and rounded like tumbled gemstones—two fighter planes improbably shred the silence. I hear the sound behind me, look up and ahead to find them. Black pointy shark shapes, wheeling and diving in games of pursuit, sporting like ravens. They vanish in ten seconds.

MH Fort Pierre (say *peer*, y'hear?), outside of Pierre, South Dakota. Nothing of it remains, but it was once the Upper Missouri Outfit's field headquarters—the biggest fort on the river, named for the company's boss, Pierre Chouteau. Its cottonwood-picket walls, with the two blockhouses at opposite corners, enclosed about twenty buildings in a space as big as a fair-sized baseball park. When the *Omega* paused here on the way up, JJA was showered with gifts by the men in charge: an enormous pair of elk horns, an elk skin, moccasins, an Indian riding whip, a collar of grizzly bear claws, Indian clothes. "More kindness from strangers," says his journal, "I have seldom received." On the way downriver at the end of summer, they stopped at Fort Pierre for a week.

The army bought this post from the fur company in 1855, as a supply depot for an expedition against the Sioux. "An army legend asserts that the place was founded by the illustrious Peter the Her-

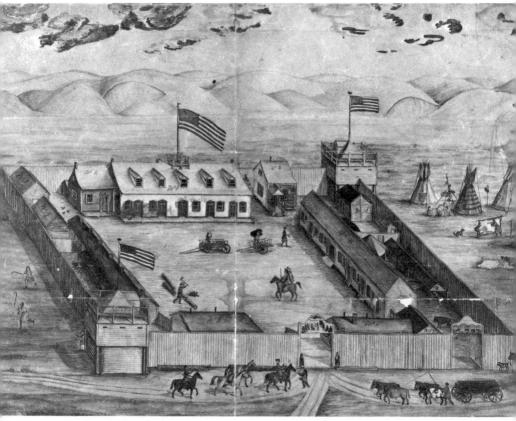

Fort Pierre, by Frederick Behman. *South Dakota State Historical Society*

mit," an officer wrote, "who . . . selected this point near the mauvais terre, because of its unmitigated dreariness and its indescribable desolation; but as this is not well authenticated we give it for what it is worth." Fort Pierre and vicinity had been so hard used for so many years that little or no good grazing or cropping land remained nearby, and the nearest firewood was twenty miles away. The Army abandoned it in 1857; it was then cannibalized for another Army post as well as pillaged; and in the autumn of 1859, sixteen years after Audubon had passed, a captain of engineers reported that "but little was left of the structure."

No one we've met knows just where we should look for the site of the old fort, but we have directions to a farmer out in the general area, near the present town of Fort Pierre. The farmer is P. C. Hamilton, a man in his mid-sixties, wearing granny glasses and a tan Stetson when I find him. He's digging a posthole, and as I introduce myself and my mission, he kicks dirt away from the edge of his hole onto my feet—not in an unfriendly way, really, but as a signal I should know this is his farm and he's busy. Then Mary comes up, and he sweetens. Yes, he knows about the old fort. The site is his land, in fact, and if we drive out that way (gesturing), and walk a bit, go through the fence, we'll be in an overgrown patch of prairie, and there's a marker, can't miss it.

As we stand chatting, Mary points to a bird that's just flown into a nearby tree and asks me what it is. "Where?" says P. C. Hamilton, whirling to look in the direction she's pointing. "Probably one of them blackbirds." Which is precisely right. P. C. Hamilton shakes his head ruefully. Those blackbirds, he says, have cost him $300 an acre of his corn crop this year, and they've been at his fruit and his vegetables too. Terrible mess. He'd like to poison them, but the state agriculture people have told him "the ecologists" wouldn't allow that.

So the land has recovered to bear corn and vegetables and fruit; and the site of Fort Pierre is now a sage-and-shortgrass pasture, which the river has deserted. Far from the road the stone marker stands in the field—a monument donated in the 1930s by an Iowa man. Unless you were looking for it, you'd never notice it, and before long even if you can find it you won't know why it's there; the inscription on the metal marker is weatherworn and difficult to read.

A county agricultural extension agent tells us that the biggest economic problem for farmers hereabouts is cattle-rustling. And the cattle business, even without that, is depressed these days. He offers a homily about two brothers: one rustled the cattle, the other stole the feed—"and even then they lost six dollars a head."

So the Galloping Party of the American Fur Company steamed slowly northwestward that spring. "Squires has been engaged in making a map of the River ever since we left the Council's Bluffs," wrote JJA to his family, "and we hope that it may assist us on our return.—Bell skins everything that is worth having of course. Sprague makes a few sketches. I write my Journal pretty full and Harris takes notes on the Geology of the shores & c." When a traveler climbs the highest hills near the river, "he finds himself on a level of others if I may thus express myself which looks as if indominable.—The soil is of the very poorest kind, and for this reason the Game . . . is obliged to resort to the equally numerous meandering Ravines which ever and anon make their way to the River crammed with under brush and scrubby Cedars, but abounding with small Birds & c."

Site of Fort Pierre; surge towers of Oahe Dam are just visible under the horizon beyond the stone marker. *MH*

And the buffaloes! They were "remarkably abundant . . . , and the snow that fell 2 feet deep on the 5th of [May] has destroyed almost all the calves and reduced the old ones to the last stage of poverty. They swim the River in vast multitudes, are drowned and left on either shores for hundreds of miles above; and many have already passed us floating, bloated and putrid!—Notwithstanding which, the Indians who are destitute and hungry actually feed upon this flesh along with the Wolves and other beasts of prey."

Audubon's edited journal has more to say about such Indian meals: "[P]rovided the hump proves at all fat, they swim to them, drag them on shore, and cut them to pieces; after which they cook and eat this loathsome and abominable flesh, even to the marrow found in the bones. In some instances this has been done when the whole of the hair had fallen off, from the rottenness of the Buffalo. Ah! Mr. Catlin [George Catlin, whose illustrated work on Indians had recently been published], I am now sorry to see and to read your accounts of the Indians *you* saw—how very different they must have been from any that I have seen!"

Is this actually Maria's prudish voice, or is it Audubon? Such remarks sound strange coming from one who had eaten maggoty cheese and unusual meat more than a few times. His journal has other things to say about the Indians *he* saw that spring of 1843. They were "thievish" and "lightfingered" and begged when they could find nothing to steal. "Squalid and miserable Devils" they were, and one small war-party had the temerity to *shoot* at the *Omega* from the bank when it would not stop as they wanted; nobody was hurt, although one rifle ball barely missed a sleeping passenger in his berth. At the fur company's Fort Clark, a few days below Fort Union, Audubon saw the Mandan village, which had recently been taken over, he reported, by nearly 3000 Arikaras. What the published journal doesn't say is that the Mandans in that village in 1837 had been almost wiped out by smallpox; when the survivors fled, the Arikaras had moved in and were still in the majority despite the subsequent return of a Mandan remnant. Not a stable situation at best. "The Mandan mud huts are very far from looking poetical, although Mr. Catlin has tried to render them so by placing them in regular rows, and all of the same size and form, which is by no means the case. But different travellers have different eyes! . . . [I]t is possible that there

Carl Bodmer's Fort Clark, 1834. *The New York Public Library, Rare Book Division*

are a hundred huts, made of mud, all looking like so many potato winter-houses in the Eastern States." We visited a reconstruction of a Mandan village at Fort Lincoln, south of Fort Clark; the "mud huts" were built of logs inside—heavy timbers, probably cottonwood, most of them set vertically; earth was mounded up over that, putting the houses virtually underground and out of the way of wind and blizzard.

"As soon as we were near the shore," the journal continues, "every article that could conveniently be carried off [the boat] was placed under lock and key. . . . The appearance of these poor, miserable devils, as we approached the shore, was wretched enough. There they stood in the pelting rain and keen wind, covered with Buffalo robes, red blankets, and the like, some partially and most curiously besmeared with mud; and as they came on board, and we shook hands with each of them, I felt a clamminess that rendered the ceremony most repulsive." He was taken, just like any tourist, to a medicine lodge and one of the smaller mud huts; he and his friends went to look at the Indians' corn-fields, then sprouting; they visited a recent Mandan graveyard, where—only as an aside—JJA mentions that the Indians buried there under heaps of earth had died of smallpox. "These mounds in many instances appear to contain the remains of several bodies and, perched on the top, lies, pretty generally, the rotting skull of a Buffalo. Indeed, the skulls of the Buffaloes seem as if a kind of relation to these most absurdly superstitious and ignorant beings." It would, he concluded, be good to get away from Fort Clark and "all this 'Indian poetry.' " A few days later, just after the *Omega* reached Fort Union, his recantation was complete—if one can trust the version of his journal published in Buchanan's "authorized" biography (this particular entry does not appear anywhere in Maria Audubon's rendering): ". . . [T]he sights daily seen will not bear recording: they have dispelled all the romance of Indian life I ever had, and I am satisfied that all the poetry about Indians is contained in books; there certainly is none in their wild life in the woods."

What has gotten into our friend? Where is the perspective, philosophy, and sorrow with which he observed the Seminoles in Florida, the Indians of Labrador, and those on the Trail of Tears through Alabama? To be fair, no man knew or could visualize exactly what was happening in fur country; events were moving too fast and haphazardly. The fur trade had revolutionized the life of the western Indians in the short space of four decades. So had the westward displacement of eastern and middle-western tribes. And in 1837— five years after Catlin visited—the smallpox had come north with the annual fur company boat and killed thousands of Indians, reducing some villages and tribes to only a few families. But where could JJA go to see nature undefiled? He had asked that question rhetorically in Labrador in 1833. He could hardly have done better than he did at this moment: travel up the Missouri when nature was still un- trimmed and uncultivated along the river's banks; when the territory was still rich with wildlife and was occupied by "savages," both white and red, after an epidemic had magnified and accelerated what the fur trade and liquor and white expansion westward had already set in motion among the Indian nations. That's nature too—man at his most raw and most ruined, greedy and desperate and careless of consequences, reduced by illness and poison and upheaval to a condi- tion vastly changed from what it had only so recently been.

Difficult, true, for a man to see this; but JJA, at least so it seems, had gone over to the other side, to the majority, without so much as a struggle. Indeed, with a sort of war-whoop against George Catlin's romantic images of Indians taken before the pox ruined them.

In tones Audubon once used himself, Catlin defended the Ameri- can Indian: "It is astonishing that under all the invasions, the frauds and deceptions, as well as force, that have been practiced upon [them], to push them from their lands and step by step towards the setting sun, these abused people have exercised so little cruelty as they have; that whiskey and smallpox . . . have been submitted to; and border warfare, until they are reduced, tribe by tribe, to mere rem- nants, and still pushed again and again to the west. . . . I feel author- ized to say that the North American Indian *in his native state* is honest, hospitable, faithful, warlike, brave, cruel, relentless—and an honorable and religious human being."

One speculation comes to mind to explain Audubon's reversal. Perhaps the Missouri river trip was one expedition too many. JJA was glad to be exploring and collecting again—"My head is actually swimming with excitement," he wrote his first morning at Fort Union—but his heart was in Minnies Land. His letters home often imagined what his family must be doing now, what stage the season had reached along the Hudson, what fish were being caught, how the garden was going, how his sons were getting on with various tasks. This was a new side to his character, that of the confirmed homebody. "Oh how happy would I be to see Dearest Mother and you all for only a few minutes, and be back again here with the swiftness of thought." He wrote such sentiments often that spring. He had once had an overpowering romantic attachment to the wilderness and to those who lived with it. He had now begun to find more romance at his civilized hearth, surrounded by grandchildren, than he did in the wilderness. That's pleasing to see—but sad too.

The territory up the Yellowstone beyond Fort Union was Blackfoot country, and the Blackfeet the least tractable and fiercest of the fur company's suppliers. They were more ill-disposed than usual toward the white man this spring because of the cruelty of one of the fur-company operatives, and JJA was advised not to go any closer to the mountains than Fort Union. So ended his last hope of seeing the Rockies. The fort would remain his base of operations for the next two months.

The Great Plains are a world of sky and weather. Westering in August to join JJA at Fort Union, we are caught in a terrific thunderstorm in Minnesota. Mounting vortices of gray cloud on gray cloud warn us; they pile high and higher with omens of the coming wind and rain and God knows what else. We stop the car in the worst of the storm—hail stones the size of marbles blowing almost parallel to the ground and whanging on the sides and windshield, hail so thick we cannot see the road. The same day two people are killed not far away when a tornado rolls their car across a wheat field.

I feel as if we cross a great tidal flat. And to be sure, wheat and soybeans and corn and sunflowers are growing on a former ocean bottom. At Minot, the land begins to buckle occasionally into sand dunes, and where the terrain is not sand dune but farms, it is also one great marshy refuge, dotted with pools, each bearing its share of coots and grebes, ducks and shorebirds.

At Stanley, North Dakota, camped against a grove of trees at the center of far-off circling horizons, with an ancient wooden water tower dripping endlessly beside our campground and another water tower across the road standing up against the wide sky, we expect to hear the sea.

And like the outgoing trickles of water across a tidal flat, which change the shape of the mud over which they flow and so change their own shapes from time to time, the Yellowstone and the Missouri flow across the plains, carve the land, and move their courses. They meet now just this side of the Montana line, about a mile east of where they met in 1843. The confluence was important in the fur trade, and the Upper Missouri Outfit of the American Fur Company built Fort Union just below it, 1829–1832. For the next thirty years the fort was the key to commerce in the region, as two competitor fur-trading forts came and went—Fort William (1833–34) and Fort Mortimer (1842–46). Then, after the Civil War, Fort Union was sold for salvage to the U.S. Army, which cannibalized it to build Fort Buford, two-and-a-half miles east, directly above the confluence. Fort Buford was abandoned in 1895.

Nothing remains of these posts except a few buildings at Fort Buford—now a North Dakota Historic Site—where the former officers' quarters is a museum; we bivouac in a cottonwood grove about a hundred yards away. Fort Union, meanwhile, has also become a National Historic Site; archaeologists have uncovered the old foundations, and the Park Service has set up a headquarters in two mobile homes; plaques spotted here and there locate parts of the fort; and the ranger in charge has put up a teepee encampment, to show visitors how the Plains Indians lived.

MD I'd had an image of the confluence of the Yellowstone and the Missouri rivers as a remote, unapproachable spot that we would have to find on our own, scratching our way cross country on foot through forest and thicket. The confluence isn't proclaimed or advertised, goodness knows, but it's clearly marked when you get there. A narrow gravel road curves down to the bluff overlooking the meeting of the rivers, and there's a small, beautifully kept picnic park, a map of the rivers' courses, swings for children, split cordwood for fires.

This was a busy place in JJA's time. My innocent image of wild country probably came from Lewis and Clark's journals. They stopped at the confluence twice—the first time in April 1805, on their way west, and in celebration at reaching this "long-wished-for spot," a dram of spirits was issued to all hands, a fiddle produced, and the evening passed "with much hilarity, singing and dancing." In August 1806, on their return trip, the confluence was the rendezvous for Lewis and Clark, who had separated for a few days of exploration on divergent routes. Captain Clark arrived first, found the mosquitoes intolerable, and left a note for Meriwether Lewis saying that he was moving down the Missouri to another campsite. The mosquitoes, in fact, were so thick that when Lewis went hunting here, he was unable to take sight on the game because of the mosquitoes swarming in his face and around his gun barrel.

This section of the Missouri river valley is a narrow corridor,

The site of Fort Union today, looking south toward the Missouri. *MH*

perhaps two miles wide, that runs east and west. A broad, raised plateau of open prairie runs parallel to the river. On both sides of the valley are ranges of steep, seamed, rounded, bare hills that look like the giant paws of crouching lions—sand-colored in mid-day light, pink and purple at sunrise and sunset.

We've walked to the top of the northern range of hills and out onto the promontary of one of the lion paws where the entire valley is laid out before you with the Yellowstone rolling in from the south-west—the view that I think of as The Visitors' View. George Catlin did a picture of it, in 1832, during his years of travel among the Indians. So did Carl Bodmer in 1833, when he came through as illustrator for the western expedition of Prince Maximilian of Wied. Both artists featured the stronghold of Fort Union in the middle distance far below, the plain covered with teepees and Indian figures. In Bodmer's painting a party of Assiniboins with horses and dogs winds away from the fort and up into the hills at our feet.

JJA came here too: "From the top of the hills we saw a grand panorama of the most extensive wilderness, with Fort Union beneath us and far away, as well as the Yellowstone River." The barren spaces, the grandeur, and the *shape* of the land here reminded JJA of Labrador. Yes! The comparison is inevitable. We three are in agreement.

Tonight, from horizon to horizon over the northern hills, the sky shimmers with northern lights. The bonfires of the gods in Eskimo mythology. To the Plains Indians, the dance of the dead enjoying themselves in the upper regions.

In the summer months when JJA was here, the weather alternated between drenching storms and merciless heat that rose above 100° Fahrenheit. We're lucky to catch these few days of autumn, a season that's almost nonexistent in North Dakota, like spring. It's either winter or summer, and winter shuts down like a steel trap, the leaves fall, streams freeze, and the snow begins. There can be ice on the Missouri from November through most of April.

Then there are the dry spells, such as this one. The rainfall last month was measured at 1/100th of an inch, and these are the times when they'll tell you that it's so dry there's nothing left for even a rabbit to feed on. It's so dry, a rabbit has to pack a lunch to cross a field.

Carl Bodmer's Fort Union, 1833. *The New York Public Library, Rare Book Division*

Winter can set in any time now—an overnight reverse in the weather—which seems to us an impossibility in these mild blue and gold harvest days. Though Lord knows the farmers are working against the clock, combines running at night, the big, one-eyed headlights bobbling across the fields, where killdeers feed in the dark and rise, calling sweetly, when we pass. Convoys of wheat trucks drive by at full throttle in a cloud of dust, one with a fresh cornstalk nailed to the box like a feather in its cap. On the radio, a commercial advertises a drying compound for sunflower seeds: "Cuts drying time by seventy per cent . . . Get your sunflower crop to Duluth before there's ice on the Lakes . . ."

Hurry, hurry, hurry.

MH It is fair to say that Audubon and his friends spent the spring and summer simply getting acquainted with the upper Missouri valley. There were innumerable distractions from the nominal task at hand, which was to collect specimens, make drawings and write notes about the quadrupeds of the west. The birds continued to hold JJA's main attention, and there were new birds and new bird questions aplenty. Audubon was fascinated, for example, by the range of plumages in the flickers that he found at Fort Union. We see it too. Only recently has the American Ornithologists Union at last decided that they are all one species—the common flicker—with wide variation in markings, but Audubon was the one who opened the Pandora's box: "Sprague went off to procure Woodpeckers' nests," he wrote as they tried to solve the mystery, "and brought me the most curious set of five birds that I ever saw, and which I think will puzzle all the naturalists in the world." Five flicker specimens, five different sets of markings.

Then there were the curiosities of the human lives around them —the Indians, the trappers, the traders. Alexander Culbertson, the boss or *bourgeois* of Fort Union, was a splendid horseman and hunter, and loved to show off his skill at loading and firing from horseback. Culbertson's young wife, a full-blooded Blackfoot, was "herself a wonderful rider," says JJA's journal, "possessed of both strength and grace in a marked degree." He spoke of an exhibition, when "Mrs. Culbertson and her maid rode astride like men, and all rode a furious race, under whip the whole way, for more than a mile

Major Alexander Culbertson, his wife Natawista-Iksana (Medicine-Snake-Woman), who was the daughter of a Blackfoot chief, and their son Joe. Circa 1862, approximately twenty years after Audubon's visit to Fort Union. *Montana Historical Society, Helena*

on the prairie; and how amazed would have been any European lady, or some of our modern belles who boast their equestrian skill, at seeing the magnificent riding of this Indian princess—for that is Mrs. Culbertson's rank—and her servant. Mr. Culbertson rode with them, the horses running as if wild, with these extraordinary Indian riders, Mrs. Culbertson's magnificent black hair floating like a banner behind her." (The fact that Mrs. Culbertson liked to eat raw buffalo brains made him squeamish, but he admired her greatly. His surviving comments about her contrast dramatically with the sweeping rejection of "Indian poetry" that comes down to us. She had remarkable "strength and grace," he said, and was handsome, courteous, and refined. He made note of the six young mallard ducks she caught for him while she swam in the Missouri one day; of a breakfast she served him and a necklace of berries she gave him; of her working on a buffalo hide using feathers from a golden eagle she had killed; and of a night in the open when a storm struck: "Mrs. Culbertson, with her child in her arms, made for the willows, and had a shelter for her babe in a few minutes.")

As a sort of grateful guest's present—one assumes—JJA painted portraits of the Culbertsons, though he complained they didn't ever sit still long enough to be decent subjects. He recorded stories of the fur country, and arranged for Culbertson and a Fort Union clerk, Edwin Denig, to make contributions to his journal, including Denig's lengthy written description of Fort Union itself. Collecting heads from Indian corpses was all the scientific rage in those days, and JJA and Denig went out and robbed a chief's coffin that was perched, as customary, in a tree—and had been so for three years. (Denig reportedly liked his liquor at least as much as JJA did, and it is difficult to imagine their going off on this risky expedition in Indian country cold sober.)

JJA hired hunters to collect animal specimens for him; he and his companions regularly went hunting themselves. But even the best hunters often come back empty-handed; that's the nature of the enterprise. And all their hunting expeditions were controlled, to a great extent, by Fort Union's constant need for fresh meat. So there were a lot of antelope and deer and buffalo brought in, and not many interesting new rabbits and squirrels and mice. Once Audubon's younger and more active companions discovered the excitement of hunting buffalo, they seemed unable to get enough of the chase; and even Audubon remarked after having a steady diet of buffalo meat that beef was practically tasteless by comparison.

There were not only animals to be collected, skinned out and preserved, but measurements and weights to be taken, observations to be noted, drawings to be done. All this in a new country, where the presence of Indians restricted the naturalists' freedom. So they had made only a beginning by the time they left.

The Fort Buford compound is in the charge of Ed Duffey, who gave up farming without regret to take over management of the museum and the grounds. A slim, wry, savvy sort of fellow, he says he's got some Indian in his background; one-sided grin on his leather-brown face—part shyness, part fun; Stetson pulled forward, eyes squinting against the light and the smoke from his cigarette. We had checked in with him briefly when we arrived, told him our mission. But our first real encounter occurred when he graciously appeared at our campsite in the cottonwoods, bearing a recent list of wildlife species identified on the reservation; at that moment Mary and I were exchanging angry opinions at the tops of our voices about how

Edwin Thompson Denig and his wife Hai-Kees-Kak-Wee-Yah (Deer-Little-Woman), the daughter of an Assiniboin chief. Circa 1855. *Smithsonian Institution*

best to set up a wet tent in a high wind. Not the ideal way for strangers to meet. His wife, Joyce—fair complexioned, gentle, capable. The Duffeys have adopted us as house guests who happen to be living in a tent near their house. They've presented us with gifts of carrots, cucumbers, tomatoes, homemade wild grape jam, a frozen sand-pike or sauger; we've had lunch in their kitchen, and they've had supper around our picnic table. Another instant friendship.

Audubon wrote of the clay hills that begin about a mile back of the fort and roll northward away from the rivers—"to the Lord knows where." The hills are dramatic and secretive in the abrupt way they rise out of the prairie, as if defending something to the rear.

Ed Duffey loves them, and knows why: specific things he experiences and finds back in the *mauvaises terres,* while "messing around" with pick and shovel. He points south in a measured gesture and tells about digging out an entire bull-buffalo skull in perfect condition, horns and all; found it in a badlands gulch on the other side of the Missouri and carried it home on his shoulders. Most of his neighbors don't mess around back in the *mauvaises terres,* and maybe they think he's a bit crazy; he goes on exploring anyway. He's the perfect guide and companion for our adventures.

We've been looking for "Pilot's Knob," a landmark JJA mentioned. Audubon and Alexander Culbertson went there one day to peer through a telescope to see how the Opposition Company at Fort Mortimer was getting along. There's no commercial river traffic here any more; the way is blocked by power dams. So there's no need for a "Pilot's Knob," and the name seems to have vanished. But Ed thinks Audubon might have meant McKenzie's Bluff, which is back from the river at a point not far from where the Opposition fort was being undercut by the current that spring of 1843. Robert Athearn, in *Forts of the Upper Missouri,* speaks of a fur trader who "recalled how one could stand atop McKenzie's Butte . . . and watch the approach of a steamer for nearly two days before she finally crabbed her way up to the Fort's landing." If the steamboat could be seen that far off, then the butte would be similarly obvious to the river pilot. Pilot's Knob. At any rate, Ed walked me to the top of McKenzie's Bluff a few evenings past, just as the sun was setting.

This landscape takes some getting used to. I knelt to photograph a flower and filled one knee with cactus spines. Ed grinned, shook his head, told me he gave his kids new bikes once, and they rode out in a field straight off; he had to throw the tires away. A bristly, parched, weather-scoured green-gray landscape, full of clay gargoyles and orange flowers and tiny seashells. The rain, when it comes, and the snow, melting, dig new folds and gullies in *les mauvaises terres* every year. As they do, they uncover—in the tops and banks of the buttes and in the bottoms of the washes—smooth brick-red globes and loaves and duckpins and hemispheres, strange and beautiful shapes that, being harder than the surrounding clay, do not melt away in runoff. They sometimes dominate a scene, as in a gully on McKenzie's Bluff where I found the ground strewn with flattish red-brown loaves, some several feet across. These "concretions" built up around an original nut of crystal or some other obstruction in the sand as minerals washed past. It took eons, obviously, for this to happen; and the last mineral coat of iron oxide gave them the color of flower pots.

We looked out toward the vast, low horizons all around us, the broad, farm-quilted river plain of the shining Missouri and Yellowstone to the south, the rutted, knobby badlands beyond, the aqua and blue sky—pink in the west—scattered with clouds. Enormous, profound space. And I thought as the sun went down, "Now *this,* my friends, is the peace that passeth all understanding."

Ed and Joyce took us back into the badlands a few days later, and Ed dug for buffalo bones at the bottom of a steep slope. He believes the ravine may once have been a "buffalo jump," toward which the herds would be stampeded and the animals killed or crippled in their fall down the unexpected pitch. He found leg-bones and ribs and the pelvic girdle of a calf, handed them to us to heft, then tossed them aside; a man who has found a perfect bull's skull gets fussy about his specimens. We kept two jawbones, complete with teeth, to go with the pieces of mica and petrified wood Ed had picked up and presented us as we walked along in the badlands, and the small cactus Mary dug to take home. (JJA promised to bring cactus plants home to Lucy.)

Only three people could fit in the front seat of the pickup truck, so coming and going I stood in back, gripping the edges of the cab-top. As we slowly crossed long stretches of hilly prairie, I felt as if I rode a tall horse. We stopped once to look at a ring of rocks in the grass—a teepee ring, the rocks having been the anchors for the hide. And we stopped again to examine some petrified sequoia stumps. This is said to be a young terrain, geologically, yet it seems as ancient as the very earth. Seen from the perspective of the sequoia —why, John James Audubon was here in North Dakota only a few minutes ago.

MD   Below the edge of the prairie where we've camped is the site of Fort Mortimer. That stretch of bottomland is now a cultivated field, newly ploughed yesterday, and Ed Duffey is walking the furrows this morning looking for artifacts—shell caps, coins, buttons, buckles, gun parts—anything that might have surfaced when the ground was turned. JJA came this way a number of times and passed by in front of our tents and our picnic table. He and Harris paid a series of visits to Fort Mortimer that summer, driving over from Fort Union in a wagon drawn by "old Peter," whom they mentioned often in their respective journals—a stolid carthorse who stood to gunfire, said JJA, "like a stump" and was eminently suited for hunting expeditions. (I compare old Peter in my thoughts to the Queen's horse, who never so much as flinches at a 21-gun royal salute or a sudden burst of pipers and drummers.)

The visits to Fort Mortimer were in the nature of errands of mercy. "We found the place in a most miserable condition," JJA wrote, "and about to be carried away by the falling in of the banks on account of the great rise of water in the Yellowstone." The swelling current from the mouth of the Yellowstone, which lay opposite this spot in those days, did indeed swallow up Fort Mortimer's ground, and to compound the destitution of the Opposition Company, their supply boat was late, their foraging game hunters unsuccessful, and the *bourgeois*, a young man named John Collins from Hopkinsville, Kentucky, fell ill. They found him one day in a sick bed under a hide tent in the sweltering sun and the next in a leaking shanty in the pouring rain. Edward Harris, who'd been pressed into service as an impromptu physician and had been treating some of the trappers for venereal diseases, ministered to Mr. Collins. Emetics, calomel, salts, Dover's powder (opium and ipecac), and quinine. Mr. Collins survived this pharmaceutical onslaught, and a few weeks later, Harris concluded that Mr. Collins "appears to suffer more for want of good wholesome nourishment than from any other cause." They brought him "some Rice and a couple of bottles of Claret Wine."

JJA also came this way on foot. The first time was two days after his arrival at Fort Union, when he and his companions had not known to follow the cart track on the high ground, but had taken the shore route. It proved to be tough going. Harris remarked in his journal on their sticky progress through bottomland thick with undergrowth. JJA declared that he found this walk "one of the worst, the very worst upon which we ever trod; full of wild rose-bushes, tangled and matted with vines, burs, and thorns . . . and encumbered by thousands of pieces of driftwood."

Months ago, before Michael and I left home, I made a pencil check in the margin of that entry, *June 14, Wednesday, 1843,* and wrote a message to myself: "Walk it."

It's not much of a distance from Fort Mortimer to Fort Union. About three miles, according to JJA and Harris, and since they'd given fair warning against walking along the shore of the Missouri, I keep to the high ground. I start upriver past the Fort Buford cemetery. In 1896, one hundred and forty-two bodies were moved to Custer Battlefield Military National Cemetery at the Little Bighorn in Wyoming, but the wooden gravemarkers that remain testify to deaths by fever, Indian ambush, and many suicides. I pick up a dusty farm road that probably follows much the same route to Fort Union as the old cart track. It dips down past a field of sugar beets and thickets of wild roses, now in haw. A fat hen pheasant flies up noisily. Two grazing deer (does) lift their heads, freeze, stare, break, and bound away toward the river. Yellow gumweed is in bloom. Spires of sweet yellow clover (melilot). Lavender asters. Thistles and milkweed gone to seed, the down-borne seeds breaking free and floating loose in the breeze. Gray-green clumps of wormwood on a dry bank. Grasshoppers leaping, crickets singing.

A freight train whistles through a mile away at the foot of the big hills, and I squint across the mown fields, counting the cars. One hundred and twenty of them, two cabooses, and three diesel engines up front. Another dip in the road and the fields are up over my head. A dozen hen pheasants whirr away out of the stubble. A rusting cutter lies in the weeds ahead, and there are rows of white beehives set back in the cottonwoods that grow along a damp gully—Hanged Woman Coulee, it is called, though no one knows any more what happened there or who she was. An Indian woman? A settler's wife? Murder? Suicide?

I pass through the cool dampness of the trees and out into the sun again on the far side of the coulee. The road bends toward a large corrugated iron storehouse that carries a NO TRESPASSING sign, "By order of the Sheriff's Department." Mourning doves, however, roost snugly on the roof. A clutter of abandoned farm machinery lies deep in burdock and goosefoot. A single hawk soars in the sky.

The road leads onto a wooden bridge that crosses an irrigation canal—pewter-colored water, bulrushes, iron wheels to open and close the sluices. The pumping station, a weatherbeaten wooden building, is on the river. I walk down to look inside. Two new chin-high Westinghouse pumps lift the water from the Missouri and spew it into the irrigation canal through a cluster of huge oldtime wooden pipes, five feet in diameter.

I turn back to the high ground. A kestrel fights the wind. The skeleton of a small rabbit lies in the dust beside the road. Wild sunflowers are in bloom and a few small pink flowers, the five petals notched at the outer rim. It's rushpink, one of the *Lygodesmia*— purely western wildflowers.

Up on the prairie, a dirt road leads to a deserted farm—a small white frame house with an inviting front porch; chicken houses, a barn with stables, a cattle chute into a narrow corral. Hayrakes, harrows, an old buckboard, empty oil drums, a "One-Minute" hand-crank washing machine, the head (or the foot) of an iron bedstead. A tin sign reading: "Bangs Area. Untested Cattle Prohibited." A dead automobile with 1970 plates; in spray paint on the trunk, "Thank you for the Kiss." A grove of wild plums where the vegetable garden used to be. I pick and eat some as I pass (sweet, sweet) and kick up another hen pheasant. A squawk of surprise from us both.

Out beyond the corral are the tumbled, overgrown remains of the dike that once damned Garden Coulee, the water supply for the Fort Union garden. In its prime, they had an acre and a half under cultivation that "produced most plentiful and excellent crops of potatoes, corn, and every kind of vegetable." It wasn't worked the year JJA visited here, because of the constant thievery by the men at Fort

Mortimer. Another smaller garden lay closer to Fort Union where they could keep an eye on it—turnips, radishes, lettuce, onions, and also green peas that JJA helped to pick one July day—"which with a fine roast pig, made us a capital dinner." He also set down a tale about one of the Fort Union men going out with a bucket to pick peas, and at the end of the first row, he came upon a large bear, also gathering fresh green peas. The man dropped his bucket and fled, whereupon the bear helped himself to those peas too.

I've been out now about an hour, I'd guess—a stop-and-go leisurely walk—and it's another mile or so to Fort Union from Garden Coulee. The big change is not the expected one: wilderness into farmland. It's the solitude. There's the difference.

When JJA was here, this stretch along the Missouri thronged with people—the men at the two forts, their Indian wives, their children, passing hunters and trappers and Indians. The Indian encampments. The river traffic—occasional steamboats, keelboats, mackinaw boats, and the Indians' tub-shaped bullboats made from animal hides. The animals themselves, elk and antelope and buffalo. The bighorns on the bluffs across the river where white-faced steer now placidly graze.

When Fort Buford was established after the Civil War, a new throng of people filled this space—the military and their families, wagon trains and settlers, and Indians everywhere, mostly war parties. Those were years when the exchange of death and massacre between the red man and the white was an everyday event, and it would have been worth your life to venture this far from Fort Buford. From the records of interments in the Post Cemetery, one entry as an example: The death of Theon Aldrich, Citizen, September 19, 1870. "Two hundred Indians in war paint rose from the tall grass, but Aldrich did not run. He commenced pumping his Winchester . . . the plunger of his rifle became misplaced and with a despairing cry he sprang forward with his gun as a club. He was instantly hacked to pieces with tomahawks and knife-pointed war clubs. 'I have helped to kill a great many white people along this river,' said Red Shirt, Unkpapa chief, 'but I never saw one fight so well or die so bravely as that boy at the mouth of the Yellowstone.' "

Here, on this deserted farm at Garden Coulee, there was a battle between the Buford men and the Sioux, who had driven off the Fort's herd of two hundred and fifty cattle. Three soldiers killed. No one knows how many Sioux. They carried off their corpses and wounded.

The Northern Overland Pony Express had a relay station at Buford. The fort served as a base of supplies for troops and railroad men surveying the route for the Northern Pacific railroad and later for the railroad work gangs. The surveying expedition that established Canadian-American boundary lines also was based at Buford. As the west was won, Indian prisoners of war passed through here by the thousands—Nez Percé, Cheyenne, Sioux. Sitting Bull surrendered at Buford. Other famous names came and went over the years: Father Pierre Jean DeSmet—"Black Robe," the Belgian Jesuit missionary to the Indians. General Philip Sheridan, then in command of the Department of the Missouri. Capt. Paul Boynton, who made a name for himself with such feats as swimming to St. Louis by way of the Yellowstone and Missouri Rivers. And in 1896, Lt. John J. "Black Jack" Pershing, on a hunting trip with fellow officers.

After that came the homesteaders and the grain fields. Buford was a fair-sized town, big enough for a bank and a schoolhouse. Up on the hill opposite the site of Fort Union was the boom town of Mondak that straddled the border between the states—the Montana side of Main Street was wet and lined with saloons, the North Dakota side dry. At the foot of the prairie, there was a ferry boat across the Missouri. Mondak is nothing but a memory these days, gone to dust up in the clay hills. The town folded during prohibition, the last remains swept by fire in 1928. The ferry boat went out of business when the railroad built a bridge over the Missouri in 1913 and established a depot named Snowden on the far side. Its lift bridge was designed to accommodate river traffic, but river traffic went out with the arrival of automobiles and trucks and the highway systems. People no longer stayed put on their small farms but moved on into urban jobs. On the farms that are left, it takes fewer hands to do more work—specialized machinery, designed to cover hundreds of acres at a clip. As the small farms closed and trucking became the modus operandi, the grain elevator depots through this valley were also dismantled. The town of Buford was reduced to a few houses. The bank became a bar, then fell to ruin. The present bar, almost all that's left at the crossroad, is in the old school building. The post office, in the corner of what was a humming general store, will shortly close. Nothing is left for sale on the shelves of the old store but a few cartons of soda pop. And around the empty room—a few turn-of-the-century antiques, ready to swim into the trade routes. A beautifully curliqued cast-iron wall hook for receipts; a handsome bench that looks like an old church pew; a magnificent grocery counter made of oak—thick moldings and fine carvings.

The Snowden bridge still stands. It serves as the back route into Montana. (Cross the Missouri and turn left.) But crossing the bridge for the first time is scary as all get out. At our first venture, we were so terrified we turned back and didn't get our nerve up till a couple of days later. It's single lane and was built only for trains, but in the early days the farmers drove their wagons across anyway, over the ties, so the railroad line planked the bridge. It's still used for both cars and trains. You pull up at the gravel embankment, peer across (and boy, it seems a long way), look behind you down the valley, and then go. We've been assured that the freight trains make their approach at 15 mph, ready to stop in case of a head-on imbroglio midstream. By now, we're as cool as everyone else around here and hesitate only for a second at the brink. *Anything coming? Nope. Onward!*—the old planks rattling and resounding under the passage of our car, then a quick side-slip, down and away off the tracks on the other shore, and onto a gravel road.

The Snowden Depot is still on the road maps, though there's nothing left of it. The last empty wooden building—"The Bar"—was burned down in a celebratory bonfire by the 1975 high school graduating class of Fairview, Montana.

I drop down off the tumbled abutment of the Garden Coulee dam and cross the gully. A sidehill wheatfield is ahead of me. The wind from the north is in my face, the sun from the south on my back. Another freight train—108 cars and 3 engines—whistles through in the opposite direction, setting up a whirlwind of doves and flickers. Fort Union should come into sight, any step now. As I gain the brow of the hill, the tepee poles with the fluttering flags of fur and cloth rise out of the plain. Five steps more and the peaks of the tepees rise. Three more steps and the encampment lifts into full view, a mile away against the horizon. It is a moment to stop and stare. The mown

Fort Union tepee village. *MH*

field is gold, the tepees white, and the sky behind them is a deep September blue.

I know what lies behind the tepees—the mobile homes of the Fort Union office—but this knowledge only heightens my awareness of solitude. The Indian encampment is an illusion, an empty, make-believe village, and on this walk, where it would once have been impossible to have gone three miles without meeting someone else or at least seeing a figure in the landscape, I have seen no one, not even from a distance.

I start across the long wheatfield. Somewhere through here, on one of their returns from Fort Mortimer, JJA and Harris came upon a wolf ambling across the prairie. They gave chase, with old Peter pulling the wagon, the wolf at a slow careless canter until he saw an Indian in his path and veered off into a ravine. There's nothing moving within my view today—except the sudden charge of our car down the road from Fort Buford. Mike is looking for me. I jump up and down and wave from the wheat field, but I'm too far away and he can't see me through the blinding bubble of dust that envelops the car.

At the Fort Union boundary, I am stopped by the government's barbed wire fence that's strung so tautly between the metal posts I can't lift the bottom strand and skin underneath. I follow the fence down to where it ends at the river bank, slide down the bluff, and crawl up the other side onto Fort Union land. I circle through the empty tepees and out into the parking lot.

"My last upper tooth fell out of my mouth the other day," JJA wrote home, "and I now must soak my biscuits &c." He assured the family, however, that he felt better than he had for years. He was fifty-eight when he made the Missouri River trip, but whatever it was that troubled him, JJA chalked it up to old age, and with his characteristic gift for prevarication, he tacked an extra decade onto his life. In one journal entry at Fort Union, he wrote: "We are now to have a regular Buffalo hunt, where I must act only as a spectator; for, alas! I am now too near seventy to run and load while going at full gallop." In a second entry, when the others were setting out on a hunting trip after bighorn sheep: "I, alas! am no longer young and alert enough for the expedition."

All aches and pains aside, he had a good time and his strength was not tried to the limit. Fort Union, in terms of frontier life in Indian country, was a comfortable place to be. The American Fur Company and the Chouteaus were first-rate hosts to visiting celebrities. Not only did they lend JJA a hundred dollars pocket money before he left St. Louis, they also hired as JJA's escort and guide the legendary wilderness-wise *voyageur*, Etienne Provost, "The Old Man of the Mountains," who had more than thirty years on the Upper Missouri under his belt and who squired Audubon from St. Louis to Fort Union and back again. (Provost also traveled with George Catlin, and he appears twice in a collection of pictures done by Alfred Jacob Miller, the illustrator on Sir William Drummond Stewart's western trip in 1837.)

JJA had his own quarters, and besides his troop of younger men at his command, he had all services, courtesies, and attentions from the staff at Fort Union. And the pleasure of a good table. Catlin had written that on his visit here every dinner was accompanied by madeira and port, served chilled in a pail of ice. Other guests wrote of their astonishment at sumptuous spreads that included wheat cakes with fresh butter, coffee with fresh cream, chocolate, omelettes made with fresh eggs, fresh bread hot from the oven, and fresh meat and vegetables. One visitor wrote in his diary that his eyes "almost ran over with tears," the first day he sat down to a Fort Union meal. Audubon also dined here on dog, a dish offered by the Culbertsons. "With great care and some repugnance I put a very small piece in my mouth; but no sooner had the taste touched my palate than I changed my dislike to liking, and found this victim of the canine order most excellent . . . Old Provost had told me he preferred it to any meat . . ."

Guests were further entertained with dances, as was JJA—an evening of cotillions and reels, with clarinet, fiddle, and drum, and the Indian women attached to the fort attired in their best. Buffalo hunts were arranged, feats of horsemanship staged on the prairie flats in front of the fort, and at sunset there was always the sport of wolf shoots from the palisades—one of Harris' favorite after-supper pursuits.

When Audubon camped out, it was no longer a matter of rolling up on the ground in buffalo robe. There were tents, mosquito netting, and inflatable rubber mattresses. One touch of "roughing it," remarked by both JJA and Harris, was an overnight trip across the river into the badlands where there was no firewood. "Mr. Audubon & I," wrote Harris, "made ourselves useful in carrying Buffalo dung to the camp to make a fire, and while so employed we would laugh outright at the idea of our friends at home having a peep at us . . . piling on one arm the *Prairie wood,* which we had to embrace very closely to prevent its falling, and when the capping piece was placed on the pile, clapping our chins upon it to secure its safe passage to the camp."

Yes, there was danger. Yes, it was wilderness and there was the chance of Indian attacks. But Fort Union wasn't a patch on the campground at the junction of the Ohio and the Mississippi in the frozen, snowbound forest twenty-five years before, with Ferdinand Rozier lying in his rug by the fire, day after day, while JJA rousted about with the boatmen and the Indian swan hunters. That had been long ago and far away. Now, he watched buffalo hunts from a carriage on a bluff. He rarely traveled on horseback, and when he did, old Peter was his choice of mount—the stolid and dependable carthorse, slow but sure, while the others rode circles around the two of them and dropped back to urge old Peter onward. I also notice in his journal the number of occasions he went fishing . . . alone.

His vanity, nonetheless, was still intact. In a description of a hunter assigned to him on the upriver journey, JJA remarked: "He wears his hair long about his head and shoulders, as I was wont to do; but being a half-breed, his does not curl as mine did."

In *The Quadrupeds of North America,* JJA spoke of the thirteen-lined ground squirrel as a creature "of exquisite beauty" that he found to be "Quite abundant near Fort Union, on the Upper Missouri." I've sat on the office steps at Fort Union fruitlessly waiting for their resident thirteen-liners to appear, but saw my first today at Fort Buford. It had been a neighbor at our campsite all along—a sleek and quick little creature, this one not more than eight inches long, including its tail, and easy to miss unless you catch it in motion. The narrow stripes of brown and yellow on the ground squirrel's back blend together, in the eye of the beholder, into a dull greenish hue that melts into the prairie, and when a ground squirrel moves, it steals

Engraving of Audubon's thirteen-lined ground squirrel. The Missouri-Yellowstone confluence is the background; Fort Union appears between the two squirrels. *Library of Congress*

through the grass like a weasel. Like all rodents, it sits up to survey
the terrain (black shoe button eyes) and it sits up nicely to eat (nib-
bling on a grasshopper as though eating an ear of corn).

Joyce Duffey says that she's always wondered what they did with
the dirt. A good question. There's not a crumb of dirt at the entrance
to the burrow, no telltale mound to give away the location as there
is at the entrance to a woodchuck's den or a prairie dog's burrow.

From our field guides in the back-seat library, I learn that thirteen-lined ground squirrels eat mice, small birds, plants, and seeds,
as well as insects. I can further report from my own experiment that
thirteen-lined ground squirrels do *not* eat granola. At least, this one
doesn't. I sprinkled some in the grass near its burrow—a tentative
taste, a thoughtful chew, and it went back to its diet of grasshoppers.

Joyce also tells us, wincing at the memory of it, that when she was
a schoolchild there was an annual event known as Gopher Day
(ground squirrels are generally called gophers around here). The
children were given a bounty of a penny apiece for "gopher" tails.
The animals were caught with nooses made of binder twine placed
around the burrow. She pantomimes the procedure—when the animal's head pops up out of the ground, jerk the noose tight; swing
gopher at end of noose to strangle it; then swing by the tail, which
comes off in your hand. She used to save the tails in her father's
Prince Albert tobacco cans and take them into town on Gopher Day
to collect her bounty.

These prairie fields churn with crickets, and our campground
seethes with them—crickets scurrying, searching, scavenging, feeding ravenously on any small tidbit. Under our picnic table, a minute
sliver of paper from a cheese wrapping is found and gobbled down.
A spot on the ground where food or fat was spilled is feasted upon.
The underground trash can that opens with a foot treadle is alive
with them. They are cannibals as well, pouncing upon and devouring
their dead fellows.

They also eat gum, a mint-flavored variety that I've taken to in
an effort to stop smoking. When I offered the crickets a chewed wad,
I precipitated a daylong battle for the possession of said gum—fierce
charges and attacks, the crossing of antennae as though crossing
swords, the winner wrapping its front legs around the prize and
clutching the chewing gum to its bosom, kicking out with its back

legs when another cricket stole up from the rear. An occasional tug-of-war, a cricket at either end of the wad of gum. Sometimes a kind of truce was declared, two or three quietly feeding on it together, share and share alike, until one of them was overcome by greed and beat off the others. Thus it went until nightfall, when the gum vanished.

The crickets nest after dark in hairline cracks in the ground, and as you tread upon their hideaways, the earth beneath your feet sings with alarmed chirpings. In the morning, they wait in their nests until the sun has warmed the prairie. As I sit inside the door of the tent with my cup of coffee, contemplating the new day, I know that when the crickets begin to emerge—antennae here, antennae there, testing the temperature—the chill of night is gone and it's time to be up and about.

Grasshoppers are plentiful too. In *The Oregon Trail* Francis Parkman wrote that the Dakota Indians called them by a name meaning "They who point out the buffalo," and he described an Indian oracle talking to a grasshopper held respectfully between thumb and finger, and saying: "Tell me, my father, where must we go tomorrow to find the buffalo?" The insect twisted about and at last pointed westward. The oracle dropped him gently on the grass, laughed with great glee, and said, "If we went that way in the morning, we would be sure to kill plenty of game."

MH   The Granddaughter's Edition of his journals includes a landscape sketch by Audubon, "Camp at the Three Mamelles." He drew it during a two-day hunt for buffalo cows at the end of July. "I hope to see a fair picture from this, painted by Victor, this next winter," he wrote.

The Three Mamelles, or Three Buttes, were a landmark. But neither Audubon's nor Harris' journal told us what direction they lay from the fort, and our guides and mentors at Fort Union and Fort Buford had never heard of the place. So this would require some of my justly famous detective work. Leafing between the two journals and their descriptions of the hunt, with a map of the confluence before me, I guessed that Audubon & Co. had gone off somewhere "between the rivers," in the broad Y marked out by the westward winding Missouri and the southwestward-winding Yellowstone. The modern survey maps I looked at didn't add any information. So late in the morning we struck off uncertainly into Montana, heading southwest along the valley of the Yellowstone. At Sydney, about twenty miles from the confluence, we stopped for lunch at a Dairy Queen, where I asked the proprietor—without much hope, I may say —if he'd heard of the Three Mamelles or the Three Buttes. Sure, he had. The Three Buttes? His daughter lived out that way, and he could give us directions. Exultant, I wrote them down and we took our junk lunch to the car, parked in the shade of the Dairy Queen. The proprietor suddenly appeared at the car window to tell us that he had checked his directions by telephone with his daughter and, in fact, had got them wrong; here were the right ones. We drove eastward on gravel roads, stones whanging against the undercarriage, and as we ascended a slight rise, three steep brown knobs began to lift above the ridgeline close on our left. There they were! The Three Buttes—not from the perspective of the drawing, but unmistakeable. Below us at the end of the road was a cluster of buildings, and there we found the flashing-eyed, silver-haired widow, Alice Prevost, mistress of Three Buttes Ranch. I began to explain our presence, waving in one hand the tattered paperback volume of *Audubon and His Journals,* open to the appropriate page. Alice Prevost caught sight of the Audubon sketch. "Where did they get a picture of *my* buttes?"

Audubon's sketch of the Three Buttes, 1843. *From* Audubon and His Journals, *1897.*

The Three Buttes. *MH*

she exclaimed, reaching for the book.

Alice Prevost already knew of John James Audubon as an historic figure, artist, and ornithologist. But with the book and sketch now in her hands, he suddenly leaped out of the pages of history onto her ranch—where he had hunted her land, drawn water from her creek, sketched her buttes, camped in her fields. She was as excited to see the drawing as we were to find the buttes, and said she wished we'd come along a few weeks earlier, since she'd just written an article about the buttes for the local newspaper.

Audubon and his companions, after a day's buffalo chase, had pitched their tents on the far side of the little creek, whose course we could trace by the line of trees running behind the Prevost house. The next morning, with "the birds singing all around us," the artist had walked up the hill back of the camp (back of the house) and while Harris and Culbertson climbed one of the buttes in the view, he sat to sketch the scene: the tent, two carts resting on their empty shafts, a standing figure, a smoking campfire, the line of trees along the creek, and—across from the slope where he sat—Alice Prevost's buttes. No, of course she wouldn't mind if we walked up the slope to find the spot where Audubon had done his sketch. She didn't think there were any steers on that part of the range. "Just watch out for rattlesnakes," she said. "They're moulting. Someone saw one last week. When they're moulting, they can't rattle and give you a warning."

We crisscrossed the dusty short-grass pasture slope above the creek for half an hour, comparing the drawing and the buttes as we went. Occasionally Mary left off to look for new wildflowers. I was never absolutely satisfied that I had found the spot. I think that time, water, winds, and use had changed the scene a little, moved a row of cottonwoods, smoothed a curve here, depressed a line there. And who's to say that Audubon's sketch was precisely faithful to the scene to begin with? Doubtless it wasn't. I myself took a number of photographs so that those who follow in *our* footsteps (should anything so heart-warming occur) will have a more precisely reliable record to go by.

We crossed the creek and its bright green tunnel of cottonwood trees (Audubon's party had found a grizzly's paw print in there), passed the house and farm buildings, and trod in Harris' footsteps, more or less, by climbing the highest butte in JJA's drawing. Underfoot were the "water rolled pebbles of great variety, such as are found in many places on the sea shore," which Harris had noted. And from the crest of the steep cone, as Harris promised, "we had a most extensive view," with the prairie and *mauvaises terres* rolling away in all directions.

Below us, three hundred feet down and nearly a half a mile away, lay the ranch. We descended to a pitcher of fresh, ice-cold lemonade in the hands of the younger Prevost boy. It was made from pure spring water, Alice Prevost assured us—not the sulphury, alkaline stuff we've found hereabouts.

We leaned on the white board fence in front of her white clapboard house, drinking lemonade and talking. Since the death of her husband two years ago, Alice Prevost has a new partner she did not expect—the federal government. She, who jointly owned the 6000-acre ranch with her husband, must pay inheritance taxes in order to keep the place—plus interest, because it will take her ten years to pay. The bright blue eyes in the handsome, patrician face are snap-

ping-angry as she tells us how her husband's father came down from
Quebec to homestead Three Buttes Ranch. She and her husband
added to the land and to the establishment, while they raised steers
and Morgan horses and poultry. "You work all your life to pay for a
place," she says, "and then the government owns it, and you have to
pay for it all over again."

The boys, still in school, are not yet big enough to do her husband's work, and hired men are hard to keep, she adds, especially if
a woman is in charge. "They won't take orders from a woman. They'll
do it their way, and if it turns out wrong, then they're mad because
I was right." So the tax-delinquent widow with two school-age boys
leases out most of the ranch to survive. Not the way she'd thought
things would go. Her sense of life's injustice is compounded by the
government's injustice. A nearby ranch is operated, mostly in ab-
sentia, by movie stars, she says (without naming names). A tax dodge.
And when a blizzard stranded their cattle herd, no one went out to
save the animals. The caretakers didn't give a damn, and as far as the
owners were concerned, it was a write-off, and they were home free.
Yet the people who care about raising animals and do so as a livelihood are in a box.

She told us of riding horseback to the Buttes with George; she
spoke of how hard he worked, and how the dog barks at everyone
since the evening George, stricken with a heart attack, was carried
from the house; and when Mary asked her the local name for a shrub
that bears white berries, Alice Prevost shook her head—didn't know
—just a weed—"but if George was here, he'd know."

Did we like beef, she asked as we were leaving. They'd just
slaughtered some beef, and she'd like us to have some. The generosity of plainspoken strangers, again. She brought her gift out of the
house in a brown paper bag. "I put in some eggs and a cucumber
too," she said. In the car on the road north, we discovered she had
given us, besides the cucumber and a dozen eggs, two big sirloin
steaks and five T-bones, frozen. Having found the Three Buttes of
Audubon's drawing, and knowing we were the first to make that
connection, I think we would have been perfectly happy with hard-
tack for supper. But Alice Prevost had given us materials for a suitable celebration. We set two T-bones on the dashboard and turned

on the defroster, so the steaks would be melted by the time we reached camp.

The Prevost ranch epitomizes the white man's history in the Dakotas: most of this land was settled by the parents or perhaps the grandparents of people living here today. It's still immediate firsthand history.

MD   On our way back to camp we met a train at the Snowden bridge, for the first time. The engineer saw us coming in a cloud of road dust, down the Yellowstone out of Montana, and he waited on his side of the river, the big diesel idling at the mouth of the bridge on the opposite bank. When we dropped down off the tracks and I leaned out my window to wave our thanks, the greeting was returned by a smiling, fashionplate of an engineer—bright red kerchief around his neck, a blue shirt with big white polka dots and an engineer's cap to match.

GOING HOME

MH In the second week of August Audubon concluded it was
time to go home. "I have scarcely done anything but write this day,"
says his journal for the ninth, "and my memorandum books are now
crowded with sketches, measurements, and descriptions." A Mackinaw boat was being built to carry him and his companions to St. Louis
with all their gear and collections; it would be forty feet long—not
big enough, Audubon believed (in fact, they would exchange it for
a bigger one at Fort Pierre), nonetheless he wanted to get started as
soon as it was ready. On the eleventh he told Harris of his decision.
Harris, he reported, was "quite startled." Well he might have been;
Harris knew as well as Audubon that they still lacked much of what
they'd come for. Five days later JJA put his back to the unknown for
the last time and started down the Missouri.

Early in September they were stopped by high winds for three
and a half days somewhere below the Moreau River in present-day
South Dakota. Banks and islands in the vicinity are drowned by the
lake that backs up from Oahe Dam, but there'd be no finding the
place anyway, for the remnants of JJA's journal do not keep close
track of the geography. He and his friends made the best use they
could of the forced halt and went hunting for food and specimens.
"Mr. J. G. Bell, on his return from a walk up the river shore, where
he had shot some [Passenger] Pigeons, started [a bird] . . . from the
ground. It flew a few yards, and [he] took it for our common Whip-
poor-will; but on its second rising and flying again before him, he saw
that it was a much smaller bird, fired at it, and fortunately brought

it to me, fresh and beautiful though dead." JJA was delighted. His friend Thomas Nuttall had reported seeing a small version of the whip-poor-will in the Rocky Mountains years before but had not collected a specimen. This bird must be the very species, said JJA, and on the spot he named it Nuttall's whip-poor-will.

Late that afternoon they moved the boat a few miles downriver to set up camp on an island. "About ten o'clock Harris called me to hear the notes of the new Whip-poor-will; we heard two at once, and the sound was thus: 'Oh-will, oh-will,' repeated often and quickly, as in our common species."

Nuttall's whip-poor-will—now just the poor-will on North American checklists—was the last new species discovered by an Audubon Galloping Party. His boat reached St. Louis well before the ice, and Ferdinand Rozier was there, up from Ste. Genevieve to greet him.

He must have known, as he crossed the Appalachians eastward that fall, that he would not go on any more expeditions. He felt he was "getting an old man"; on his way down the Missouri he had "missed my footing on getting into the boat" one evening "and bruised my knee and my elbow, but at seventy and over I cannot have the spring of seventeen." Seventy and over—though he was not yet sixty! But he felt old, all right. He'd come tantalizingly close this summer but had not seen the Rockies; he had not seen the Pacific coast of his "own dear Country." He had proved to himself that he was not up to the physical or spiritual demands of collecting for the *Quadrupeds;* his specimens and notes from the west were spotty, given the one short season he'd just spent and the inevitable fascination he and his companions had felt for the big-game hunts and other sights on the American wilderness frontier. Now he would have to face the insatiable scientific curiosity and certain disappointment of the stay-at-home Bachman over what had not been accomplished or learned; in fact, it would be years before he let his friend read the journal of the expedition, even as they worked on the project— Bachman in Charleston, JJA in New York.

A young naturalist, who met Audubon along the way, described him as hale, erect, sharp-eyed, wearing a white beard down to his chest—and given to long silences punctuated by impulsive and fragmentary conversation. To me this does not sound like our garrulous companion of earlier days—as if he were not altogether pleased with himself and his lot. . . . But perhaps his mind was already luxuriating at Minnies Land.

The meeting took place on a canal boat between Pittsburgh and Philadelphia, on that amazing, ill-considered engineering tour-de-force, the Pennsylvania Canal, which went up over the mountains and down the other side. This route consisted only partly of canals and locks—sixty-six locks in one hundred and four miles on the western side and one hundred and eight locks in one hundred and seventy-two miles on the east slope. The capstone of this edifice was indeed at the top; for between Johnstown and Hollidaysburg, a distance of about thirty-five miles, a climb of more than a thousand feet had to be negotiated on each side. By 1843, this was accomplished on the Portage Railroad. "There are ten inclined planes," wrote Charles Dickens, who made the trip in 1842, "five *as*cending and five *de*scending; the carriages are dragged up the former and let slowly down the latter by stationary engines . . . Occasionally the rails are laid upon the extreme verge of a giddy precipice; and . . . the traveller gazes sheer down without a stone or scrap of fence between, into the mountain depths below."

At the very top was an inn, a halfway house, built of stone; the canal was soon put out of business by the rise of less fanciful railroading, and most of its course has been obliterated, but the inn still stands and is a National Historic Landmark. We saw it on a dark, snowy December afternoon—the handsome gray house, and on either side, tracks laid downhill, west and east, along broad avenues through the gray-and-white woods.

MD   On the last leg of our journey, we also cross the mountains —to the south in Virginia. It is mid-May. We're here to visit one of our last Audubon landmarks, the Natural Bridge, where he won a wager once upon a time. He tells the story in his essay on phoebes —an essay in which five pages are devoted to a tender and total recall of the phoebes he studied and banded in the little cave on Perkiomen Creek at Mill Grove. (What other memories of Mill Grove surged at that writing?)

The Natural Bridge, a limestone arch over Cedar Creek, is two

This sketch, done from memory in the 1880s by George W. Storm, a local artist, shows the inn Lemon House, at the highest point on the Allegheny Portage Railroad. *American Canal and Transportation Center, York, Pennsylvania*

hundred and fifteen feet high and spans ninety feet. Because of the contour of the gorge and the many trees, one cannot see any part of the arch from the road above. "My companion," said Audubon, "who had passed over this natural bridge before, proposed a wager that he could lead me across it before I should be aware of its existence." They trotted on. JJA heard the notes of a phoebe. They were nearing the bridge, he announced. "The surprise of my companion was great. 'How do you know this?' he asked." It was simple, JJA replied. Since he knew the nesting habits of the phoebe, he knew that a cave or a deep rocky creek was at hand. And indeed, phoebes "rose from under the bridge in numbers." The bet was won.

Motels and hotels. A convention center. A mammoth parking lot. Neon signs. Lift rides. Souvenirs. A winding walk down to Cedar Creek, the limestone bridge arching above. When George Washington came this way as an apprentice surveyor, aged sixteen, he climbed up into the arch and carved his initials on a rock. In 1774, Thomas Jefferson bought the bridge and one hundred and fifty-seven acres from the Crown for twenty shillings and built a cabin here for two slaves who served as hosts and guides for visitors. During the Revolution and the War of 1812, the bridge was used as a shot tower, molten lead dropped from the heights above into the cold water of the creek. A later owner, one Captain Lackland, suspended an iron carriage from the bridge, and visitors were lowered by windlass while a Negro musician played appropriate airs on a violin.

The Indians had called it The Bridge of God, and Jefferson wrote that "so beautiful an arch, so elevated, so light, and springing, as it were, up to heaven," aroused the most sublime of emotions. The present management plays up this religious theme. Old-fashioned hymns whoofle from loudspeakers in the rocks. An after-dark light show is advertised—a dramatization of the seven days of creation accompanied by an eclectic musical score that ranges through *La Traviata* and *Tannhauser* to "The End of a Perfect Day."

Kenilworth ivy grows on the walls, swallowtail butterflies hover. Washington's initials are still there, thirty-five feet above the creek. Wood thrush, Carolina wren, Louisiana waterthrush, rough-winged swallows, nighthawks, least flycatcher, cardinals, and robins feed around the bridge. And in the ledges up under the arch—the mud nests of Audubon's phoebes. The young have hatched and are grown enough to begin exercising their wings. The parent phoebes fly in with food, occasionally resting to sing a few notes. The music of the hymns reverberates over all, amplified by the sounding board of the arch and drowning out the natural sounds of the water and the birds. It was amusing at first to hum along and sing along. "The Doxology." "What a Friend We Have in Jesus." "The Old Rugged Cross." But enough is enough. Give sublimity a chance. For heaven sakes, turn off that confounded recording!

Notes from our last campsite, Cave Mountain Lake, Jefferson National Forest, Virginia:

May 16. Overhead, a spectacular sky-fight between two hawks, a redtail and a sharpshin, the redtail doing barrel rolls and flipping onto its back to defend itself against the smaller hawk. Then they leave our patch of sky and carry the fight over the ridge and out of sight. A babbling brook. Purple skullcap, showy orchis, and Deptford pinks in bloom. Peepers singing. Catbirds, scarlet tanagers, Swainson's thrush. No one else is here. Perfection.

After tonight, we'll be in cities all the way (Washington, Philadelphia, New York) and this perfect place has plunged both of us into a black melancholy. Mike snarls at the fire, swears at the pots and pans, sits down at the picnic table, chin in the palm of his hand, and stares fixedly into the woods. I mope in grim silence over my dinner.

Fireflies come out. One shooting star falls down the sky. I open my notebook and write in heavy, slashing, capital letters—I DON'T WANT TO GO HOME.

MH This trimmed-down existence suits us. Mary likes to tell the exemplary tale of the piano-player and the tent. We had set up camp one afternoon in North Dakota next to a big Winnebago, which proved to be the traveling home of a touring jazz pianist who went by the name Sunshine. The morning we left, he came out to see us off. I packed the car, Mary struck the tent, and it all took only a few minutes. As Mary was finishing, Sunshine said. "Will you look at that. That woman has just rolled up her house and put it in a sack." "I loved it," says Mary, and she means not just the comment but the fact.

I wish our traveling companion Mr. Audubon had had the chance to cross the Rockies to the Pacific, and to get to Arizona, for instance,

The Natural Bridge, engraved by W. J. Bennet after a painting by J. C. Ward.
The New York Public Library, Prints Division

and Hudson's Bay, James Bay, northwestern Canada . . . Oh, I could write him a wonderful itinerary.

MD When Audubon returned to the house on the Hudson (embraces and kisses for everyone waiting on the verandah—Lucy, sons, daughters-in-law, grandchildren) the town of New York was still well to the south. "That crazy city," as he called it. "I wonder that men consent to swelter and fret their lives away amid those hot bricks and pestilent vapors . . . Great New York with all its humbug, rascality, and immorality." Out in the country at West 155th Street, the family lived in a rural Eden. Oaks, chestnuts, pines, tulip trees. A brook. A waterfall. Fruit orchards and gardens. A stable, dairy, poultry yards, enclosures for deer, elk, wolves, fox, marten and other wild animals. A landing on the river. Boats. "Fish—whenever we draw the seine." Near the main house, a studio barn. And eventually, two more houses built by John and Victor as their families grew. (Both men had married again after their first wives, the Bachman sisters, died of TB.)

The driving project was the completion of *The Quadrupeds of North America.* There was data to gather, pictures to be painted with his son John as co-illustrator, and subscriptions to be raised for the work in progress. Audubon hated the business trips—the canvassing for subscribers—although he was wined and dined by the great, the famous, and the influential. He once wrote from Baltimore that the amount of attention he received was "bewildering" to him: "The very streets resound with my name, and I feel quite alarmed and queer as I trudge along." But for the rest, his letters and journals spoke of "fatigue beyond description," of his feet swollen from pounding the pavements, of homesickness and anxious dreams. On a selling trip to the north, the Albany steamer passed the house on the Hudson, handkerchiefs were waved from the shore, JJA waved his hat in return, his sons came out in their sailboat to bid him adieu, as the steamer pulled away upstream. The sailboat faded in the distance; Audubon bent his head and wept.

The *Quadrupeds* project, however, was in dire straits. Scientific notes that Bachman needed were not forthcoming from the Audubon household. Field studies that should have been completed on the Missouri River trip had been neglected. Bachman was in alternate despair and rage, writing letter after letter for reference books and

The Audubon house, lithograph, *Valentine's Manual,* 1865. *Museum of the City of New York*

for specimens of quadrupeds that never arrived: "Wake up and work as you used to," he wrote to JJA, "when we banged at the Herons and roared at the fresh-water Marsh hens." But the unthinkable was coming to pass. Audubon now spoke of himself as "a poor old man." His eyes began to trouble him, he would not wear glasses, he could no longer paint, and then—as though the drives and passions that possessed him for a lifetime had burned out the circuits of his brain —JJA drifted off into the never-never land of senility.

Bachman did not know the truth of the situation until he came to New York in 1848 and saw for himself. From a letter (now in the Bachman Collection at the Charleston Museum):

"My Dear Maria—The Girls say I have been snoring loud & strong in an arm chair with my feet on the hot fender this chilly evening . . . I had best try to shake off lethargy by writing a few lines to you. . . . The old Gentleman has just gone to bed after having eaten his eleventh meal, handed his [snuff] box all round, kissed all the Ladies & heard his little evening song in French. . . . The old Lady is as straight as an arrow—in fine health but much worried—what with her particularity in house keeping—her looking over the advertisements for maids—(plenty of trouble in these changes) & taking care of the poor old Gentleman.

"His is indeed a most melancholy case. I have often sat down sad & gloomy in witnessing a ruin, that I had seen in other years in order & neatness, but the ruins of a mind once bright & full of imagination is still more melancholy to the observer. The outlines of his countenance & his general robust form are there, but the mind is all in ruins. But why dwell upon it. Imagine to yourself a crabbed restless uncontrollable child—worrying & bothering every one & you have not a tythe of a description of this poor old man. He thinks of nothing but eating—scarcely sits down two minutes at a time, hides hens' eggs—rings the bell every five minutes calling the people to dinner & putting the old Lady into all manner of troubles. But I turn away from the subject with a feeling of sadness. . . . Mrs. Aud. is going to town maid hunting & I will send this by her."

The following year Victor wrote to the Bachmans: "My poor old father is apparently comfortable, and enjoys his little notions, but has no longer any feelings of interest for any of us and requires the care of a man—This is the hardest of all to bear, among the trials in store for us." Meanwhile, the family kept news of "his melancholy case" as quiet as possible, for fear of tarnishing his public image.

Audubon died on January 27, 1851, aged 65, and was buried in the Trinity churchyard on the hill.

Michael and I come up out of the day-glo spray-decorated subway at Broadway and 157th Street and walk two blocks south to West 155th Street and up the steep front steps of the Trinity Chapel of the Intercession—a cool, high-vaulted, Gothic building. Ecclesiastical banners are hung from the clerestory in the medieval fashion, rich splashes of blue from the stained glass windows are strewn across the flagstone floor. We go out through a side door into the green forested sanctuary of the graveyard. Fresh spring grass touched with white clover. Sycamore, maple, oak, and beech trees dappling the grass and the headstones with tender shadows. Squirrels. Nesting birds—robins, starlings, house sparrows, pigeons. A soft breeze. Soft spring sunshine.

The last daguerreotype of Audubon, taken in New York City about 1850. *From National Audubon Society*

The monument, placed on JJA's grave by the New York Academy of Sciences in 1893, is in the design of a Celtic cross (a curious choice to commemorate a man of French descent). The Henry Inman head of Audubon is carved on the base. Another surface carries an artist's palette with brushes, another shows a huntsman's gear—the powder-horn, crossed rifles, a game bag. Birds and animals decorate the tall shaft. A dove, great horned owl, pelican, hawk, crow, swallow, cormorant, prairie chicken, roseate spoonbill, albatross, wild turkey, vulture; a bat, squirrel, rabbit, opossum, wolf, mountain lion, deer, bear, caribou, bison, badger. The legend reads: "All ye beasts and cattle, bless ye the lord, praise him and magnify him forever."

Michael takes photographs. I take notes—white chickweed in bloom at the base of the monument, a drift of dry maple-seed wings—and at that moment I realize for the first time that I know more about John James Audubon than I do about anyone else in the world, except myself. I know more about him than I do about my husband, my children, my parents. I've read his journals, his mail, his anecdotes, his essays, the complete accounting—the vanities, lies and

Audubon's grave. *MH*

blather, follies and furors, the triumphs and the failures. We've stood in his tracks, tramped his woods and marshes, his riverbanks and seashores, climbed his hills, seen his vistas, slept under his skies and his moon. We have followed him down the arches of the years, and this moment, at his gravesite, is the day of his death. It's done.

My throat tightens and my eyes fill with tears. I don't say a word to Michael (my voice would break and I'd burst into tears for fair), but put on my dark glasses to hide my eyes and wander away for a walk through the rest of the cemetery, away from the image of self weeping at Audubon's tomb. (*There* would be a tableau for the yard-men and anyone looking out the windows of the parish office.)

Near a tool shed, at the end of leafy winding path, I meet Mr. Buchanan (his name on the pocket of his green jumpsuit), who apparently is in charge of the grounds. He tells me there are lots of robins this year. "They like the rain," he explains. "It softens the ground. Makes it easier to catch earthworms." He points out a catalpa tree, a Japanese pine, a tulip tree, and a mulberry tree that grows on a sharp ridge sheered away on the far side of the cemetery wall to accommodate 153rd Street. In the Battle of Washington Heights on November 16, 1776, the redoubt on that ridge was the second line of defense, held by the 3rd Pennsylvania Battalion and the Connecticut Rangers. (*A battle. The dead.* More tears well up behind my dark glasses.)

On the south side of Broadway, toward 156th Street, is Audubon Terrace, built on what was once their woodlands. An open plaza, a row of handsome buildings in the classical mode: The Museum of the American Indian, The American Geographical Society, The American Numismatic Society, The American Academy of Arts and Letters, and The Hispanic Society of America.

On the north side of Audubon Terrace is a pool (empty) and a surrounding sculpture court, magnificent figures in bronze and lime-stone by Anna Hyatt Huntington. El Cid, mounted on a warhorse, holds aloft a bannered spear. Don Quixote. Boabil (the last Moorish king of Granada). Animal groups—a red stag, a red doe and fawn, jaguars, wild boars, vultures, lions, brown bears.

From the Manhattan phone book:

Audubon Auto Club
Audubon Auto School
Audubon Ballrooms Inc.
Audubon Billiards Club
Audubon Cycle Shop
Audubon Film, Inc.
Audubon Freezair Service
Audubon Garage
Audubon Gas Range & Refrigeration
Audubon Health Bldg.
Audubon Health Offices, Inc.
Audubon Ignition Co.
Audubon Magazine
Audubon Metalwove Belt Corp.
Audubon Plumbing Co., Inc.
Audubon Society
Audubon Touring Service
Audubon Travel Agency
Audubon TV Service
Audubon Uptown Florist
Audubon Welding & Boiler Service, Inc.

There is an Audubon Avenue in uptown Manhattan. There used to be an Audubon telephone exchange before the numbers went digital. The portrait of General Andrew Jackson in the New York city hall is half Jackson, half Audubon. JJA posed for the torso in 1824 when Vanderlyn was painting the portrait, "since my figure resembled that of the General, more than any he had ever seen." In the American Hall of Fame, at the Bronx Community College, is a bronze bust of Audubon done by Alexander Stirling Calder, who also did the bust of William Penn there. (Calder, the father. Not his sculptor son whose forte was mobiles and stabiles.) Otherwise, the only monument to him in Manhattan is on his grave, though a year after his death it had been proposed that a statue be erected in Audubon's honor in Central Park. Somehow or other, the grand plan was lost in the shuffle.

In 1932, the Audubon house, on a last shred of its original forty acres, still overlooked the Hudson from a wooded grove in the shadow of the uphill curving arm of Riverside Drive. There had been

John Vanderlyn's protrait of Andrew Jackson for which Audubon posed for the figure. In her biography of Audubon, Alice Ford suggests that Vanderlyn also used Audubon's profile for the young officer in the background. *Art Commission of the City of New York*

passing flurries of schemes to save the house—to restore it, to create a park around it, to float it upriver to Fort Washington Park. But 1932 was the end of the line, though a last-minute effort was made to raise funds, even as a wrecking company began demolition to make way for the Riverside Drive Viaduct.

God knows there had been enough prodding over the years. Back in 1917, the *New York Tribune* ran an angry article on the city's "disheartening" indifference to the Audubon house: "It apparently hasn't a friend in the world. Tin cans, old papers, debris of all kinds clutter up the immediate yard. The porch is falling into decay and the erstwhile trim little fence and gate are in the last stages of final ruin."

The *Evening Sun* raised the issue again in 1920 with an article headlined: Audubon's Home Nearing Ruin. There was a fresh outcry in the New York papers in 1927 when it was learned that JJA had done paintings and drawings on his studio wall and that these last tokens of his work had only recently been obliterated with lead paint and wallpaper by a railroad worker named McGrath, who made his home in the old house and used the studio as his kitchen.

Today, at 155th Street and Riverside Drive, as one looks upriver into what had been the Audubon property, the sense of a river bluff is gone, the landscape gigantically rearranged. The city, at this intersection, is built on superstructures of masonry, steel, and concrete. But on the south side of 155th Street is a second large swath of the Trinity Cemetery (barred and locked at the Broadway entrance). Lean over the wall at this corner, look below through the treetops. The land rambles downhill toward the river. The bluff, the trees, the natural order of things.

With us this afternoon at 155th and Riverside are three disparate gatherings of New Yorkers on the stone benches in the sun. Gathering One: four politically, sociologically, and intellectually minded people (white, two male, two female), who discuss ghettos, welfare, and what-should-be-done. Gathering Two: a pair of neatly dressed senior citizens (Negro, male), who discuss and agree on the undercover agencies of government—the omnipotent "they" who can have anyone they wish killed off, removed from the scene, put out of commission. Gathering Three: a trio of housewives (white), who are stretched out semi-naked, greased and oiled, one to a bench, stealing a march on their summer suntans.

The family finances had been shaky before Audubon's death, but John and Victor also had made bad investments that came home heavily to roost. In a later effort to recoup, they contracted for new editions of *The Quadrupeds* and *The Birds of America.* The majority of their subscribers were in the southern states, the Civil War broke out, and the family finances were blown to bits by debts to the printing and publishing company.

Within the family, tragedy struck. Victor injured his spine in a fall, was invalided, and died (aged 51) only six years after his father's death. Five years after that, John died (aged 49) from a "heavy cold," presumably pneumonia. The property was heavily mortgaged. Lucy rented the main house, then sold it. The family set of *The Birds of America* went to John Taylor Johnston, railroad tycoon and a founder and first president of the Metropolitan Museum of Art. He got a bargain. The original price was $1000. Mr. Johnston paid $600.

In 1863, Lucy sold the original paintings for *The Birds of America* to the New-York Historical Society for $2000. (Her asking price had been $5000.) The paintings were held in basement storage for 108 years. The first full exhibition was not mounted until 1971. She had also hoped that the Historical Society would buy the remaining copies of the *Ornithological Biography.* "I assure you the world is too busy to care for the wants and grievances of an old and lone widow," she wrote to the chairman, Frederic De Peyster. "I find it impossible to keep the rats from the boxes of the 'Ornithological Biographies.' Therefore I have concluded to sell them for what I can, being in real want. Will not your Historical Society give me something for all I have, say even a dollar a volume rather than have them destroyed."

She sold the copper plates of *The Birds of America* to the only buyer she could find—a brass and copper firm that proceeded to melt them down as scrap at a furnace in Ansonia, Connecticut. In one of those storybook flukes of fate, the general manager's fourteen-year-old son, who was keen on birds and taxidermy, noticed the engravings as they were being thrown into the furnace and raced manfully to the foreman, to the superintendent, to his father, and, at last, to his mother, who came down to the factory to look at her son's find. She recognized them as Audubons, and the destruction was stopped. Some three dozen plates were rescued.

Lucy taught school for a while (private classes for neighborhood children, one of whom was George Bird Grinnell, founder of the first

Audubon Society in 1886). She then lived in a New York boarding house under the eye of a granddaughter, who was earning *her* way giving music lessons. "It would seem to me," Lucy wrote to a relative, "as if we were a doomed family."

She was next taken in by former neighbors, the family of the Reverend Charles Coffin Adams, who helped her prepare *The Life of John James Audubon, the Naturalist*, published in 1869. She moved on to the care of a granddaughter in Louisville (also a teacher) and finally to Shelbyville, Kentucky, where she stayed with her brother William's wife. There Lucy died, aged 86, in 1874.

We stopped in Shelbyville on our Kentucky travels—a pleasant country town east of Louisville. Her sister-in-law's house had been leveled by fire the year after Lucy died and her remaining possessions there lost. Among them, the death mask of John James taken by his sons. There was no Lucy Audubon file in the town library, no Lucy Audubon mementoes, no handed-down recollections that we could find, except from an elderly lady of old Shelbyville lineage, who had only one comment to offer: "As I understand it, she was Miss Lucy Bakewell and she was married to Mr. John James Audubon and he was away from home all the time."

We walk along the Riverside Drive Viaduct, past the crawl of apartment buildings occupying the space where the Audubon house had stood, and try to catch an imaginary glimpse of trees, a brook, a waterfall, the colonnaded front porch with its view of the river and cliffs of the Palisades on the New Jersey shore. For Audubon's grandchildren, who spent their childhood here, it was probably the happiest time of their lives—despite the trials and tragedies that overwhelmed the family. Shortly before she died in 1925 at the age of 83, his granddaughter Maria Audubon wrote a few heart-wrenching lines of reminiscence: "When any of the four remaining children of my father, J. W. Audubon, speak or write of 'home,' we mean the house on the Hudson, where we learned to swim, and row, and go crabbing and fishing, and do all the rest of the delightful things one can do if fortunate enough to live near a river. Seven of my father's nine children lived to maturity, and all uncle Victor's six, and I can hear the call on summer evenings, 'Sunset, children!' which meant that the boats must come in, and the wandering children assemble to see the sunset."

Far below on the river side of the Viaduct is a patch of parkland, the abandoned West Side Highway, and the railroad tracks along the shore, "that confounded railroad," which cut through the property in 1847 and separated the house from the river. Upstream, the George Washington Bridge and the little red lighthouse on the promontory at its feet. Downstream, a pall of smoke. Something is burning on the Jersey shore. A jogger huffs by. The day wanes. We head home.

Sunset, children.

AUTHORS' NOTE

The first of the standard Audubon biographies is Francis Hobart Herrick's two-volume *Audubon the Naturalist: A History of His Life and Time*—the second edition, published in 1938 by D. Appleton-Century Company and republished by Dover Publications in 1968. More recent scholarship is embodied in Alexander B. Adams' *John James Audubon: A Biography* (G. P. Putnam's Sons, 1966) and in Alice Ford's *John James Audubon* (University of Oklahoma Press, 1964). Stanley Clisby Arthur's *Audubon, An Intimate Life of the American Woodsman* is valuable for Arthur's firsthand knowledge of Audubon territory in Louisiana. Other biographies have been published, of course, but they are not works of the first rank.

Among the primary sources are the British and American editions of Audubon's bird biographies and his literary sketches of American life. Various journals and collections of his letters have been published, including *Journal of John James Audubon Made During His Trip to New Orleans in 1820–21* (Howard Corning, editor; The Club of Odd Volumes, 1929) and *The 1826 Journal of John James Audubon* (Alice Ford, editor; University of Oklahoma Press, 1967). Despite its many failings, another essential work is *Audubon and His Journals* by Maria R. Audubon (two volumes; Charles Scribner's Sons, 1897, and Dover Publications, 1960). Alice Ford compiled and edited a collection of delightful, little-known drawings, *Audubon's Butterflies, Moths, and Other Studies* (Studio Publications, Inc./Thomas Y. Crowell Company, 1952). American Heritage Publishing Company issued in 1966 a superb two-volume collection, *The Original Water-*

color Paintings by John James Audubon for The Birds of America,
with an introduction by Marshall Davidson. Waldemar H. Fries' *The
Double Elephant Folio* (American Library Association, 1974), traces
the histories of all the known copies of the Audubon-Havell work.

Students who wish to delve more deeply into Audubon's life,
work, and times will find good bibliographies in the Herrick, Adams,
and Ford biographies. But one work not mentioned therein, which
we found especially useful, is Robert G. Athearn's *Forts of the Upper
Missouri* (University of Nebraska Press, 1967). Another is Richard C.
Wade's *The Urban Frontier: Pioneer Life in Early Pittsburgh, Cincinnati, Lexington, Louisville, and St. Louis* (Phoenix edition, University of Chicago Press, 1964; originally published by Harvard University Press, 1959, as *The Urban Frontier: The Rise of Western
Cities*); among other things, that helped put Audubon's early business experiences into perspective.

The lengthy segments of Audubon's 1820–21 journal are published
by permission of the Houghton Library, Harvard University, and of
The Club of Odd Volumes, Boston. Robert Todd's letter was found
at the Cincinnati Historical Society. The letter from Audubon to
Lucy from Bradore Bay is in the John J. Audubon Papers of the
Missouri Historical Society. Some of the material in Michael Harwood's entries about our towboat trip down the Mississippi River
appeared in *The New York Times Magazine.* We wish to thank all
these organizations and institutions.

And now that we've reached the thank-yous, let us begin by
saying that this book depended on a cast of hundreds. To thank
everyone is impossible. We are, of course, deeply indebted to all
those whose names appear in the preceding pages. Among those not
yet named but who gave us material, art, opinions, advice, and other
crucial help are: Rhoda Addison, Chester E. Allan, Robert S. Arbib,
Jr., James Baird, Gene Balsley, Kenneth E. Biglane, Gregoria Carr-
era, William Chess and the late Virginia Chess, William C. Coles, Jr.,
Neil Currie, Sylvia S. Donohue, Henry Gibson, Martha Hootsell, Ben
and Jane Innis, Griffith and Margaret Jones, Mary Kreid, Mrs. André
Lapeyre, Albert and Betty Milton, Edward Montgomery, Rita Montgomery, Roger Pasquier, Marion Smith, Robb Smith, Augusta Talbot,
David and Rachel Titus, Mark Titus, Penny Titus, Art Tomerlin,

Geoffrey Truly, William E. Wellman, and Reshelda White.

Small community libraries, local historical societies, and historical museums are often gold mines for the visiting researcher, and dozens of them helped us. We would like especially to thank the Charleston Museum in South Carolina; the Cincinnati Historical Society; The Filson Club of Louisville, Kentucky, and its librarian, Martin F. Schmidt; Mrs. Florence Nordquist of the Halifax Historical Society, Daytona Beach, Florida; the Monroe County Public Library in Key West, Florida, and Betty Bruce of its Local and State History Department; the Historic Natchez Foundation; the Pensacola, Florida, Historical Museum; the Pictou, Nova Scotia, Heritage Society; the St. Augustine Historical Society in Florida; Edward F. McGuinness, president of the Washington Heights Historical Society in New York City; and the West Feliciana Historical Society, St. Francisville, Louisiana—in particular Mary Ellen Young and Elizabeth Kilbourne Dart.

Other institutions, organizations, and people that made key contributions to our work and have not been acknowledged in picture credits or been mentioned in the text include the Academy of Natural Sciences, Philadelphia; the American Philosophical Society, Philadelphia; the Library of the Boston Athenaeum; the College of Charleston Library; the Division of Recreation and Parks, Department of Natural Resources, Florida; the Georgia Historical Society; the Louisiana Historical Society; the Louisiana State Museum; the Office of State Parks in Louisiana; the library of the National Audubon Society and its librarians, the late Nancy Turel and Michelle Inviene Epstein; the National Museum of Natural History, Smithsonian Institution; the Princeton University Library; the South Dakota Historical Society; the Wisconsin Barge Line; the State Historical Society of Wisconsin; and Archibald Hanna, curator of the Beinecke Rare Book and Manuscript Library at Yale University.

Many individuals, besides, gave us meals and places to sleep, acted as guides, became our friends. William Hedden, with inexplicable courage and generosity, gave us his camera equipment for more than a year; many of the photographs in the book were made with that equipment, and thousands more served as an *aide-memoire* as we wrote. The GAF Corporation contributed much of our color film.

And Ellen Moore was able to make sense of the most illegible, tangled thickets of copy and turn them into a manuscript.

To all of the above, our thanks. Whatever may be the faults of this book, the blame is ours.

Mary Durant &
Michael Harwood

Washington, Connecticut
February 12, 1980

GENERAL INDEX

Adams, Alexander, 213
Adams, Charles Coffin, 615
Alabama, 492, 564
Allegheny Portage Railroad, Pa., 599; illus., 600–601
alligators, 200, 243, 368, 373, 374, 514
Alpha, Flossie, 506–8
American Fur Company, 539–41, 546, 557, 560, 567, 587
American Museum of Natural History, 292, 537
American Ornithological Union, 198, 379, 572
André, ——— (Mme.), 272
Arikaras, 561
Arkansas, 161, 164–68, 192–202
Arkansas River, 192–95
armadillos, 197, 245, 518
Armstrong, ——— (Mr.), 300–301
Arthur, Stanley Clisby, 229, 231–32
Assiniboins, 569, 575
Athearn, Robert, 576
Atlantic Ocean shore, 300–318
Audubon, Eliza, 121
Audubon, Jean, 1–2, 15, 17, 79, 266–69, 276
Audubon, John James:
  appearance, 238–40, 286, 292
  artistic tastes, 288–89
  attitudes toward Indians and slavery, 291, 485–87, 564–65
  bird names used by, 178–81, 471, 498–500

birds kept by, 87, 413, 441
books and equipment used by, 177
dogs owned by, 477
drawings and paintings of, xiii, 3–4, 34–36, 55, 59–60, 80, 81, 83, 91, 105, 109, 111, 114, 120, 138, 162–63, 198, 203, 208, 218, 229–30, 233, 245–46, 259–60, 284–85, 297–98, 300, 326–28, 339, 342, 346, 354, 358, 381, 386, 398, 413–15, 439, 441, 449, 474, 574, 588–90, 593, 615
  "Chute de L'Ohio" (1808), 35
  Immature Rose-breasted Grosbeak (1810), 81
  Great Horned Owl (1814), 83
  "Thomas W. Bakewell" (1820), 109
  Bonaparte's Gull (1820), 116
  "John Cleves Symmes" (1820), 117
  Eagle with a Catfish (n.d.), 163
  Black Vulture (1820), 167
  "Eliza Pirrie" (1821), 225
  Swallow-tailed Kite (1821), 231
  Black-necked Stilt (1821), 263
  Hawk-owl (n.d.), 297
  Long-billed Marsh Wrens (1829), 312
  Osprey (1829), 315
  Bachman's Warbler (1833), 342
  Long-billed Curlews (1831), 346
  White-crowned Pigeons (n.d.), 381
  Brown Pelican (n.d.), 398
  Golden Eagle (1833), 415
  Gannets (1833), 439

623

Audubon (*Cont'd*)
Horned Larks (1833), 449
Black Rats (1842), 537
Western Fox Squirrel (1843), 538
Thirteen-lined Ground Squirrel (1843), 588
"Three Buttes" (1843), 593
as "failure," 177
French accent and words of, 88, 178, 258
handwriting of, 121
health of, 527, 586, 608
interest in flowers and trees, 11, 55, 92, 217–18, 245–46, 285, 455, 474, 525
interest in mammals, 3, 55, 88, 537, 557, 588, 590, 610
journals, xiii, 121, 178–182, 231, 246, 286–93, 328, 419, 427, 434–35, 455, 460, 466–67, 472, 478, 486, 541, 560–61, 564, 572, 591–94, 597; illus., 122, 280–83
portraits and statues of, 9, 87, 92, 94, 104–5, 265, 414, 610, 612; illus., 10, 93, 266, 290, 609
as sportsman, 209–12
as taxidermist, 4, 65, 67, 111
techniques of, 7, 118–19, 211–12, 284–85, 355, 357, 413–14
writings of, xiii, 3, 8, 30, 40, 56, 73–75, 80, 90, 92, 115, 211–12, 245–47, 262, 279, 284, 300–302, 328–29, 331–32, 344, 348, 350, 368, 382, 384, 414, 483, 485, 535–36, 539, 552, 588, 598–99, 606–7, 614–15
Birds of America, The, 3, 8, 30, 35, 92, 115, 211–12, 245–46, 262, 279, 284, 300, 338, 344, 348, 350, 382, 384, 485, 536, 615
"Journey Up the Mississippi," 41
"Kentucky Barbeque, A," 30
Ornithological Biography, 56, 74, 80, 178, 301–2, 328–29, 331–32, 368, 414, 483, 485, 536, 552, 615
"Prairie, The," 73–74
Report on the Agriculture and Geology of Mississippi, 247
Viviparous Quadrupeds of North America, 539, 588, 598, 606–7, 615

Audubon, John James:
birth (1785), x, 266–72, 275–77
at Mill Grove Estate, Pa. (1804–1806), 1–16, 17
childhood and adolescence, x, 1–2, 4–7, 9, 11, 14–16
initial studies, 1, 4, 6–7, 11, 33–34, 36, 82, 87
courtship of Lucy Bakewell, 14–16
marriage to Lucy Bakewell, 19, 36, 37
in Louisville, Ky. (1807–1810), 17–36
in Henderson, Ky. (1810–1819), 37, 64, 73, 79–110
early business career with Ferdinand Rozier, 17, 20–22, 34, 36, 38, 55, 64–65, 68
in Ste. Genevieve, Mo. (1810–1811), 37–38, 64–72
reconnaissance trip to Ste. Genevieve, 37–78
business partnership with Thomas Bakewell, 79–80, 82, 107–8
declares bankruptcy, 82, 84, 108, 111, 115, 485
in Cincinnati, Ohio (1819–1820), 111–20
hired by Western Museum, 111–20
teaches drawing, 111, 115, 217
Ohio River-Mississippi River trip (1820–1821), 121–42, 143–204
in Natchez, Miss. (1820–1824), 205–19
teaches dancing, 215–16
at St. Francisville, La. (1821–1829), 220–58
becomes accomplished painter of wildlife, 221, 279
at Oakley plantation, La. (1821), 222–28
at Beech Woods and Beech Grove plantations (1821–1822), 230–32, 234–35
in New Orleans, La., 259–78
in England (1826–1829), xi, 3, 92, 198, 230, 234, 247, 279–99
in Europe (1826–1829), 279–99
in Camden and Great Egg, N.J. (1829), 300–318
in Mauch Chunk and Great Pine Forest, Pa. (1829), 319–29
in England (1829), 327–28

in Charleston, S.C., 330–49
in East Florida (1831–1832), 350–73
in Florida Keys and Dry Tortugas
 (1832), 374–410
in Labrador (1833), 411–84
in Texas and Gulf Coast area (1837),
 485–534
Missouri River trip (1843), 535–96, 606
final years, 597–616
in New York, N.Y., 4, 11, 485, 606–16
death (1851), 608
Audubon, John Woodhouse, 79, 205, 217,
 252, 275–76, 296, 298, 327–28, 331–32,
 340, 367, 411, 414, 438, 472, 485, 487,
 535–36, 539, 606, 614–16
Audubon, Lucy (née Bakewell), 14–16, 19–
 22, 29, 36, 37–38, 79, 87, 94, 104, 106,
 108, 115, 122, 205, 217, 230, 232, 234, 239–
 40, 258, 265, 267, 269, 327–28, 330, 333,
 338, 340, 347, 350, 353, 354, 359, 365,
 367–68, 382, 403, 411, 414, 418, 471–72,
 485, 487, 535–36, 539, 547, 565–66,
 577, 606, 615–16; illus., 240, 241
Audubon, Maria R., 121, 287–88, 291, 403,
 419, 427, 434, 561, 564, 591, 616
Audubon, Victor Gifford, 22, 36, 38, 205,
 209, 217, 232, 252, 296, 298–99, 327–28,
 331, 347, 367, 411, 418, 487, 535–36,
 539–40, 591, 606, 608, 614–15
Audubon and his Journals, 287
Audubon, Pennsylvania, xiii
Audubon Society and chapters, 11, 84, 86,
 96, 105, 109, 126, 177, 225, 608, 616
Audubon Terrace, N.Y., 611, 614
Auk, The, 121, 275
Aumack, Jacob, 120, 160, 176, 178, 182–83,
 192–93

Bachman, John, 330–34, 337–41, 343–45,
 377–78, 414, 467, 485–87, 489, 500,
 535–36, 598, 606–7; illus., 336
badlands (Dakota), 556, 577, 588
Bakewell, Gordon, 271, 276, 295
Bakewell, Thomas W., 79, 82, 367; illus.,
 109
Bakewell, William, 15, 367, 616
Ballast Key, Fla., 386
banding, bird, 11, 357–58, 393, 395

Bartett, William Henry, 416
Bartram, William, xii, 368, 374
Baton Rouge, La., 172–73, 175
Bayou Sara, La., 221, 234–35, 252, 328;
 illus., 236–37, 238
Beargrass Creek, 30
Beaudoin, Leo Paul, 468
Beech Grove plantation, La., 234–35
Beech Woods plantation, La., 230–32, 234
Behman, Frederick, 558
Bell, John Graham, 540, 552, 557, 560,
 597
Belle Isle, Strait of, 444, 446, 448, 452, 471
Benét, Stephen Vincent, xiii
Bennet, Philip, 475, 477
Bennett, W. J., 412, 605
Bent, Arthur Cleveland, 45–46
Berthoud, Nicholas, 82, 107, 177, 208, 219,
 232
Best, Robert, 115–16
Bingham, Caleb, 173–74
Birch, Thomas, 13
Birds of America, The (Audubon), 3, 8,
 30, 35, 92, 115, 211–12, 245–46, 262, 279,
 284, 300, 338, 344, 348, 350, 382, 384,
 485, 536, 614–15
Blackfeet, 566, 573
Blanc Sablon, Que., 457–61, 464, 468–70
Bodmer, Carl, 125, 551, 563, 569, 571
Bonaparte, Charles Lucien, 116, 232–33,
 339, 400
Boone, Daniel, xii, 33, 49, 60
Boston, Mass., 411, 413–14; illus., 412
Brackenridge, Henry Marie, 57, 64
Bradford, Mary Fluker, 265, 267–68
Bradore Bay, Lab., 447–54, 457, 459, 463,
 465, 471; illus., 451
Brecher, Leonard, 27, 30, 33
Brewer, Thomas M., 527
Briggs, Richard A., 32
Brunet, J. H., 425–27
Buchanan, Robert, 293, 564
buffalo, 561, 564, 574, 575, 577, 581, 587–
 88, 591
Bulow, John J., 361–65, 367
Bulow Ville, Fla., 361–65, 368, 373; illus.,
 366
Burnham Island, Ill., 186–88

Burr, Aaron, 30, 138
Bush Key, Fla., 390, 392, 396; illus., 393

Cache (Cash) Creek, 41–44, 52, 57, 141
Cairo, Ill., 146, 148, 153, 160
Cajuns, 496–500, 509
California, 328
Camden, N.J., 300–318
Campbell, 492–93, 495, 504–5, 519, 521, 528, 534
Canada, 4, 47, 411–84, 486–87, 527, 564–65
Canso, Strait of, N.S., 421–22; illus., 421
Cap-aux-Meules, Que., 424, 427
Cape Breton Island, N.S., 421–23, 479
caribou, 453–54
Carl Ross Key, Fla., 408
Carlisle, Ruth, 149–51, 158, 168, 170–71, 176
Catesby, Mark, 185, 344
catfish, 162–63, 313–14, 316
Catlin, George, 491, 561, 565, 569, 587
Cave-In-Rock, Ill., 125–26, 128, 130, 133, 135–37, 141; illus., 125, 127
Chappell, Edward, 476–77
Charleston, S.C., 329, 330–34, 336–45, 347–49, 411, 485–87, 598; illus., 335, 346
Charleston Museum, 334, 337, 339, 607
Cheyennes, 582
Choctaws, 275
Chouteau, Pierre, 539, 557, 587
"Chute de L'Ohio" (Audubon), 35
Cincinnati, Ohio, 111, 114–20, 367; illus., 112–13, 118
Cincinnati College, 111
Claiborne, F., 275
Clark, David, 91
Clark, George Rogers, 28–29, 52
Clark, William, xi, 552–54, 567–68
cod, 460–61, 466
Coffin, Francis J. H. (Mrs.), 343–45
Collins, ——— (Mrs.), 58
Collins, Antoine, 492
Columbia River, 328
Columbus, Ky., 188–90
Comanchees, 486
Coolidge, Joseph, 414, 438, 478
coral snakes, 360–61

Coste, Napoleon, 492–93
Cote Blanche Bay, La., 505–8
cottonmouths, 514–15
Creeks, 487
crickets, 590–91
Croghan, William, 29
Cruikshank, Frederick, 240
Culbertson, Alexander, 572, 574, 576; illus., 573
Cumberland Island, Ill., 138–39
Cummins, Caleb, 45
Cummins, Dan, 45, 47, 49
Cummins, Joe, 45, 47–50
Cuvier, Georges, 210
Cyr, Aristede, 429–31, 433–40; illus., 432

Dakota Territory, 4, 549
Dana, C. A., 545
Darwin, Charles, 197, 279
Day, Robert, 387
De Peyster, Frederic, 615
DeCuir, Guy, 508–512
DeHart, Martin and Marjorie, 511–16, 518; illus., 517, 519
Delaware River, 300–301
Delta National Wildlife Refuge, La., 494–95
Denig, Edwin Thompson, 574; illus., 575
Dotson, Ron, 84–85, 96
Drake, Daniel, 111, 114–15
Drummond, James, 489, 525
Dry Tortugas, Fla., ix, 329, 374–410
Duffey, Ed and Joyce, 575, 576–78, 590
Dunlap, William, 232

Eager, William, 481
Eastport, Me., 418, 484; illus., 416
Edwards, George, 344
Egan, James, 399, 403
1826 Journal of John James Audubon, The, 286–87
Elmer, George T., 306–9, 313–14, 316–17
Emery, Henry Tilton, 416, 418, 427, 478; illus., 417
England, 3, 92, 198, 230, 234, 247, 279–99, 327–28, 411, 485, 535–36
Everett, Edward, 328
Everglades, Fla., 390, 402–10

Fatland Ford farm, Pa., 14–16
Fearon, Henry Bradshaw, 22
Featherstonhaugh, G. W., 329
Fichter, George S., 75
Filson Club, 18, 33
fire ants, 244–45
Fish and Wildlife Service, U.S., 392, 494
flatboats, 120, 160, 173–74
flies, 454
Florida, 302, 329, 350–410, 485–87, 489, 492, 564
Floyd, Charles, 553–54
Forbush, Edward Howe, 46
Ford, Alice, 268, 286, 613
Forest Service, U.S., 341, 345, 348
Fort Buford, N.D., 567, 575, 579, 581–83, 586, 588
Fort Clark, S.D., 561, 564; illus., 562–63
Fort Jefferson, Fla., 388, 390–91, 396–97; illus., 389, 393
Fort Leavenworth, Kan., 546, 549; illus., 547
Fort Livingston, La., 503–5
Fort Massac, Ill., 139–40
Fort Mortimer, N.D., 576–79, 582, 586
Fort Moultrie, S.C., 347–49
Fort Pierre, S.D., 557, 559, 597; illus., 558, 560
Fort Union, N.D., 549, 561, 564–67, 569, 572–74, 579–83, 586–88; illus., 568, 570–71, 584–85
fox squirrels, illus., 538
France, 286, 291
Francis Marion National Forest, S.C., 333, 345, 348
Fremont, John C., 546
Fundy, Bay of, 483

Galveston, Texas, 519–21, 523–29; illus., 522
Garden Key, Fla., 388, 390–91; illus., 393
Garneray, Ambroise Louis, 261
Geiger, John H., 379, 382–84
Georgia, 350–51, 353
Glassel, James, 377, 382–83
Gmelin, Johann Friedrich, 177
gnats, 75–76
Godwin, George, 420, 434

Gordon, Ann Bakewell, 293, 295; illus., 294
Gordy, Michael, 506–8
Gould, John, 344
Graham, Edward W., 9, 11
Grand Isle, La., 496–97, 500
Grand Terre, La., 496, 500–502
Grand Tower, Mo., 61, 64, 152, 155; illus., 62–63
grasshoppers, 590–91
Great Egg, N.J., 300–305, 307, 309–18; illus., 306, 308
Great Pine Forest, Pa., 319–29
Greenly Islands, Que., 467–69
Grinnell, George Bird, 615
ground squirrels, 588, 590; illus., 599
Gulf Islands National Seashore, Ala., 489

hackberry trees, 98–99
Hai-Kees-Kak-Wee-Yah, 578; illus., 576–77
Haiti, 266
Halifax River, 362, 368
Halifax, N.S., 478, 483
Hall, Basil, 26, 260
Hall, H. B., 10
Hamilton, P. C., 559
Harlow, William, 98, 124
Harpe brothers, 128
Harris, Edward, 487, 492, 539–40, 556, 578–79, 587–88, 591–94; illus., 488
Harvard University, 92–93, 121–22
Havell, Robert, 91–92, 230, 245, 329, 339, 344, 414, 536
Havre Aubert, Que., 424, 426–29; illus., 425
Haw Creek, 368–70
Henderson, Ky., 37, 64, 73, 79–110, 126
Hernandez, Joseph, 359, 361, 365, 367; illus., 360
Herrick, Francis Herbert, 92, 268–70, 276
Hickory Run State Park, Pa., 323–25
Himely, —— (Mr.), 261
Hobbs, Leonard, 453–59, 462–63
Hog Bayou, La., 513
Holley, Mary Austin, 531
Homochitto National Forest, Miss., 208–9, 219

Hone, Philip, 358
Houghton Library, 121–22
Houston, Sam, 529, 532
Houston, Texas, ix, 528–29, 532–34; illus.,
    530–31
Hudson's Bay Company, 441, 443
hurricanes, 500, 502, 504, 547

Illinois, x, 11, 53, 72–78, 124–30, 134, 137–
    42, 186–88, 541
Indian Key, Fla., 397, 399–402
Indiana, 81, 123–24
Indians, 38, 40–41, 43–45, 50, 55–56, 59–
    60, 73–74, 88, 90–91, 185, 194, 196, 275,
    303, 358, 360–61, 363–64, 367, 370–71,
    443, 447, 454, 474, 478, 485–87, 489–
    91, 497, 499, 529, 546, 552–53, 557, 561,
    564–67, 569, 572–77, 581–82, 586, 588
Ingalls, William, 416, 418, 465, 478, 484
Inman, Henry, 9, 10, 87, 415, 610
Iowa, 549, 553–54
Irish, Jediah, 320, 325–26
Irving, Washington, 195–96

Jackson, Andrew, 487, 612; illus., 613
Jardine, William, 279
Jefferson City, Mo., 541, 546; illus.,
    544–45
Jefferson National Forest, Va., 603
Jestico Island, N.S., 422–23
John James Audubon State Park, Ky., 91,
    96–97
Johnson, William Garrett, 234
Johnston, John Taylor, 615
Jolly, Sid, 198–202, 220
"Jolly Flatboatmen" (Bingham), 173; illus.,
    174
Jones, ——— (Mr.), 448, 450–53, 466
"Journey Up the Mississippi" (Audubon),
    41

Kansas, 546–47, 549
Keeton brothers, 147–48, 152–58, 162,
    164–66, 168, 170, 172–73, 175, 185–86, 190
Kelly, Stephen, 218
Kemble, Fanny, 411
Kentucky, 17–36, 37, 44–45, 53, 64, 79–
    110, 118–19, 131, 134, 141–42, 161, 186–90,
    616

Kentucky Barbeque, A (Audubon), 30
Key West, Fla., 374–76, 378–79, 382–87;
    illus., 377, 380
King, Thomas Butler, 350–51; illus., 352
Kinney, Joyce Emery, 417–18

Labrador, ix, 411–84, 486–87, 527, 564–65
Lafitte, Jean, 497, 500–501, 522–23
Landry, Frederic, 427
Latapie, Ralph, Jr., 501–3
Lawson, Thomas, 232–33
Lehigh River, 319–21, 326
Lehman, George, 329, 346–49, 350, 353–
    54, 356, 359, 373, 396
Lenapes, 454
Lesueur, Charles A., 238
Lewis, Henry, 206, 237, 543
Lewis, Meriwether, xi, 552–54, 567–68
Lichtenstein, Martin Heinrich, 339
Licking River, 118–19
Life of John James Audubon, the Natu-
    ralist, The (Lucy Audubon), 615
Lincoln, Thomas, 414, 416, 438, 465, 469,
    471–72, 484
Lind, Jenny, 31
Linnaeus, Carolus, 177
Lizars, William Home, 26, 260, 279, 296
Locust Grove estate, Ky., 29
loggerheads, 409
Lorimier, (Pierre) Louis, and son, 38, 52,
    59–61, 152
Louisiana, 4, 148, 172, 200, 204, 220–78,
    493–519, 534
Louisiana Territory, 546
Louisville, Ky., 17, 19–25, 27–36, 108, 111,
    123, 327–28, 367, 616; illus., 18, 26
Lowery, George H., Jr., 251
Lutz, Frank, 75

MacGillivray, William, 328, 354, 403
Magdalene Islands, Que., 423–40
Maine, 411, 414, 416, 418–19, 484
Mandans, 561, 564
Mandeville, La., 270–72, 275–77; illus.,
    268
Marigny, Bernard de, 267–72, 275–77;
    illus., 273, 274
Marion, 374–75, 377, 382–83, 387, 395,
    397

Martin, Maria, 333, 338–40, 342–44, 356
Mason, Joseph, 120, 148, 192, 221–24, 228–30, 261
Massachusetts, 411
Matthews, Lucy, 228–29
Matthiessen, Peter, 57
Mauch Chunk, Pa., 319, 321–29; illus., 320
Maximilian of Wied, 125, 569
McCuish, Murdoch, 482
McCulloch, Thomas, 479, 481–82; illus., 480
McDermott, John Francis, 40
McLane, Lewis, 328
Meade, Charles, 101–4
Memphis, Tenn., 165
men-of-war, Portuguese, 526
Mexico, 105, 328
Mexico, Gulf of, 485–534
Mic-Macs, 474, 478
Michaux, François André, 456
migrations, bird, 11, 300, 332, 465, 477, 498
Mill Grove estate, Pa., 1, 3–11, 15–16, 108, 599; illus., 2, 12–13, 14
Miller, Alfred Jacob, 587
Minnesota, 566
Mississippi, 166, 169, 204, 205–19
Mississippi River, ix, 38–41, 44, 46, 52–57, 72, 75, 120, 139, 142, 143–204, 493–95; illus., 542–43
Missouri, 37–72, 143, 162, 164, 539–46
Missouri River, ix, 535–41, 544–49, 552–95, 606; illus., 542–43, 550–51
mistletoe, 141–42
Monro, Daniel, 480
Montana, 549, 567, 582–83, 592, 596
Moussier, Jean-Baptiste, 501
Mud Island, N.S., 420
Muscarilla, —— (Mr.), 216
Musée des Iles, 427
Museum of Comparative Zoology, 92–93

Natashquan, Lab., 440, 465
Natawista-Iksana, illus., 574
Natchez, Miss., 177, 183–84, 205, 208–13, 215–19, 261; illus., 206–7, 214
National Audubon Society, *see* Audubon Society and chapters
National Park Service, 348, 388, 408, 567

Natural Bridge, Va., 599, 602–3; illus., 604–5
Nebraska, 549, 552–53
Nedd, Billy, 157, 159–60, 169–72, 176, 192
New Brunswick, 411
New Jersey, x, 300–318
New Orleans, La., 148, 185, 205, 221, 259, 262–64, 267–78, 493, 495, 501; illus., 260, 261, 265, 266
New York, 4, 11, 465, 485, 606–16
New York, N.Y., 4, 11, 465, 485, 606–16; illus., 616
New-York Historical Society, 9, 357
Newfoundland, x, 443–48, 456, 463, 472–78
Nez Percés, 582
North Carolina, 330
North Dakota, 4, 549, 566–96, 603
Nova Scotia, 419–22, 444, 478–84
nutrias, 513–19
Nuttall, Thomas, xii, 411, 598

Oakley plantation, La., 221–26, 229–30; illus., 227, 228
Ohio, 111–20
Ohio River, ix, 17–21, 24–31, 33, 35, 37–41, 44, 46, 51–54, 75, 79, 104, 121–42, 154
Omahas, 552–53
Omega, 540, 546–49, 552–53, 555, 557, 561, 564
optical equipment, 177
Ord, George, 116
Ornithological Biography (Audubon), xiii, 56, 74, 80, 178, 301–2, 328–29, 331–32, 368, 414, 483, 485, 536, 552, 615
ornithology, xii, 6, 24, 33–34, 105, 116, 121, 176, 178–84, 198, 210–11, 264, 284, 328, 395, 437, 527
Osages, 55
Ozarks, 130–31, 135

Paducah, Ky., 186–87
Parker, Anne Wetherill, 8–9, 288
Parkman, Francis, 591
Parkman, George, 413
Paroquet Island, Que., 467–68
Passamaquoddy Bay, Me., 416
Peattie, Donald Culross, 57, 357
Penn, William, 486

Pennsylvania, 1–16, 17, 80, 198, 233, 319–
    29, 485, 599–601
Pensacola, Fla., 489, 492
Percy, Robert (Mrs.), 230, 232, 234–35,
    238, 242
Perkins, Thomas Handasyd, 411
Perkiomen Creek, 1, 4–6, 11, 14
Perrine, Henry, 401
pesticides, 502–3, 559
Philadelphia, Pa., 485
phlox, 489
Pictou, N.S., 478–79, 483; illus., 481
Pirrie, Eliza, 222–24, 226–28, 293, 383;
    illus., 225
Pirrie, James (Mrs.), 222–23, 226–27, 235,
    238, 242
Pope, John, 37, 55–56
Pope, Nathaniel Wells and Martha, 235,
    238–39, 242–43, 267
Post of Arkansas, 192–98
Postal Service, U.S., 104–5
Prairie, The (Audubon), 73–74
Prevost, Alice, 592–96
Prince Edward Island, 423, 444
Proby, Kathryn Hall, 358
Profilet, Emile, 218
Provost, Etienne, 587

*Quadrupeds, see Viviparous Quadrupeds
    of North America*
Quakers, 3, 14, 258, 289, 291
Quebec, 423–40, 445, 447, 452, 458, 464
Quinn, Melicent, 94–95, 344

Rabbit Island, La., 508–9
Rabin, Jeanne, 268–69, 271, 275
Rafinesque, Constantine Samuel, 80, 85,
    378
Rankin, Adam, 88, 108
rats, 88–89, 121, 615; illus., 537
Ravenel, Henry, 333, 347
Ray A. Eckstein, see towboats
*Report on the Agriculture and Geology
    of Mississippi* (Audubon), 247
Retreat plantation, Ga., 350–51; illus., 353
Ripley, 416, 418–23, 425, 429, 437, 439–
    40, 443–44, 460–61, 472, 474–75,
    478–79

Roberts, Frank, 252–54; illus., 255
Roberts, William, 31
Robertson, Bill, 390, 392, 395–96
Rochers des Oiseaux (Bird Rocks), Que.,
    429, 431, 433–35, 437–40; illus., 436
Rockin Cave, *see* Cave-In-Rock
Rocky Mountains, ix, 328, 539, 546, 566,
    598
Roquette, Adrien, 275–76
Rousseau, Jean Jacques, xii
Roy's Island, N.S., 478–79
Rozier, Constance (née Roy), 65, 70
Rozier, Firmin, 65
Rozier, (Jean) Ferdinand, 17–22, 34, 36,
    37–40, 55, 64–65, 68, 70, 73, 152, 588,
    598; illus., 66, 67
Rozier, Joseph Jules, Jr., 68, 71–72, 152;
    illus., 69

St. Augustine, Fla., 350–51, 353–54, 359,
    365, 373
St. Francisville, La., 205, 327
St. George's Bay, Nfld., 474, 478
St. Lawrence, Gulf of, 4, 422–23, 433–34
St. Louis, Mo., 143, 148–49, 185–86, 598;
    illus., 539, 540
St. Simon's Island, Ga., 350–51, 353
Ste. Genevieve, Mo., 37–38, 64–72, 90,
    152, 598
Sanders, Albert, 334, 339
Sandy Key, Fla., 402–5, 407–10; illus., 406
Sandy Point, Nfld., 474–75, 477–78; illus.,
    476
Sanson, ———— (Dr.), 269
Santo Domingo, 266–69
Scharf, John Thomas, 548
Scotland, 279, 286, 293, 485
Seal Island, N.S., 420–21
seals, 453, 461
Selby, Prideaux John, 279, 344
Seminoles, 358, 359, 361, 363–64, 367,
    485, 564; illus., 490–91
Sharp, Mary Rozier, 71
Shattuck, George, 413, 416, 471, 552
Shawnee National Forest, Ill., 131
Shawnees, 40–41, 43–45, 50, 55, 60, 88, 90
Shawneetown, Ill., 76–78, 79, 124–26, 139
Shelbyville, Ky., 616

Shippingport, Ky., 25, 27, 29, 108, 232, 252; illus., 26
Shuler, Jay, 341, 343
Sioux, 557, 582
Sire, Joseph, 546–47, 552–53; illus., 548
Smith, Perley, 423
South Carolina, 329, 330–49
South Dakota, 4, 549, 554–65, 597
Spinney, Ashton, 420–21
Sprague, Isaac, 540, 557, 560, 572
Squires, Lewis, 540
squirrels, 588, 590; illus., 538, 589
Stack Island, Miss., 158, 166
steamboats, 146, 176
Stewart, William Drummond, 587
Stirling, Sarah Turnbull, 252
Stites, Robert, 102–3
Storm, George W., 601
Stresemann, Erwin, 357
Strobel, Benjamin, 377–78, 382–83
Sugg, William, 99–100; illus., 101
Sullivan's Island, S.C., 347–48
Sully, Thomas, xi
Swainson, Edward, 340
Sykes, ―― (Sgt.), 377–78, 382–83, 399
Symmes, John Cleves, illus., 117

Tarascon, ―― (Mr.), 25
Tawapatee Bottom, Mo., 54, 56–58
taxidermy, 4, 65, 67, 111, 540
Tennessee, 162, 165, 191–92
Texas, 485–86, 497, 519–34
thirteen-lined ground squirrels, 588, 590; illus., 589
Thorpe, Jim, 321
Three Buttes Ranch, N.D., 592–93, 595–96; illus., 594
Thruston, Alfred, 399, 402
Todd, Robert, 111, 114
Torrence, Timothy S., 497–98, 500, 503
towboats, 143–76, 185; illus., 145, 147, 175
Towles, Susan Starling, 85–88, 95, 102, 252
Towles, Thomas, 85–86
Traill, Thomas S., 198
Tuckahoes, 303

Turton, William, 177
Twain, Mark, 146, 155, 161, 376

Valentine, Edward Virginius, 265–66
Van Buren, Martin, 487
Vanderlyn, John, 260–61, 612–13
Vieux Carré, La., 261–62
Virginia, 599, 602–5
Viviparous Quadrupeds of North America (Audubon), 539, 588, 598, 606–7, 614

Wabash River, 123
Ward, Henry, 329, 350, 354–55, 359, 373, 403
Ward, J. C., 605
Warren, John Collins, 413
Warren, Robert Penn, xiii
water hyacinths, 369
weakfish, 314–15
Webster, Daniel, 411, 413
Welty, Eudora, xii–xiii
West Feliciana, La., 231, 234–35, 247–51, 254, 257–58, 291
West, Jessamyn, xiii
West Point, Ky., 30–31; illus., 32
Western Museum, 111, 114–15, 117–20
Wetherill, Henry, 15–16
Wetherill, Herbert, 8–9
Wetherill, John, 8
Wetherill, Samuel, 3, 8
Wetzel, Fred, 355–58, 373
White River, 192–95
Widman, O., 275
Wild, J. C., 113
Wilson, Alexander, xii, 33–34, 177, 181–82, 211, 232, 247, 300–301, 304, 319, 326, 331, 339–40, 428
Woodbury, Levi, 328, 489
Woodville, Miss., 216
Wyoming, 579

Yazoo River, 182–83, 185
Yellowstone River, 538–40, 546, 566–69, 577, 578, 582, 589, 592, 596
Young's Inn, Ky., 30–31; illus., 32

BIRD INDEX

Acadian flycatchers, 300
albatrosses, 610
alder flycatchers, 198
"American Buzzard," *see* red-tailed hawks
American kestrels, 179, 391, 505
"American Teal," *see* green-winged teals
arctic terns, 392, 419, 465
auks, 436
"Autumnal Warbler," *see* pine warblers
avocets, 123, 528

"Bachman's Pine-Woods Finch," *see* Bachman's sparrows
Bachman's sparrows, 340, 344
"Bachman's Swamp-Warbler," *see* Bachman's warblers
Bachman's warblers, 339-41, 343-45; illus., 342
bald eagles, 11, 61, 64, 152, 154, 179, 189, 405, 502
Baltimore orioles, 67
barn owls, 3
barred owls, 3, 123-24, 180, 192, 246-48, 317
Bell's vireos, 552
bitterns, 116, 118, 317
black-backed gulls, 420, 441, 471
black-backed three-toed woodpeckers, 326
black-bellied plovers, 406
black-crowned night herons, 28, 499
black ducks, 47

black guillemots, 425, 427, 441
"Black Hawk," *see* rough-legged hawks
black-legged kittiwakes, 437
black-necked stilts, 302, 313, 494; illus., 263
black pelicans, 178
black skimmers, 305
black terns, 123
black-throated blue warblers, 326
black-throated magpie jays, 105
black vultures, 166, 179; illus., 167
black and white sea swallows, 387, 390
blackbirds, 96, 122, 124, 180, 186-88, 192, 386, 494, 496, 513, 528, 559
Blackburnian warblers, 326
blackpolls, 300
"Blue Crane," *see* great blue herons
blue-headed quail-doves, 378-79
blue herons, 179, 195, 284-85, 332, 347, 406-7, 428, 499
blue jays, 9, 96, 105, 180, 196, 245, 479
blue warblers, 326
blue-winged teals, 48
bluebirds, 124, 180
boat-tailed grackles, 180, 184, 494, 521
bobolinks, 246
bobwhites, 65, 115, 148, 179, 525
Bonaparte's gulls, 179, 233; illus., 116
boobies, 387
brants, 305; illus., 306
"Brown Eagle," *see* bald eagles; golden eagles
"Brown Lark," *see* pipits

brown pelicans, 178, 358, 386, 391, 397, 402, 407, 502–3; **illus.**, 398
brown thrashers, 180
buffleheads, 179, 356
"bullbirds" (dovekies), 471
buntings, 180–81, 339, 428, 442, 552
buzzards, *see* vultures

Canada geese, 24–25, 39, 47, 84, 179, 305
Canada warblers, 14, 326
canvasback ducks, 47–48, 499–500
caracaras, 354–55
cardinals, 87, 96, 124, 180, 193, 196, 402, 505, 514
Carolina parakeets, 41, 179, 184
Carolina wrens, 96, 124, 180, 246, 254, 277–78, 514
carrier pigeons, 337
"Carrion Crow," *see* black vultures
Caspian terns, 409
catbirds, 180, 479, 603
cattle egrets, 369–70, 391, 407–8
"Cedar Bird," *see* cedar waxwings
cedar waxwings, 78, 98, 178, 180
chickadees, 514
chickens, 248, 337
chimeny swifts, 333
"Cincinnati Gull," *see* Bonaparte's gulls
clapper rails, 305, 310, 317, 496
clay-colored sparrows, 552
cliff swallows, 119
Collie's magpie-jays, 105
"Columbia Jay," *see* black-throated magpie-jays
Cooper's hawks, 179
coots, 196, 520, 566
cormorants, 179, 182–85, 407–8, 441–42, 610
cranes, 139, 179, 181, 194, 332
crested flycatchers, 67
"Crested Titmouse," *see* tufted titmice
crows, 161–62, 177, 179–80, 194, 402, 610
curlews, 313, 332, 347, 349, 436, 456, 460, 466, 472, 499; **illus.**, 346

dark-eyed juncoes, 181, 246, 257
dickcissels, 180, 193
"Diver," *see* loons

double-crested cormorants, 179, 182–84, 407
dovekies, 471
doves, 179, 247, 375, 379, 580, 583, 610
downy woodpeckers, 230, 514
ducks, 5, 47–49, 84, 87, 138, 148, 154, 164, 179, 181, 189, 200, 208, 264, 324, 337, 411, 413, 436, 477, 498–500, 513, 527–28, 566, 574
"Dun Diver," *see* mergansers
dunlins, 305

eagles, 3, 9, 11, 39, 61, 64, 84, 152, 154, 162, 164, 178, 189, 327, 405, 413–414, 502, 574; **illus.**, 163, 415
eastern bluebirds, 124, 180
eastern meadowlarks, 124, 180, 193, 200, 528
eastern phoebes, 11, 180, 196
eastern towhees, 7, 181
eastern wood pewees, 300, 303
egrets, 304–5, 311, 313, 333, 345, 353, 369–70, 407–8, 494, 505, 520; **illus.**, 306
Eskimo curlews, 436, 456, 460, 466, 472
European house sparrows, 369
European starlings, 369
evening grosbeaks, 98

falcons, 84, 178–79, 356, 391, 502, 505, 581
fantail pigeons, 337
finches, 180, 339, 428
fish crows, 180
"Fish Hawk," *see* ospreys
flickers, 67, 96, 124, 180, 185, 200, 514, 552, 572, 583
"Florida Cormorant," *see* double-crested cormorants
flycatchers, 121, 198, 300, 375
Forster's terns, 528
fox sparrows, 456, 465
"French Mocking Bird," *see* brown thrashers
frigatebirds, 383, 390–91, 397
fulmars, 419

gadwalls, 499
gallinules, 402
gannets, 435–37; **illus.**, 439

geese, 24–25, 39, 47, 84, 92, 164, 179, 194, 305, 324, 477
glossy ibises, 368
godwits, 402, 406
golden-crowned kinglets, 180
"Golden Crowned Thrush," *see* ovenbirds
"Golden Crowned Wren," *see* golden-crowned kinglets
golden eagles, 3, 9, 39, 61, 179, 413–14, 574; illus., 415
golden plovers, 179
"Golden Wing Woodpecker," *see* flickers
goldeneye ducks, 84
goldfinches, 180
goshawks, 84, 327
grackles, 122, 180, 184, 187, 494, 496, 520–21
gray-backed ducks, 498
gray-cheeked thrushes, 428
great auks, 436
great black-backed gulls, 471
great blue herons, 179, 195, 284–85, 332, 406, 499
"Great Footed Hawk," *see* peregrine falcons
great horned owls, 3, 97, 123, 180, 192, 303, 317–18, 357–58, 555, 610; illus., 83
great white herons, 386, 406
greater shearwaters, 419
greater yellowlegs, 122, 179, 310, 354
grebes, 122–23, 566
green-winged teals, 48, 123, 179, 500; illus., 163
greenshanks, 353–54
"Grey Snipe," *see* willets
grosbeaks, 98; illus., 81
grouse, 246, 441
guillemots, 419, 425, 427–28, 441–42
gulls, 179, 181, 233, 302–3, 353, 406, 408, 420, 441, 471, 477, 496, 503–4, 521; illus., 116, 308

harriers, 179, 181–82, 203, 513, 520
Harris' sparrows, 552
hawk-owls, illus., 297
hawks, 101, 178–179, 194, 230, 247, 300–301, 355–56, 391, 466, 520, 603, 610

"Hemlock Warbler," *see* Blackburnian warblers
Henslow's sparrows, 246, 345
hermit thrushes, 122, 180, 428
herons, 28, 121, 179, 181, 284–85, 302, 332, 347, 353, 358, 386, 402, 406–8, 428, 477, 499, 504–5, 513, 525, 607
herring gulls, 420, 471, 496
horned larks, 180; illus., 449
horned owls, 3, 83, 97, 123, 180, 192, 303, 317–18, 357–58, 555, 610
house sparrows, 369
"Hudsonian curlews" (whimbrels), 466
hummingbirds, 266, 267, 285, 368, 479, 498

ibises, 368, 402, 499
"Intrepid Hawk," *see* Cooper's hawks
"Iowa Bunting," *see* dickcissels
"Irish Goose," *see* double-crested cormorants
ivory-billed woodpeckers, 84, 162, 180, 184–85, 200

jays, 9, 96, 105, 180, 196, 245, 479
juncoes, 96, 124, 181, 246, 257

kestrels, 179, 391, 505, 580
"Key West Pigeon, or Dove," *see* Key West quail-doves
Key West quail-doves, 378–79
killdeers, 179, 305, 356–57, 513, 557, 572
king birds, 65
kingfishers, 6–7, 11, 180, 513
kinglets, 67, 180, 254, 339
kites, illus., 231
kittiwakes, 437

Labrador ducks, 411, 413, 436
larks, 180, 552; illus., 449
laughing gulls, 303, 406, 503, 521; illus., 308
"Lawyer," *see* black-necked stilts
Le Conte's sparrows, 552
least bitterns, 116, 118–19
lesser yellowlegs, 347
Lincoln's sparrows, 455, 465

little blue herons, 347, 407
long-billed curlews, 347, 349; **illus.,** 346
long-billed marsh wrens, 311; **illus.,** 312
longspurs, 180, 552
loons, 138, 178, 194, 441–42, 469, 474, 477
"loppers" (short-eared owls), 428, 471
Louisiana herons, 358, 407, 504–5, 513

magnolia warblers, 326
magpie-jays, 105
mallards, 47, 179, 189, 194, 500, 574
marbled godwits, 402, 406
"Marine Vulture," *see* frigatebirds
"Marsh Hawk," *see* northern harriers
marsh hens, 302, 607
marsh wrens, 311, 353; **illus.,** 312
"Maryland Yellowthroat," *see* yellow-throats
meadowlarks, 124, 180, 193, 200, 528, 552, 557
mergansers, 178, 181, 499
merlins, 441
Missouri red-moustached woodpeckers, 552
Missouri (western) meadowlarks, 552, 557
mockingbirds, 39, 73, 99, 124, 180, 245, 267, 285, 333, 500
mourning doves, 179, 247, 533–34, 580
mourning warblers, 340, 428
mud hens, 67
murres, 437, 441, 471
Muscovy ducks, 208

night herons, 28, 499
nighthawks, 300–301
noddies (noddy terns), 387, 390–93, 395; **illus.,** 394
northern harriers, 179, 181–82, 203, 520
nuthatches, 96, 303, 327
Nuttall's whip-poor-wills, 598

"Oregon Junco," *see* dark-eyed juncoes
orioles, 67
ospreys, 11, 29, 303, 309–10, 313–14, 408, 502; **illus.,** 315
ovenbirds, 180, 300

owls, 3, 24–25, 28, 97, 123–24, 179–80, 191–92, 246–48, 264, 303, 317–18, 357–58, 428, 471, 555, 610; **illus.,** 83
oystercatchers, 343

palm warblers, 180, 407
parakeets, 41, 179, 184, 200, 285, 467
"Partridge," *see* bobwhites
passenger pigeons, 30–31, 78, 84, 187, 200, 466, 597
peacocks and peahens, 230
peepers, 603
pelicans, x, 84, 178, 182–83, 194, 353, 358, 386, 391, 397, 402, 407–8, 502–4, 610; **illus.,** 398
peregrine falcons, 84, 178–79, 356, 502
petrels, 419–20
"Pewee Fly Catcher," *see* eastern phoebes
pewees, 300, 303
phoebes, 11, 180, 196, 599, 602–3
pigeons, 30–31, 78, 84, 187, 200, 337, 378–79, 382, 386, 400; 402, 466, 597; **illus.,** 381
pileated woodpeckers, 180, 184–85, 200, 230, 326
"Pine Swamp Warbler," *see* black-throated blue warblers
pine warblers, 230, 326
pintail ducks, 47, 138, 179
pipits, 180
plovers, 179, 305, 356–57, 406
pouters, 337
prairie chickens, 84, 87, 610
"Prairie Hawk," *see* northern harriers
prairie warblers, 407
prothonotary warblers, 250–51, 257, 392
ptarmigans, 448, 455, 460
puffins, 441, 467–68
purple finches, 180

quail, 148
quail-doves, 378–79

rails, 305, 310, 317, 353, 496, 515
Rathbone's warblers, 35
razorbills, 437, 471
ravens, 326, 425, 428

red-bellied woodpeckers, 96, 124, 407
red-breasted nuthatches, 327
"Red Breasted Thrush," *see* robins
red-headed woodpeckers, 180
"Red Owl," *see* screech owls
"Red Poll Warbler," *see* palm warblers
red-shouldered hawks, 179, 230
red-tailed hawks, 101, 179, 187, 194, 356, 603
red tanagers, 65, 324–25, 603
red-throated loons, 474
red-winged blackbirds, 122, 124, 180, 186–88, 494, 496, 529
"Red Winged Starling," *see* red-winged blackbirds
redbirds, 526
reddish egrets, 407
redpolls, 464
ring-billed gulls, 353
ring-necked ducks, 47
robins, 28, 78, 96–98, 180, 192, 200, 252, 257, 264, 285, 428, 514, 611
roosters, 248
rose-breasted grosbeaks, **illus.**, 81
roseate spoonbills, 402, 405–6, 528, 610
roseate terns, 392, 399–400
rough-legged hawks, 179
royal terns, 409
ruby-crowned kinglets, 254
ruddy turnstones, 353, 406
ruffed grouse, 246
rufous-sided towhees, 7
rusty blackbirds, 180
"Rusty Grackle," *see* rusty blackbirds

sanderlings, 305, 353
sandpipers, 87, 246, 305, 353, 471, 477
sapsuckers, 65, 99
savannah sparrows, 246, 345
saw-whet owls, 3
"Scarlet-headed Swallow" (nonexistent), 81
scarlet tanagers, 65, 324–25, 603
scaups, 47, 498
screech owls, 3, 179, 192, 317
sea eagles, 61, 64, 152
sea parrots, *see* puffins
sea swallows, 387, 390

seaside sparrows, 310–11, 317
sharp-shinned hawks, 179, 391, 603
sharp-tailed sparrows, 310–11, 317
"Shattuck's Bunting," *see* clay-colored sparrow
shearwaters, 419
"Shore Lark," *see* horned larks
short-eared owls, 428, 471
siskins, 450
skimmers, 305
"Slate Colored Hawk," *see* sharp-shinned hawks
Smith's longspurs, 552
snipes, 65, 67, 264, 345, 428, 528
"Snow Bird," *see* dark-eyed juncoes
snow buntings, 180
snow geese, 84
snowy egrets, 304–5, 311, 313, 347, 407, 494; **illus.**, 306
snowy owls, 24–25, 28
song sparrows, 479
sooties (sooty terns), 390–92, 395
sora rails, 515
"Sparrow Hawk," *see* American kestrels
sparrows, 39–40, 96, 181, 193, 196, 246, 303, 310–11, 317, 339–40, 344–45, 369, 455–56, 465, 479, 514, 552
speckled snipes, 65, 67
spoonbills, 402, 405–6, 528, 610
spotted sandpipers, 477
Sprague's pipits, 180
"Sprig Tail Duck," *see* pintail ducks
starlings, 180, 184, 187, 369
stilts, 302, 313, 494; **illus.**, 263
storks, 370
summer tanagers, 397
Swainson's thrushes, 428, 603
Sainson's warblers, 340
swallow-tailed kites, **illus.**, 231
swallows, 33, 81, 119, 387, 390, 407, 513, 610
swamp sparrows, 181
swans, 43–47, 87, 164, 179, 284–85
swifts, 3, 33, 333

tanagers, 65, 324–25, 397, 603
teals, 48, 123, 178–79, 500, 513; **illus.**, 163

"Tell Tale Godwit," *see* greater yellowlegs
terns, 123, 179, 302, 310, 383, 387, 390–92, 394–96, 399–400, 408–9, 419, 465, 528; illus., 393
thick-billed murres, 471
thrashers, 180
thrushes, 97, 122, 180, 428, 603
"tickle-asses" (spotted sandpipers), 477
"tinkers" (razorbills), 437, 471
titmice, 180, 254
"Towe Bunting," *see* eastern towhees
towhees, 7, 181
Trail's flycatchers, 198
tree swallows, 513
trumpeter swans, 43–47, 179, 284–85
tufted titmice, 180, 254
tumblers, 337
"Turkey Buzzard," *see* turkey vultures
turkey vultures, 177, 179
turkeys, 55, 87, 91–92, 115, 138, 179, 198–202, 220, 229, 247, 338, 610
turnstones, 305, 353, 406
"turres," *see* murres

upland sandpipers, 246

"Variegated Grosbill," *see* rose-breasted grosbeaks
veeries, 428
vesper sparrows, 303
vireos, 300–301, 552
vultures, 166, 177, 179, 354–55, 513, 610; illus., 167

"Wagtail," *see* ovenbirds
warblers, 14, 35, 180–81, 230, 245, 250–51, 257, 300, 326, 339–41, 343–45, 386, 391–92, 407, 428; illus., 342
warbling vireos, 300–301
"Washington Sea Eagle," *see* sea eagles
water pipits, 180
waxwings, 78, 98, 178, 180
western meadowlarks, 552, 557
whimbrels, 466

whip-poor-wills, 300–301, 303, 597–98
whistling swans, 179
white-breasted seagulls, 302
"White Crane," *see* whooping cranes
white-crowned pigeons, 382, 386, 400; illus., 381
white-crowned sparrows, 456, 465
white egrets, 520
white-eyed flycatchers, 121
white-fronted geese, 84
"White Headed Eagle," *see* bald eagles
white herons, 386, 406
white ibises, 402, 499
white pelicans, 84, 178, 503–4
white-throated sparrows, 39–40, 514
whooping cranes, 139, 179, 332
wigeons, 47, 499
"Wild Goose," *see* Canada geese
wild turkeys, *see* turkeys
willets, 260, 310, 318, 406
willow flycatchers, 198
willow ptarmigans, 455, 460
"Winter Falcon," *see* red-shouldered hawks
"Winter Hawk," *see* red-shouldered hawks
winter wrens, 180
wood ducks, 84, 87, 179, 200
wood pewees, 300, 303
wood storks, 370
wood thrushes, 428
woodcocks, 191–92
woodpeckers, 84, 88, 96, 124, 162, 180, 184–85, 200, 230, 326, 407, 514, 552, 572
wrens, 96, 124, 180, 246, 254, 277–78, 311, 317, 339, 353, 514; illus., 312

yellow-bellied sapsuckers, 65
yellow-crowned night herons, 28, 332
yellow-rumped warblers, 180, 257
yellow warblers, 35, 245
yellowlegs, 122, 179, 310, 347, 354
yellowthroats, 180, 246, 254, 513

Zenaida doves, 379